Learning Theory

and the

Symbolic Processes

O. HOBART MOWRER

Research Professor of Psychology
University of Illinois

New York · JOHN WILEY & SONS, INC. · London

To

JOHN P. SEWARD

RICHARD L. SOLOMON

and

M. E. BITTERMAN

with appreciation

It is such significant symbols, in the sense of a subset of social stimuli initiating a co-operative response, that do in a certain sense constitute our mind, provided that not only the symbol but also the responses are in our own nature. What the human being has succeeded in doing is in organizing the response to a certain symbol which is a part of the social act, so that he takes the attitude of the other person who co-operates with him. It is that which gives him a mind (p. 190).

G. H. Mead (1934)

By our definition of man as an *animal symbolicum* we have arrived at our first point of departure for further investigations. . . . That symbolic thought and symbolic behavior are among the most characteristic features of human life, and that the whole progress of human culture is based on these conditions, is undeniable. But are we entitled to consider them as the special endowment of man to the exclusion of all other organic beings? Is not symbolism a principle which we may trace back to a much deeper source, and which has a much broader range of applicability? If we answer this question in the negative we must, as it seems, confess our ignorance concerning many fundamental questions which have perennially occupied the center of attention in the philosophy of human culture (p. 27).

Ernest Cassirer (1944)

Now that the transcript of science has become so large that a single individual cannot hope to encompass a hundredth part of it in the course of a lifetime, the problem of order and economy in learning, that is, the transmission of the transcript into the image of the scientist, becomes of overwhelming importance. . . . We must re-examine the whole process of formal education from the point of view of what is the *minimum* knowledge, not the maximum, which must be transmitted if the whole structure is not to fall apart. Any economizing of learning, therefore, is highly desirable. Eiconics may be more of a contribution to this restructuring of the universe of knowledge than it is a new science in the sense in which the old sciences are sciences. If a single theoretical principle can be shown to apply over a wide area of the empirical world, this is economy in the learning process (pp. 162–163).

Kenneth Boulding (1956)

Preface

Within the whole range of the behavioral sciences, few developments have been so striking and significant during the past decade as those pertaining to the symbolic processes. Primitive Behaviorism had no place for nor interest in such phenomena. Speech, like behavior in general, was seen as grossly instrumental, not informative; and the whole concept of knowledge and communication languished. However, as Behaviorism has come of age, attention has been irresistibly drawn, once again, to these phenomena and to a broad spectrum of problems with which earlier behavior theory was not at all concerned. The present book describes and interprets these developments.

Many collateral influences, extending from technical philosophy to the new branch of engineering known as cybernetics, have importantly stimulated and shaped contemporary thought concerning the symbolic, or representational, processes. But we shall here be particularly concerned with the unfolding of potentialities which lay within Behaviorism itself. While originally repudiating all that was subjective and cognitive, this scientific movement has recently shown itself unexpectedly competent to deal therewith, in a framework which is at once more systematic and seminal than any approach previously available. In the beginning avowedly opposed to the study of "mental life," Behaviorism has, paradoxically, provided a new, firm foundation and powerful inducement for just such study.

The reader who wishes a detailed account of the scientific developments which are antecedent to those delineated in this book should consult a companion volume, *Learning Theory and Behavior* (John Wiley & Sons, Inc., 1960). In it the systematic conception of learning which, thanks to the combined efforts of many workers, has gradually emerged during the last twenty years is presented, against the backdrop of earlier and less adequate, but still provocative, theories. Today this newer, more inclusive scheme provides the conceptual substructure for the contemporary analysis and better understanding of the "higher," symbolic processes with which this book is especially concerned. And the last chapter of *Learning Theory and Behavior,* which deals with generalization, constitutes a natural transition to the topic of mediation, as developed in Chapter 2 of this book. It is, however, by no means essential that the first book be read as a prerequisite. Chapter 1 of the present volume summarizes the argument of the antecedent one, so that the advanced student need be at no disadvantage in going to work on this book directly. Also a phonographic recording, which briefly summarizes the thesis of the preceding book and exemplifies the effect of delayed auditory feedback on ordinary speech, is available from the author upon request, with the compliments of the publisher of these two volumes.

Because the widespread interest in symbolic operations and communication is of relatively recent origin and still growing, the question of scope and organization of this book has been a difficult one. The reader will find that some much-publicized developments, e.g., those pertaining to so-called "information theory" and "general semantics," receive scant attention, whereas certain unconventional topics, e.g., statistics and probability theory, have been accentuated. The writer has no strong defense for this particular pattern of inclusion and exclusion. The whole arrangement is frankly experimental, and suggestions and criticisms from readers will be gratefully received.

Some readers may be surprised that only in the final chapter of the book is any extended attempt made to consider the field of psychopathology. Because of frequent past efforts to explore the relationship between learning theory and psychopathology, this limitation may seem particularly odd. But as one immerses himself in the history of the psychology of learning, it becomes ever clearer that many of the earlier attempts to "apply" learning theory to this realm were, of necessity, premature and naive, if for no other reason than that our understanding of learning in general, and of the symbolic processes in particular, has been so partial and so incomplete. Some of the conceptions of learning which have been used most confidently in this connection are, in the present work, found to be seriously deficient and misleading. Besides, the specific and detailed issues of psychopathology lie beyond the scope of the title of this volume, properly speaking. It is hoped that this book may nevertheless be "propaedeutic" with respect to the field in question.

Because of the exploratory nature of this book and the general fomentation of the field which it represents, its "audience" cannot be precisely forecase. However, its possible uses as a supplement to *Learning Theory and Behavior* and as a basic text in more advanced work in the psychology of learning are obvious. Moreover, special courses in communication and the symbolic processes ("Psycholinguistics") are beginning to appear in both the collegiate and graduate curricula, for which this book can also appropriately serve as a text; and specialists (and students) in such cognate areas as education, speech, logic, human engineering, psychiatry, and the social sciences generally should find relevant "collateral" reading here. The writer will be grateful for readers' comments as to how the cogency and usefulness of this volume can be expanded.

Here I also wish to call attention to the various acknowledgments previously made in the Preface of *Learning Theory and Behavior*, which apply with equal cogency to the present volume, and to indicate, in addition, my appreciation to those authors and publishers (fully recognized in the Bibliography) who have generously granted permission for the reproduction of quotations and illustrations in these two books. As is so often the case in book making, the end result is a broadly *social* product.

O. HOBART MOWRER

Urbana, Illinois
June, 1960

Contents

Résumé and Introduction

Readers who are familiar with the author's *Learning Theory and Behavior* (1960) may wish to omit the present chapter, beginning the systematic study of this volume with Chapter 2. Or, they may wish to use this chapter as a means of reviewing and consolidating their knowledge of the earlier book and of tying it in, the more directly, with what is to follow. But in any event, their perusal can be rapid and in no way arduous. On the other hand, persons who have not previously read *Learning Theory and Behavior* will find this chapter more essential and warranting quite careful study. With close attention, they will find it a sufficient preparation for the ensuing ones. And if not, they can revert to the antecedent volume, whose central argument is most fully expounded in Chapter 7. Other chapters in the preceding book can then be read, or not, as special interest and need suggest.

I. From Introspection to Behaviorism

The beginning of the 20th Century found American psychology undergoing a major transformation. Since its founding as an independent science, some twenty-five years earlier, psychology had been largely preoccupied with "the study of consciousness, *per se*," and its method was mainly that of introspection. Some systematic knowledge was thus acquired, especially as regards sensation and perception; but, for the most part, the approach had proved limited and unproductive. This was particularly true of the psychology of learning.

Already, in 1896, Dewey had predicted that the New Psychology would be based upon the concept of the reflex arc—a prediction which proved to be well founded. Soon the work of Pavlov on "conditioned reflexes" was to arouse world-wide interest, and Thorndike was to introduce a theory of habit which, in a rather different sense, was equally reflexological.

Both of these developments were stimulated and influenced by the evolutionary thought of Charles Darwin. Pavlov (1927) directly acknowledged his debt to Darwin and was at pains to show how the type of learning which he termed conditioning aids an organism in its struggle for existence. Thorndike was less explicit on this score, but Campbell (1956a, 1956b) has recently pointed out that the Law of Effect is concerned with the survival and nonsurvival of particular *actions*, just as the theory of evolution is concerned with the survival or nonsurvival of individual organisms.

The psychology of introspection (or so-called Structuralism) had been concerned with consciousness. Pavlov and Thorndike were concerned with objectively observable stimuli and responses. It was therefore not surprising that Watson (1914, 1919) should have coined and popularized the name, "Behaviorism," for the new movement.

Although they were alike in that they were both behavioristic (and essentially "reflexological"), the views of Pavlov and those of Thorndike were in other respects quite different. Learning, as Pavlov conceived it, was entirely a matter of *stimulus substitution*. By the paired presentation or occurrence of two stimuli—an originally neutral, or "meaningless," one with another which already has the capacity to elicit a particular reaction—this reaction, according to Pavlov, gets connected with, or "conditioned" to, the formerly neutral stimulus. And since, in order for this process to take place, the originally neutral (ineffective) stimulus must occur first, somewhat in advance of the other (already effective) stimulus, the originally neutral stimulus may be said to act as a *signal;* so that, in conditioning, the organism learns to respond to signals, as well as to the things thus *signified.* Hence, it is understandable why Pavlov stressed the adaptive, life-preserving implications of this type of learning or behavior change.

In contrast, Thorndike saw learning as a matter of *response substitution*. It was not, he believed, so much a matter of an organism's coming to make the *same* response to a *new* stimulus as it was of its coming to make a *new* response to the *same* stimulus. If, for example, a particular stimulus (such as hunger) causes an animal to make a response which is rewarding (hunger reducing), well and good: the connection, or "bond," between that stimulus and that response ought to be, and presumably is, strengthened. But what a misfortune it would be if an organism kept repeating a useless or actively harmful response! Obviously organisms need and apparently have a device for getting rid of, or "disconnecting," such responses. This Thorndike called punishment or "stamping-out." Thus it is, reasoned Thorndike, that if one response to a particular stimulus does not work or works adversely, the organism can get rid of it and, through "trial and error," find and fixate a better one.

II. Both Pavlov's and Thorndike's Theories Inadequate

Here, then, were two almost diametrically opposed conceptions of how learning operates, with a body of scientific as well as commonplace observations to support *each* of them. Psychologists, here in America and the world over, either "took sides" and sought to defend one position to the exclusion of the other or wondered if, despite their seeming incompatibility, they might not *both* be true. The latter possibility is what may be termed the first *two-factor* or *two-process* conception of learning.

In 1932, E. C. Tolman published a book in which he took the position that all learning is *sign* learning, i.e., that it is simply a matter of new meanings or "cognitions," rather than overt responses, getting connected to appropriate stimuli. Given such a change in the "cognitive structure" or "psychological field" of the learner, more or less appropriate changes in behavior were assumed, somehow, to follow. Just how mere "knowledge" could instigate and control behavior was never fully explicated, a fact that prompted Guthrie (1952) to remark that Tolman's theory left the subject "lost in thought" instead of getting him to his goal.

Roughly a decade later, Clark L. Hull (1943), eschewing the subjectivism which Tolman (while still calling himself a Behaviorist) had allowed to creep into his theory, made an effort to unify the observations of Pavlov and Thorndike in a different way. Whereas Tolman had taken conditioning (he called it *sign* learning) as basic and tried to derive trial-and-error behavior therefrom, Hull, turning the tables, took trial-and-error (Thorndikian) learning as basic and tried to make conditioning a by-product thereof.

Here it will not be necessary to indicate just how Hull approached this task or wherein his endeavor was unsuccessful. It will suffice to say that in 1947, the present writer, incorporating the research and thinking of a number of investigators, suggested a *second* version of two-factor theory (actually the first to carry this designation), which continued to posit a fundamental distinction between *sign learning*, on the one hand, and *solution learning* on the other, but which also involved certain important departures from the way in which Pavlov and Thorndike had, respectively, defined them. Some of the work on so-called "avoidance learning" was particularly influential in shaping this newer two-factor position. Various studies had by then made it clear that neither the Pavlovian nor the Thorndikian hypothesis, taken alone, could explain all the relevant facts. Pavlovian theory fell down in that the final behavior shown by a subject in avoidance learning may be quite unlike the behavior which the organism manifests in response to the "unconditioned" (traumatic) stimulus, in the event that this latter stimulus is *not* successfully "avoided." Hence, the idea that learning is just a matter of one and the same response being shifted to a new stimulus seemed to collapse. And Thorndike's notion that learning is instead a matter of response substitution also was impugned by the fact that, in avoidance learning, apparently the *first* thing the subject learns is to *be afraid* of a formerly neutral stimulus; and this, obviously, does not occur on the basis of trial and error: it is a matter of straight conditioning or "contiguity" learning. The subject evidently reacts to the "danger signal," purely and simply, because that signal has been temporally associated with (made "contiguous" to) the thing or event it signalizes. Here, it seems, is a clear and undeniable instance of stimulus substitution, i.e., conditioning. These considerations prompted the formulation of the "second" two-factor theory along lines to be sketched in the next section.

III. The Two-Factor Position (Second Version)

When a buzzer sounds in the presence of a laboratory animal and the animal then receives a brief but moderately painful electric shock, we can be sure that the reaction of *fear*, originally aroused by the shock, will, after a few pairings of buzzer and shock, start occurring to the buzzer alone. Here the buzzer becomes a *sign* that shock is imminent, but no "solution" is yet in sight. Only when the subject, now motivated by the secondary (acquired, conditioned) drive of fear, starts *behaving* (as opposed to merely feeling) is he likely to hit upon some response which will "turn off" the danger signal and enable the subject to avert the shock. This, however, is no longer conditioning, or stimulus substitution, but habit formation. Here it seems that the subject first learns to *be afraid* and then what to *do* about the fear. These stages or steps were assumed to involve two separate and distinct *kinds* of learning: sign learning, i.e., the process whereby the fear gets shifted from the unconditioned to the conditioned stimulus; *and* solution learning, i.e., the process whereby an organism acquires the correct, effective instrumental response needed to lessen or eliminate the fear.

This revised "two-factor" or "two-step" way of thinking about learning had some important advantages, chief among which is that it provides an improved theory of "punishment." If an external, experimenter-controlled stimulus, like a buzzer, acquires the capacity to arouse fear as a result of having been paired with electric shock (or some other form of painful stimulation), would there not also be a form of fear conditioning which would occur when a shock follows something the subject *does?* Thorndike had assumed that when a stimulus-response sequence is followed by punishment, the latter acts in such a way as to *weaken* the pathway between stimulus and response, just as a reward was supposed to strengthen this "connection." But it is obvious, even to casual observation, that the most immediate and reliable "effect" of behavior is neither punishment nor reward but, rather, the stimuli (sensations) associated with the occurrence of the behavior itself. Now if these response-correlated forms of stimulation are followed by an event such as electric shock, they will, by the principle of conditioning, themselves become capable of arousing fear, which can be allayed only if the subject *inhibits* the response which arouses them. In other words, if a response has been "punished," when the subject later starts to repeat that response, it will arouse proprioceptive, tactile, visual, or other forms of stimulation which will act as "danger signals" and will tend, through the fear they elicit, to block the response.

This interpretation of punishment was an improvement over Thorndike's stamping-out conception thereof, for it took into account the possibility of *conflict.* If a punishment acted as Thorndike supposed, then a habit, when subjected to punishment, would quietly fade away, deteriorate, whereas we know that living organisms do not give up established modes of gratification without a struggle. The notion that punishment causes fear to become connected to response-correlated stimuli is compatible with the observed facts and provides common ground, which had not existed before, between learning theory and clinical psychology.

Although "avoidance" learning was first studied in situations in which the "warning" stimulus comes from the external environment, it was soon evident that, in principle, the situation is no different where the warning stimulus or stimuli are inherently associated with the subject's own activity. In the one case, fear gets conditioned to an independent stimulus or situation which the subject can perhaps flee from or manage in some other way, while in the other the fear gets conditioned to *response-aroused* stimuli which can occur only when a particular response occurs and can best be eliminated by cessation of the activity in question. Both of the forms of behavior cited involve "avoidance" but, in the one case, avoidance by "doing something" and, in the other, by *not* "doing something." In the one situation the subject may be said to get "punished" if he *does not* perform a particular response, whereas in the other he gets punished only if he *does* perform some specified response. The first may be termed *active* avoidance learning and the second, *passive* avoidance learning.

Here, clearly, is a way of thinking which has "power": by means of the same principles (fear conditioning followed by solution learning), one can account for two such seemingly diverse phenomena as flight and behavior inhibition. But there are also some inherent weaknesses; and in order to see these most clearly (in Section IV), it will be desirable to note the salient ways in which this second version of two-factor learning theory differed from the first. The first version had taken the views of both Pavlov and Thorndike more or less at face value, whereas the second version made certain important modifications. Pavlov had completely by-passed the problem of motivation and had tried to derive a wholly objective science of behavior from the concept of stimulus-substitution; in the second two-factor theory, it was assumed that what conditioning does, pre-eminently, is to attach *fears* to formerly neutral (independent or response-dependent) stimuli and that these fears then instigate trial-and-error behavior along lines very similar to those suggested by Thorndike. However, trial-and-error theory was also modified in two important ways: (1) whereas Thorndike had been interested almost exclusively in primary drives, such as hunger and thirst, the new two-factor position stressed the possibility of trial-and-error learning in response to secondary, as well as primary, drives; and (2), on the assumption that fears (once conditioned) may act as motivators and their reduction as reinforcers, a new conception of punishment (as well as active avoidance) emerged which was very different from the one advocated by Thorndike.

Although this second version of two-factor theory thus had much to recommend it, it, too, was incomplete in certain important ways, which will be considered in the next section.

IV. Secondary Reinforcement as "Hope"

The two major weaknesses in the second version of two-factor learning theory were (a) that it did not adequately deal with what is now known as secondary reinforcement and (b) that it continued to accept, essentially unmodified, Thorndike's "bond" (reflexological) theory of habit. As already indicated, Thorndike's "stamping-out" conception of punishment has been generally replaced by a conflict, or "feedback," theory thereof; and Tolman, Lashley, Lewin, and other influential psychologists had for years been pointing out that most of the supposedly "habitual" (learned) behavior of man and beast alike is far more flexible and richly variable than a strictly connectionist view could account for (see also Woodworth, 1958). According to Thorndike's view, an organism can learn only what it *does,* i.e., a particular stimulus-response connection has to "occur" before it can be strengthened (or weakened); but experiments on latent learning and extinction, insight, and other mediated forms of behavior modification (see Chapter 2) have shown that learning can occur *without* "doing," thus impugning the generality of the connectionistic position. Yet, for want of a better conception of what is involved in habit formation, two-factor learning theory (although rejecting his theory of punishment) continued to accept Thorndike's rather manifestly inadequate conception of habit as an S—R bond which is strengthened by reward. As it turns out, recent studies which have served to clarify the nature of secondary reinforcement have also provided the basis for a new and superior theory of habit.

Many years ago, Pavlov and his collaborators demonstrated what they called *second-order* salivary conditioning. If, for example, a blinking light is presented just before a hungry dog receives a bit of food, the salivary response which the food elicits (more or less reflexly) "moves forward" and starts to occur to the light alone. This is the familiar phenomenon of having one's "mouth water" at the sight, smell, or sound of food and represents what Pavlov called *first-order* conditioning. Then it was found, to continue with the same laboratory example, that the light, once the salivary response has been conditioned to it, can be paired with a *new* stimulus, e.g., the ticking of a metronome, and that, by this means, the salivary response can be transferred to the sound of the metronome, without the latter having ever been paired with the "primary" or original reinforcer, food. In other words, Pavlov showed that once the salivary response has been conditioned to a "first-order" conditioned stimulus, that stimulus can serve as the "unconditioned" stimulus for "second-order" conditioning.

Then, somewhat later, particularly as the result of researches in this country, it was found that a first-order conditioned stimulus can serve as a "secondary reinforcer" (the terminology is unfortunate but now conventional) in yet another sense. Let us suppose that a hungry dog has been taught, by the procedure indicated, to salivate upon the occurrence of a blinking light. And let us further suppose that provision is now made so that the dog himself can *turn on the light*. If given a convenient opportunity, will he do so? He *will*, repeatedly—thus indicating that a first-order conditioned stimulus can serve as a secondary reinforcer, not only in the sense of establishing higher-order salivary conditioning, but also in the sense of setting up *new habits*. If the blinking light can be turned on by nosing a "button" or pressing a lever with its paw, the dog will show a much more marked tendency to make such a response than if it produces no such stimulus. What is happening here is that the dog learns a new bit of behavior, not because that behavior produces (is rewarded by) food, but because it produces merely a sign, or *promise*, of food. How can this finding be explained?

In their study of salivary conditioning, Pavlov and his co-workers had been zealously objective and had meticulously limited their observations (or at least their scientific reports) to the action of the salivary gland, to the neglect of the dog-as-a-whole. As a result of conditioning experiments which were conducted and reproduced as motion pictures by Carl Zener (1937), it was demonstrated that a hungry dog, upon hearing or seeing a stimulus that signalizes food, not only salivates; the dog looks interested, hopeful, even "happy" and, if not physically restrained, will move bodily *toward* the place where the food is likely to be delivered.

From this and related observations it was justifiably inferred that, in a situation of the kind described, a conditioned stimulus not only makes the subject salivate: it also makes him *hopeful,* just as surely as a stimulus which has been associated with onset of pain makes a subject *fearful.* And if a fear-arousing stimulus elicits the two forms of *avoidance* behavior previously discussed, it might be surmised that a hope-arousing stimulus would be capable, likewise, of producing either of two forms of "approach" behavior, one of which has already been alluded to and which, in ordinary life, is exemplified by the family dog coming "when called." Just as an organism wishes to get *less* of a stimulus that makes it afraid (cf. Holt's concept of *abience,* 1931) and may do so by fleeing, so will an organism try to get *more* of a stimulus that arouses hope (Holt's *adience*) and may do so by going toward the source of that stimulus. Hence we emerge with an understanding of what has been called positive and negative *place* learning (spatial approach and avoidance).

But there is manifestly more to the story, which leads to a new conception of habit formation.

V. A Feedback Theory of "Habit"

In Section III of this chapter we have seen how the study of "place-avoidance" learning led to a new and apparently improved conception of punishment (response avoidance or inhibition). And in the preceding section, reference has been made to recent work on secondary reinforcement as it pertains to "place-approach" learning. Does not this work on, and way of thinking about, secondary reinforcement now suggest a conception of positive behavior modification or "habit formation" which is as radical as was the change from Thorndike's "stamping-out" theory of punishment to the "conflict" model which is now so widely accepted?

If a formerly neutral stimulus is paired with a rewarding state of affairs (drive reduction), that stimulus acquires the capacity to act as a secondary reinforcer and to *attract* the subject toward it. The subject acts as if it wants to get *more* of the stimulus; and since the stimulus is commonly one which is located at some point remote from the subject, the subject's reaction is, of necessity, often one of approach (Mowrer, 1960, Chapter 9). The biological utility of such a predisposition on the part of living organisms is obvious: it carries them into the vicinity of probable primary reinforcements and rewards.

But now let us suppose that the stimulation which precedes a rewarding state of affairs is *response-produced*, rather than environmentally produced. Let us suppose, that is to say, that a hungry animal makes a particular response, thereby stimulating itself in a characteristic manner, *and obtains food*. By principles already enunciated, we would expect the response-correlated stimulation to take on secondary reinforcement properties and that the subject, when again hungry, would now try to "get more" of *these* ("promising") stimuli. What would be the result? Since these "promising" stimuli are not located in space, the subject could not get more of them by going to any particular place. The only way to arouse or intensify them is for the subject to make or accentuate the *response* that has previously produced them! *And the tendency to make a particular response, in the presence of a particular drive or need, is what is ordinarily termed a "habit."*

According to Thorndike's classical statement of the Law of Effect, a habit consists of a strong "connection" between a particular stimulus or drive and a particular response. Although this connection was often said to be merely "functional" (or even "mathematical"), without necessarily implying anything about *neural* pathways, it was very natural to assume that the theory did presuppose the direct strengthening of neural connections. How otherwise was one to interpret the notion of a "connection"? The conception of habit just suggested is different in that it presupposes only that there is an improved or strengthened connection (a specifically neural connection rather than just a vaguely "functional" one) between certain end organs which are excited in specific ways by a given response *and the emotion of hope.* Hope is something which motivated organisms like to have (since it implies imminent drive reduction), just as fear is something they do *not* like to have (since it implies a threat of drive increase), so that we may legitimately infer that a motivated organism will show a strong tendency to make those responses which have, as one may say, a *hopeful* "feedback." The tendency to seek response-correlated stimulation which arouses hope is biologically useful in that it disposes a motivated organism to make responses which in the past have led to (or produced) satisfaction. Thus, as between the tendency noted earlier for living organisms to seek *external* stimulation which has been associated with reward and the tendency, just described, for them to seek *self-produced* stimulation which has been associated with reward, we have at least the rudiments of an explanation for goal-seeking behavior in general.

VI. Symmetry and Scope of the System

Behavior, we thus discover, consists of two types of approach and avoidance tendencies. If an *independent stimulus* arouses fear, flight is likely to follow; whereas *response-correlated stimuli* which arouse fear produce inhibition. And if an independent stimulus arouses hope, approach will occur; whereas response-correlated stimuli which arouse hope produce response facilitation or "habit." And where response facilitation or response inhibition is concerned, it is not that a direct drive-behavior bond is either strengthened or weakened; instead it is a matter of the hope or fear that has gotten conditioned to the stimuli which are typically aroused by the occurrence of a particular pattern of action.

Stated most concisely, the thesis is that much of the adjustive, self-regulatory behavior of living organisms can be subsumed under four rubrics: the *avoidance* of places and the *inhibition* of responses which have been negatively (incrementally) reinforced and the *approach* to places and the *facilitation* of responses which have been positively (decrementally) reinforced. Thus the question of whether living organisms learn "responses" *or* "places" is resolved by the discovery that they are capable of and constantly manifest *both* forms of learning, which, however, involves one and the same set of principles: namely the conditioning of hopes and fears, under the impact of drive decrements and drive increments, to either independent or response-dependent stimuli. This way of thinking cuts the ground from under the controversy between "reinforcement theorists" and "field theorists" and provides the basis for a conceptual scheme of considerable generality and power (Mowrer, 1960, Chapter 9).

This is still a two-factor, or two-process, conception of learning, but it differs from the preceding (second) version in certain important ways. The earlier version distinguished between sign learning and solution learning; the new version assumes that *all* learning is sign learning, or conditioning, and that solution learning (including inhibition) is a derivative or special case thereof. Wherein, then, is the theory still two-factored? It is still two-factored in that it assumes that there are two quite different forms of reinforcement: drive decrement (reward) and drive increment (punishment). In this respect the theory is congruent with common sense and with important aspects of many other psychological systems (see Section XII); but it deviates from the thesis of Hull (also favored for a time by Thorndike, 1931, 1932) that all reinforcement is decremental; and while agreeing with Tolman that all learning is sign learning, it is more "dynamic," less purely "cognitive." Finally, the new conception accepts "Pavlovian conditioning" as basic, but it goes considerably beyond Pavlov in stressing the essentially emotional (motivating and reinforcing) nature of conditioned responses; and it also holds that overt, instrumental behavior is much more complexly determined than Pavlov's (essentially reflexological) position assumed.

Thorndike's bond theory of habit was, in one respect, perfectly straightforward and scientifically impeccable. It assumed that a stimulus impinging at one end of an S—R connection or "channel," as *cause*, produced at the other end, *as effect*, a behavioral reaction of some kind.

In this sense, then, it could not be accused of implying *teleology* (causation from the future); but the charge often leveled at it—and with good reason—was that it made living organisms, per theory, "blind" and "stupid" to a degree which their actual behavior belies. In insisting that animals (including human beings) learn only by *doing*, the theory precluded insight, foresight, and "latent" learning in general, which phenomena the present theory accommodates very comfortably (see Chapters 2 and 6 especially). But, in accomplishing this, the theory may seem to have lost its mechanistic moorings. However, as will be seen in Chapter 7, the new science of cybernetics (Wiener, 1948), with its emphasis upon "feedback," gives us now an excellent model for explaining (and, indeed, producing) "teleology" in a thoroughly "mechanical" way. Pending the fuller discussion of this problem in the chapter cited (see also Mowrer, 1960, Chapter 7), the reader will perhaps wish to suspend judgment concerning it. But a crude, intuitive grasp of what is involved can be had from the proposition, derived from the new theory, that, for example, an organism engages in food-seeking and food-consuming behavior not only because it is *hungry* but also because, in instituting (or perhaps just "contemplating") such behavior, the organism already "feels better" (see Section XI). Thus, in a manner of speaking, the organism is not only pushed but also "pulled" toward previously successful activity, in the sense that the "pressure" (to shift to a pneumatic analogy) becomes *less* when there is movement (of at least a symbolic kind, see Chapter 6) toward the goal and again *greater* when the movement is stopped or reversed. Because we have been so accustomed to think about behavior in terms of the mechanics of the 19th century, it is difficult to assimilate the implications of the new conceptions suggested by 20th-century mechanical and electronic "control systems"; but these, as a little study will show, are vastly more relevant to the understanding of the behavior of living organisms than are the "push-button" models of an earlier day.

VII. Two-Factor Theory and the Present System Compared

Because it is not always easy to see precisely how the present conceptual scheme differs from the earlier "two-factor" positions, and because it is important that there be no ambiguity about this difference, this section will reproduce a discussion from an earlier study (Mowrer, 1956) which goes into this matter in some detail.

The original [actually the *second*] version of two-factor learning theory now appears, in retrospect, as a sort of stepping stone, intermediate between monistic interpretations and the revised two-factor position here presented. The systematic relationships here involved may be summarized as follows:

Thorndike's Law of Effect is schematized in Fig. 1–1 and the Pavlovian conception of conditioning is represented in Fig. 1–2. Each alone, according to its exponents, was capable of accounting for the basic facts of learning; but others felt that both conceptions were necessary. Two-factor learning

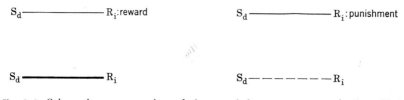

$$S_d \text{————————} R_i\text{:reward} \qquad S_d \text{————————} R_i\text{:punishment}$$

$$S_d \text{————————} R_i \qquad S_d\text{— — — — — —}R_i$$

Fig. 1–1. Schematic representation of the two halves, or aspects, of Thorndike's Law of Effect. It held, in essence, that if some drive stimulus S_d produces some instrumental (behavioral) response R_i, and if R_i is then followed by reward, this S_d—R_i sequence, or *bond*, will as a result be strengthened (diagram at left) and that if such a stimulus-response sequence is followed by punishment, the bond will as a result be weakened (diagram at right).

Fig. 1–2. Schematic representation of conditioning, as conceived by Pavlov. S_c is a stimulus which, initially, is not capable of eliciting response R, but which as a result of contiguous occurrence with S_u (above, left), acquires this capacity (above right). The subscripts c and u are used to designate, respectively, what Pavlov termed the "conditioned" and the "unconditioned" stimulus.

theory, as envisioned a decade ago, accepted, essentially unmodified, the "first half" of the Law of Effect, which held that reward strengthens habit; but it departed from the Law of Effect in holding that punishment achieves its action, not by simply reversing the effects of reward, but by causing fears to become attached (conditioned) to stimulation associated with the occurrence of the punished response. This version of two-factor theory is shown in Fig. 1–3. Here habit formation, or solution learning, is conceived essentially as Thorndike suggested; but punishment is seen in more complex terms. Instead of simply reversing the effect produced by past reward, punishment is here thought of as providing the basis for the conditioning of fear, which then produces conflict and, if the fear is strong enough, inhibition.

The details of this interpretation of punishment are shown at the right in Fig. 1-3. Here a problem situation or drive, S_d, produces an overt, instrumental response, R_i. R_i is followed by punishment, which is here represented as S_p. The punishment elicits a response R_p of which r_f, or fear, is a component. But when R_i occurs, it not only produces the extrinsic punishment, S_p; it also produces a number of other stimuli, s, s, s, which are inherently related to the occurrence of R_i. The result: a part of the reaction produced by S_p, namely fear, gets conditioned to these response-produced stimuli, s, s, s. Consequently, when S_d recurs and the organism starts to perform R_i, the resulting stimuli "remind" the organism of the antecedent punishment, i.e., cue off r_f, which tends to inhibit R_i.

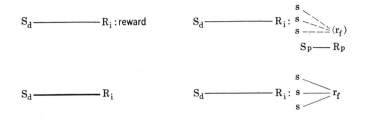

Fig. 1–3. Schematic representation of the second version of two-factor learning theory. According to that formulation, habits were made by reward, as shown at the left, in essentially the way suggested by the Law of Effect. However, punishment was assumed to involve fear conditioning, as shown at right, with ensuing conflict and probable inhibition (see text).

Two-factor learning theory, in its middle version, thus accepted Thorndike's conception of habit formation but derived the phenomenon of punishment from fear conditioning, rather than attributing it to a process which simply reversed the effects of past reward. As has been shown, this theory of punishment involves the same principles as have been found most satisfactory for explaining so-called avoidance learning. In both instances, fear becomes conditioned to stimuli, either external or response-produced, and the organism then makes whatever type of adjustment will most effectively eliminate these stimuli and reduce the attendant fear.

Current two-factor theory is diagrammed in Fig. 1-4. Here it is assumed that habit formation is a matter of conditioning no less than is punishment. If a stimulus, S_d, produces a given response R_i, and if R_i is followed by reward S_r, then it is assumed that a part of the total response, R_r, which is produced by S_r will become conditioned to the stimuli inherently connected with R_i. Here the conditionable component of R_r is r_h, the "hope" (secondary reinforcement) reaction; and it becomes connected to stimuli, s, s, s, just as fear does in the case of punishment. The result is that whenever R_i starts to occur, it is facilitated rather than inhibited (pp. 121–123).

Perhaps the best way to epitomize the difference between the second and the present version of "two-factor" learning theory is as follows. The second version was "two-factored" in two different ways: it distinguished between sign learning and solution learning *and* between incremental reinforcement and decremental reinforcement, sign learning being associated with incremental reinforcement and solution learning with decremental reinforcement. Now the theory is two-factored in *only one* way, namely, with respect to *types of reinforcement,* incremental and decremental. With regard to the other principle

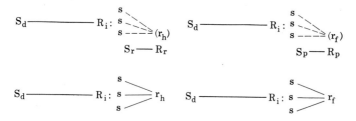

Fig. 1–4. Schematic representation of revised two-factor theory. Here the changes produced in behavior by reward, as well as those produced by punishment, are derived from conditioning plus the feedback principle.

of classification employed in the earlier versions, the theory is decidedly one-factored: that is, it assumes that all learning is sign learning and that solution learning (as well as response inhibition) is a derivative thereof. In short, as far as "types of learning" are concerned, the current version is "one-factored"; but it remains definitely two-factored as regards reinforcement. This is perhaps not a very good or sufficient basis for deriving a *name* for the present theory; but, for the time being at least, two-factor learning theory can serve as well as any other, provided that it does not imply two kinds, or forms, of *learning,* simply two kinds of *reinforcement.*[1]

[1] Another terminological matter should be mentioned here. The reader may find it awkward to use the term "incremental" to designate the form of reinforcement involved in punishment (drive induction) and thus likely to produce active or passive avoidance behavior, and to use the term "decremental" to designate the reinforcement which reward (drive reduction) provides and which typically results in behavior facilitation. In other words, confusion may arise from the fact that decremental reinforcement commonly produces what is sometimes called "response increment" (habit) and incremental reinforcement often produces "re-

VIII. The Nature of Unlearning

Thorndike had a definite and simple, though probably mistaken, conception of unlearning. It was the process of "connection" weakening which resulted, as he believed, from punishment. And Pavlov saw unlearning as involving either of two processes: extinction *or* counterconditioning. A conditioned response, he found, will eventually stop occurring if it is not occasionally confirmed, or "reinforced," by the occurrence of the unconditioned stimulus. That is to say, if a promise (sign of reward) or a threat (sign of punishment) is repeated over and over again and not at least occasionally substantiated, or "made good," one would certainly expect the subject to stop responding: to continue indefinitely to react to no longer valid signs would not be biologically useful. And Pavlov repeatedly showed, by laboratory experiment, that extinction is a very definite and real phenomenon. Also, what is equally plausible, he showed that the response to a conditioned stimulus or sign can be modified by means of counterconditioning. Thus, if a sign has originally meant reward and if conditions are changed so that it now means punishment, we would expect the reaction produced thereby to change from hope (salivation, in Pavlov's experiments) to fear (Pavlov spoke of "defense reactions")—or vice versa. But as we have now seen, neither Thorndike's nor Pavlov's original formulation is entirely satisfactory; and having evolved a new and different conception of the learning process, we also must now come to grips with the problem of unlearning within this new system.

Revised two-factor learning theory assumes, as already indicated, that all learning, in the final analysis, is sign learning or conditioning—

---

sponse decrement" (or inhibition). This ambiguity is unfortunate; but, for the moment, nothing can apparently be done about it. The reader, to avoid confusion, only needs to bear in mind that when we speak of decremental or incremental reinforcement (or reinforcers), the reference of the qualifying words is to the correlated *direction of change* in the assumed underlying *drive state* and has nothing to do, necessarily, with either the augmentation or diminution of activity or behavior, per se. *That* is determined by other considerations, notably whether the conditioned stimuli or signals in the situation are independent or response-dependent and on how and when the reinforcement is applied. For example, by the sagacious use of reward it is possible to teach an animal to "be still" as well as to "work," and by the use of punishment to be active as well as "inhibited." The nature—that is, the *direction* (up or down)—of reinforcement is thus, it seems, of greater systematic importance than is the question of whether the resulting *behavior* is "incremental" or "decremental."

not conditioning in the sense of overt responses (or as mere "cognitions") but in the sense of positive and negative emotions, notably those of hope and fear, which then mediate and guide actual behavior (but see also Chapters 2 and 5). And since extinction and counterconditioning are the recognized forms which unlearning takes where conditioned reactions are concerned, we here accept the assumption that these are the major (perhaps only) forms of unlearning. In the final analysis, extinction and counterconditioning may come down to the same thing, for a hope that is not confirmed is said to involve *disappointment* (which is a form of punishment) and a fear that is not confirmed provides *relief* (which is a form of reward). Therefore, it may be more precise to say that unlearning always involves counterconditioning, and that extinction is merely a species thereof. But, for the moment, this is not a pressing issue.

What is much more critical is the question of how one can accept a counterconditioning theory of unlearning and still be able to account for the manifest phenomenon of *conflict*. As already noted, one of the serious weaknesses of Thorndike's Law of Effect was that it had stimulus-response bonds being directly strengthened or weakened by reward and punishment, respectively, with no possibility of the subject ever experiencing frustration, confusion, or a sense of contradiction. And if we now assume that unlearning is simply a matter of the *sign* ("direction") of signs being changed, from positive to negative (hope to fear) or the reverse, there might seem to be here also equally little grounds for the experience of conscious conflict. A stimulus or situation would, presumably, be either "good, bad, or indifferent," but never "ambivalent." It would be strongly or mildly negative for the subject, strongly or mildly positive, or neutral; but it could not be positive and negative *at the same time,* and this, at least superficially, is the essence of conflict.

Although this problem cannot be said to have been fully solved, a promising possibility lies in the fact that any one response or any one situation involves a great number and variety of stimuli, some of which may, at a particular point in time, be conditioned to hope and others to fear. Thus, as the subject "attends" (Chapter 5) now to one, now to another set of stimuli, first one emotion (attitude) will predominate, then another. This could easily account for the back-and-forth vacillation sometimes seen in a conflicted organism and also explain why it is that such an organism is said to be of "two minds" about the situation (or action) in question. Only when all or at least a clear majority of the stimuli associated with a particular response or place become positive or negative does the individual become one-minded, unified, organized (cf. Mowrer, 1960, Chapter XI).

It seems, therefore, that the question of unlearning offers no serious difficulties to revised two-factor theory and helps clarify the form which the theory, of necessity, must take—although this treatment of conflict needs to be carefully checked against N. E. Miller's (1944, 1958b) studies of approach-avoidance behavior. It is believed, however, that Miller's findings lend themselves rather nicely to reinterpretation along the lines suggested.

IX. "Paradoxical" Resistance to Extinction

In order to have the proper background for the section which is to follow, it is necessary to say a word here about a paradox, sometimes known as the "Humphreys effect" (Skinner, 1938; Humphreys, 1939a, 1939b). If a stimulus is followed by reward, it acquires the capacity to arouse hope; if followed by punishment, the capacity to arouse fear; and if a stimulus which has been followed by either reward or punishment is now followed by "nothing," i.e., is not confirmed, it tends to lose the meaning it has previously possessed. Such at least would seem to be reasonable assumptions.

However, some 20 years ago it was discovered that if, during training, reinforcements occur *intermittently*, i.e., if reinforced trials are interspersed with nonreinforced trials, then in the *test* situation there will be greater "resistance to extinction" than if reinforcement has occurred on each and every training trial. For example, if a hungry rat learns to press a little bar as a means of obtaining food, this "habit" will be more persistent after food has been discontinued if, during the training period, the subject has sometimes pressed the bar and received no food. From a common-sense point of view, this outcome does not seem very remarkable: persons, we observe, who have had a "hard time" are often more persevering, in the face of adversity, than are those who have "had it easy." But, in the light of learning-theory logic, the phenomenon has been puzzling.

On the assumption that hope (secondary reinforcement) is built up through the conjunction of a response (response-correlated stimulation) with reward and that hope is weakened by nonconfirmed occurrences of the response, then, for instance, 50 successive pairings of response and reward ought to produce more "habit strength" (hope) than 50 comparable rewarded occurrences of the response intermingled with, say, 50 nonrewarded (extinction) occurrences thereof. Consider the situation thus: if each rewarded occurrence of the response produces a certain increment of habit strength and if each nonrewarded occurrence produces a certain decrement, then any given number of successively rewarded occurrences of the response should "add up" to more habit strength than the same number of rewarded occurrences intermixed with any number of nonrewarded occurrences. That is to say, if each rewarded occurrence of the response is thought of as a + ("plus") and each nonrewarded occurrence as a — ("minus"), then any given number of +'s alone will sum to *more* than will the same number of +'s with —'s (however few) included.

Several different conjectures have been advanced to explain the Humphreys effect, of which the most satisfactory, until recently, was the so-called "discrimination hypothesis" (Mowrer & Jones, 1945; Bitterman, Feddersen, & Tyler, 1953). It goes as follows. When a subject has been intermittently reinforced during training, he continues to react, at least for a while, during the test period as if "nothing has happened," for the reason that response without reward is no novelty to him. That is to say he cannot, for a while, "tell the difference" between the conditions of intermittent reinforcement (which prevailed during training) and no reinforcement whatever (extinction); whereas if, during training, reward has been forthcoming on every trial, then the very first nonrewarded (extinction) trial is different and the subject quickly senses that something is "wrong" and soon "stops work."

From a common-sense, intuitive standpoint, this interpretation seems very plausible; but its acceptance has been seen as something of a defeat for reinforcement theory in that the "discrimination hypothesis," as ordinarily formulated, is highly "cognitive" and seems to transcend ordinary reinforcement concepts (Woodworth, 1958, p. 265). But thanks to a recent paper by Amsel (1958; see also Section VIII), it now seems that the Skinner-Humphreys effect was "paradoxical" because the whole process of extinction (unlearning) had been misconceived. As Amsel has been able to show, on both logical and empirical grounds, nonreinforcement is not a purely neutral (merely nonreinforcing) experience; it is, instead, a *frustration*. And what intermittent reinforcement during acquisition does, apparently, is not to produce a stronger habit (as increased resistance to extinction has been taken to mean) but rather to make extinction (*consistent* nonreward), when it finally comes, *less frustrating*—because the experience of nonreward has previously been interspersed with reward and its "sting" removed. In short, intermittent reinforcement seems to produce, not greater habit strength, but *diminished frustration effectiveness*.

Here, then, is an interpretation of the Humphreys effect which is in no way paradoxical but is, instead, fully in accordance with expanded reinforcement principles. They are expanded to the extent of assuming, not unreasonably surely, that the threat of punishment produces *fear*, that promise of a reward produces *hope*, and that a promise which has been made but not fulfilled produces *frustration* or *anger* which, along with fear, can serve to obliterate (countercondition) hope. And from this it follows that when, during so-called intermittent reinforcement, frustration (due to nonreward) on one trial is shortly followed by reward on the next, then the reaction of frustration or anger on the nonrewarded trials gives way to *hope*, which is all that is needed to provide the basis for a highly parsimonious and "objective" explanation of the Humphreys effect. (There is an instructive complication here, which is raised by certain findings reported by Weinstock, 1954; but this, as we shall see in Chapter 5, merely stimulates our theory to healthy, new growth and in no way invalidates it.)

Thus, the "discrimination hypothesis," which has usually been formulated in frankly cognitive terms, can be reformulated in a more systematic way: one which, to be sure, somewhat expands, but does not in the least impugn, our general "reinforcement" position.

X. How Real is Secondary Reinforcement?

The point has sometimes been made that a satisfactory theory of habit cannot be based upon the concept of secondary reinforcement (see Section V) for the reason that the latter is so transitory and feeble. Habits, as we know, can be extraordinarily stable and resistant to extinction; and if they are really dependent upon the secondary reinforcement, or "hope," that gets conditioned to the stimuli aroused by the response in question, then secondary reinforcement must be capable of greater durability than most experiments have demonstrated. In the laboratory this phenomenon has been typically studied as follows. A buzzer is paired a number of times with the presentation of food to a hungry rat; and a bar is then made available to the rat, depression of which will cause the buzzer to sound but will produce no food. Typically, the rat will press the bar a few times (not many, but demonstrably *more* times than if the bar did not produce the buzzer), and then will stop. Here the bar-pressing habit is established exclusively on the basis of secondary reinforcement; but it is not much of a habit, as indicated by the comparatively few times it occurs. Thus it has been argued that secondary reinforcement cannot be said to provide the basis for habits in general, which often are exceedingly strong and stable.

This objection is not well founded. In the first place, the bar-pressing habit cited for illustrative purposes involves *second-order* conditioning which, as Pavlov showed, tends to be transitory and unstable. That is to say, in this example the buzzer, as a result of its conjunction with food, acquires secondary-reinforcement properties, by first-order conditioning; and then the sensory feedback from the bar-pressing response, as a result of its conjunction with the buzzer, acquired secondary-reinforcement properties, but now, by second-order conditioning. The response-correlated stimuli are therefore "once removed" from the primary reinforcement provided by food; and the conditioning, instead of being direct (as when bar pressing is immediately associated with food), is indirect or *mediated*, by means of the buzzer. The fact that a habit which is established through second-order conditioning is weak is certainly no grounds for assuming that a habit, established through *first*-order conditioning, cannot be strong and still dependent, as the theory assumes, upon secondary reinforcement.

Moreover, Zimmerman (1957, 1958a) has recently shown that even in the relatively unfavorable case of second-order (mediated) conditioning, a habit of surprising durability can be set up, if certain special conditions are observed. As already noted, one can markedly increase resistance to extinction (or, rather, lower frustration effectiveness) if training involves intermittent reinforcement; and since one of the great difficulties in setting up a new habit solely by means of a secondary reinforcer is the tendency of the latter, through extinction, to lose its potency, it becomes particularly desirable to use any expedient which will offset this tendency. Accordingly, what Zimmerman did was to present a buzzer to a thirsty rat and then have it followed by water, at first fairly regularly, but then less and less so, until finally an average reinforcement-nonreinforcement ratio of about 1–10 was reached. Under these conditions, when the buzzer sounded, the rat would still promptly "check" to see if water was going to appear; but it became well accustomed to finding no water, following buzzer, although it could never be sure when water *might* be present.

Hence, by the technique of intermittent reinforcement, we may say that the buzzer acquired quite strong and persistent secondary reinforcement properties. This assumption was confirmed by the fact that when Zimmerman made it possible for the rat to produce the buzzer (though never any water now) by pressing a bar, it did so a *great many* times; and this number, Zimmerman found, could be increased still further if bar pressing produced the buzzer, not on every trial, but only part of the time. Thus, by means of what may be termed a *double* intermittent-reinforcement procedure, it has been found possible to set up an extremely stable and resistant habit, even though habit strength (secondary reinforcement) is acquired by the comparatively unfavorable method of second-order conditioning.

Altogether, then, it seems that the phenomenon of secondary reinforcement, or hope, is real enough and quite strong enough to give to responses that degree of persistence and durability which "habits" typically have. The revised two-factor interpretation of habit appears to be buttressed by solid experimental data.

XI. The Nature of Secondary Reinforcement More Precisely Identified

At this point a source of confusion needs to be considered, namely, the fact that the term "secondary reinforcement" is commonly used to denote two phenomena which, at least superficially, are quite different. Because fear is generally regarded as a *secondary* (conditionable) drive and because it has been demonstrated, over and over again (Section III), that its termination (relief) has reinforcing power, many writers (see, for example, Miller & Dollard, 1941) have referred to fear reduction, of the kind that occurs when a danger signal is terminated, as *secondary reinforcement.*

While this usage seems entirely legitimate, it is at variance with another usage which also has good precedent and justification. As indicated in the preceding section (and in Section IV), Hull, following a line of thought suggested by Pavlov, used the term "secondary reinforcement" to denote the reinforcing power of a stimulus which has been associated with the termination of some primary or secondary drive, such as hunger or fear. Hull's formal statement of this conception was that: "A receptor impulse [stimulus] will acquire the power of acting as a reinforcing agent if it occurs consistently and repeatedly within 20 seconds or so of a functionally potent reinforcing state of affairs, regardless of whether the latter is primary or secondary" (Hull, 1943, p. 95).

Although the mechanism whereby this form of secondary reinforcement is mediated was not made entirely clear by either Hull or his followers, it was supposedly related in some way to the notion of *anticipatory goal reaction* which they commonly designated as r_g. But the paradox which was involved here was that, basically, *reinforcement* was conceived of as involving drive reduction; yet *secondary* reinforcement, as represented by the r_g notion, involves stimulation increment, not decrement. Gradually the r_g conception of secondary reinforcement has given way to a more explicit and more consistent way of thinking about the problem, which can be summarized diagrammatically. Fig. 1–5a shows the well-known phenomenon of fear conditioning. Some originally neutral stimulus is converted into a "danger signal" by virtue of its being paired a few times with some painful, noxious stimulus such as electric shock which can be depended upon to elicit the emotional response of fear. Under these circumstances the subject soon starts "anticipating" the shock as soon as the danger signal appears and reacting with fear, as shown by the dashed line.

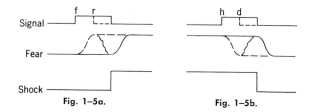

Signal

Fear

Shock

Fig. 1–5a.   Fig. 1–5b.

Figs. 1–5a and 1–5b. Graphic representation of the operational ("situational," see Hunt, Cole, & Reis, 1958) definition of four major emotions: fear, relief, hope, and disappointment (f, r, h, and d, respectively). Fear and relief, on the one hand, and hope and disappointment on the other are, in some ways, just "mirror images" of each other; but they differ in another respect as well. Fear and relief, although always having an implied reference to some primary noxious event (such as electric shock), may occur in the *absence* thereof; whereas hope and disappointment are, at least per theory, possible only when some such drive, or "problem," is *present*. This inference is supported by considerable empirical evidence (Mowrer, 1960, Chapter 5).

Now, once a conditioned fear reaction of this kind has been established (it can be objectively indexed by the psychogalvanic skin reaction), it can function as a *secondary drive;* and if the subject does something which causes the danger signal to "go off" (see dotted line) and prevents the shock from occurring, the secondary drive of fear will be reduced (see wavy line) and the subject will experience *secondary reinforcement,* in the sense in which Miller & Dollard and others have used that expression. This is the conception of secondary reinforcement (which can be conveniently designated as secondary reinforcement *type-*

1) which has proven so useful in explaining active avoidance learning
and which gave rise to the new conception of punishment (passive
avoidance learning) which has been described in Section III.

But what of that conception of secondary reinforcement (which
may be termed secondary reinforcement *type-2*) which Hull has presented? Fortunately a clear understanding of it, too, can be obtained
by "extending" Fig. 1–5a as shown in Fig. 1–5b. When the primary,
noxious stimulus (shock) is finally terminated, its termination will be
followed by a subsiding of the emotional upset or fear reaction. And
if a signal shortly precedes these events, it is reasonable to suppose
that the fear reduction which follows shock termination will also soon
become anticipatory, as suggested by the dashed line. This effect, we
conjecture, is what is ordinarily meant by *hope* and is the substance of
what has become known, among psychologists, as secondary reinforcement (type-2). Once established, it alone can produce higher-
order conditioning (as Pavlov demonstrated) and can mediate habit
formation without the occurrence of primary drive reduction (as
Hull and many others have shown).

This way of thinking has many advantages, prominently including
the fact that it makes type-2 secondary reinforcement contingent upon
secondary drive reduction no less than is type-1 secondary reinforcement and that it provides an extremely satisfactory way of thinking
about the phenomenon or *disappointment* or *frustration*. The latter
typically occurs when a "promise" is made but is not fulfilled—see the
dashed line in the "safety signal" and the wavy line in the fear response.

Here then we have, in systematic relation to each other, the four
major affects: *fear, relief, hope,* and *disappointment*. And earlier sections have suggested the several roles which these "dynamic" factors
play, in combination with the primary drives, in the instigation and
control of behavior. There are, to be sure, some questions concerning
this schematization which have not as yet been fully answered (Mowrer,
1960, Chapters 4–6); but the obstacles to its acceptance are now trivial
in comparison to the advantages.

XII. Unifying Power of the Present Theory

One of the major aims of this (and the preceding) volume is to
delineate a psychology of learning capable of reconciling and uniting
rival hypotheses. Two-factor learning theory, in the revision that is
here presented, appears to have considerable potency in this respect.
Confidence in its integrative possibilities is especially strengthened by

the fact that many other writers, quite independently, are moving toward much the same position.

In addition to its incorporation of some of the basic thinking of Pavlov and its explanation of many of the phenomena which particularly interested Thorndike, revised two-factor theory (another name would serve as well, or better) is compatible with many of the premises of "field theory" and psychoanalysis. Here we may note especially the positive and negative "valences" which Lewin (1936) attributed to objects in psychological space and the positive and negative "cathexes" of which Freud (1920) often spoke. A positive "valence" or "cathexis," it seems, is simply that attribute ("hope" in our terms) which a stimulus acquires by virtue of its conjunction with important satisfactions; and a negative valence or cathexis, by the same token, is simply that attribute ("fear") which a stimulus acquires

	Decremental (+) reinforcement	Incremental (−) reinforcement
Response-correlated stimuli	I Response facilitation ("habit")	II Response inhibition ("punishment")
Independent stimuli	III Place approach behavior	IV Place avoidance behavior

Fig. 1–6. Schematic representation of the symmetry and scope of two-factor learning theory.

by virtue of its conjunction with discomfort or pain. Revised two-factor theory likewise is congruent with common-sense (and social-psychological) notions about positive and negative "interests" and "attitudes" (Allport, 1935; Thorndike, 1935).

The accompanying diagram shows the four categories of behavior which revised two-factory theory takes into systematic account. Most of the behavior in which Clark Hull and his followers have been interested in falls into categories I and, to some extent, III. Thorndike was mainly interested in I and II. On the other hand, Tolman, Lewin, and other "field theorists" have emphasized behavior falling into categories III and IV. "Response" theorists and "place" theorists have, it seems, engaged in quite unnecessary controversy in this connection. Our present view suggests that both types of learning are valid and important, and must both be included in any conceptual scheme which aspires to completeness.

XIII. Delayed Reinforcement, Generalization, Discrimination, and Skill

In the scheme which is here under discussion, six forms of reinforcement have been identified: (1) primary drive decrement, (2) primary drive increment, (3) secondary drive decrement type-1 (relief), (4) secondary drive decrement type-2 (hope), (5) secondary drive increment type-1 (fear), and (6) secondary drive increment type-2 (disappointment). Reinforcements (1), (3), and (4) are "positive" and reinforcements (2), (5), and (6) are "negative"; and each of these can function with either independent or response-produced types of stimulation, giving thus 12 "learning situations" in all.

Now the picture takes on yet another dimension when it is realized that learning occurs most readily when a stimulus and a reinforcing event occur in close "temporal proximity" but that learning is still possible when there is an intervening interval of not to exceed 30 or 40 seconds. Following a suggestion made by Pavlov, Hull (1943) was able to derive the "gradient of reinforcement" from the phenomenon of *stimulus trace* (or immediate memory). It appears that every stimulus, however brief its objective duration, "lives on" for a time ("reverberates") in the nervous system and that it is this fact which makes delayed reinforcement possible. Reinforcement, strictly speaking, is thus always here-and-now, never really "delayed"; and this "contemporariness" is made possible by the phenomenon of stimulus trace.

There is now extensive research to document the foregoing assumptions; but this has been reviewed earlier (Mowrer, 1960, Chapter 10), and will not be further considered here. And the fact that much longer intervals than those mentioned can be "spanned" by means of *mediating stimuli* will be discussed in the chapter immediately following the present one.

However, learning is complicated and refined in yet another way. When a living organism learns to react (emotionally) to a particular signal or conditioned stimulus, it has a tendency to react also to similar stimuli (without specific experience with them) according to a bell-shaped curve known as the (double) *generalization gradient*. The biological economy in such an arrangement is obvious; but it also happens that such extension of learned reactions is sometimes not warranted—it may, in fact, be decidedly maladaptive; and so living organisms are capable of *discrimination,* which is a means of correcting generalization which has "gone too far."

In one sense, learning itself involves "generalization," of what may be called the *once-always* variety. Conditioning may be said to consist of an inductive process which, in verbal terms, goes as follows: "Event A was followed by event B once, twice, . . . ; event A is *always* (or at least frequently) followed by event B." And when *this* form of learning has "gone too far," i.e., is no longer functional, the phenomenon of *extinction* sets in as a corrective. In like manner, what may be called *one-many* generalization, while basically useful, must also be capable of correction when it is no longer so. This is the role of discrimination.

Against the background of this way of conceiving generalization and discrimination, one is in a position to think about the phenomenon of *skill* in an improved way. The older "bond" conception of habit implied that a skill was just a well-practiced and somewhat over-learned habit. If we now adopt the "feedback" conception of habit, which holds that behavior is "selected" and "guided" by the positive and negative emotions which have become conditioned to response-correlated stimuli, skill reduces to a matter of discrimination. Evidence from many sources now suggests that the musical virtuoso, the athletic prodigy, or the "artist" in some other type of behavior differs from the duffer mainly in being able to make very fine distinctions (discriminations) between the feedback from a performance that is *exactly right* and one that is only approximately so. They know, in other words, more precisely "what they are doing." This is not to say, of course, that there are not congenitally determined factors that are essential to the attainment of unusual skill; but to these must always be added a highly trained, highly "discriminating ear" or other means of sensing what is "going on." Without this perceptiveness and sensitivity, if our theory is correct, there can be no high artistry or unusual "motor" accomplishment.

And from this same general orientation also comes a helpful suggestion concerning the nature of so-called *response* generalization. As already noted, "ordinary" generalization is *stimulus* generalization, in the sense that a response which has been conditioned to one stimulus is capable of being elicited (somewhat less vigorously) by similar stimuli. By contrast, response generalization is said to involve the tendency for a stimulus or situation which has become capable of eliciting a given response to be capable also of eliciting a family of related or "similar" responses. (Sometimes this phenomenon is known as "transfer of training" or, more simply, "transfer.") If, now, it turns out that the selection and control of behavior is dependent, not upon the stamping-in of S—R bonds in the Thorndikian sense, but upon the making of conditioned "connections" between response-correlated stimuli and certain emotions, then so-called response generalization becomes, in the final analysis, merely a special case of *stimulus* generalization. The full implications of this inference remain to be explored; but, from preliminary examination, they look very promising.

XIV. Tasks for Later Chapters—and for the Future

Because the theory of learning which has been outlined in this chapter (and more fully developed in *Learning Theory and Behavior*) is, in many ways, unusually comprehensive and inclusive, it may at first seem odd that a second, elaborating volume is deemed necessary. For some purposes, it is not. But the very fact that this new approach *is* comprehensive and fraught with far-flung implications means (a) that it can be fruitfully extended into avenues where a less adequate theory would be "lost" and (b) that, inherent in it, there are also some difficulties which call for further consideration.

As already intimated in this chapter, there is now a growing body of fact and conjecture concerning *mediating functions* which could not be properly considered in the earlier book and which lead, very naturally, into the *psychology of language*. Here, in turn, we find a limitation—but also a challenge—in that the phenomenon of *meaning* manifestly involves learned reactions which transcend those thus far discussed and calls for a reconsideration of *imagery*. And, over and beyond all this, is the fact that in abandoning the connectionist conception of habit, one is thrown back upon that ever-puzzling problem of *consciousness*. The emerging science of *cybernetics* gives promise, however, of unusual assistance here and calls for careful attention.

Finally, if a more adequate conception of the total learning process thus emerges (largely from the study of animal behavior), it is natural to ask what its implications are for those distinctively human problems which are denoted by such terms as "personality," "social learning," and "psychopathology." Even at the end of this volume, many questions will remain unanswered; and we shall see, in retrospect, that although we have come a long ways, the road is *still* opening before us, inviting further inquiry.

2

Latent Learning, Punishment, and Extinction and the Concept of Mediation

With the concept of mediation we make the transition from "simple" behavior to the more complex, "symbolic" processes. But this concept is broadly adumbrated in phenomena which are ordinarily thought of as strictly "instrumental," or nonsymbolic. For example, in Chapter 10 of the companion volume, *Learning Theory and Behavior*, there is considerable reference to stimuli (both independent and response-produced) which serve to span or "bridge" temporal intervals which exceed the natural gradients of primary reinforcement and thus "mediate" learning which would otherwise not occur. And in Chapter 12 of the same volume, an explanation is given of so-called "response generalization" in terms of ordinary stimulus generalization; and the latter, in turn, implies a primitive form of "mediation" (see also Postman, 1958). If a human subject, as a result of exposure to paired presentations of a tone (of given pitch and intensity) and an electric shock, has been conditioned to respond to that tone with fear (as indexed by the galvanic skin response), we expect him, as a matter of course, to show the same response (though not so strongly) to somewhat different (higher and lower or louder and softer) tones. The factor of "similarity" may be said to "mediate" or "carry" the subject's reaction from the original (specifically conditioned) tone to the other (not specifically conditioned) tones. Here, in the instances cited, is a mechanism which, when elaborated, provides the basis for some remarkable behavioral and "intellectual" feats.

In this chapter we shall examine this mechanism as it has been identified and studied in the learning laboratory.

I. Early Studies of Latent Learning

Few topics have a history as dramatic, and as tortuous, as that of "latent learning." The problem of selection and organization of material for a chapter on this subject which will do justice to the intricacies of fact and theory and at the same time not be unduly long is an acute one. While it will thus not be feasible to review the history of this topic comprehensively, we can be thorough at least to the extent of beginning at the beginning. Then we shall soon discover that recent theoretical developments throw new light upon the old, established facts. Here we find particularly convincing evidence for the notion that "habit" is a set of "valences" rather than a drive-response "bond" and that the concept of response (really "stimulus") mediation is a powerful and versatile one.

The first systematic study of "latent learning" was carried out at the University of California in 1929 by H. C. Blodgett, who was also the first to employ the term. The objective of his study Blodgett stated thus:

> The purpose of this investigation was to study the efficiency of units of practice when unaccompanied by rewards. The method devised was that of running two groups of rats through the maze: an *experimental group* which received no reward during the first part of learning, but which suddenly had reward introduced in the latter part of learning, and a *control group* which received reward throughout the whole of learning. The answer to the question as to the efficiency of non-rewarded units of practice was sought in a comparison of the learning curve of the experimental group (both before and after the introduction of reward) with that of the control group (p. 113).

In referring to the literature which was relevant to his study, Blodgett found it necessary to cite only three previous investigations. One by Simmons (1924) had only an indirect bearing and will not be described here; but a study by Lashley (1918) and one by Szymanski (1918) are closely related to Blodgett's work and are summarized by Blodgett as follows:

> Lashley, in a maze experiment upon distribution of practice, throws some light upon our problem. There were only 25 rats in all, divided into four

groups: Group A was allowed to run about in the maze for 20 minutes the day before the first run. During training, this group was given reward at the end of the run. Group B was a control, run once a day with the incentive of food; Group C was run the same as A but was not allowed to correct errors; and Group D was run with the incentive of food screened in the food box [cf. the Watson and the Warden-Haas experiments, cited in Chapter 10 of *Learning Theory and Behavior*]. The quickest learning was made by Group A, the group which explored the maze for 20 minutes before the first run. The record of the control group, Group B, was next best, Group C was third, and Group D, last.

Szymanski has published a series of articles upon the learning of maze habits with various kinds of reward. One of his experiments is closely related to our problem. Three rats were run through a maze to their home cage in which food had been placed. The rats were not hungry. At the end of 61 trials there was no reduction in time and error scores. Then the condition of experiment was changed so that the rats were run when they were hungry. They ran the maze perfectly in one or two trials (p. 114).

The Blodgett study was divided into several parts, but the one of most immediate importance for us was carried out, in the maze shown in Fig. 2–1, as follows:

Group I. *Control*—This group consisted of 36 rats run once a day for seven days and allowed to eat for *three minutes in the food box at the end of each run.* They were then removed to another cage (not the living-cage) and allowed to finish their day's ration, after which they were returned to their living-cages.

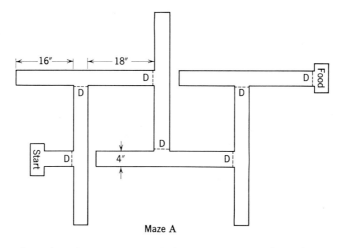

Maze A

Fig. 2–1. Floor plan of maze used by Blodgett (1929, p. 117) in study described in text. Doors, indicated by the letter "D" and dotted line, were closed behind rat as it moved through the maze from Start to Food Box.

Group II. *Experimental*—This group also consisted of 36 rats. (They were litter mates of Group I. . . .) *For the first six days*, Group II found no food in the food box and were kept in it without reward for two minutes. They were then removed to another cage (not the living-cage) where they were fed after an interval of approximately one hour. Only then were they returned to their living-cages. *For day seven and the two subsequent days* they were treated exactly like Group I; that is, they found food in the food box for three minutes and finished their day's ration immediately afterward in another cage.

Group III. *Experimental*—This group consisted of 25 rats. Like Group II, they began with no reward at the end of the maze. But for them such reward was introduced at the end of the third day rather than at the end of the seventh day (pp. 119–120).

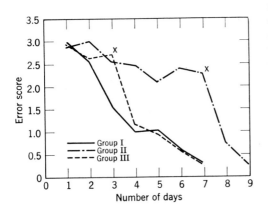

Fig. 2–2. Results of Blodgett's original study of latent learning (1929, p. 120). The solid curve shows the rate of maze learning by a group of 36 hungry rats which received food reward on each day's run. Point X on the other two curves indicates the introduction of food reward for the first time in comparable experimental groups. The precipitous improvement in performance thereafter is supposedly a reflection of prior learning which had remained "latent."

The results, in terms of errors made in getting through the maze on the successive daily trials, are shown in Fig. 2–2. Here it is apparent that in both Group II and Group III there was a decided (and statistically significant) drop in errors on the trial immediately succeeding the first rewarded one (indicated by the letter "x").

Do these sudden drops in errors which come after the introduction of reward indicate that something to be called *latent learning* developed during the non-reward period—latent learning which made itself manifest after the reward had been presented? (p. 122).

After a statistical analysis of his results, Blodgett concludes:

Taking these two results together, the hypothesis that the periods of non-reward in groups II and III really produced *latent learning* which became manifest when a reward was introduced seems well supported (pp. 123–124).

At the time the original Blodgett study was carried out, little was known about the operation of secondary reinforcers, either incremental or decremental. Therefore, when Blodgett spoke of "practice unaccompanied by reward," he meant, obviously, the *primary* reinforcement, or reward, provided by food and hunger reduction. The question therefore arises as to the extent to which "latent learning" may be due, not to primary reinforcement, which Blodgett excluded, but to subtle sources of secondary reinforcement.

In 1929–30, G. W. Haney (1932), also working at the University of California, repeated Blodgett's experiment with a view to checking on the following possibility. He said:

> Blodgett removed his rats from the maze at the end of each run; hence there is the possible criticism that there may have been an element of reward even for the so-called non-rewarded rats in always going through the maze in the forward direction and in the fact of the mere removal from the maze and the return to the home cages at the end of each such forward run (p. 320).

In order to obviate this difficulty, Haney performed a different type of experiment, one rather similar to a part of the investigation by Lashley, previously referred to. In it, on four successive days rats were allowed to wander about, without restriction, in a maze for a period of 18 hours. They were then returned to the home cage but not fed for three hours; at the end of six hours, following return to the home cage, they were again put back into the maze. Animals in a control group were treated in the same way, except that their 18-hour periods of exploration were in "a simple rectangular maze."

When tested in what may be called the *experimental* maze, by being put into and released from the starting box, with food in the goal box, the animals which had become familiar with this maze did significantly better, in terms of error scores, than did the control animals, which had explored in the rectangular maze. Haney concluded:

> 1. Under the conditions of this investigation, error differences between rats having previous general familiarity with the maze and those having none, seem to be real differences. The critical ratio of 8.8 is indicative of a significant difference.
> 2. Under the same conditions the time score differences are not so significant (p. 333).

Since Haney's findings are in essential agreement with those of Blodgett (and Lashley), it seems clear that whatever secondary reinforcement may have been derived by Blodgett's experimental subjects by being lifted out of the maze following each day's no-food run was

not responsible for the results obtained. Indeed, the operation of secondary reinforcement would not, in any case, account for *latent*
learning, since the effects of such reinforcement, whether decremental
or incremental, would have been no less *manifest* during training than
would performance changes brought about by primary reward or
punishment. Therefore, further analysis of this problem along these
lines does not seem very promising.

It is not surprising that the experiments just reviewed released a
flood of new research. In an article published by Thistlethwaite (1951)
and entitled, "A Critical Review of Latent Learning and Related Experiments," there is a bibliography of 76 titles; and the number of pertinent
studies since published is probably equally great. These studies make
fascinating reading, but we cannot hope to review all of them, even in
outline form. Instead, we shall turn for the time being to studies of
latent *punishment* and then revert, later, to latent learning in the positive or decremental sense.

II. Latent Punishment and the Mechanism of Mediation

In 1933 Tolman published a highly readable and intriguing paper
with the title, "Sign-Gestalt or Conditioned Reflex?" The reader can
put himself in the proper mental "set" for appreciating this study by
asking this question: What would have happened, in the Blodgett investigation, if on the seventh day the animals in Group II, instead of
receiving reward (for the first time) as a result of *running* through the
maze, had been *placed* (by the experimenter) in the goal box with
food present?

Says Tolman:

The general fact that specific acts tend to be learned or not learned according to the "goodness" or "badness" of their consequences is an empirical generalization with which, I suppose, we would now all agree. Our dis-
putes will arise not with respect to this empirical fact but rather with regard
to the hypothesis we would adopt for its underlying explanation. The "trial
and error" psychologists would explain this influence of consequences upon
the learning by their laws of "effect." They would say that those stimulus-
response connections which are followed by "good" effects, whether these
latter be conceived as pleasure, increased sensory consequences, or what not,
will be strengthened, whereas those which are followed by "bad" effects will
be weakened. And they will hint at various neurological concepts to explain
this back-action of effects upon learning. But it is not this trial and error
doctrine, in any of its forms, in which I am interested in this paper. Rather
I wish now to draw your attention to a conditioned response doctrine of
consequences (p. 246).

In a moment we shall return to Tolman's discussion; but it is well to pause long enough to indicate why such extended quotation from this study is desirable. In the first place, we shall here again see (cf. Mowrer, 1960, Chapter 9) how closely Tolman has come to the conception of learning which underlies our present approach. Here, in the paragraphs which are to follow, he lays the basis for deriving trial-and-error learning from conditioning and for thus reducing all learning, in the final analysis, to conditioning—or what he preferred to call sign learning. At the same time, he also advances some of the historically important logical considerations out of which the concept of response (stimulus) mediation eventually emerged. Tolman continues:

At first blush it might seem that the conditioned response psychologists could have no doctrine of consequences. For in their original and pristine statement they seem to assert that a response gets learned (i.e., attached to a new stimulus) in so far as that new stimulus has been presented enough times preceding or just simultaneously with an original stimulus. Good or bad consequences do not come into the picture. It is the mere concatenation of the two stimuli which does the work. And yet the conditioned response psychologists, at least those in this country, do have a doctrine of consequences. And one can but admit that they, in achieving it, have been both "as wise as serpents and as harmless as doves." For they have invented a way of allowing for the different effects of good and bad consequences and yet at the same time of apparently still adhering to their original *bona fide* conditioning principles. Let me illustrate in terms of a concrete experiment.

[Figure 2–3] shows the ground plan of a discrimination box similar to one which I have been recently using. B and W are black and white curtains hanging just behind the two exits from the choice box. They are interchangeable. The task is always to choose the white curtain. D is a door which in each trial is so placed that, if the animal chooses the white curtain he gets to the food, whereas, if he chooses the black he runs into a blind alley and also he can be given an electric shock in this blind alley. How do our conditioned response friends explain such a discrimination learning?

They argue somewhat as follows: Learning consists in conditioning a positive response to the white curtain and a negative response to the black curtain. The rat learns to enter the door which, in the given trial, has the white curtain behind it because this white-curtained door, as a stimulus, is followed by a free open path and by food. And to such free open path and food the positive responses of approach and of eating are already attached. That is, the unconditioned positive responses which the animal makes to the food or to the free open path get conditioned back to the stimulus, white-curtained door, which always precedes them. Similarly the rat learns *not* to enter the black-curtained door because this latter, as stimulus, is always followed by the further stimuli of blind end and electric grill to which latter negative responses are already attached. And these negative responses get conditioned back to the black curtain which just precedes them.

It appears that what our conditioned response friends really do is to divide

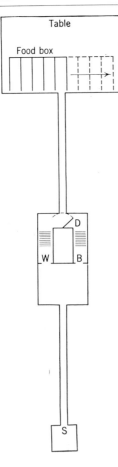

Fig. 2–3. Floor plan of apparatus used by Tolman (1933, p. 247) in testing deductions concerning "sign-gestalt expectations."

all responses into two sorts—positive and negative. And they argue that in a trial and error situation the acts which get learned are those which result in bringing the animal into the presence of further stimuli to which positive responses are already attached. And the acts which do not get learned are those which result in bringing the animal into the presence of further stimuli to which negative responses are already attached. These resultant positive and negative responses get conditioned back to the cue stimuli. It must be noted, however, that the positive and negative responses which thus get conditioned back may in concrete terms be as different from the original responses from which they are supposed to be derived as entering is from eating or as non-entering is from jumping back and squealing. But this last is a little point which is not stressed by the theory. Our conditioned response friends are truly both serpentish and dovelike (pp. 248–249).

Again we interrupt the flow of Tolman's argument in the interests of clarification. Obviously the classical conception of conditioning, which Tolman is describing here, is much too simple to account adequately for the observed facts. As elsewhere indicated (Mowrer, 1960), it is not overt behavioral responses themselves that get "conditioned" but rather certain emotional (autonomic) reactions, notably those of hope and fear, which then in turn goad, guide, and correct behavior so as to make it move along sensible and biologically useful lines. This modification makes ample provision for the flexibility of behavior to which Tolman alludes; and it also provides a fuller and more explicit basis for the "doctrine of consequences" which he is here describing.

But let us not be too captious. For it must be admitted that this conditioned response formula, even though it be thus a bit—shall we say—jesuitical, is really surprisingly workable. It can be applied usefully to most discrimination box and maze problems and, as such, it seems to provide a helpful schema for holding together past results and for predicting future ones. Nevertheless my purpose here must be to show that there are (or at any rate there ought to be) types of maze or discrimination box findings for which this all-useful though emasculated conditioned response formula will not hold.

By way of a first example, let me return to an experiment of my own which used a discrimination box like that just shown. After having, as part of another problem, overtrained rats in this discrimination box, I tried putting them directly into the food compartments and shocking them then and there. Then I carried them immediately around to S and started a run in the usual fashion. My assumption was that as a result of all their preceding training, in which they had been running through the box as the way to get food, the rats would have built up what in my barbarous terminology I have called sign-gestalt expectations.[1] These sign-gestalt expectations I assumed would be to the effect that the earlier parts of the discrimination apparatus would have become a sign or a set of signs to the rats that the encountering of the food compartments was to be achieved by running through this discrimination apparatus. And, if the rats had built up such sign-gestalt expectations, I assumed further that a single experience of the changed character of the food compartments (or, as I should put it, this changed character of the significates of the sign-gestalts) should have been enough so that upon being reintroduced to the signs (that is, to the first parts of the discrimination box) the rats would at once have inferred or remembered this new changed character in the goal compartments. And hence they should have refused to run.

[1] This elaboration [says Tolman] of the conditioned reflex formula is probably to be credited in the first instance to Smith and Guthrie (1921), to Wilson (1924) and to Frank (1923). See also Guthrie (1930). Recently it has been further elaborated in a series of striking articles by Hull (1929, 1930a, 1930b, 1931, 1932). Finally, for a criticism of it see Williams (1929).

But alas, no such thing. Each rat (I must confess that I tried it with only four), after having been shocked in the food compartment and then carried to the starting point, immediately dashed off gaily and just as usual through the whole discrimination apparatus and bang whack into the very food compartment in which he has just been shocked. If the rats had sign-gestalt expectations, then sign-gestalt expectations are not as intelligent as I have supposed them to be (pp. 69–72).

In 1935, in a paper entitled "A Reply to 'Sign-Gestalt or Conditioned Reflex?'" N. E. Miller reported positive findings in a situation similar to that outlined by Tolman, but suggested a different way of interpreting them. Miller began by saying:

In a very interesting and provocative paper, Professor Tolman has maintained that, on the basis of sign-gestalt theory, "insightful" behavior ought to occur in a certain learning situation. He has also expressed the opinion that, if this behavior actually does occur, it will be unexplainable in terms of conditioning (p. 280).

Then, after briefly describing the Tolman experiment, Miller continued:

The apparent stupidity of the rats might seem to be wholly in line with the principles of conditioning. However, it is our opinion that such a view would be based on a misconception of the potentials of conditioned-response mechanisms. It is true that the intelligent behavior expected by sign-gestalt would not itself be a simple conditioned reaction. But there is reason to believe that it should be produced, as something new, by the interaction of several familiar principles of conditioning. In fact, a conditioned-response analysis of the sign-gestalt experiment reveals a probable reason for the negative results and leads one to predict that the insightful behavior should appear when the experiment is appropriately modified. . . .

The discrimination apparatus, which happened to be a part of Professor Tolman's set up, is not essential to the issue at stake. So let us eliminate it and consider the case of the hungry animal running down a single alley for food. The animal already possesses responses to joint stimulation from hunger and food. Following Professor Hull's (1931) terminology, we shall call these responses, such as eating, salivating and related behavior, the goal responses. Since the goal responses, reinforced by food, regularly take place immediately following and during stimulation from cues in the food box, they should become conditioned to these cues.

But the reinforced goal responses also occur regularly a short interval after stimulation by the cues from the starting box and from the several portions of the alley. Now, it is well known that if reinforcement regularly occurs a short interval after a given stimulus, a trace conditioned reaction to that stimulus tends to be set up and that there is a strong tendency for this trace conditioned reaction to antedate its reinforcement (Pavlov, 1927; Switzer, 1934). Thus there should be a strong tendency for the goal responses to occur in the alley and in the starting box.

This theoretical expectation is given convincing empirical support by the well established fact that even reactions near the goal, such as the last turn leading to food, show a strong tendency to intrude into the earlier portions of a maze sequence (Spence & Shipley, 1934; Spragg, 1934). However, it is practically impossible for the complete goal reaction to take place without the actual presence of food. So one would expect only some parts of the goal reaction to take place in the starting box, the alley, and in the section of the end box preceding the food. These might be such items of behavior as incipient mouth and head movements. Let us follow Hull's (1931) terminology again and call these antedating, fractional components of the goal response which would occur in the starting box and the alley, *anticipatory goal responses*.

Now, the principles of physiology lead us to expect these antedating responses to produce a certain amount of characteristic interoceptive stimulation. Thus, when the animal is placed directly into the food box and then shocked, the cues there will necessarily be expected to arouse anticipatory (or complete) goal responses and the stimuli from these responses must precede and coincide with the shock. The responses to the shock will therefore be conditioned to these interoceptive [response-produced] stimuli.

When the hungry animal is placed in the starting box, the cues there will, as has been shown, lead to similar anticipatory goal responses. These responses will produce some of the interoceptive stimuli to which the reaction to shock have just been conditioned. The animal should, accordingly, be expected to exhibit in the starting box or the alley certain components of the withdrawing, crouching, sitting behavior which characterizes a rat's conduct following shock.[2] Thus, we have deduced from strict conditioned response principles that behavior related to the shock should appear in a situation (the starting box and alley) which, to state it anthropomorphically, might on the basis of past experience be expected to lead to the shock even though this situation has *never* itself directly preceded the shock. This type of transfer of training [note the term!] is commonly called foresight.

Let us restate our analysis in brief, dogmatic form. The laws of trace conditioning demand anticipatory goal responses. The fact that the same reinforcement follows both the food box and the alley requires that the anticipatory goal responses to these two be at least partially identical. The interoceptive stimulation from these similar anticipatory responses is the common element by which the conditioning of the shock is transferred from the food box to the alley (pp. 281–283).

There is much food for thought in the preceding paragraphs, so let us pause in order to analyze and assimilate what is being said. First of all, we see that Miller is proposing a formula which is applicable to a considerable range of phenomena. In the passages quoted, Miller himself refers to *insight* and *foresight*, but his hypothesis seems to apply equally to instances of behavior which are termed "latent learning"

---

[2] Here Miller, too, is expositing the classical conception of conditioning. We would now say that it is *fear* which is conditioned in this situation and that it then *motivates* overt acts of the kind described.

and "reasoning" (see Chapter 6). And the key concept is what has since been termed *response mediation*. As Miller suggests, "transfer" of learning from one situation to another quite different situation can be expected to occur *if some item of behavior*, implicit or overt, *is common to both*. Actually, of course, it is not the communality of behavior, as such, in the two situations that provides the basis of transfer of training but, as Miller shows, the *communality of stimulation* which the occurrence of the same or similar behavior in the two situations produces. Hence it is more accurate to speak, not of response mediation, but of *stimulus mediation*, or, more exactly still, of response-produced-stimulus mediation. (That this is inherently the same logic as employed by Miller is indicated by his use of such terms as "transfer," "partially identical" responses, and "common elements." Note also his reference to "interoceptive stimulation.")

This way of thinking can be made more readily comprehensible, perhaps, by the following analogy. Suppose that a rat has been trained to find food at the end of a black L-maze. Suppose also that the goal box of the maze (not visible from the starting point) is painted white. But now suppose that the rat, after the training just described but while *satiated*, is *placed* in the white goal box, with a barrier to prevent escape, and given one or more electric shocks. Later, after the rat has been removed from the maze and allowed to get hungry, it is put back into the maze, at the usual starting point. But now, as the rat looks down the first leg of the maze, suppose that, instead of seeing the uniform black interior, it sees, on the wall, immediately back of the turning point, a large patch of *white*. It would be in no way surprising, certainly, if the rat, though hungry, would show conflict in the first leg of the maze or perhaps completely refuse to leave the starting area. Here one of the stimuli which had been associated with the electric shock has "moved forward" in the maze and effectively inhibits the rat with respect to a type of behavior (running the maze) for which it has *never been punished*. The white area seen down the alley, at the turn, "reminds" the rat of the shock received in the goal box and immobilizes it. Or, to be more precise, the fear conditioned to the white end compartment in which shock was experienced generalizes to the white area, near the turn, and produces anticipatory or "foresightful" inhibition.

Such "foresight" (in the quite literal sense!) is manifestly an instance of stimulus mediation. If, on the other hand, the interior of the maze is left completely unchanged (i.e., all black) following shock in white goal box, the animal may still, as suggested by Miller, show foresight.

But now the inhibition of behavior must be produced by fear which is conditioned, not to some external stimulus, but to some response-produced stimulus or stimulus pattern. Hence one would expect that, under these conditions, the rat would have to be hungry and to have made some of the "goal responses" just as the shock was applied, so that *they,* when later occurring in the starting box or maze, would produce stimulation to which fear had been conditioned and would thus arouse fear and inhibit behavior which, in the ordinary sense of the term, had never itself been punished.[3]

Thus we arrive at one of the major unifications of field (sign-gestalt) theory and stimulus-response (conditioning) theory. Tolman was eminently right in predicting the phenomenon; but Miller, as a representative of the stimulus-response school, gave the first fully explicit *rationale* for such behavior. Tolman, it will be recalled, in the paper cited speaks at some length about the wide applicability of conditioning principles but holds them to be incapable of explaining behavior of the kind described. Miller's analysis quite straightforwardly deduces the phenomenon from conditioning principles, though in introducing the concept of anticipatory (mediating) responses and the concept of fear one is going somewhat beyond the type of conditioning theory which was prevalent when Tolman wrote his paper and Miller replied to it.

---

[3] Mediated (foresightful) behavior of the kinds just described would, if real (see Sections III–V), have such obvious biological value that it has apparently not occurred to anyone previously to ask if they might ever be maladaptive. But a student, Mr. Jerry Griffith, upon reading the galley proof of this chapter, *has* asked this question. The answer seems to be that, although very generally useful, such behavior *can* be useless, nonfunctional, misleading. Let us revert, for the sake of simplicity, to the hypothetical L-maze experiment, in which the mediating stimulus is provided by the environment, rather than being response-produced. Although a patch of white at the turn, which is visible from the starting point, would almost certainly tend to operate, psychologically, in the manner suggested, there is no inherent reason why the appearance of such a patch would *necessarily* indicate that shock would now again be experienced in the goal box. Its presence *might* mean, quite specifically, that goal-box shock would *not* occur. Therefore, if the subject, on the basis of stimulus generalization, reacted to the patch as to the whiteness of the goal box itself, such a reaction would, under these conditions, be quite "wrong." But this rather special example does not in the least impugn the supposition that response (stimulus) mediation is, in general, highly advantageous and helpful. What it does show is that, in some situations, response-mediated generalization has to be corrected by further (discriminative) learning (see Mowrer, 1960, Chapter 12). Cf. the subsequent discussion in this chapter of response-mediated discrimination; also, in Chapter 6, the idea of wrong "insights."

III. A Theoretical Deduction Empirically Confirmed

Now that Miller has given us such an excellent *theory* of "latent learning" (incremental type) and related phenomena, it might be nice to know if it is *so*. Fortunately, in the same paper Miller also reports confirmatory data. We return to Miller's account of his work.

But the sign-gestalt [Tolman's] rats did not exhibit the foresightful behavior demanded by the conditioned response analysis. How can this be accounted for? It will be remembered that the foresightful behavior was deduced from the assumption that a distinctive response, affording a characteristic pattern of interoceptive stimulation, was present in the food box. If this response was absent during the original training to run the alley, components of it could not become anticipatory. If this response was absent or only weakly functional when the animals were placed directly into the food box and shocked, the reactions to the shock could not become conditioned to any characteristic pattern of interoceptive stimulation. In either case the insightful behavior would not manifest itself. If, on the other hand, an experiment should be arranged in which the distinctive response affording the crucial interoceptive stimulation was sure to be present in gross form, the insightful behavior should appear.

Fig. 2–4. End boxes employed by Miller (1935*a*, p. 284) requiring subject to make distinctive responses just before and as reward was obtained.

To test this logic, several experiments were set up in which the reward devices illustrated [in Fig. 2–4] forced the animals to make very gross and distinctive responses in order to secure the lure after entering the end box of the alley. In one reward device the animal was forced to climb up and make a sharp turn to the right to secure food; in the other he must go straight in and make a sharp turn to the left to secure water.

In the first experiment seven animals, motivated by both hunger and thirst, were trained to run down a short alley at the end of which they found only the special reward device containing food. At other intervals during this preliminary learning these animals were placed in a special cage, isolated from the alley, and given separate training to use both the food and the water reward devices there, one at a time. . . .

Then three of the seven animals were put through the following procedure: The rat was placed in the special isolated cage which contained only the food in its reward device. As soon as he had climbed up, turned to the right in the accustomed manner and taken his first bite of food, he was shocked for one second. Then he was given time to get off the grid and was kept in this special cage for a two-minute period during which he was given an additional immediate shock each time he touched the grid. At the end of this period he was taken out and placed in another cage for three minutes in order to allow the general disturbance from the shock . . . to subside somewhat. After this, he was placed in the starting box of the alley. The length of time it took him to reach the last curtain [there were four curtains in the alley, the last just before entry into the food box] was recorded. The reward device was now absent from the box at the end of the alley. Thus, the animal could be put back into the starting box and given a total of five test runs without danger of secondary conditioning.

The other four rats were put through a similar procedure except that they were shocked in the isolated special cage while using the water reward device.

The experimental results confirmed the deduction from the conditioned response theory. The animals that had been shocked in the isolated food device while performing the act identical with the one ordinarily following their alley behavior sequences, required longer on the average for their first test run through the alley than those that had been shocked in the water-reward device while performing the act *not* associated with the alley (pp. 283–286).

There is more to the Miller study, including other experimental results and statistical analysis of their reliability, but the gist of his argument and findings has been given. His paper ends:

In conclusion, the results of the first two experiments demonstrate that there is generalization of conditioning (in other words, a transfer of training) from the reward device to the alley, which is dependent upon the previous association between the two. A comparison of these results with the negative results of the sign-gestalt experiment (Tolman, 1933) suggests that the distinctiveness of the goal (or near goal) reaction is an important factor in determining the amount of the transfer. The third experiment suggests that the results of the first two would have been still more striking if the reactions in the two reward devices had been more dissimilar.

In the situation used in these experiments, the generalization of conditioning, dependent upon previous association is commonly called foresight. A deduction of this foresightful behavior has been made from strict conditioned-response principles. This conditioned-response analysis may be said to have reduced the concepts used in the sign-gestalt description of foresightful behavior to more basic ones which are amenable to direct investigation and which already have been found useful in the description of hosts of other, quite different situations. The theoretical analysis using these stimulus-response concepts tends to be confirmed by the fact that it suggested the modification which produced the positive experimental results (pp. 290–292) (see also Miller, 1951b, pp. 464–466).

Several years later, Tolman & Gleitman (1949b) published a paper entitled "Equal Reinforcements in Both End-Boxes, Followed by Shock in One End-Box," which was in certain important respects a replication of the Miller study—and which also produced positive results. Tolman & Gleitman summarize their study by saying:

 1. Twenty-five hungry pigmented M and M Tryon stock rats were run in a covered T maze [see Fig. 2–5] to equal food reinforcements at the two ends of the T. The two end-sections were strongly differentiated. The end-boxes were of different size and one had a bright light shining into it and the other was dark. The two entrance sections to these end-boxes also differed. One had baffles and the other a hurdle, and the doors into the end-boxes were somewhat different in size and manner of being hinged.

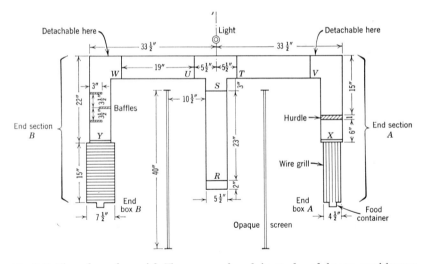

Fig. 2–5. Floorplan of special T-maze employed in study of latent punishment published by Tolman & Gleitman (1949b). As will be apparent from the drawing, the end boxes and the entries thereto were different for the two wings of the maze. The point of these differences was to provide the subjects (rats) with distinctive impressions of the two wings which might mediate foresightful behavior at the choice point (see text).

2. After equal training on the two sides—one free trial and one forced trial per day for nine days—the two end-sections were placed in another room. Half of the rats were shocked in one of the end-boxes and half in the other.

3. When placed back on the maze, 22 out of a total of 25 rats immediately avoided the side leading to the box in which they had just been shocked. In this test trial all animals were run under equal drive strength—i.e., 26 hours of food deprivation.

4. In the original training the total group had been divided into two motivation groups—one 48 hours hungry when originally trained in the maze and the other 12 hours hungry. No differences in the later avoidance of the side leading to the box in which the animals had been shocked appeared between the two motivation groups.

5. Our general theoretical position is that, although the Spence and Lippitt (1946), Kendler (1947), Kendler & Mencher (1948), and Walker (1948) experiments have indicated that "latent learning" under the conditions of their experiments did not appear, this does not disprove the possibility of latent learning appearing under other conditions. All that the sign-Gestalt (or field expectancy) theory of learning assumes is that under some conditions, latent learning—that is *learning which does not involve the differential reinforcement of responses*—can nevertheless take place.

6. The present experiment now seems to have clearly provided such a set of conditions.

7. It is suggested that many further experiments varying such factors as the type of maze set-up, the amounts of initial training, degrees of motivation, forced or non-forced trials, the presence or absence of a reward object for the drive under which the animals are initially trained, and the like are needed in order to discover the precise conditions under which a non-differentially rewarded picking up of discriminanda and discriminanda relationships (i.e., latent learning) will or will not tend to appear (pp. 818–819; italics added).

IV. Seward's Study of Latent Learning

At this point it may be useful to pause and ask: Just what is implied when one speaks of "latent learning"? Several different kinds of "mazes," including a discrimination apparatus, were employed in the studies thus far cited in this chapter; and the common element in all the types of resulting behavior may not be immediately evident. Tolman & Gleitman, in the passage just quoted, give a definition of latent learning when they say: "latent learning—that is the learning which does not involve the differential reinforcement of responses." In the decremental, or reward, sense of reinforcement, the right- and left-turning tendencies of the Tolman-Gleitman subjects were not "differentially reinforced" in that, during the preliminary training, *both* right- and left-going tendencies were reinforced equally. But what about the *incremental* reinforcement, or punishment, employed in the experiment? Was it also applied with equal impartiality? It is true that no animal was ever subjected to shock after having just gone from the starting box in the T-maze to either the right end box or the left end box. Therefore, strictly speaking, one must again say that these responses were not "differentially reinforced." But this does not exclude the possible—indeed, the very probable—operation of the type of mechanism postulated, and apparently demonstrated, by Miller. Of this possibility, Tolman & Gleitman say:

> It is to be recalled that some years ago Miller (1935a) performed an experiment which had features similar to ours, the results of which he explained in reinforcement terms plus the assumption of anticipatory goal-responses. . . .
>
> An especial feature of Miller's argument is that the two very distinctive goal-responses made by the animals in the two end-boxes produce two very distinctive anticipatory goal-responses with two very different resultant proprioceptive stimuli. One of these sets of proprioceptive stimuli gets conditioned in the shock situation to avoidance [fear] and the other does not.
>
> Now it must be admitted that our own experiment involved a somewhat similar set-up. . . . [Therefore] we cannot altogether deny the possibility of such an explanation. Absolutely to settle the issue it would be necessary to repeat our experiment where the two end-boxes differ in "perceptual" characters only and where absolutely no differences in goal response in the two boxes would be involved. However, it may be noted in Seward's experiment (1947a) it was found that white and black goal boxes, when the rats were fed in one and not in the other, gave as positive latent learning results as did a pair of goal boxes which did produce different types of overt responses.
>
> However, it may be asked what about blinking, pupillary reactions or the like? Is it possible to have a perceptual "awareness" of any sort without concomitant motor responses? If it is Miller's (or Seward's) argument that there are such differentiating motor accompaniment for all perceptual processes, then these authors can perhaps hold, if they want to, that what we have called sign-Gestalten are based upon chains of minimal anticipatory responses going on at a very covert level. We, personally, are interested in the functional significance of latent learning and the resultant functional concept of sign-Gestalten and not in extremely hypothetical notions concerning the underlying neurology (pp. 817–818).[4]

[4] It may not be immediately evident to the reader what it is that Tolman objected to in the Miller-type analysis. Manifestly it applied neatly to the experiment which he and Gleitman have here reported. From a general knowledge of Tolman's systematic thinking we may, however, infer that he was privately convinced that foresightful behavior *can* occur without any form of *stimulus* mediation (whether independent or response-produced), i.e., *can* occur, at least under optimal circumstances, on the basis of *pure cognitions* (memories, images, "knowledge")— cf. Chapters 5 and 6.

It may seem that the experiments of Tolman, Miller, and Tolman & Gleitman, just reviewed, have departed considerably from the investigation by Blodgett previously described in this chapter. These experiments have departed, perhaps most indisputably, in that they have all involved punishment, whereas the Blodgett study did not. But these investigations have been selected for special consideration because they, probably better than any others, show the development and explanatory power of the concept of *response mediation* or, more accurately, *response-produced-stimulation mediation*. With the mediation, or transfer, notion now well in mind, let us turn from experiments on what might be called "latent punishment" to further consideration, in the same general frame of reference, of latent learning where the main result is produced, not by incremental reinforcement, but by decremental reinforcement or reward. Here a study published by Seward (1949) and entitled, "An Experimental Analysis of Latent Learning," comes conveniently to hand. The author begins:

How does a rat learn a maze? According to reinforcement theory (Hull, 1943), when a rat chooses the correct path his responses lead more directly to food and thus receive a greater share of primary or secondary reinforcement than when he enters a blind alley. In later trials he reacts on the basis of differential strengths of habit thus produced. According to sign-Gestalt theory (Tolman, 1932) a rat learns a maze by running it; he then chooses on the basis of anticipated consequences. If hungry he takes the path that leads, in his experience, to a food place. To decide between these views we must separate running the maze from feeding in it; learning should then be retarded by the first view but not by the second. The latent-learning experiment is thus a crucial one. In it the rat first explores an empty maze; he then finds food at some point in it; whereupon he has been found to run the maze as well as if fed there from the beginning (Blodgett, 1929; Tolman & Honzik, 1930).

Elsewhere I have tried to envisage the essential mechanism of maze learning as revealed by the latent learning experiment (Seward, 1947b). It involves two stages: (1) the rat builds up differential anticipatory responses to the right and left cues at the choice point; (2) one of these responses becomes associated with food. As a result the rat now reacts to the appropriate cue because response to it is "reinforced" (i.e., facilitated) by food anticipation [or, in terms of the thinking evolved in *Learning Theory and Behavior*, secondary reinforcement, in the sense of hunger-fear reduction]. To test this interpretation let us suppose that a rat is allowed to explore a simple T-maze with all outside cues removed and with endboxes clearly differentiated but out of sight from the choice point. He is then put directly into one of the endboxes, where he finds and eats food for the first time. After this experience he is placed in the starting box and allowed to choose either arm of the maze. The above interpretation leads us to predict that the rat will go directly to the box in which he has been fed. There is one important proviso: the endboxes must be distinguished in such a way as to arouse *different responses* which can be partially reinstated at the choice point on the critical trial. Otherwise the rat will be left with no medium to serve as a connection between choice-point cues and anticipated food (p. 177).

Before reviewing Seward's empirical findings, it is well to remark briefly upon certain features, expressed and implied, of the foregoing paragraphs. It is apparent, first of all, that Seward's conception of latent learning follows along lines very similar to those laid down by Miller in his 1935 paper. The "different responses" stressed by Seward clearly serve as *mediators* for the transfer of learning from one part of the maze (the goal box) to another (the choice point). Seward does not speak explicitly of response mediation (nor does Miller, for that matter); but his intention is clear and he comes very close to the term itself in saying that without these "different responses," the rat "will be left with no *medium* to serve as a connection between choice-point cues and anticipated food."

One other point should also be considered. As already noted in connection with the problem of latent punishment, it would be in no way surprising if, after being shocked in a white goal box, a rat avoided going to that box if an area of white could be *seen* from the choice point; indeed, the rat might even refuse to go to the choice point, if an area of white could be seen just beyond it (cf. Section II). Let us now apply this type of stimulus mediation (or generalization) to latent learning, rather than to latent punishment. In the type of situation described by Seward, the procedure might consist of first letting the subjects freely explore a T-maze, as proposed, then feeding the rats (individually) in one of the goal boxes, which is painted *white*. Later, if a patch of white were placed near the white goal box and in such a position that it could be *seen* from the choice point, it would not be at all surprising if the rats made a high percentage of "correct" choices on the first trial, i.e., with no "practice" (see Mowrer, 1960, Chapter 10, Section X). The correct performance would be stimulus-mediated, but this is not to say that it occurred without "differential reinforcement." It is true, of course, that no particular *response* has been "differentially reinforced"; but a *stimulus* has been—and this, it seems, is all that is necessary to produce "latent learning." Thus, the negative definition of latent learning, given by Tolman & Gleitman, as "learning which does not involve the differential reinforcement of responses" needs to be supplemented by a positive statement. This might take the following form: latent learning occurs (and will later be *manifested*) when some stimulus which will later be produced by a given response is first produced independently and conditioned to either hope or fear, such a stimulus being properly known as a *mediator*.[5]

V. Latent Learning Analyzed Further

Now this type of thinking, suggested by Seward's experiment and by earlier discussion in this chapter, may have an interesting bearing upon the findings reported by Blodgett. In his experiment there was, to be sure, only *one* goal box, but there were many blind alleys. Suppose, then, that on the seventh day of experimentation, instead of being allowed to *run* through the maze into the alley containing the goal box and there, for the first time, finding food, the rat had, on this day, been passively carried to and *placed* in the now baited goal box. Suppose that, in addition, as the rat ate it "noticed" (see Chapter 5) certain features of the experimental room which could be seen *directly above* the goal box. On the basis of familiar and well-established principles, we would expect these visual stimuli to take on some degree of secondary reinforcement. What, then, would be the most likely result when, next day, the rat was allowed to *run* the maze? If some of the extra-maze stimuli which had been seen and thus secondarily reinforced while the rat ate in the goal box could now be seen *from other*

[5] If the foregoing sentence is not entirely clear to the reader, let him take comfort: on rereading it, in galley proof, the writer is not certain he knows exactly what it means, either. Perhaps these additional comments will help. First of all, let it be observed that in all forms of mediated learned behavior, what happens is this: the mediating stimulus (either response-produced or independent) occurs in a "new" situation and makes it sufficiently similar to, or reminiscent of, an "old" situation that there will be a generalization, or transfer, of learning from the old situation to the new one. In other words, the mediator makes the new situation enough *like* the old situation that it produces the same or at least a somewhat similar type of behavior. Here, presumably, is the essential and common feature of latent learning (and punishment), foresight, sensory preconditioning (Section VI), and insight (see Chapter 6). This position will be given further support in the section which follows. But one thing more needs to be said here. In experiments of the kinds presently under discussion, the "new situation" is usually one that is physically (often spatially) different from the original one: for example, the difference between the goal box and the starting box or alleys of a maze. The difference might, however, be entirely *internal*: e.g., a change in drive state or in the neural trace from prior stimulation (see Mowrer, 1960, Chapters 10 and 12). But this qualification does not, it seems, alter the basic principles which have been postulated, although it may be that there are aspects of the problem which have not yet been thoroughly analyzed and that a more felicitous terminology could be developed for the whole area.

parts of the maze, we might reasonably expect the rat's maze responses to be differentially satisfying, depending upon whether they carried the rat *toward* or *away from* these "cues," or secondary reinforcers.

If this were the way "latent learning" operated in the Blodgett experiment, it would not be a case of the *maze* being learned at all, not even "latently," during the trials which were not food-rewarded, but rather simply a case of the rat, after one experience of eating in the goal box, being *guided* through the maze, on the next trial, by extramaze cues which had thus taken on secondary-reinforcing, or goal-attraction, properties.

This type of reasoning is purely hypothetical as far as the Blodgett experiment is concerned, since no reference to extra-maze cues is made in the report thereof.[6] But in the Seward experiment, already alluded to, such cues were studied and found to be effective, along with response-produced stimuli, in mediating the occurrence of performances which had never been directly reinforced. Says Seward, by way of summarizing his investigation:

An experiment was devised to test a hypothesis about the essential requirements for latent learning at a choice point. The hypothesis was that these consist of two separable factors: (1) associations between choice-point stimuli and alternative consequences of going right or left, giving rise to differential anticipatory reactions at the choice point; (2) association between one of these consequences and a satisfier. To test this hypothesis extra-maze cues were largely [but not entirely!] excluded from a simple alley T-maze. Rats were allowed to explore without food; they were then [placed and] fed in one endbox and immediately thereafter given a free choice in the maze. Twenty-eight out of 32 rats, or 87.5 percent, chose the path to the endbox in which they had been fed.

Three control experiments were run in an attempt to delimit more precisely the factors involved in this performance:

1. A control group prefed and tested without previous experience in the maze failed to exceed chance.

2. To isolate the critical cues operating on the test trial, all differences between the right and left endboxes were eliminated for one control group; all cues *outside* the endboxes were removed for a second group. In neither case did the score exceed chance. These results indicated that successful performance depended in part on differential anticipatory reactions to endbox cues.

3. The main experiment was repeated with fresh rats, but they were placed in both endboxes, one with and one without food, just before their free choice. Twenty-six of 32 rats, or 81.4 percent, chose correctly, thus establishing the role of the food incentive (p. 185).

[6] For an experiment bearing upon related but not precisely the same considerations, see Meehl & MacCorquodale (1953); also Desiderato (1956) and Honzik & Tolman (1936).

The most important sentences in the above quotation are these: "To isolate the critical cues operating on the test trial, all differences between the right and left endboxes were eliminated from the control group; all cues *outside* the endboxes were removed for a second group. In neither case did the scores exceed chance." Elsewhere (Mowrer, 1960, Chapter 9) we have reviewed the controversy as to whether place learning or response learning is the more basic and have concluded that the question is not meaningful—or at least of no theoretical importance. Adaptive behavior, as we have repeatedly seen, can occur on the basis of either place-produced *or* response-produced stimuli or on the basis of *both*. Therefore, it would seem reasonable that *mediating* stimuli can likewise be either place-produced or response-produced. In the experiments on latent punishment reported by Miller and by Tolman & Gleitman, the mediating stimuli were obviously response-produced; whereas, in the experiments on latent learning of the more "positive" kind, reported by Blodgett and by Seward, the indications are that the mediating stimuli (or at least some of them) were place-produced.

Here again there is no theoretical issue. If either a punishment or a reward is experienced in conjunction with stimuli that are provided either by the environment or by the subject's own behavior, and if *these same stimuli* are then experienced (perceived) *at a distance* from the point where the reinforcement occurred, the subject will have a tendency to avoid or to approach the place of reinforcement, without having ever been previously punished or rewarded for doing so. This, it seems, is the essence of so-called "latent" learning (be it inhibitory or facilitory) and of "foresight." This conclusion is in accord with the point of view arrived at in Chapter 7 of *Learning Theory and Behavior* in connection with the discussion of what was there termed *learning without doing*. Latent, or mediated, learning is just another term, it seems, for the same basic phenomenon.[7]

This conclusion can be perhaps clarified, and further substantiated, by recalling the procedure (Mowrer, 1960, pp. 106–108) which Skinner began using more than 20 years ago to facilitate a rat's learning to press a bar as a means of obtaining food. Here the procedure, in brief,

---

[7] For further experimental analyses of this problem along interesting dimensions, see Meehl & MacCorquodale (1953), Muenzinger & Conrad (1953), Thistlethwaite (1951), Spence (1951a, pp. 275–281), and Spence (1956). It is noteworthy that Spence (1956) credits difficulties "that showed up in experiments on latent learning" with finally convincing him of the untenability of the S—R bond conception of habit (cf. Section VII).

is this. With no bar yet present in the experimental apparatus, the rat learns to go to the food trough whenever it *hears* the noise which is produced by experimenter activation of the food-delivery mechanism. Then, after 20 or 30 such trials, the bar is made available and the rat itself can produce ("make") the noise—and the attendant pellet. According to the definition previously suggested—"some stimulus which will later be produced by a given response is first produced independently and conditioned to either hope or fear"—this is a very simple and explicit case of "latent learning."

Perhaps the misleading thing about the Blodgett experiment, and the reason it is a less good paradigm than the Skinner procedure—is that in the former *the response* (maze running) occurred first and the secondary reinforcement was *then* set up (presumably by virtue of food being received at and associated with a particular place). If hungry rats were first placed and fed, for example, in a gentle beam of light on the floor of an otherwise dark room, it would not be at all surprising if they later moved toward the beam when released at other places on the floor of the room. This procedure would more nearly parallel the Skinner paradigm—and better illustrate "latent learning" in pure form.

This is not to say, of course, that place learning was the *only* learning that occurred in the Blodgett experiment. During the exploratory runs in the maze, the rats undoubtedly learned much about it, despite the fact that there was as yet no primary reinforcement. However, we must remember that the rat was probably being *secondarily* reinforced by little frustrations and satisfactions inherently (or adventitiously) associated with the exploratory behavior (Mowrer, 1960, Chapters 6 and 11). Thus we arrive at the conclusion that the term "latent learning" should not be used to refer, loosely, to any and all learning that occurs without primary reinforcement; instead, if it is to have precision and technical utility, it should be restricted to situations wherein a stimulus which is later to be response-correlated is "baited" in advance, by being "preconditioned" to hope or fear, thus predisposing the subject to make or not make some particular response or approach or avoid some particular place. Here the "transfer of training," or generalization, which is so prominent in so-called latent learning, is from the situation in which the stimulus in question is independently produced (and conditioned) to a situation in which it occurs (or is increased) as a consequence of something which the *subject does*. Here, as is generally the case, the "transfer" is "mediated" by a *common element* (stimulus similarity).

VI. Other Examples of Response
(Stimulus) Mediation

Because the mechanism of mediation is so essential to the understanding of latent learning and because it plays so important a role in the "higher" (language and thought) processes to be considered later, it is desirable to make this phenomenon as explicit and vivid as possible. To this end we shall reproduce a portion of a previously published paper entitled, "The Psychologist Looks at Language" (Mowrer, 1954). This material to some extent presupposes notions which will not be fully elaborated until Chapter 4; but the allusions made here to those notions will prepare the way for their more extended discussion and better understanding later.

As Osgood has remarked, the concept of mediation is not devised "solely to meet the needs of semantics; it is the application of a general theory of learning to this particular class of phenomena" (1953, p. 696). One of the experiments which is most relevant in this connection has been concisely summarized by Osgood as follows:

"Fortunately [he says] there are cases in which the mediation process is specifiable with some accuracy. Shipley (1933) paired a faint light with a sudden tap on the cheek, which elicited winking; then the tap was paired with shock to the finger, eliciting withdrawal; on subsequent tests, the light flash (never paired with shock) evoked finger withdrawal. Since this did not occur unless the light and tap had initially been paired, any sensitization explanation is ruled out. . . . It becomes evident that the only difference between this experiment and those on sensory conditioning lies in the specificity of the mediating reaction—here, the winking movement" (1953, pp. 461–462).

This experiment is schematized [in Fig. 2–6] and provides a nice example of how it is that a response, in this case the eye blink, can "carry" another response, finger flexion, from one stimulus (tap on cheek) to another (light) without the latter having ever been used either as a conditioned or an unconditioned stimulus for the elicitation of the flexion response. This, in essence, is the mechanism posited [see Chapter 4] to explain how it is that, in a sentence, a meaning conditioned to another meaning, i.e., to the mediating response, can generalize or transfer back to the object presented by the sign that elicits the mediator or, more precisely, the *response* elicited by that object.

As will be more fully seen in Chapter 4, the Shipley experiment does not provide an exact parallel of what happens in language behavior. There the new meaning is acquired by the mediating reaction as produced by a word (conditioned stimulus) and generalizes to the thing (unconditioned stimulus); whereas, in the Shipley experiment, the new response (finger flexion) is conditioned to the mediating reaction (blink) as produced by the tap (unconditioned stimulus) and generalizes to the light (conditioned stimulus). Experiments cited later in this section show that "semantic generalization" of conditioned reactions occurs from thing to cognate word as well as from word to thing. But ordinarily, in language, we are more concerned with the latter occurrence than with the former. For the Shipley paradigm to have been strictly parallel to this type of generalization, finger flexion should have been conditioned to blink as elicited by light (a conditioned stimulus) so that the flexion could have generalized to the tap (or unconditioned stimulus).

(1) Light
(2)   Tap ⇒ Blink
(3) Light — Blink
(4) Tap — Blink
(5)   Shock ⇒ Finger flexion
(6) Tap — Blink — Finger flexion
(7) Light — Blink — Finger flexion

Fig. 2–6. An example of response mediation discovered, rather accidentally, by Shipley (1933). The assumption is that in the second stage of conditioning (lines 4 and 5) the finger flexion gets attached, not directly to the tap stimulus, but to the response (blink) produced by the tap (see line 6). (More precisely said, the finger flexion becomes conditioned to the proprioceptive and other stimuli produced by the blink—or to the central equivalents of the blink.) And since light, as a result of the first stage of conditioning, is also capable of producing the blink reaction, it follows that the light, through the intermediation of the blink, will produce finger flexion (see line 7), even though the light has itself never been paired with shock, the unconditioned stimulus for finger flexion.

In trying to understand the Shipley experiment, students are sometimes puzzled to know why it is not interpretable, quite simply, as a case of higher-order conditioning (Mowrer, 1960, Chapter 4). It is certainly true that much the same result could have been produced by such a procedure. Suppose that tap had been paired with shock (as in lines 4 and 5 of Fig. 2–6) so that tap alone would become capable of eliciting finger flexion (line 6). Then suppose that light and tap had been paired (lines 1 and 2), so that the first-order conditioned finger-flexion response to the tap is now elicited, as a second-order conditioned response, by the *light* (line 3). Here the response of finger flexion is, so to speak, transferred from shock to light without these two stimuli having ever been directly associated. This, from one point of view, was all that was accomplished in the Shipley experiment, so why the concern about a mediating response or stimulus?

There is, however, one small but highly significant difference. Whereas ordinary higher-order conditioning would involve first the pairing of tap and shock and then the pairing of light and tap, the actual sequence in the Shipley experiment was just the *reverse:* light was paired with tap and *then* tap was paired with shock. The fact that light *still* proved able to elicit finger flexion can therefore apparently be accounted for only in the manner suggested, by means of a *mediating* response (blink); it *cannot* be understood in terms of merely higher-order conditioning.[8]

Let us now return to the article from which the preceding quotations came:

> However, since the Shipley experiment was done without reference to the mediation hypothesis and with no particular attention being paid to the blink reaction in the second stage of conditioning, it is important to ask, as does Osgood:

[8] Or, might it not be interpretable as an instance of so-called *sensory preconditioning?* Here two presumably "neutral" stimuli, e.g., a light and a bell, are temporally paired; and then the bell is paired with a prepotent, or unconditioned, stimulus such as food or electric shock. If, subsequently, the light is presented and elicits a response appropriate to the unconditioned stimulus that has been used, "preconditioning" is said to have occurred. In the Shipley experiment the light and the tap would correspond to the light and the bell (in the above example) and the tap and the shock to the bell and the unconditioned stimulus, so that the similarities are indeed striking. However, mediated generalization seems to be well established as a phenomenon, whereas there is considerable doubt about sensory preconditioning. Although a number of experiments on sensory preconditioning which have recently been reviewed by Rozeboom (1958) have given positive results, the reviewer concludes that "any attempt to evaluate the magnitude of the effect strongly suggests that the phenomenon is a minor one, at least judging from the published studies. Thus the empirical importance of preconditioning is still problematic" (p. 30). The one obvious difference between the format for sensory preconditioning and for mediated generalization is that the second, or intermediate, stimulus is supposedly neutral in the one case, i.e., produces no clearly defined response, whereas in the other case it is not neutral, e.g., the tap in the Shipley experiment reliably produces an eye blink. This difference suggests that instead of mediated generalization being an instance of sensory preconditioning, it is more accurate to say that sensory preconditioning is an (inferior) instance of mediated generalization and that the reason so-called sensory preconditioning does not ordinarily work very well is precisely the fact that the "middle" stimulus does not produce any very clear-cut response to serve the mediation function. (Cf. Mowrer, 1960, Chapter 8, Section VII; also Kendler, 1959, p. 54.)

"But did this mediating winking reaction actually occur? Lumsdaine (1939, cf. pp. 230 ff. in Hilgard & Marquis, 1940) has repeated Shipley's experiment with detailed graphic recording. His records indicate that, in most cases the light *did* elicit a winking movement which was closely followed by finger withdrawal. There were some cases, however, in which the withdrawal reaction antedated the eyelid movement, and this suggests that the winking movement may be only an overt index of the actual mediation process. This is what would be expected according to the mediation hypothesis: in the original training, the light (sign) was presumably becoming associated with the fractional anticipatory portions of the reaction to tap-on-cheek (stimulus-object), and it is this mediation process which is more or less faithfully indexed by the overt winking" (1953, p. 462).

Elsewhere in his book, Osgood (see also Cofer and collaborators) cites a number of other instances of response mediation, reported mainly by Russian investigators, in which responses conditioned to words readily generalized to the objects they represent and in which responses conditioned to objects generalized to cognate words. Against the background of these findings, it is not surprising to discover, as has Razran (1939), that a salivary response conditioned to one word, e.g., "style," will readily generalize to another word, viz., "fashion," which is physically very different but which elicits much the same meaning or mediating reaction. In fact, this investigator found that considerably more generalization of conditioning (59% as opposed to 37%) occurred on the basis of similarity of meaning (synonyms) than on the basis of similarity of sight or sound (homophones, e.g., in the present instance, to a word like "stile"). That some transfer occurred on both bases suggests that, in the Razran experiment, the salivary response was conditioned not only to the meaning reaction produced by the word "style" but also, to some extent, directly to the word itself. To the extent that this occurred we may say that salivation replaced the meaning response previously attached to this word, i.e., its meaning was *changed;* but this was not the only, or even the main effect, since transfer on the basis of the mediation mechanism was greater.

No, the notion of response mediation—Hull (1930b) spoke of "pure stimulus acts," Hilgard and Marquis (1940), of "intermediate responses"—is by no means invented "to meet the needs of semantics." It is a common and well-established phenomenon whose centrality in language can hardly be doubted and which apparently can alone explain, broadly yet simply, how it is that what we learn through sentences can generalize, or transfer, despite absence of any sensory similarity or continuum, both to other words of similar meaning and also to the realities thereby denoted.

Since the above was written, in 1954, many new studies have appeared confirming the notion of mediation, both logically and empirically. Goss (1960) has done an excellent historical review; and Griffith, Spitz, & Lipman (1959), Jefrey & Kaplan (1957), Lipman & Blanton (1957),

Ray (1958), Rozeboom (1956), Staats & Staats (1957), and many others (see Kendler's 1959 review) have reported experimental confirmation of deductions made from the theory. We may therefore confidently say that the concept (phenomenon?) of mediation is here to stay, with only a few competent students of behavior still questioning it.

At the 1959 meeting of the American Psychological Association (see the *American Psychologist* for July, 1959), there was a symposium on "Mediating Processes in Verbal Behavior," in which there was some debate, not about the reality of mediation, but concerning the mechanism thereof. In contrast to the position taken by Staats (1959a) and most workers in the field, Bousefield (1959) and Russell (1959) took the position that so-called verbal mediation involves verbal (vocal or subvocal) response of an "associative" nature rather than meanings or representational reactions (see Chapters 5 and 6). In so doing, they overlooked, for example, the experimental findings of Razran (cited earlier in this section) on synonyms and homophones and other pertinent sources of evidence, apparently out of a feeling that the one type of explanation is much more "objective" than the other. And Skinner and his followers have, rather generally, also rejected the concept of meaning as a source of mediation, apparently for much the same reason. Even in his recent work on the use of machines for teaching arithmetic and other common school subjects, Skinner has insisted that "meaning" and "understanding" have nothing to do with the case and that, in the final analysis, what one is still doing (no less than in the training of lower animals) is progressively "shaping behavior" (1958b).

Also at the 1959 meeting of the APA there was a paper presented by Gagné on "Teaching Machines and Transfer of Training," in which the author took active issue with Skinner on this score and persuasively argued that in teaching a subject such as mathematics, whether by machine or human instructor, we must work, not for mere "predictability of response" (i.e., "well-shaped" behavior), but for "breadth of applicability" of what is learned, for transfer, "understanding." And this one can account for, on theoretical grounds, only if one posits the principle of mediation. At a special conference at which Professor Skinner described his ideas and program for the use of teaching machines, one listener's considered appraisal of the approach was: "Stepwise and leap-foolish." Certainly we want students to be able to make "original applications" of what they learn, to be able to "think for themselves," to make "leaps," "transfers," and not to be mere automata.

This is not to say that one cannot use teaching machines to achieve this end; but, as Gagné was at pains to point out, we have to have mediated generalization—and the practical results it makes possible—in mind when we *program* such machines; otherwise, the results are likely to fall far short of the desired goal.

But we are getting somewhat ahead of the story. In succeeding chapters we shall again be talking about mediation in the more specific context of language, reasoning, and the like. Before we can resume our discussion at this level of discourse, there are, however, more background and lower-order phenomena which need to be analyzed.

VII. Latent Extinction

As is well known, behavior can be modified positively (facilitated) by reward and modified negatively (inhibited) by punishment. Moreover, *both* of these forms of learning can be undone by extinction, i.e., by nonconfirmation of expectations previously established. In other words, a bit of behavior which has previously been followed by reward tends to disappear if the accustomed reward is eliminated; and behavior which has previously been followed by punishment tends to reappear if the accustomed punishment is eliminated. These and related facts have been considered more fully in Chapter 1 (see also Mowrer, 1960, Chapter 11); but they have an immediate relevance in the following way. It has been established that latent learning, i.e., change in behavior without full performance thereof, can be made to occur with both decremental and incremental reinforcement. The question now is: Can "extinction" also come about on the latent-learning basis, i.e., without performance?

Seward & Levy (1949), in a paper entitled "Sign Learning as a Factor in Extinction," were apparently the first investigators to bring this question to an empirical test. They summarize their study thus:

An experiment was designed to test the sign-learning theory of extinction; the theory, namely, that when reward is removed CS becomes a sign of non-reward and CR drops out through lack of incentive. The deduction tested was that CR could be weakened without itself being elicited, provided that the situation formerly associated with reward was now experienced without it.

The response selected was to traverse a narrow elevated path [30 in. long] from one platform to another; the reward was found on the second platform. Thirty-three rats were given 10 training trials in this habit. They were then divided into two groups, experimental and control. Group E spent time on the goal platform without food both before and between extinction trials;

Group C spent equivalent periods on a neutral platform. Both groups were extinguished to a criterion. The results were as follows:

Group E reached the [extinction] criterion [of two successive refusals to leave the starting platform] in a mean of 3.12 trials, group C in 8.25 trials; the difference was significant at the .01 level (p. 667).

The most striking thing, of course, about these findings as far as the latent-learning issue is concerned is that animals in the experimental group showed a reduced tendency to run the maze on the *first trial* after exposure to the goal box without food therein. This "habit" was thus not weakened by nonrewarded *performance*—which is what extinction is usually thought of as involving—but by merely allowing the subjects to find the goal box empty when passively put therein. This finding is therefore comparable to the results obtained, by Miller and Tolman & Gleitman, by the use of active punishment, rather than mere nonreward, in the goal box. By the same logic, one would expect it to be possible to release an *inhibited* response by re-exposing subjects, without punishment, to that part of an experimental situation in which punishment had previously been received. This would be the counterpart of the type of "latent extinction" demonstrated in the Seward-Levy study. If this type of experiment has not already been carried out, a report thereof—with positive results—can be expected shortly.

The validity of the Seward-Levy findings, just described, was questioned in a paper published in 1952 by Bugelski, Coyer, & Rogers, but these findings have since received substantial support from studies reported by Deese (1951), Gleitman, Nachmias, & Neisser (1954), Moltz (1955), Moltz & Maddi (1955), Coate (1956), Moltz (1957), and Hurwitz (1955).[9] We may therefore assume, at least tentatively, that latent extinction, no less than latent learning (in both its decremental and incremental forms), is an established phenomenon. The question then becomes: How is it to be explained? In the studies reported by Miller and by Tolman & Gleitman, which involved punishment, it was apparently necessary, in order to obtain positive results, to require the subjects to make certain *distinctive responses* in connection with the experience of punishment (at one place) and the experience of non-punishment (at another place).[10] In the experiment carried out by Seward (Section V) latent learning was obtained solely by means of

[9] For recent negative evidence, see studies by Scharlock (1954) and Rozeboom (1957).

[10] Cf. a later study of Gleitman (1955) entitled "Place Learning without Prior Performance."

reward; and no such responses were necessary, although Seward did find that the two end boxes of the T-maze which he employed had to be, in the absence of extra maze cues, visually distinctive. Whether the sudden change in behavior noted by Seward after exposure of his subjects to the baited end box was mediated by the anticipatory occurrence, at the choice point, of some sort of distinctive response made to the appearance of the baited goal box, or whether the changed behavior was mediated, as Tolman prefers to think, by some immediate cognition or purely sensory memory, seems to be an open question (see Footnote 4, p. 46).

However, the interpretation of the Seward-Levy findings on latent extinction is simplified at least in this regard. In this study there was *only one* goal box, and the experimenters tested latent learning simply by noting the tendency of their subjects to go or not to go to this box. Hence the existence of response-mediated cues which might set this goal box apart from some other goal box is not an issue: *any* goal-box response which would occur anticipatorily, in the starting box or in the maze runway, could mediate learning (or unlearning) which had occurred in the goal box and thus affect runway performance. Miller has already been quoted as saying:

> Reinforced goal responses also occur regularly a short interval after stimulation by the cues from the starting box and from the . . . alley. Now, it is well known that if reinforcement regularly occurs a short interval after a given stimulus, a trace conditioned reaction to that stimulus tends to be set up and that there is a strong tendency for this trace conditioned reaction to antedate its reinforcement. Thus there should be a strong tendency for the goal responses to occur [at least in attenuated, or "token," form] in the alley and even in the starting box (1935a, p. 182).

Reference has been made (footnote 7, p. 51) to the fact that Spence credits difficulties "that showed up in experiments on latent learning" with finally persuading him of the untenability of the S—R conception of habit and of Hull's general conception of reinforcement. Recently, however, Moltz & Maddi (1955) and Moltz (1957) have specifically defended the applicability of Hull's principles here. They say: "If S were placed directly in the goal box without the presence of the reward object (a procedure . . . called 'latent extinction') this would reduce or eliminate the secondary-reward value of cues present in the goal box, and this would, in turn, lead to extinction through nonreinforcement or a decrease in reinforcement" (p. 71). And empirically, these investigators found that the *hungrier* subjects (rats) are when subjected to "latent extinction," the greater is the extinction of the secondary reinforcement acquired by stimuli previously associated with primary reinforcement. Thus do the investigators cited derive an explanation of latent extinction consistent with Hullian principles: in latent extinction, so-called, there is *real* extinction of important secondary reinforcers, which extinction is then reflected by a corresponding loss of vigor in the habit with which they have been associated. Our own interpretation would differ in only one major way: Instead of assuming that some overt response or habit (conceived as an S—R bond) is "reinforced" by secondary reinforcers and that extinction of the latter would thus remove a source of further "strengthening" for the former, we conjecture that the secondary reinforcement which has become attached to response-correlated stimuli *is* the "habit" and that if *it* is extinguished so also, automatically and forthwith, is the habit (see Chapter 1, Sections V and VIII; also Mowrer, 1960, Chapters 7 and 11).

Habit theory, as developed by Thorndike and elaborated by Hull, does not, of course, deny—in fact, definitely affirms—that extinction (by withdrawal of primary reward) can be retarded by the operation of secondary reinforcers. But this type of theory does hold that a habit has some irreducible and inherent "strength" of its own, quite aside from that provided (subsequently) by secondary reinforcers. Therefore, if it could be shown that a previously well-rewarded response could be *completely nullified* either by the elimination of all stimuli having secondary-reinforcement power *or* by extinction of that power, the notion of inherent "habit strength" would be hard to maintain (cf. Mowrer, 1960, Chapter 8). The evidence derived from research on latent learning generally, and on latent extinction in particular, seems to point in this direction. It is not that a habit has first to *occur* and then be weakened by the absence of secondary reinforcement (as the Moltz-Maddi interpretation would imply): in latent extinction the habit is weakened *without* occurring, a circumstance which seems strongly to favor the view that secondary reinforcement and habit strength are one and the same thing.[11]

---

[11] Lewis & Cotton (1958) have interestingly related the phenomenon of latent learning (and extinction) and that of partial reinforcement (Chapter 1; see also Mowrer, 1960, Chapter 12). How, they have asked, does intermittent latent reinforcement (or intermittent latent nonreinforcement) compare in its effects with those of consistent latent reinforcement (or consistent latent nonreinforcement)? The problem is obviously a complicated one, and it is not surprising that the investigators cited obtained some complicated results. These will not be discussed here, except to say that this is a promising area for future inquiry.

VIII. Mediated Discrimination or Distinctiveness

The quintessence of mediation, as thus far considered in this chapter, is that it is a mechanism whereby a response which has become attached (through a mediator) to one stimulus can be made to generalize to other *quite different* stimuli (provided that they, too, elicit the mediator). Since N. E. Miller was among the first to understand this phenomenon clearly, it is natural that he, in collaboration with Dollard (1950), should also have elucidated the notion of mediated discrimination. These writers say:

Attaching the same cue-producing response to two distinctive stimulus objects gives them a certain *learned equivalence* increasing the extent to which instrumental and emotional response will generalize from one to the other (Birge, 1941; Foley & Cofer, 1943; Miller, 1935a). This may be illustrated from our previous example of counting change. Five dimes and a fifty-cent piece present cues that are innately quite different. Since they both elicit the same label (i.e., verbal cue-producing response), "fifty cents," they have a certain amount of learned equivalence in our culture. . . . Similarly, the label of "Doctor" tends to mediate the transfer of confidence and response to anyone to whom it is attached.

Conversely, attaching distinctive cue-producing responses to similar stimulus objects tends to increase their distinctiveness. To use the example of counting change again, an array of nineteen nickles is sufficiently similar to an array of twenty nickles so that few people would be able to make the discrimination by merely looking. Whenever the nickles are counted, however, they lead to the distinctive cue-producing responses "nineteen" and "twenty," so that the discrimination is easy. . . .

To cite another example, a faculty member was anxious, disappointed, and annoyed at not being invited to a large party given by a close friend. These painful emotions motivated problem-solving behavior. Turning it over in his mind, he suddenly noticed that all of the guests were members of the friend's department, which was different from his own. As soon as he labeled it "a departmental party," his fear that he had offended his friend or had been ungenerously neglected, and his ensuing disappointment and aggression, were eliminated; he no longer had an emotional problem (pp. 101–102).

Just as naturally dissimilar objects or situations are, on occasion, made artificially (but none the less usefully) "similar" by means of mediated generalization, so are naturally similar objects or situations made artificially (but, again, often very usefully) "dissimilar" by means of mediated discrimination. The *logical* justification for the latter conception is therefore very good; but thus far there are fewer empirical demonstrations thereof than we have for mediated generalization. Recently, however, Grice & Davis (1958) have reported an ingenious experiment in which both of these phenomena clearly appear. They say:

Much of the work in this area has dealt with behavior of a rather high level of complexity and the cue-producing responses have been regarded more often as inferred entities than as variables under experimental control (e.g., Lawrence, 1949, 1950; Osgood, 1953). The experiments reported here represent an attempt to investigate the problem of mediated stimulus equivalence and distinctiveness at the level of conditioning and with experimental manipulation of the cue-producing responses (p. 565).

The authors describe the Shipley-Lumsdaine experiments which have already been considered in this chapter (Section VI) and outline their own study thus:

The basic design involves a procedure of differential conditioning. There are three clearly discriminable tones varying in frequency which may be called "High," "Medium," and "Low." The medium tone is the CS [for an eyeblink response in human subjects], always paired with the UCS, a puff of air. The high and low tones are negative stimuli never paired with the UCS. Now if, during conditioning, S is instructed to make one manual response to the CS and one of the negative tones and a different manual response to the second negative tone, a paradigm for both mediated equivalence and distinctiveness is provided. Equivalence should be mediated between the CS and the negative stimulus to which the same response is made, and distinctiveness should be mediated between the two negative tones and between the CS and the tone to which the response is different. In other words, the generalization gradients would be asymmetrical.

One may suppose (actually this was controlled by a counter-balanced experimental design) that there would be just as much inherent tendency for a human subject to show a generalization of eyeblinking from the Medium tone, let us say, to the High tone as from the Medium tone to the Low one. However, the High tone was made more "similar" to the Medium tone by virtue of the subject's being told to make the same *manual* response to these two tones; and the Low tone was made "different" from the Medium tone by instructions to the subject to make a *different* manual response thereto. Therefore, reasoned these investigators, if mediated generalization is a reality the tendency for the eyeblink response to occur to the High tone ought to be increased (over its "normal" generalized tendency) and the tendency for the eyeblink response to occur to the Low tone ought to be decreased; i.e., "the generalization gradients would be asymmetrical."

Grice & Davis describe their findings thus:

There were [reliably] more conditioned eyeblinks to negative stimuli to which the Ss made the same manual response as to the CS than to those to which they made a different response. The results are interpreted as being in general agreement with a theory of response mediated stimulus equivalence and distinctiveness (p. 570).

There is, however, an ambiguity about this experiment which Grice & Davis fully recognize. In order for the proprioceptive and tactile stimuli produced by the two manual responses to serve as mediating cues, these responses would have to occur *before* the conditioned eyeblink response. Otherwise, they could not mediate either generalization or discrimination. The conditioned eyeblink can be extremely rapid—in fact, is commonly classified among the so-called short-latency conditioned reflexes—and so might well precede rather than follow a voluntary response to the same objective stimulus (i.e., tone). Therefore, in an effort to obviate this difficulty, Grice & Davis allowed an interval of 500 milliseconds (one-half second) between the onset of the CS and the UnCS (in the hope of somewhat slowing up the conditioned eyeblinks) and excluded from their tabulations all eyelid responses that occurred less than 150 milliseconds after the onset of the CS, thus providing a greater opportunity for the distinctive manual responses to occur before, or at least *with*, the occurrence of the eyeblink. There are, however, still complications here which prompt the authors to suggest that perhaps just the "set" to make a particular manual response which is centrally aroused by the CS "may have a mediating effect" (p. 570). The authors indicate (personal communication) that they now have research in progress which is designed to deal more definitely with these problems—perhaps the solution would be to use an emotional response rather than a short-latency reflex; but, in any event, the experiment aptly illustrates the *principles* which are at issue here; and, despite the difficulties, it still produced results of the predicted kind.[12]

IX. Summary

Several experiments have been reported which show that, given the right circumstances, behavior can be facilitated, extinguished, or inhibited *without occurring*. These findings go counter to the dictum that organisms learn (or unlearn) "only by doing"; and such results cannot be explained on the basis of any simple stimulus-response, or "bond," conception of habit. But neither do they demand that we

---

[12] For an interesting, but somewhat different, approach to the problem of mediated generalization and discrimination, see Goss (1955). And see also the articles cited in the literature review near the end of Section VI.

revert to a cognition psychology. They can be handled, quite nicely, by means of the concept of *mediation*. In the final analysis, mediation is always *stimulus* mediation; but the mediating stimulus may be independent, or it may be response-correlated, in which case we are likely to speak (somewhat misleadingly) of "response" mediation. An illustration will be useful.

Suppose that our object is to teach a hungry rat to go to the right-wing goal box of a T-maze for food, but "without practice." Generalizing from experiments actually performed and reviewed in preceding sections of this chapter, we may infer that if a rat were passively carried (without vision) to the right goal box, placed therein, and fed with a distinctive tone sounding nearby, the rat would be more likely, when subsequently put into the maze at the base of the stem, to go to the right-wing goal box, i.e., *toward* the tone, than it would be to go to the left-wing goal box, i.e., *away* from the tone.

Or, suppose that our object is to *inhibit* a well-practiced response of some sort, without "punishment." First we allow the rat, when hungry, to discover that it can obtain food in either of the two goal boxes of a T-maze. Then we place the rat in one of these boxes, say the left one, and shock it, in the presence of the tone. When later placed in the starting box, this rat will (with tone again sounding near the left goal box) be considerably less likely to go to the left goal box and more likely to go to the right goal box, although it has previously shown no such predisposition and has certainly never been "punished" for going from the starting box to the left goal box.

In both of the instances just described, the phenomenon of stimulus mediation (or generalization) is extremely obvious: An emotion of hope or fear is conditioned to a tone in one situation; and later, when the tone is heard *at a distance*, the hungry subject will be more or less disposed to go to that situation, depending upon whether the emotional conditioning has been positive or negative.

Stimulus mediation becomes subtle, and interesting, only when the mediating stimulus is response-produced, rather than provided by the environment. But it is still easy to see that if, in one situation, an organism makes some distinctive response and experiences a particular pattern of "feedback" and is then either rewarded or punished, and if, in later moving toward this situation the organism "anticipates" being in the situation, i.e., makes some part of the response previously made (and rewarded or punished) therein, then this response and its correlated stimuli will call out either hope or fear, and the organism's progress toward the situation in question will be adaptively speeded or slowed (stopped), as the case may be. By thus appropriately responding *at a distance* (generalizing), the subject is said to show *fore*sight.

Thus, by the examples given, one sees that overt behavior can be either "stamped in" or "stamped out" without having been *directly* associated with either reward or punishment; and the indications are that an inhibitory effect, similar to that produced by incremental reinforcement, can be produced by mere nonreward (disappointment, frustration, "extinction").

Several instances of so-called latent learning, latent punishment, and latent extinction have been analyzed in this chapter in terms of either response-produced or independent stimulus mediation; and it would appear that mediation is the key to an understanding of all such phenomena. Manifestly we are here dealing with mechanisms similar to those involved in "semantic generalization" (Chapter 4), in "insight" (Konorski, 1950, explicitly equates it to "latent learning"), and other higher mental processes (Chapter 5), and in the control of behavior through feedback (Chapter 8). Also we see, once more, the advantage of thinking of habit strength as a function of whether fear or hope is attached to response-correlated stimuli, rather than in "connectionistic" (S—R bond) terms.

The various instances of latent learning (including extinction and punishment) which have been considered in this chapter are dependent upon mediated *generalization,* i.e., some stimulus (independent or response-dependent) which makes the test situation *more like* (gives it something in *common with*) the situation in which the original learning (extinction or punishment) occurs. However, it is now known that *discrimination* can also be "mediated"; i.e., where an original learning situation and a test situation are naturally somewhat alike and therefore likely to show generalization, they can be made artificially *different,* by means of distinctive cue-producing responses made to each. This phenomenon has been clearly conceptualized by Dollard & Miller and empirically exemplified by Grice & Davis. However, misunderstanding should not be allowed to arise here. The term mediation, as it is ordinarily used, implies *a medium,* something that goes between or is common to two or more situations. So-called mediated discrimination implies, in one sense, exactly the reverse picture: one in which two situations which are inherently alike are made different. And in order for this to occur, not a "mediator," but two distinct and disparate stimuli are introduced. They do *not* "go between" (mediate) two different situations; each, so to say, "stays put" and so increases the uniqueness of the situation in which it occurs.

Therefore, one can say that the term, mediation, is applicable only where generalization is "artificially" produced and that some other term should be available for the situation where discrimination is, in like manner, "artificially" produced. Only the artificiality (provided by response-produced cues) is common to both generalization and discrimination of this kind; otherwise they are quite different. But there is probably no harm, established usage being what it is, in continuing to speak of both mediated generalization and mediated discrimination, providing that we remember that the generalization is "mediated" in a much more literal sense than is the discrimination.

A word should also be said about another minor ambiguity in this chapter. The bulk of our discussion has dealt with the mechanism whereby two objectively different situations can be rendered more nearly equivalent, psychologically and functionally, by means of response-produced mediating stimuli. However, as intimated in the introduction to this chapter, it is also possible for mediation to function in the purely *temporal* dimension. Often a situation at t_1 (in time) will be *objectively the same* as at t_2; but at t_1 the stimulus trace of some recent event will still be present, whereas at t_2 it will have disappeared, thus rendering situation t_1 and situation t_2 *subjectively different*. This change, or loss of "equivalence," between t_1 and t_2 becomes highly important in circumstances involving delayed reinforcement (decremental or incremental), wherein a stimulus event which has occurred (and left its trace) just prior to t_1 is functionally related to events that occur at t_2. However, because of the disappearance of the stimulus trace of the antecedent event, the two objectively identical situations (t_1 and t_2) will have become subjectively different; and, as a result, the "connection" between the antecedent stimulus event and the subsequent reinforcing event will be "lost." As indicated in Chapter 10 of *Learning Theory and Behavior*, such an interval can be spanned in a variety of ways; but the one most interesting from the standpoint of the present discussion is that in which *the subject* introduces behavior ("pure stimulus acts") which will make the situation at t_2 "artificially" *more like* the situation at t_1 than it otherwise would be. In the chapter cited, an animal experiment by Ferster (1953) is described which nicely exemplifies this phenomenon. And it is even more remarkably and pervasively illustrated by the use of language by human beings, to which topic we shall shortly turn in the two following chapters.

However, before proceeding with the study of symbolism in its more elaborate forms, a few further observations should be made concerning the idea of mediation. Anyone who has read the companion volume, *Learning Theory and Behavior*, or who knows this field from other sources, is familiar with the concept of *intervening variables* and may, at this point, quite reasonably find himself wondering about the relation of this concept to that of *mediation*. A mediator obviously is a "variable," and it also "intervenes" between an objective situation and overt behavior. But are *all* intervening variables also mediators; and if not, wherein do they differ?

In 1948 MacCorquodale & Meehl devoted a long article to a discussion of intervening variables (as conceived by Tolman) and their relationship to "hypothetical constructs" (particularly as employed by Hull). But no one, it seems, has addressed himself systematically to the question of the relation between intervening variables and mediators. Nor shall we here attempt to deal with this problem in any exhaustive fashion. We may, however, usefully break ground for later exploration by looking, once again (cf. Mowrer, 1960, especially Chapters 3 and 9), at this matter of intervening variables. As MacCorquodale and Meehl properly note, an intervening variable is a variable that intervenes between a so-called independent variable and a dependent variable, i.e., between a manifest cause and an observed consequence or effect of some sort. Now the concept of intervening variable arose, in psychology at least, out of the patent inadequacy of simple S—R theory. It was soon found, for example, that the response (conceived as overt behavior) which a conditioned stimulus, or signal, elicits may be very different from the response made by the subject to the unconditioned stimulus; and this difference is likely to be especially striking when the unconditioned stimulus is painful, noxious. The only satisfactory way, it seems, to account for this discrepancy is to assume that what gets conditioned, directly, to the danger signal is *fear* and that it may then motivate any of a variety of overt behaviors, depending upon what the organism's prior experience has been in dealing with this drive. Here the reality of the fear, as an intervening variable, is easily demonstrated empirically as well as subjectively; and its postulation has gained general acceptance in contemporary behavior theory.

Some 15 years ago, the author wrote to Professor Tolman asking if the concept of fear, as it was then coming into systematic use, would qualify as an intervening variable, in the sense in which he used the term. Tolman's reply was equivocal. He did not deny that fear is *one kind* of intervening variable, but he distinguished it from the kind of intervening variable in which he, personally, was most interested, namely, cognitions (see Chapter 5) rather than emotions. What can now be done by way of relating these two kinds of intervening variables, or "mediators"?

In a certain limited sense, *all conditioning*, as that phenomenon is conceived in this work, may be said to involve "mediation." If, for example, the combination of a signal and a noxious stimulus (such as electric shock) is thought of as the learning, or acquisition, situation, then the occurrence of the signal alone may be termed the *test* situation; and fear, as elicited therein, may be said to provide a common element, or to "mediate," between these two situations. The fact that the fear now occurs in the test situation makes that situation *more like* the learning situation and prompts more or less appropriate anticipatory behavior therein. Therefore, in at least a loose, general sense of the term, fear is not only an intervening variable, but also a "mediator." And in this sense, we can argue that other emotions, to the extent that they are conditionable, are likewise mediational. They are what make it possible for living organisms to react to a signal (really to an emotional "mediator") more or less as if it were the "real thing," to their decided biological advantage.

But it is also evident, from earlier sections of this chapter, that not all mediators are emotions; many, in Hull's apt phrase, are "pure stimulus acts," with no motivational or reinforcing properties in their own right. These "acts" are nevertheless important and useful because the stimuli which they produce *do* arouse emotions, and thus prompt and guide ensuing behavior.

Thus we arrive at the suggestion—perhaps a rather significant one— that there are different kinds, or levels, of mediation. An emotion is a mediator of the *first order;* a pure stimulus act (or a mediational stimulus supplied by the environment) to which an emotion (or first-order mediator) is conditioned is a *second-order* mediator. And we may later discover that it is possible to have "purely mental" (cognitive) surrogates for pure-stimulus acts (as Tolman has proposed) which might be said to constitute mediators of the *third order*. Mediators of the latter kind will be given special consideration in Chapter 5 (see especially the discussion of images); and in Chapter 7, we shall find a parallel notion in the work of Powers, McFarland, & Clark (1957), on a cybernetic model for "personality" and the higher mental processes. The problem, in very general terms, will also be considered in Chapter 6.

3

Learning Theory
and Language Learning:
The Problem of "Imitation"

As the preceding chapter indicates, the phenomenon of *mediation* provides a "bridge" or transition from the relatively simple principles that govern animal behavior to the more elaborate "intellectual" or "symbolic" processes found in man. Words are, in fact, "mediators" *par excellence;* and it is natural for us now to undertake a systematic study of their acquisition and function.

Language and learning have a curiously interactive, or reciprocal, relationship: language is itself learned; but, once learned, it then importantly facilitates and guides further learning. These two aspects of the relationship seem to be sufficiently important and sufficiently different to warrant separate chapters, the present one being devoted to language learning and the following one to learning *through* language. The systematic analysis of language learning, we shall find, generates a surprisingly satisfactory conception of imitative behavior in general, and one that articulates easily and meaningfully with the concept of "habit" as it emerges in revised two-factor learning theory.

I. The Understanding and the Use of Words

The learning or acquisition of language breaks down into two phases: understanding and reproduction, references and responses, meanings and motions. Bertrand Russell, a good many years ago (1927), suggested that words acquire, or are given, meanings through conditioning: "ball" (word) is associated with *ball* (thing), and at least a part of the reaction evoked by the latter gets connected with the former. On the other hand, learning to *make* the noises which we call words depended, according to Russell, upon what has commonly been called trial-and-error learning: An infant, more or less accidentally, says "ball" (or something like it), is objectively rewarded in some way, and becomes disposed to repeat the response. This distinction clearly corresponds to what, in the earlier version of two-factor learning theory (see Chapter 3), were termed sign learning and solution learning. Words, as heard, are signs; as made by ourselves to others, solutions.

But now, in terms of the revised two-factor position adopted in this book, which reduces all learning to sign learning or conditioning, type-I and type-D, what happens to this distinction? There is no problem as far as the learning of word meaning, reference, or significance is concerned. If a word, as heard, is temporally contiguous with a thing, person, or event which is itself "meaningful," a part of that meaning will become attached to the word. Things and events are meaningful mainly in the sense of being good or bad, helpful or harmful; and it is precisely these two effects that have, as we have seen, the capacity to act as reinforcing agents and to cause stimuli which are contiguous therewith to take on the surrogate properties of secondary reinforcement and secondary motivation, respectively.

There is, of course, manifestly more to the meaning of words than this purely evaluative aspect. Thus "apple" implies beauty, good smell, good taste, and hunger reduction; but it is also uniquely designative of a particular category of real objects, i.e., it has certain properties which are seemingly independent of its affective implications (Carroll, 1953, pp. 95–97). As yet we are not prepared to discuss these (see Chapter 5). But present indications are that the affective, evaluative element in word meaning is, in any case, basic. A study of the meanings of words, made possible by an objective method described by Osgood and Suci (1955), shows that the good-bad dimension accounts for about 70% of all the meaning which words have. So the reaction of fear, or of hope, aroused by a word is a good place to start in studying meaning; and two-factor theory, as now conceived, provides a specific basis for the acquisition of these affective aspects of meaning (see Fig. 1–5).

But what of two-factor theory and the process whereby the human infant learns to reproduce, or *say*, words? The most widely accepted view is that word learning, like other instances of "habit formation," is dependent upon trial and error. This is the assumption put forward by Russell in the work already cited; and it permeates the writings to be found on this problem in a variety of fields—psychology, philosophy, speech, etc. To borrow an expression used by Thorndike in a different context (see Section V), we may term it the "babble-luck" theory, since it presupposes that the infant, in the course of *babbling*, has the *luck*, once in a while, to make a noise that to others sounds like a word. Such a noise, or "word," elicits attention and other rewarding behavior on the part of the parents; and in this way, supposedly, the responses, or "habits," involved in speech are learned.

This is not an illogical theory, but it is improbable. Most parents apparently do not look upon what they do to get their children to talk in quite this way: instead of passively waiting for the baby to make a conventional word noise, they themselves *talk to* the baby and then rely upon something which they term "imitation" to do the rest. What does this "imitation" imply?

If we adopt the revised two-factor assumption that all learning is, in the final analysis, a form of conditioning, what implications does such an assumption have for the problem of language learning? The early conception of conditioning obviously will not work in this connection. When Behaviorism was most popular, during the 1920's, conditioning was seen mainly as a process whereby an external, behavioral response of some sort, which could be reliably elicited by a so-called unconditioned stimulus, would become capable of being elicited by a new, formerly neutral stimulus, as a result of paired presentation of this and the unconditioned stimulus. Such a conception of learning is, of course, not very useful in explaining word acquisition, for the reason that there *are* no "unconditioned" stimuli which can be relied upon to elicit words, on an unlearned, reflexive, nativistic basis. The knee jerk can be reliably produced by a blow on the patellar tendon, and it can be conditioned (at least in some subjects) to another stimulus which is associated with the tendon tap. But words (like most behavior), not being reflexive to begin with, cannot be acquired as "conditioned reflexes" (see Section VIII).

How, then, can conditioning, as defined in two-factor theory, account for word learning—if at all? Oddly enough, the present version of two-factor theory was worked out and first applied in relation to the problem of language learning, before it was understood and stated in its more general form. The background facts are these. In view of the many divergent hypotheses which had been advanced concerning the nature and course of language learning by human infants, it seemed that something more specific and definite might be learned if a systematic study was made of the circumstances under which parrots and other species of birds learn to make human, word-like sounds. This work has been reported in detail elsewhere (Mowrer, 1950, Chapter 24), but the upshot was this: In order for a bird to learn to make a particular word sound, that sound has first to be heard, repeatedly, in a pleasant, agreeable context. Varied evidence indicates that if a sound, such as "Hello," is uttered as the trainer comes into the presence of the bird after an absence, or if the sound is repeated as the trainer gives the bird food and water, scratches its head or neck (an attention particularly appreciated by parrots), or amuses or comforts the bird in some other way, the bird will sooner or later start using the word, both in the absence of (as if calling for) and in the presence of the trainer, as a means of securing "services" which the trainer can provide.

When this research on training birds to "talk" was being carried out (1946–48), enough was already known about secondary reinforcement to suggest that this phenomenon was importantly involved. The explanation seemed to go like this: As a result of being repeatedly uttered by the trainer in conjunction with some dependable, "primary" form of decremental reinforcement, a given word or phrase, as heard, takes on secondary-reinforcement properties. When, subsequently, in its verbal play or "babbling," the bird makes—and itself *hears*—a sound somewhat like the word, there will be ready-made, or "built-in," reinforcement of the response; and the more nearly the sound made by the bird approximates (or "imitates") the sound made by the trainer, the more it will be, in this way, reinforced and repeated. Imitation, as thus interpreted, becomes a sort of automatic trial-and-error process, one which is dependent upon reward from another organism, or "parent person," only in an indirect, derived sense. The response has become "baited" so that whenever the bird makes it, satisfaction and reinforcement will be powerful and prompt—and self-administered!—provided appropriate motivation is present.

Another, perhaps clearer, way to put this idea is to say that the secondary reinforcement which has become conditioned to the word stimulus as made by the trainer *generalizes* to the word stimulus as made *by the bird itself*. And since our supposition is that habit is just the secondary reinforcement, so-called, which has become attached to response-correlated stimulation, then, in "imitation," the bird acquires the "habit" of making a particular sound, not by making it, but by merely *hearing* it made. This, obviously, is just a special case of the

principle of latent *learning* discussed in the preceding chapter. As we
have seen, latent learning, in the final analysis, is simply a matter of
generalization or transfer of training. This, it seems, is also what is
involved in imitation.[1]

Sometimes the phenomenon of imitation has been interpreted as due
to a special "instinct" (cf. Thorpe, 1956). Thus, if one organism "imitates" and another does not, this is said to be because of the presence
or absence of an "instinct of imitation." We have reduced the phenomenon to very general learning principles, yet it is well known that word
learning is possible only in human beings and certain species of birds
(with chimpanzees and dogs having the capacity in only very rudimentary degree [2]). So if it is not an "instinct of imitation" that varies,
how then can the observed wide variations in performance be accounted for? The answer, apparently, is that the "motor connections"
required for making word-like responses are simply not present in
most living organisms and no amount of teaching or learning can bring
them into existence. Chimpanzees seem to have all the physical equipment required for word formation; the deficit is manifestly neurological
(see Section VIII). And even the generally "talkative" little parakeet
finds some sounds naturally difficult.

II. Word Learning and Other Instances of "Habit Formation" Compared

The two following illustrations, with which we have already become
familiar, may help clarify and concretize the view of word learning
which has just been sketched. Knowledge of how to teach a dog to
"shake hands" (see Mowrer, 1960, Chapter 7) is commonplace. This
is *not* ordinarily done by showing the dog, visually, how to shake
hands; nor is it done by waiting, tid-bit in hand, for the dog to lift one
of his front paws in a particular manner. The procedure consists instead

[1] As will be made more explicit in Chapter 7, this way of thinking about learning in general and imitation in particular is compatible with the basic assumptions
underlying the new discipline of cybernetics. For a discussion of language and
related problems in the context of cybernetic theory, but without reference to
any of the seemingly very naturally related ideas considered here, see a series of
papers appearing in a volume edited by Von Foerster and published in 1951. For
an appreciation of this relationship, see Peterson (1955).

[2] In 1956 Will Rogers, Jr., on his TV "Morning Show," offered cash prizes for
each clearly distinguishable word uttered by "talking dogs." Several dogs that
were exhibited by their masters received two or more such prizes. For a report
on "talking chimpanzees," see Section VIII.

of passively moving the leg and at the same time petting the dog or perhaps giving it some preferred food. In this way, the particular pattern of stimulation from muscles, tendons, and joints which is produced by the passive flexion of the leg takes on secondary-reinforcement properties; and when, after several repetitions of this training procedure, the dog himself starts to move his leg in the same way, the movement somehow "seems right," "feels good," and will be carried through to completion, because it maximizes the attendant secondary reinforcement or derived, "autistic" satisfaction.

At this point, the dog's master begins to notice the apparently spontaneous, or "voluntary," occurrence of the response, himself feels rewarded for his efforts, takes the paw and again rehearses the response, all the while lavishing new approval upon and perhaps more concretely rewarding the dog. Hence, just as a word, acquired on an autistic (self-satisfying) basis by a bird or baby, may then become "instrumental" in producing predictable behavior on the part of others, so does the gesture on the part of a dog of "offering" to shake hands come to have a social, or *signaling*, function; and we are likely to say that the dog is now "begging" for food or for some other form of "attention." However, in both word learning and "hand shaking," it is to be remembered that the response is "conditioned," or "*pre*conditioned," in the sense that certain stimuli which will occur when the response is voluntarily performed are first produced through the efforts of *others* and in a context which will cause them to acquire secondary-reinforcement power. Hence, when the organism which has received this kind of training itself happens to behave in such a way as to produce roughly the same pattern of stimulation, the secondary reinforcement transfers or generalizes—and a "habit" will be discovered to have come into existence.[3]

As already suggested, a response may be tried again and again by the subject, so as to make the pattern of stimulation produced by voluntary performance of the response correspond as closely as possible to the pattern of stimulation which has originally acquired the secondary reinforcement (see Mowrer, 1960, Chapter 12 for a discussion of "skill"). In this sense it is indeed true that "practice makes perfect"! And once the action is recognized by others as "imitative," it

---

[3] Suppose that a dog's foreleg naturally made a *squeaking* sound when acutely flexed. If *this* sound was produced "artificially," either by flexing the dog's leg passively or in some other way, and followed by food, it would not be surprising if the dog started "making it himself." This is all that is presumed to be involved in word learning or in "hand shaking."

may receive new, direct, primary reinforcement. But the basic notion here is that, originally, learning does not necessarily involve *doing*, as has so often been maintained. The important thing is simply that, in order to acquire secondary-reinforcing properties, a given pattern of stimulation be contiguous with primary (or secondary) reinforcement. It not uncommonly happens, of course, that a particular pattern of stimulation can be experienced *only* when the subject himself behaves in a particular way. In such a case, about all the would-be teacher or trainer can do (with nonverbal, animal subjects) is to wait for the response to be made (or at least approximated) by the subject and then, as we say, "reward it." But this is the limiting case, not the most general one. It seems that the mechanics of "habit formation" are most transparently seen when a given pattern of stimulation can be produced *by others* and thus brought into repeated contiguity, for the subject, with reinforcement. Then, whenever the subject (properly motivated) himself behaves so as to reproduce this pattern of stimulation, such behavior will immediately have the properties of a "habit." Hence we see that the basic condition for learning is not necessarily *doing*, but rather contiguity of a particular constellation of sensation with reinforcement.

Reference has repeatedly been made in *Learning Theory and Behavior* to the technique developed by Skinner as a means of getting a laboratory rat to push a bar more quickly as a means of obtaining food. The trick here consists of giving to some of the stimuli inherently associated with the occurrence of this response S^r potency before the response ever occurs. Then, when the bar is made available and, in the course of random exploration, is pressed, the habit is already in force and "ready to go." This procedure involves precisely the same principles as does the procedure according to which talking birds and human infants learn to make (imitate) words. In the Skinner situation the bar-pressing response is ordinarily followed, not only by the stimuli which have already acquired S^r power, but also by primary reinforcement (food). The same is true in the word learning situation: when a bird or baby begins to "do it himself," important and satisfying things, of a very tangible nature, are likely to happen to him. But this is by no means essential, at least not immediately so. Skinner himself and others have shown that a very respectable little "habit" can be set up on the basis of secondary reinforcement alone; and the indications are that the same holds for words.

There is, however, this difference. In the case of a rat and a Skinner bar, the technique of "baiting" is merely an advantage, not a necessity;

whereas, in teaching small children and birds to say words, this is the *only* procedure that works. Trial-and-error methods, with primary reinforcement alone, are too slow and uncertain to be at all practical.

In some ways it is surprising that the "autism" theory of word learning and, indeed, the entire new conception of habit which is delineated in this book did not suggest themselves to those who have used the method of "pretraining" just mentioned. It is, so to say, "all there." However, as far as Skinner is concerned there has been a singular preconception: that in no organism other than man is it possible for vocal responses to function as what he calls true "operants," i.e., voluntary, instrumental, habitual responses.[4] This has prevented serious consideration of the talking birds as experimental subjects in this connection, to say nothing of other organisms. When J. Konorski was in this country, late in 1957, he reported that some of his fellow researchers have confirmed in the laboratory the common impression that dogs can be taught to bark, instrumentally (cf. Lawicka, 1957a). There was, however, this difficulty. When a dog is taken into a strange experimental situation, he is likely to become very quiet and indisposed to bark. It may, in fact, be *so* long before he emits such a response that, for all practical purposes, one may say that the response does not occur; and, in terms of ordinary habit-training methods, the response has to occur before it can be strengthened.

The expedient reported by Konorski and his colleagues was this: In the living quarters, several dogs are housed together, with the result

[4] In an unpublished but much publicized dissertation written by Greenspoon (1950) at the University of Indiana, evidence has been presented for believing that adult human verbal behavior obeys the same principles as does "operant" (instrumental) behavior in general: namely, that it can be selectively facilitated by rewards (in this case, grunts or nods of social approval) and that, moreover, changes in the types of words "emitted" can be produced *without awareness* on the part of the subjects of such a change. Verplanck (1956) has worked out a more refined and reliable method of studying this phenomenon; and an extensive program of research in this field is now being carried out by Dulany (1955, 1960). The exact nature and import of the results is still under debate; but it seems likely that truly "unconscious" learning has now been demonstrated in this connection. If so, this fact poses certain problems for the autism theory of word learning and for our general conception of learning, with its stress on "central" concomitants of the learning process. An example of apparently unconscious motor learning is cited near the end of Chapter 12 of *Learning Theory and Behavior* and poses the same sort of difficulties. Although revised two-factor theory satisfactorily accounts for a wide range of phenomena, we count it no discredit to the theory that certain observations appear to challenge it. This fact at least indicates that the theory is testable—and therefore scientifically meaningful (cf. Chapter 6, especially Section X).

that there is a good deal of spontaneous barking, occasioned by the general social ("emotional") situation. Here a hungry dog will be singled out and whenever, under the stimulation of this situation, he barks he is fed. The result is that his barking, in this situation, will be facilitated, to the point that eventually it is so well established—not just as a social response, but as a specific device for "begging" for food—that it will transfer to other situations.

An instructive variation of this procedure would be the following. By means of a tape recorder one would obtain some exhibits of a dog's own barking in his living quarters. Then both the dog and the tape recorder would be moved to an experimental room. Here the dog, now hungry, would periodically be allowed to hear some of his own *recorded* barking and then be given a bit of food. The stimulus consequences of the desired response would thus acquire S^r potency, and it would be very surprising if the dog himself did not soon start making the barking response. Since the recorded bark would be something which the dog would very much wish to hear (because it would indicate the imminence of food), the dog would have every incentive for wishing to *hear himself* make the response—and this, we conjecture, is the essence of habit. The fact that the "model" is here provided by a recording of the dog's own performance (in another situation), rather than by a vocal noise (word) made by a human being, does not, of course, mean that the principles involved are any different from those involved in the imitation that occurs in language learning—or, as we have seen, in instances of latent (mediated) learning in general.

We are dealing, apparently, with principles of wide generality.[5]

---

[5] Since this chapter was written, Zimmerman, (1958b), under the author's direction, has performed an experiment with dogs of the kind indicated. The results were *completely negative!* Despite intensive training, over a period of several weeks, not one of five kennel-bred Brittinary Spaniels and four assorted house-pet dogs learned to bark when hungry as a result of hearing their own recorded barks and then being fed. In light of the varied evidence already cited and more to be cited, this finding is most remarkable. Whether it discredits the theory which the experiment was designed to test or tells us something special about the psychology (and neurology) of dogs will be left for the reader to decide. But this much is clear: if human words were tape recorded and the experiment repeated with properly motivated parrots, myna birds, or children, imitative learning would be a foregone conclusion. The writer's best guess is that in the dog experiment we were working against a neurological defect or powerful instinctive mechanism of some sort. Incidentally, the situation is made all the more puzzling by the fact that some house dogs are apparently able to bark ("speak") on command (see footnote 3); yet, as a supplement to the experiment in question, a professional dog trainer was unable to establish such behavior in any of our subjects.

III. The "Autism" Theory of Word Learning Restated and Extended

The view that words are learned, by "talking" birds and by human infants, neither by trial and error nor by simple reflex conditioning, but by the mechanism outlined in the preceding section has been developed, somewhat differently and more fully, in a paper entitled "The Autism Theory of Speech Development and Some Clinical Applications" (Mowrer, 1952). A portion of that paper is reproduced below.

Recently there has emerged, as a deduction from learning theory and psychoanalysis, an hypothesis concerning normal speech acquisition which promises to have interesting applications in the field of speech pathology.

More particularly this hypothesis comes from an investigation which the author started some five years ago in an attempt to see what could be learned about language and its development in human beings from a study of the so-called talking birds. From an analysis of such anecdotal literature as is available and our own observations with a small number of birds (including two parrots, a Mynah bird, two common crows, two Western magpies, and a number of Australian parakeets), it is apparent that birds learn to talk when and only when the human teacher becomes a *love object* for them. This interpretation is consistent with expectations generated by the principle of secondary reinforcement (learning theory) and the principle of identification (psychoanalysis).

Operationally, the first step in teaching a bird to talk is to make a "pet" of it, which is to say, tame, care for, and "baby" it in such a way as to deflect the interests and emotional attachments of the bird away from members of its own species to another species, namely *homo sapiens*. This is commonly done by isolating the bird from its own kind and making it dependent for food, water, and social attention and diversion upon its human caretakers.

But there is another step involved which only a few species of birds—and apparently no mammal save man—can make. As one cares for and plays with these creatures, one makes certain characteristic noises. These may or may not be parts of conventional speech; any kind of a noise will do—be it a word or phrase, a whistled or sung fragment of a tune, a nonsense vocalization, or even a mechanical sound like the creaking of a door or the opening of a food box—anything so long as it is intimately and consistently associated with the trainer and his care-taking activities. As a result of the association of these sounds with basic satisfactions for the bird, they become positively conditioned, i.e., they become *good sounds;* and in the course of its own, at first largely random vocalizations, the bird will eventually make somewhat *similar* sounds. By the principle of generalization, some of the derived satisfaction or pleasure which has become attached to the trainer's sounds will now be experienced when the bird itself makes and hears like sounds; and when this begins to happen the stage is set for the bird's learning to 'talk.'

In terms of learning theory, what has happened is that initially neutral sounds, by virtue of their occurrence in temporal contiguity with primary reinforcements, have acquired secondary reinforcing properties. When the bird itself happens to make somewhat similar sounds, it is now secondarily rewarded for having done so and tries to perfect these sounds so as to make them match as exactly as possible the original sounds, and thus derive from them the maximum of pleasure and comfort.

In terms of psychoanalytic theory, the bird, as a result of developing "positive cathexis" (love) for its human trainer, or "foster parent," identifies with and tries to *be like* that person. Birds cannot do much by way of making themselves *look like* human beings, and even if they could they would not ordinarily enjoy this resemblance [since they could not usually *see* themselves]; but they *can* make themselves *sound like* human beings, and this they do, under the conditions indicated, with evident satisfaction.

Once words, phrases, whistles, snatches of song, or other distinctively human sounds have been perfected on the autistic or self-satisfaction basis just described, these same responses can, of course, be employed socially or communicatively. Birds that have learned human sounds on an autistic basis can later use these sounds instrumentally, as a means of indicating some desire or need or perhaps just as a device for assembling and holding an admiring and reassuring audience. But the essential first step in this developmental sequence, in the author's belief, is one in which the reproduction and perfection of human sounds occur, not because of their objective utility, but because of the *subjective* comfort and satisfaction they provide.

So far as can be determined at present, essentially the same account holds, at least up to a point, for acquisition of speech by human infants. Words or other human sounds are first made by infants, it seems, because the words have been associated with relief and other satisfactions and, as a result, have themselves come to sound good. Human infants, like birds, are vocally versatile creatures and in the course of random activities in this area will eventually make sounds somewhat similar to those which have already acquired pleasant connotations and will, for reasons indicated, have a special incentive for trying to repeat and refine these sounds.

Soon, however, the infant discovers that the making of these sounds can be used not only to comfort, reassure, and satisfy himself directly but also to interest, satisfy, and control mother, father, and others.[6] Up to this

---

[6] One may thus say that words are first reproduced by infants, when parents are not immediately available, as a means of recapturing some of the pleasures which parents have previously provided. In a very primitive and rudimentary sense, they are trying to re-present the mother, i.e., make her present again, in an autistic, quasi-magical way. This they do, not with a conventional word for her, but with *her sounds*. But then, as the infant thus learns to make conventional word sounds, the *second* stage of word functioning emerges. Now he utters a specifically meaningful word which serves, literally, to re-present the mother, recall, recapture, recreate her; and in so doing the infant reduces the necessity for relying upon the autistic, self-supplied satisfactions. Now, instead of merely *playing* with words, the infant makes them *work*. It is well known that small children who have "re-

point the speech learning of birds and babies seems to be virtually identical; but before long, somewhere around 18 months or two years of age, human infants begin to do something of which birds, even the most talented of them, are incapable. It is always a big event for the rest of the family (and probably for the baby, too!) when a baby begins to "put words together," i.e., to make original, functional sentences. Birds may learn to repeat, "parrot fashion," phrases, sentences, or even longer sequences of human speech but the indications are that these are never understood and used by birds with their full import and meaning. As De Laguna (1927) has remarked, *predication* is the thing that gives language at the human level its most distinctive quality, and it seems that this is never achieved by infrahuman organisms (pp. 263–265) [see Chapter 4; also a series of papers on language and "personality" as they appear in Newcomb & Hartley, 1947].

Saying that one must first make a "pet" of a bird (or a baby) in order to provide the conditions necessary for the development of words is not, of course, the same as saying that it should be "spoiled." The writer once received a letter from a woman who owned a myna bird which was thoroughly "loved" in the sense of being indulged, but still it would not talk. From details supplied in the letter, it was apparent that the bird never knew a moment of want: it had a constant supply of water and preferred food and was even taken to work by its owner rather than being left alone. The reason, obviously, why the bird did not talk was that, since it was never allowed to want for anything, its mistress could not reward it and, as a result, was unable to cause her utterances to take on S^r potency. On advice, the bird's mistress changed the regime and wrote, in less than two weeks, to say that the bird had started to talk. He had, figuratively speaking, learned to "say Uncle." But the lady added (facetiously) that, although the bird was learning to talk, the training procedure was so hard on *her* that she didn't know how much longer she would be able to keep it up.

IV. Autism Theory Applied Clinically

The theory of word learning outlined in the preceding sections of this chapter is supported (a) by the fact that it is simply a special case of a broader set of principles and (b) by empirical evidence derived from the observation of word learning by birds and babies. Still further

sponsive" and "attentive" parents do not rely upon fantasy (and other forms of autistic behavior) so extensively and protractedly as do neglected children. Here, as elsewhere, it seems that good parenthood involves a judicious balance between indulgence and deprivation. If the child never wants for anything, he lacks motivation for speaking; but if he speaks and no one responds, this too can deter normal language development.

credence is given to the theory by the success reported in the following paragraphs (Mowrer, 1952) in making clinical application thereof.

Two years ago a young woman reported that tests had recently confirmed what she and her husband had suspected for some time, namely that their two-year-old daughter was very hard of hearing and that as a result her language development was being seriously retarded. In fact, the child had no real words and showed no interest in and refused to wear a hearing aid. The mother was convinced that the little girl had *some* hearing, as evidenced by the fact that if she were engaged in some forbidden activity and the mother shouted "No," the child, even though her back was turned to the mother, would respond.

It was apparent from these meager facts that the only sounds that were getting through to this child were "bad" sounds; and one could conjecture that the less often she heard them the better it suited her. There was, in short, no "appetite" for the vocalizations of others and consequently no desire to make similar sounds herself.

When the situation was interpreted to the mother in these terms, she quickly consented to a regime in which vocalizations would not be used for disciplinary purposes at all but would instead be associated as often and as deliberately as possible with *agreeable* experiences. Ordinarily one announces pleasant events in a soft tone of voice reserving the raised voice for warnings and condemnations. The prescribed plan thus called for a reversal of the usual situation. The mother was able to carry through, however, and very quickly the child became *interested* in words, was soon willing to tolerate a hearing aid so that she would be more clearly aware of them, and within six months was herself effectively making and using quite a number of words.

More recent follow-up data are not available on this case, nor has there been opportunity to test this type of thinking systematically, with a statistically meaningful number of cases.[7] One case can serve as well as many, however, to illustrate a remedial procedure and the rationale behind it. Other investigators, with more numerous cases of a similar kind at their disposal, may be able to validate the procedure. Even though the theory be entirely correct, one cannot of course, expect success in all instances. The method's effectiveness presupposes, above all else, parents—and in particular a *mother*—who can and will make the indicated changes in vocal habits. Not all parents have the requisite degree of flexibility and motivation to accomplish this end, but it seems likely that the demands which the method places upon parents will usually be acceptable; and in such cases the method, given other favorable circumstances, should work as well as in the case described.

Sanger (1955), in an unpublished study directed by the author, observed the relationships of a number of mothers and their infants over a period of

---

[7] Since the above was written, the author chanced to meet the little girl's father in another city. He reported that "L—— is chattering like a magpie now. In fact, if anything, she talks too much—we can't answer all her questions." And informal reports from speech clinics indicate that the method is working out well in other cases (cf. Rigrodsky, 1958; Morkovin, 1960).

many months, with special reference to the role of vocalization by mother and by infant. One of the first things discovered was that most mothers —and particularly those who, by other criteria, seemed to be the *good* mothers—kept their infants "bathed in sound" most of their waking hours. While caring for their infants or just spending leisure time with them, these mothers vocalized almost continuously; and even when other duties took them to adjoining rooms, they would commonly sing or call to the baby intermittently (cf. Rheingold, Gewirtz, & Ross, 1959).

This pattern of behavior is well calculated to make the mother's voice a welcome and reassuring sound, and it seems probable that much of the motivation for the babbling and cooing that infants normally engage in stems from the fact that the human voice, by virtue of the circumstances just described, has taken on pleasurable (secondary reinforcing) properties. Although baby's voice does not sound exactly like mother's voice, the similarity will usually be sufficient to cause a carry-over of some of the pleasurable qualities of one to the other; and we may surmise that the production of mother-like sounds, in the form of babbling, is a first and highly useful step in the child's progression toward fully articulate speech.[8]

The fact that congenitally deaf babies babble very little, if any, and do not, without highly specialized instruction, learn to talk at all indicates how crucial is the capacity to hear and inwardly enjoy first the pleasant, reassuring voices of others and then one's own somewhat similar sounds. Although congenitally deaf children usually have completely normal voice organs and although their parents would only too gladly reward them [in keeping with the trial-and-error learning principles] for using these organs to make word-like noises, the fact that such responses, because of the deafness, are not autistically satisfying to the child is a crucial handicap.

It is usually only after a normal infant has had many months of experience with the mother's voice as a good sound that he begins to hear it, on occasion, with implications of warning and threat. That this is an unwelcome development is dramatically indicated by the fact that when parents are scolding or admonishing them, small children will sometimes be seen to put their fingers in their ears, thus shutting out the now distinctly unwelcome human voice. But ordinarily, by the time parents begin to discipline their offspring by means of speech, the speech-learning process will have already gained sufficient momentum to be able to withstand the shock of this negative use of voice; and the impact of this discipline, however else it may be reflected, almost never has a permanently harmful effect upon language functions.[9]

[8] Because a woman's voice is more like that of an infant or small child than is a man's voice, it is probably more efficient for women to have primary responsibility for the verbal development of children than it would be for men to have this responsibility.

[9] So many different guesses have already been made about the possible cause(s) of stuttering that another, equally questionable one, cannot be objected to. Conceivably, in *some* instances, the trouble arises from a conflict between wishing and *not wishing* to hear one's own voice. This might arise, through generalization, from a strong ambivalence toward the voices of *others*. Or, where the stutterer himself feels chronically *guilty about* something, the conflict could arise from the

When, however, the gentle, loving sounds which good mothers make to their infants have been missed, due to hearing defects, and when the first human sounds to get through to the child are shouts of displeasure and proscription, it is almost axiomatic that the child thus handicapped will not *want* to hear, will not want to *use* even that small portion of his hearing equipment which may still be functional. When this abnormal course of events has occurred, the theory here explored would dictate the corrective procedure already described, and with reasonably favorable attending circumstances, one should expect results comparable to those obtained in the case reported (pp. 266–268).

It is an interesting and instructive circumstance that infants who are born totally deaf do not *babble*, or do so very little. In terms of our present thinking, there are two reasons for this, the first being that, since such children are unable to hear the sounds which *others* make in rewarding contexts, there is no secondary reinforcement to generalize to their own vocalizations (Mowrer, 1950, Chapter 24). But, as indicated in a preliminary way in Chapter 7 of *Learning Theory and Behavior* and more fully in Chapter 7 of this book, it is also probable that so-called voluntary control (or initiation) of a response is contingent upon sensory feedback therefrom; and since the major and, by all odds, most discriminating awareness of vocal responses is normally through the *ear*, it is likely that the control, as well as motivation, of these responses is seriously impaired. There is clearly an important relationship between the type of theory under consideration and practical methods of teaching the deaf (see, for example, Silverman, 1954; Fairbanks, 1954; and Dicarlo, 1958).[10]

Somewhat parenthetically, it is also interesting to note how nearly identical the sensory consequences of vocalization are (in normal individuals) for both the speaker and the hearer. Actually, of course,

---

self-accusatory—or self-revealing—potentialities of his own voice. For somewhat related thoughts about this problem, see Wischner (1952a, 1953b), Goss (1952), Sheehan (1953), and Sheehan & Voas (1954).

[10] One other brief word needs to be said about the business of *babbling*. Commonly it is said to be a prelude to or precursor of speech. In a certain sense, it *is* speech, i.e., an imitation of the *undifferentiated* voice sounds which the infant constantly hears around him. Young parakeets, before beginning to say separate and distinct *words*, often engage in what is called "little bird talk," namely a kind of babble or jabbering; and parrots, even after they learn to say definite words or phrases, will sometimes give an astonishingly good imitation of the conglomerate sound of voices in a roomful of people. A mixture of distinct words and babble occurs in this sequence of utterances which a neighbor's Myna bird often engages in: "Hel-loo. . . . Jabber, jabber, jabber. . . . Jabber, jabber, jabber. . . . Ha, ha, ha, ha hah! . . . Jabber, jabber, jabber. *Good*-bye!" The original model for this performance is not hard to identify.

both are "hearers," and *what* they hear differs only in minor ways (which become apparent when one hears one's voice in recorded form, rather than directly). In *most* forms of behavior, kinesthesis is the principal sensory result—which, of course, can be perceived only by the performer—i.e., only he knows what he is "doing." Only when a (nonvocal) action can be *seen*, both by performer and by others, do we begin to approximate the special conditions required for language; and even here what the performer sees (and the angle from which he sees it) is considerably different from what another person sees (see next section for further discussion of gesturing). Only by watching himself in a mirror or some other "reflecting" surface can the performer get a "feedback" which closely approximates the pattern of visual stimulation reaching others. But there is another means, which has been of enormous historical importance, of achieving much the same end: If a person moves a hand (or foot) in such a way as to leave a *mark* on something, what *others* see when they exchange places with the mark-maker is exactly the same. And it is this simple and important fact which has made possible that other, nonvocal form of language which we call *writing*. How extensively this form of communication is utilized and cultivated in the education of the deaf, as a substitute for or an adjunct to speech is, of course, well known (Myklebust & Bruttan, 1953). But it is also known how extremely difficult the establishment of language is where hearing and sight are both absent. Here *touch* becomes the principal medium, or mediator, of learning; but it is not nearly so satisfactory and efficient as either hearing or seeing (see Keller, 1902).

An objection to the autism theory of language learning is sometimes raised on the grounds that it cannot explain how infants learn to utter and use *negative* words. If words are reproduced because their original pronunciation by others occurs in the context of pleasure and gratification, how, it is asked, can one explain the fact that infants also learn to say "No" and to reproduce other forbidding, negative, *un*pleasant words? Such an objection is easily answered. We begin with the observation, and ready admission, that if the *only* words which an infant hears are negative (fear arousing, frustrating) ones, then he will indeed not learn to speak, as the case of the little girl cited above clearly indicates. But in the normal situation, the infant has relatively enormous experience with human sounds (especially those uttered by the mother) in all kinds of positively reinforcing contexts, long before there is any negative use of voice; and on the basis of the word responses which are thus learned (on an autistic basis), the child soon discovers the great practical utility of words, as a means of instrumental and social control, with ensuing reinforcements which are no longer merely autistic. Therefore, by the age of two or three the child sees what a "good thing" language is and actively works at getting more of it and is now able, and strongly disposed, to reproduce words "voluntarily" (in much the same way that he makes other overt responses), if it suits his purposes to do so. Just as an adult can (within limits) deliberately repeat a heard vocal sound if he wishes, so may a child, after the basis for language has been laid, autistically. In other words, if a child sees that other children (or adults) can protect themselves or otherwise control a situation by uttering the word, "No!", there is no reason to suppose that such a response has to be learned on the original, primitive autistic basis.

And, more than this, negative, prohibitive terms are often used by a child in the management of his own behavior. Not infrequently youngsters, when in a conflict situation (i.e., when tempted to do something for which they have previously been scolded or punished), are heard to say, "No, no! Johnny mustn't do that." Thus, once language is fairly launched (by the autistic mechanism), we see that there can be quite powerful incentives and reinforcements for utterance of the so-called negative words and that this fact is in no way at variance with our assumption about the mechanism underlying the earlier, more fundamental stage of word learning (cf. Mowrer, 1958).

V. The Origin of Language, with Special Reference to Gesturing

During the eighteenth and nineteenth centuries the *Societé Linguistique* received so many communications on "the origin of language" that, some 75 years ago, it put a ban upon further papers on this topic. The difficulty, of course, was that there is no very good way to check speculation against the historic—or, more precisely, the *pre*historic —facts. Writing is our oldest means of recording speech, and its invention dates back only about six thousand years, whereas the true beginnings of human language probably go back to the Stone Age, 80,000 to 100,000 years ago (Bodmer, 1944; Stewart, 1946). Admittedly, the methods available for disciplining, much less crucially confirming, speculation along these lines are poor; yet the problem is a fascinating one and warrants our asking if the autism theory of word learning, as it applies in a social group already possessing language, can throw any light upon how man *probably* started using certain sounds as words rather than other equally possible ones.

In a book called *Man and His Works*, by E. L. Thorndike (1943), there is a delightful chapter entitled, "The Origin of Language," which gives a quite excellent summary of the various theories which have attracted most interest and credence in this connection.[11] With certain unimportant omissions, this summary follows.

We must first glance at three time-honored and then dishonored theories, now known by these opprobrious names: ding-dong theory, bow-wow theory, and pooh-pooh theory.

The ding-dong theory assumed a mystical power of certain things to evoke certain sounds from men. Since each such sound was associated with the experience of the thing, it came to mean it. And since men were alike in their responses to things by sounds, one of these sounds meant more or less the same thing to all in the group, and easily became a vehicle of communication. All the evidence is against the existence of any such mystical power, and only extremely strong evidence would induce any scientific student of psychology or of language to put any faith in so extremely unlikely an origin of language (pp. 84–85).

Implicit in the ding-dong theory, as Thorndike describes it, is the notion of conditioning in its classical guise: the *direct* "experience of the thing" is the UnCS and produces a reflexive vocal reaction of some sort in the subject; and since we often see things before they impinge upon us, the *sight* thereof would serve as a CS and elicit the same reaction, which, as a conditioned response, could now serve the function of indicating or *naming*. Although our reasons are not precisely the same as Thorndike's, we can quickly agree with him that this is not a very plausible hypothesis. This writer goes on to say:

The *bow-wow* theory supposed that men formed habits of using the sounds made by animals, things, or events to mean the respective animals, things, and events, and that these habits started them on the road to inventing other sounds as signs of animals, things or events. For various reasons this theory is discredited. Doubtless after man has language he will often make the sounds that animals and things make, but it is doubtful how often he will do so in a languageless group. Possibly he will do so only accidentally as a part of his general vocal play. There might be little agreement in the ideas evoked in the members of a human group by hearing the varying sounds which its various members made when they thought of a dog, a cow, thunder, and the like (p. 85).

Actually, as we shall see presently, there is much to recommend the bow-wow theory; and Thorndike summarily rejected it, it seems, less from lack of evidence than from the inability of his own theory of

[11] More recent treatments of the same topic may be found in Cassirer (1944), Pumphrey (1951), and Estrich & Sperber (1952).

learning to account for it, *if* true. But we should get Thorndike's argument more fully before us before entering our objections in detail.

The *pooh-pooh* theory, or interjectional theory, supposed that the instinctive unlearned cries of man as a wordless animal, which already are sounds that are evoked by certain situations and evoked in human hearers certain equally unlearned responses of action and feeling, came to possess meanings also, and that on the basis of this vocabulary of familiar sounds meaning pain, surprise, fear, affection, and the like, early man here and there used other sounds to mean other facts.

Nobody should doubt that part of this is true. To a mother whose baby cries and seeks her breast that cry probably *means* that the baby wants to be fed if anything means anything to her. If she can think of anything she will think of that, as well as react appropriately to it. But for various reasons students of language have decided that the attachment of meanings to the hearing or the making of these sounds of instinctive nature is not adequate to originate articulate speech. So-called animal language plus the power of thinking meanings would not produce human language.

An ingenious theory has been set forth by *Sir Richard Paget,* a physicist and student of phonetics, who argues that the total behavior of a man to a situation includes characteristic movements of the tongue and lips and other organs of speech. These gestures of the mouth parts became specially important when a man's hands were "in continual use . . . for craftsmanship, the chase, and the beginnings of art and literature," so that he could not gesture with them. Sounds were added to these "mouthings," and finally came to play the leading role (pp. 84–87).

Paget's book (*Human Speech*) is so recent (1930) that his theory has not yet received a pet name. Using the first illustration that he gives we might call it the yum-yum theory. This, however, really misrepresents and unduly favors it; for the theory requires the mouth parts to pantomime not eating, drinking, sipping, blowing, and other acts of the mouth parts themselves (nobody doubts that), but movements of other parts of the body. A truer nick-name would be the "tongue-tied" theory, meaning that the tongue is yoked with the body by subtle bonds of mimetic kinship. The theory has been accepted by at least one psychologist, Eisenson, but it has not been accepted generally. Personally, I do not believe that any human being before Sir Richard Paget ever made any considerable number of gestures with his mouth parts in sympathetic pantomime with gestures of his hands, arms, and legs, still less that any considerable number of men in any local community made the same oral gestures in such pantomime (p. 90).

Although it is something of a digression, there is more that can and probably should be said here about the relation of *gesture* to both language and learning theory. In another paper (Mowrer, 1954), to which repeated reference will subsequently be made, this problem has been analyzed as follows:

One aspect of the problem of the origin of words which is of special interest here has to do with the tendency, under favorable conditions, for instrumental acts, or "habits," to become foreshortened into mere behavior tokens, or "gestures." I shall always remember the following experience with the little girl mentioned earlier in this paper. Having learned to sit alone on the floor when about six months of age, she would occasionally cry to be picked up; and often, in anticipation of such action on the part of her parents, she would hold up her arms flexed in preparation for being lifted. One day she was seen looking hopefully in the direction of her father, arms flexed, but not crying. She was picked up, and her mother's cooperation was elicited in seeing what would happen if we let this gesture replace crying as a signal for being taken up. Being more effortful, apparently, the crying quickly gave way to the arm flexing; and, then, this response itself underwent further involution. Soon the little girl was lifting only her right arm, and finally she would just hold up the right hand or forefinger.

The tendency for actions which an experimenter has arbitrarily defined as "correct" in a problem-solving situation to deteriorate has been commented on by various writers. As early as 1898, Thorndike, having taught cats and dogs to lick or scratch themselves as a means of getting out of a problem box, remarked: "There is in all these cases a noticeable tendency, of the cause of which I am ignorant, to diminish the act until it becomes a mere vestige of a lick or scratch" (p. 28). And some forty years later, Lorge (1936), having performed a similar type of experiment, wrote:

"In addition to reducing the time required to make these responses followed by rewards irrelevant to them, the animals *short-circuited* these responses. With successive trials, the responses became more perfunctory and stereotyped. The 'face-washing' changed from a vigorous wash to a rapid movement of both forelegs to the face; the 'scratch' changed to a rapid flexion of the hind-leg to the flank, only remotely reminiscent of the first response to irritation" (p. 110).

This "strain toward inertia," a phrase used by Sumner, Keller, and Davie (1928), or tendency toward economy of effort can be observed to special advantage under the circumstances shown in the following motion picture (Movie). Here we see how readily an initially complete instrumental response, involving a rat's going about two feet from a food trough to push a Skinner bar and then returning thereto for the food thus produced, will, if given an opportunity, deteriorate, first in the sense of the bar pressing turning into mere bar touching; then the rat will begin running well down toward the bar but turning around and going back to the trough without touching the bar; then these "loops" are seen to get shorter and shorter; until, finally, the rat, after finishing a pellet of food, will simply move his head around and "look" in the direction of the bar. Thus, he may be said merely to "give us the nod" to indicate his wish for another pellet.

It goes without saying that in order for gesturing to replace fully instrumental behavior, there must be, somewhere in the situation, a second organism which is able and willing to do some of the first organism's work for it, on the basis of a mere sign or "command." In the present instance, this second organism was the experimenter, who took over the function of activating the food delivery mechanism which had previously been done by the rat's bar pressing. Thus, what was originally a fully instrumental action, involving only the rat and the physical world, was changed into a *social situation* and what was originally an instrumental act became a *social act* involving, minimally, two organisms.[12]

The protracted helplessness of the human infant and the necessity for the mother to display, in response to signs, what Courtney (1949) has called mediating behavior creates a strong natural predisposition for human beings to be inveterate sign users. Because of this long period of dependence and indulgence, perhaps it is not too much to suppose that we spend a good deal of the remainder of our lives trying, by means of signs, to get others to do things for us or, at least, cooperate with us. Infantile helplessness very likely gave the human race one of its most powerful pushes toward both language and sociality, generally speaking.

The Law of Least Action, as Wheeler (1929) called it, which we have seen exemplified in the foregoing discussion, is a very pervasive behavior principle, whose special applications in certain areas of language have been documented in detail by Zipf (1949). However, it has a major limitation with respect to our present concern. We find that the signs most commonly employed in human communication are not gestures, which are visually transmitted, but rather the particular noises we call words.[13] And since a great many instrumental actions are essentially silent to begin with, we cannot very plausibly look upon words as condensations, or foreshortened versions, of originally fully instrumental, nonsocial behaviors.[14]

---

[12] The writer also recalls the development of an interesting gesture on the part of a myna bird. When offered food, this bird was sometimes not able to determine if she liked it or not merely from its appearance, so would take it into her mouth and taste it. If she did not like it, she would then shake her beak vigorously back and forth in order to eject the food. On numerous occasions it was observed that when this myna was offered food previously found objectionable, she would shake her head *as if* the food were in her mouth. Here we see perhaps an ancient historical root of the corresponding human gesture of negation. Cf. Darwin (1873); Wolff (1945); F. H. Allport (1924, p. 179).

[13] Perhaps the most elaborate visual sign and gesture language known in historical times was the *Lingua franca* of the American Indians. In comparison with any known spoken language it was, however, apparently very awkward and inefficient.

[14] At the risk of overcomplicating an argument which is already far from simple, the writer is tempted to inject the following thought at this point. Granted that words probably did not stem directly from the foreshortened instrumental acts which we call gestures, there is still a sense in which language is a *substitute* for grosser, more effortful action. In fact, one of the powerfully reinforcing things about language is that it so often, and so effectively, *saves us trouble*, the trouble of going somewhere else and doing something ourselves which another person, who is already *there*, can more economically *do for us*. (Being "somewhere else" may be interpreted either geographically or in terms of special skills which only a few acquire because of the "long road" of experience and learning that is involved

Some words may very well have originated as copies of sounds associated with particular actions, as, for example, the word, "patter," to represent or suggest running. But even here the responses involved in saying "patter" have nothing in common with the responses involved in actually "pattering," so even in this case we must look for a different principle (pp. 676–678).

The theory of the origin of language which Thorndike, in the chapter already cited, himself advanced is intricate and, to this writer, improbable; so no attempt will be made to describe it in detail. It involves, as one might expect, basically a trial-and-error procedure (see p. 72); but Thorndike recognizes some of the difficulties inherent in such an approach and makes the following summarizing, as well as somewhat deprecatory, statement:

It is perhaps time to attach a name to the theory I am expounding. Let us save everybody trouble by giving it an opprobrious name from the start! Since it relies on the miscellaneous vocal play of man instead of his alleged mimetic or emotional utterances, it could be called the "babble-babble" theory. Since it starts with languages private to single persons, and progresses gradually toward speech in the full speaker-hearer relation (which, indeed, my exposition has not yet reached) it could be called the "onety-two" theory. Since it depends on successive selections of chance variations in sound-reality connections, it could be called the "chancy-chance" or "luck-luck" theory. Or we may combine its two main dynamic features and call it the "babble-luck" theory (p. 97).

Thorndike extrapolated this theory into an explanation of how, in his opinion, an infant, born into a society which already has words, learns those words. In the course of its random vocalizations, the young child has the luck to make a sound that is recognizably like some accepted word; reward, from mother or some other person, follows; and

---

in mastering them.) When we think of how much "lost motion" is thus avoided, i.e., how much more we can accomplish ("get out of life") if we are "in contact" with others at more or less remote points in space (or who have specialized skills) than we could if we had to "go and do" everything for ourselves, the implications of language become almost overwhelming; and we see, especially clearly, how intimate and indispensable a role it plays in creating and perpetuating what we call *society*, or "sociality," both transversely and longitudinally, through space and through time. These remarks will recall what has already been said and, at the same time, indicate that there is at least a superficial inconsistency between the conception of language as a means of social coordination and control and the view, more especially stressed in this paper, that the main function of the sentence is to produce second-order conditioning in others, which will then be generalized to the referent, or significate, of the sentence subject. In the one case we are primarily interested in "*getting action*" and, in the other, in *giving information*. How these two aspects of language process, both of which seem real enough, are systematically related invites independent consideration (Chapter 4).

the likelihood of this sound's subsequent occurrence is gradually increased. This, of course, is strictly in keeping with Thorndike's conception of learning by *doing*.[15] Or, should it be said that, having arrived at this conception of word learning from his general theory of learning, Thorndike then constructed the foregoing notion of how language originated, in the history of the race? In any case, Thorndike's views on both language origin and individual language learning were consistent with (and probably dictated by) his over-all notions about the learning process.[16] Already we have examined the quite different view of word learning to which our own conception of learning in general leads; and in the section which follows we shall consider that theory of language origination which is most congruent therewith.

[15] Of the making of theories concerning language origin there seems to be no end. Since the foregoing section was written, Bixler & Yeager (1958) have published yet another one. Their paper, entitled "It May Have Begun with 'Mama',", notes the well nigh universal use of "mama" (or some variant thereof) as the small child's name for its mother. The authors say: "Our proposal may be stated as follows: The earliest vocalized syllables associated with discomfort, especially hunger, consist of variations of 'ma ma ma muh.' At the time speech would have originated it seems likely that only the mother could have relieved hunger pangs. Thus the cry, 'ma, ma ma muh,' when it occurred was followed most frequently all over the world by the mother relieving the child's distress and, in turn, gaining relief from distention of her breast. At this point either or, more likely, both mother and child could learn (become 'operantly conditioned' to) the sound 'ma ma' in some variation as designating the mother. Support for this idea is found in the observations of Gesell & Amatruda (1947) and Lewis (1948), the apparent universality of 'ma ma' as an infant designation of mother, and Skinner's (1957) research in operant conditioning" (p. 474). Although the ubiquity of "mama" is indeed impressive, the theory is somewhat less so. This footnote is being written on a train; and a few seats removed is a crying infant. What the writer seems to hear is predominantly "wa wa" and "owh owh," and he cannot recall ever hearing an infant (prior to the onset of conventional language development) cry with the syllables "ma ma ma." Perhaps a more likely surmise would be that the mouth movements involved in saying "ma ma" (and perhaps "pa pa" as well) get reinforced in process of nursing and thus, when phonated, produce the familiar sounds. Even if the Bixler-Yeager thesis were valid as regards "mama," it could hardly be expanded into a *general theory* of word acquisition, either in the race or the individual. *That* is our objective.

[16] Cf. also Skinner's (1958a) conception of response "shaping" by the judicious use of reward for successively closer and closer "approximations" of the required act. This procedure works well enough in some situations; but it would be manifestly inefficient in teaching a myna bird to say, for example, "How are you today?" In fact, one may reasonably doubt that it would be even remotely effective here (cf. Skinner, 1957).

VI. The Bow-Wow (Onomatopoetic) Theory and Autism Theory Compared

After the foregoing survey of various theories of language origin, we are in a position to ask: Which of these theories, if any, is most congruent with, and would be most favored by, the psychological principles (of learning and language) which have been thus far enunciated in this book? In the paper already cited (Mowrer, 1954), an attempt has been made to answer this question, thus:

Of the various classical theories of word origination, the one most closely related to this scheme is obviously the "onomatopoetic" or so-called "bow-wow" theory. This conception of word genesis can be illustrated in a crude but probably valid way as follows. Suppose that just before or as we give a laboratory rat a bit of food, we sound a tone of standard pitch and intensity. This tone, as we know from numerous studies, will take on secondary reinforcing properties. And if the rat could, with its own vocal cords, make a noise reasonably like the tone, we would predict, on the basis of principles already cited, that it would soon begin to do so. Unhappily, in view of the severe limitations on vocalization in the rat which have already been mentioned, we cannot expect this to happen. However, if we place the electronic oscillator used by the experimenter in producing the tone at the disposal of the rat, on the basis of movements which the rat can easily make, we should not be in the least surprised if the rat, under *these* circumstances, is disposed to "make" the sound. So let us, after the rat is well trained with respect to tone associated with food, make a Skinner bar available, depression of which will have the same effect, with respect to producing the tone, as the telegraph key previously used by the experimenter. [Fig. 3–1] shows the behavior of a hungry rat toward such a bar during a 20-minute period, in the course of which bar pressing produced no food but the "promise" of it, in the form of the tone and the secondary reinforcement it had acquired from prior pairings with food (p. 679).

This experiment is reminiscent of the Skinner procedure (previously described) for getting a rat to make a particular (bar-pressing) *response*. But we are here not so much concerned with the subject's response *per se* as with the *stimulation* (sound) which the response produces. In other words, our frame of reference is different: instead of being interested in the direct utility (to the rat) of the bar pressing, we are concerned with its effectiveness in *signaling* to another organism.

How energetically a rat, trained in the manner just described, will continue using the tone as a *signal to the experimenter*, if the experimenter will only cooperate, is suggested [in Fig. 3–2]. Here will be seen what happens if, when the rat pushes the bar and produces the tone, another organism responds to it as a sign that the rat wants food—and obliges.[17] A stimulus which was originally made by the environment to the rat is thus "taken over" by the rat and "made back" to the environment; and if another organism will respond thereto, it becomes a "social act," or true sign.[18] Of course, on the basis of trial-and-error learning alone, without the presence of a signal of any sort, a rat would eventually learn to press the bar if it produced food. But the precipitous nature of the learning shown [in Fig. 3–2] suggests, and experimentation reported elsewhere (Mowrer, 1950, Chapter 11) confirms, that the intermediation of a stimulus with previously acquired secondary reinforcing properties produces a performance markedly superior to what can be expected on the basis of trial and error alone (pp. 679–680).

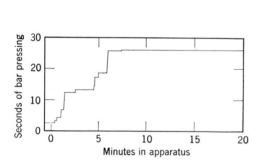

Fig. 3–1. Graphic record of bar pressing by rat, where this performance produced a tone which had been previously associated with food. The bar-pressing "habit" was thus learned solely on the basis of the secondary reinforcement provided by the tone. As the secondary reinforcement extinguished, the animal ceased to press the bar. In this situation the experimenter may be said first to have made the signal to the rat as a means of indicating that it was going to get food. The rat, when given an opportunity to push a bar which turned on the tone, made the signal "back" to the experimenter, but the experimenter did not respond (cf. Fig. 3–2).

[17] The reader may be struck by a crude analogy between the performances shown in Figs. 3–1 and 3–2 and the two stages of language development in the child as proposed by Piaget (1926): the "ego-centric" stage wherein the child "talks to himself," and the stage of social communication, wherein the child talks to someone else.

[18] A somewhat parallel instance is reported by Hollingworth (1928). Having trained a pet terrier to "sit-up" on command, with food as a reward, Hollingworth observed that the dog was soon "sitting up" on its own initiative, now not as an act of obedience but as a way of "begging," i.e., signaling its desire for food.

But perhaps the relationship of the foregoing discussion to the onomatopoetic theory of language origin is still not fully apparent. The
tone, in the experimental situation described, may seem too "artificial"
to suggest how *natural* sounds may have become the starting point for
human language development. The following quotation, taken from
the same study, provides a partial answer.

A particularly rich source of sounds which might then be transformed
into "words" are those which living organisms characteristically make during
consummatory behavior of any kind [cf. footnote 15]. This possibility
was called to the writer's attention under the following circumstances. A
number of rats were being fed, seriatim (but at rather long intervals), in
separate compartments so constructed that the rats could not see each other
but could easily hear any noises which the other rats made. The particular
manner of feeding involved inserting food up into each animal's compartment, "under its nose," so to say, on the end of a small metal rod, between

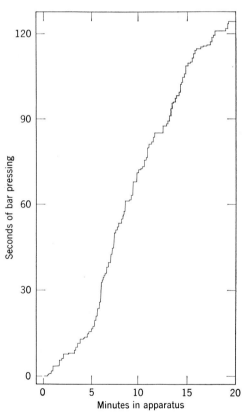

Fig. 3–2. Graphic record of bar pressing by a rat where this performance produced a tone previously associated with food and caused the experimenter to provide food. After several trials, there was something like an "insight" (see upward inflection of curve at about 5 minutes). As the animal became satiated, toward the end of the recording, the rate of responding declined. In this record we see what happens if an organism learns the meaning of a signal, is then permitted to make that signal, and some other organism responds appropriately thereto. See text for discussion of possible bearing of this demonstration on the question of where human beings first got the noises they used as words and how infants learn to speak.

the bars constituting the floor grill of the compartment. While eating, the rat would hold the rod in its front paws and inadvertently "rattle" it against the grill bars. Because this "rattling"—which itself sounds as if it might have had an onomatopoetic origin—accompanied eating, it became a "sign" to which the rats not having the rod responded with much interest and apparent anticipation. It rather clearly had come to "mean" *food*, and one could imagine that in a comparable situation involving prehistoric men such a sound might well have supplied the model for some vocal reproduction (p. 679).

In a course on the psychology of learning, taught in the Summer Session of 1957 at the University of Illinois, the writer was explaining the natural relationship between the autistic theory of word learning and the onomatopoetic theory; and in the discussion which followed, a Turkish student, Mr. Ahmet Enc, related the following story. At one stage of World War I, French airplanes repeatedly bombed certain Turkish cities. In order to do so they had, of course, to fly over open countryside, where they were a source of much interest to the peasants, who had never before seen airplanes and, indeed, had no name for them. They were, however, soon christened "girgirs"—and the source of the word is obvious: several old-style propellered planes, flying along together, make an unmistakable sound of "gir, gir, gir, gir." And this word came into widespread usage, although there was already another word for airplane in the Turkish language, namely "Ucak." [19]

Here, however, the sound from which the word was developed was a "bad," rather than a good, one; and it might seem to go against our theory that such words develop, as well as words which are predicated upon good sounds. We conjecture that man, or protoman, was indeed first drawn into play with "words" because, by means of them, he could reproduce sounds which he *liked* to hear and that, in the beginning, he was very careful *not* to reproduce bad sounds. But later, when man had begun to discover the marvels of language, he became more venturesome and found that even "bad" sounds can have a good effect, when properly used (as will be more fully explained in Chapter 4; (cf. also Section IV).

We thus see that there is a good deal of support for the view that those *natural* sounds which, in the course of ordinary daily experience, had taken on secondary-reinforcement value for members of some pre-

---

[19] Cf. also the English-American terms, "buzz-bomb" and "bazooka." For renewed interest in and an experimental approach to the onomatopoetic theory of word origin, see Wissemann (1954); also Brown (1955) for an English review of this work. Cassirer (1944) likewise gives the onomatopoetic theory considerable credence (pp. 112–114).

historic human group probably provided the models, or prototypes, for those *social* sounds which we now call words. There is, however, at least one superficial objection to this theory which remains to be mentioned, namely, the fact that different groups developed *different* languages, different vocabularies and sentence structures. Assuming Nature to be uniform and her sounds and their significances to be relatively constant throughout the world, would we not expect, on the basis of the foregoing analysis, the emergence of a *universal* language, rather than the innumerable languages which actually exist?

There are two, rather obvious, rejoinders which can be made to this objection. (1) It is, first of all, highly arbitrary to assume that human experiences, in widely separated and diverse parts of the world, *are* the same. Pretty clearly, both the environment and man's activities therein vary considerably with geography; hence, language variability, rather than uniformity, would be the expectation. (2) Moreover, in the preceding paragraphs we have been speaking only about the *most primitive* origins of words. Once a human, or protohuman, group had discovered the magic of language from the use of a handful of words modeled upon natural sounds, it would almost inevitably come about, human ingenuity being what it is, that new words would then begin to be created, more or less *ad hoc;* and, in the course of time, these "artificial," though no less useful or effective, words would numerically overshadow the onomatopoetic words and thus create a quite misleading impression about "word origins." The fact that a good many clearly onomatopoetic words are still found in various languages and that new ones continue to come into contemporary use every now and then certainly leaves considerable basis for supposing that onomatopoeia may, indeed, have provided the "start" for human language development, historically speaking.

VII. The Problem of "Imitation" as Viewed by Thorndike

As will now be clear, the analysis of language learning (both individual and racial) which is put forward in this chapter prominently emphasizes *imitation*. Such an emphasis is, of course, far from new. But the difficulty commonly involved in earlier discussions of the problem was that "imitation" was largely just a word, which carried potency only in the sense of explaining what its definition already implied. Thus, word learning might be said to be "due to imitation," and imitation would then be defined, by example, as a situation in which one individual *copies* what another says or does. It is, of course, the very *fact* of copying that calls for explanation; and it is believed that such explanation is achieved, in preceding sections, in a strictly non-circular manner. In other words, it appears that we have evolved a genuine *theory* of imitation.

Although a considerable literature exists on the topic of imitation, no attempt will be made here to review it systematically. Instead, reference will be made to only three specimen treatments of the problem, an early one by Thorndike and, in the following sections, recent ones by Miller & Dollard and by Hayes & Hayes. In a monograph entitled "Animal Intelligence" and published in 1898, Thorndike reports some highly cogent, but little-cited, observations. He says:

> To the question, "Do animals imitate?" science has uniformly answered, "Yes." But so long as the question is left in this general form, no correct answer to it is possible. It will be seen, from the results of numerous experiments soon to be described, that imitation of a certain sort is not possible for animals, and before entering upon that description it will be helpful to differentiate this matter of imitation into several varieties or aspects. The presence of some sorts of imitation does not imply that of other sorts.
>
> There are, to begin with, the well-known phenomena presented by the imitative birds. The power is extended widely, ranging from the parrot who knows a hundred or more articulate sounds to the sparrow whom a patient shoemaker taught to get through a tune. Now, if a bird really gets a sound in his mind from hearing it and sets out forthwith to imitate it, as mocking-birds are said to do, it is a mystery and deserves closest study. If a bird, out of a lot of random noises that it makes, chooses those for repetition which are like sounds that he has heard, it is again a mystery *why*, though not as in the previous case a mystery *how*, he does it. The important fact for our purpose is that, though the imitation of sounds is so habitual, there does not appear to be any marked general imitative tendency in these birds. There is no proof that parrots do muscular acts from having seen other parrots do them. But this should be studied. At any rate, until we know what sort of sounds birds imitate, what circumstances or emotional attitudes these are connected with, how they learn them and, above all, whether there is in birds which repeat sounds any tendency to imitate in other lines, we cannot, it seems to me, connect these phenomena with anything found in the mammals or use them to advantage in a discussion of animal imitation as the forerunner of human. In what follows they will be left out of account, will be regarded as a specialization removed from the general course of mental development, just as the feathers or right aortic arch of birds are particular specializations of no consequence for the physical development of mammals. For us, henceforth, imitation will mean imitation minus the phenomena of imitative birds (pp. 47–48).

Then follows a discussion of various commonplace phenomena which are usually regarded as "imitative" but which Thorndike was persuaded were "indirect results of instinctive acts." And, finally, he says:

At any rate, whether previous authorities have agreed that such a process is present or not, it is worth while to tackle the question; and the formation of associations by imitation, if it occurs, is an important division of the formation of associations in general. The experiments and their results may now be described (pp. 47–50).

According to Thorndike's view and conviction, the upshot of these experiments, with chickens, cats, dogs, and one monkey, was that animals do *not*, in general, imitate and that they do not *learn* by imitation. Instead, Thorndike believed that learning was always, or at least most commonly, due to "trial and error."

While among the most astute of modern behavior theorists, Thorndike was handicapped in two ways. In 1898, and for a good many years to come, psychologists placed more explanatory reliance upon the concept of "instinct" than is today thought justifiable, with the result that they sometimes interpreted as "due to instinct" behavior which would now be analyzed in terms of the more subtle learning processes. Thorndike's recognition of the obvious fact of imitation in the parrot but his dismissal of it as a peculiarity (instinct?) of the species is an illustration of this common tendency.

At the same time, Thorndike knew little or nothing about the phenomenon of secondary reinforcement. If he had, he might have been more disposed to interpret the imitativeness of parrots in terms of learning (rather than instinct); and he might also have been less inclined to deny the occurrence of imitation in other species. So strong, in fact, were his preconceptions on this score that he was inclined to discount the contrary testimony of professional animal trainers— though, with true scientific integrity, he *reported* it. Said he:

> It seems arrogant and may seem to some unjustifiable thus to discard testimony, to stick to a theory based on one's own experiments in the face of these opinions. If I had wished to gain applause and avoid adverse criticism, I would have abstained from upholding the radical view of the preceding pages. At times it seems incredible to me that the results of my experiments should embody the truth of the matter, that there should be no imitation. The theory based on them seems, even to me, too radical, too novel. It seems highly improbable that I should be right and all the others wrong. But I cannot avoid the responsibility of giving what seems to my judgment the most probable explanation of the results of the experiments; and that is the radical explanation already given (pp. 63–64).

Perhaps Thorndike erred in giving too much generality to his observations with cats, which he used especially often in his researches. He was very possibly correct in holding that these animals cannot easily be taught by putting-through procedures; but cats are curiously remote and independent creatures and seem to resent direction and interference. The dog, on the other hand, which in terms of docility is much closer both to the laboratory rat and to man, benefits and benefits greatly by being put through responses which are problem-solving but otherwise unlikely to occur. We have already discussed the familiar procedure of teaching a dog to "shake hands," and many other instances could be added. For example, the common practice in teaching a dog to "roll over" involves passively rolling the dog over and then rewarding it with food. Professional animal trainers are often a little jealous of their special knowledge and skill, so that we do not know precisely how it is that they get their subjects to do many of the remarkable tricks one commonly sees; but it is a safe surmise that "putting through" plays a significant role in at least the early part of such training. Moreover, it is entirely possible that after much training and experience a dog, chimpanzee, or other intelligent type of animal might begin to show genuinely imitative behavior, even though naive animals of the same species do not. Harlow (1949) has brilliantly demonstrated the development of what he calls *learning sets* or "learning to learn" in monkeys, with central emphasis upon discriminative learning (Mowrer, 1960, see Chapter 12). It would seem equally possible that when the solution to a problem lies, not in discrimination, but in so-called imitation, there might likewise be a progressive improvement as the subject moves from one such task to another, and another, and another (cf. Section X and Chapter 5, Section IX).

What are we to make, then, at this vantage point in time of Thorndike's treatment of the problem of imitation? Surely it is difficult to avoid the surmise that his perception of the facts was heavily colored by a theoretical bias. If Thorndike's version of Connectionism was valid, it followed that living organisms learn only by doing: that is, the only way an organism can learn is to *do* something ("exercise a connection") and then experience reward or punishment. In this, and *only* this, way could bonds, or connections, presumably be modified. Imitation, if real *qua phenomenon*, constituted a major embarrassment for Thorndike; and it was apparently easier for him to question the facts than to formulate a new and more adequate theory of learning in general. The bond notion of learning was a great stumbling block and had to be discarded before real progress could be made along these lines. In the last section of this chapter, we shall see just how liberating and potent revised two-factor theory is by comparison.

But it will first be necessary to follow certain other lines of development. In the section immediately following we shall review efforts which have been made, again without much success, to derive an explanation of imitation in terms of classical Pavlovian conditioning principles. Next, in Section IX, we shall examine the approach which Miller & Dollard make to this problem in their book, *Social Learning and Imitation* (1941). Because Hull's theory of learning was basically Thorndikian, and since the position taken by Miller & Dollard draws heavily upon Hull (but is also at least obliquely influenced by classical conditioning theory), we are not surprised to find some of the same limitations in their treatment of this problem that characterize Thorndike's analysis. In Section X will be described the remarkable observations of Hayes & Hayes on imitation in a domestic chimpanzee, which no prior theory seems able to encompass. But for revised two-factor theory they are made-to-order.

VIII. Imitation and the Conditioned Reflex (Humphrey, Holt, and Piaget)

To the best of the present writer's knowledge, the first systematic attempt to explain imitation in terms of conditioning principles was made in 1921 by Humphrey. After noting the ubiquity of imitative behavior in both man and animals (in contrast to Thorndike's position), Humphrey came to grips with his subject as follows:

There is here presented an analysis of the seemingly simple process of imitation and an attempt to show that it consists of highly complex integrations of a peculiar type of conditioned reflex. . . . The fundamental thing about an imitative response is that it is similar to the stimulus which produces it. . . . In each case the response I make is in some way similar to the stimulus (pp. 2–3).

This writer then refers to the familiar notion of reflex chains or sequences which have a beginning and an end, and he also speaks of *circular* sequences of action such as that involved in many repetitive performances, such as hand-feeding a printing press.

But suppose that our unit is very small so that the response acts as a direct stimulus for an identical response. . . . There is the case of the crying baby. Originally the stimulus was perhaps a pain, but as the child cries he hears himself crying. Then we have S producing R, and with it the auditory stimulus S_2, the sound of the baby's own crying in the baby's ears. Hence by the law of substitution of stimuli, S_2, the auditory stimulus, produces R, the reaction, and the more the baby cries the more he cries. . . . A similar phenomenon may be observed with animals. One restive dog will keep the whole dog population of the district barking. A crowing cock will start all other cocks crowing. Action of this type may be regarded as the elementary unit of imitation. It depends upon the fact that man and animals have *senses by which they can perceive the reactions to stimuli from the same or other senses.* It is a particular kind of conditioned reflex, where the response acts as a secondary stimulus. It comes from a psychological in-breeding, a kind of parthenogenesis of behavior (pp. 3–4, italics added).

Here was an adumbration of the notion of the *reflex circle* which E. B. Holt was soon to popularize; but the palpable difficulty with it was that it accounted for *too much.* That is to say, as Miller & Dollard (1941) have observed, there was no way of explaining how a reflex circle, once activated, ever stops. The passage just quoted is neverthe-less a significant one, particularly because of the words in italics. Here we see a clear recognition of the phenomenon of response-correlated stimulation, or sensory feedback from behavior, which is so essential, not only to an adequate understanding of imitation, but of habit forma-tion in general. But without a better grasp of reinforcement (and of what it is, precisely, that gets conditioned) than was available in 1921, this analysis was severely handicapped.

The point has also been made against the conditioned-reflex inter-pretation of imitation, and particularly as it applies to language learn-ing, that there is no unconditioned stimulus for words and thus no way of getting the infant to imitate *others.* This objection cannot be met in an entirely satisfactory manner, but Humphrey gave a partial answer in the following observations:

Breed (1911) reports that pigeons placed in a cage where they could see other pigeons eating, pecked the ground although no food was given them [cf. Section VI]. The sight of other birds pecking had become a conditioned stimulus for pecking. Here the imitation is direct from other animals, and does not depend on the animal's own activity. . . .

If the mother happens to gurgle at the same time as the child is gurgling and making few other movements, and gurgles more frequently when the child gurgles, then after a time the gurgle from the mother will call forth the "imitative" gurgle from the child. Here the original secondary stimulus comes from without, and we have a kind of converse of type one. There may be other types, but all will be found to depend, as these do, upon the establishment of a conditioned reflex where the secondary stimulus is similar to the reaction. Imitative action may be defined as *action involving a condi-tioned reflex the secondary stimulus of which is similar to the reaction* (pp. 4–5).

In 1924 F. H. Allport (pp. 183–189) attempted to handle the prob-lem of language learning along much the same lines; and in 1931, in his *Animal Drive and the Learning Process,* E. B. Holt wrote as follows:

There is an amusing and instructive little game that can be played with a child, say of five years, that illustrates three points that I would bring out.

At a moment when the child is in good humour and not keenly bent on any special activity, one stands up in front of the child smiling, and copies whatever movement the child happens first to make. The child will almost infallibly (smile and) repeat his movement. One repeats after him. He will repeat again, and with each repetition the child's movement becomes more energetic and longer in sweep. . . . Now when the game is in full swing, if the older person introduces a new movement the child will almost infallibly *imitate* it, and this will start a new sequence. . . .

The little game brings up more points than the three that I wish to emphasize here. Of these three, the first is that the increasing vehemence of the child's repetition of his own and the other person's movement is directly due to echo. . . .

Secondly, when the game is in full swing, and the older person introduces some *new* motion, the child will copy it. . . .

Thirdly, our game with the child sheds some little light on the process known as "leadership." When the game is in full swing it becomes at times ambiguous as to which individual is leading, and which is copying, the other (pp. 117–119).

The experiments of Miller & Dollard which are to be discussed presently seem obviously to have been inspired by these observations by Holt. But at least the *theory* behind these experiments came more directly from the Thorndike-Hull tradition, so we shall deal with them independently rather than in the present context. More in line with the immediately preceding discussion are the views of Piaget on the subject of imitation as set forth in his 1951 book, *Play, Dreams, and Imitation in Childhood*. But first one word more, of a somewhat parenthetical nature, concerning the "game" described by Holt. It is easy to verify that children *are* intrigued by, and easily involved in, such a procedure. But the interpretation Holt gives of it seems much too simple. Note, first of all, that the child used in the example is five years old, and therefore a quite highly socialized little creature. Having an adult do what *it* does must be quite a novelty, indeed; and we can hardly be surprised if some interest and excitement ensue. It seems most unlikely, however, that anyone could ever get a bird to "talk" by this device; and it seems equally improbable that anyone could, for that matter, succeed in teaching language to a human infant in this way. But we nevertheless discover that such an expert on child development as Jean Piaget, in the work already cited, subscribes to a virtually identical doctrine. He says:

In order to stimulate the baby's voice, the other voices must either reproduce certain familiar sounds already uttered by the child, or certain intonations known to him. Moreover, the child must be interested in the sounds he hears, in which case the contagion is in no way automatic, but is a kind of spontaneous circular reaction. In a word, vocal contagion is mere stimulation of the child's voice by another voice, without exact imitation of the child's voice.

Secondarily, there is mutual imitation, which is apparently exact imitation, when the experimenter imitates the child at the very moment when he is uttering this or that particular sound. The child then redoubles his efforts and, stimulated by the other voice, imitates in his turn the sound his partner is imitating. . . . The child makes no effort to adapt himself to the sound he hears, but merely has to retain the sound he himself was making a moment earlier, and his imitation is only a continuation of the circular reaction (pp. 10–11).

When the child now hears others making sounds similar to those he himself makes, accommodation to these sounds is inseparable from a schema of assimilation already formed, and thus at once sets the schema in motion, the result being imitation (p. 14).

Despite the fancy vocabulary, it is clear that Piaget is saying (and saying rather less well) substantially what Holt, Humphrey, and others have said much earlier. Since Thorndikian theory was so completely inadequate to account for imitation, it is not surprising that various writers should have tried to explain this phenomenon along Pavlovian lines. But since the very heart of Pavlovian theory has had to be modified to make it viable as far as a general psychology of learning is concerned, one would hardly expect a theory of imitation derived from the classical form of this theory to be anything very different from what it manifestly is: Namely, a feeble fabrication which is neither logically consistent nor empirically well supported.

Therefore, we leave this line of inquiry and speculation with a somewhat paradoxical evaluation: Although conditioning is the core of the learning process, traditional conditioning theory has taken its advocates on a proverbial wild-goose chase as far as the understanding of imitation is concerned. The line of developments to be considered in the next two sections points in a far more promising direction.

IX. Miller & Dollard on Imitation and Language

Thorndike, as we have seen in Section VII, in effect repudiated the whole problem of imitation; and the attempts to derive a satisfactory explanation thereof in terms of classical conditioned-reflex principles were likewise unavailing. Therefore, the effort made by Miller & Dollard, in 1941, to approach this problem in terms of Hull's attempted synthesis of Thorndike's and Pavlov's views (Mowrer, 1960, Chapter 3) attracted much interest and attention. The following excerpts, taken from the Miller-Dollard book, carry us quickly to the heart of their analysis.

Two children . . . were playing in their bedroom, which was adjacent to the family kitchen. The kitchen opened upon a back stairway. It was six o'clock in the evening, the hour when father usually returned home, bearing candy for the two children. While playing in the bedroom, Jim heard a footfall on the stairs; it was the familiar sound of father's return. The younger child, however, had not identified this critical cue. Jim ran to the kitchen to be on hand when father came to the back door. Bobby happened on this occasion to be running in the direction of the kitchen and behind Jim. On many other occasions, probably many hundreds, he had not happened to run when Jim did. He had, for instance, remained sitting, continued playing with his toys, run to the window instead of the door, and the like; but on this occasion, he was running behind his brother. Upon reaching the kitchen, Jim got his candy and Bobby his.

On subsequent nights with similar conditions, the younger child ran more frequently at the mere sight of his older brother running. When he ran, he received candy. Eventually, the behavior, under pressure of continued reward, became highly stabilized, and the younger child would run when the older ran, not only in this situation but in many others where time and place stimuli were different. He had learned in this one respect to *imitate* his older brother, but he had not learned to run at the sound of his father's footfall (94–95).

Miller & Dollard, using their familiar drive-cue-response-reward paradigm, then make the following theoretical analysis of the foregoing example of imitation. They say:

The relationship between the acts of leader and imitator can be put together into one diagram as follows:

	Leader		Imitator
Drive:	Appetite for candy		Appetite for candy
Cue:	Father's footfall	– – –dependent– – – – – – –→	Leg twinkle of leader
Response:	Running – – – – – – –matched– – – – – – –→		Running
Reward:	Eating candy		Eating candy

It will be noted above that the responses are *matched*, thus fulfilling one important condition of imitative behavior. It is further clear that the response of the imitator is elicited by cues from the act of the leader. His behavior is therefore *dependent* on that of the leader. Simple, or simple-minded, as an analysis so detailed of an incident so humble may seem, it represents, nevertheless, a large class of cases of social behavior which is called imitative. Such cases are frequently encountered when the history of the act is not known, and therefore the observer cannot be certain that the imitative act was learned. Every case ought at least to be examined to see whether the variables called for by the learning hypothesis are not in fact present.

The chapter immediately following the one from which the fore-going excerpts are taken begins thus:

An analysis of an observed example of imitative behavior has led to the conclusion that certain conditions of social life reward the learning of imitation. An attempt will be made to verify experimentally the deduction that imitation will actually be learned whenever these conditions are present (p. 98).

The experiments carried out in this connection are summarized by Miller & Dollard as follows:

In this series of experiments, albino rats that had been living together in a conventional type of wire cage were first tested to see if they had any initial tendency to perform a very simple type of imitative response. The response selected was that of turning in the same direction as a leader at the junction of a T-maze. It was found that animals raised under these conditions had no marked initial tendency either to imitate by going in the same direction as the leader or to non-imitate by going in the opposite direction. Then the animals were divided into two groups. One group was rewarded for going in the same direction as a leader; the other group was rewarded for going in the opposite direction. Under these conditions, it was found that the two groups gradually learned to imitate and to non-imitate, respectively.

In order to make the situation more parallel to many of the social situations in which imitation would be expected to be learned, the responses of the leaders were guided by black and white cards which they had learned to use as cues. Control tests, in which the cards were removed and leaders were used that had been trained to make either right or left turns, indicated that under the conditions of the experiment the animals learned to use the response of the leader as their cue.

After this simple type of imitation had been learned in one situation, tests indicated that it generalized, that is, appeared without additional training in other similar situations. The two groups trained to imitate and non-imitate white leaders showed a highly reliable tendency, respectively, to imitate and non-imitate black leaders. After the two groups had learned to imitate and non-imitate when motivated by hunger, they showed a highly reliable tendency to imitate and non-imitate when motivated by thirst. After learning to imitate and non-imitate on the long, narrow runway of the T-maze, they showed a tendency, which, however, was not statistically reliable, to imitate and non-imitate in stepping off a small, square starting platform onto one of four adjacent square platforms.

That animals can learn the response of imitating (or non-imitating) under appropriate conditions of drive, cue, and reward, and that this response learned in one situation generalizes to other similar situations, confirms the theoretical analysis made in the preceding chapter (pp. 119–120).

The Miller-Dollard analysis of imitation has sometimes been criticized along these lines. It has been pointed out that their experimental animals "imitated" (see also the example of the two children) only in the sense that one subject gets its *cue* for a particular action from like (or unlike) action on the part of another subject. Hence, it might be said that Miller & Dollard were not really studying imitation at all, but simply discrimination in which the cue stimulus is provided by the behavior of other organisms. Their rejoinder would probably be that imitation *is* "simply discrimination" of the kind just described; and they might then point out that what they have done, in effect, is to show that so-called imitative behavior is just a special instance of quite general principles.

The over-all theory of learning on which the Miller-Dollard analysis of imitation is based may be summarized as follows. It holds that there are four aspects or elements involved in learning: *drive, cue, response,* and *reward.* Said otherwise, for learning to occur, the subject must *want* something (drive), *notice* something (cue), *do* something (response), and *get* something (reward). Thorndikian theory specified only three of these four elements: drive, response, and reward. The Miller-Dollard formulation is therefore closer to that of Hull (Mowrer, 1960, pp. 66–74), where we see the same four elements represented. And because of the introduction of this fourth element, it becomes possible to derive at least a limited theory of imitation, which is not possible with the simpler, less fully elaborated theory of Thorndike. However, there is a question as to whether the Miller-Dollard analysis of imitation is adequate.[20] Can it, for example, account for word learning, as this phenomenon occurs in birds and human infants? Here it is hardly a question of the subject's learning to listen to what the "leader" (mother, trainer) *says* as the basis for determining what he says as a means of solving some practical problem (like getting food). As we have seen, all that is necessary for word learning in birds is to have the word said, by the trainer, and then *followed* by food (or some other reward). The bird does not have to say the word and then *be* rewarded by food; the secondary (autistic) reinforcement provided by the sound of the word is alone sufficient to bring it into existence.

The position of Miller & Dollard with respect to language learning is suggested in the following paragraph:

A mother was worried because her child seemed to be retarded in learning to talk. Brief questioning revealed that she was adept at understanding the child's every want as expressed by its gestures. Having other successful

[20] Schein (1954), using adult human subjects, has confirmed the general Miller-Dollard thesis, *re* imitation, "but Ss' reactions were highly complex" (p. 395); cf. also pp. 110–112.

means of responding, the child was not in a dilemma. He only learned his old habits of using gestures more thoroughly and consequently did not perform that type of *random vocal behavior which would lead to speech*. By gradually pretending to become more stupid at understanding gestures, the mother put the child in a dilemma and probably facilitated the learning of speech. At least, under these modified conditions, this child rapidly learned to talk (p. 34; italics added).

At the time *Social Learning and Imitation* was written, the authors were well aware of the phenomenon of secondary reinforcement and made extensive use of the concept. Although they may not have seen its full implication for word learning, it is interesting that they did anticipate it to some extent, as the following paragraphs indicate:

At the same time that the child is practicing his own crying responses, he is learning to respond to the voices of others. Adults who are feeding, fondling, and otherwise caring for infants usually talk to them; thus certain tones of the human voice acquire a reward value and may later be used to soothe the fretful child. It seems possible that this acquired reward value of the sounds in the language generalizes to sounds which the child makes while he is babbling and helps to reinforce his babbling behavior.

It would be interesting to compare the babbling behavior of different children after an attempt had been made to give different phonemes a special acquired reward value. One child would be talked to with a certain phoneme while being fed and with a different but equally pronounceable phoneme while being dressed or having some other routine performed which seems to annoy him. A second child would be talked to with the first phoneme while being dressed and the second while being fed. Each child would be talked to with both phonemes for an equal length of time. The babbling behavior of the two children would then be compared. The prediction would be that the child would learn to babble with the phoneme which had been given an acquired reward value more than with the other (p. 81).

Here one sees a clear adumbration of the autism theory of word learning; but it was made ancillary to trial-and-error (the second paragraph just quoted is really a footnote), instead of being put forward as the first and most basic mechanism involved in the acquisition of word responses. Subsequent developments, as regards both theory and research findings, seem to give greater support to the autism theory of language learning than to "babble-luck" theory, of which the main Miller-Dollard theory is a variant.

X. Imitation and "Speech" in the Chimpanzee

In September, 1947, Dr. and Mrs. Keith Hayes "adopted" a three-day-old chimpanzee baby from the Yerkes Laboratories of Primate

Biology, at Orange Park, Florida, where Dr. Hayes was employed as a research psychologist. Dr. and Mrs. Hayes took "Viki" into their home and treated her, as nearly as possible, as they would have a baby of their own. She was clothed, fed, played with, toilet trained, and disciplined in the conventional human ways; and the result was that she developed some remarkably human characteristics. In 1951 Mrs. Hayes published a delightful account (with pictures) of this venture, in a book called *Ape in Our House*. Here, in a chapter entitled "Monkey See, Monkey Do," Mrs. Hayes graphically indicates what an inveterate little imitator Viki had become by the time she was about three years old.[21]

Viki showed her first evidence of imitation at sixteen months of age, when she began crudely copying my household routine—dusting, washing dishes, pushing the vacuum cleaner about. In a very short time, however, we began to wish that Viki were not quite so enterprising. For instance, one day she claimed the grater from my lemon-pie-making residue, helped herself to a lemon from the refrigerator, and grated it all over the living-room rug (p. 181).

As Viki matured, both physically and in terms of her experience in the Hayes household, her "aping" became even more remarkable:

Sometimes she saw us using materials to which she would not have access until hours later. Nevertheless, by "delayed imitation," she must try her skill. One night she watched me dab furiously with a washcloth, trying to remove spilled milk from my skirt. The garment was left hanging in the bathroom, and Viki was shortly put to bed; but the next morning she took down the skirt, wet the washcloth, and rubbed at the spots (p. 182).

Mrs. Hayes then goes on to say:

It was not necessary to teach Viki to imitate; she had already done so in play. What we had to teach her was the meaning of the command "Do this!" so that she would imitate our actions even when they seemed pointless (p. 182).

Mrs. Hayes says that Viki's imitativeness developed as a part of her *play*, i.e., as activity engaged in because it was self-rewarding rather than objectively instrumental. The same assumptions underlie what we have called the "autism" theory of word learning. But just as Viki soon reached the point, with training, where she would imitate on command, so do children reach a similar stage with respect to the imitation of words. When they have reached the point that they repeat

[21] For a more technical description of this research, see Hayes & Hayes (1951, 1952).

words on command, then they can be given names and other instrumentally useful words; and their language acquisition can proceed by
leaps and bounds (or, should we say, by verbs and nouns). Thus, it
will be clear that our view does not limit word learning to the autism
principle; we hold that it is merely the mechanism whereby word
acquisition *gets started*.

That Viki's imitativeness was not just some inherent, instinctive
tendency was proved by the fact that a young chimp, of the same
age, which was borrowed from the colony at Yerkes Laboratories for
the purpose, showed none of the spontaneous imitativeness so characteristic of Viki and failed completely at special problem-solving tasks
where the solution could be learned by watching Dr. or Mrs. Hayes.

The major finding of this series of problems was that Viki was able to
do the various kinds of imitation approximately as well as children. Since
we used only one educated chimpanzee, our study is not offered as a quantitative evaluation of anthropoid imitative ability. But it does show that her
species has the innate factors necessary for imitation. This was not true
of speech, where no amount of training could make up for Viki's innate
deficit (pp. 188–189).

As explained by Mrs. Hayes in a preceding chapter, Viki, at an early
age and in spite of her total separation from other chimpanzees, exhibited "standard chimpanzee vocalizations," which are "instinctive,
appearing in all chimpanzees, and persisting into adulthood with little
change" (p. 61). These were an apprehensive "Oo oo, oo oo," a scolding bark "rhow!" and a special food sound, "a staccato stream of *e*'s
(as in wet), the lips drawn back over the teeth" (p. 61). But Viki did
very little babbling of the kind which is so characteristic of human
infants; and her foster parents had the impression that vocalizations,
other than the instinctive ones, were not at all easy for her to make.

Suddenly, one day when she was ten months old, she began making a
very strange new sound. The first time we heard it we were surprised and
vaguely displeased for it was an ugly sound, hoarse and strained. It was
like someone whispering "ah" as loudly as possible and with great effort.
When Viki said it her face contorted while her eyes assumed the tense
preoccupied stare of a stutterer. Then from her lips burst this rasping tortured "ahhhh." She then confidently reached for the milk, so that we concluded she had at last gotten the idea of speaking for food. From then on,
whenever we told her to speak, she replied with this straining "ahhh,"
and we came to call it her "asking sound."

Why was it so terribly hard for Viki to make this sound? As we pon-
dered this question, and re-examined our notes on Viki's "speaking" for
food, we realized an astonishing fact. Before our coaching *Viki had been
completely unable to make any sound at all on purpose.* She made chimp

noises, yes, but these were *beyond her control*. They were merely reflex expressions of her feelings. If she could have uttered even these voluntarily, she would have spoken up more quickly to get her food. As it was, she had to be disturbed before these burst out, and except for the chimp noises, Viki had been noiseless!

Why was Viki unable to vocalize when she wanted to, when her supper demanded it? Perhaps because the ape, for all its humanlike vocal apparatus, lacks the neural organization necessary for voluntary speech; perhaps because she did not babble; perhaps some interdependent combination of the two was responsible for Viki's shortcoming. In any case until now she could not vocalize on purpose. She had lacked *the motor skill of vocalization* (pp. 65–66).

These observations are consistent with the conjecture, expressed earlier, that birds alone are able to reproduce human word sounds with some success because they are unique (among infra-human organisms) in possessing the special brain-to-muscle "wiring" needed for flexible control of the vocal apparatus. And it can hardly be doubted that the greatest single "mutation" which separates man from other anthropoids consists precisely of this: new and more abundant neural connections between the speech center in the brain and the speech organs! (See also Chapter 4, Section II.)

That language failure in the chimpanzee cannot be attributed to any lack of "intelligence," in the sense of general learning ability, is clear. The paragraphs quoted show what an energetic and clever imitator Viki was with respect to her foster parents' nonvocal behavior. And presumably the same learning principles were involved that we have postulated as being responsible, in human infants and birds, for successful word learning: Viki learned to *love* her foster parents, particularly her "mother"; the latter's activities, because they mediated important primary satisfactions for Viki, took on powerful secondary-reinforcement properties; and there was a generalization thereof from the sight of "mother" performing them to the sight (sounds, and feel) of *Viki* performing them. But, as Dr. and Mrs. Hayes shrewdly surmised, Viki simply was *not capable* of doing the things "mother" did in the area of vocalization, and so never learned to "talk." With great patience and effort on the part of all concerned, Viki did learn to whisper "mama" and "cup." But this is where the matter ended.

Certainly the Hayes' observations with Viki show the error of Thorndike's contention that imitation does not occur in mammals other than man. Where it was *really* absent was in his theory; and because of this deficit, he never was inspired, either in the laboratory or out, to create the conditions necessary for the occurrence of this phenomenon.

Also we see that the Miller-Dollard analysis of imitation, in terms of doing something *on cue*, is unsatisfactory: Viki not only showed "*delayed* imitation"—it is also clear that the activities imitated, instead of being instrumental means to other (primary) satisfactions, provided their own (secondary) reward.[22] On the other hand, *all* the observations reported by Hayes & Hayes seem to be consistent with and supportive of the "autistic" theory of word learning and imitation generally and of the over-all conception of habit formation (both direct and mediated) with which this book is concerned.

XI. Concluding Comment

The autistic conception of word learning, as elucidated in this chapter, provides a particularly good illustration of revised two-factor theory in action. However, it would be a mistake to suppose that it was deduced from this theory. The truth is that the autistic interpretation of word learning came *first* (Mowrer, 1950, Chapter 24) and was not followed by a statement of the general theory which it exemplifies until considerably later (Mowrer, 1956). The advantages of research on talking birds (alluded to in Section I) were even greater than originally supposed!

Now we not only have a new and improved theory of habit formation; we also see more clearly than before the relation of this phenomenon to so-called imitation. In imitation the initial "model" for an act is supplied by organism A, but the reward (reinforcement) goes to organism B. In other words, to revert to the work with the talking birds, the *trainer* makes a particular noise and the *bird* gets fed, watered, or in some other way rewarded. The result is inevitable: the *stimulus consequences* of A's action, as they impinge on B, take on secondary reinforcement; and B, when properly motivated, tries to re-create them—in short, "imitates." This, when one thinks of it, is a remarkable phenomenon: what is at first a stimulus produces a response which *reproduces* that stimulus.

But imitation, so conceived, is really no more remarkable than is "ordinary" habit formation. The principal difference, it seems, is simply this, that in habit the learner himself provides the original "model."

---

[22] At this level of "imitation" one is probably justified in also using the psychoanalytic term, *identification*. The emotional conditions in Viki and in her relation with the foster parents were apparently right for her to become, fully and completely, their "child." There was only one, crucial difficulty: Viki could not learn to *talk*.

That is to say, an organism acts in a particular way (with certain stimulus consequences); its action (we assume) is followed by reward; and the result is that these stimulus consequences (or response-correlated stimuli) take on secondary-reinforcing (hope-arousing) capacity; and, when again properly motivated, the organism "imitates"—except that we now usually say "repeats"—what *it* (rather than some other organism) *did before*.

In imitation and in habit alike, then, we can say a model for or *image of* desirable, attractive, cathected, promising action emerges (see Chapter 5 of this book; also the discussion of skill in Mowrer, 1960, Chapter 12). The sensory consequences of such action have taken on secondary reinforcement as a result of having been first produced by another organism (in imitation) or as a result of having been first produced by the organism itself (as in regular habit). In both instances the response-correlated stimulation has "worked" in the sense of "producing" (being followed by) reward for organism B. And when B wants more of this reward or wants it again, we would expect B to attempt to reproduce this stimulus constellation (by means of the appropriate action), in much the same way regardless of whether the stimulus pattern or model was originally produced by organism A or by organism B.

But now an important distinction must be made. When an organism recreates a constellation of stimuli which, as a result of past action by the organism itself, has acquired secondary-reinforcement potential by virtue of that action having produced reward of some sort—when this occurs, the organism will, of necessity, also have reproduced the previously effective *action*, which will now again be likely to produce the desired satisfaction. But what of imitation? By reproducing the pattern of stimulation originally provided by organism A, organism B may be able to re-experience (autistically) some of the satisfaction previously associated with this stimulation. But will the reproduction thereof have the same likelihood of being instrumentally effective, i.e., of producing again the desired satisfaction, as does a regular "habit"? The answer seems to be that, in general, imitative action is instrumentally effective only if a second organism is present to act as an intermediary, as in the original learning situation, except that instead of A producing a given pattern of stimulation and then rewarding B, B now provides the stimulation and A reacts to it. Thus a child, if our analysis in this chapter is correct, first reproduces a word because of the indirect, autistic satisfaction which the word provides; but *then* the word may prove efficient in a more practical way in that it causes the parent again to supply the satisfaction with which his original pronunciation of the word was associated. In ordinary habits the situation is a little different: since the reinforcement is initially not socially mediated, it does not have to be subsequently. But this difference does not detract from the basic similarity of the principles involved in the two situations.

Interestingly enough, in his book, *Mind, Self, and Society*, G. H. Mead (1934) has a footnote which reads as follows:

> An attempt was made by Baldwin (1912) to carry back imitation to a fundamental biological process—a tendency on the part of the organism to reinstate a pleasurable sensation. . . . In the process of mastication the very process of chewing reinstates the stimulus, bringing back the flavor. Baldwin would call this self-imitation. This process, if it takes place at all, does not by any means meet the situation with which we are dealing (p. 64).

Here, it seems, was a remarkable anticipation of the analysis presented in the preceding pages. Both imitation and habit ("self-imitation") were made to depend on the same principles, and these importantly involved the notion that any stimulation which is associated with pleasure (today we say reward or reinforcement) will take on a derived pleasure and will cause the subject to try to "reinstate" this stimulation.[23] But Baldwin's shrewd suggestion never "took hold," as evinced by Mead's casual rejection of it. The reason, very probably, was that it was made at a time when reflexological and "bond" learning theory was coming into vogue; and as we have seen earlier in this chapter, the bond theory of habit (particularly as developed by Thorndike) automatically excludes the possibility of imitation. But now that we have a revised, and seemingly more realistic, conception of habit, we find it does indeed articulate with imitation, in very much the way Baldwin suggested.[24]

[23] Much the same idea is expressed by Humphrey (1921) when he says: "The general connection between imitation and repetition [habit] is very marked. In fact it is hard to say where one ends and the other begins, whether repetition is not 'self-imitation' just as often as it is response to repeated stimuli. Here we have repetition of an action imitated from others; this may be either response to repeated stimuli or imitation of self, the primary and secondary stimuli being identical. In either case the examples show the way in which integration adds step-by-step to the system" (p. 6).

[24] It goes without saying that exactly the same reasons can be applied to explain the *negative* imitation—not to be confused with the inverse or nonmatching behavior of Miller & Dollard's (1941) experiments—which results when the action of organism A is followed by *punishment* to organism B. Here the same principles are operative as in "ordinary" punishment, i.e., punishment applied to B for something B (rather than A) has done.

It is, patently, an advantage thus to have a common set of assumptions from which imitation and habit formation (in both their positive and negative aspects) are equally derivable. Moreover, having arrived at this point, one can go even further and note yet another possible form of "vicarious" learning. Suppose that organism A not only provides the "model" but *also* experiences the reinforcement. If an observing organism, B, experiences some of the same immediate sensory consequences of A's behavior as A experiences it and also "intuits" A's satisfactions (or dissatisfactions), then we may suppose that B will be rendered more or less likely to repeat A's behavior, although, to what is involved in simple imitation, is here added the element of *empathy*. The extent to which this "higher-order" vicarious learning occurs in animals is perhaps open to debate; but it occurs very commonly at the human level and is verbalized by the remark: "If that kind of behavior is good (or bad) for others, it will probably be good (or bad) for me; I think I will (will not) try it myself." [25]

Thus, our basic principles provide a satisfactory and unified explanation of *habit formation* (response, with resulting stimulation, provided by individual B and reinforcement experienced by individual B), *imitation* (response, with resulting stimulation, produced by individual A and reinforcement experienced by individual B), and *empathetic learning* (response, with resulting stimulation, produced by individual A and reinforcement experienced by individual A but with B also experiencing the reinforcement, vicariously). *Putting through* (Mowrer, 1960, Chapter 7) is logically between habit formation and imitation, in that individual B experiences the reinforcement and also "performs" the response *but passively*, under the initiative and guidance of individual A. Obviously putting through, empathetic learning, and imitation all involve *latent learning* of sorts, in that the secondary reinforcement (positive or negative) acquired by the stimuli produced by a

---

[25] Since the above was written, two animal studies have appeared which represent at least the beginnings of systematic research in this area. Church (1959) has shown that rats experience fear (as indexed by behavior inhibition) in the presence of other fearful rats; and Miller, Murphy, & Mirsky (1959), having taught monkeys to operate a lever when afraid, have demonstrated that such behavior can be activated by the mere sight of another monkey in a state of fear. In fact, these investigators even report that: "The enhancement of avoidance behavior by presentation of pictures of monkeys reacting fearfully indicates that exposure of a fearful stimulus animal elicits, through some empathic process, fear in the viewer" (p. 158). Although these studies do not involve imitative *behavior*, they clearly reflect an imitation of *affect* which is the essence of empathy (cf. Luchins, 1960; also Chapter 10, Section V).

given response as performed by another *generalizes* to the stimulation produced by that response as performed by the individual himself, and in this sense a kind of "mediation" is involved; but there are many instances of mediated learning which are not, of course, in any sense imitative (Chapter 2). In the chapter which follows, mediation will be examined in yet another context and form.

4

Language and Learning: The Psychology of Signs and Sentences

At the outset of the preceding chapter, language was referred to as a mediator of learning, as well as a product thereof. The processes whereby language is learned, as regards both word comprehension and word production, have now been reviewed. In the present chapter, we shall explore the way, or ways, in which language, once mastered as a tool, may then function as a means of producing the special kinds of learning that we call *communication*.

As a result of preceding discussion, we now have some notion of how human infants learn to reproduce and to know the meanings of the words they hear about them. But this knowledge, alone, gives us a very incomplete understanding of the *dynamics* of language. Let us therefore ask: Why did the race, or why does the individual, *want* language? What *good*, what practical *use* is it?

I. Earlier Theories of Language in Action

E. L. Thorndike is one of the few major learning theorists who have been seriously interested in language. In the preceding chapter we have reviewed his thinking about the origin and learning of language. Here we shall consider his views concerning its *function*.

In one respect, virtually all writers are agreed: language, they concede, has been transcendently important in the evolution of human culture and mentality. Thorndike (1943) evaluates it thus:

> Language is man's greatest invention. It is a social tool more important than the community, the state, the law, the church, or the school. It is an intellectual tool as important as observation and experiment, and more important than logic. It is more important than all the physical tools invented in the last two thousand years. These assertions may well seem extravagant, but they can be justified.

Thorndike then proceeds simultaneously to criticize a common conception of language and to develop the one which he believes more defensible. He says:

> Let us consider first the function of language. It is commonly said that the function of language, the service it performs in satisfying human wants, is to express thoughts or feelings. This statement is inadequate. Language is used not only to express but also to arouse thoughts and feelings and still more to arouse movements. The relation of most importance is not the parallelism between the words and the inner life of the one who uses them but the effect upon the one who hears or sees them. The function of language is fundamentally just the same as that of pushing, pulling, paying money to, feeding, clothing, knocking down, or helping up an animal. It is to produce responses on the animal's part, to get him to think or feel or do something. We do not talk exclusively for the sake of expressing our mental condition any more than we pay men money exclusively to express our satisfaction with their services (p. 60).

But after this vigorous and promising start, Thorndike's discussion of language in action becomes diffuse and uninstructive. And a moment's reflection upon this writer's assumptions concerning the basic circumstances of learning will suggest why this should be the case. Thorndike, it will be remembered, though often referred to as an "associationist" (in the "connectionist" sense), really did not take much stock in the principle of conditioning.

Thorndike argues, persuasively enough, that the central objective of language is to produce a modification or redirection of behavior in others. But he never comes to grips with the question of precisely *how* this influence is achieved. Granted that habits of *speaking* might be developed in the way suggested by Thorndike in the passages quoted in the preceding chapter, we are still left with the question of precisely how speech affects the *hearer*. Here we must face the problem of *meaning;* and it would now appear that for a systematic and genuinely adequate treatment of this phenomenon, the concept of conditioning is indispensable. It is small wonder, then, that Thorndike's discussion of language strikes us today as one-sided and incomplete.

Only a little less remarkable than the extent to which psychologists have neglected the field of language as a whole is the extent to which linguists themselves have also by-passed its more dynamic implications. During much of his highly influential career, Leonard Bloomfield dismissed efforts at "psychologizing" language as a waste of time. But in his well-known book, *Language*, published in 1933, there is a chapter entitled "The Use of Language" in which Bloomfield himself takes a turn at this activity. Here he says:

> Suppose that Jack and Jill are walking down a lane. Jill is hungry. She sees an apple in a tree. She makes a noise with her larynx, tongue, and lips. Jack vaults the fence, climbs the tree, takes the apple, brings it to Jill, and places it in her hand. Jill eats the apple.
>
> This succession of events could be studied in many ways, but we, who are studying language, will naturally distinguish between the *act of speech* and the other occurrences, which we shall call *practical events*. Viewed in this way, the incident consists of three parts, in order of time:
> A. Practical events preceding the act of speech.
> B. Speech.
> C. Practical events following the act of speech.

There then follows an elaboration of what Bloomfield means by A and by C, after which we read:

> If Jill had been alone, she might have been just as hungry and thirsty and might have seen the same apple. If she had sufficient strength and skill to get over the fence and climb the tree, she could get hold of the apple and eat it; if not, she would have to stay hungry. The lone Jill is in much the same position as the speechless animal. If the animal is hungry and sees or smells food, it moves toward the food; whether the animal succeeds in getting the food, depends upon its strength and skill. The state of hunger and the sight or smell of the food are the *stimulus* (which we symbolize by S) and the movements toward the food are the *reaction* (which we symbolize as R). The lone Jill and the speechless animal act in only one way, namely
>
> $$S \longrightarrow R.$$
>
> If this works, they get the food; if it does not work—if they are not strong or skillful enough to get the food by the reactions R—they must stay hungry (pp. 23–24).

We now see the direction in which Bloomfield's analysis is moving; and shortly he speaks of Jill's words to Jack being a *substitute* for R and represents them as r. For Jack they are in turn a substitute for S (his own hunger or thirst which might make him seek the apple) and are represented as s. Hence, what Bloomfield calls a "speechless" reaction ($S \rightarrow R$) becomes transformed into a "reaction mediated by speech: $S \rightarrow r \cdot \cdot \cdot \cdot s \rightarrow R$."

Here Jill feels the stimulus S and makes the reaction r; Jack receives the stimulus s and makes the response R, which involves not only getting the apple (as if for himself) but also *giving* it to Jill.

The difference between the two types [of stimulus-response sequence] is evident. The speechless reaction occurs always in the same person as does the stimulus; the person who gets the stimulus is the only one who can make the response. The response, accordingly, is limited to whatever actions the receiver of the stimulus can make. In contrast with this, the reaction mediated by speech may occur in a person who did not get the practical stimulus; the person who gets a stimulus can prompt another person to make a response, and this other person may be able to do things which the speaker cannot. The arrows in our diagrams represent the sequence of events within one person's body—a sequence of events which we think is due to some property of the nervous system. Therefore the speechless reaction can take place only in the body which received the stimulus. In the reaction mediated by speech, on the other hand, there is the link, represented by a dotted line, which consists of sound-waves in the air: the reaction mediated by speech can take place in the body of any person who hears the speech; the possibilities of reaction are enormously increased, since different hearers may be capable of a tremendous variety of acts. *The gap between the bodies of the speaker and the hearer—the discontinuity of the two nervous systems —is bridged by the sound-waves* (p. 26).

The implications of this analysis for a theory of social action and interaction are far-reaching. Here is a basis for explaining division of labor, cooperation, and other powerful cohesive forces in human groups (see De Laguna, 1927). Bloomfield then continues and concludes his discussion thus:

The important things, biologically, are the same in both the speechless and the speaking occurrence, namely S (the hunger and sight of the food) and R (movements which get the food or fail to get it). These are the *practical* phase of the affair. The speech-occurrence, s · · · · r, is merely a means by which S and R may occur in different individuals. The normal human being is interested only in S and R; though he uses speech, and thrives by it, he pays no attention to it. Saying the word *apple* or hearing it said, appeases no one's hunger. It, along with the rest of speech, is only a way of getting one's fellowmen to help. As students of language, however, we are concerned precisely with the speech event (r · · · · s), worthless in itself, but as a means to great ends. We distinguish between language, the subject of our study, and *real* or *practical* events, stimuli and reactions. When anything apparently unimportant turns out to be closely connected with more important things, we say that it has, after all, a "meaning"; namely, it "means" these more important things. Accordingly, we say that speech-utterance, trivial and unimportant in itself, is important because it has *meaning:* the meaning consists of the important things with which the speech-utterance (B) is connected, namely the practical events (A and C) (pp. 26–27).

Basically, Bloomfield's treatment of language is just an extension and explication of Thorndike's. Both by-pass the concept of meaning as an internal conditioned reaction; and both are thoroughly behavioristic. Thorndike argues that the "expressive," or subjective, value of language is trivial in comparison with its objective, interpersonal utility; and Bloomfield agrees by saying that language is "worthless in itself" and valuable only as a means to "practical" ends. However, as we shall later see, it seems that in disregarding certain of the subjective aspects of language, these writers cut themselves off from an understanding of language in its most truly and uniquely "practical" sense.

Philosophers and logicians have, in some ways, been quite attentive to the language problem but usually not in ways which bear upon the *psychology* of language. However, a book by Susanne K. Langer, entitled *Philosophy in a New Key* (1951), offers an interesting departure from the more traditional treatments of language. The chapter on "Language" begins with these now widely quoted words:

Language is, without a doubt, the most momentous and at the same time the most mysterious product of the human mind. Between the clearest animal call of love or warning or anger, and a man's least, trival word, there lies a whole day of Creation—or in modern phrase, a whole chapter of evolution. In language we have the free, accomplished use of symbolism, the record of articulate conceptual thinking; without language there seems to be nothing like explicit thought whatever (p. 83).

Animals . . . are one and all without speech. They communicate, of course, but not by any method that can be likened to speaking. They express their emotions and indicate their wishes and control one another's behavior by suggestion. One ape will take another by the hand and drag him into a game or to his bed; he will hold out his hand to beg for food, and will sometimes receive it. But even the highest apes give no indication of speech (p. 84).

. . . Even though Professor Yerkes's young apes, Chim and Panzee, met their food with exclamations like "Kha!" and "Nga!" these are like a cry of "Yum-yum!" rather than: "Banana, today." They were sounds of enthusiastic assent, of a very specialized emotional reaction; *they cannot be used between meals to talk over the merits of the feast* (p. 85) [cf. Cassirer, 1944].

Langer then reviews certain untenable theories of language origin and function, in human beings, and concludes that in the following paragraph, quoted from Sapir (1933), there lies the germ of a far more promising approach to the problem.

The primary function of language is generally said to be communication. . . . The autistic speech of children seems to show that the purely communicative aspect of language has been exaggerated. It is best to admit that language is primarily a vocal actualization of the tendency to see reality symbolically, that it is precisely this quality which renders it a fit instrument for communication and that it is in the actual give and take of social intercourse that it has been complicated and refined into the form in which it is known today (pp. 88–89).

Langer takes her lead from Sapir's reference to the tendency of human beings "to see reality symbolically." But then she asks, why is it that we have this tendency so abundantly and our closest of kin among the apes have it not at all? Here, after a brilliant beginning, she falls back upon a "difference of natural proclivities."

The ape has no instinctive desire to babble in babyhood. He does not play with his mouth and his breath as human infants do; there is no crowing and cooing, no "goo-goo" and "ba-ba" and "do-de-la" in his otherwise unroarious nursery. Consequently there are no sounds and syllables that please or frighten him by their sheer aesthetic character, as he is pleased, frightened or conforted by purely phenomenal sights. Oddly enough, it is just because all his utterances have *signification*—all are pragmatic or emotional—that none of them ever acquire *significance*. He does not even imitate sounds for fun, as he imitates gestures, and gravely mimics practices that have no utility for him (p. 94).

Although the rest of Dr. Langer's chapter is engaging and, at points, highly suggestive, it ends without having developed a well-knit theory of either language origination or use. One has the feeling that the author was looking in decidedly the right direction; but because certain experimental facts and theoretical concepts from the learning laboratory were not at her disposal, she was unable to capitalize upon a sound intuition. In contrast to Thorndike and Bloomfield, who stress the *practicality* of language, Langer underscores its *subjective* qualities:

A genuine symbol can most readily originate where some object, sound, or act is provided which has no *practical* meaning, yet tends to elicit an emotional response, and thus hold one's undivided attention (pp. 94–95).

Or again:

Young children learn to speak, after the fashion of Victor [the "Wild Boy" of Aveyron], by constantly using words to bring things *into their minds*, not *into their hands*. They learn it fully whether their parents consciously teach them by wrong methods or right or not at all (p. 98).

Hence we see a decided difference of opinion between Thorndike and Bloomfield, on the one hand, with their emphasis upon the objective and utilitarian function of language, and Langer, on the other, who stresses its subjective and autistic aspects. Is there not, in the preceding chapter of this book, the basis for a happy reconciliation? There we have advanced and empirically supported the view that word-making reactions are initially learned on an autistic basis but are then stabilized and perpetuated because they prove to be "practical," instrumentally effective. Or, in stricter terminology, word-making "habits" are acquired because the response-correlated stimuli have acquired *secondary reinforcement* potency (that is, words "bring things *into their minds*"); but these "habits" also turn out to be "practical" and are stabilized and perpetuated through the action of *primary reinforcement*. Bloomfield and Thorndike had only the concept of primary reinforcement ("practical effects"), whereas Langer had an intuitive grasp of the concept of secondary reinforcement but did not understand its systematic relationship to primary reinforcement.

Thus, on the basis of revised two-factor learning theory, we arrive at a more complete, more integrated conception of language. But a large and important issue remains. In the preceding chapter we have worked out the theoretical details, i.e., the mechanism, of word learning. In the present one, we have acknowledged the practical, interpersonal function of words, once learned; but we have as yet no clear and precise understanding of how this effect is achieved. It might seem that we should be able to find an answer in either of two recent movements that have attracted considerable attention: namely, General Semantics and Information Theory. But the latter, we find, is not at all concerned with language in the more general sense of the term; and General Semantics, despite its name, is concerned with a really quite specific and probably not very important point. Wilson (1954) has recently appraised Information Theory incisively yet fairly in these words:

> As the previous discussion has indicated, information theory's chief contribution to the study of language is a set of descriptive measures and a unit, the *bit*, which are much more broadly applicable than to language processes themselves. It serves chiefly, therefore, as a quantitative tool for describing language processes. It is not a theory of information in the usual sense, nor does it provide us with a theoretical model which can provide hypotheses about or explain the phenomena of human communication (p. 24).[1]

Although much has been written under the rubric of General Semantics, the key notion has been dramatized by Hugh Walpole (1941) in the following story (see also Korzybski, 1933, and Hayakawa, 1942). There was, it seems, a farmer who each day called his chickens into

---

[1] Garner (1958; see also Garner & McGill, 1956) has, in fact, recently suggested that the term "information theory" be abandoned, because of its misleading implications, and replaced by the semantically more neutral and statistically more precise term, "uncertainty principle."

the chicken house and fed them. Then came a day when he called them into the chicken house and fed them, as usual; but as they ate he closed the doors, presently caught them, put them into coops, and sent them off to market. The chickens had made the error of *"over-generalizing"*; because the farmer's call had in the past been followed by food and nothing else, the chickens did not *discriminate* between his friendly calls and the calls he made when he wanted to catch and market them (how *could* they?), and so lost their freedom—and probably their lives. As indicated elsewhere (Mowrer, 1960, Chapter 12), discrimination, under some circumstances, is indeed highly important; but, under other conditions, the capacity to generalize is equally vital. So it would seem that the General Semanticist's main point is not only limited but, possibly, quite misleading (see Winthrope, 1946); and it leaves us still looking for the touchstone of a truly general theory of language operation.[2] This, it seems, we shall have to construct for ourselves on the basis of facts and principles already discussed or implied in preceding chapters.

II. On Signs and Signaling: The Biological Background of Human Speech

Because revised two-factor theory reduces all learning to sign learning, we have already, in this (and the preceding) book, devoted a good deal of attention to the psychology of signs. And from this approach we have seen that inherent in the theory of sign learning, or conditioning, are the notions of "information" and "meaning." A formerly neutral stimulus which is temporally contiguous with either drive increment or drive decrement takes on the capacity to arouse fear or hope and thus provides the reacting organism with *memory* of the past and *knowledge* of things to come (see also Chapter 5). When a formerly neutral or indifferent stimulus is associated with a significant (reinforcing) one, the first stimulus takes on a *representational* function, coming to mean or *stand for* the second one. This moving forward in time of a part of the reaction evoked by a biologically important situation, so that the organism can make an anticipatory response of either an approach or an avoidant nature, is clearly one of Nature's most ingenious inventions and is a crucial aspect of what we call "intelligence" and "foresight" (cf. Chapter 2).

Hence from our study of learning in lower animals we obtain a sound

[2] For an excellent, brief history of the General Semantics movement and a critical yet impartial evaluation, see Carroll (1953, pp. 160–168); see also Weinreich's (1959) bibliography.

conceptual underpinning for the study of language in human beings, which is just an intricate system of sign functions. There are, however, some rather serious limitations in the extent to which a study of animals can guide us to a fully adequate theory of communication at the human level. Animals, it seems, are often extremely well equipped for the detection of remote and subtle stimuli and for learning, through conditioning, to attach special meanings to them. But they are much less well prepared or disposed themselves to *make* stimuli that may have sign, or signaling, value. Animals, of course, inadvertently provide some stimuli which may then be reacted to by other organisms, for purposes of either pursuit or flight. They may be seen, heard, smelled, etc.—all of which is usually a disadvantage to the first organism; so

"*I'm going to take a chance
and answer that one. They can't all be hunters.*"

Fig. 4–1. A drawing by Rea, reproduced with permission from *The New Yorker* (Nov. 3, 1945). An alternative legend might be, "Hunters or no hunters, I'm going to *answer* that one!"

that nature (evolution) has tended to put a premium, through color, camouflage, foot-padding, etc., upon *inconspicuousness*. Whenever an organism engages in *displays* of any kind, through appearance, vocalization, or odors, it is usually as a means of signaling to other members of the *same* species, commonly for sexual purposes; so that the survival of a species often depends upon a subtle balance between inconspicuousness and conspicuousness, between silence and signaling. The essence of this dilemma has been captured (as is so often the case) by a *New Yorker* cartoon, which is reproduced here as Fig. 4–1.

How effectively "muted" the laboratory rat is in certain situations is brought out in a study published a few years ago by Mowrer, Palma, & Sanger (1948). It has been shown by numerous researches previously cited in this book that if some stimulus or situation is conditioned to the response of fear, rats can learn to do any of a wide variety of things as a means of relieving the fear and, hopefully, avoiding the thing feared. Also well established is the fact that rats squeal vociferously when subjected to even fairly mild pain, such as that produced by an electric shock. So it occurred to the authors cited to wonder if rats could likewise learn to use *this* reaction "instrumentally," as a means of terminating a danger signal and averting shock. Fig. 4–2 gives the results. As the figure shows, when circumstances were such that rats could terminate a danger signal and avoid shock by *running*, this response was readily learned; but when the rats were required to *vocalize* as a means of achieving the same ends, there was no change in performance.

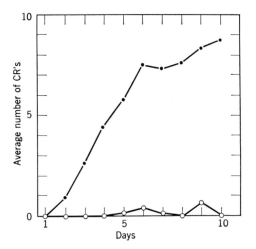

Fig. 4–2. Curves contrasting the ease with which two types of response—a simple running reaction and vocalization—can be elicited in laboratory rats on the basis of so-called avoidance conditioning. The curve with the solid circles shows the high proficiency of one group of subjects in learning to run in response to a warning signal, whereas the curve with the open circle shows the very low proficiency of a group of comparable subjects in learning to vocalize in response to the same signal.

Mowrer, Palma, & Sanger go on to suggest that in rats, and perhaps in many other animals, there is an instinctive mechanism which ensures their vocalizing when "caught," as a means of warning other members of their species of the presence of danger, but which prevents them from vocalizing out of fear alone. The authors say:

The rat which only sees, hears, or smells an enemy will do well, no matter how terrified, to remain silent, either as it crouches in hiding or slinks to safety. . . . If an animal is "caught," it does not much matter if it squeals both to actual pain (shock) and to the mere threat of pain (the danger signal); but if an animal is "free," it makes a great deal of difference whether it squeals to the mere prospect of pain (thus calling, "Here I am," to the hungry pursuer), or squeals only in response to pain itself (thus urging other members of its species to bolt from a possibly similar fate).

Support for the thesis that animals do well in a state of nature to "suffer in silence" and not to cry out when frightened, except when "caught," in indicated by Darwin (1873) in the following passage:

"We have seen . . . that when the sensorium is strongly excited, the muscles of the body are generally thrown into violent action; and as a consequence, loud sounds are uttered, however silent the animal may generally be, and although the sounds may be of no use. Hares and rabbits for instance, never, I believe, use their vocal organs except in the extremity of suffering; as, when a wounded hare is killed by the sportsman, or when a young rabbit is caught by a stoat. Cattle and horses suffer great pain in silence, but when this is excessive, and especially when associated with terror, they utter fearful sounds. I have often recognized, from a distance on the Pampas, the agonized death-bellow of the cattle, when caught by the lasso and hamstrung. It is said that horses, when attacked by wolves, utter loud and peculiar screams of distress" (pp. 83–84).

Thus we see the reasonableness of the assumption that nature (evolution) has taken pains to control and, indeed, *suppress* vocalization in anmials, except in special circumstances. As already indicated, about the only state aside from that of capture in which vocalization is allowed, in many species, is that where reproduction of the species is at stake. Again, to quote Darwin:

Although the sounds emitted by animals of all kinds serve many purposes, a strong case can be made out, that the vocal organs were primarily used and perfected in relation to the propagation of the species. . . . The chief and, in some cases, exclusive purpose appears to be either to call or charm the opposite sex (p. 290).

In support of the latter argument Darwin (1885) points out that "the sounds produced by fishes are said in some cases to be made only by the males during the breeding-season" (p. 196). Beach (1944) reports that the alligator "breeds during the early summer, and it is at this time that roaring is most frequently heard" (p. 481). Others have remarked on this correlation in other species, but reference is seldom made to the fact that even in human beings there is no "change of voice" in the male until the advent of puberty. Presumably it is only at this time that vocal differentiation of the sexes becomes functional.

The circumstances, then, under which terrestrial mammals vocalize can be quickly enumerated. As adults, animals which are preyed upon are likely to be silent save (a) when, as we have seen, they are caught, (b) when a mother is separated from her young, (c) when seeking a mate, and occasionally (d) when fighting. Predatory animals seem to have slightly greater vocal freedom in that they may vocalize, not only under the four circumstances just mentioned, but also (e) when attacking an intended victim.[3] Thus, says Darwin (1873):

> Rage leads to the violent exertion of all the muscles, including those of the voice; and some animals, when enraged, endeavour to strike terror into their enemies by its power and harshness; as the lion does by roaring, and the dog by growling. I infer that their object is to strike terror; because the lion at the same time erects the hair of the mane, and the dog the hair along its back, and thus they make themselves appear as large and terrible as possible. Rival males try to excel and challenge each other by their voices, and this leads to deadly contests (p. 85).

Thus, from varied lines of evidence we see that vocalization, in a state of nature, ordinarily occurs only under fairly specific and critical ("emotional") circumstances. How, then, did man, or protoman, ever achieve the vocal freedom and versatility required for voluntary speech? Numerous writers have remarked that, under conditions of domestication, various species of fowl, dogs, and other animals have become somewhat more vocal. This has occurred, presumably, (a) because domestication provides considerable, if not complete, protection against natural enemies and hazards and (b) because man, the domesticator, probably likes a certain amount of vocalization in his pets and other "live stock" as a means of knowing where they are, if they are safe, etc. But there was no one to "domesticate" and thus protect *man*, so we are still faced with the question of how *he* won through to vocal freedom. Mowrer, Palma, & Sanger offer the following hypothesis in this connection:

> In human beings voice is under exquisite voluntary control. How, we may ask, did proto-man ever secure the safety from predators needed to allow this function to pass from instinctive control over into the realm of responses which are controlled by individual learning?

---

[3] Howard's highly original study (1920) of the use of song by birds to establish "territoriality" warrants perhaps another category. See also the observations of Tinbergen (1953) reported in Chapter 10, Section II.

Without proposing in any sense to exhaust the possible answers to this question, we wish to suggest one line of thought and briefly indicate some of the relevant evidence. We know that birds and arboreal primates are the most vocal of living creatures. Only birds and monkeys are said to "chatter." What do they have in common? In the one case by flight and in the other case by specialized climbing skills, they have both escaped the dangers that beset terrestrial mammals. They alone seem to have attained enough security so that it does not matter if they are "noisy," and only with such security does it seem possible for the enormous experimentation to occur which must have been the precursor of articulate speech.

By this route we are led to the conclusion that man, as a speaking terrestrial mammal, could have evolved as such only as a result of having spent a protracted period of time "in the trees." Whether we wish to call the first creature with articulate speech "man" is perhaps a debatable question; but there appear to be good grounds for suspecting that man, or his immediate ancestor, was already "talking," or at least capable of it, when he descended from the trees and became an earth-dweller. Man seems to have survived on the ground by virtue of peculiar vocal, intellectual, and manipulative skills which developed in connection with arboreal life and which made possible the development of a considerable degree of social integration and perhaps an impressive "culture" before he could hazard existence on the ground. Some anthropologists believe that human culture, in the complexity which we find in even the most primitive contemporary peoples, could never have developed in a tree-dwelling species; but this is not to say that man may not have had an excellent start as a talking and culture-bearing organism before becoming able to exploit the advantages, as well as cope with the dangers, of a terrestrial habitat.

These, of course, are highly speculative thoughts, but thoughts to which our initial laboratory observations seem not unreasonably to lead us (pp. 38–42).

The foregoing analysis leaves some questions unanswered. Why, for example, have not the birds developed a form of communication comparable to human language? As we have seen (Chapter 3), many avian species are quite capable of reproducing human words, but they do not seem able to *use* them in the same way. This may be because birds, in order to fly, have sacrificed the possibility of developing *hands;* and perhaps only a handed creature can develop a technology and culture in which fully articulate speech becomes highly functional. But monkeys and apes have hands quite as good as our own; and their oral and vocal equipment seems completely adequate for speech. Why have *they* not developed linguistically, beyond the few stereotyped sounds previously discussed? Here one can only surmise that the remarkable mutation with respect to the "speech centers" of the brain which manifestly took place in the evolutionary line from which man has descended did not occur in these species.

III. Signaling and Quasi-Predication

As later sections of this chapter will show, *predication* is the most distinctive feature of human language. It seems not to occur in infra-human organisms; and it takes quite some time for it to make its appearance in the human infant (see Section V), despite its continuous occurrence in the infant's social environment. At the same time, there is something similar to be found in lower animals which is highly instructive, namely what may be called *quasi-predication*.

In the preceding section we have seen that most of the signaling reactions made by lower animals have an instinctive, emotional, non-voluntary basis. Thus there are danger and distress cries, snarls and growls of warning, sex calls, food calls, and, very likely, not much else; and these signals, such as they are, are largely if not wholly intended for intraspecies consumption. But how, precisely, do they operate?

If it be granted that the *making* of the signaling responses is instinctive rather than learned (it seems that nature could not depend upon the chancy learning of such important social actions), the principal remaining question is how the *response* to these sources of stimuli is acquired. As we shall see presently, there seem to be some instances in which these stimuli are not only made but also reacted to instinctively; but a simpler and more instructive situation is one in which the *meaning* of a signal has to be learned. If an older dog and a pup are fed from the same bowl, the pup will at first innocently and brashly rush up to the bowl, along with the older dog, as soon as food is put into it. The older dog, having no inclination to share the food until his own hunger has been allayed, will resent the pup's intrusion, growl at him, to no avail, and then, likely as not, nip him. After a few repetitions of this sequence, the growl alone is enough to keep the pup at a respectful distance; and, eventually, the mere *sight* of the situation (older dog eating from bowl) in which the pup has been growled at and, on occasion, nipped will have the same effect.

There is, of course, nothing either novel or particularly instructive in the foregoing illustration, since it is readily interpretable on the basis of well-known principles. But let us consider an extension of the illustration. Suppose the older dog is jealous of his relationship with his master and that whenever he sees the pup making friendly, affectionate overtures to him, the older dog growls. If the master does not intervene and silence the older dog, it is quite possible that the pup will become *afraid of the master*, not because of any mistreatment or punishment he has received *from* the master himself but because he has been conditioned to fear, or at least to fear approaching, him by means of a *mere signal (or "warning") from the older dog.*

Here again, in terms of principles, there is nothing new—merely an instance, we would say, of second-order conditioning. But the situation is nevertheless interesting, for we see in it a rudimentary example of "teaching" or "instruction" by means of a signal. By associating, in the pup's experience, sight of master and sound of growl, the older dog can change the pup's attitude and behavior toward the master in a quite significant way. Here we have *quasi*-predication. By this is meant that the *subject* of a "sentence" is physically present ("understood"), with only the *predicate* symbolized, verbalized. The "predicate" (growl) is, a half-sentence, which carries the "message," (Master) *is dangerous.* As it happens this sentence is not "true," in that the master (presumably) is *not* dangerous; but if the pup saw the master only in the presence of the older dog and had no opportunity to "reality-test" (i.e., to extinguish his fear) in another situation (and thus discriminate between master-with- and master-without-older-dog-present), the sentence would be true *for him*—and serves, perhaps all the better, to suggest how "language" operates.

Many other examples of the same sort of phenomenon could, of course, be cited. When a mother hen, sighting a soaring hawk in the sky, gives (instinctively?) her long, shrill alarm cry and her chicks react (instinctively?) with fear and flight, conditions are right for them to learn that: (Hawk) *is dangerous.* To the extent that they have perceived the hawk when the alarm cry sounds, they will come to react to sight of hawk much as they do to sound of the hen's distinctive cry.[4] Or, when the hen finds food, she gives a series of quick "chirps," which serve to call the chicks to the location of the food and presumably help them later to recognize and locate edible substances on their own.

Or, at the human level, we see much the same sort of thing occurring as a result of the use of so-called "one-word sentences." After cer-

---

[4] Hartley, a British zoologist, has recently (1950) reviewed a number of studies on the reactions of hand-reared wild birds to predator birds of various kinds and concludes, on the basis of this evidence, "that the process of recognition by a configuration of visual clues is innate" (p. 335). And the present writer has observed that myna birds which have been taken as nestlings and thereafter reared in captivity are instantly alerted and often thrown into apparent panic by the sight of any soaring object in the sky. Perhaps the common chicken, through its long domestication, has lost some of this instinctive wisdom and (like man) has to be individually "instructed."

tain sounds, such as "No, no," "Stop," "Hot, hot," "Come," "Nice, nice," have through conditioning acquired meaning for a child, they can be associated with persons, things, or situations which are physically present; and the result is that the child's attitude and behavior toward the latter is changed, without any *direct* experience therewith which would justify the change. In other words, by means of such signs or signals, the person making them can "go between" the child and certain inherently painful or pleasurable experiences in such a way as to dispose the child either to avoid or to seek such experiences. Here learning is *vicarious* or *mediated* (see Chapter 2), which is one of the hallmarks of "language."

But thus far, in all the examples given, there has been a serious limitation: the "subject" of the so-called sentence has been in some sense *present* rather than re-present-ed. Only when the subject, as well as the predicate, of a sentence is representational or symbolic can we say that we have language in its fully developed, fully "articulate" form; and this is a level of achievement apparently found nowhere in the animal world.

But perhaps the illustrations cited do not do full justice to language in animals. Perhaps other species are more accomplished in this regard. Since language and social development are often linked together, perhaps the so-called "social insects" have transcended the limitations which we have just noted. Fortunately, Karl von Frisch (1950) has meticulously studied and beautifully described for us what he calls the "language" of bees. In reporting on an experiment in which sugar water is placed a few meters from a bee hive with special provision for observing activity in the hive, von Frisch says that it takes some little while before the first bee locates the sweetened water. Then bees, all from the same hive, shortly start arriving in large number. "Evidently," says von Frisch, "this bee must have announced its discovery at home" (p. 53). How, precisely, is this done? Von Frisch continues:

"After she has returned to the hive, our marked bee is first seen to *deliver most of the sugar-water to other bees*. Then she begins to perform what I have called a round dance" (p. 55; italics added).

"During the dance, the bees near the dancer become greatly excited; they troop behind her as she circles, keeping their antennae close to her body. Suddenly one of them turns away and leaves the hive. Others do likewise, and soon some of these bees appear at the feeding place. After they have returned home they dance, and the more bees there are dancing in the hive, the more appear at the feeding place. It is clear that the dance inside the hive reports the existence of food" (p. 56) (Mowrer, 1954, p. 674).

Later investigation showed that the round dance is used by bees to indicate the presence of food within a radius of 50 to 100 meters from the hive, without reference to direction. It is, in short, an invitation or command to go out and "cruise" around the hive. Food sources beyond 100 meters, on the other hand, are reported by means of what von Frisch calls "wagging dances," which indicate, apparently with considerable precision, both distance and direction. Here we shall not be concerned with the intricacies of the latter, but rather with the fact that in both the round dance and the wagging dance, the returning bee brings some of the newly discovered food and *distributes it to other bees*. This behavior is of special importance for purposes of language analysis, for it suggests that, for all its ability to execute sentence predicates, sometimes of remarkable complexity, the bee has no signs for sentence subjects and has to use a bit of *the thing itself* for this purpose. Therefore, one may conclude that even the industrious and ingenious bee has not, in any basic sense, transcended other animals with respect to language function: it, too, is limited to "sentences" of the thing-sign variety. And experiments either conducted or cited by Schneirla (1950) with the ant show that here, despite the intricacy of social organization, "language" is even less highly developed than in the bee. However, it should be noted that the distribution of bits of the sugar water to other bees in the home hive is a *sort* of "representation" and is only one step removed, obviously, from "true" predication.

But what of the "talking birds"? There are many authentic instances of parrots, parakeets, or myna birds learning to say "complete sentences" and even reciting short poems. For example, in a phonograph record obtainable from Mr. and Mrs. G. William Smith, Hickman Mills, Missouri, one can hear a talented parakeet, "Blueboy," reciting the first stanza of "Mary Had a Little Lamb." Here, in terms of physical sounds, we have three relatively long sentences which are linguistically complete. But it seems most unlikely that "Its fleece was white as snow," means to "Blueboy" anything like what it means to us. In other words, although parakeets and many other types of birds are capable of learning to "parrot" long verbal sequences, there is no indication that they are doing anything more than amusing themselves or trying to entertain and thus keep close to them some beloved human being.

In summary, then, we may say that although the phenomenon of quasi-predication occurs among infrahuman organisms, true predication—which is the genius and hallmark of human language—does not (cf. Cassirer, 1944). However, our analysis of the former provides a solid underpinning of the understanding of the latter, as it will be depicted in the next section.

IV. From Signals to Sentences
(True Predication) [5]

Since the actual historical origin of language is lost beyond any hope of recovery, we are left with only more or less plausible surmises, or fictions. The following one has the advantage of giving us, by implication, also a good working definition of language. In his book, *Man, An Autobiography*, George Stewart (1946), Professor of English at the University of California, goes about the problem in this way. He supposes that a sound like "Ouch" may have developed as a half-reflexive reaction to sudden pain. And then, says Man, speaking autobiographically:

After awhile, when a creature had as good a brain as mine, [such] sounds would be more standardized, and their meanings fitted to the situation. Thus, "Ouch!" might be used playfully, when the individual felt no real pain, or it might warn a child not to pick up a bee (pp. 31–32).

Again, [says Man], something which could start more for playfulness than for "use" might soon come to be of value in other ways. When the band was foraging, one of them might signal his position by calling "Coo!" like a dove, to let the others know where he was.

Eventually came the union of the noun-idea and the verb-idea. It may be that a woman came back without her companion, and much troubled. All attempts at gesture failed to tell what had happened. In desperation, naturally enough and yet with a stroke of genius, she cried, "Coo-ouch!" Then they knew that he who was called Coo had been taken with a sudden pain. Such a combination of two ideas was more than mere expression of personal feeling, and more also than mere pointing-out of an individual. It was the setting of two ideas into a new relation, and thus the beginning of real language (pp. 32–33).

The foregoing passages are the relevant ones for our immediate purposes, but they are followed by a brief paragraph which must also be added:

I like to think that mothers may first have made and practiced language, and that for some generations the fathers still sat around merely grunting while the mothers chattered happily. At least I notice that girl-babies are still quicker to speak than boy-babies, and that they grow up in general to be more fluent talkers.[6] Besides, there has always been in language a great

---

[5] This and the following sections are adapted from "The Psychologist Looks at Language" (Mowrer, 1954).

[6] Stewart might also have observed that women are still the first language teachers of both boy and girl infants. On the basis of an analysis of language published elsewhere (Mowrer, 1950, Chapter 24), it seems likely that very few, if any, children learn to speak from their fathers, save in the most exceptional circumstances. See Thompson (1952, pp. 366–367).

deal of an illogical and emotional quality. I might say, "Women invented language, but men invented grammar" (p. 33).

With the male ego thus saved, let us return to our inquiry. What Professor Stewart has done here, following Grace De Laguna (1927) and others, is to make the phenomenon of *predication*, i.e., the combination of two (or more) signs into a so-called sentence, the bedrock of true language development. Certainly anyone who has been present when a child starts, as we say, "putting words together" knows what a momentous event it is. The author will never forget when his own first child, a little girl, met him at the door one evening and excitedly exclaimed: "Pammy-kitty! Pammy-kitty!" He knew that his daughter had visited a little neighbor, Pammy, that afternoon. Therefore, "Pammy-kitty" clearly said, "Pammy (has a) kitten," and the enthusiasm which accompanied the statement also implied the qualifying clause, "which is really quite wonderful." [7]

No, there can be no doubt that the act of putting words together in novel and informative combination is of enormous importance, both in the history of the race and in the development of each individual. And the product, which we call the sentence, can usefully serve as the central fact in our definition and analysis of language. However, an instructive complication at once arises, namely, the existence and relatively frequent use of the so-called one-word sentence, already alluded to.[8] And with this we are back where we started: with single, noncombined signs.

It is certainly a commonplace observation that small children, well before they start speaking in formal sentences, communicate quite effectively—though, as we shall see, with definite limitations—by means of single words. And even at the adult level, we often make single words function as full sentences, in what Skinner (1957) has called "mands," i.e., demands, commands, exclamations, etc. But, if we look closely at these so-called one-word sentences, we discover an interesting characteristic, namely, that they always, or at least com-

[7] Wyatt (1960) has noted and analyzed some 26 of the sentences first used by a little girl whom she systematically observed. She concluded: "The first appearance of these phrases was quite striking. At fifteen and a half months it seemed absolutely impossible for Nana to put words together. . . . Then suddenly, overnight, so to speak, the faculty to put words together or to produce two words in succession, emerged (age sixteen months)" (p. 29).

[8] *Webster's New Collegiate Dictionary* speaks of "*full sentences*, as distinguished from *minor sentences*, which generally consist of a completive word or phrase" (1951, p. 771). Fowler says that where the subject or the predicate of a sentence is "understood," one has an "elliptical sentence" (1926, p. 523).

monly, *imply* something else and thus *function*, in a restricted way, as a two-sign complex or true sentence. "Mands," it seems, always refer to, or imply, some thing or person which is physically present at the moment. Thus, if a baby says, "Bottle," it implies, "*I* want bottle"; and if an adult cries, "Stop," he implies, "Discontinue what *you* are now doing." Or, to revert to the passage quoted from Stewart, the "Ouch" which the primitive man (or woman) uttered as a child was about to pick up a bee implied the bee and said, in effect, "Take care! *That object* is dangerous, will cause—pain." We may say, therefore, that although a single word or phrase can tell us something (and thus function as language) with respect to *something physically present*, it cannot tell us anything about what Hull has aptly referred to as "the not here and the not now" (Hull, 1930b, p. 524). To say anything about a physically or temporally remote thing, event, or person we must represent it symbolically—there is, apparently, no other option; and this involves a *second sign*, or term, to which conventionally—and probably for very sound psychological reasons (see Section V)—we give first place in the two-sign sequence. Thus, as Stewart so insight-fully observes, language comes into its own only with the develop-ment of the "noun idea," i.e., when sentences have "sign" subjects as opposed to "thing" subjects. And this is a feat which no infrahuman organism seems to have achieved, and one which it takes even the human organism a little while to get the hang of.[9]

[9] This analysis helps explain why it is that some writers (e.g., Hunter, 1928; Hollingworth, 1928) make language equivalent to *any* use of signs. As we have seen, if the "subject" of a sentence is physically present, a single sign can "com-plete" the sentence. Thus, without careful scrutiny, single and combined signs may appear to serve essentially the same function. But the one-sign sentence has, as we have seen, the serious disadvantage of restricting communication to the here-and-now. For communication concerning the there-and-then, we must go to the two-sign sentence as a minimum. Cf. McCarthy (1954, pp. 544–551) for a dis-cussion of the "one-word sentence" in small children. A few pages later, McCarthy, citing various investigators, makes the point that it is only when the child's speech becomes more complex that it also becomes "abstract." She says: "Lewis (1951) brings out that at first the language of the child is concerned exclusively with the immediate situation in which it is spoken and that gradually it begins to deal with things that are absent. This matter of reference to things absent has also been emphasized by both K. and C. Buhler (Buhler, C., 1930; Buhler, K., 1930). Lewis relates the child's use of past and future tenses to the functions of his earlier undifferentiated speech. It is because of the child's use of speech as an instrument to draw others into his social circle that he begins to speak of absent things and events" (McCarthy, 1954, p. 557). "Ames (1946) reports that children first speak of the present, then of the future, and that references to the past occur later" (p. 558). Of course, by pre-arrangement, a single stimulus (like the lantern

In summary of our inquiry thus far, we may say, then, that the transition from the use of single signs to multisigns or *sentences* is, in some ways, insignificant but in other ways momentous: It enables us to go from the concrete to the abstract, from the here-and-now to the "not here, not now." Our next task is to clarify and expand this assumption and to indicate in more detail just how the grammatical unit or complex which we call the sentence works.[10]

V. Psychological Analysis of the Sentence

In the preceding discussion we have asked, and in at least a preliminary way answered, the question: What is the *nature* of a sentence? We have tried, that is to say, to determine what sentences, scientifically considered, *are*. In this section an attempt will be made to discover what sentences *do*, i.e., how they *work*, psychologically speaking.

There is a very widespread assumption, which we shall later have occasion to question, that in the process of spoken or written communication we, somehow, transfer meanings from mind to mind. To communicate, it is suggested, is to make something common, shared; and this something is meaning, understanding, thought, knowledge,

---

in the Old North Church of Boston) can be made to convey—or, perhaps more accurately, *confirm*—a highly complex message. But such "code" stimuli, by their very nature, cannot be combined, in nonprearranged ways, with other signs; they thus fall outside the realm of language as we here conceive it.

[10] There remains, however, an incidental problem which ought to be discussed in the present context in at least a preliminary way. It pertains to the problem of the "parts of speech." In the foregoing, we have made the subject-predicate relationship, or "predication," the essence of language. And we have seen that this approach demands a minimum of two signs. The question is: Do these two signs, the so-called subject and predicate, differ in any intrinsic or scientifically meaningful way? Subjects are commonly thought of as "nouns" and predicates as "verbs." And it is certainly true that, in English—with the exception of words like "murder," "table," and "bridge," which can be either a noun or a verb —we can often identify a word (if it is not some other "part of speech") as one or the other. However, no less a student of linguistics than Whorf (1952, p. 6), on the basis of comparative data, questions the validity of the noun-verb distinction; and several examples which will be given later in this chapter, as well as the "Pammy-kitty" sentence already cited, suggest that there is not a one-to-one relationship between subjects and "nouns" and predicates and "verbs" (see McCarthy, 1954, p. 530). If the general psychological approach to the phenomenon of language suggested in this chapter proves valid, it may provide a new frame of reference in which to re-examine the whole question of speech parts. (Cf. Fries, 1952, Chapters V–VIII; see also Section IV of this chapter.)

ideas, information. One writer puts the matter this way. He says that language, broadly speaking, is characterized by a "transfer of meaning." It is the device "by which men have conveyed significant messages to one another since the dawn of history." "Meaning may be transferred by devices that have nothing to do either with the spoken language or with its written counterpart, and this basic proposition few will be so hardy as to deny" (Pei, 1948, p. 10).

Another writer says:

When the day arrived on which one person could make such movements, gestures, or grimaces as would lead another person to avoid or to accept an object, that is to say, when a meaning could be transferred to one mind from another, language was created (Griffith, 1924, pp. 207–208).

Yet another says:

The philosophy of language, we may then say, to begin with, is concerned with *the evaluation of language as a bearer of meanings, as a medium of communication and as a sign or symbol of reality* (Urban, 1939, p. 37).

And to this the same writer later adds:

On the question as to what linguistic fact is not, linguists are in general agreed. They are also agreed upon what it is that constitutes positively linguistic fact. The *sine qua non* of language is precisely the *meaning* of which the sounds, the motor processes and tactual sensations, are the bearers (p. 66).

The first of the writers just cited is a linguist, the second a psychologist, and the third a philosopher. We thus see how widely accepted is the notion that the basic function of language is to transfer or bear meanings from person to person, from mind to mind.[11]

It is not hard to understand how this conception of language has arisen; and, as we shall see later, there is a certain limited sense in which it is undoubtedly correct. But in another, more basic sense, this notion seems to be wide of the mark and to have been a barrier to the development of a psychology of language with real "power." [12]

[11] In Greenough and Kittredge's book, *Words and Their Ways in English Speech*, published in 1906, we find the same general thesis formulated thus: "Language is the expression of thought by means of words" (p. 2). And even in Fries' otherwise very adventurous book, *The Structure of English: An Introduction to the Construction of English Sentences*, published in 1952, we find the author saying that he does not "deny that the chief business of language is to communicate meanings of various kinds" (p. 8).

[12] Contemporary "information theory," in the manner of Shannon & Weaver (1949) seems to be based, at least obliquely, upon the person-to-person-transfer-of-meaning notion. Perhaps this is why some of the original promise of the theory has not been fulfilled (see Section I).

Let us explore now, instead, the proposition that in communication we are not transferring meanings from person to person as much as we are transferring meanings *from sign to sign* within a given person, within a single mind. Said a little differently, the suggestion is that in order for us to communicate effectively with another person, he must already *have* the meanings with which we shall be dealing and that in the communicative act we are, for the most part, merely changing the signs to which particular meanings are attached, merely shifting or transferring meanings from one sign to another. One person, by the use of appropriate words or other signs, can *arouse*, or "call up," particular meanings in the mind of another person; but he does not "transfer" or implant them there. The communicative act, in its most salient aspect, lies rather in the combination, juxtaposition, or association of the meanings thus aroused in *novel, "informative" ways.*

A rudimentary sentence will illustrate this notion. Let us assume that John is telling Charles that: *Tom is a thief.*[13] It is clear that for the intended effect to be produced by this sentence, Charles must already know Tom and must know about thieves and thievery. In other words, Charles must already have meanings attached to the words, *Tom* and *thief*. What, then, is the function of the sentence, "Tom is a thief"? Most simply and most basically, it appears to be this. "Thief" is a sort of "unconditioned stimulus"—we shall later want to qualify this term, but for the moment it will suffice—a sort of "unconditioned stimulus" which can be depended upon to call forth an internal reaction which can be translated into, or defined by, the phrase, "a person who cannot be trusted," one who "takes things, steals." When, therefore, we put the word, or sign, "Tom" in front of the sign

Fig. 4–3. Diagram illustrating how the sentence, "Tom is a thief," can be recast in the vernacular of conditioning theory.

"thief," as shown in Fig. 4–3, we create a situation from which we can predict a fairly definite result.[14] On the basis of the familiar principle

[13] Lest there be any ambiguity about the identity of the particular Tom here referred to, let it be said that he is Tom, the Piper's Son, of fable and song.

[14] In the above analysis the copula and indefinite article are omitted on the assumption that, in a present indicative sentence, they are really unessential. Sup-

of conditioning, we would expect that some of the reaction evoked by the second sign, "thief," would be shifted to the first sign, "Tom," so that Charles, the hearer of the sentence, would thereafter respond to the word, "Tom," *somewhat as he had previously responded to the word, "thief."* Thus, in the Stewart example of the prehistoric woman saying "Coo-ouch," some of the quality of "ouchness" presumably gets attached to the word, "Coo," and in the case of the little girl saying "Pammy-kitty," the hearer likewise comes to make some part of the "kitty" reaction to "Pammy."

Although the notion that the essence of language involves predication, i.e., the temporal conjunction of something called a *subject* with something called a *predicate*, is ancient and widespread,[15] there has recently been considerable tendency to replace it with the view that single words and sentences do not differ basically. In their book, *The Meaning of Meaning* (1923), Ogden & Richards, while accepting the hypothesis that words *arouse* but do not "convey" or "bear" meanings,[16] nevertheless take the position that a sentence is just a complex sign. They say:

port for this position is provided by the following excerpts from a recent letter from Professor Gregory Razran. He says: "The Russian equivalent of the English, 'I am a thief,' is 'Ya vor.' The copula is always omitted in modern Russian in the present indicative, but is not omitted in Czech and Polish. The copula was not omitted in Old Slavic. Yet it would be incorrect to attribute such omissions to modern developments, since such copulas are also absent in ancient Hebrew. Moreover, . . . such copulas may also be omitted in Latin and Sanskrit (one may say in Latin, 'Ego fur sum,' as well as, for emphasis, 'Ego fur.'). As far as I know, Slavic languages have neither a definite nor an indefinite article, while Hebrew has a definite but not an indefinite article. The indefinite article in Teutonic and Romance languages seems to have developed from 'one,' as notice their identity in German, French, Spanish, and Italian, and, I believe, also in Old English. However, there is the differentiation of 'a' and 'an' from 'one' in modern English." (A foreign student also reports that in modern Turkish one would not say "Tom is a thief" but merely "Tom thief," "*Tom hirsiz.*")

[15] "Thus Sapir is voicing a view very prevalent among philologists, when he writes, 'There must be something to talk about and something must be said about this subject of discourse once it is selected. . . . The subject of discourse is a noun. . . . No language wholly fails to distinguish noun and verb" (Ogden & Richards, 1923, p. 260). "For centuries it has been insisted that, for completeness, every sentence must have a word 'asserting' or 'saying something' about that person, place or thing. There must be a 'subject' and a 'predicate'" (Fries, 1952, p. 14).

[16] Malinowski (1938) wrote an essay entitled "The Problem of Meaning in Primitive Languages" which Ogden and Richards published as part of their book and which Osgood, in discussing the notion that words "carry" meanings from person to person, evaluates as follows: "Malinowski aptly dubbed this naive conception the 'bucket theory' of meaning—words like little buckets are assumed to pick up their loads of meaning in one mind, carry them across intervening

Thus the reference of "larks sing," since it has two components, will differ from that of "larks" just as do "soaring larks" or "lark pie," being also dual references. This difference is therefore unessential, though most complex references do in fact use the propositional form (p. 259).

In his *Signs, Language, and Behavior*, Morris (1946) says:

The fifth criterion requires that language signs be combinable with each other in certain ways, and not in others, and that these combinations form a complex sign. . . . Hull has suggested that such combinations are to be explained in terms of simultaneous and temporal stimulus patterning, since ". . . In reading, each letter is a complex visual pattern, each word is a complex pattern of these letter patterns, and each sentence is a temporally patterned sequence of printed word patterns" (p. 58).

And more recent and more explicit still is the following formulation by Dollard & Miller (1950):

As has already been pointed out, a person can learn to respond to specific combinations of stimuli or relationships among them and to make different responses to the same cues in different contexts. This is called patterning. A person's responses to the words that he hears someone else speak obviously involve patterning. Thus a parent will respond quite differently to the following two reports containing the same words in different sequences: "Jim hit Mary" and "Mary hit Jim." This is an exceedingly simple example. Although scarcely a beginning has been made toward the study of language from the point of view of learning theory, it is obvious that man's great innate capacity and rigorous social training have produced marvelously intricate and subtle patterning in his responses to spoken language (p. 100).[17]

The notion under examination in this chapter is different. It is that the sentence is, pre-eminently, a *conditioning device*, and that its chief

---

space, and dump them in another mind. 'This attitude in which the word is regarded as a real entity, containing its meaning as a Soul-box contains the spiritual part of a person or thing, is shown to be derived from the primitive, magical uses of language and to reach right into the most important and influential systems of metaphysics. Meaning, the real "essence" of a word, achieves thus Real Existence in Plato's realm of Ideas. . . .'" (Osgood, 1953, p. 680).

[17] The notion that language is merely a form of interpersonal stimulation and response is undoubtedly a product of the era of Behaviorism; and it achieved one of its earliest, clearest, and most influential formulations in the writings of Bloomfield (see Section I). Here the recipient of the speech stimulation is what Courtney (1949), in discussing the child-mother relationship, has called a "mediator" (not to be confused with "mediating response," Section VI). (Perhaps "intermediatary" would be a better term.) While widely accepted (see Fries, 1952, Chapter III), this conception of language seems greatly oversimplified: it ignores the phenomenon of predication (by making a sentence basically the same as a stimulus) and bypasses the whole problem of meaning, knowledge, information, i.e., mediate as opposed to immediate behavior, predispositions to action as opposed to direct response.

effect is to produce new associations, new learning, just as any other paired presentation of stimuli may do. This position is congruent with the traditional notion that predication is the essence of language and may indicate, perhaps more precisely than purely linguistic research has done, the basic nature of this phenomenon.

This notion is presented here in a frankly exploratory manner, as a hypothesis which others are invited to consider and test against the prevailing concepts and facts of their particular specialties. So far as the writer has been able to determine, no similar conception of the sentence has been previously put forward. In their otherwise illuminating discussions of language, Russell (1948, see especially Chapter VI), Cassirer (1944, see Chapter VIII), Skinner (1957, Chapter 14), and Carroll (1953) make no allusion to such a notion, although many of the linguistic phenomena to which they refer go unexplained for lack of it. Because of the special promise of this hypothesis, the next two sections will be concerned with its further analysis and elaboration, with special reference to the problem of mediation and a laboratory analogue.[18]

[18] The writer has recently discovered a very closely related, but unelaborated, conception of the communicative process. In a paper by Carpenter (1953), entitled "A Theoretical Orientation for Instructional Film Research," there is brief reference to the "releasor-organizer hypothesis," which is "that the signals, signs, and symbols of sound motion pictures function principally as releasors and organizers of meanings and responses in human subjects" (p. 42). The releasing function of signs is said to be "both dependent (or interdependent) on the stimulation and on the activated brain process ('engrams') of the experiencing subjects. Thus, it may be reasoned that the functions of signals, signs, and symbols is to *release responses in subjects*. . . . Signs and symbols *do not transmit meanings;* they release meaning when and only when the subjects respond. The characteristics of these responses relate closely to personal life history differences" (pp. 42–43). The same author continues: "The releasor concept of signs and symbols must be supplemented by the related *organizer* concept. Previously learned 'engrams' may be modified by new stimulation, and even new *related* elements may be 'imprinted.' New relationships may be shown, and old responses modified, by film-mediated stimulation. The results are conceived principally of the *re-organization* of previously learned neural-organic patterns which intervene between film stimulation and the subsequent actions or reactions of the individual" (p. 43). The notion that signs release, or arouse, meanings *in* rather than "bear" them *to* another individual, as stated by Carpenter, is identical with the position taken in the present analysis. The "organizer" conception, while stated in somewhat different terms, is also believed to be essentially congruent, at a relatively abstract level, with the theory of sentence function as here developed. Whether the notion of "re-organization" can, without injustice, be analyzed in terms of conditioning and mediation (see next section), or whether more holistic principles are required, is uncertain.

VI. The Problem of Mediation

Perhaps the most generally accepted criterion as to whether a sentence has or has not done its work is this: If, as a result of hearing or reading a sentence, an individual's behavior, on some future occasion, with respect to some person, thing, or event not present when the sentence occurred, is different from what it would otherwise have been, then that sentence may be said to have been "understood" and to have functioned effectively. If, for example, John tells Charles, in the absence of Tom, that Tom is a thief and if, when Charles subsequently encounters Tom, he reacts toward Tom with distrust and apprehension, communication has clearly taken place.

But this criterion of linguistic action poses an interesting problem for the behavioral scientist. Everyone is familiar with situations in which an organism learns, or is taught, to react to a sign more or less *as if* it were the thing or event signified. In the vernacular of the conditioning laboratory, the organism, after conjoint exposure to the conditioned stimulus and the unconditioned stimulus, reacts to the CS somewhat as if it were the UnCS. Or, as we may equivalently say, the meaning of the UnCS "moves forward" and becomes anticipatory.

This phenomenon seems to occur in language, true enough, as when the predicate meaning of a sentence "moves forward" and gets connected to the sentence subject. But in language something else, of a different nature, is also involved. This is the remarkable, and indeed somewhat paradoxical, phenomenon of an organism, after exposure to a sentence, reacting to some thing, event, or person as if *it* were the corresponding sign or symbol which was the subject of the sentence. In other words, the new meaning attached, by means of predication, to the sign constituting the subject of a sentence has a tendency to shift or transfer "back," so to say, to the thing, event, or person which the subject of the sentence represents, or "stands for." This phenomenon—sometimes referred to as *semantic* generalization—has received comparatively little attention but can be satisfactorily accounted for on the basis of well-known principles (see Chapter 2).

Let us note, first of all, that what we are positing here is something quite different from so-called backward conditioning. This is fortunate, for backward conditioning is a questionable, controversial type of event (Mowrer, 1960, Chapter 10), whereas the phenomenon with which we are here concerned seems, as phenomenon, not to be in the least questionable. We are, however, in need of a precise explanation.

Let us begin by making a more detailed diagrammatic analysis of the sentence, "Tom is a thief." In Fig. 4–3 we have already seen how the familiar principle of conditioning can explain the fact that some part of the reaction evoked by the word "thief" gets connected to the word "Tom," but we have not as yet said anything about the sequence of events whereby "Tom" and "thief" originally acquired their meanings.

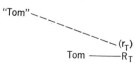

Fig. **4–4**. Schematic indication of the way in which the word "Tom," through the process of conditioning, comes to denote, mean, or imply a certain person, Tom.

As Fig. 4–4 shows, the word "Tom" acquired its meaning, presumably, by being associated with, and occurring in the context of, Tom as a real person. Tom himself has elicited in John and Charles and others who have had first-hand contact with him a total reaction which we can label, R_T, of which r_T is a component. And as a result of the paired presentation or concurrence of "Tom"-the-word and Tom-the-person, the component, or "detachable," reaction, r_T, is shifted from the latter to the former.[19]

Fig. **4–5**. Replication of Fig. 4–4, showing how the word "thief," acquires its distinctive meaning.

And similarly for the word "thief." As indicated in Fig. 4–5, this word is likewise presumed to have acquired its distinctive meaning by having been used in the presence of, or to have been, as we say, "associated with," actual thieves. Therefore, when we make the sentence, "Tom (is a) thief," it is in no way surprising or incomprehensible that the r_t reaction gets shifted, as originally shown in Fig. 4–3, from the word, "thief," to the word, "Tom." This is seemingly a straightforward instance of second-order conditioning: By first-order conditioning some part of the total reaction elicited by real thieves is shifted to the word, "thief"; and by second-order conditioning of the type provided by the sentence, this same reaction, with some attenuation or weakening, gets further transferred or shifted to the word "Tom."

Our analysis thus far is, however, either incomplete or faulty; for if language worked precisely as suggested, it would pretty obviously not do what we want it to do and what, a good deal of the time, it manifestly does. If language worked as thus far indicated, the sentence, "Tom is a thief," would serve merely to *change the meaning of "Tom,"* so that when Charles, as the recipient of this sentence, subsequently heard this word, it would remind him less or perhaps not at all of Tom but rather of *thieves.* It would, in other words, become just a synonym for the word, "thief," and we would have simply an instance of *reconditioning* or "redefinition," a procedure whereby the noise, "Tom," would lose its old meaning and acquire a new, different one. This type of conditioning, or reconditioning, would, pretty obviously, not serve our communicative needs at all and would soon lead to utter chaos. Clearly, something essential is missing here; fortunately, the difficulty can be quickly remedied.

In drawing a diagram of conventional type to represent conditioned-response learning, we are likely to represent the UnCS and the response it elicits and then, in adding the CS, to say something like this: "This is an originally neutral stimulus. Oh, to be sure, it probably evokes *some* reaction, but for our purposes it is not important." Thus we end with a drawing something like that shown in Fig. 4–6.

Fig. 4–6. Conventional conditioning diagram, indicating the common neglect of the reaction originally produced by the conditioned stimulus.

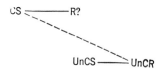

But if we are to succeed in making conditioning theory account for the basic facts of language, we must proceed a little differently at this point. As already indicated, particularly in Fig. 4–3, the subject, or "CS," in our specimen sentence has, by assumption, a very definite reaction potential or meaning, which we have designated as r_T. Let us, therefore, redraw Fig. 4–3; but, instead of ignoring r_T, let us give it rightful recognition in the diagram. Figure 4–7 is the result.

Assuming now, as we reasonably may, that the "Tom"—r_T con-

[19] It may be helpful to think of the R_T reaction, mentioned above, and the so-called "detachable component," r_T, as analogous, respectively, to the total reaction produced by an electric shock in a rat and the reaction produced by a stimulus which is merely a sign of shock. Shock produces sensations of pain, fear, and physical agitation; but it is only the fear that gets conditioned, or "detached," and occurs anticipatorily, to a mere signal or sign of shock. (See also Chapter 5.)

nection is a relatively stable one, we will expect the conditioning outcome shown at the bottom of Fig. 4–7. Instead of r_t, the thief-meaning, getting connected *directly* to the word, "Tom," and more or less replacing the r_T reaction, we may infer that r_t will be conditioned rather to the reaction—or, more accurately, to the stimuli or sensations produced by the reaction—which the word "Tom" produces, namely r_T. This internal reaction, or meaning, thus becomes what Lumsdaine (1939), Foley and Cofer (1943), Osgood (1953), and others have recently called a *mediating response* (see Chapter 2); and its importance is indicated by the felicity with which it delivers us from the difficulties into which a too simple, too abbreviated analysis of language in terms of conditioning plunges us.

"Tom (is a) thief."

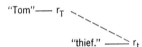

Fig. 4–7. Replication of Fig. 4–3, but with the mediating response, r_T, included rather than omitted.

"Tom"——r_T ————r_t

We have already posited (Fig. 4–3) that the meaning reaction, r_T, which gets connected to the word, "Tom," is a component of R_T, which is the reaction or reaction complex evoked by Tom himself; and we have also posited (Fig. 4–7) that the sentence, "Tom (is a) thief," will cause the thief-meaning, r_t, to get connected to r_T. Therefore, when Tom-the-person is subsequently encountered by Charles, Tom will elicit in Charles the R_T reaction, of which r_T is a part, which will in turn elicit the thief-meaning, r_t. Q.E.D. This mechanism for the occurrence of semantic generalization or meaning transfer from sign to thing is shown schematically in Fig. 4–8 and is characterized

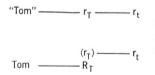

Fig. 4–8. Indication of how r_T, in the example given, functions as a "mediating response." (Cf. Figs. 4–3 and 4–7.)

by relative simplicity yet also possesses, seemingly, considerable generality and explanatory vigor.[20]

[20] Interestingly enough, this hypothesis has at least verbal similarity to the "identical-elements" theory of "transfer of training" as advanced by Thorndike

If our specimen sentence worked as Fig. 4–3 implies, i.e., if the thief-meaning, r_t, got conditioned directly to the word, "Tom," and thus more or less replaced the Tom-meaning, r_T, then there would be only one apparent way in which the thief-meaning could get transferred to Tom as a person, namely for Tom-the-person, when encountered, to elicit in Charles *a labeling reaction*, which would involve his saying, at least subvocally, the word, "Tom," which in turn would then elicit the thief-meaning, r_t (see Fig. 4–9). While this hypothesis

Fig. 4–9. A possible, but not entirely satisfactory, conception of how a meaning acquired by a word ("Tom") can get transferred to the thing or person (Tom) represented by the word.

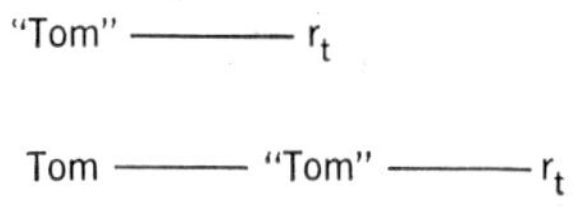

$$\text{"Tom"} \longrightarrow r_t$$
$$\text{Tom} \longrightarrow \text{"Tom"} \longrightarrow r_t$$

is logically tenable and may in some cases correspond to reality, it has, as will be shown in the next section, rather limited applicability. Moreover, as we have seen (Figs. 4–7 and 4–8), the type of mediation mechanism already posited takes care of the known facts very nicely, without entailing any of the limitations of the labeling hypothesis.[21]

VII. Further Analysis of the Sentence as a Conditioning Device

The essence of the argument advanced up to this point is that the subject-predicate complex which we call a sentence is, in effect, simply an arrangement for conditioning the meaning reaction produced by the predicate to the interoceptive stimulation aroused by the meaning reaction elicited by the sentence subject.[22] The following laboratory

---

(1925) and others. A mediating reaction, such as r_T in the above example, is an "identical element" in the reaction produced by both the word, "Tom," and the person, Tom. Therefore, if, by means of the Tom-is-a-thief sentence, we get a new meaning-reaction, r_t, conditioned to r_T as elicited by the word, "Tom," we will expect it to generalize to r_T as elicited (in the context of the total R_T) by the person, Tom.

[21] Dollard & Miller (1950, see especially Chapter VI) have developed in considerable detail the notion of response generalization and transfer (as well as discrimination) through "labeling." However, they agree that such generalization may occur on the basis of "labeling or other cue-producing-responses" (p. 105). Thus they do not exclude as a possibility the mechanism which is to be emphasized in the following discussion. See also Chapter 2, Section VI.

[22] Since this statement was written, Staats, Staats & Heard (1959) have reported a direct experimental confirmation of this hypothesis. They say: "The hypothesis that a meaning response can be conditioned to a meaning response was sub-

paradigms will help put this way of thinking about language function into a broader, more systematic perspective and, at the same time, will provide a summary of this chapter as a whole.

Let us assume that our objective is to train a rat not to eat a certain preferred food. Cheese is such a food for rats, which they will readily take even though fully satiated on such a well-balanced ration as Purina Laboratory Chow. The most direct way, and the one to be first considered here, of teaching chow-satiated rats not to eat cheese is to punish them while in the process of eating or starting to eat the forbidden food. It goes without saying that by using a harmless source of pain like electric shock, it is possible in this way to make cheese itself, as well as the actions involved in taking and eating it, so fear-producing that rats will turn away from it instead of moving toward and taking it. This procedure for accomplishing a purely heuristic objective is represented diagrammatically in Fig. 4–10 and is, of course, analogous to the practice, not uncommonly employed in child training, of catching the child, as we say, "in the act" and administering some sort of primary punishment forthwith.

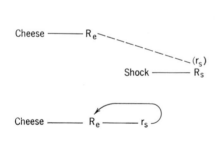

Fig. **4–10.** A "thing-thing" conditioning sequence, or "sentence," R_e is the eating reaction elicited by the cheese (and hunger), and R_s is the total reaction elicited by the shock, of which r_s is the "detachable component," *fear*. Since r_s gets conditioned to R_e (or, more exactly, to its proprioceptive "backlash"), R_e tends to become inhibited as shown in the lower line of the diagram. (There is also some fear conditioned to the cheese itself, but for simplicity of analysis, this connection is not represented, and for present purposes is not relevant. For support, derived from experimentation with human subjects, for this kind of analysis, see Razran, 1939b.)

---

stantiated. Thus, Mowrer's conception that communication takes place by the meaning of the predicate becoming conditioned to the meaning of the subject is given support. . . . The mediated conditioned meaning effect was significant at the .005 level [of significance]. It was concluded that meaning responses can enter into multi-link mediating chains of responses, without Ss' awareness" (pp. 5–6). See also Staats & Staats (1957).

While the most direct and in some ways most efficient way of inhibiting a particular form of behavior, the procedure just described—which we shall refer to as a *thing-thing* sentence—is only one of four ways in which the same objective can, at least in principle, be achieved.

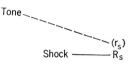

Fig. 4–11. Conventional procedure for conditioning a fear reaction, r_s, to tone.

Suppose that we now take naive rats and first pair a tone with electric shock a few times (Fig. 4–11). Now let us present cheese and as the rat starts to take it, we sound the tone (Fig. 4–12). This involves the use of what may be called *secondary*, or fear, punishment and will serve only a little less effectively than does primary punishment to inhibit the act with which it is associated. A recent study by Bixenstine (1956) shows that this means of controlling behavior can be used quite effectively with rats; and it is clearly parallel to the parental practice of warning, or "speaking to," a child when engaged, or about to engage, in some disapproved action. This procedure may be conveniently dubbed a *thing-sign* sentence.

Next there is a procedure which we may, in the same vein, call a

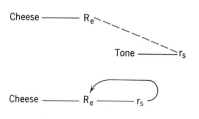

Fig. 4–12. Illustration of how cheese eating can be inhibited by paired presentation of cheese and a fear-eliciting tone.

sign-thing sentence. Suppose we have paired a blinking light several times with the presentation of cheese so that it elicits a confident "expectation" of cheese and appropriate anticipatory movements (Fig. 4–13). If the rat is placed on a grill-like floor and if cheese is presented vertically on the end of a stylus a little to one side of the rat and the blinking light is presented a few seconds in advance of the cheese, the rat will soon start making horizontal pendular, or "groping," movements in anticipation of the presentation of the food. (Albino and therefore partially blind rats have been used in this study and are probably better, for this particular experiment, than rats with pigmented eyes.)

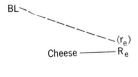

Fig. 4–13. Procedure for getting a part (r_e) of the total eating reaction (R_e) elicited by cheese conditioned to a blinking light (BL).

A sharp discrimination between the experimental situation with and without the blinking light is necessary and is achieved by leaving the animals in the situation for relatively long periods of time between presentations of the blinking light and cheese. In other words, the sign value of the experimental situation as such is thus thoroughly extinguished. For reasons to be mentioned shortly, such a clear-cut discrimination is necessary in this type of investigation.

If we now present the blinking light, which elicits the "searching" or "groping" head movements, and follow it with shock, we will expect these movements to be punished and to be inhibited, as suggested in Fig. 4–14.[23] And since the same movements are part of the

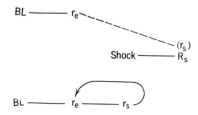

Fig. 4–14. Procedure for getting fear attached to the anticipatory, food-seeking response (r_e), which is produced by the blinking light (see Fig. 4–13).

total response called forth by cheese itself, we will expect this training to generalize to cheese, as shown in Fig. 4–15. It will be seen that we are here employing exactly the same assumptions about the role of mediating reactions as advanced in earlier parts of this (and in the pre-

[23] The reason, alluded to above, why the head movements need to be conditioned quite specifically to the situation-plus-blinking-light is that if they occur also with any frequency to the situation-alone, then any attempt to determine, in a control group, the effect of administering a shock not combined with the BL would be invalidated: an animal might be in the act of making the head movements, "spontaneously," just as the shock came on, which would produce an effect not greatly different from that obtained where the BL and shock are paired.

ceding) chapter and that the situation is parallel to one in which a parent reinstates verbally some form of misbehavior and then administers primary punishment.

Fig. 4–15. Indication of how it is that inhibitory tendencies acquired at the symbolic level (see top line) generalize, through the mediating response r_e, to the "reality" level (bottom line).

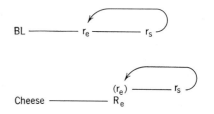

Finally, we come to a procedure which parallels what is presumably involved in language proper, i.e., in a *sign-sign* sentence. Let us assume that our subjects have had the kinds of training shown in Figs. 4–11 and 4–13 and then the kind shown in the upper part of Fig. 4–16. The first behavioral result we would expect from this type of sign-sign conditioning is that the anticipatory, exploratory responses formerly elicited by the blinking light (r_e) will be inhibited (lower line, Fig. 4–16), because of the fear that has gotten attached to them. And as a further consequence, we would expect this inhibitory effect to generalize to the behavior produced by the *thing* represented by the blinking light, namely cheese. This would involve the now familiar mechanism of response mediation, as already shown in Fig. 4–15. Exploratory experiments give empirical support for these inferences.

Fig. 4–16. Diagram showing how fear (r_s) is connected, by a "sign-sign" sentence, to the anticipatory food reaction, r_e, and tends to inhibit it.

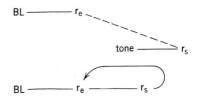

This paradigm seems to fulfill the criterion of true language: By means of a two-sign complex, or sentence, namely BL-tone, we cause a living organism to be so modified, in the absence of something (cheese), that when it later encounters that thing it behaves differently from the way it would have behaved without the intervening training. The parallel to our earlier analysis of the English sentence, "Tom is a thief," will be evident. In both cases we see once again, and perhaps more clearly now, that what we call a sentence is basically a device for producing associative shifting, or conditioning, but that in order for the sentence completely to fulfill its intended function there must also be the phenomenon of response mediation (Fig. 4–15), whereby the new meaning which thus gets connected to the sentence subject can generalize, or transfer, to the thing thus symbolized.

VIII. What, Then, Is a "Symbol"—and the Essence of Language?

After having the foregoing material presented to them in the class-room, students often ask: "Now just what *is* a 'symbol'?" This is a fair question; and somewhere, surely, in a book on the *symbolic processes*, it ought to have a clear and explicit answer. As it happens, however, our approach to this problem in the context of contemporary learning theory is still so new that thinking about it has not yet been fully consolidated. An able young psychologist who read a preliminary draft of this chapter admirably high-lighted the situation as follows:

Since language is an area which learning theory has never dealt with very adequately, a fuller discussion of certain issues would be desirable. It seems to me that the concept of mediation behavior is the key which opens up this field for learning theory and permits the solution of many pre-viously perplexing problems. More attention should be given to the ways in which this approach differs from other approaches to language (such as that of Skinner) which do not assume mediational processes. Also there are some distinct points of difference between this approach and that of other mediational theories, such as that of Osgood. The Osgood formula, although assuming mediating stimuli and responses, still retains the Hullian conception of bonds or connections; and reinforcement is an operation for strengthening them. . . . It is interesting that the most ambitious attempt by a philosopher to deal with the *pragmatics* of language (cf. Morris' *Signs, Language, and Behavior*, 1946) did not at all employ the mediational notion, but stayed close to the ideas of Hull and Tolman. Bertrand Russell's writings on language seem benighted with respect to learning theory.

It is possible that the key to understanding language lies in the develop-ment of mediation processes generally rather than in vocalization specifically. Perhaps mediation processes evolved first, then only later speech and com-munication. Consider an aggregation of near-human beings many of whom had developed little fragments of "thought" and symbolism, which were in various ways functional in their own behavior alone. This would represent a sort of unstable situation which could be "triggered" into further rapid evolution, much as a super-saturated solution is triggered into crystallization by a small stimulus. As soon as a few vocalizations began to take on meaning, there would be a wholesale rush of meanings and ideas from one individual to another; the little fragments of thought would now be "shared," resulting ultimately in culture.

In contrast to this evaluation of the role of mediation in understand-ing the nature of language is the disparaging view of Brown as set forth in his book, *Words and Things* (1958b). He says:

What evidence is there for the existence of such fractional implicit responses? Jacobson's work demonstrated that some words sometimes evoke implicit responses. This study does not demonstrate that the implicit responses are fractional components of reactions to stimulus objects that may be considered referents for the words used. The evidence for actual conditioning of fractional implicit reactions has all been obtained with autonomic reactions to shock or with salivation to food powder. And there are good reasons to doubt that either of these is sufficiently covert and abbreviated to be a meaning. There are many studies in which one or the other of these reactions has been conditioned to a number of different words. If we were to take these responses for the meanings of the words it would follow that the words had been given identical meanings by this conditioning procedure and that is patently absurd. It is necessary to say that these responses are at most only a part of the total mediating reaction, the remainder of the reaction not having been observed in any of these studies. In sum, *there is scarcely any direct evidence for the existence of mediating responses elicited by linguistic signs* (p. 101, italics added).

Finally, behavioral meanings are found cheek-by-jowl with imaginal meanings inside the organism—neither revealed in action nor available to introspection (p. 102).

The reason for this rejection of the concept of mediation (in the face of much empirical evidence not cited by Brown) becomes more apparent when one discovers that the author has immersed himself in formal linguistics (probably more fully than any other American psychologist) and is operating within the slogan of that discipline: "Language is a system" (viii). Here the central assumption, as Brown interprets it, is that an "utterance" (the term "sentence" is not in favor among linguists at present) consists of "systematic sign contingencies" (p. 183). And as one reads further it emerges that this expression implies "configurational conditioning" and "contextual dependency." In short, Brown completely disregards the phenomenon of predication and has taken the position that an "utterance" is just a more or less complex *combination of stimuli* (cf. Section V of this chapter) which human beings learn to make and to react to in accordance with the rules of the linguistic system which is dominant in their particular society. Once they have learned this system, they supposedly have a "disposition" to know how to construct and interpret such utterances. Says Brown:

It seems to me that when one comes to understand a linguistic form his nervous system is partially rewired (in the sense of changes in synaptic resistances or neurone process growth) so that one is disposed to behave appropriately with regard to that form. For the psychologist [?] meaning is not a particular response. It is the disposition to behave in varying ways with regard to the form as the contingent circumstances are changed. The disposition has no substantial character other than the structure of the nervous system. It is not a learning, a beginning, a miniature reaction. It is a response potential. A disposition is discovered by creating various contingencies and observing responses.

Within a linguistic community there are standards (not necessarily formulated) for the usage of an utterance and for total behavior with reference to the utterance. These standards define appropriate behavior, the conventional disposition. A child born into the community does not at first conform to these standards, but he eventually does so and is then said to speak and understand the language.

I am satisfied that the disposition theory gives a more sensible account of linguistic meaning than any variety of particular reaction theory (p. 103).

Although this brief excerpt may not do full justice to Brown's thesis, it indicates the direction in which his approach points; and for reasons previously advanced in this chapter, it seems that this direction is not a promising one. Brown's analysis entirely by-passes the problem of predication and in so doing leaves no place for the concept of mediation; and when mediation is rejected, so also, apparently, is the heart of the problem of meaning (see Chapter 5). But the Brown book, despite its theoretical bent, makes good reading and is, in many ways, highly informative.

As already noted, N. E. Miller has made some of the basic contributions to our understanding of mediation; and in his 1950 book collaboratively written with Dollard, there is considerable reference to this phenomenon. Here the authors say:

In order to talk about the higher mental processes we need to make the distinction between instrumental and cue-producing responses (Hull, 1930b). An instrumental act is one whose main function is to produce an immediate change in the relationship to the external environment. Opening a door, lifting a box, jumping back on the curb are examples of instrumental acts. A cue-producing response is one whose main function is to produce a cue that is part of the stimulus pattern leading to another response. Counting [cf. Chapter 2, p. 62] is a cue-producing response (p. 98).

And later Dollard & Miller continue:

Having made the distinction between instrumental and cue-producing responses, we can improve our description of the distinction between the "lower" and "higher" types of adjustment. In the former, the instrumental response is made directly to the pattern of external cues and internal drives; in the latter, one or more cue-producing responses intervenes (p. 100).

But this distinction, useful as it is for some purposes, does not provide the basis for the understanding we are now seeking. Infrahuman organisms engage, not uncommonly, in "cue-producing responses" ("pure-stimulus acts"), as has already been indicated in Chapter 2 and will be further seen in Chapter 6. Such organisms do not, however, have *language;* and it is the defining characteristics of the latter that we are here trying to derive. For Dollard & Miller this problem was still an unsolved one, as indicated by the following statement:

It should be noted . . . that by emphasizing the hypothesis that verbal and other cue-producing responses play an essential role in the higher mental processes, *we are not denying the fact that the organism must possess certain capacities, the exact nature of which is still unknown, before such responses can operate in this way.* A parrot can learn to imitate words but not to become a greater thinker (p. 101)

IX. The Views of Certain Philosophers

In some ways the most seminal mind to deal with the problem of symbolism in this century was that of G. H. Mead; and the essence of his thought on this score is captured by the following quotation from his book, *Mind, Self, and Society* (1934):

The sentinel of a herd is that member of the herd which is more sensitive to odor or sound than the others. At the approach of danger, he starts to run earlier than the others, who then follow along, in virtue of a herding tendency to run together. There is a social stimulus, a gesture, if you like, to which the other forms respond. The first form gets the odor earlier and starts to run, and its starting to run is a stimulus to the others to run also. It is all external; there is no mental process involved. The sentinel does not regard itself as the individual who is to give a signal; it just runs at a certain moment and so starts the others to run. But with a mind, the animal that gives the signal also takes the attitude of the others who respond to it. He knows what his signal means. A man who calls "fire" would be able to call out in himself the reaction he calls out in the other. In so far as the man can take the attitude of the other—his attitude of response to fire, his sense of terror—that response to his own cry is something that makes his conduct a mental affair, as over against the conduct of the others. But the only thing that has happened here is that what takes place externally in the herd has been imported into the conduct of the man. There is the same signal and the same tendency to respond, but the man not only can give the signal but also can arouse in himself the attitude of the terrified escape, and through calling that out he can come back upon his own tendency to call out and can check it. He can react upon himself in taking the organized attitude of the whole group in trying to escape from danger. There is nothing more subjective about it than that the response to his own stimulus can be found in his own conduct, and that he can utilize the conversation of gestures that takes place to determine his own conduct. If he can so act, he can set up a rational control, and thus make possible a far more highly organized society than otherwise. The process is one which does not utilize a man endowed with a consciousness where there was no consciousness before, but rather an individual who takes over the whole social process into his own conduct. That ability, of course, is dependent first of all on the symbol being one to which he can respond; and so far as we know, the vocal gesture has been the condition for the development of that type of symbol. Whether it can develop without the vocal gesture I cannot tell.[24]

I want to be sure that we see the content put into the mind is only a development and product of social interaction. It is a development which is of enormous importance, and which leads to complexities and complications of society which go almost beyond our power to trace, but originally it is nothing but the taking over of the attitude of the other. To the extent that the animal can take the attitude of the other and utilize that attitude for the control of his own conduct, we have what is termed mind; and that is the only apparatus involved in the appearance of mind (pp. 190–191).

Mead is here obviously painting on a large canvas with broad strokes and includes territory which lies beyond the scope of our present inquiry; but his analysis points in the direction in which behavior theory must ultimately move and, for immediate purposes, serves to highlight the distinction, previously suggested, between the use of signs *as signals* and *as symbols*. An animal may, advertently or inadvertently, make a sign to which *other* animals react meaningfully, i.e., with a conditioned (usually emotional) response; but the first animal will not, argues Mead, necessarily react similarly. On the other hand, human beings, as a result of their membership in a more complex social group, react to their own signs very much as they expect others to; and therein, says Mead, is the essence of the symbolic (as opposed to the mere signaling) function.

Mead's lectures and writings have had a stimulating and inspiring effect throughout the social sciences and are probably more influential now than they were during Mead's own lifetime. But his analysis of the symbol, shrewd as it is in many ways, still seems incomplete; and we turn to a modest but unusually penetrating treatment of this subject by the French philosopher and scholar, Ernst Cassirer, in his book *An Essay on Man* (1944). Here, in a chapter entitled "From Animal Reactions to Human Responses," we find a line of reasoning which coincides well with the one followed in this volume and which, when combined therewith, enables us to take at least one additional forward step toward the resolution of the riddle of symbolic function.

[24] Elsewhere in the same volume Mead has significantly observed: "It is this which gives such peculiar importance to the vocal gesture: it is one of those social stimuli which affect the form that makes it in the same fashion that it affects the form when made by another. That is, we can hear ourselves talking, and the import of what we say is the same to ourselves that it is to others" (p. 62). For a similar emphasis, see Chapter 3; Cassirer (1944, see especially Chapter 3) treats this matter somewhat differently. See also Chapter 10, Section II.

Many of the writers previously cited in this chapter have graphically reconstructed the emergence of language and what it has meant for human beings in general; and we have also commented on the excitement which a small child shows when he or she gets the "hang" of language and through it finds himself entering into a far more extensive and wonderful "world" than he ever before supposed to exist. But no one has done better in capturing this marvel of language in words than Cassirer when he says:

In the mental development of the individual mind the transition from the one form to the other—from a merely practical attitude to a symbolic attitude—is evident. But here this step is the final result of a slow and continuous process. By the usual methods of psychological observation it is not easy to distinguish the individual stages of this complicated process. There is, however, another way to obtain full insight into the general character and paramount importance of this transition. Nature itself has here, so to speak, made an experiment capable of throwing unexpected light upon the point in question. We have the classical cases of Laura Bridgman and Helen Keller, two blind deaf-mute children, who by means of special methods learned to speak. . . .

In order to arrive at such an understanding the child had to make a new and much more significant discovery. It had to understand that *everything has a name*—that the symbolic function is not restricted to particular cases but is a principle of *universal* applicability which encompasses the whole field of human thought. In the case of Helen Keller this discovery came as a sudden shock. She was a girl seven years of age who, with the exception of defects in the use of certain sense organs, was in an excellent state of health and possessed of a highly developed mind. By the neglect of her education she had been very much retarded. Then, suddenly, the crucial development takes place. It works like an intellectual revolution. The child begins to see the world in a new light. It has learned the use of words not merely as mechanical signs or signals but as an entirely new instrument of thought. A new horizon is opened up, and henceforth the child will roam at will in this incomparably wider and freer area. . . .

The principle of symbolism, with its universality, validity, and general applicability, is the magic word, the Open Sesame! giving access to the specifically human world, to the world of human culture. Once man is in possession of this magic key further progress is assured (pp. 34-35).

Granted, then, that it is the "symbolic attitude" and the capacity for *naming* which mark the transition from infrahuman mentality, we are still not entirely clear as to how this comes about and of precisely what it consists. Cassirer attacks this problem as follows:

It is necessary, first of all, to find a correct logical starting point, one which can lead us to a natural and sound interpretation of the empirical facts. This starting point is the *definition of speech* (Révész, 1940, 1941). But instead of giving a ready-made definition of speech, it would be better perhaps to proceed along tentative lines. Speech is not a simple and uniform phenomenon. It consists of different elements which, both biologically and systematically, are not on the same level. We must try to find the order and interrelationships of the constituent elements; we must, as it were, distinguish the various geological strata of speech. The first and most fundamental stratum is evidently the language of the emotions. A great portion of all human utterances still belongs to this stratum. But there is a form of speech that shows us quite a different type. Here the word is by no means a mere interjection; it is not an involuntary expression of feeling, but a part of a sentence which has a definite syntactical and logical structure (Sapir, 1921). It is true that even in highly developed, in theoretical language the connection with the first element is not entirely broken off. Scarcely a sentence can be found—except perhaps the pure formal sentences of mathematics—without a certain affective or emotional tinge (Bally, 1936). Analogies and parallels to emotional language may be found in abundance in the animal world. As regards chimpanzees Wolfgang Koehler states that they achieve a considerable degree of expression by means of gesture. Rage, terror, despair, grief, pleasing, desire, playfulness, and pleasure are readily expressed in this manner. Nevertheless one element, which is characteristic of and indispensable to all human language, is missing: we find no signs which have an objective reference or meaning. "It may be taken as positively proved," says Koehler, "that their gamut of *phonetics* is entirely 'subjective,' and can only express emotions, never designate or describe objects. But they have so many phonetic elements which are also common to human languages, that their lack of articulate speech cannot be ascribed to *secondary* (glosso-labial) limitations. Their gestures too, of face and body like their expression in sound, never designate or 'describe' objects (Bühler)" (Koehler, 1921, p. 27; also see Koehler, 1927, p. 317).

Here we touch upon the crucial point in our whole problem. The difference between *propositional language* and *emotional language* is the real landmark between the human and the animal world. All the theories and observations concerning animal language are wide of the mark if they fail to recognize this fundamental difference.[25] In all the literature on the subject there does not seem to be a single conclusive proof of the fact that any animal ever made the decisive step from subjective to objective, from affective to propositional language. Koehler insists emphatically that speech is definitely beyond the powers of anthropoid apes. He maintains that the lack of this invaluable technical aid and the great limitation of those very important components of thought, the so-called images, constitute the causes which prevent animals from ever approaching even the least beginnings of

[25] An early attempt [says Cassirer] to make a sharp distinction between propositional and emotional language was made in the field of the psychopathology of language. The English neurologist Jackson introduced the term propositional language in order to account for some very interesting pathological phenomena. He found that many patients suffering from aphasia had by no means lost the use of speech but that they could not employ their words in an objective, propositional sense. Jackson's distinction proved to be very fruitful. . . . (For details see Cassirer, 1923, III, pp. 237-323).

cultural development. . . . If we proceed from a clear and precise definition of speech, all the other forms of utterances, which we also find in animals, are automatically eliminated (pp. 29–30).

X. Symbolism—and Language—a Matter of "Abstraction"

Here, apparently, is an analysis which permits us to bring all our other observations into orderly relationship. Stewart (1946) was right in insisting that the discovery of *nouns* marked the advent of real language; for they and they alone make sentences (propositions) possible. The sentence, we find, can be understood psychologically only if the concept of *mediation* is employed. And as the next chapter will show, *imagery* as well as emotion is an important aspect of *meaning*. But there is still a mystery. As we have repeatedly seen, mediation is by no means absent in infrahuman organisms and cannot, therefore, account for the fact that full-fledged language is found only in human beings. We now have reason for supposing that animals experience a wide range of emotions, and there is no compelling reason for supposing that they do not also have at least some imagery (Chapter 5). So perhaps the issue comes down to the matter of "nouns"; but then we recall the hypothetical experiment described in section VII of this chapter, wherein a blinking light is made to "stand for" cheese and to function, in all essentials, as a noun. It is true that this experiment has not been fully carried out; but there are no *a priori* grounds for thinking it would not work. And if it did work, would we not have eliminated the last remaining logical reason why animals cannot "talk"? [26] Not quite, for we must remember that such a "sentence" would be expected to function only if the subject were *hungry* and actively *wanted* cheese. Then and only then, so far as we can gather, would the blinking light *mean* anything to a rat, rouse his "interest," and elicit a response that could mediate the "message" provided by the buzzer "predicate." When animals have no immediate, "practical" need for an object, they likewise have no interest in a *sign* thereof—and thus fall short of exhibiting symbolic behavior.[27] They are, in other

[26] Brown (1958b, viii) quotes "a distinguished learning theorist" as saying that, for him, the remarkable thing is not that human beings can talk but that animals *cannot* (see also Brown, p. 156 ff.). Small children take it for granted that animals can talk and often show far less astonishment than do adults upon hearing a "talking bird." The child's expectation is by no means an unnatural or naive one.

[27] A possible misapprehension should be anticipated at this point. As demonstrated elsewhere (Mowrer, 1960, Chapter 5), animals do not have to be hungry, i.e., motivated by a primary drive, in order to be interested in food; if they merely

words, like the aphasic human subjects of Jackson (see footnote 25) who have lost their "propositional sense," i.e., the ability to use (and perhaps even understand) words in their abstract, referential, purely "informational" sense. What the aphasic human being has *lost*, neurologically, infrahuman organisms apparently have *never possessed*. They lack, in other words, not only the "symbolic attitude" but also the very *capacity* for such an attitude; and since even the most intensive efforts (e.g., those of Dr. and Mrs. Hayes) to provide the requisite *social* conditions and encouragements for the development of this capacity have been unavailing, we may legitimately conclude that the defect is *neurological*.

Skinner (1957) insists that the difficulty is, quite simply, that no creature other than man has gained voluntary control of his vocal cords and for this reason has never developed language.[28] This hypothesis has two serious weaknesses: (1) In the passage quoted from Cassirer, reference is made to Koehler's pertinent observation that if lack of voluntary control of the vocal apparatus were the only barrier to language in chimpanzees (or other animals), they would resort (as human beings do when there is vocal incapacity) to *gestures* made by

---

have *hunger fear*, they may still seek and "hoard" it. Therefore, in saying that an animal is not "interested" in an object unless he has a "practical" need for it, we are not excluding the possibility that this need may be derived (secondary), rather than primary, as these terms are now used in psychological parlance. In saying that an animal has no *practical* interest in food, we mean that the animal, at the moment, has neither hunger *nor* fear of hunger.

[28] Coverage of the relevant literature may seem to have been in some ways eccentric in this chapter. For example, only passing attention has been given to the just-cited major work of Skinner. This is because (1) Skinner is not interested in mediation and predication, which are our central concerns, and (2) his whole approach is so primitively Behavioristic that there is little conceptual contact between it and our own, although many of the experiments performed by Skinner and his followers are extraordinarily useful. (For reviews of Skinner's book on language, see Osgood, 1958; Morris, 1958; and Chomsky, 1959.) Osgood and his students have done yeoman service in developing objective methods for studying the phenomenon of meaning (cf. Chapter 5); and there is obviously much in common between his approach and the present one. Osgood has not, however, as yet written a systematic, general treatment of language, so it remains to be seen just what his ultimate position here will be. (For reviews of *The Measurement of Meaning*, by Osgood, Suci, & Tannenbaum, 1957, see Brown, 1958a; Gulliksen, 1958; and Weinreich, 1958.) Carroll (1953), Johnson (1946, 1956), G. A. Miller (1951), Piaget (1952), Whorf (1956), and Zipf (1949) have also written perceptively in this field but from specialized standpoints, such as Information Theory or General Semantics, which limit the relevance of their works for the present discussion. For a review of recent books by Johnson and Whorf, see Mowrer (1957).

parts of the body which are unmistakably under voluntary control; and (2), this explanation would not, in any event, apply to many species of birds, in which vocalization is quite as versatile and voluntary as is any other form of behavior. The far more basic and general explanation of the failure of animals to develop language lies, it seems, in the fact that when a sign is of no immediate ("practical") interest to them, they simply cannot be induced either to attend to it or to make it. For this reason they have no "nouns" (in the sense of signs with a purely abstract, referential function); and having no nouns, they have no sentences; and lacking sentences, they do not have language.

The term, *abstract*, is interesting in this connection. It comes from two Latin words meaning separated, apart from, or, more literally, *to draw away*. In the above analysis, it is suggested that animals cannot "abstract" in the sense of making or reacting to a sign when they have no interest in the significate. In other words, they cannot separate or detach the sign and employ it for reasons which are motivationally unrelated to the object or event which the sign represents. Thus, we may say, a *symbol* is an *abstracted* sign. And here, perhaps, lies one of the reasons why its precise identification and definition has been so difficult: a symbol is not distinguishable from an ordinary sign in terms of its *form;* it is only when the *motivation* behind its usage is taken into account that the difference clearly emerges. When a thirsty child cries, "Water, water!" he is using a sign, in much the same way that lower animals do; but, when not thirsty himself but instead questioned by a playmate, he says, "Water is in the pitcher," he is using a symbol. Here the child's motivation is quite unrelated to personal thirst. This is not to say that in using words symbolically human beings are *un*motivated; they are rather behaving in response to motives which are separated, abstracted from the referents themselves. Therefore, the absence of symbolism in animals may be due, in part at least, to deliminations in their motivational systems, perhaps along lines suggested in the passage quoted from G. H. Mead.

Elsewhere (Mowrer, 1954) much the same notion has been phrased as follows: Before man could develop language he not only had to get the "noun-idea" (Stewart, 1946), he also

had to have achieved enough social organization to make "helping others," through speech, a rewarding activity. The notion that language is used to "help others" calls attention to two quite different conceptions of its function. One common view of language is that it is used primarily as a means of helping oneself; this view is discussed [in Section I]. Here language is seen as serving mainly to coerce or cajole someone else into doing something useful for the speaker (or writer). By contrast, there is the view that language is the medium by which "gifts" are bestowed upon others; we are said to "give them information," which *they* will find useful. In fact, perhaps the best definition of "education" is that it is a means whereby one person (usually through language) helps another solve some problem more quickly than he himself could do on an unaided (trial-and-error) basis. Ontogenetically, the "selfish" use of language comes first and the "altruistic" use later [cf. Chapter 3, and especially the autism theory of word learning]; and perhaps this was also true historically. But in any event we can say that both uses of language presuppose considerable social co-operation (p. 675).

This is not to say, of course, that the altruistic, "unselfish" use of speech is not motivated and reinforced, but simply that speech, at this level, is disconnected (abstracted) from the motivations to which it most directly pertains and occurs because of more remote, more "refined" drives and interests. A high degree of social co-operativeness, or helpfulness, is achieved in the "language" of bees, as already noted; but this may reflect more of an instinctive arrangement than conscious motivation and satisfaction. In any case, the bees lack true nouns and are thereby barred from a truly abstract (freely propositional) language.

In other words, it appears that *two* conditions, both of which are presumably found only in human beings, must obtain before *bona fide* language is possible: (1) certain *neurological* developments which make it possible for an individual to utter a word pertaining to one motive or interest system under the impact or pressure of a *different* motive or desire; and (2) a degree of *social* development which will provide and activate the latter type of motivation. A subtle interplay of neurological and social evolution thus seems to have provided the (extremely unlikely) conditions for the development of the "symbolic attitude" and fully articulate ("free") speech. Language is thus truly a miracle, not only in terms of what it can do, but also in terms of the improbability of its emergence.

In this analysis, we are not, of course, saying anything which has not been said before in more general terms; and we still leave unanswered the question of precisely what it is, neurologically, that makes fully symbolic activity possible. But perhaps we have here focused the problem a little more sharply, in a way that will generate new researches and will help us to penetrate further into this fascinating field of inquiry.

5

Imagery, Memory, and Attention (Observing Reactions)

For psychologists whose graduate training dates back to the 1920's or 1930's, the terms which constitute the title of this chapter were then and perhaps are still, in some measure, *taboo*. Many of us were taught, under pain of banishment from professional psychology, never to use these terms, at least not during "working hours." In our discourse with laymen it was permissible, indeed essential, to use them (or their equivalents); but such language was deemed completely unsuited to the purposes of science.

The situation is, of course, changing, as the preceding chapters of this book attest. But it is slightly ironical that those very methods of analysis and research which radical Behaviorism introduced are now leading us, ineluctably, back to concepts which Behaviorism was determined to ignore—or even destroy.

In the two preceding chapters we have seen that our earlier analysis of the psychology of learning (Mowrer, 1960) has laid a useful foundation for an improved understanding of language. With the concepts and principles now available, we have a better grasp than formerly of how children learn to utter words and perhaps also of how, in the history of mankind, words originated and evolved. And we have, within the same theoretical framework, a new and seemingly quite powerful basis for explaining the operation of those word constellations which we call sentences. However, in one important respect our discussion of language has been inadequate—or, more precisely, our discussion has revealed an inadequacy and incompleteness in the psychological underpinning of language. This crucial defect has to do with the phenomenon of *meaning*, which will be the first topic of special concern in this chapter. This will lead naturally to consideration of the other concepts comprising the title of this chapter.

I. The Problem of Meaning, Imagery, and Reinforcement

In a graduate seminar, a bright—and slightly impish—female student once asked this disconcerting question. She wanted to know, she said, just what *is* this "mediating reaction" which we had been stressing as so essential in explaining the operation of sentences. As in the preceding chapter, we had been speaking, light-heartedly, of *meanings;* but the only definition we had given of them was an operational one: When a word is associated with a thing (in the nominative or naming relationship), it acquires the capacity, alone, to arouse *some part* of the total reaction produced by the thing itself. This conditionable component of the total reaction to the thing is, by assumption, the word's meaning.

But elsewhere (Mowrer, 1960) we have rejected the notion of the conditionability of overt, behavioral responses and have concentrated instead upon the *emotions*—and, more particularly, upon hope and fear. Therefore, what the student was asking, really, was whether these two emotions could be reasonably supposed to perform all the functions we were attributing to the so-called mediators. The answer, manifestly, is that they *cannot*. And we have already suggested (Chapter 4) the direction in which one may look for a more complete type of explanation. As Osgood & Suci (1955) and Spitz (1958) have shown, a considerable portion of the meaning of many words is indeed evaluative (good-bad, emotional); but this leaves a sizable remnant of the meaning "variance" (as measured by the "semantic differential") unaccounted for (see also Noble, 1958). Here, presumably, lies the specifically denotative or "cognitive" aspect of meaning. Thus, the word "apple" not only carries the implication of something liked or disliked but also of an object with certain purely *sensory* qualities. And, thus far, our account of learning contains no provision for explaining *this*, as opposed to the purely emotional, evaluative aspect of the meaning reaction.

There is, one quickly discovers, excellent precedent for distinguishing between the *evaluative* and the *cognitive* aspects of meaning. Cassirer (1944), in a passage already quoted in Chapter 4, says:

The first and most fundamental stratum [of speech] is evidently the language of the emotions. A great portion of all human utterance still belongs to this stratum. But there is a form of speech that shows us quite a different type. Here the word is by no means a mere interjection; it is not an involuntary expression of feeling, but a part of a sentence which has a definite syntactical and logical structure (p. 29).

Bertrand Russell, in *Human Knowledge: Its Scope and Limits* (1948), draws the distinction thus:

Music may be considered as a form of language in which emotion is divorced from information, while the telephone book gives information without emotion. But in ordinary speech both elements are usually present (p. 59).

Or, consider a formulation by Carroll (1953):

In our discussion of the implications of a theory of language and meaning for education in the advanced language skills, we have already alluded to another direction in which Ogden and Richards's work has had an influence. This is the use of semantics in interpretation, which in this context may be defined as the analysis of the total content and effect of any verbal communication into elements relating to its "plain sense," its "feeling," its "tone," and its "intention." In this way, both the symbolic and the emotive contents with which a message is charged are to be taken account of (p. 163).

And the contrast is made particularly clear in a recent book by Boulding (1956):

The subjective knowledge structure or image of any individual or organization consists not only of images of "fact" but also images of "value." . . . If I say "Stanford University is in California," this is rather different from the statement "Stanford University is a good university, or is a better university than X, or a worse university than Y." The latter statements concern my image of values, and although I shall argue that the process by which we obtain an image of values is not very different from the process whereby we obtain an image of fact, there is clearly a certain difference between them (p. 11).

The emotions of fear and hope are obviously examples of what Boulding is referring to as "images of values," i.e., fear is an "image" or anticipation of something bad, punishing, whereas hope is an "image" of a good, rewarding experience. But what is a *factual* "image"? The answer, it seems, is precisely that phenomenon which has been historically known, quite simply, as *an image*. Behaviorism banished not only the concept of imagery but also that of emotion. The latter, by the route already traced in this book (and the preceding one), has been re-admitted into psychological science; and it appears that a similar fate may now be in store for the former as well. So the issue is: How can the phenomenon of imagery be conceptualized, if at all, within the general framework of two-factor learning theory?

Many years ago, the following incident occurred in connection with an experiment which the writer was conducting for quite a different purpose (Mowrer, 1938a). Human subjects were being given an electric shock (through wrist electrodes) which started at zero and gradually increased in intensity. Subjects were instructed to press a key as soon as the shock became perceptible, at which point the shock reset to zero and the cycle started again. On this particular occasion, the programming apparatus broke down while a subject was being run; but since he was located in an adjacent sound-proofed room, he did not know of this. The experimenter, while re-adjusting the stalled apparatus, was surprised to find that the subject was still periodically pressing the key, although obviously (to the experimenter) receiving no shock. What, clearly, had happened was that the subject had developed a *temporally conditioned sensation of shock*, or a sort of periodic "hallucination." A survey of psychological literature (see, for example, Perky, 1910) showed that similar findings had been reported previously, usually under the rubric of "suggestion"; and not long thereafter Ellson (1941a, 1941b) reported the deliberate reproduction of this type of phenomenon.

Particularly relevant is a paper by Leuba, "Images as Conditioned Sensations," which appeared in the *Journal of Experimental Psychology* in 1940, and which concludes with these two sentences:

> Our experiments indicate that after an inadequate stimulus has been presented a number of times, while an individual is experiencing certain sensations, it will by itself automatically, and without the intervention of any conscious processes, produce those sensations. An image can, therefore, be considered as a conditioned sensation (p. 351).

Although cast in the vernacular of the modern conditioning laboratory, the notion that an image is a conditioned sensation (see also Cason, 1936) squares not only with common sense but also, as we shall presently see, with certain classical psychological notions. An image, in common parlance, is some object which an individual "sees" or otherwise "perceives" without the object being objectively present. By a word, another image, or some other stimulus, the individual is *reminded* of the object and reacts somewhat *as if* it were actually present. In other words, a *part* of the total experience produced by the object itself is here being aroused as a learned, conditioned response;

and this response we call an image—and the process of its arousal, *imagination*.[1]

As will be discovered in Boring's *History of Experimental Psychology* (1929), all this seems to have been well understood by the early English psychologist, David Hartley (1705–1757), as indicated by this sentence which Boring quotes:

Sensations, by being often repeated, leave certain Vestiges, Types, or Images, of themselves, which may be called, Simple Ideas of Sensations (p. 199).

Thus, without further ado, we shall postulate that images are indeed conditioned sensations and that, as such, they are an important part— the *cognitive* or *representational* part—of the meanings which words (and quite possibly certain other stimuli) characteristically come to possess. But if in this way we gain in realistic understanding of the genesis and nature of meaning, we also introduce a considerable complication for learning theory.

Since about 1930, a distinction has grown up between so-called *reinforcement* theory and *contiguity* theory in the field of learning. Although the term "reinforcement" was originally used by Pavlov to denote the learning that occurs when a conditioned stimulus immediately precedes an unconditioned stimulus, the term became gradually identified, at least in this country, with the special views and formulation of Clark L. Hull. For him, all learning was contingent upon drive reduction, or what he called "primitive reinforcement," of some kind; and sheer stimulus contiguity was not alone deemed a sufficient condition for learning. In two-factor theory, something of a reconciliation has already been achieved in this connection. Learning, in the sense of emotional conditioning, is here assumed to occur under two different conditions of "reinforcement," drive decrement and drive increment; so that stimulus contiguity and reinforcement (of one form or the other) are *both* seen as essential. But now, with the

---

[1] What is being assumed here is analogous to the fact that an electric shock produces pain *and* fear but that only the fear, generally speaking, is conditionable. Thus it is legitimate, it would seem, to speak of an image as the conditionable fraction of a sensation. One would not want a sensation, in its totality, to be conditionable; for this would lead to a full-scale hallucination. When, therefore, things work out right, we experience just enough of the original sensation to know what it is but *not* enough to make us think that we are actually having it again. In other words, we know it is "all in your head" instead of "out there." See Section XII; also Chapter 7, Section II.

admission of the concept of an image as a conditioned sensation, we seem to be dealing with a form of learning which presupposes only stimulus contiguity, "pure contiguity" as it is sometimes called, without the occurrence of either drive increment or decrement.

Because a so-called unconditioned stimulus often has either rewarding or punishing properties (at least in mild degree), it is not always a simple matter to demonstrate "pure contiguity" learning; but experiments on "sensory preconditioning" are sometimes cited in this connection (cf. Mowrer, 1960, pp. 281–282). For example, Bitterman, Reed, & Kubala (1953) begin an article on this subject as follows:

As Birch and Bitterman (1949) noted in a recent analysis of the nature of reinforcement, the phenomenon of sensory preconditioning poses a rather difficult problem of Hullian theory. Consider, for example, an experiment by Brogden (1939). Two stimuli, a tone and a light, are repeatedly paired in the first stage of training [with dogs as subjects], and in the second stage one of these stimuli, say the light, is paired with shock to the forelimb until it comes to elicit a flexion response. Finally, the tone is presented alone and the flexion response appears despite the fact that tone and flexion have never before occurred in temporal contiguity (p. 178).

From this type of observation it has sometimes been reasoned that the mere concurrence of two presumably neutral stimuli such as the bell and light produces associative learning, no less than does the pairing of one such stimulus and a more "meaningful" stimulus such as electric shock or food. Because, in the example cited, the tone proves capable of eliciting the flexion response, it is held that, in "sensory preconditioning," the tone came to "stand for" the light, so that as soon as the light, as a result of regular conditioning, came to stand for the shock, then tone also was premonitory of shock and so produced the flexion-reaction. Some investigators have dismissed such findings as artifacts, attributing them to sensitization or "pseudo-conditioning." Here it will not be necessary for us to enter into the merits of the argument, on either side (for a sophisticated new study, see W. J. Coppock, 1958); for there is an overriding consideration of a purely theoretical nature. The difficulty with the notion of pure contiguity, or S—S conditioning as it has sometimes been called, is that it "explains" all too much. We know, quite well, that mere conjunction of stimulation is by no means a guarantee of learning. Consider, for example, the case of Mr. Jones, who has, for years, paid bills, by mail, to certain places of business without, however, ever learning their addresses. Here, if learning were a matter of pure contiguity, he should learn the "connection" between each business concern and the address to which he monthly remits. But he does not learn, and if one asks Mr. Jones *why* he does not, he will say: "It's because I'm not interested. I don't *need* to remember the addresses—they're always *on* the bills. If I had a reason, a motive for learning, then, of course, I could and would."

Compare, for example, the man who drives an automobile to work each morning and has to park, as opportunity affords, in different places. Occasionally he may misremember where his car is at the end of the day; but, in general, he will do surprisingly well in keeping its location "in mind," a performance which, superficially, may look like perfect learning, in *one* trial. But the image, or memory, of where the car is located can be, and probably is, recalled or "rehearsed" from time to time during the course of the day. Here, clearly, the car owner (unlike Mr. Jones) has a lively incentive for remembering, and does so. But the basis on which this feat occurs is obviously *not* "sheer contiguity"—motivation also importantly enters into the picture.

Thus, in this commonplace example and many other instances that might be cited, mere conjunction of stimulation does *not* provide the sufficient conditions for learning; and one is left, in terms of a "sensory-sensory contiguity theory," with no guiding principle for deciding when contiguity will and when it will not result in learning. In ordinary conditioning, where the second stimulus is definitely rewarding or punishing, contiguity is a necessary condition for learning; but the indications are that it is not sufficient. If it were, then living organisms would form countless associations which would be perfectly useless and meaningless. Interest, meaning, motivation, significance, "reinforcement" must, apparently, be in some way involved, though this "dynamic" factor can apparently operate in very subtle and unaccountable ways.

More specifically, this argument means that we have no way as yet for determining when a sensation will or will not be "conditioned" and thus elicitable as an image; but the indications are that here, as elsewhere, mere contiguity is no guarantee of learning and that some element of reinforcement is a crucial, though as yet often obscure, determinant.[2]

---

[2] In his doctoral research at the University of Buffalo, Mr. Steven Finesmith (1959) has recently obtained laboratory support for the foregoing conjectures. His subjects were required to learn a series of nonsense syllables, presented as paired associates, at the same time that psychogalvanic readings were being taken. In the early stages of learning, presentation of the first of a pair of syllables would produce a slight PGR, which reached a peak on the trial on which the

II. Imagery, Memory, and Knowledge

In 1956 the present writer published, in one of the technical journals, a preliminary version of the argument which is summarized in Chapter 1 of this book but, in advance, invited Dr. K. S. Lashley to comment thereon. The latter's reply reads, in part, as follows:

> I agree with your basic idea but think it a mistake to call it a theory of learning; it is a theory of motivation of action but seems to me irrelevant to the formation and retention of associations. I was recently served a very bad meal at a restaurant. I shall not go there again but I remember in detail the arrangement of the dining room, the appearance of the waitress, the flavor of the bad coffee, even the decorations on the dinner ware.
>
> Motivational theories were developed from studies of animals, in which it is very difficult to demonstrate memory without motivating action. But even with rats one can observe bits of behavior which suggests that in the course of training the animal learns many things unrelated to the motivation of the experiment. Like me, the animal learns his motives but learns a great deal besides. I feel sure that the learning problem would be much clarified, if this distinction were emphasized. The key to learning is in the phenomena which Thorndike called "Belongingness," but I don't seem able to make any progress here.[3]

Here Dr. Lashley put his finger on a major weakness toward the elimination of which efforts are being made in this chapter. In the preceding section we have posited a mechanism whereby sensations may become converted into images; and once the reality of images is established, so also is the phenomenon of *memory*. Once we have recognized the possibility that sensations can be conditioned to words or other psychological events that can serve to "recall" them, then the basis is laid both for memory, as it applies to things past, and for imagination, as it applies to things to come. (And "forgetting" might be accounted for in terms of reconditioning or counterconditionings, along lines suggested in Chapter 11 of *Learning Theory and Behavior*.) Here, presumably, we have a basis for the phenomenon which Lashley (with others) has referred to as the "formation of associations," but

---

associated syllable was first recalled and then, on ensuing trials, declined. Although the "content" of nonsense syllables is inherently about as unemotional as anything can be, yet emotion seems to accompany the actual learning process. Precisely how it operates is still a mystery, but Finesmith's results substantiate the view that even the most "cognitive" types of learning probably involve motivation and reinforcement.

[3] Lewin, in 1942, made a very similar plea for the recognition of two kinds of learning: the learning of motivations *and* the learning of cognitions.

the underlying mechanism proposed is the familiar one of conditioning, not the gestalt-like concept of Belongingness advanced, but never very effectively developed, by Thorndike. As indicated earlier (Mowrer, 1960, Chapter 8), Tolman has, of course, long stressed the reality and importance of "pure cognition" in animal learning, which Guthrie has cogently criticized on the grounds that while it may lead to all manner of wisdom in a rat, it never *gets* him anywhere. Having posited cognition, we must also get motivation into the picture. Our procedure in the present work has followed this course: we have started with the motivational aspect of learning and have found that it will carry us far but that eventually the cognitive or mnemonic aspect must also be considered. The concept of the image as a conditioned sensation seems to provide a solid linkage between these two domains. E. B. Holt (1931) once remarked that the phenomenon of conditioning "brought mind into existence." If, as now seems likely, conditioning can be made to account for both motivation and cognition, it goes a long way in this connection. Although Pavlov's (and Watson's) attempt to make the conditioned reflex the unit from which all behavior is constructed was a failure, the concept of conditioning nevertheless provides us with the basis for understanding both motivation and cognition and thus arriving at a more adequate and more sophisticated picture of behavior than Behaviorism itself was able to provide.[4]

It is not without significance that the economist, Kenneth Boulding, after spending a sabbatical year recently at the Ford Center for Ad-

---

[4] The notion that an image is a conditioned sensation suggests a somewhat altered way of thinking about the conditioning process in general. It is conventional to assume that the response in question is initially produced by a so-called unconditioned stimulus, UnCS, and that, by virtue of its temporal conjunction with the UnCS, the conditioned stimulus or CS in some way acquires the capacity to produce the response, R, *directly*. It is, however, entirely conceivable that conditioning operates in a different way: namely, that the CS acquires the capacity to produce R, not directly, but by virtue of first producing an *image* of the UnCS to which R is already "connected" (just as it is to the UnCS itself). Thus, the apparent conditioning of R to CS would be achieved, not directly, but through the *mediating* action of the conditioned image of the UnCS. Instead of emotional and imaginal conditioning being parallel phenomena, the former, according to this view, would be derivable from the latter; and all conditioning (learning), in the final analysis would be "cognitive." The writer is indebted to Mr. In-Mao Liu for the suggestion that this conception of learning may be close to that implied by Hebb (1949). This idea (see also Eriksen, 1958, p. 206 ff.) generates some very definite expectations concerning the neuro-physiology of conditioning; it will be explored more fully in Chapter 7, especially Section IX (cf. Mowrer, 1960, p. 260; Schönback, 1958).

vanced Study in the Behavioral Sciences, at Stanford University, decided to summarize his year's work there in the small book (already cited) called *The Image*, the historical background of which he gives as follows:

Psychology started out with an image of the mind as a sort of jigsaw puzzle of ideas. The science took a firmly antieiconical turn, however, with the development of behaviorism. It is a little difficult to believe that Dr. Watson actually believed what he is supposed to have believed, namely, that Dr. Watson was an epiphenomenon. It is, however, in the record that this is what psychologists used to believe. The attempt to interpret the organism as a stimulus-response slot machine was terribly good for the rat business, but it certainly was not eiconics. With the coming of the Gestalt school, however, psychology began to take a sharply eiconical direction. Psychologists began to conceive the organism not merely as a jigsaw puzzle or as a slot machine but as an organization (p. 151).

As a result of his year of special study. Dr. Boulding thus concluded that the "behaviorial sciences" have moved on beyond Behaviorism and are ready to take a broader view of psychology and life. It is not possible or necessary here to review his argument in detail, but the following excerpt gives some of the high lights of Boulding's thinking.

What I have been talking about is knowledge. Knowledge, perhaps, is not a good word for this. Perhaps one would rather say my *Image* of the world. Knowledge has an implication of validity, of truth. What I am talking about is what I believe to be true; my subjective knowledge. It is this Image that largely governs my behavior. . . . *The first proposition of this work, therefore, is that behavior depends on the image* (pp. 5–6).

Here, certainly, is a point of view which is radically different from Behaviorism but one which squares well with the approach followed in this book (see also McClelland, 1955). Although, prior to this chapter, we have not specifically used the term, image, it has been in several ways implied. For example, in Chapter 8 of *Learning Theory and Behavior*, in discussing the procedure of teaching a dog to "shake hands," it might have been said that what we thus do, when we move the dog's leg passively (and then provide a reward), is to give the dog an *image* of the particular response *we* wish him to make and which he also, as a result of our training, later wishes to make. In Chapter 12, under the rubric of skill, we spoke of the accomplished musician or athlete having a clear picture, or "image," of what he (and others) regard as a good performance. And in Chapter 3 of the present volume the same logic was applied to the process whereby human infants learn to utter conventional word noises, and other organisms come to "imitate" in other ways. Hence, the notion that "behavior depends on the image" is by no means foreign to us, and our detailed analysis of the learning process provides a rather more explicit explanation of the genesis of images than does Boulding's discussion. "The image," he says, "is built up as a result of all past experience of the possessor of the image" (p. 6); and he specifically attributes its origin to the "stream of messages entering the organism from the senses" (p. 6); but his analysis in this connection is otherwise somewhat indefinite. The experimental facts cited in the preceding section, it would seem, give substance and specificity to Boulding's views. Along with other writers cited in that section, Boulding, in stressing the imaginal or cognitive aspect of learning and experience, also acknowledges evaluation and motivation; and, using gestalt-like, organizational concepts, he tries to show throughout his book how the two relate and interact. This is also a challenge to the more segmental, neobehavioristic approach being followed in the present study; and the next section will be devoted to a sort of "case study" of this problem and its proposed solution. But what has already been said will indicate that our approach is one which, while firmly based upon principles which are empirically demonstrable with rats, also meaningfully articulates with those more intricate and more readily demonstrated operations in men which go under the name of knowledge, memory, imagination, and the like.[5]

However, over against this growing recognition of the legitimacy of the concept of imagery in systematic behavior theory (see also Miller, 1959, and Woodworth, 1958) is Brown's (1958b) repudiation thereof. As indicated in Chapter 4, Brown quite rightly holds that emotions alone cannot provide an adequate basis for word meanings; and we can equally well agree that Watson's theory that "meanings are implicit [speech] responses originally elicited by referents and then, through association, by words" (p. 97) is also untenable. Having long since rejected the notion that overt behavioral responses are directly conditionable, we would be on weak ground to accept a covert version thereof. But Brown goes further than this and maintains that the situation is not improved by the introduction of imagery as a vehicle of meaning. He says:

[5] For an excitingly similar approach to these and related problems, see *Plans and the Structure of Behavior*, by Miller, Galanter, & Pribram (1960). Working in complete formal independence, these writers have produced a book with almost uncanny resemblance, in certain important ways, to the present one. Although there is now no opportunity to make more than this brief allusion to it here, the reader will profit greatly if he uses the Miller-Galanter-Pribram book for collateral reading in connection with this and the two following chapters, particularly.

A man who has heard dogs named becomes able to identify dogs for himself and to distinguish them from other kinds of things. It is natural to suppose that this performance is possible because the man has formed a mental image of the dog which he can match against any animals presented to his vision. The next step is to suggest that the meaning of the word *dog* is the same mental image; the click of comprehension is the image that the word evokes. However, there is a second change of behavior to be seen in the man who has heard dogs named. He begins to respond to the word as he formerly responded to the referent, to treat the word as a sign of the thing. If, for example, he has always run away from the animal he may now run when someone simply shouts out the word. Ordinarily when we understand words in reading or in listening to speech we do not make any obvious response like running away but perhaps we do make some internal sign reaction, perhaps the click of comprehension is some subtle response of a muscle or gland. It will be argued in this chapter that neither of these notions of meaning is acceptable. If there is an immediate effect that constitutes understanding of a meaningful form that effect must be neurophysiological. There is nothing in consciousness or in behavior that is set off whenever the comprehended form occurs. Psychological semantics must operate for the present with regard to the two kinds of overt action that are produced by reference and leave the "click" to neurology (p. 83).

Brown then gives a detailed account of the whole theory of imagery, particularly as developed by Titchener (1909a) and his students, and advances various criticisms of which many are patently trivial. For example, he ridicules, quite justifiably, Titchener's reported image of the word, "but." "Titchener's image of 'but' was of the back of the head of a speaker who often used this word while Titchener sat behind him on a platform." And when Brown says that such ("accidental") images are "unacceptable as the meanings of words," we can only agree. But the point is, "but" is not a noun and not a symbol in the fullest sense of the word. It could never be the subject of a sentence (except if, as in metalinguistics, we were referring to the *word*, "but") and therefore does not *need* to have a meaning in the referential sense. It is, rather, a sort of verbal *signal* which does not *represent* anything but instead says to the hearer (or reader): "Hold on a moment, a qualification is needed. More is to come."

Brown also goes wide of the mark in tacitly assuming that images must necessarily be *visual*. Theoretically they can occur in *any* sense modality, and taste and odor imagery seem especially common. Only a few days ago the writer and a colleague were discussing this problem, and the latter remarked that, as a result of having been given castor oil in orange juice as a little girl, his wife can still sometimes "taste" it when she drinks pure orange juice. And many similar examples could be cited. Thus, the fact that a particular word does not call up a visual image does not prove that no imagery whatever is involved.

But Brown is hardly a disinterested observer as far as images are concerned. As indicated in section VIII of the preceding chapter, he favors a "dispositional" theory of meaning which makes meaning contingent upon word constellations rather than upon a special reaction of some sort to a specific word. However, our whole approach to language is different, and we find the concept of imagery highly useful rather than superfluous. It is fortunate that someone with Brown's interests and skills has explored the approach which he advocates; but his rejection of imagery is not such, on either empirical or logical grounds, as to lessen substantially its usefulness and validity for our purposes. A specific, nonlinguistic example of its relevance in contemporary behavior theory will be given in the following section.

III. The Image and Weinstock's Interpretation of Partial Reinforcement

As already indicated (Mowrer, 1960, Chapter 12), the fact that intermittent, or "partial," reinforcement during acquisition produces a habit with heightened resistance to extinction has stimulated and challenged contemporary concepts of learning in a variety of ways. At face value, this phenomenon seems to impugn the whole notion of reinforcement and to demand the introduction of cognitive principles. In Chapter 12 it has been shown that the so-called "discrimination hypothesis" seemed to be the most adequate explanation of this effect advanced to date; but at that stage of development of our analysis certain issues remained unresolved which may now be handled more adequately, so we return to this problem with special reference to a study reported in 1954 by Weinstock. As also noted in Chapter 12, this investigator has shown conclusively that the partial-reinforcement effect is not contingent upon the massing of acquisition trials (as the theories of Hull, 1943, and Virginia Sheffield, 1949, would seem to require). In fact, Weinstock found that successive trials may be separated by as much as 24 hours and still show this effect, as indicated in Fig. 5–1 (see also Wilson, Weiss & Amsel, 1955). Weinstock's own interpretation of these findings runs as follows:

The author [assumes] that the competing responses which the animal makes in the goal box [at the end of a straight alley] on a nonreinforced trial habituate during the course of a series of nonreinforced [acquisition] trials. Thus, partially reinforced animals, which have had some number of nonreinforced trials during acquisition, will have their competing responses to an empty goal box habituated to some relatively low level. The competing responses, having habituated, will occur with a low frequency, and there will be little decrement in the strength of the original response due to the presentation of a nonreinforced trial.

The decrease in frequency of competing responses seems to be visible in the behavior of the partially reinforced animals. On early nonreinforced trials they go to the food place, find no food, and run about the goal box. On later nonreinforced trials the running-about behavior has dropped out and the animals remain in the vicinity of the food place (p. 321).

Although couched in a somewhat overly "objective" terminology, this statement contains the nub of a potent idea. In Chapter 11 of *Learning Theory and Behavior*, the suggestion has already been advanced that extinction is really a form of counterconditioning, in which hope (habit strength) is counteracted by the frustration which results from the nonfulfillment of the subject's expectations. Recast, then, in these more subjective terms, what the Weinstock hypothesis means is that in intermittent reinforcement, the subject's tendency to be disappointed or frustrated when reaching the goal box and finding it empty (i.e., when primary reward is completely eliminated) has itself been largely "extinguished" during acquisition, and the reaction of

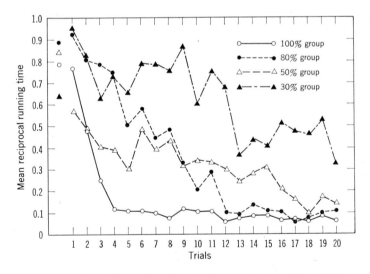

Fig. 5–1. "Mean reciprocal running time during extinction. The initial, unconnected points are the means of the last block of five acquisition trials" (Weinstock, 1954, p. 320.)

frustration which normally counterconditions hope has likewise been extinguished so that hope continues relatively unabated (cf. Zimmerman, 1959, for a related interpretation). It is, in fact, almost axiomatic that if, in the face of continued failure, an organism can be kept from becoming frustrated and hopeless, it will remain hopeful and "habitful." This apparently, then, is what intermittent primary reinforcement during the acquisition of a habit does: it habituates out the frustration reaction before "extinction proper" starts and so eliminates the factor which, in extinction following continuous reinforcement, rapidly counterconditions the hope reaction (see Chapter 8, Sections VII and VIII).

But this explanation, intuitively appealing as it is, glosses over a crucial question: namely, if extinction is a matter of counterconditioning, what is it that is responsible for the extinction of the frustration reaction during intermittent reinforcement? It must, per hypothesis, be the reaction of hope; and yet, in the Weinstock experiment, successive trials are so far apart that it is unthinkable that the frustration experienced as a result of finding an empty goal box on one trial could be in any way influenced by the experience of finding food therein on the next trial, 24 hours later. Hull (1943) and Virginia Sheffield (1949), in studies cited by Weinstock, had in fact hypothesized that partial reinforcement might owe its special effectiveness to a persistence of a stimulus trace from one (nonrewarded) trial to the next (rewarded) one. But a stimulus trace 24 hours long is out of the question; and Weinstock is quite right in holding that his data invalidate any such hypothesis. However, by introducing the concept of imagery (not to be confused with r_g or r_s), a new hypothesis emerges with none of the difficulties just cited.

One may reasonably suppose that after a rat has run down an alleyway a few times and received food in the goal box, it will begin to have an image of goal-box-with-food as it later negotiates the runway. But now the rat, for the first time, makes a run and finds *no food*. Lively frustration will presumably ensue. On the next trial, as the rat runs down the alley it *remembers* (images) the empty-box experience from the preceding trial and, immediately, enters the goal box and *finds food*. Thus image-of-empty-goal-box is closely associated with reward; and when, on a later trial, the goal box is again found to be empty, there will be a *generalization of the hope reaction from the image to the real thing*. The result? The subject will react to the empty goal box much as if its last experience therein had been shortly followed by a trial in which food was found! In other words, by positing the imagery mechanism previously described in this chapter, one can account for the effects of partial reinforcement where acquisition trials are widely distributed in time, no less well than when they are temporally massed.[6]

But do we not have an embarrassment of riches, as far as possible explanations of this phenomenon are concerned? In Chapter 12 of *Learning Theory and Behavior* considerable evidence has been advanced in support of what is there called the Discrimination Hypothesis; and now we have derived a seemingly quite different type of explanation. But are they really so different? Where reinforcement during acquisition of a habit has been contiguous, the only image the subject has of the consequences thereof is one of reward; and once extinction has started, that image is suddenly and consistently controverted by the fact of nonreward. Discrimination is precise, and counterconditioning of the hope built up during acquisition is maximal. On the other hand, where reinforcement during acquisition has been intermittent, the subject's image of what will follow a particular action is highly ambiguous: acquisition and extinction are hard to discriminate; and, as we have seen, the frustration response to the experience of nonreward has been associated with subsequent reward and therefore rendered ineffectual as a source of counterconditioning of the habit's original strength.

Thus it would appear that we are here describing one and the same process in two different vocabularies. And the use of the concept of image as a conditioned sensation has been crucial in enabling us to make this integration.

IV. Reflex Arc or Image?

In 1896 John Dewey wrote an article, "The Reflex Arc Concept in Psychology," which was strangely prophetic. In Chapter 1 of *Learning Theory and Behavior* we have already quoted from this paper to the effect that, in its writer's opinion, the reflex-arc idea then held promise of becoming the model on which psychology would be re-

[6] If it seems that we are going too far in attributing imagery to animals, see Chapter 11 of *Ape in Our House*, entitled "The Very Strange Case of the Imagery Pulltoy" (Hayes, 1951); also Freides (1957), Kendler, Pliskoff, D'Amoto, & Katz (1957); and Petrinovitch & Bolles (1957). The latter, for example, say: "Traditional S—R mechanisms do not appear capable of explaining this behavior. Therefore, it seems reasonable to assume that some sort of symbolic process underlies it. We suggest that rats can remember where they went last, and that this memory serves as the cue for the correct response" (p. 365).

systematized. That promise was fulfilled in the movement which was to be known as Behaviorism. But, most remarkable of all, the author went on to point out certain crucial ways in which the reflex arc is conceptually incomplete and inadequate, ways which only today, more than sixty years later, are being seen and fully appreciated.

Conditioning, as conceived by Pavlov, was frankly a form of reflexology and, implicitly at least, so also was Thorndike's connectionism. Step by step, in earlier chapters, we have traced out the weaknesses of these two conceptual schemes, as originally formulated, and have concluded that what Thorndike thought of as a "connection," or "habit," probably involves (a) the conditioning of certain emotions to certain patterns of stimulation and (b) something we can hardly avoid calling volition or choice (see Chapter 6). Here the notion of continuous feedback from action is crucially important; and we come to see that not only does stimulation cause response (through the mediation of consciousness) but also that response causes, and is inherently associated with, stimulation. It is true that the reflexologists made a good deal of "reflex chaining," as they called any sequence of actions wherein one response produced stimuli that cued off the succeeding response. But this is something quite different from the notion that an action, *while in progress,* is under the control of its own stimulus consequences. This Dewey saw with prescient clarity.

Dewey's paper is closely reasoned and not easily paraphrased or summarized. Perhaps his argument is most concisely stated, in his own words, thus:

The distinction of sensation and movement as stimulus and response respectively is not a distinction which can be regarded as descriptive of anything which holds of psychical events or existences as such. The only events to which the terms stimulus and response can be descriptively applied are to minor acts serving by their respective positions to the maintenance of some organized coordination. The conscious stimulus or sensation, and the conscious response or motion, have a special genesis or motivation, and a special end or function. The reflex arc theory, by neglecting, by abstracting from, this genesis and this function gives us one disjointed part of a process as if it were the whole. It gives us literally an arc, instead of a circuit; and not giving us the circuit of which it is an arc, does not enable us to place, to center, the arc. This arc, again, falls apart into two separate existences having to be either mechanically or externally adjusted to each other (p. 364).

How amazingly modern all this sounds! The older machines, of the nineteenth century, which were man-operated, did indeed involve "reflex arcs" with the "circuit" having to be completed by the operator. But in present-day automata, the circuit is completed *within the machine,* thus providing the capacity for *self-regulation* which, as Dewey knew full well, living organisms have long possessed. And how, precisely, is this achieved? In any final and complete sense, we do not know. But we have now firmly identified *three* important variables: primary motivation (comparable to the "driving force" of a machine); secondary drives and rewards which control and guide action as it occurs; and a *standard* or *"image"* of some sort which is being constantly compared with actual performance (cf. Chapter 7). As earlier chapters of this book indicate, a good deal is now known about the relationship between primary and secondary drive; but we are less clear as to how images fit into the picture. On this score Boulding has the following to say:

> In a sense, we may say that the concept of the "image" begins in a very rudimentary form at this [the physical and physiological] level. The thermostat has an image of the outside world in the shape of the information regarding its temperature. It has also a value system in the sense of the ideal temperature at which it is set. Its behavior is directed toward the receipt of information which will bring its image and its value system together. When its image of the outside world is "right," that is, conforms to its value system, it ceases to act. As long as the image, as confirmed by the messages received, does not conform to its value system it acts in order to bring the two together. Here, therefore, even below the biological level we see a concept something like that of the image in operation (p. 22).

While the foregoing may leave something to be desired in the way of explicitness, yet the conception toward which the author is pointing is clear enough: behavior is not just a matter of "blind power"—it also involves intelligence and knowledge. In the following section an attempt will be made to be more specific about this point of view.

V. All Behavior as Scanning or Sensory Search

It is manifestly true that some activities are more conspicuously "sensory" while others are more conspicuously "motor," but each has both its sensory and its motor aspects. When an organism moves its eyes (or head) about so as to survey its visual environment, it is said to be *looking;* and here the matter of seeing, or perceiving, is accented, although no one would deny that the subject is also moving, acting, behaving. Contrariwise, when a man moves his arm, he is said to be *doing* something; but his arm, too, carries sense organs which, by virtue of the arm's movement, are stimulated. When the sense organs are prominent and the manipulating muscles small, we use one vocabulary; and when the muscles are large and the sense organs small, we use another. But surely it is sufficiently evident that perceiving involves doing and that doing involves perceiving, sensing. One without the other is futile. Saying that an individual "doesn't *know* (perceive) what he is *doing*" is tantamount to charging him with idiocy or madness; and to perceive without being able to do is to be paralyzed.[7]

The view that all behavior is thus inherently sensory or perceptual is, in fact, virtually demanded by the conception of habit which has been developed earlier, wherein action is guided and directed, not by fixed sensory-motor pathways, but by hopes and fears that have become conditioned to response-correlated stimuli—or to what we may now think of as good and bad "images." But the applicability of this way of thinking to so-called perceptual activities did not suggest itself until the author chanced to read the opening sentences of an article by Fredericson (1950) entitled "Cognitive Maps and Reinforcement."

> Reference to a type of disruptive activity which occurs when a previously obtained goal object is no longer accessible has been made by Tolman (1938). He described the rat's behaviour under such conditions as a form of searching and exploration (p. 253).

This passage, particularly the last sentence, suggests that, if our basic assumptions in this book be true, *all* behavior is "a form of searching and exploration." This searching may be gross and obvious, as in so-called trial-and-error behavior; or it may be refined and delimited, as in a violinist trying to get just the right quality of tone and shading as he performs (plays) a strictly prescribed series of reactions (notes). But, in principle, both involve "searching and exploration." Stanley & Aamodt (1954) have recently reported a study (cf. Mowrer, 1960, Chapter 11) which provides experimental illustration of and support for this point of view. They state their problem thus:

> Two article (Applezweig, 1951; Maatsch, Adelman, & Denny, 1954) have recently criticized experiments designed to test the fatigue (Miller and Dollard, 1941; Mowrer and Jones, 1943) or reactive inhibition (Hull,

---

[7] It may at first appear that this fusion of perceiving and doing is invalidated by differences in the extent to which these activities are "informative" as opposed to "instrumental." Looking at or seeing something does not change that thing— it merely *informs* the looker; whereas, in *doing* something, we are likely to change the external world, not just ourselves. While there is here unquestionably a difference in degree, it is by no means categorical. In adjusting a sense organ, we inevitably "disturb" the environment in at least some minimal way; and when we set out to produce more striking effects of the latter kind, perception, as we have seen, is still involved. Thus the interplay between doing and perceiving seems to be continuous and inescapable.

1943) theories of extinction because these experiments failed to control "habit strength"—specifically, force requirement per response during conditioning. According to this criticism, two studies (Mowrer and Jones, 1943; Solomon, 1948) interpreted as supporting fatigue or inhibition theories of extinction may be regarded as demonstrating that requiring forceful responses during conditioning yields forceful responses during extinction. It is a further implication of this criticism that if a reinforcing stimulus is made contingent on weak responses, then weak responses should occur during extinction.

It was the purpose of the present experiment to determine the validity of both these hypotheses. Specifically, it was expected that force requirement during conditioning would be positively related to forcefulness of responding during extinction (p. 462).

In the experiment which Stanley & Aamodt carried out, it was indeed found that their subjects (laboratory rats) showed greater resistance to extinction with regard to a bar-pressing habit if, during extinction, it took the *same force* to operate the bar as had been required during the original (food-reinforced) training; if the force requirements were different during extinction, there was a reduction in the resistance to extinction. What these findings seem to mean is that during acquisition a specific pattern and intensity of kinesthetic stimulation had taken on secondary reinforcement properties. When, during extinction (absence of primary reinforcement), a response recreated this same pattern of stimulation, it produced more secondary reinforcement (hope) and was therefore more resistant to extinction than when a response resulted in a different pattern of kinesthetic stimulation. All of which suggests that the bar-pressing habit here consisted of a tendency to *search* for, and to be secondarily reinforced by, a particular type and intensity of stimulation or sensation.

A modification of the Stanley-Aamodt experiment would make the point even more clearly. Suppose, for example, that one group of rats were trained to press a bar for food which required 20 grams of effort and that the bar used with a second group required 100 grams of effort. Now, during extinction, the bar is no longer counterbalanced by a weight but by a *spring*. This would mean that the bar could be pushed with whatever amount of effort the subject desired to use. The experimental findings already cited, as well as common sense, would certainly lead us to expect that, in the extinction procedure, the subjects would *search out* that particular pattern of kinesthetic and tactile stimulation which, during training, had been reinforced and would avoid making responses that resulted in a different sensory pattern. This expectation derives from the principle (discussed in Chapters 7 and 11 of *Learning Theory and Behavior*) which holds that "habit strength" is a function of the extent to which a response continues to reproduce the same stimuli that were produced when the response previously occurred and received primary reinforcement.

In Chapter 6 we shall discuss the head-wobbling that a rat tends to engage in at the choice points in a maze or a discrimination apparatus. This has commonly been referred to as *vicarious*, or diminutive, trial-and-error behavior. Here the element of "searching and exploration" is obvious, as it is in other activities whose most patent function is the play of sensory organs, as is "looking around" or "listening." But now we also have empirical as well as logical justification for supposing that behavior generally functions in much the same way; it, too, is a form of searching, a searching for the particular stimuli which, on prior occasions, have been followed by basic satisfactions. Thus, an organism which has a "habit" or a "skill" is simply an organism that "knows what he's looking for." Otherwise, if he *doesn't* know, his behavior is random and aimless. What the skillful, informed, habitful organism does, in effect, is to seek those stimuli (response-correlated and independent) which, in Tolman's terms, are now "demanded" or, in other words, can provide secondary reward and will, in all likelihood, lead the organism to primary satisfaction. This way of thinking carries us considerably beyond the reflex-arc concept and behavioristic thinking generally and points to problems which will be further considered in the ensuing sections (see also Chapter 7).

VI. Perception, Performance, and Evolution

Repeatedly in this book we have found that contemporary writers, with the most divergent backgrounds and on the basis of seemingly quite independent data, are tending to converge upon a common point of view concerning learning and behavior theory. An interesting example of this confluence is found in an article by Campbell (1956a) on "Perception as Substitute Trial and Error." This writer's own summary of his argument runs as follows:

Selective survival among random variations is taken as a general paradigm for instances of organismic fit to environment. Darwinian theory of natural selection applies the model to the fit between the inherited characteristics of organisms and the opportunities provided by their habitats. Trial-and-error doctrines apply the model to learned fit between organismic response and environment. Ashby (1952) and Pringle (1951) have independently noted the formal parallel between evolution and learning [see also Skinner, 1953a].

Attention is called to a third level of organismic fit to environment, in the adaptive responses employed in the flexible execution of well-learned habits. For blind organisms, the trial-and-error component in the carrying out of a habit may be obvious; but for organisms with distance receptors, the smoothly guided yet flexible character of the execution of learned responses seems quite out of keeping with the random variation required by the model. An effort is made to resolve this incongruity by characterizing perceptual processes as substitute trial and error, containing a search component which takes the place of blind overt motor movements. The notion is a more primitive one than that of "vicarious trial and error." It seems relevant for the empirical inconsistencies in the problems of "what is learned" and "insight." As related to servo-mechanism models, the notion is to be clearly distinguished from the simple negative-feedback regulators, like thermostat or governor, in which the feedback comes from the outcome of the primary effector. But a suggestive parallel is available in complex servo-systems such as the radar-controlled guiding of a ship or projectile, in which a blindly emitted beam is selectively reflected, and is used to substitute for a trial and error of ship movements or projectiles (p. 341).

Campbell's argument might be paraphrased somewhat as follows. In organic evolution there is a struggle for existence, or "trial-and-error" process, in a *population of individuals*. Some individuals, showing favorable organic (structural) variations, survive best and reproduce themselves most abundantly, thus differentially "strengthening" or "reinforcing" these variations. In trial-and-error learning much the same principle is involved: successful responses are perpetuated and unsuccessful ones are discarded, i.e., they do not "reproduce themselves." Here, however, the competition, selection, or "struggle" is between a *population of responses*, rather than of individuals; and the deviations involved are *functional* rather than structural. It was therefore a great advance when this type of variation became possible; for in organic evolution an "error," being structural and uncorrectable in the individual, meant death or at least serious disadvantage; whereas, with learning, an error can often be abandoned and replaced by more suitable action. Epitomizing, we may thus say that learning is a form of *in*organic evolution, or change, in the sense that it involves no gross bodily modifications and such modifications (in the nervous system) as are required can occur very quickly—millions of them, in fact, within the lifetime of each individual.

Surely, despite significant differences, the similarities between the theory of organic evolution and Thorndike's theory of learning are striking. In a footnote Campbell says:

The parallel between natural selection and trial-and-error learning seems obvious, once pointed out, and yet it is an important and profound

intellectual achievement. It is interesting to note that Lloyd Morgan and
E. L. Thorndike, who were imbued with the Darwinian heritage and were
proponents of the trial-and-error doctrine, seemed to miss it, or at least
did not make it explicit. Ashby and Pringle, both participating in the intellectual ferment out of which cybernetics and information theory have
developed, seem to have noted the parallel independently (p. 331).

But Campbell, in the article cited, is saying something more. While
structural variation was useful to a species in helping it fit more snugly
into a particular physical environment, the "searching and exploration" thus involved was of a drastic and often, literally, fatal kind. In
plants, where structure is maximally important and "behavior" minimally so (see Fuller, 1934), change occurs almost entirely by means of
the evolutionary mechanism; but in animals, with nervous systems and
the attendant possibility of response variation, there is the capacity
for another kind of "evolution" or change, namely learning. But this,
says Campbell, is not the end of the matter. Learning by actual *doing*
involves hazards; and a still higher level of advantage accrues to organisms which can explore their environments, not only in terms of
actual, overt performance, but also *perceptually*. What, more precisely,
does this involve? Campbell's answer runs as follows:

Let us consider a blind person who has learned the task of sorting mixed
machine parts into separate bins. The response of reaching is for the most
part a body-consistent response, guided in terms of body orientation and
memory. The final phase of the grasping, however, involves an observable
blind, random groping, varying in extent depending upon the accuracy of
the initial movement. Without the trial-and-error component, the object-
consistent adaptive fit of the response would not be achieved. An example
of a blind, fumbling, yet object-consistent response for a seeing person
might be finding a cigarette lighter in a pocket. But even for a blind
person's behavior, this random trial-and-error aspect of executing well-
learned behavior may not be too apparent. In part, this is due to the fact
that, in a simple stable environment, body-consistent responses may approach fit quite closely, leaving the random trial-and-error component to
a minimum. Thus in walking on a well-known level floor, the blind person
may place each foot without hesitation, or visible trial and error. And on an
uneven terrain, the random trial-and-error component may be safely
limited to one dimension, and appear only as a hesitant feeling for the
ground. But if we are to follow the logic of Ashby's presentation, and
avoid any unexplained prescience on the part of the organism, the random
trial-and-error component must be present in every object-consistent
response.

Let us follow further our blind subject in his well-learned performance.
He identifies the piece by a random scanning of its surface with his fingers.
He places it without apparent hesitation in the correct bin, if the bins are
large enough for a body-consistent response to be adequate. But if we

observe him more closely, we note that he has searched out the correct bin with his left hand, and that this has given confidence and precision to the response of the right. Somehow, the random trial and error of the left hand has vicariously served for the right one. Similarly, he may in walking use a blind trial and error of cane movements to search out steps, walls, and doors, reducing the trial-and-error component in his walking.

But most object-consistent responses have a smooth, accurate, guided quality which seems quite out of keeping with the prescribed random trial-and-error process. If the formal model for adaptive fit is to be retained at this level, the only resolution seems to be to locate the trial-and-error process in the function of the sensory organs. It is the burden of this paper that perception serves this function of trial-and-error exploration, substituting for the motor trial and error found in the blind object-consistent response.

It is probably easiest to accept this point of view for an organ of vicarious exploration like an insect's antenna, or the blind man's cane. The analogy of the radar screen as an aiming device is of help. The radar beams scan the sky in a blind sweep, blind in that it is not modified by any prior knowledge of the location of objects. When in this search a beam reflects from a plane, a gun is then appropriately aimed. The trial and error of a radar beam has substituted for a trial and error of expensive bullets. In a parallel way, a ship's radar vicariously explores the waterways, by a trial and error of radar beams learning the location of obstacles that might otherwise have been located by a trial and error of ship movements and collisions.

It is an easy transition from the radar model to the bat's supersonic echo location—in which sound waves emitted in all directions provide the substitute random trial-and-error process. Similarly, the lateral line organ of fishes seems to have the purpose of registering waves of water pressure change in such a fashion as to locate objects in terms of the echo of the fish's own swimming, and Pumphrey (1950) has suggested the radar and echo-location analogy for this process [see also research on porpoises by Kellogg, 1958].

The case for vision is most important, but cannot be made with the clarity and completion possible for the radar and echo-location examples, since the emitting process is missing. However, the notion of vision as a surrogate trail-and-error process seems not only required by the formal model but supported by other considerations. If in visual search the gross eye movements are not blindly searching it is because other sources of information such as touch, memory, or hearing have been employed to narrow the range of search. Hebb (1949) has assembled impressive data on the active searching movements that typically characterize the simplest seeing process, and his facts belie the implicit notion of the passive, fixed-focus eye implicit in both Gestalt and conditioning theories. But even without temporally extended scanning, the eye in a single glance provides spatial information which can substitute for motor trial and error, which can lead to smooth, guided, object-consistent responses (pp. 334–336).

In this section we have conjectured that, despite their apparent differences, "perceptual" and "motor" responses are fundamentally similar, serving the same functions and being controlled by the same laws. There is, however, a difficulty which arises in this connection which will be considered in the following sections.

VII. "Information" and Learning Theory

As we now see, there is considerable justification for believing that the behavior involved in the scanning, focusing, and related "adjustments" of sense organs is not basically different from so-called instrumental or habitual behavior in general. In this section we shall review some of the experimental evidence for and against this assumption.[8]

In 1952, Wyckoff published a seminal paper on "observing responses" in the pigeon which may usefully serve as our point of departure. This investigator found that pigeons would step on a small treadle which in no way influenced the accessibility of primary reinforcement but which did provide certain "information" about the conditions under which reinforcement could be obtained. And Wyckoff (following suggestions previously put forward by Skinner, 1938, and Dinsmoor, 1950; see also Mowrer, 1960, Chapter 12) concluded that the treadle response was learned because information (in the sense of cues) has secondary-reinforcement properties. However, the details of both the theoretical and the empirical aspects of Wyckoff's study are too intricate for full examination here, so we turn to a somewhat simpler attack on the problem published by Prokasy in 1956. He sets forth the objective of his study as follows:

> The present study was designed to determine if exposing a rat to discriminative stimuli in a maze also has a reinforcing effect. More specifically, the purpose was to test the hypothesis that rats would show a preference for conditions enabling them to "anticipate" the presence or absence of food over conditions not enabling them to "anticipate" the presence or absence of food, when the average amount of food resulting from a choice of either condition was the same. Since a response which allows "anticipation" is analogous to an observing response in Wyckoff's study, this experiment is another test of Wyckoff's basic hypothesis (p. 131).

The maze employed by Prokasy was shaped like the letter E, with the starting box in the center stem and goal boxes at the ends of the two wings. Food was available in each of the two goal boxes on 50% of the trials, and there was a delay chamber in each wing, just anterior to the goal box, where the subject was detained briefly, on each trial,

---

[8] It goes without saying that the present chapter does not provide anything like a complete account of the topic of perception. For more comprehensive treatments, see F. H. Allport (1955) and Bartley (1957).

before being allowed to proceed to the goal box. On one side of the maze the delay chamber was always the same color as the rest of the maze, namely gray; whereas, on the other side, the delay chamber was white on trials when food was to be obtained in the goal box and black when it was not (or *vice versa*). The results are shown in Fig. 5–2

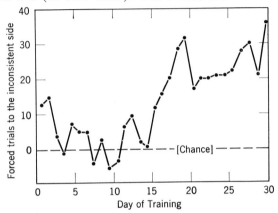

Fig. 5–2. Curve showing the emergence of a preference (on the part of rats) for that side of an E-maze in an experiment wherein there was foreknowledge of presence or absence of reward in the goal box (Prokasy, 1956, p. 132).

Here it is apparent that the subjects (rats) eventually developed a decided preference for the side of the maze where they were "tipped off," by the color of the delay chamber, as to whether reward would be forthcoming on any particular trial—and this despite the fact that no more food was, on the average, available on this side of the maze than on the "noncommittal" side. In other words, the subjects seem to have been rewarded by "advance notice" of whether reinforcement would or would not be available in the goal box. This finding confirmed Wyckoff's hypothesis that "information" is rewarding, but it did not greatly explicate theory.[9]

Perkins (1955) has suggested that information is rewarding for the reason that it helps an organism *prepare* for future events. But we can be considerably more explicit in this connection if we think along the

[9] Cf. Dashiell's (1938) remark regarding the Muenzinger shock-right effect (Mowrer, 1960, Chapter 11), that "we have let ourselves be surprised at this 'shock-right' phenomenon; but the surprise is due to our having emphasized the word 'shock' and not the word 'right'" (p. 213). (Cf. also Osgood, 1953, pp. 424 ff.; Deese, 1952, p. 116.)

following lines. We may reasonably suppose that in the Prokasy experiment the information received in the delay box on nonrewarded trials would keep the frustration reaction in the goal box from being as intense as it was on the nonrewarded trials on the other side of the maze. Therefore, in keeping with inferences drawn in connection with the Weinstock experiment (see also Mowrer, 1960, Chapter 11), the effects of nonreward on the informative side of the maze would cushion the resultant frustration and lessen the extent to which it would countercondition the phenomenon of hope (habit strength). The result would be that the secondary reinforcement or hope involved in going to one side of the maze would become stronger than that involved in going to the other side of the maze because the nonrewarded trials would be less frustrating on the first side than on the second. Thus, what at first appears to be a tendency on the part of rats to "seek information" can be reduced to differential extinction of two initially equal response tendencies (see Chapter 9, Sections VII and VIII).

VIII. Observing Reactions in Situations of Danger

However, "news" can be bad as well as good, and we must therefore confront what is at least superficially a dilemma: If "observing reactions," like behavior in general, are controlled by reward and punishment, then if such reactions commonly result in the observing organism being frightened or perhaps more vitally "hurt," one might expect such reactions to be inhibited, to stop occurring—and thus expose the organism to even greater danger and possible death.

In the winter, when there is snow or ice on the ground, the writer's wife puts sunflower seeds on a feeding platform for the cardinals that live in our neighborhood. Also, one of our neighbors keeps a cat that is an excellent hunter. Therefore our cardinals, when eating, behave as follows. The head is lowered, the seed is taken between beak and mandible and quickly husked and swallowed, and the head is then raised so that the bird is in a better position to "look around." After thus making sure that the "coast is clear," the bird again lowers its head, and the cycle is repeated. Certainly the cardinals do not *want* to see the cat, yet we are faced by the puzzle of why they nevertheless *keep looking for him.*

In a recent paper Liddell has collected a number of instances of "vigilance" in animals and human beings (see also Deese, 1955), of which the following, supplied by a seal hunter, is particularly striking:

"When the sun becomes hot, the seal who is a chilly animal, will emerge from its hole and stretch out on the ice. There, three feet away from the opening, it sleeps, ready to slip back in at the slightest danger. Every eight to ten seconds, the seal wakes up, lifts its head, looks around and goes back to sleep. The Eskimo approaches on the flat empty plain. He waits for the animal to go to sleep and then runs for about four or five seconds. After which, he lies down on the ice and waits for the animal to wake up. And so it goes. Eighty yards away from his prey, the hunter changes his tactics. Whenever the seal lifts its head to look around, the Eskimo lifts his head like the seal, he looks right and left with the same astonished expression. Being nearsighted, the seal believes that it is face to face with another of its kind. In this manner, the man can, if he is clever, come right up to the animal, grab one of its fins, and with his free hand, plunge his knife in the seal's heart" (Liddell, 1950b, p. 185—quoted from de Poncins, 1949).

One possibility is that such vigilant reactions as those just described are essentially instinctive.[10] In what follows we are not at all excluding this possibility; but it will be our purpose to show, alternatively, how a reinforcement explanation might also apply. Here, to use the example first given, we start with the not unreasonable premise that a cardinal, upon alighting on the feeding platform, is (a) hungry and (b) somewhat apprehensive. So, upon alighting, the bird looks around, sees no cat, and feels safe enough to lower its head and take a sunflower seed. During the latter act, visibility is reduced, fear presumably mounts slightly, and the bird presently raises its head and looks about. What it sees is *reassuring* (fear-reducing); and it now feels safe enough to lower its head and again eat, and so on. This, it seems, is a conflict situation in which two antagonistic responses are being alternately reinforced: the lowering of the head and eating, by hunger reduction, and the lifting of the head and looking about, by fear reduction. Here, looking (vigilance) is far more frequently reinforced positively (by relief of fear) than negatively (by seeing the cat), and so the dilemma is presumably solved.[11]

[10] For a fascinating account of the "observing reactions" of wild animals in Africa, see Moorehead (1957).

[11] Elsewhere (1959b) the writer has suggested the same idea as follows. "Because living organisms sometimes 'look for trouble,' in the sense of making 'observing responses' which may involve unpleasant discoveries, Woodworth (1958, p. 249) sees here further support for his behavior-primacy and environment-learning principles, in opposition to homeostasis [see also Schlosberg & Solomon, 1943]. . . . It is entirely possible that the observing reactions which are prompted by apprehension usually result in reassurance (Nothing there!) and that the occasional 'punishment' which comes when trouble is actually spotted is more than offset thereby. Many wild things, when captured and confined, do abandon their watchfulness; for *nothing* is then reassuring, they experience only 'alarm' when

It will be recalled that in Chapter 12 of *Learning Theory and Behavior* an experiment by Mowrer & Keehn (1958) was cited in which rats periodically turn a revolvable cage a few inches as a means of averting electric shock. One would not ordinarily think of such behavior as involving "observing reactions," but the underlying mechanism seems to be much the same: in both cases the organism does something which makes it feel reassured, it then engages in some other form of behavior (during the course of which its fear mounts), and it again performs the reassuring action. The same investigators, in a different experimental situation involving the recurrent presentation of a visual danger signal, have been interested in the extent to which laboratory rats will go to a particular place as a means of "watching for" this stimulus and will then go to another point and push a lever as a means of eliminating the danger signal (which can now no longer be seen) and averting shock. Although rats show some prospect of being able to solve a problem of this kind, it seems to be extremely difficult for them. Perhaps this problem will be attacked in the future with improved techniques—and more striking results. But already enough has been done to show that the problem is amenable to experimental study and does not (as Coppock, 1954, has argued) necessarily carry us beyond the principles which the study of ordinary instrumental behavior has revealed (see Section IX).

In a paper entitled "The Influence of Complexity and Novelty in Visual Figures on Orienting Responses," Berlyne (1958) has reported some findings with human subjects that are congruent with those already cited. Using visual figures which were (a) simple and unambiguous, (b) complex, and (c) ambiguous, this investigator found that the subjects spent most of their time looking at figures in the (b) and (c) categories. One interpretation which Berlyne suggests is that human beings have a "tendency to fixate a part of the environment that is a

---

they 'observe,' and, likely as not, they close or otherwise cover their eyes and plaster down their ears" (p. 131). The importance, for the reinforcement of observing responses, of the subject's being able to *do* something when trouble is discovered is further emphasized by the following experience which the writer soon thereafter recorded as follows: "I was taking two postal cards to the Departmental letter box. In casually glancing at them, I found that I had failed to put air-mail postage on them—and it was urgent that they go air mail. My first reaction was one of startle, then of relief: an undesirable event had been *avoided*. By seeing (observing) the effects *in advance*, I was able to circumvent them!" Thus, even on those occasions when observing responses spot trouble, corrective action may occur which is very rewarding and reinforces not only that action but also the observing behavior which made it possible.

relatively rich source of information in preference to one that is a relatively poor one" (p. 294). But perhaps a more telling hypothesis is that complexity and incongruity (e.g., a bird with four legs or a cat with an elephantine trunk) are puzzling, "uncertainty-laden" (Berlyne's term), and therefore somewhat threatening until they are fully explored and "understood." Pavlov's conception of an "investigatory reflex" (1927) usefully denotes the facts but does not provide an explanation. Such stimuli presumably make the subject slightly uneasy, and he continues to explore them until he feels reassured. Here, it would seem, much the same principles are involved as those cited earlier in this section (cf. also the concept of "mastery")

IX. Observing Responses and Reinforcement: Empirical Findings and a Theoretical Issue

Since the foregoing sections were written, two pertinent experiments have appeared in the periodical literature and a third one has been carried out, by Mr. Mohammed Akhtar, in the University of Illinois laboratories. Lyman (1959), in a paper entitled "Signal Vigilance Level and Conditioned Avoidance Acquisition in the Goat," after a brief historical introduction, reports a high correlation between "orienting responses" on the part of his subjects to the danger signal and learning of avoidance leg retraction. Says Lyman:

> The more vigilant the organism during signal period, the fewer trials required for avoidance acquisition. In addition, the results show that the organism is more vigilant or alert during avoidance-response than during UR-signal periods (p. 90).
> The data suggest that vigilance plays an important facilitating role in avoidance learning (p. 91).

However, the theoretical analysis of this study is weak, as indicated by the concluding statement: "The suggestion is offered that vigilance allows for a more ready association of CS and sustained avoidance flexion" (p. 91).

The details of the experiment recently reported by Darby & Riopelle (1959) are complicated, but the over-all purpose and outcome can be quickly indicated. Various efforts have been made to get animals to learn by watching other animals, but the results have been unimpressive. However, taking some leads from Harlow's work on learning sets (Mowrer, 1960, Chapters 10–12), these investigators found that by exposing one monkey to several hundred exhibits of another monkey working on different discrimination problems, the observer monkey definitely profited by such exhibits in his own approach to the same problem. Moreover, the extent to which such profiting occurs *increases* with practice and experience. Here, once again, we see an indication of the fact that observing (perceptual, "cognitive") behavior follows principles apparently quite similar to those which control more overt, gross types of behavior and that reinforcement theory, as described in this volume, readily articulates with problems of this kind. This study also has the virtue of involving observing reactions in a situation wherein the primary reinforcement is decremental rather than incremental, as it is in the Lyman experiment and in the experiment by Akhtar which is now to be described.

Near the end of the preceding section, reference has been made to a preliminary study by Mowrer & Keehn in which rats received a visual warning signal in a situation so arranged that this signal could not be seen from the place where the actual avoidance behavior (a modified bar-pressing response) had to occur. Although there was some tendency for the subjects to "go and watch" for the danger signal, this behavior never became highly proficient, in part, no doubt, because the danger signal "went off" (and type-1 secondary reinforcement was experienced), not as the subject made the instrumentally effective response of pushing the bar, but in advance of this, as the animal left his observing post and the danger signal (though still "on") was lost from sight.

In order to investigate the same problem but under improved conditions, Mr. Akhtar, under the writer's direction, carried out the following experiment. At irregular intervals (which averaged about a minute and a half), a rat received electric shock from the grill floor of a revolvable cage, and this shock had to be turned off by the rat's revolving the cage a minimum of two inches, *in either direction*, by running. However, if the rat, just before the shock came on, was facing in one direction in the revolvable cage, it received a warning signal in the form of a tone; whereas, if the rat was facing in the other direction, there was no warning signal. The theoretical question was simple, as was the empirical answer: Will rats orient in such a way that they will receive the warning tone, rather than in a way in which they will not; and the answer is clearly, yes. Receiving 15 trials per day, four of five animals reached the criterion of proper orientation and successful avoidance of shock on all 15 trials on a given day, in 9, 13, 14, and 34 days, respectively. The fifth animal, at the end of 55 days, had not yet reached criterion and was discontinued. The more or less "typical" performance of the 14-day animal is shown in Fig. 5–3.

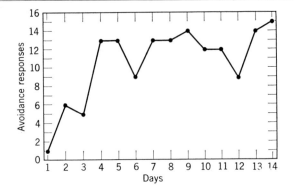

Fig. 5–3. Curve showing the increasing proficiency (learning) of a rat in orienting in a revolving cage in such a way as to receive an auditory warning signal and make a response which avoids an electric shock. In thus "looking for trouble" (warning signal), the animal has *less* of it (in the form of shock) in the long run.

Why did these animals learn to orient in the revolvable cage in such a way as to receive the danger signal, in preference to the reverse orientation in which they would not thus be "bothered"? The fact is that the danger signal was, in the final analysis, not a "bother" in this situation; it was, in fact, decidedly helpful. When orienting in the wrong direction, an animal never "knew" when he might be shocked and so was more or less chronically apprehensive. When the shock came, the rat could, to be sure, always turn it off by running; but avoidance was impossible. When, however, the rat oriented in the *right* direction, it could not only respond to the fear thus aroused with an anticipatory run (which would avert the shock); it could *also sharply discriminate* between the brief periods when it was in real danger (i.e., when the tone was on) and the rest of the time, when the rat was perfectly safe and could well afford to "relax." Hence, the reinforcements for being "realistic" and *watching* for the danger signal, rather than engaging in so-called ostrich-like behavior, are clear-cut and obvious. The only surprising thing is that there was one rat, out of the five, which for some reason did not see the situation in quite this light.

In the hope of devising a still simpler way of attacking this problem, Mr. Akhtar carried out a second version of this experiment. A conventional Miller-Mowrer shuttle box was divided in the middle by a board with a small hole in it in which there was a swinging door (hinged from above), which was easy to pass through but which excluded vision into the other side of the apparatus. Again the warning signal was a tone; and it was available in only one side of the apparatus. On alternate days, each rat was put into the apparatus on opposing sides; and all it had to do to solve the problem was to go to (or stay on) the side where shock was preceded by the tone and, when the tone came, to leap into the air slightly. In 23 and 35 days, respectively, two out of four animals solved this problem to criterion; but two other animals did not. However, it was noteworthy that, although failing (refusing?) to make the necessary avoidance response of jumping, they nevertheless showed a clear preference for the side on which the shock was preceded by warning. Although, for some reason, failing to terminate the danger signal by jumping and preferring not to jump until forced to by shock, they nevertheless apparently "felt better" on the side with the warning signal (as indicated by more time spent there), for reasons already indicated in connection with the first version of this experiment.

Preliminary and crude as these two experiments were, they nevertheless serve to indicate that observing reactions, even where a "negative" or "danger" signal is involved, follow expectations generated by revised two-factor learning theory and do not, at least at this stage of our understanding of this type of problem, call for new or different principles. The paradox of behavior that seems to involve "looking for trouble" is resolved by the thought that if one looks for trouble, not in the sense of creating it for himself, but of knowing when to *expect* it and what to do then to *avoid* it, one is much better off in the long run. Somewhat more analytically and formally, one may say that in being willing to be frightened occasionally (secondarily motivated), one is often able to avoid the greater evil of being more seriously hurt. Thus, we stay well within established reinforcement principles and also within the conceptual framework of homeostasis in general.

As an after-thought it occurs to the writer that some readers may feel that the outcome of the Akhtar research was a foregone conclusion and that the attendant theoretical analysis is aimed at a straw man. "Of course living organisms, if they have any sense at all, will make use of warning signals!"—might seem a reasonable view of the matter. But critics of reinforcement (homeostatic) theory have often voiced at least intimations of skepticism in this connection. For example, Sidman & Boren (1957), in an article entitled "A Comparison of Two Types of Warning Stimulus in an Avoidance Situation," have this to say:

Almost without exception, theoretical formulations of avoidance behavior place great stress upon the conditioned aversive function of the
warning stimulus. Termination of the stimulus is generally held to provide
reinforcement for the avoidance behavior, either directly (e.g., Dinsmoor,
1954; Schoenfeld, 1950; Skinner, 1953b) or through mediation of postulated
drive reduction (e.g., Miller, 1948; Mowrer, 1939). Such reinforcement
would indicate that the stimulus itself becomes aversive. [But see Mowrer,
1960, p. 50.] It was, therefore, somewhat surprising to note the inability of
the warning stimulus [used in this experiment] to maintain a higher rate of
avoidance responding prior to its onset. The present investigations aimed at
a more detailed elucidation of the discriminative and aversive functions of
warning stimuli in the avoidance situation (p. 282).

The Sidman-Boren experiment is intricate and, for anyone not intimately familiar with their theoretical presuppositions and somewhat
cryptic vocabulary, perhaps also not entirely intelligible. But understanding and mastery of the details of their experiment is not, for our
purposes, necessary. The quoted passage serves, in any case, to show
that questions *are* sometimes raised in this general area—and it also
helps to sharpen an interesting paradox. The results of the Akhtar
studies indicate that organisms commonly seek out a place or assume
a bodily orientation which permits them to receive a warning signal,
thus suggesting that the signal has *positive* value or motivational significance for them; and yet, as Sidman & Boren cogently note, the general assumption, backed by much empirical research, is that warning
signals are "aversive," i.e., fear-arousing and therefore disagreeable,
objectionable, motivationally *negative*. Fortunately, the Akhtar studies
are of such a nature as to point to a solution of this problem. Even in
those rats which most systematically "sought" the warning signal, it
is not in the least necessary for us to assume that this signal was positive or rewarding, per se. These animals were undoubtedly "punished"
by the appearance of this signal and rewarded for making the responses
that turned it off. *Why*, then, did they "go for" it? The answer, literally, is that they didn't. They did not seek the warning signal as such;
instead, they sought the situation in which the warning signal occurred, because (as we have already noted) they experienced less
total fear here than in the no-signal situation. Or, if this phraseology
seems tainted with teleology, let it be said that for these animals the
no-signal situation, *as a whole*, was more fear-provoking than was
the signal situation; and so the animals experienced type-1 secondary
reinforcement of the responses that took them from the former to
the latter and so developed a "habit."

However, to repeat, this is not to say that the signal as such was
in any way "positive." Actually what the signal does is to concentrate,

or "collect," all of the animal's fear in the one situation into one brief period and leave the rest of the intertrial interval relatively pleasant, whereas in the no-signal situation the entire intertrial period is fear-laden and, in balance, decidedly less attractive than the signal situation. Perhaps at no one instant, in the no-signal situation, is the subject's fear as high as it is, in the signal situation, when the signal comes on; but the *total amount* of fear experienced in, and therefore conditioned to, the no-signal situation will still be much greater than that experienced in and conditioned to the signal situation (by which is meant the situation in which the signal occurs but is not, for the most part, present).

Epitomizing still further, one may say that no organism *likes* to get a danger signal; but between two situations which involve danger, the one in which there is a signal will be preferable to the other.

In prompting this additional clarification of a really very nice theoretical issue, the Sidman-Boren study, whatever its other ambiguities may be, is very useful.

X. Perceptual Vigilance and Defense

It could, of course, be argued that in the immediately preceding sections of this chapter we have been "talking around" the point at issue. Thus far we have largely equated "perception" with "observing *reactions*"; and it could be objected that what is really important is not what an organism does with his sense organs but rather what gets through to him, subjectively, in the form of sensations and "percepts."

Some years ago Bruner & Goodman (1947) reported that objects having positive value for the individual (e.g., "coin of the realm") tend to be seen as physically larger than they actually are; and other investigators reported, at about the same time, that it is more difficult to see briefly exposed words with a "threatening" meaning than words of neutral or positive connotation. From these and similar observations (for reviews see Hilgard, 1951; Murphy & Solley, 1957; and Dulany, 1955, 1957), the inference was drawn by some that perceptions are palpably influenced by our "wishes" and that we learn to "perceive as we *wish* to perceive." [12] But wishes, as we know, can diverge from reality; and the basic, biological function of perception (and sensory reception generally) is to tell us what is *really there,* and not just

[12] This inference was undoubtedly prompted in part by the promises underlying the use of the so-called "projective" tests (cf. Piotrowski, 1957); see also Hallowell (1950) on perception and culture theory.

what we would like to *believe* (cf. the emphasis of Gibson & Gibson on what they call "veridicality"). So it is not surprising that the resulting literature has been a conflicted one, as regards both fact and interpretation (Postman & Crutchfield, 1952; Gardner, Holtzman, & Siegal, 1956; Jenkins, 1957).

If one attempts to go further in the study of "perception" than the mere observation of the way in which living organisms play their sense organs over the environment, and thus try to get at what the subject is experiencing subjectively, there is a great temptation to fall back upon verbal report. This, of course, can be used only with human subjects; and, even here, there is a serious complication. For example, who can say for certain that a college sophomore really did not "see" a tachistoscopically presented obscene word or simply felt inhibited from reporting (pronouncing) it? Although experimental techniques are now available which may be capable of handling this and some of the related difficulties, we shall make no effort to review or evaluate them here, except as regards one special consideration which may be approached as follows.

During World War II, one of the writer's students enlisted in the Navy and, after attending officer-training school, was commissioned and put in charge of a small coastal patrol craft. In his first letter he described his and his crew's assignment as that "of looking for submarines—and being scared to death that we'll *find* one!" Their predicament, obviously, was much like that of the cardinals and the cat (Section VII); but in one respect it was more difficult. If, in the course of its observing responses, a cardinal found what *it* was "looking for," it would undoubtedly have been momentarily dismayed; but then, by taking to flight, it could probably have quickly put itself safely out of range of the cat. Although the particular look that led to the discovery of the cat would have thus been "punished," the great majority of such responses would, as already noted, have been rewarded, and so might well be expected still to have considerable "habit strength" when the bird's hunger later brought it back to the feeding station. Moreover, having thus seen the cat would have served to reinforce the bird's fear and thus, indirectly, the observing responses; and the fact that even the one negatively reinforced observing response was shortly followed by escape from fear would presumably have tended, in some measure, to have offset the transitory negative reinforcement. Thus we arrive at a plausible explanation, consistent with established reinforcement principles, of why vigilance responses may be perpetuated even though the "cue" be a negative one.

By contrast, the members of the crew of the CP boat were confronted by a more serious situation: if *they* found what they were "looking for," honor and duty required that they approach and attack it. Most of the time, as they scanned the horizon, the report came back, "Not there, not there," with a reassuring effect which presumably rewarded and strengthened the observing action. But now suppose that a submarine were sighted and attacked, with traumatic consequences. The survivors of such experiences (if there are any) sometimes suffer, as we know, from "battle fatigue" and become unable to *face* further duty. Here not only does the individual become incapable of again attacking the enemy—he cannot even look for or think about him. And such an incapacitated individual may now unconsciously "defend" himself in any of various ways, including hysterical blindness, paralysis, hallucinations, and so on; but here we have clearly passed over into the realm of psychopathology, and the growing impression seems to be that "perceptual defense" results only in those circumstances which, as in the one cited, involve essentially *insoluble conflicts* (cf. Stagner & Karwoski, 1952, pp. 501–502).[13] Normally, as we have seen, observing reactions are capable of being reinforced and perpetuated when the cue involved is negative, quite as well as when it is positive; and so, from the standpoint of ordinary principles and mechanisms, there seems to be no serious dilemma here. We may reasonably doubt that, in a state of nature, living organisms are any more prone to perceive distortedly, because of motivational factors, than they are to stop making observing responses because such responses are sometimes punishing. Only, it seems, when an individual is "trapped," with ordinary possibilities of escape cut off, is he likely to resort to reactions, either sensory or psychic, which cut him off from his environment. Recently captured wild animals, unable to flee and hide from the world, may sometimes be seen "hiding the world," i.e., closing their eyes, standing with their face in a corner, putting their head under cover. But this is an exceptional situation and, presumably, highly atypical behavior (cf. Eriksen, 1958, pp. 204–209).

At the 1959 meeting of the American Psychological Association there was a symposium on "A Decade of 'New Look' Perception," which admirably summarized the current status of the issues in this area. Here Bruner remarked that "we now see better the great effectiveness of perception," which in context seemed to imply an increasing

---

[13] Much the same logic might be expected to apply, also, as regards "repression." Here, presumably, it is not a sensation that is defended against but an idea, a memory, an *image* (see Chapter 10).

recognition of the essential stability and accuracy of perception and its relative immunity to the influences which were formerly emphasized. Perloe defended the concept of perceptual defense (as opposed to the mere inhibition of report). But Eriksen took the position that in perception there are "two concurrent, parallel response systems—the one affective, the other cognitive," and added: "I put the inhibition on the response level, not on the perceptual level." Perceptual defense, he held, "is purely a response phenomenon, subject to ordinary principles of reward and punishment. These effects are not really perceptual; they are exclusively response effects" (cf. Dulany & Eriksen, 1959).

Here three trends are noteworthy:

1). A tapering off in the excitement about motivated modification of perception, which was so pronounced a decade ago.

2). Growing recognition of the essential stability (veridicality) of perception.

3). And recognition of the fact that perception (meaning) is both a cognitive and an affective phenomenon, in keeping with the basic assumptions of this chapter.

This field is obviously still somewhat unsettled, but there is no compelling factual evidence in it at present to contradict any of our major assumptions. Attention, in the sense of sense-organ adjustment, is obviously influenced by reinforcement factors, as are verbal reports in human beings (and *behavior* in general); but perception as sensation, and even as image, seems to follow the "reality principle" much more closely than they do the "pleasure principle."

XI. A Note on Masochism and Compulsions

It may not be at first apparent how "masochism" is related to the other topics discussed in this chapter. Perhaps the phrase, "looking for trouble," will suggest the connection. From the standpoint of learning theory, such an expression implies a paradox which, at least as far as so-called perceptual vigilance is concerned, has been satisfactorily resolved. But what of the clinical concept of masochism? Do we not here have a clear violation of Freud's pleasure principle and of homeostatis in general?

While there may still be grounds for disagreement, there are growing indications (Mowrer, 1938a; Whiteis, 1956) that masochism is more apparent than real. As viewed clinically, it seems always to involve a situation where there is mounting anxiety or guilt which can be reduced most effectively either by self-inflicted pain or by the individual's doing something that elicits punishment from others. An experimental analogue of this situation is suggested in the following quotation:

In an analysis of the learning process as exemplified in conditioning, which has appeared elsewhere (Mowrer, 1938a), the writer has posited (on the basis of the spontaneous comments of subjects used in an investigation of the galvanic skin reaction to electric shock) that if a stimulus is presented recurrently, at regular temporal intervals, expectation of that stimulus rises and falls in the manner indicated in the schematic diagram reproduced [in Fig. 5–4]. The assumption that was made at the time of the original publication of this diagram, but not incorporated in it, was that if a stimulus does not occur at the expected point, expectancy may remain constant for a time, or perhaps even mount a little higher than usual, and then undergo a relatively gradual decay (Mowrer, 1940, p. 5).

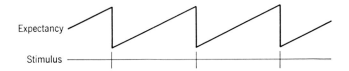

Fig. 5–4. Schematic indication of the way in which "expectancy" (e.g., fear) will rise and drop as a function of the recurrent presentation of a "stimulus" (e.g., momentary electric shock). (Reproduced from Mowrer, 1938, p. 72.)

In the example cited (which has been empirically confirmed), we see that under some conditions pain (or punishment) can indeed have the effect of *reducing* rather than arousing fear;[14] and this fact has prompted laboratory workers occasionally to see if the subject can be induced to *give himself* the "shock" (or other form of painful stimulation) which is needed to reduce the fear. However, with one exception—the experiment of Whiteis, cited in Chapter 12 of *Learning Theory and Behavior*—none of these efforts has succeeded: a human being (or other living organism) apparently will not "hit himself on the head with a hammer because it feels so good when you stop." Ordinarily there must be a source of guilt or anxiety *outside* the immediate situation to "prime" masochistic behavior (Dulany & Tsushima, 1959). Thus an individual may *seek* one form of punishment as a sort of sub-

[14] This, of course, is because the shock has acquired, in addition to its inherent negative reinforcing properties, the capacity to act as a *sign*—a sign that a period of no-shock is to follow. Cf. the discussion (Mowrer, 1960, Chapter 12) of the sign value of food or its absence in situations where the subject is hunger-motivated. See also Baker (1959).

stitute for another, more serious form and use it as a form of "symptomatic relief," in an effort, apparently, to *avert* the latter (see, for example, Wischner's analysis of stuttering, 1952). But in this and all the other instances cited in this chapter which superficially seem to violate the homeostatic principle, we find that, upon closer examination, the violation is more apparent than real. At least, as of the present writing, there is no known compelling example of pure "pleasure in pain"; [15] and in Chapter 10 we shall see that even in those instances where moral principle prevents an individual from taking the easy road of pleasure or sloth, there are still ample grounds for interpreting such behavior within the homeostatic framework.

Originally this section dealt only with masochism; but Mr. Jerry Griffith (a graduate student in the Department of Speech at the University of Illinois) has made a suggestion which invites some additional comment. As a result of reading this chapter (in proof), Mr. Griffith reported that the cyclic, repetitive behavior involved in observing reactions reminded him (and he cited particularly the case of the hungry cardinals and the cat) of "compulsions" as seen clinically, which are also repetitive and cyclic in nature. For reasons which will be elaborated in Chapter 10, it is not a major objective of this book to make clinical application of the principles which are here under discussion; but it will do no harm, at least in passing, to look at such a classical compulsion as Lady Macbeth's recurrent hand washing and ask wherein it resembles or differs from the recurrent "looking" of the cardinals.

One might be tempted to say that the looking "accomplished something," whereas the hand washing did not. But this is not a very pene-

---

[15] It goes without saying that a mild shock can be made to acquire secondary-reinforcement capacity. Experiments carried out in Pavlov's laboratory by Eroféeva show that an electrical shock (if introduced at a low intensity and gradually increased) can serve as a conditioned stimulus for salivation in very hungry dogs (Pavlov, 1927); and from this one would infer that the shock, in the process of its association with food, had also acquired secondary-reinforcement power. If given an opportunity, the subjects in this experiment would presumably have performed some act as a means of "getting" this stimulus, even though it was now not followed by food. An observer who saw a dog thus shocking himself and who did not know the learning that had preceded such a performance might well be tempted to make a diagnosis of "masochism." But if our general analysis of secondary reinforcement is correct, the sounder view would be that the *hope* generated by the shock in a situation of this kind would (at least for a few trials—perhaps a great many if an intermittent-reinforcement training procedure had been used) be sufficiently rewarding to more than offset the negative effect of the shock itself.

trating distinction; for if our principles are valid, the hand washing, if *not* in some sense functional, would have soon extinguished. In other words, we do not believe in "habits" as purely automatic actions which, once started, continue without motivation or reward. The compulsive hand washing must accomplish *something*, we would assume, in order for it to persist. Nearer to the heart of the matter perhaps is whether what it accomplished was or was not *obvious*. The birds were presumably looking to see if the cat was "there," and the looking served this function very nicely—and presumably no other. But in periodically washing her hands, was Lady Macbeth *really* washing them or doing something else? Manifestly, she could not be motivated by the fact that her hands were dirty in any ordinary sense of the term, so we say the function was in some way symbolic, or symptomatic. The washing of her hands presumably acted as a sort of token confession and expiation, which gave momentary but not enduring relief; for it did not alter the fact that she stood guilty of having participated in the treacherous murder of the king.

Thus, the main similarity between Lady Macbeth and the cardinals is that in order to remain tolerably comfortable and "secure" they both had to "keep doing" something, which may be termed a phenotypic resemblance. But genotypically, i.e., in terms of *genesis*, the actions were very different, the one realistic, frank, just what it seemed to be; the other devious, distorted, symptomatic. Many behaviors are, of course, repetitive—in fact, repetitiveness is one of the hallmarks of "habit." But not all habits are "compulsive." The point of the difference is that the motivation and reinforcement which keep "normal" habits going are clear and recognizable. The more *obscure* they are (to others and perhaps to the actor himself), the more likely we are to say that the resultant behavior is "compulsive," rather than merely "habitual."

And much the same distinction, incidentally, can be made between an "obsession" and *normal thought*, which will be our topic for consideration in the next chapter.

XII. Images, Phase Sequences, and Cognitive Dissonance

Once the concept of imagery has been admitted into systematic behavior theory, its implications ramify in profusion in many directions, as the preceding sections of this chapter attest. So at this point it would not be unnatural if the reader wished for a nice, tidy summary statement. This, at least from the present writer, is not possible. Instead, we shall only complicate the picture further by exploring other facets of the problem—and we shall investigate still others in later chapters. The precise mapping of this territory can come at another time. Just now we have to establish major landmarks and general terrain.

Everyone has probably had the experience of being, as we say, lost in reverie and then finding that it takes a moment, and perhaps a little effort, to "come back to reality." A graduate student in psychology once reported that as an undergraduate he sometimes would day-dream in class and then have the experience of the instructor's voice "gradually getting louder again as the daydream or fantasy passed." This phenomenon reminded him, he said, of current work on the reticular formation which shows that as an organism concentrates on stimuli in one sensory modality, there is often a blanking-out of impulses from other modalities (Hernandéz-Péon, 1956; Lindsley, 1957; Sutton *et al.*, 1959). Therefore, it seems entirely possible that vivid imagery can likewise "suppress" the centers concerned with actual sensory imput.

Several years ago a young woman who had become alarmed about her sanity consulted the writer because she found that what had originally been deliberate day-dreaming was getting out of control, with some difficulty on her part at times in telling what was real and what was not. And in psychopathology in general the problem is a common one, termed *hallucination*. This phenomenon, in simplest form, is simple indeed and hinges upon the question of how sensations and images can be reliably differentiated. Half a century ago, Titchener, in his *Textbook of Psychology* (1909b), went at the problem in this way:

> The facts of synaesthesia lead up to the question of the nature of the image, and of its differences from sensation. It is usually said that the image differs from the corresponding sensation in three respects: its qualities are relatively pale, faded, washed out, misty; and its intensity and duration are markedly less [cf. Section I].
>
> Since these differences are all differences of degree, and not of kind, it should be possible to find experimental conditions under which the sensation and the image are confused. Experiments have, in fact, been made, and with positive result, in the fields of sight, sound and touch (pp. 197–198).

Experiments are then described in which images are sometimes taken to be sensations and sensation to be images, after which Titchener continues:

> How is it, then, that we so rarely confuse image with sensation in our everyday existence? Well, the confusion may not be so uncommon as we suppose. However, if it is, the distinction may be accounted for, at any

rate in large measure, by the differences of conscious context or setting in which the two processes appear. Images, for instance, seem to be less sharply localized than sensations; they change and shift more rapidly, and in a meaningless way; they move with movements of the eyes. . . .

Individual minds differ widely in the nature and frequency of their characteristic image-processes (pp. 199–200).

As Titchener then proceeds to show, visual and auditory imagery are common, kinesthetic and tactile imagery less so. "Images of taste and smell have been reported, but only exceptionally play any considerable part in consciousness. Organic images are rare" (p. 200).

If, per hypothesis, images are a conditioned version of sensations, it need not surprise us that there is often striking similarity between them; and if imagery is to do its work effectively, we must obviously be capable (Section III) of generalization from one to the other. McKellar (1957) has recently reviewed the sizeable, and growing, literature on imagination and thinking in a book with this title (see also Barber, 1959, and Nash, 1955); and we shall have occasion in ensuing chapters to examine the so-called representational function of images. Here, however, we shall largely limit ourselves to the phenomena specifically mentioned in the title of this section. Fortunately, Hunt (1960) has reviewed the pertinent literature in this connection, and we can rely heavily upon his exposition. He says:

Hebb's (1949) theorizing is physiological in that he conceives the residues of past inputs to be stored in semi-autonomous, reverberating cerebral circuits which he terms *cells assemblies*. These cell assemblies are the neural analogue of concepts, and they get sequentially integrated into what he calls *phase sequences*. The sequential organization in time provides for the subjective phenomenon of expectation. When markedly incongruous receptor inputs disrupt this sequential organization, behavior is changed and the process is felt as unpleasant emotion. Slight degrees of incongruity, which can readily be accommodated, lend interest and may provide attractive problems, but the larger ones are repelling and perhaps even devastating (pp. 22–23).

Hebb's particular phraseology is not an attractive, or particularly intelligible one, to the present writer (and the notion of reverberating circuits as the basis of memory is almost certainly wrong, factually); but the import of Hunt's last remarks is clear. One is sitting at his office desk typing. There is a door to his right and slightly forward. From hundreds of past experiences, this person has the expectation that if he opens this door, he will see a hallway, stairs, etc. Suppose, now, that upon opening the door, this person sees Lake Michigan! If such a thing happened, it would indeed be "devastating." [16] And experiences of this kind occur frequently in psychosis. Commonly termed disorders of thought or hallucinations and attributed to some biochemical disbalance, might not such phenomena instead represent a form of self-punishment, even more exquisite than depression whose retributory function can hardly be missed? Take the case of the schizoid girl referred to a few paragraphs earlier. Suppose that her daydreams were of a guilt-inducing nature (as they indeed were: of an affair, thinly disguised as physical examinations, with a middle-aged physician). If conscience could not control this behavior with the affect of depression (or anxiety), is it inconceivable that it might try to do so "cognitively," by disrupting normal "phase-sequences" or "expectations"? The upshot of this young woman's seeking "help" was that she abandoned the fantasied sexual gratification (or "mental masturbation"), and secured a divorce from a joyless marriage, and in a few months remarried, successfully. Was the "unconscious" disruption of established "phase-sequences" a mark of "deep pathology" in this girl, or of profound health and strength? But we are digressing. Hunt continues:

Jean Piaget (1952b, 1954) utilizes very much the incongruity notion to account for the development of intelligence and concepts in human children. . . .

Helson (1947, 1948) has called the residues of immediate past experience in the typical psychophysical experiment an *adaptation level*. Both he and McClelland (1953) have seen affective arousal to be a matter of the size of the discrepancy between receptor imputs and the adaptation level. Small discrepancies may be attractively pleasant, large ones repellingly unpleasant. Some of you will readily recall having experienced the affective startle that comes when you have been set to pick up what you thought was a full pail, only to find it empty.

Leon Festinger (1957) has recently written a book entitled *A Theory of Cognitive Dissonance* in which he shows that a discrepancy between belief about a situation and perception of that situation acts like a drive. The subject acts to reduce the *dissonance* by either withdrawing from the incredible situation or by changing his beliefs, and, incidentally, finding the dissonance highly unpleasant.

[16] Manifestly, the situation is this. In normal "phase-sequences," each familiar sensation arouses an image, or expectation, of what is to *come next*. And such expectations are ordinarily confirmed, i.e., the ensuing sensation is congruent with the image aroused by the just preceding sensation. When sensation does *not* match image or expectation, there is obviously surprise, not to say dismay. We have talked much, in recent decades, about the anticipatory or expectancy function of emotions (especially fear). Hebb has done us a service in calling attention also to the essentially expectant nature of many cognitions.

Carl Rogers (1951) has described the basis for anxiety as discrepancy between the phenomenological field and perceived reality. . . .

George Kelly's (1955) *Psychology of Personal Constructs* refers to the
ways in which individuals construe and anticipate events. . . .

Perhaps it is worth noting that this incongruity-dissonance principle
makes both motivation and reinforcement intrinsic to the organism's relation with its environment, intrinsic, if you will, to the organism's informa-
tion-processing. It is as if the organism operated like an error-actuated,
feedback system where the error is derived from discrepancy between re-
ceptor-inputs of the present and the residues of past experience which serve
as the basis for anticipating the future. The dominant view of the past half
century has seen both motivation and reinforcement as extrinsic to information processing (pp. 23–25).

Obviously there is much ferment in this field at the present time.
The next two chapters rest directly upon the groundwork laid in the
present one.[17]

---

[17] After this book was in page proof, an extraordinarily pertinent paper came
to the author's attention. Written by Staats, Staats, & Heard (1960) and entitled
"Language Conditioning of Denotative Meaning," it provides direct empirical
confirmation of a number of assumptions made in this chapter (see especially
Sections I and II). Similarly persuaded that there is more to word meanings than
mere emotion (evaluation, connotation), these authors have been able to show
"that what is commonly called denotative meaning may be conditioned to nonsense syllables to form their meaning. Moreover, the principles of denotative
[cognitive] meaning conditioning appear to be the same as those involved in the
conditioning of connotative meanings" (p. 10). And later they add: "Thus, if
the term 'denotative meaning' is to be used, it is suggested that it refer to the
implicit, mediational, representational responses which can be classically conditioned to words, as were the responses in the above studies. The unconditioned
stimuli used in the two studies were sensory stimuli and the implicit responses
involved would presumably be elicited on the basis of the sensory characteristics
of the stimuli" (p. 12). "In a recent article Staats (1959b) proposed that one type
of representational mediating response which can be conditioned to words to
form their meanings may consist of sensory responses originally elicited by a
stimulus object. These conditionable sensory responses [i.e., sensations which,
when conditioned, become images] could be visual, auditory, or tactual responses,
i.e., components of the 'seeing,' 'hearing,' and 'feeling' sensory responses elicited by
the appropriate stimulus. A number of studies (e.g., Leuba, 1940; Phillips, 1958;
Lipton & Blanton, 1958; and studies of sensory preconditioning) indicate that
sensory responses may be conditioned, and two of them (Phillips and Lipton &
Blanton) indicate that these responses may constitute the meanings of words"
(p. 12). There are many other passages in this important paper which further indicate the marked congruence between the authors' findings and the general
theoretical position here adopted.

6

Learning, Thought, and Insight

Structuralism, or so-called Faculty Psychology, compartmentalized mind into thought, feeling, and action. In *Learning Theory and Behavior* it has been shown that the modern conception of learning unifies and fuses feeling and action into an organic whole; and in the immediately preceding chapters, the concept of "action," or response, has been broadened to include mediators and images. Now we turn to a consideration of that special form of *exploratory* and *anticipatory* action known as "thought," which also, like action in general, is found to be intimately related—not opposed—to feeling. Thus will we achieve a still more integrated conception of the functioning of the "total organism," which will then provide the basis for a discussion, in the following chapter, of that ever enigmatic but manifestly important topic, consciousness.

But first a disclaimer: the present chapter in no sense purports to give a complete account of the psychology of thought (see Flavell & Draguns, 1957, and Bartlett, 1958). It is merely an *approach* to the subject, from the particular vantage point provided by our general systematic position. While avowedly incomplete, this approach may, however, have the virtue of suggesting new experimental problems and fresh theoretical perspectives.

I. The "Thoughtlessness" of Behavioristic Theories of Learning

As noted in several earlier chapters, behavioristic conceptions of learning were commonly presented in such a way as to make the organism itself appear unimportant. In both response substitution (trial-and-error learning) and stimulus substitution (conditioning), S—R bonds were drawn straight "through" the organism, without so much as bothering to note the organism's existence, however incidentally, with an interpolated "O." This, of course, was no mere inadvertence. The aim was to have an *entirely objective* psychology, a true *science of behavior,* which would not be plagued by any subjective agencies or activities.

The central idea of behaviourism was that all animal and human behaviour should be studied only empirically and that any reference to what the animal thinks or feels is superfluous (Konorski, 1958, p. 1106; see also Troland, 1928, and Pillsbury, 1950).

In all seriousness, thought could not, of course, be entirely disregarded; and Watson made a gesture in the direction of acknowledging it as a form of subvocal speech. Osgood (1953) has neatly put the matter thus:

It was Watson, in *Behavior: An Introduction to Comparative Psychology* (1914), who first made a comprehensive defense of the thesis that thoughts, ideas, and images are merely implicit verbal responses. As the most vigorous sponsor of a nascent behaviorism, he was crusading against mentalism in psychology, and such concepts as "thought" and "image" are certainly mentalistic in connotation. This materialistic position was not original with Watson; many thinkers before him had stated its essence. Bain, for example, had said, "Thinking is restrained speaking and acting." But Watson's statements were made at a time when experimental psychology was taking root, and the proposition—*thought is implicit speech*—was an open invitation to the gadgeteer (p. 648).

Osgood then reviews various experiments which were instigated by the implicit-speech theory of thought, experiments which, while ingenious, led to somewhat uncertain results. Fortunately, the issue does not hinge entirely upon the results of such research, for there is a logical issue which is in many ways more compelling. It is agreed that animals other than man do not have speech; and if it is then further agreed that thought is implicit speech, it follows that *no animal other than man thinks.* Descartes had, of course, long before been forced into a somewhat similar dilemma (see Chapter 10), and it was no less awkward for the Behaviorist.

Clear evidence for "thought" in animals will be obtained *in situations in which the relevant cues are not available in the external environment at the time the correct response is required, but must be supplied by the organism itself.* Several situations that meet this criterion have been devised and extensively studied. Two of the earliest animal experimentalists, Lloyd Morgan (1900) and Thorndike (1911), did conclude that animals are incapable of higher mental processes, have no ideas or thoughts as such. More recent investigators have refuted this position; yet—and this is an interesting bow to the classic tradition—they have cautiously referred to "representational factors" rather than to "thought" when describing symbolic processes in animal subjects (Osgood, 1953, p. 656).

In the same year that Osgood's book appeared, the then president of the Canadian Psychological Association opened an address to that organization, entitled, "On Human Thought," with the following remarks:

> In the topic of human thought I have chosen what is indubitably the central problem of psychology—at once the most difficult and the most important that scientists face. Its difficulty is the burden of my address; as for its importance, this can be seen both in the technical field of research and in the practical world of affairs.
>
> Thorndike tried to dispose of the difficulty fifty-five years ago by denying its existence. He buried thought in 1898, but the ghost insists on walking. Often we decline to say that animals think; but comparative psychology has been unable to avoid concluding that animals have expectancies, insights, hypotheses, conceptual activities, a variable attention, and so forth. These are but aspects of thought; and if we cannot deal with the comparatively simple behavior of animals without taking account of thought, how adequate can a thought-less human psychology be? (Hebb, 1953, p. 99).

It is not difficult to see why Thorndike should have tried, as Hebb puts it, to "bury" thought. The main business of thought, surely, is to guide and control action, to make it intelligent, adaptive, efficient, precise. Thorndike's Law of Effect proposed an alternative means of achieving the same end. Effects, i.e., rewards and punishments, were seen as stamping actions "in" or "out," and thus selectively, intelligently, adaptively determining behavior. The effects of a given action thus altered, redirected, controlled subsequent conduct and left no place or need for "thought" or "intellect."

As will be recalled from the beginning chapters of *Learning Theory and Behavior*, Pavlov's formulations, though different in principle from those of Thorndike, were similar in goal. Pavlov was likewise interested, not just in a theory of "learning," but in the organism's *total behavior*, in what Hull was later to refer to as the *principles of adaptive action*. Both trial-and-error learning and conditioning imply adaptation to the environment, but this end was achieved, in both cases, "mechanically," nonmentalistically, *without thought*.

Two-factor learning theory, in its second version, accepted Thorndike's theory of habit formation, essentially unmodified; and, in doing so, necessarily aligned itself with the thoughtless psychologies, or "behavior-ologies." At the same time, in admitting fear conditioning and in developing a feedback conception of punishment, the theory disposed itself toward what has become explicit in the revised (third) version. Now we see response facilitation (habit formation) as no less a matter of conditioning and meaning change than is response inhibition (punishment). And, what is more immediately important, this new position, while in some ways just as mechanical and automatic as were the views of Thorndike and Pavlov, is nevertheless thoroughly hospitable toward—in fact, logically demands—some such notion as "thought." Hopes and fears (as the prototypes of "knowledge" in general) are internal events and, as such, are assumed to be learned and, after learning, to occur in a purely automatic, "involuntary" manner. Here are "mechanism" and "determinism," pure and simple. But, if our hypothesis be correct, there is no simple and direct relationship between what an organism *learns* and what it *does*. Action, we conjecture, is the result of more or less intricate and elaborate processes *intervening between the end results of learning and the execution of behavior*.

The concept of "thought" fell into disrepute among the Behaviorists precisely because it implied that behavior was, in the main, "voluntary," i.e., governed by thought, knowledge, judgment, "conscious choice." And to imply choice, it was inferred, was to imply indeterminancy, freedom, free will, i.e., a break in strict causal sequence and succession. Our present platform is (a) that learning is fully determined, in the ways already indicated; (b) that learning ("knowledge" as defined above), in turn, determines, "conditions," controls behavior; but (c) that this control involves the not inconsiderable complication which we call "thought," rather than being achieved in a purely "reflexive," unconscious or nonconscious manner. Choice, it is held, is a real phenomenon and is, in general, intelligent; but it is a determinate (lawful) rather than indeterminate (capricious) procedure. In fact, the essence of "thought" surely is that it attempts to make conduct *more* reasonable, *more* realistic, *more* congruent with inner needs and outer circumstances. It is, so to speak, decidedly "task-oriented," is by no means "free" in the sense of being idle, irrelevant, yet makes possible a kind of freedom and flexibility not to be approximated by any purely reflexological arrangement (see Chapter 7).

Behavior, then, is determined—determined by the results of experience, of learning; and learning is automatic. But this is not to say that behavior is "automatic" in the same sense. "Thought" intervenes and adds new and important dimensions to the whole adjustmental, self-regulatory process. Is the concept of thought incompatible with that of determinism? Not at all—it is simply a question of the complexity, and flexibility, of the determinism.

In the next section we shall make at least a preliminary attempt to indicate what thinking, as opposed to learning, is.

II. Vicarious Trial and Error as "Overt Thinking"

If it is not already evident from common observation, reviews by Johnson (1950) and by Taylor & McNemar (1955) show unmistakably that the terms, "thought" and "thinking," are used, at the human level, to refer to a wide variety of "higher mental processes" which have long defied exact analysis. However, a promising lead to the field as a whole is provided by a bit of behavior which, being behavior, is objectively observable but which is also typical of "thought."

In an experiment reported in 1931 under the title, "Tone Discrimination in White Rats," Muenzinger & Gentry observed a type of activity in their subjects which, though noted before, had not previously been given much attention. Writing in 1946, Muenzinger says of the earlier study:

> Several years [ago] Dr. Evelyn Gentry and I studied the auditory sensitivity of the white rat. In doing so we made a special effort to record minutely the behavior of each animal at the point of choice. A rat would stop before entering either one of the choice alleys and turn his head to the left and right, often several times in succession. The frequency per trial of this type of behavior increased as the animal was nearing the phase of perfecting his habit, and it disappeared as soon as the habit was automatized. Since this turning of the head *seemed to replace the actual entry into the wrong alley*, we named it "vicarious trial and error," or VTE. I shall not be able to tell you all of this fascinating story of the exploration of what appears to be *a primitive kind of thinking* (p. 12; italics added).

From what has been said thus far, it may seem a trifle forced to refer to the slow, lateral head "wagging" here described as a form of "thinking." Would it not be simpler and generally more defensible merely to say that the rat, in "looking" (or listening) now to the right, now to the left, is trying to decide which of two stimulus specimens, or *cues*, is the correct one, i.e., which indicates an open route (on any given trial) to the goal and which indicates a closed route and no reward? But at once we see that something more must be involved here. The cue stimuli (tones, colors, visual patterns, or whatever) have *cue properties* only by virtue of prior learning, i.e., the fact that, on past trials, one has been followed by food and the other by no food (and frustration), and have in this way acquired distinctive *meanings*. So what the subject is really doing is *comparing the two different internal (conditioned) reactions which the cue stimuli arouse*. Hence the comparison that really counts is the one being made between two internal ("mental") states, and the playing of the distance receptors (ears, eyes, etc.) back and forth is merely the necessary means of arousing these inner states, successively (see Chapter 5).

All this can be made clearer still by examining the VTE that occurs in a somewhat different type of situation. In so-called discrimination experiments with animals (such as performed by Muenzinger & Gentry), there are always two (or more) external stimuli or signs which "lead to" different consequences. However, as previously noted (Mowrer, 1960, Chapter 12), these stimuli "move around" from trial to trial, so that the correct "response" does not involve either making a particular set of movements or going to a particular place (*op. cit.,* Chapter 8). Instead it involves learning to *go toward* one stimulus (no matter where it is or what movements have to be made to get there) and *away from* another stimulus (*op. cit.,* Chapter 9).

Let us now consider what is in some ways a simpler, and more instructive, situation. Suppose that the task set a rat is that of learning to go to the right at the choice point in a T-maze. That is to say, food will always be found in the goal box at the end of the right wing, never in the left wing, so that the animal is learning both to go to a particular *place* and to do so by means of a particular *response*. But now, unlike the usual "discrimination" set-up, there are no external "cues." The right and left wings of the maze look, sound, smell, and feel as nearly alike to the rat as human ingenuity can ensure; and, what is more, all so-called "extra maze" cues will be strictly balanced and equated. Yet the animal still has to "decide" which way to turn when it gets to the choice point. With no objective cues available, this might logically seem like a difficult thing to do. Yet, intuitively, we know that the rat will have no more—in fact, probably less—trouble here than in the "discrimination" situation.

Careful observation of the actual performance of a rat in a learning situation of the kind just described reveals a remarkable fact: the rat will make VTE movements, even though there is absolutely no difference in what he sees, hears, or smells in either direction! Nevertheless, one has the impression that the subject is making some sort of discrimination, some sort of comparison. What could it be? Then we recall that, on each preceding trial, *turning right* has been followed by one result (reward) and that *turning left* has been followed by a different result (no reward). Therefore the *response-produced stimuli* associated with these two different consequences (decremental versus incremental reinforcement) become conditioned, respectively, to hope and fear. Thus, when the rat "turns right" or "turns left" *in miniature*, as it does in VTE, it is, so to say, "sampling" the consequences which will follow if it actually turns one way or the other. The rat, in moving its head back and forth, is thus engaging in a very simple but real type of "reasoning"—it is, quite literally, "using its head." [1]

Now wherein does the experimental situation just described differ from the so-called discrimination apparatus or situation? Obviously, if our surmises be correct, the rat is making a "discrimination" in the T-maze no less than in the other situation; and in both instances the discrimination is between the anticipated consequences of one course of action as opposed to another. The difference, rather clearly, is that in the one case differential cue stimuli are provided by the environment, whereas in the other case the subject has to *make them himself*.

III. VTE, Further Evidence and Theory

In one of his earliest theoretical papers, Hull (1930b) displayed an excellent grasp of the foregoing problem and coined an apt phrase—"pure-stimulus acts"—to refer to those responses which an organism makes solely for the purpose of providing itself with much needed cues. But because Hull's theory as he later developed it was, like Thorndike's, basically behavioristic, basically thought-*less*, Hull made little systematic use of the pure-stimulus-act notion. Says Osgood (1953):

> In the Hull paper already cited we find the following: "A reflective consideration of the habit mechanisms involved in anticipatory defense reactions reveals a phenomenon of the greatest significance. This is the existence of acts whose sole function is to serve as stimuli for other acts. We shall accordingly call them *pure stimulus acts*" (p. 515). And in the summary of this paper Hull declares: "Such behavior sequences have great biological significance because they enable the organism to react both to the not-here and the not-now. Incidentally it accounts for a great deal of the spontaneity manifested by organisms. The concept of the pure stimulus act appears to be the organic basis of symbolism . . ." (p. 524). For a number of reasons,

[1] Freud (1911) has likened thought to a general moving lead soldiers about on a miniature battle field, in preparation for a real battle to follow. And Osgood (1953) has spoken of thought involving "light" (i.e., easy and *safe*) responses which help the individual determine what course of overt ("heavy," important, fateful) action to pursue.

chiefly the extensiveness of the research program he set for himself, Hull never did fully explore the implications of this mechanism (pp. 395–396).

The perceptiveness of Hull's analysis is rendered all the more remarkable because it came before the careful empirical work of Muenzinger and his students. However, the phenomenon of VTE, though not so named, has long been familiar to animal experimenters; and the interest and research work it has more recently generated is indicated in the opening paragraphs, quoted below, from the very competent and complete recent survey, "Vicarious Trial and Error and Related Behavior," by Goss & Wischner (1956).

A number of experimenters have reported a more or less typical and frequent pattern of behavior which occurs at the point of choice in the discrimination box, maze, or during the choice process in visual discrimination studies employing jumping stands. This pattern has been variously described as "choice by negation or comparison," "looking to the right or left before choice," "swaying back and forth," "head movements," "partial elimination," etc. To this general pattern of behavior Muenzinger and Fletcher (1936) have given the name "vicarious trial and error," abbreviated "VTE."

Although first used to label choice-point behavior of rats prior to spatial or non-spatial discriminative responses, the term VTE has subsequently been extended to vacillatory behavior in conditioning (Girden, 1938), reasoning (Maier, 1940), place vs. response learning (Ritchie, 1947; Ritchie, Hay & Hare, 1951; Tolman & Gleitman, 1949a; Tolman, Ritchie, & Kalish, 1947), delayed reaction (McCord, 1939b), conflict (Barker, 1942), and even non-choice (Taylor & Reichlin, 1951) situations. Moreover, not only the choice-point or choosing behavior of rats but also of dogs (Girden, 1938), monkeys (Kluver, 1933), children (Barker, 1942; Gellerman, 1933a, 1933b), and adults (Tolman, 1941) in various of these situations has been labeled "VTEing." Thus VTE behavior now refers to the vacillatory behavior of various types of Ss at points of choice in a wide range of situations.

On the theoretical level, VTE has been interpreted as a behavioral definition of consciousness (Tolman, 1926, 1927, 1932), a catalytic process which aids learning (Tolman, 1938, 1939, 1941, 1948), a form of symbolic exploration (Mowrer & Ullman, 1945), an analogue or mechanism of reasoning (Maier, 1938; Muenzinger, 1938), "overt thinking" (Dashiell, 1949), a behavioral index of conflict (Barker, 1942; Brown, 1942; Hovland & Sears, 1938; Miller, 1944; Sears & Hovland, 1941; Underwood, 1949), or a preparatory response (Taylor & Reichlin, 1951). Tolman (1938, 1939, 1941), particularly, and Barker (1942), Schlosberg and Solomon (1943), Taylor and Reichlin (1951), and Austin (1953) have advanced relatively complex and systematic explanations of the VTE phenomenon (p. 35).

That the phenomenon of VTE should have had a special interest and attraction for Tolman and his students is almost axiomatic. He has long held that what is learned are *expectancies, not performances,* and that there are important "intervening variables" or processes between "stimulus" and "response." In VTE we seem to see such intervening processes clearly at work. That the rat should engage in some degree of reasoning or thought at a choice point, whether in a maze or on a discrimination stand, is certainly consistent with Tolman's whole approach. But, as Guthrie (1952) has observed, we must be careful not to *leave* the rat at the choice point *"lost* in thought." We must somehow get him "going" again, and eventually to his goal. If, in thought, we are merely dealing with expectancies in the sense of "pure cognitions," there is an acute problem here. But if, instead, we view these expectancies more dynamically (as hopes and fears), then we have a basis for expecting thought to be closely related to, and to eventuate in, overt motion. As the rat symbolically samples, successively, the probable consequences of one course of action as opposed to another, he is not experiencing mere cognitions but actual *motivating states,* with reinforcing properties; and we may plausibly conjecture that what happens is something like this. Each turn of the head to the right produces, let us say, a little feeling of hope, while a turn to the left produces slight fear. The head responses are repeated a few times more, with their attendant experiences; and presently, as a result of *"on-the-spot"* conditioning, turning head to the left, even in token form, becomes disagreeable, while turning the head to the right is pleasant. The rat is now "all set" (Tolman would say "cognitively structured"), and all he *can* do is to "follow his nose." [2]

Perhaps the difficulty inherent in Tolman's analysis arises from a false antithesis which has long been made (at least since classical Grecian times) between *intellect* and *emotion.* Emotion has been regarded as a *low* order of activity, to be distrusted and shunned, whereas intellectual processes are said to occur on a higher order and to be more worthy of cultivation. Hence, if this antithesis is accepted, one would be inclined toward a "purely cognitive" rather than affective analysis of *thinking.*

That there is reason to distrust this antithesis is now evident on many sides; but McGill (1954), in a recent book on *Emotions and Reason,* puts the matter especially well when he says:

[2] Parenthetically, one might say that the purpose (function) of thought is to *end* thought. It helps one to decide, to "make up one's mind," to stop thinking and *act.* One thinks when in doubt; thought (reasoning) is a means of resolving doubt, gaining certainty (cf. Bartlett, 1958).

It was Plato in the *Phaedrus*, who first gave expression to this dualism of emotion and reason. Reason is depicted as a noble steed "straight and well-knit, with high neck and arched nose, in color white, with black eyes, a lover of honor in all temperance and modesty, a friend of true glory, . . ." whereas desire, or emotion, is a horse of a different color—"crooked, lumpish, ill-jointed, with a stiff neck, a short throat, a stub nose, in color black, with gray eyes, sanguineous, a friend of lust and boastfulness, . . ." Whereas the noble white horse follows the path of truth, goodness and beauty of its own bent, the bad black horse of desire is perverse and impetuous, striving might and main to drag the white horse and the charioteer down some dark road where destruction is certain, and must be continually chastised and corrected.

Those who divorce emotion and reason have sometimes forgotten that this is only a myth, and that Plato himself, as in *Philebus*, presents quite a different picture. There, emotion is the complement of reason and falls into error only when true knowledge fails. Aristotle also saw that emotion and reason are not opposites but integral parts of one process and inseparably associated in the good life, or happiness. Emotions are to be restrained in some cases, but strengthened and cultivated in others. Spinoza showed, even more clearly, that emotions involve reason and reason, emotions; and that the narrowness and stupidity of the passions is also a privation and confusion of knowledge. The evil of the passions is to be cured only by summoning other emotions which are contrary to them (p. viii).

In summary, then, we may say that the simplest and clearest instance we have of "thought" in animals suggests that this phenomenon, rather than being unrelated to emotions and motives and reinforcers, is associated with them very intimately. Emotions are, in fact, the core of thought in that they *mediate* between primary drives and the real consequences of various possible actions. In VTE, as exhibited by rats and certain other animals, what the organism tries to do, apparently, is to sense and compare two (or more) stimuli which have previously been temporally contiguous with reward or punishment. These stimuli may either be "in the environment," as in so-called discrimination experiments; *or* they may be available only if the subject himself produces them, by means of tentative, "exploratory" movements, as in a maze where external cues have been eliminated. But the point is, simply, that these stimuli are sought or "consulted," not for "information" inherent in them, but because they are conditioned to affective states which will then serve to *guide* the subsequent course of overt behavior. As Muenzinger has long since observed, VTE is not immediately evident in a rat, in its initial trials in a discrimination apparatus or a T-maze—presumably because the cues have not yet become sufficiently conditioned to "good" or "bad" anticipations. Moreover, as Muenzinger has also noted, VTE "tends to disappear as soon as the habit [is] automatized." What the latter statement presumably means is that clear anticipations of one as opposed to another course of action become conditioned to stimuli which occur prior to the subject's reaching the "choice point" and so *sets* the animal for the correct turn in advance, thus eliminating the necessity for head-wagging debate at this point. In a T-maze, well-trained rats can be seen "hugging the wall" on the same side of the *stem* of the maze as the correct wing is located, thus indicating that their "minds are already made up" as to what they are going to do at the choice point, thus making VTE superfluous.

Rarely are the experimental facts so abundant or their implications so clear as they appear to be in respect to vicarious trial-and-error behavior. Goss & Wischner, in the review cited, describe in considerable detail the many aspects of VTE which have now been systematically studied; and they promise a later review of theories concerning this phenomenon. But the central fact stands out, unopposed, that we have here a superb illustration of an activity which is at one and the same time both symbolic (in a limited way—see Chapter 4) and yet grossly observable.

IV. An Electromechanical Analogue of VTE

As a result of reading a preliminary draft of this chapter, Mr. L. D. Hagenbook was reminded of the operation of a "tracking" device known as a *Rawin set*. This he has kindly described as follows:

In weather prediction, aircraft flight, and artillery and missile firing, precise measurements of atmospheric conditions at different altitudes are needed. Some rather complex electronic equipment has been evolved to meet this need.

A high-frequency radio transmitter attached to a balloon is sent aloft. The transmitter, being carried higher and higher, sends back information about temperature, air pressure, and humidity. Besides the vertical ascension, winds carry the balloon horizontally. By tracking this horizontal movement with a very accurate radio direction finder, information about wind speeds and directions are also obtained. The radio direction finder currently in use is an entirely automatic servo-mechanism called a Rawin set. (A servo-mechanism is roughly any self-regulating electro-mechanical device.) The following is a description of how it tracks the radio transmitter sent aloft.

The antenna assembly of a Rawin set employs a large movable, parabolic reflector having the appearance of an over-sized salad bowl. The goal in tracking is to keep the axis of the parabolic reflector oriented on the transmitter. To do this the Rawin set must get information telling it when it is off target and in which direction it must rotate the antenna assembly to get back on target. As shown in the diagram below, there is a small dipole antenna located in front of the reflector. Over the antenna is a round cup which rotates on an off-center axis. A signal being received by the antenna assembly bounces off the reflector directed toward the rotating cup; it is then reflected off the rotating cup and picked up by the antenna. The off-center cup rotates at a speed of 30 revs. per second and its effect is to modulate the incoming signal at a frequency of 30 cycles per second. Coupled to the motor (M) which drives the rotating cup is a generator (G). The generator also puts out a 30 cps. signal. When the antenna assembly is "tracked-in" and the axis of the parabolic reflector is lined up with the balloon transmitter, these two signals are exactly in phase (i.e., they vary together). When the antenna assembly is not tracked-in, the modulated signal from the transmitter will be out of phase with the signal from the generator. The amount of phase difference is a function of the location of the transmitter in relation to the axis of the parabolic reflector. The modulated signal from the transmitter and the signal from the generator are fed into a phase-discriminating network. This electronic circuit measures the difference in phases between the two signals, and by means of four different outputs (error signals) drives motors to turn the antenna system in any of the four possible directions on its two rotating axes. Thus, if the antenna system is not on target, it will track-in by turning on either its horizontal axis, its vertical axis, or both.

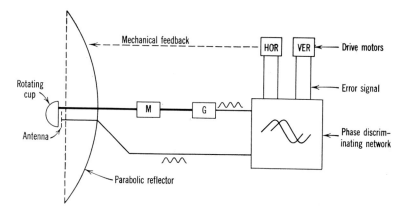

Fig. 6–1. Schematic diagram of a Rawin tracking apparatus (courtesy of L. D. Hagenbook, Jr.).

To summarize: A 30 cps. signal from the transmitter is compared to a 30 cps. reference signal. Differences in phase between these two result in an error signal activating drive motors to move the antenna assembly on target and subsequently to follow any course the transmitter might describe. This is analogous to a rather complex stimulus-response relationship.

It may be interesting to note that a characteristic problem in servomechanisms is "time lag" caused by the inertia of the mechanical parts. This results in a slowness of response both in starting and stopping, a lagging of the mechanical "effect" behind the electronic "cause." To help counteract starting inertia in the Rawin tracking mechanism, each drive motor has current flowing through it in opposing directions even when not moving. This yields a dynamic equilibrium analogous to muscle tonus making possible finer and more rapid starting responses.

The other effect of time lag, slowness in stopping, results in mechanical oscillation. In this device, so long as the reflector is off target the drive motors operate to move it on target. The error signal will decrease and then stop as the antenna assembly gets on target; but due to inertia, the antenna assembly will over-shoot and swing off target again. The drive motors then operate in the opposite direction and again there is an over-shoot. Oscillation occurs sustained by boosts from the drive motors. To prevent oscillation, braking or damping devices have been employed. In the Rawin set the damping is a signal tending to drive the motors in the opposite direction they are being driven by the error signal. This damping signal is a constant fraction of the *speed* of the motors. When the error signal is strong it over-rides the damping signal and the motors drive toward the target, but when the error signal decreases as the target is approached, the damping signal over-rides and throws the motors in reverse. By this anticipatory action, movement is effectively braked. Since damping devices are needed in all fast acting servo-mechanisms, and since the human body with its nervous system and muscle tissue is exactly analogous to a servo-mechanism, it is interesting to wonder what kind of damping devices are employed in the human body.

Like servomechanisms in general, the Rawin set is "error-actuated" (see Chapter 7). Whenever there is a discrepancy between the ideal and the actual, the apparatus is "motivated" and moves to correct this discrepancy. Thus, we have self-regulation of the same "homeostatic" (drive-reduction, stabilizing) sort as is found in living organisms. When the apparatus is off target, there is a marked phase difference between the reference signal and the signal generated by the rotating cup; and this phase discrepancy then activates "adjustments" which eliminate the phase discrepancy and, in the process, put the apparatus on target, just as motives in living organisms normally function so as to eliminate themselves and, in the process, achieve other ends, i.e., those of keeping the organism alive and healthy. According to Mr. Hagenbook, a Rawin set can "track-in" when as much as 6 degrees off target to begin with and, once "on the beam," can track with an error of less than .03 of a degree.

In terms of the purpose for which it was designed, this apparatus is obviously highly efficient, highly "intelligent," and Mr. Hagenbook says that those who work with it easily fall into the practice of attributing "mental" qualities to it—it behaves so much like a living organism. But wherein does it instruct us in the psychology or strategy of thought? Is not the little wabbling cup in the Rawin apparatus reminiscent of the rat's wabbling head in a discrimination or choice situation? When the antenna assembly is off-target, the cup ("head"?) feeds more of the signal to the antenna, and the phase discrimination network ("consciousness"?) is in a position 180 degrees removed. And, as a result of continuously "sampling" back and forth, the "head" thus tells the "organism" (apparatus) as a whole which way to turn. First the head goes this way and that; differential information is obtained; and orders are then issued to the "muscles" (motors) to move the whole body (antenna assembly) in the direction favorably explored by the head alone.

Various biologists and neurologists (e.g., Sherrington, 1906; McCulloch, 1951) have been interested in the fact that the heads of living organisms are normally the *foremost* part of the organism as it moves through space.[3] It "gets there first" and alters the line of progression of the rest of the body if the "there" is not good. Of course, heads have become highly specialized in terms of the "special receptors" they contain, notably receptors which are capable of detecting stimuli *at a distance*, viz., eyes, ears, nose. But these specializations must have been preceded by the special organs of *"touch"*—such as provided by taste buds and vibrissae. And perhaps even more primitive are the receptors which report which way the head is turned, or "headed." If heading in one direction gets the organism into trouble, it would seem highly prudential for an organism to be troubled (secondarily, emotionally) just on the basis of the stimuli produced by a token turn, i.e., of the head alone.

Efficient and versatile as it is, the Rawin set is, of course, in one important respect decidedly inferior to organisms, even quite lowly ones: It does not *learn*. Perhaps, in one respect, this is an advantage: it does not *have* to learn since all it needs to "know" is, literally, wired-in by its maker. By virtue of the way the apparatus is constructed it "automatically" operates "intelligently," i.e., given one form of in-put signal it does one thing, given another form of signal it does another; and both actions are correct. Living organisms are to some extent similarly blessed in the form of *instincts;* these are, supposedly, re-action potentials which are "ready to go" on the basis of the very

---

[3] The author recalls, from his days in government service during World War II, the picture of a turtle prominently displayed in one of the staff rooms, with this legend: "Remember the turtle—he makes progress only when his 'neck is out.' " The moral, for both a government worker and the student of behavior, is clear!

construction of the organism, as opposed to *experience*. The difficulty with instincts is, of course, the same as the "difficulty" with a Rawin set: they may do what they were originally designed to do superbly well, but if conditions and demands are altered slightly, their adaptive function may break down completely. Living organisms, with their capacities not only for thought and action but also for learning, have, in the long run, a considerable advantage. This is what Ashby means (Chapter 7) when he refers to the principle of "ultra-stability" manifested by living organisms, i.e., the capacity for a system to reorganize itself and re-establish functioning after a change in either environmental conditions or (through illness or damage) in the system itself.

Our discussion thus far has shown that thought and action are intimately interrelated. Thought-less behavior is, in general, very poor behavior; and thought, at least in some instances, is itself a form of behavior—miniature or token behavior. But we now see that a system can have the capacity for both thought and action without necessarily having the capacity to learn. Although, as the next section will show, it is possible to learn by means of thought, thought tends to presuppose learning. As we have seen, learnings, meanings, significances can either be built in (Rawin sets, instincts)[4] or they can be derived from experi-

---

[4] Revised two-factor learning theory raises some interesting possibilities concerning the nature of instinct. Some of the apparent mystery of instinctive activity has been dispelled by careful and detailed studies, such as those carried out by Wheeler (1928). It had been known for a long time that in at least certain species of ants, there are so-called "nurse" ants whose "duty" it is to feed and otherwise care for the colony's "nursery," containing the developing eggs and young larvae. In the steadfast way in which the nurse ants feed the larvae we seemed to have a striking example of instinctive altruism. Day after day they carry great quantities of leaf cuttings and other coarse food to the larvae and stuff them to capacity, with no evident reward. However, the persevering Wheeler finally saw something which others had overlooked. Around the larvae's mouth are glands which manufacture a sugary substance; and when the mouth of the larvae is well stuffed, the sheer pressure of the stuffing causes this "nectar" to be exuded, which is then lustily licked off by the altruistic(?) nurses. There are, however, many other instances of behavior where it is much more difficult to demonstrate a pleasure-principle type of explanation and where the notion of inherited "connections" of some sort seems about the only alternative (see, for example, Thorpe, 1956). But in this connection Dr. Norman Ginsburg, in a recent seminar, has made this suggestion: If revised two-factor learning theory is valid, does it not suggest a revised theory of "instinct" as well? If so-called habits are dependent, not upon drive-behavior bonds, but upon the particular meanings that have become conditioned to response-correlated stimuli, may it not likewise be that instincts are *inherited* neural connections between response-correlated stimuli and certain meanings (hopes and fears) rather than such connections between drives (or other vaguer forms of stimulation) and specific responses? Some of the differential predictions that

ence. But, in either case, it seems that their principal function is then to affect thought and thus guide action, rather than to determine action in the more immediate sense implied by "habit" theory, as developed by Thorndike and Hull.

V. Thought as Planning or "Preconditioning"

At the human level one of the commonest and most important forms of thinking involves principles we have already explored in Chapters 3 and 4, which deal with language. Because the psychology of the sentence is the prototype for this kind of thinking and because sentences apparently are never made by infrahuman organisms and only rarely, if ever, fully understood by them, we may infer that the type of thinking under discussion here is very limited, or completely nonexistent, in animals. In principle, however, it is in no way incompatible with the type of animal thinking described in the two preceding sections.

The gist of the notion to be conveyed here has been put forward in a previous study (Mowrer, 1954), in the following words:

What I would like to say here about the nature of *thought* will be avowedly incomplete and no more than suggestive. Let me begin with an example. A few weeks ago, I took home to my seven-year-old son a box of small blocks and other scrap lumber from our departmental machine shop. I knew the box, after the blocks were taken out, ought to be returned to the shop and so took it back to the psychology building; but, at the time, the shop was locked so I put the box in a storage room—and, then, forgot about it for several days. Later, at home, I remembered the box and thought, "Machine-shop door, box. Machine-shop door, box." In more elaborate terms I was, I suppose, saying to myself something like this: "The next time I pass the *machine-shop door* I must remember to get and return that *box* to the shop." Later, when walking down the hall on the way to my office, I passed the door, was reminded of the box, got it, and returned it to its accustomed place.

What I had done, evidently, was to *condition myself in advance* to the door, by using a symbol thereof, so that it would cue off the reaction of getting and returning the box. I had, in other words, in the absence of the door (and the box, too, for that matter)—i.e., in the realm of the "not here, not now"—conditioned myself so that the door, on the basis of generalization from symbol to thing, would bring to mind, or remind me, that I ought to do a particular think. In effect, I had "talked to myself" and pro-

---

flow from a bond vs. feedback theory of habit have already been explored. Whether a feedback theory of instinct would lead to expectations logically different from those generated by a bond theory of instinct must be determined by others particularly equipped to investigate the problem (cf. Chapter 10, Sections II and III).

duced a result apparently quite comparable to that which we have here made the basic criterion of objective sentence formation and interpersonal communication.

I would not hold that this is the only or even the most typical pattern which thinking takes. Certainly planning and the consideration of alternatives would have to be carefully examined in this connection and may turn out to involve something rather different. More formal reasoning, e.g., that involved in mathematics, may also depart more or less critically from this pattern. However, enough has been said to suggest that in at least some types of thinking, there is a process of self-stimulation and response, involving the subject-predicate relationship, which is similar to that involved in interpersonal stimulation and behavior alteration of the kind achieved by objectively expressed sentences. In other words, in the light of the present analysis of sentence psychology, it now appears that we can "talk to ourselves" as well as to others and achieve thereby much the same outcome, namely, that of affecting (conditioning) an organism (oneself) in the presence of a mere symbol for something so that when that thing itself is later encountered, there will be a manifest change in behavior with respect to that thing.[5]

Perhaps the kind of "thinking" just described is more likely to intrude itself upon our attention when it *fails* than when it succeeds. Normally the writer, in riding his bicycle from home to office in the morning, takes the same route. One morning, however, an errand made it desirable to take an unaccustomed turn. The unusual turn was rehearsed "in thought," much as in the foregoing illustration; but then, when the time came, it was not *made*. Soon thereafter the oversight occurred to the rider and he said something of this sort to himself: "I forgot to take that turn, after all!"

If asked why he had "forgotten," the cyclist would have probably said, "Oh, I just wasn't thinking." But now what does "thinking" mean in this context? If the earlier "thinking" had done its work, the result should have presumably followed automatically, but it did not. A

---

[5] What we know about the role of *repetition* in language corresponds moderately well with common facts from the conditioning laboratory. A signal and an electric shock usually have to be paired at least twice before an animal such as the rat seems to "get the connection." It is as if the chances are too great that one conjoint occurrence may be mere coincidence (Chapter 9), so that the reality of the relationship has to be established by at least a second conjunction of the two stimuli. Small children seem to learn very quickly that a sentence twice repeated —"Pammy-kitty, Pammy-kitty"—is more effective than a single repetition thereof. When we are trying to *remember* something, through a process such as described above, the association is also usually repeated at least two times, as a minimum. This is not to deny that single repetitions of sentences often "do the trick," but we have no way of knowing how often this is because the recipient "picks up" the sentence, so to say, and fixes and confirms it by subvocal rehearsal.

Freudian might hold that such a "lapse" or "error" is dynamically determined: the individual did not respond as he had planned or *intended* because he was really "ambivalent" about the action involved. There were, within his personality, opposed, competing "wishes" which expressed themselves, not openly, in defiance of the original plan, but subtly, at the critical moment of execution.

The possibility cannot, however, be totally ignored that some episodes of the kind described, perhaps a great many of them, are truly accidental. In other highly complicated "systems" there are sometimes failures of operation which presumably cannot be explained as due to "unconscious wishes"; and it would be very surprising if an "apparatus" as compact as the brain and a "process" as intricate as the human mind did not occasionally fall short of perfection. If one permits oneself to become preoccupied with thoughts about other matters, or if there is unanticipated distraction, or if there are "psychological" disturbances, such an oversight or failure might well occur without any unconscious countermotivation. The very fact that one has "programmed" a given action for a particular time and place (to borrow a bit of "computer" parlance) prompts one to feel free now to "think of other things," on the assumption that the action, having been preset, will run itself off "automatically" or at least that there will be an automatic reminder when the propitious moment arrives. All this is not, of course, to say that conflicting motivation may not, on occasion, express itself precisely as Freud suggested; what the facts do suggest is that not *every* error of this sort calls for an expedition into the unconscious for a Freudian wish.

In our study of VTE we arrived at the conclusion that this fascinating type of behavior is a device for helping an organism get organized —get "set" with respect to immediately imminent action—in answer to the question, "What to do *next?*" In contrast, the type of thinking we have just explored is concerned with "getting set" *for more remote behavior.* The question of whether this type of presetting or preconditioning can occur only in human beings or has at least some prototype in lower organisms will be considered in the next section.

VI. Thought and the Delayed-Reaction Experiments

The kind of presetting of action, or preconditioning, discussed in the preceding section is, in a sense, a form of *delayed reaction.* This is the essence of "planning": One cannot do it *now* but will at a later time. And we have seen how, by means of their elaborate symbolic skills, human beings can get set for a specific action well in advance of its actual occurrence. The assumption has been, moreover, that infrahuman organisms, lacking symbols, are much less effectively planful. Although not usually placed in just this context, there is a large experimental literature on delayed reaction in animals which provides a clear-cut answer to the question here implied. This literature has been admirably summarized and interpreted by Osgood (1953), as follows:

The delayed reaction. In an early approach to this question, Hunter (1913) tested the ability of both rats and human children to make delayed reactions. The rats were first trained to run to whichever of three doors was lighted. After this habit was well established, a delay interval was inserted between flashing a light over one of the doors (distinctive cue) and releasing the animal, the rat being held in a glass-sided box throughout this period. With the children, an attractive toy was dropped into one of three boxes and, after a delay interval, the child was allowed to look into one of three boxes for the toy. In both cases the distinctive cue is not available at the time the correct response must be made; to the extent that correct responses are made beyond chance frequencies, some symbolic, representative processes must be functioning. Hunter found that the maximal delay for the rat was about 10 seconds and even then success seemed to depend upon the animal's maintaining bodily orientation toward the correct door. Children, on the other hand, were not only capable of much longer delays but could respond successfully without maintaining any specific overt orientation. That the actual length of delay for the rat depends upon specific experimental procedures is shown by the results of other investigators. Honzik (1931) allowed his animals to run toward the relevant cue before it was removed, thus insuring that the rat actually received the stimulus, and he obtained delays of 45 seconds or more. McCord (1939a) found rats capable of delays of 4 or more minutes. He used a square enclosure with distinctive cards on each of the four sides, the rats being required to jump from a central stool at the form under which the experimenter had previously held and withdrawn a food cup. The fact that the four alternative cues were separated by 90° angles in this case, thus minimizing the likelihood of interference from conflicting response tendencies during the delay period, probably facilitated the maintenance of the correct set.

Other species have been used as subjects in delayed reaction experiments, and maximum delays are highly variable. The cat has been found capable of delays of from 3 to 17 hours (Adams, 1929), the monkey 15 to 20 hours (Tinklepaugh, 1928), and the chimpanzee as long as 48 hours (Yerkes and Yerkes, 1928). These values can only be considered suggestive since experimental procedures varied widely. Nevertheless, a certain trend in data is apparent: *the length of the delay interval increases with the phylogenetic level of the organism.* Another general conclusion seems warranted as well. Hunter (1913) had observed that his rats could delay successfully only if they maintained bodily orientation toward the correct door; McCord (1939) increased the discriminability of the alternative cues and obtained longer delays; the capacity of both human children and adults to make delayed reactions is known to depend upon the character of the intervening activity. *The length of the delay interval varies with the nature of the interpolated activity.* We shall return to this point again (pp. 656–657).

A few pages later this writer again picks up the matter of delayed reaction and deals with it thus:

Animals can perform delayed reactions and double alternations successfully and they can learn through observation and insight; all these activities seem to share a dependence upon certain symbolic processes, termed "representative factors." Since the relevant cue is not present at the time the correct response is made, the animal must supply itself with some distinctive cue, some mode of representing what is lacking in the present external environment. The frontal lobes have been shown to play an important role in such performances—whether as the locus of mediation processes or merely as a facilitative agent is not yet clear. From introspective reports we are led to believe that the human animal stimulates himself with distinctive verbal cues in situations of this sort. By what process does the subhuman organism mediate between past and present experiences?

Overt motor orientation. A simple explanation, attributing little in the way of higher level capacities to subhuman species, is that the animal maintains an overt muscular "set" toward the relevant cue until the correct response can be made. Hunter (1913) believed that rats and dogs were limited to this level of performance. These animals "pointed" toward the light which flashed and held this motor orientation until released. Forcing them to change position resulted in failures. Although this is undoubtedly one method of bridging a temporal interval, it is clearly not the only possibility for an animal. Raccoons and preverbal children did not need to maintain a motor "set," and even the humble rat may be able to perform delayed reactions when their motor orientations are disturbed (Honzik, 1931). Furthermore, this explanation would not explain successes in double alternation, observational learning, and insightful problem-solving.

Implicit motor orientation. There is, of course, no reason why a mediating motor "set" should be either overt or obviously related to the goal-object in question. When the human adult thinks "it's behind the *third* door," the observer cannot see the response, and there is no essential relation between thinking "third" and the actual goal-place beyond the representing relation itself. The animal might conceivably maintain an increased tension in the muscles about the left eye after a light has flashed on that side, the stimulation from this response serving as the distinctive cue once the delay interval is over (cf. Hull's "pure-stimulus act," 1930b). Such a hypothesis, attractive, though it may be, is practically untestable. Where in the organism are we to look for the specific muscle system being used for mediation? In any case, what meager evidence exists is in the negative: Loucks (1931) administered a general anesthetic during the delay period and found his rat subjects still capable of successful delayed reactions.

Representation and retention. Is it actually necessary that any activity persist through the delay interval in order that successful mediation occur?

The only requirement is that some distinctive cue be given *at the time the correct response must be made*. If our human subject learns to say "it's behind the third door" at the time of original presentation, he does not need to keep repeating the phrase during the retention interval; all he must do in order to demonstrate a delayed reaction hours or even days later is to *recall* "it's behind the third door" when again brought into the test situation. Similarly, the rat does not have to maintain tension in the muscles about the left eye throughout the delay period; it merely has to "remember" to make this response at the time of release and thus provide itself with the distinctive cue. This interpretation clearly places "representative factors" on a continuum with ordinary retention. Are there any differences? There appear to be two salient ones: (1) Only a single trial is provided for original impression (except for whatever implicit repetitions are made by the organism during the interval). (2) The stimulus in the test situation is not identical with that during original learning (the relevant cue is missing). The latter difference between original and test situations is probably bridged through generalization (pp. 663–664).

That animals can, relatively successfully, make plans for future actions, where such plans are based upon *spatial* arrangements, seems clear from the foregoing evidence and discussion. They have, as Osgood puts it, fairly adequate representational or mediate processes by means of which prior spatial learning can be retained and reinstated. But here the matter seems to end. Yerkes, for example, working with chimpanzees, asked (in effect) this question: Can these organisms "make plans" where the execution of the intended (delayed) action is dependent upon *non*spatial cues? As the following discussion, quoted from Yerkes (1943), indicates, the answer appears to be No.

In each of four corners of a large room there was placed a small wooden box with hinged lid. The boxes were identical in size, shape, and surface texture, but they were painted white, black, red, and green respectively. The chimpanzee subject was tied to a post in the middle of the room equidistant from the boxes, while the experimenter ostentatiously put its breakfast into one of them and closed the lid. The animal was then taken away to its living quarters and during its absence the boxes were interchanged. After a definite interval the animal was brought back and from its central position in the room given opportunity to choose from among the boxes the one in which the food had been hidden and to approach it, and in case of correct choice take the food. Under the circumstances, successful choice seemingly must depend on memory for the visual appearance of the box. With a short period of delay, say five minutes, between seeing the food concealed and opportunity to try to locate it, this problem would seem to us very simple and we should naturally suppose that the hungry ape would rarely miss its breakfast. Normal human subjects ordinarily would find such a test easy to meet successfully. What actually happened in the experiment is more than surprising; it is indicative of a highly significant perceptual characteristic of the chimpanzee.

Actually when a subject responded in the four-box situation it chose, irrespective of color, the box which happened to be in the corner where the food had been concealed, and despite the severe penalty of missing breakfast, this same type of incorrect response tended to persist and might be repeated several times in succession, with increasing emotional disturbance, violence of protest, and either prolonged delay for a comparison of the boxes prior to choice or refusal to make a choice. I recall instances in which a subject, having opened the box which was in the position where it had seen the food placed, searched thoroughly within and without the box as if unwilling to trust its senses, and then, throwing itself on the empty box, cried piteously.

That in this experiment the dominance of the spatial factor was amazingly strong is evident, but one may suspect that the subject either was unable to distinguish the boxes by their color or, finding it very difficult to do so, made its choice on the basis of position or location in the room (pp. 104–105).

In the passage already quoted from Osgood, reference is made to the fact that the capacity to hold a response "in suspension," for a delay period after the cue stimulus has been given and has disappeared, appears to be specifically related to the functioning of that part of the brain known as the frontal lobes. This is inferred from two sources of evidence: (1) as one ascends the evolutionary scale one finds (a) progressive development of this capacity and (b) elaboration of the frontal lobes; and (2) surgical assault upon the frontal lobes typically impairs this capacity. The results of an experiment by Lawicka (1957b) are typical. In a large rectangular room, a dog would be tethered on one side and three food trays fanned out in front of him, some feet away. A light would be flashed or a buzzer sounded near one of the trays (the baited one); and, after a delay, the dog would be released. If it immediately went to the correct tray, the presumption was that it had in some way held that tray "in mind" during the delay period. Normal (unoperated) dogs were able, under these conditions, to respond correctly after delays of as much as 10 minutes. During the delays they did not have to maintain a fixed bodily orientation; they were not disturbed by intervening stimulation of various kinds; and they could even be briefly removed from the experimental situation without impairing their ability, when released, to make the correct choice.

The dogs [with prefrontal lesions] differed strikingly in the performance of any of the above tests.

1). They were unable to choose the correct foodtray even after a delay of several minutes, but they did so only if during the whole delay period the orientation of their body towards this foodtray had not been changed.

2). If during the delay period they changed their posture for one reason or another, they would go to the foodtray towards which they had been oriented when released.

3). All extraneous stimuli sufficiently strong to orient the animals in another direction disturbed the right delayed response.

4). The prefrontal dogs were unable to make a correct choice when moved away from the starting place (p. 108).

Here is a clear indication that the central processes involved in delayed reaction are mediated by the frontal lobes and that, when they are disconnected, the dog is limited to a much more primitive and less efficient peripheral mechanism, involving posture fixation.

Thought, like love, is a "many-splendored thing"; and there is no guarantee, because one form thereof is associated with a particular part of the brain, that all its forms are also thus localized. But, in general, there is a tendency for the more complex psychological operations to be mediated by the most recently evolved parts of the nervous system, the correlation just reviewed being typical of many others.

VII. Insight or "Putting Things Together"

Insight, as the experience of having ideas suddenly "click into place," is familiar to everyone. Yet psychologists have had difficulty deciding how to classify and explain it. The Gestalt school has attempted to make insight a substitute for learning, holding that solutions to problems are really arrived at suddenly, if at all, and that the progressive, little-by-little nature of learning is an illusion. This position, as ongoing research and theory construction have pretty conclusively shown, is too sweeping in its implications. On the other hand, learning theorists of the stimulus-response camp have been reluctant to recognize insight as in any way unique or distinctive and have tried to derive the cited instances from simple S—R principles (see, for example, N. E. Miller on the problem of mediation, Chapter 2).

Pending a more definite settlement of this issue, one may tentatively adopt the position that insight and learning are different, even antithetical (cf. Maier, 1931; Hilgard, 1956, p. 6). As suggested previously (Mowrer, 1950), learning may be regarded as essentially an *inductive* (experiential) process, whereas insight is more *deductive* (logical) in character.

In its simplest form, deduction is nothing but an instance of the individual's deciding, "This is a case of that." Thus, in the familiar syllogism previously referred to, if we know that "All men are mortal," as soon as we decide or discover that "Socrates is a man," we immediately know that "Socrates is mortal." Socrates may be an entirely new experience to us, as such, but as soon as we can *classify* him, as soon as we can relate him to other members of a category with which we *have* had experience, we can then bring our past learning to bear upon him and properly feel that, in some measure, we "know" him too—and what expectations we may properly have with respect to him. Obviously, this may save us a lot of time and trouble over what would be involved if we had to start fresh with every new organism or situation we encounter (p. 335).[6]

It is, however, perhaps not quite fair to equate insight to logical deduction, especially in view of the harsh things that have often been said of the latter and the obvious importance and refreshing quality of the former. Let us, for example, listen to Bertrand Russell:

> [Deductive] inference is supposed to be a mark of intelligence and to show the superiority of men to machines. At the same time, the treatment of inference in traditional logic is so stupid as to throw doubt on this claim, and syllogistic inference, which was taken as the type from Aristotle to Bacon (exclusive), is just the sort of thing that a calculating machine could do better than a professor. . . . I have never come across any . . . case of new knowledge obtained by means of a syllogism. It must be admitted that, for a method which dominated logic for two thousand years, this contribution to the world's stock of information cannot be considered very weighty.
>
> The inferences that we actually make [inductively] in daily life differ from those of syllogistic logic in two respects, namely, that they are important and precarious, instead of being trivial and safe [see Chapter 9]. The syllogism may be regarded as a monument to academic timidity: if an inference might be wrong, it was dangerous to draw it. So the mediaeval monks, in their thinking as in their lives, sought safety at the expense of fertility (1927, pp. 79–80).

In what sense, then, is insight more truly exciting and significant? The early but never surpassed observations of Köhler (1927) provide many dramatic instances, of which we select a classic example. Sultan, a young chimpanzee, is in a large enclosure separated by bars from an adjacent area. In the latter the experimenter places a banana, just out of reach, through the bars, by means of either of the two sticks with which the ape has been provided. Says Köhler:

> His sticks are two hollow, but firm, bamboo rods, such as the animals often use for pulling along fruit. The one is so much smaller than the other, that it can be pushed in at either end of the other quite easily. Beyond the bars lies the objective, just so far away that the animal cannot reach it with either rod. They are about the same length. Nevertheless, he takes great pains to try to reach it with one stick or the other, even pushing his right shoulder through the bars. When everything proves futile, Sultan commits a "bad error," or, more clearly, a great stupidity, such as he made

---

[6] For discussion of the role of labeling or classifying in concept formation and mediation, see Mowrer (1960, Chapter 12) and Chapter 2 of this book; also Section VIII of this chapter.

sometimes on other occasions. He pulls a box from the back of the room towards the bars; true, he pushes it away again at once as it is useless, or rather actually in the way. Immediately afterwards, he does something which, although practically useless, must be counted among the "good errors": he pushes one of the sticks out as far as it will go, then takes the second, and with it pokes the first one cautiously towards the objective, pushing it carefully from the nearer end and thus slowly urging it towards the fruit. This does not always succeed, but if he has got pretty close in this way, he takes even greater precaution; he pushes very gently, watches the movements of the stick that is lying on the ground, and actually touches the objective with its tip. Thus, all of a sudden, for the first time, the contact "animal-objective" has been established, and *Sultan visibly feels* (we humans can sympathize) *a certain satisfaction* in having even so much power over the fruit that he can touch and slightly move it by pushing the stick. The proceeding is repeated; when the animal has pushed the stick on the ground so far out that he cannot possibly get it back by himself, it is given back to him. But although, in trying to steer it cautiously, he puts the stick in his hand exactly to the cut (i.e., the opening) of the stick on the ground, and although one might think that doing so would suggest the possibility of pushing one stick into the other, there is no indication whatever of such a practically valuable solution. Finally, the observer gives the animal some help by putting one finger into the opening of the stick under the animal's nose (without pointing to the other stick at all). This has no effect; Sultan, as before, pushes one stick with the other towards the objective, and as this pseudo-solution *does not satisfy him any longer*, he abandons his efforts altogether, and does not even pick up the sticks when they are both again thrown through the bars to him. The experiment has lasted over an hour, and is stopped for the present, as it seems hopeless, carried out like this. As we intend to take it up again after a while, Sultan is left in possession of his sticks; the keeper is left there to watch him.

Keeper's report: "Sultan first of all squats indifferently on the box, which has been left standing a little back from the railings; then he gets up, picks up the two sticks, sits down again on the box and plays carelessly with them. While doing this, it happens that he finds himself holding one rod in either hand in such a way that they lie in a straight line; he pushes the thinner one a little way into the opening of the thicker, jumps up and is already on the run towards the railings, to which he has up to now half turned his back, and begins to draw a banana towards him with the double stick. I call the master: meanwhile, one of the animal's rods has fallen out of the other, as he has pushed one of them only a little way into the other; whereupon he connects them again."

The keeper's report covers a period of scarcely five minutes, which had elapsed since stopping the experiment. Called by the man, I continued observation myself: Sultan is squatting at the bars, holding out one stick, and, at its end, a second bigger one, which is on the point of falling off. It does fall. Sultan pulls it to him and forthwith, *with the greatest assurance*, pushes the thinner one in again, so that it is firmly wedged, and fetches a fruit with the lengthened implement. But the bigger tube selected is a little too big, and so it slips from the end of the thinner one several times; each time

Sultan rejoins the tubes immediately by holding the bigger one towards himself in the left and the thinner one in his right hand and a little backwards, and then sliding one into the other [Fig. 6–2]. The proceeding *seems to please him immensely;* he is very lively, pulls all the fruit, one after the other, towards the railings, without taking time to eat it, and when I disconnect the double-stick he puts it together again at once, and draws any distant objects whatever to the bars (pp. 125–128; italics added).

Fig. 6–2. The ape, Sultan, making a double-stick (Köhler, 1927, opposite p. 128).

As we look back over this graphic description, what "insights" suggest themselves concerning *insight?* What, more precisely, *is* it? Sultan clearly wanted a longer stick. If he had had a longer one, he would undoubtedly, in the course of variable behavior, have used it. But the fact was that he had only two *short* sticks. Neither alone could enable him to solve the problem; and so eventually, as Köhler says, the subject gave up "for the present" and reverted to playing "carelessly with them." Now where, exactly, did the insight take place? Did Sultan suddenly "have the idea," or "realize," that he could *make* a longer stick by joining the two short ones together? "It happens," says the keeper, "that he finds himself holding one rod in either hand in such a way that they lie in a straight line; he pushes the thinner one a little way into the opening of the thicker. . . ." Thus far it does not sound as if the ape has had any great Ah-Haa! experience. It was not that he was sitting quietly "thinking" and suddenly jumped up and ran to the sticks and picked them up and confidently joined them. No, he was playing with them *carelessly* and inserted one into the other only *a little way*. Up to this point, Sultan's behavior seems to have been characterized by the vagueness and variability of bafflement. But then, suddenly, something happened and Sultan "is already on the run towards the railings . . . and begins to draw the banana toward him with the double stick." The *in*sight was apparently largely a matter of *sight:* suddenly the ape *saw* that he, in fact, *had* a long stick (cf. Hilgard, 1956, p. 226). This fact now completely altered the situation, from "hopeless" (Köhler's own term) to *hopeful,* and released the banana-seeking behavior again.

If we are to make further progress with this analysis, the time has now obviously come to note that there are two levels of need, drive, or "problem" involved here: one, the primary need for food and the *derived* need for a long stick. That the ape was enormously pleased at finding himself (unexpectedly?) in possession of a long stick seems clear. Therefore the stimuli associated with the more or less random, accidental joining of the sticks must, per theory, have taken on strong secondary-reinforcing potency, with an ensuing tendency to repeat this action: "Each time Sultan rejoins the tubes immediately by holding the bigger one towards himself in the left and the thinner one in his right hand and a little backwards, and then sliding one into the other. The proceeding seems to *please him immensely*." No banana yet, just stick! No hunger reduction, just relief: "*Now* I can get the banana!"

That sudden "insight" often involves sudden, secondary, *reward* is suggested by an experiment carried out some years ago by two of the writer's students, Dorothy Kunberger and Kaya Kardash (Mowrer, 1950, Chapter 11). Hungry rats, placed in an oblong compartment, found that whenever a tone sounded, a pellet of food would appear in the food box located at the left end of the compartment. As soon as the rats had reached the point that they would immediately run to the food trough upon hearing the tone, they were divided into two subgroups. A small brass bar was made available at the *right* end of the apparatus, approximately 30 inches from the food trough. Depression of the bar would, in any case, now cause a pellet of food to roll (noise-lessly) into the food trough; but the procedure followed with the two subgroups of subjects differed in that, with one group (experimental), whenever the bar was pushed it would cause the tone to sound (as well as deliver food into the trough), while with the other (control) group, bar depression produced food but *no* tone.

Under these circumstances the control-group rats failed to acquire the bar-pressing "habit." In the course of their exploratory wanderings, they would occasionally push the bar and cause the food to roll into the trough; but such a long interval would usually elapse before they got back to the trough that they would not "see the connection," be-tween bar pressing and food delivery. What got reinforced, instead, were the responses *last made* before finding food in trough, which in-cluded approaching the trough and certain irrelevant bits of behavior.

By contrast the animals in the experimental group learned to press the bar as a means of obtaining food, very rapidly. The *instant* they pressed the bar they experienced the secondary reinforcement pro-vided by the tone, so that the tendency to press the bar was in this way strengthened; and, more than this, the hearing of the tone also released, or cued off, the response of running to the food trough and thus also receiving, relatively quickly, primary reinforcement from the food itself.

It will be immediately clear that this was a situation in which the temporal interval between an instrumental response and a delayed pri-mary reward was "bridged" by means of a secondary reinforcer (cf. Mowrer, 1960, Chapter 10). But what, one may ask, does all this have to do with "insight"? The parallels to the case of Sultan and the sticks are not uninstructive. Suppose that Sultan had been incapable of experi-encing any secondary reinforcement upon first (randomly) joining the sticks? How long would it have been, one wonders, before he would have found that the compound stick would reach the banana? Then and only then would Sultan have been primarily rewarded for putting the sticks together; and so many other actions would probably have intervened that *they*, rather than the stick-joining, would have been strengthened. After a great deal of further experience in the situation, Sultan might eventually have learned, on the basis of primary reinforcement alone, how to fit the sticks together and then get the banana; but the chances of success are obviously much better if there can be an immediate secondary reward for this action.[7] The analogy

[7] A consideration which has thus far been merely implied should now be made explicit: namely the *source* of the secondary reinforcement in the Sultan experi-

to pressing the bar and getting or not getting the tone in the Kunberger-Kardash experiment will be obvious.

Prior to 1925, stimulus-response learning theorists, if they spoke of drive and drive reduction at all, spoke only of primary drives, such as hunger and thirst. Köhler saw that Sultan was rewarded ("pleased") well before he got the banana and realized the inadequacy of S—R theory (as then conceived) to explain what he so clearly witnessed. Whether Professor Köhler would today accept the notion of immediate secondary reinforcement as satisfactorily accounting for Sultan's behavior or would still insist upon invoking "insight" in some more abstruse form is not certain. But this much is clear: as S—R learning theory has become more and more fully elaborated, Gestalt psychology has lost much of its peculiar cogency and appeal. As indicated both here and repeatedly in other parts of this volume (see, for example, Chapter 2) and in the companion volume (see, for example, Chapter 9), we seem to be moving, at last, toward a truly unified conceptual scheme.

VIII. Rudimentary Reasoning and Concept Formation

As will already be apparent to the reader, terminology concerning the "higher mental processes" is not very exact. Certainly "thought," "insight," and "reasoning" have common features and overlap in their meanings. It is therefore not surprising to find that the use of one rather than another of these terms in a particular context is often more dependent upon historical accident than logic. VTE has been called "overt thinking." The behavior of Köhler's ape, Sultan, has been termed "insight." And certain other experiments have been said to show *reasoning* in primitive form, although the terms "thought" and "insight" would seem, perhaps, equally applicable.

Beginning in 1929, Maier has published a long series of ingenious experiments with rats which he has interpreted as showing "reasoning." However, because of somewhat greater simplicity, we shall consider here a similar type of experiment reported by Tolman in 1932. With admirable clarity, Garrett (1955) has summarized this experiment as follows:

---

ment. It has already been noted that Sultan was pleased when he found he had, in fact, *made* a longer stick. This could only have occurred, presumably, as a result of prior experience with such a stick. Or at any rate he knew he *needed* a longer stick; and when he found he *had* one, this may be assumed to have provided the immediate, secondary reinforcement—and the "insight" that he had done the right thing in putting the sticks together.

Some psychologists believe that reasoning can be inferred when animals solve problems which demand the ability to see relations, combine past experiences in new ways, and make generalizations from observations. [Fig. 6–3] illustrates a maze used in the study of reasoning in the white rat.

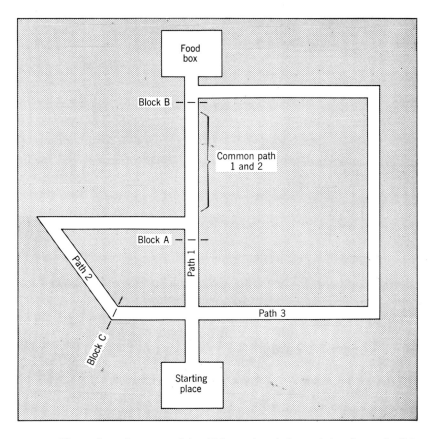

Fig. 6–3. Floor plan of maze used by Tolman (1932) in studying "reasoning" in rats (from Garrett, 1955).

There are three pathways from the starting point in the maze to the food box. Path 1 is the shortest and most direct, path 2 is somewhat longer than 1 (because of the detour), and path 3 is the longest. Note that paths 1 and 2 have a *common section* not traversed by path 3. In preliminary training, path 1 is blocked at A, and the rats must learn to retrace path 1 and take path 2. When 2 is also blocked at C, the rats must take path 3. In the final tests (after training), paths 1 and 2 are blocked at B, just below their common section. Nearly all of the rats, finding path 1 blocked in the final tests, retraced their course and took path 3, not path 2. This result led the experimenter to conclude that since path 2 had been preferred to path 3 previously, the rats had "inferred" that B blocked the common path. Expressed differently, the rats had "put two and two together" and come out with four; that is, had "figured out" the right answer.

Animals can learn many complex tasks which require the sensible organization of elements in such a way as to reach a correct solution. But since animals do not possess language, it seems unlikely that they employ verbal symbols or set up hypotheses in the way human beings do. Although reasoning does not always have to be carried on by means of symbols such as words, numbers, and maps, the solution of many problems, especially those in mathematics, is virtually impossible unless acceptance and rejection of alternatives can be expressed in symbols (pp. 418–419).

The expression, "putting two and two together," is obviously used here in such a way as to mean something rather different from "putting things together" in the way exemplified by Sultan. In that experiment there was a literal putting together of things, two physical things. In the experiment just cited,[8] what are the "two" and "two" which are said to be related? By the use of a syllogism the question can be answered very nicely:

Path 1 and path 2 have a common segment.
Path 1 is blocked in the region of this segment.
Therefore path 2 is blocked.

But how, precisely, does a *rat* make such an inference? As Garrett points out, animals do not possess language and hence cannot set up propositions of the kind involved in the foregoing syllogism. Yet, in practice, rats seem to have some equivalent, nonverbal means of coping with a situation of this sort. And, in fact, it is not at all difficult to derive an explanation of this phenomenon from formal theory, though we cannot be sure that such a derivation is very similar to what happens in terms of the rat's own view of the matter. Briefly, path 1 and path 2 are *more alike,* by virtue of the rather long common segment, than are paths 1 and 3 or paths 2 and 3 (where there is also a common segment but it is extremely short). Hence, if, as a result of encountering a barrier at B, the rats develop a negative "attitude" toward path 1, this attitude (emotion, meaning) will generalize more strongly to path 2 than to path 3.[9]

---

[8] For other experiments of a related kind, where the attempt to demonstrate "reasoning" has not always been successful, see Crannell (1940), Dove & Thompson (1943), Keller & Hill (1936), Kuo (1937), Evans (1936).

[9] At several earlier points in this chapter, as well as in the above paragraph, the reader will no doubt have sensed a relationship between the phenomena presently under discussion and the concept of *mediation,* as developed in Chapter 2. There it was concluded that, in the final analysis, mediation involves a form of *transfer*

A possible check on the foregoing interpretation could be carried out as follows. Suppose, again, that there are three routes to a common goal, but that now the communality consists of the *color* of the pathways rather than identical segments. Two of the paths, let us say the middle one and the one at the left, are *black*, while the third path, the one at the right, is *white*. Now block the middle (black) path; if *our* "reasoning" is correct, rats will be more likely to resort to the white path than to the other black one, although both are equally open and accessible physically.

If "reasoning" of the kind just described is dependent upon generalization, then we should examine *concept formation* in the same context; for it, too, seems to be related to generalization in a special way.[10] Here again we quote from Garrett:

Experiments (Goldstein, 1939) have shown that a person who has suffered brain injury may lose the capacity to think in abstracted terms, even when his ability to take a "concrete attitude"—one controlled by immediate sense impression—is unimpaired. Suppose that objects of different form, color, material, or use are presented to a subject who is told to "put together those things that belong together." The subject's method of classifying reveals whether he is employing concrete or abstract concepts. Grouping on the basis of form or color (using a general category) is taken to indicate an abstract attitude—that is, the use of an abstract concept. If, on the other hand, the subject groups only identical or nearly identical objects, or those that belong together by virtue of some *specific* use, his attitude is "concrete." To illustrate, a subject takes the abstract attitude when, for example, he puts into the one category of "tools," hammers, screw drivers, saws, and nails of different size and shape. The subject takes the concrete attitude if he selects one hammer and one nail, stating that one hammer is enough to drive one nail. Again, the attitude is abstract when pipe, cigar, matches, and ashtray are all classified under smoking materials; it is concrete when the subject selects one cigar and one match on the grounds that after dinner one match is enough to light one cigar.

The test blocks shown [in Fig. 6–4] have been widely used in the experimental study of concept formation. This test (E. Hanfmann & J. Kasanin, 1937) consists of twenty-two blocks in five colors, six shapes, two heights (tall and flat), and two sizes (large and small). On the hidden underside of each block is printed a three-letter nonsense syllable which serves to define a block type. All *lag* blocks are tall and large; all *mur* blocks tall and

---

or *generalization*. Such generalization is manifestly involved in the above example of "reasoning." For an excellent discussion of and review of the literature relevant to "mediational processes" in relation to reasoning and problem solving in general, with special reference to the role of *verbal* factors, see Cofer (1957).

[10] The reader may wish to relate the following discussion to the notion, developed in Chapter 4, that the sentence can be thought of as a *reclassification device*.

small; all *bik* blocks flat and large; and all *cev* blocks flat and small. Color and shape are irrelevant as far as classification is concerned and are really distractors, size and height being the important variables. The examinee is told that there are *four* kinds of blocks and that he is to find the four kinds and put them together. As a starter he is given one block of a kind (a *lag*, for instance), and is told to sort out all of those blocks which belong with it.

Fig. 6–4. Hanfmann blocks, designed for the investigation of concept formation (reproduced through courtesy of the C. H. Stoelting Co.).

The subject is free to proceed as he pleases, except that he is not allowed to invert a block or read its name. After a sorting in which perhaps all blocks of the same color or shape have been grouped, the experimenter points out one wrongly selected block and tells the subject to try again. The test continues, with the same directions for the other three types, until all four classifications have been made correctly. The experimenter seeks to determine whether the subject has used a logical hypothesis (all *lag* blocks are tall) or has followed a trial-and-error or guessing procedure. Like the tasks described above, the object is to discover how quickly the subject is able to detect the basis of classification—that is, whether he can grasp an abstract concept. Young children and low-grade adults, as well as patients suffering from mental disease (for example, schizophrenia) or brain injury, usually take the concrete attitude: each block is treated as a separate stimulus-object, and there is an inability to generalize or to group in terms of abstract quality (pp. 421–423).

What then, more precisely, *is* concept formation? We are told in the quotation that, in the Hanfmann test, *color* and *shape* are not admissible as bases for classifying the blocks. Surely these are the most obvious, most concrete dimensions in which the blocks vary; but they are ruled out, for the very reason that they are so obvious. Here a category, or class, or "concept" depends upon quite *simple* forms of "similarity." Color and form are *immediately* discernible and do not require much in the way of "thought" or "abstraction." On the other hand, in classifying the blocks in the four required ways, as large-tall, small-tall, large-flat, and small-flat, the subject has to generalize or classify on the basis of characteristics which are not so immediately apparent or common. Thus there is a tendency to speak of concept *formation*, for the reason that the generalization has to be *made*, as a result of some sort of psychological activity. In Chapter 12 of *Learning Theory and Behavior* we have examined the phenomenon of *sensory* generalization; in so-called concept formation, we are dealing instead with generalization which is more subtle, not so simple or immediately evident. As previously noted, sensory generalization seems to occur on the basis of some largely innate mechanism; "concept formation," by contrast, is harder to come by, takes more "gray matter." Here capacity to *use symbols* seems crucial. If one could not *say* "Large and tall," "Large and flat," etc., it seems unlikely that he could *see* the four "classes" of blocks which the test calls for. Here generalization and classification depend not so much upon the properties of the objects themselves as upon the *symbols* applied to them. If there are certain objects to which one can say, "Large and tall," then they become "alike" even though differing radically in other respects, notably color and shape. Hence we emerge with the deduction that so-called concept formation is really a matter of *mediated*, rather than "immediate," generalization. What this means is that instead of making the over-all judgment of like or unlike on the basis of *direct* sense impressions (i.e., sensory generalization or "classification"), the subject applies certain *verbal* terms to the blocks and then makes the classification on the basis of *their* similarity (or difference; see Dollard & Miller, 1950).

Although there is much more to reasoning and concept formation than indicated in this section (see, for example, Brunner, Goodnow, & Austin, 1956; Miller & Murphy, 1956b), enough has been said to show how even these more complex psychological phenomena are analyzable in terms of principles developed in connection with the study of simpler phenomenon. These principles are thus seen to have generality and power.

IX. Mathematical Reasoning and the Transposition Experiment

It had been the writer's original intention not to make any systematic reference in this book to the subject of mathematics. But now (as the book goes to press) it seems desirable to alter this plan and to deal with this topic in at least a preliminary way. As Chapters 3 and 4 indicate, we today have a very respectable psychology of language which stems directly from basic learning principles. In Chapter 5 the psychology of meaning has been examined; and in Chapter 2, we have also rather intensively studied the phenomenon of mediation. With this background, plus the material on insight and reasoning which have been reviewed in this chapter, it would seem natural to venture at least a little way into what may be called the *psychology of mathematics*. Moreover, it has been the writer's privilege in recent months to be associated, in a peripheral way, with the work of the Committee on School Mathematics, at the University of Illinois, and from this a number of new interests and hypotheses have emerged. But it should be re-emphasized that what is said in this section is indeed preliminary and will leave many challenging questions quite untouched.

In the section on "Mediated Discrimination or Distinctiveness" in Chapter 2 of this volume, we have already seen how successfully Dollard and Miller (1950) have used the concept of response mediation to explain the dramatic improvement in discrimination of multitude (and, in so-called measurement, or magnitude) which *counting* makes possible. And there are many further applications of basic learning principles which are fairly begging to be made to other aspects of what today is, rather happily, being called "number behavior." But these are not our immediate concern. Instead, we wish to proceed directly to some more intricate instances of number behavior which are particularly pertinent in a chapter such as the present one and which have the additional virtue of providing the occasion for at least brief allusion to a phenomenon, namely that of "transposition," which is not otherwise considered in this work.

How, then, to start? Perhaps the best way is to imagine Professor Max Beberman teaching a group of twelve-year-old boys and girls in one of his famous demonstration classes in mathematics. On this particular morning he begins by asking the class to tell him at least two numbers which will "factor," or divide into, the total for the expression, $(4 \times 29) + (3 \times 29)$. The children are encouraged to look for some "easy way" of finding the answer, instead of using pencil and paper. Various numbers are suggested by the class, and there is general discussion as to which ones are correct; but the instructor "plays dumb" and seems somewhat unsure about it all. A few of the children think that 7 and 29 are the two correct numbers, but the rest of the class is uncertain and at a loss to know how these numbers were arrived at.

Dr. Beberman then gives the following series of "*similar*" problems:

$$(1 \times 5) + (2 \times 5)$$
$$(2 \times 7) + (3 \times 7)$$
$$(2 \times 13) + (1 \times 13)$$
$$(3 \times 11) + (2 \times 11)$$
$$(3 \times 41) + (8 \times 41)$$
$$(11 \times 31) + (2 \times 31)$$
$$(9 \times 43) + (2 \times 43)$$

By this time nearly all the class is able to give the two correct numbers for each new "problem," and the instructor asks them to "make up" other examples, for themselves. He does not tell them any "rule" and the students are admonished not to announce any rule or "general principle" to each other. By merely looking at example after example, they begin to "*see* what to do." [11]

Obviously what is going on here, behaviorally, is a little complex; but there is at least an analogue to be found in a well known type of experiment, commonly carried out with animals but sometimes also with very small children. For our purposes a particularly illuminating example of this type of research is Margaret R. Kuenne's (1946) study on "The Relation of Language to Transposition Behavior in Young Children." Her report begins thus:

The phenomenon of transposition in the discrimination behavior of animals and young children has received a considerable amount of attention from psychological theorists. The Gestalt psychologists, in particular, have made much of this ability of Ss to transfer a learned differential response, e.g., a response to the larger of two stimuli, to a new combination of stimulus objects differing in the same property (e.g., size), and they have cited it as conclusive evidence that the response was to the relative properties of the stimulus situation (p. 471).

[11] For further discussion of this type of classroom activity, see Unit 1 of the Teachers' Edition of *High School Mathematics* (Beberman, Vaughn, *et al.*, 1959). Here we need only say that such activity is not aimed merely at providing "shortcuts" for certain types of computation; it helps lay a basis for the use of algebraic notation, set theory, and other important mathematical devices, as well as a lively set of attitudes toward mathematical activities in general (see end of this section).

Then, after a review of the most directly relevant literature, this author states the specific problem she proposes to investigate as follows:

As a basis for an attempt to extend our understanding of discrimination behavior and the phenomenon of transposition in human *Ss, the working hypothesis is here adopted that the mechanisms assumed by Spence* [1937; see also Hilgard & Marquis, 1940, pp. 188–194] *to underlie this behavior in animals are also operative in the young child, and that with the development in older children of the capacity to employ verbal responses in such behavior situations, a shift occurs to the verbal type of control* (p. 474).

The experimental procedure involved, first of all, allowing 44 children with mental ages ranging from three to six years to work to obtain a succession of small toys from one or the other of two adjacent boxes, which could be rendered distinctive by placement of a square, white board (with a surface of 68.0 sq. in.) on top of one box, with a similar though smaller board (37.8 sq. in.) on the other one. The smaller of the two squares was the positive cue, indicating the box in which the toy, on any given trial, was to be found. The box with the negative cue was locked. As in a Lashley-type discrimination apparatus (used with rats), the positive and negative cues were randomly alternated with respect to the two (otherwise identical) boxes.

The subjects were then divided into two matched groups and, after the training just described, were "tested in counter-balanced order . . . with two pairs of still smaller stimuli (21.0 vs. 37.8 sq. in., and 2.0 vs. 3.6 sq. in.). All spontaneous verbalizations of the size aspect of the stimuli were recorded throughout the experiment, and attempts were made at the conclusion, through questioning, to elicit verbalization of the general principle of solution" (pp. 488–489). What the investigator wished to see was whether the children, when given pairs of cues smaller than the original pair, would respond to the larger of the smaller pair, because it was more nearly the absolute size of the original positive (smaller) cue, or would react to the cues *relatively*, i.e., to the *smaller* one of the pair, no matter what their absolute size might be.

Analysis of the results revealed a highly significant relationship between mental age and the occurrence of far transposition [involving the 2.0–3.6 cues], and a low relationship between mental age and near transposition [the 21.0–37.8 cues]. The median number of responses on the far transposition test increased with age from 50 per cent at mental age three years to 100 per cent at six years. The corresponding value for the near transposition test was 90 per cent or above at all four age levels (p. 489).

In other words, all the older children did about equally well in "transposing," i.e., were equally successful with both near and far transpositions, whereas the younger children did decidedly better at transposing with the 21.0–37.8 cues than with the 2.0–3.6 cues. Since verbal development was further advanced in the older children than in the younger ones, the original hypothesis was thus upheld: "with the development in older children of the capacity to employ verbal responses in such behavior situations, a shift occurs to the verbal type of control." From other studies it is known that infrahuman subjects transpose much more easily when the test cues are similar to the original cues than when the test cues are very different. Therefore, the performance of the small children in Kuenne's experiment was quite similar to that of animals, whereas the older children—presumably because of their superior command of language—were equally proficient in *both* types of test.

At this point, many intriguing thoughts suggest themselves, only a few of which will be explored here. It may be that animals and small children "transpose" successfully when the two cues are only slightly different from the original pair, in absolute terms, because the subjects do not perceive them as really "different." In other words, the apparent transfer or generalization of the original discrimination training may occur so well because the subjects have no very clear way of remembering or conceptualizing (symbolizing) the absolute size of the stimulus objects (cf. the problem of "absolute-pitch discrimination" in music), and hence do not perceive the test cues as different from the original cues. But when the difference is flagrant, it becomes impossible for them to ignore the absolute difference, and subjects must then truly "transpose," or else make serious errors of some sort. Subjects who can say, "Oh, I know; it's the *smaller* one that's correct" (or something equivalent) would seem to have crucial advantage over those who cannot so verbalize. In other words, they can now "transpose" or generalize much more widely, because a mediating response ("it's the *smaller* one") helps make the positive test stimulus now "*more like*" the positive training stimulus (despite their "objective" difference), than they would be to "direct perception." That is to say, the verbal mediator, or concept of "smaller-ness," now provides the cue and tells the subject "what to do" (cf. Weir & Stevenson, 1959).

With the transposition paradigm before us, we can now advantageously return to the classroom example. Success with this type of problem clearly involves a sort of "transposition," i.e., the finding of *a kind of "similarity"* between the various "examples" which does not depend upon the *size* of the specific numerical values involved. Students must see, for one thing, that all the numbers involved in the answers are "primes" (capable of being divided only by themselves or by one); and they must also see that one number is common to both pairs of numbers in the examples. Then, eventually, they see that "7 and 29" is the answer to the problem which was first presented because 29 is the common number and 4 and 3 make 7, i.e., seven 29's. And seven 29's (one doesn't need to know what it comes to otherwise) *must* be divisible by both 29 and 7, and by no smaller numbers.

In order to solve an ordinary transposition problem successfully (at least where a "big" transposition is called for), the subject must, apparently, have or be able quickly to form the *concept* of larger-smaller and then to note that all stimulus pairs are alike in that one is larger, the other smaller—and that, in the experiment described, it is *always the smaller* that is the correct cue.

This analysis is obviously rough, but it suggests a rather broad continuity between "mathematical reasoning" and basic learning principles: a "discrimination" generalizes more widely if there is a mediator (common element) which the subject can introduce in going from the original training situation to the test situation, wherein the "specific elements" are different. In other words, once you "get the principle" or "find the rule," i.e., find the common element or mediator, the solution (transposition, or transfer, of the "correct answer") becomes easy.

There is, at the moment, a lively controversy going on between mathematicians, or at least mathematics teachers, in the area under consideration. The traditional assumption has been that, in keeping with the experimental findings of Kuenne, the capacity to verbalize or articulate "the rule" (i.e., find the common element, get the mediator) is not only helpful but essential in the development of mathematical skill and competence. Hendrix (1947, 1950), on the other hand, has stressed the importance of "nonverbal awareness"; and Haslerud & Meyers (1958) have published what appears to be experimental support. Verbalization, or formalization—particularly if it "comes too soon" (a phrase which, of course, somewhat begs the question)—is thus regarded as a hindrance rather than an asset.

Although it is much too early to be confident on this score, the present writer is inclined to the view that the point of the method employed by Beberman (and by a number of other investigators using somewhat similar approaches) hinges not so much upon the occurrence or nonoccurrence in the student of verbalization as upon certain simple, but often overlooked, *motivational factors*. Certainly in terms of excitement and adventure, there is no comparison between a method which typically involves giving students a formal rule and then requiring them to "apply it" in the solution of routine exercises and a situation in which they are first confronted with the "examples" and encouraged (almost "dared") to develop, or discover, "the rule" themselves. The amount of secondary reinforcement experienced in the second situation, other factors being anything like equal, would intuitively seem very much greater and the chance of spontaneous rehearsal and perseveration of "mathematical thinking" would seem enormously enhanced.

But, again, it should be stressed that the foregoing discussion is included here, not as necessarily providing final answers, but more as a means of showing that there *is* common ground ("mediators"?) between basic learning principles and "number behavior." It is the writer's prediction that in the years immediately ahead notable progress will be made in this general area, comparable to or perhaps even exceeding what we have already been able to point to with respect to the psychological analysis of word learning and sentence function (cf. Newell, Shaw, & Simon, 1958b; Wertheimer, 1959).

X. Other Approaches to the Psychology of Thought

Because scholars have long been interested in the psychology of thought, there is naturally an imposing literature on the subject; and if no cognizance were taken of it, the present treatment could justly be regarded as narrow and provincial. Actually, some narrowness can be defended. Here it is not our purpose to write a general treatise on the nature of thought or even to deal exhaustively with the relationship between thought and learning. Rather are we concerned, primarily and specifically, with what revised two-factor learning theory has to suggest concerning this particular topic. That assignment having been completed, albeit sketchily, at least a token attempt should be made to put this chapter into context as far as the more conventional literature on the subject is concerned.

In his *Principles of Psychology* (1890), William James included a chapter on "The Stream of Thought" which has been widely read and very influential. Having in preceding chapters presented a point of view (largely derived from physiology) which foreshadowed Behaviorism, James introduces his discussion of thought thus:

We now begin our study of the mind from within. . . . I use the word thinking, in accordance with what was said [earlier], for every form of consciousness indiscriminately. If we could say in English "it thinks," as we say "it rains" or "it blows," we should be stating the fact most simply and with the minimum of assumption. As we cannot, we must simply say that *thought goes on* (pp. 224–225).

So far so good, says the modern reader; but then we find that the chapter is going to be divided into five parts dealing with the following propositions:

1. Every thought tends to be a part of a personal consciousness.
2. Within each personal consciousness thought is always changing.
3. Within each personal consciousness thought is sensibly continuous.
4. It always appears to deal with objects independent of itself.
5. It is interested in some parts of these objects to the exclusion of others, and welcomes or rejects—*chooses* from among them, in a word—all the while (p. 225).

And the full-scale development of these assertions is carried out in a way which leaves the modern reader "cold." A psychology of thought which is purely descriptive, in an introspective sense, cannot be saved from unspeakable dullness and futility, it seems, by even so lively a style as that of William James. Only in a quotation from the biography of a congenitally deaf man, which bears upon "the question whether thought is possible without language" is the modern reader's interest likely to pick up. And even here interest is short-lived, for James makes nothing of the passage which articulates with contemporary theory except to say: "The reader sees by this time that it makes little or no difference in what sort of mind-stuff, in what quality of imagery, his thinking goes on" (p. 269). In other words, although the individual in question, as a boy, neither spoke nor wrote, he had a rich, varied, and essentially normal thought life and later, when he learned to read and write, was able to describe it with great clarity. But then James lapses into a haze of obscurity and we soon lose him (or *vice versa*) as he goes on to say:

The only images *intrinsically* important are the halting-places, the substantive conclusions, provisional or final, of the thought. Throughout all the rest of the stream, the feelings of relation are everything, and the terms related almost naught. These feelings of relations, these psychic overtones, halos, suffusions, or fringes about the terms, may be the same in very different systems of imagery . . . (p. 269).

Published in 1906, J. Mark Baldwin's imposing three-volume work on *Thought and Things* represents a beginning of transition. As the author remarks in his Preface, "The inroad of evolution and developmental theories, under the general notion of genesis, upon various 'preserves' of the old disciplines, is resulting in a certain obliteration of boundaries and readjustment of methods." And Baldwin significantly subtitles his work: *A Study of the Development and Meaning or*

Thought, or Genetic Logic. But the body of the work itself consists largely of that elaborate and arid descriptiveness which characterized Structuralism rather than the evolutionary psychology which came to be known as Functionalism. However much one may dissent from Watson's Behaviorism, one cannot but sympathize with his impatience with the kind of "psychology" which Introspectionism produced. "Words, words, words!" one is tempted to exclaim. Will readers another half century removed find our own productions of today equally vapid?

Passing reference has already been made to Watson's attempt to deal with thought as implicit speech—and to the difficulties to which it leads. But he at least makes a contribution in the *negative* sense of showing the futility of sheer speculation and introspection.

Watson's influence was felt not only in psychology proper but also in adjacent disciplines. So that when Markey (a sociologist) wrote a small book, in 1928, the imprint of Behaviorism was deep and clear. Now we see objective *experimentation* and new, more dynamic concepts emerging. Conditioned-reflex theory has suggested the notion of *sign;* and *symbol* and social *interaction* are "just around the corner." John Dewey and George Herbert Mead have by now both published influential works; and the *social* aspect of self and consciousness is being stressed. The exact conclusions at which Markey's book arrives are not easily located; but its general orientation and aim are clear, as the following sentences, excerpted from the Preface, indicate.

Attempts to locate the origin of the symbolic process and "thinking" in the separate individual are bound to make them appear an enigmatic gift. But most of those who endeavour to make such explanations have little hesitation in assuming that, if the search be long and careful enough, such phenomena will be located in hidden sources somewhere inside the organism —perhaps cotton-packed to prevent injury. . . . Scientific advance bids fair to dislocate such ideas and to emphasize interdependent and social characteristics.

The recent Gestalt theorists, in spite of their brilliant work, have gone in regard to the problem under consideration little beyond pointing out mysteries which require explanation, their next and most difficult task—a task which greater attention to social interaction will facilitate. Recent behaviouristic explanations have also suffered from ignoring important social factors, which, if cognizance were taken of them, would have furnished a very effective defence for the behaviouristic position, but which, when ignored, have left such explanations open to attack at their weakest point. But theories do not stay as hot as they are baked; cooler analysis discloses the parts not well done. Considerably more must come off the scientific griddle before intellectual nourishment is properly taken care of on these points. . . .

The main task of this book is an explanation of the social processes in the genesis, integration, and functions of symbols. There is an obvious need for such a systematic treatment, and a clearer statement of these processes (pp. ix–x).

There can be no denying that man *is* a social animal and that much of mentality and experience is socially determined and socially oriented (see Chapter 10); but this is not to say that there are no propensities and capacities which are given by the very nature of an organism's heredity and structure. As we have seen, one of the difficulties which the implicit-speech theory of thought encounters is the fact that thought and speech are not strictly co-extensive; animals, without speech, show clear indications of "thinking"; and there are similar difficulties if one makes thought completely contingent upon sociality. Certainly we have no clear evidence that thinking as we see it in rats and apes is particularly dependent upon social experience or relationships. For example, a rat reared in social isolation would seem just as likely to VTE at a choice point as one which had had extensive social experience. Human speech and human sociality are, of course, intimately connected; and there is no question that they influence both the content and the modes of human thought; but clearly, a general psychology of thought cannot be predicated upon either of them. Thought, at least in its rudimentary forms, is a more primitive affair.

The more recent literature on thinking has been organized and evaluated in a volume by Johnson (1955), entitled *The Psychology of Thought and Judgment.* This is a very large undertaking and it is referred to here, not for purposes of review, but rather as a source which the reader may wish to consult in the original.[12] Of his own work Johnson says:

> To anyone with a practical or theoretical interest in human beings the status of the psychology of thought is distressing. Such fields of psychology as perception, learning, and personality are being explored thoroughly and systematically. But the scientific investigation of thinking is unsystematic and, in general, unsatisfactory.
>
> Many psychologists express an interest in thinking, and some make raids on it. The field is littered with disabled wisdoms cast off by hit-and-run theorists. The purpose of the present work is to tidy up and remap this field, charting what is known and pushing a step or two ahead (p. 1).
>
> The principal purpose of this book is an integration of present knowledge of the psychology of thought, aiming at breadth rather than the exploitation of any special theoretical approach (p. 21).

[12] For surveys of the field from other vantage points, see Blanchard (1940), Leeper (1951), Rappaport (1951), Révész et al. (1954), and Bartlett (1958).

How important man's thought life is to him is indicated, not only by the extended literature and researches, but also by the following sentence which Johnson quotes from W. P. Montague: "Man began to think in order that he might eat; now he has evolved to the point where he eats in order that he may think" (p. 56). This evolution is truly momentous; and if we have in this chapter been mainly concerned with "thinking" as an adjunct to "eating," it is not because we do not recognize or appreciate the "higher," more autonomous aspects of thought. Instead our purpose has been to examine only those activities which can be legitimately included under this rubric and which, also, articulate fairly directly with our main theoretical concerns. As learning theory is refined and elaborated, it is hoped that the progression from the simpler processes which have here been explored to the more intricate ones, such as invention, logical problem solving, artistic creation, and dreaming will prove continuous and smooth.

7

Learning Theory, Cybernetics, and the Concept of Consciousness

Most psychologists of today have perfectly succeeded in developing a coherent science based on behaviour, taking no account of consciousness. Is it not puzzling to encounter such negative attitudes at the time when neurosurgeons are beginning, so to speak, to "experiment" on consciousness and raise the question of its localization within the brain? The recent multiplication of symposia devoted to problems of consciousness is an expression of our present need, for scientific purposes, of a better understanding of a phenomenon which is indeed the most mysterious in the whole universe (Fessard, 1954, p. 201).

The "negative attitudes" just mentioned are, as we know, deeply rooted historically. The attempt to make a science of psychology by means of introspection, which occupied psychologists during the latter part of the nineteenth century, was a failure; and the movement known as Behaviorism stemmed directly from the attendant frustration and exasperation.

But in one respect Dr. Fessard's otherwise apt statement is in error: Behaviorism has *not* produced a completely "coherent science." Repeatedly in this volume we have explored the blind alleys into which it has led us and from which we have found deliverance only by recourse to "intervening variables" and the concept of "feedback." The time has now come to look more systematically at the implications of these developments and to relate them to collateral developments in other sciences and to human experience generally.

I. Current Interest in the Physical Correlates of Consciousness

In its ultimate sense, the phenomenon of consciousness is as mysterious as life itself; and no one seems to be very sanguine about the prospect of completely "explaining" it in the near future. However, it *can* be studied; and it will be our purpose in this section to look at some of the fruits of recent investigation (see Footnote 17, p. 292).

As Magoun (1954) has observed, one important line of research has developed, opportunistically, from the fact that consciousness is periodically interrupted by sleep and from the "chance observation that direct electrical excitation of the reticular formation of the brain stem induces changes in the EEG seemingly identical with those observed in awakening from sleep, or alerting attention, and which have been referred to variously as activation, desynchronization, EEG arousal or the blocking reaction" (p. 1).

These findings quickly led to an experimental assault upon the brain area in question, with results which Magoun has summarized thus:

The great functional importance of this non-specific reticular system in the brain stem is indicated by the consequences of lesions in its cephalic part. Monkeys with such experimental injury remained throughout survival in a comatose state, in which the absence of all behaviour associated with wakefulness contrasted sharply with the alertness and activity which this animal normally displays. The EEG's of such preparations were chronically hypersynchronous and could no longer be affected by peripheral stimuli, emphasizing the importance of collateral over direct corticipetal paths in EEG arousal induced by afferent stimulation. Results in general similar to these have followed injury to the cephalic brain stem in the cat; and the findings are in good agreement with Bremer's fundamental observations that transection of the upper brain stem leaves the cerebral hemisphere in a state of sleep, with which current investigations of this problem may be said to have begun (p. 6).

Naively, the conception of brain functioning has been that consciousness was pervasively "located" in the uppermost or cortical areas of this organ, where incoming messages from the sense organs were received and orders for bodily action issued. Now the evidence is that, deep down in the brain stem, is an *activating system* which pours a stream of impulses into the cerebral hemispheres and "puts them to work." During the emission of these impulses the organism is awake, conscious; and when they are inhibited, the organism is asleep, unconscious. As a result of this view of the matter, the phenomenon

of sleep has taken on particular significance and is being investigated
with renewed interest. This function has been given special attention
by W. R. Hess (1954), who prefaces his discussion with these remarks:

> The more differentiated an organism, the more it depends on conscious
> elaboration of, and appropriate reaction to, signals from the external world
> in its struggle for survival. During sleep these capacities are depressed and
> the individual is left defenseless. The fact that all highly organized creatures
> accept this risk for a considerable part of their life suggests that sleep must
> have a vital function. We consider it a reparative process which obviously
> cannot take place in the highest centres while they are active (p. 117).

Considering that the whole adaptive "intelligence" of an organism is
dependent upon the state of arousal or alertness known as consciousness, the periodic occurrence of sleep is indeed paradoxical; and only
the most urgent of physiological considerations could have commanded
such a sacrifice in the matter of security. But be this as it may, the
fact of sleep dramatically focuses our attention upon the reality of
consciousness as something of great biological importance (and far
from an epiphenomenon) and shows how unrealistic and deliberately
self-restrictive any theoretical system is that ignores it. Hess summarizes current thinking with respect to consciousness and sleep as
follows:

> The organism's state of general excitability—which includes alertness and
> consciousness—is regulated by two antagonistic functional centres: the
> ergotrophic centre which aims at maximal alertness and readiness for de-
> fensive or aggressive action, whenever such action is needed in the struggle
> for survival, and the trophotropic centre which instigates inhibition of such
> activity, bring about sedation and eventually sleep, in order to preserve
> energy and allow tissues to recuperate. From absolute prevalence of the
> former centre to maximal predominance of the latter, shades of intermediate
> states exist, such as relaxation, drowsiness, light sleep and so on, each linked
> to a corresponding level of consciousness. These states are the result of a
> balance between the two antagonistic centres and conform to the needs of
> the environment (p. 125).

It should not be inferred, of course, that wakefulness and sleep correspond exactly to consciousness and unconsciousness. The fact that a
person is asleep is no guarantee that he is unconscious, as witnessed by
the phenomenon of *dreams*. And, conversely, the fact that an organism
is "awake" is no proof that he is *conscious*. The latter point has been
aptly made by Kleitman (1957):

> In the new-born infant, or older anencephalous child, as in the decorti-
> cated dog or cat, the level of consciousness is close to, if not at, zero. Their
> responses to stimuli do not meet the criteria for consciousness. Yet they

show definite alternation of sleep and wakefulness. . . . In delirium, fugues, icteral or posticteral automation of psychomotor epilepsy, a person may be judged to be behaviorally awake, but his level of consciousness is very low, and he may have a complete amnesia of events (p. 358).

In hypnosis the question of when the individual is asleep and when awake, when conscious and when unconscious becomes extremely complicated. Moreover, as will be shown in Section X, there is reason to believe that, whereas the reticular formation (or "lymbic system") is importantly involved in emotional learning, the cortex may be the "seat" of cognitive learning (Chapter 5). This would square with the notion that an organism may be "awake" and capable of affective reactions without, however, really "knowing" anything, as is apparently the case in the "sham rage" of decorticated cats (see Bard, 1934). However, for many purposes, consciousness and wakefulness may be treated as synonymous; and the lately renewed interest in this general field has understandably stimulated much new research on anesthetics and sedatives (see, for example, the review by Brazier, 1954); and psychologists (e.g., Miller, 1958; Brady, 1957; Skinner, 1958a) have come forward with ingenious behavioral techniques for assaying their more subtle and distinctive effects. The fact that those pathological states of consciousness (and unconsciousness) associated with Jacksonian epilepsy can often be remedied by brain surgery has opened up to Penfield and his associates the possibility of studying the effects of careful electric stimulation of the brain during such surgery. They have been able to produce, in fully conscious patients (operated on under local anesthetic), elaborate "memories" (in various sense modalities) which have more the qualities of images than of sensation, although to a limited extent they have also been able to produce "hallucinations." Stimulation of the motor areas of the cortex produces an infinite variety of more or less intricate bodily movements; but, says Penfield (1954):

When a motor area of the cortex is stimulated, conscious patients do not believe that they have willed the action. They recognize invariably that movement occurs independent of, or in spite of, their own volition (p. 286).

The integrating mechanisms prerequisite to voluntary planned action are subserved by to-and-fro cortico-subcortical neurone circuits.

There is a kind of fundamental dilemma in psychology in its efforts to be science. If it attempts to take a "centralist" position, i.e., to focus upon brain and consciousness, its data are global and relatively unanalyzable. On the other hand, if it attempts to take a "peripheralist" position, i.e., focuses upon reflex arcs and specific stimulus-response connections, its units of analysis become more manageable, but there is the danger that it will forever neglect those capacities for organized and integrated functioning that are so characteristic of living organisms. As Konorski (1958; see also Mowrer, 1960, Chapter 7) has pointed out, Sherrington made a masterful study of the mammalian nervous system as far as its peripheral response systems (reflexes) are concerned; but, despite the fact that his great work was entitled *The Integrative Action of the Nervous System*, Sherrington actually had very little to say about integration. The researches cited in this section represent attempts to attack this aspect of the problem more directly, but consolidated knowledge is still meager and conceptualizations tentative.

In psychology proper, the opposition has been between the so-called S—R psychologists and those who have stressed cognition, organization, and Gestalt-like notions generally. K. S. Lashley has repeatedly made statements such as the following:

> Attempts to express cerebral function in terms of the concepts of the reflex arc, or of associated chains of neurons, seem to be doomed to failure because they start with the assumption of a static nervous system. Every bit of evidence available indicates a dynamic, constantly active nervous system, or, rather, a composite of many interacting systems, which I have tried to illustrate at a primitive level of rhythm and the space coordinates. Only when methods of analysis of such systems have been devised will there be progress toward understanding of the physiology of the cerebral cortex (1951, p. 135).

And Hebb (1949), among others, has called for renewed efforts to understand behavior in terms of the total brain rather than in terms of segmental stimulus-response pathways (cf. James', 1902, expression, "The Field of Consciousness" and Köhler & Wallach's "Field Theory of Cortical Integration," 1944; but see also Thomas & Stewart, 1957). While there can be no doubt—and this has been repeatedly documented in this book—that the S—R bond is a greatly oversimplified abstraction and that we must not rest content with this level of analysis, the fact is that the segmental, not the global, approach has yielded the more solid research findings and has grown in the more orderly and progressive manner.

This is not to say that everyone should necessarily be working on the problem in the same way. It is certainly useful to have some investigators who are willing to adopt different perspectives and research strategies; but it is entirely possible that the segmental approach in psychology has been leading us toward a better understanding of the organism-as-a-whole than we have fully realized. At least this pre-sumption is strengthened by a line of thought which will be followed in the next section and by recent developments in the area of physical automation, which will be considered presently.

II. Representation and Consciousness

It is one thing to agree that the Behaviorists were, in a sense, "wrong" in denying or ignoring consciousness, but it is something else again to find a truly fruitful way of studying this phenomenon psycho-logically. The study of "consciousness per se" (or "conscious states"), by means of introspection, netted us very little (Mowrer, 1960, Chap-ter 1). In fact, it created a sort of scientific scandal.

> The concept of consciousness still remains associated with one of the most traumatic experiences in the life history of scientific psychology, i.e., intro-spectionism. The wound has not yet healed; consciousness still means to many people a menace to behavioral science (Nuttin, 1955, p. 349).[1]

But the same writer then proceeds to make a case for consciousness which is consistent with "behavioral science" and, quite specifically, with concepts developed in the present volume. There is, he notes, a "representational theory of consciousness" which holds that external reality has an independent "existence" and that perception or con-sciousness serves to reproduce or represent this reality on the *inside* of the organism or individual.

> The object perceived is considered only a representation or a duplicate of that unknown reality as it is supposed to exist in itself, independently of the behaving subject. From the behavioral or psychological viewpoint, however, there is no doubt that man perceives the things themselves, that is, the world itself. Perception does not give him a *representation* of the world, but a direct *presence* of the world itself (p. 350).

The issues here involved seem somewhat philosophical, i.e., without predictable consequences or testable implications, and therefore need not directly concern us here. However, from them Nuttin moves on to a discussion of the utmost cogency to our present interests. He says:

> The problem of consciousness, however, becomes complicated by the fact that the world can be present to us in different ways. Man is able to find himself in the presence of an object or a situation which is not im-

---

[1] Brown (1958b) makes the same point, even more graphically, when he says: "In 1913 John Watson mercifully closed the bloodshot inner eye of American psy-chology. With great relief the profession trained its exteroceptors on the labora-tory animal" (p. 93).

mediately presented to him from the outside. This is what I call the *vicarious presence* of an object. This possibility of vicarious presence of things to us, via images, concepts, and symbols, is a capital behavioral fact. It enlarges to an enormous extent the world in which man is living and, consequently, the possibilities of behavior. By this vicarious presence man's dealing with situations goes far beyond the limits of responding to actually present things [cf. Chapters 5 and 6]. . . . This inner, cognitive dealing with situations is intrinsically directed to, or projected toward, an outside world and it is, as a rule, preparatory or compensatory to effective external behavior (p. 352).

This, as Nuttin agrees, is also a "representational" view of consciousness; but the distinction is between the older view that a *present* reality is re-presented perceptually or consciously and the view, just stated, that a reality which is *not* present perceptually can nevertheless be represented, "via images, concepts, and symbols." [2] The great and disastrous trouble with radical behaviorism was that it was so completely *non*representational, in Nuttin's second sense of the term. Rather obviously there was nothing representational about the Law of Effect, as conceived by Thorndike. In fact, it was designed to provide a *substitute* for representational functions, as we have seen in the preceding chapter. In later sections of this chapter we shall find that the Law of Effect has potentialities for expansion in a direction which Thorndike seems not to have at all envisioned; but these are not directly relevant to our present discussion.

On the other hand, from the beginning, conditioning theory carried an implication of representationism. Pavlov himself (1927) stressed the fact that the conditioned stimulus or signal comes to stand for, or "represent," the unconditioned stimulus which, on earlier occasions, has followed the conditioned stimulus. This representation is indicated by the fact that the subject responds to the CS *as if* it were the UnCS. But here the representational function is all on the "stimulus side," and it is only when we examine the subject's *responses*, rather more carefully than Pavlov did, that we begin to find representationism in its most significant form. For Pavlov there was nothing particularly representative or symbolic about a conditioned response. It was, in fact, exactly the *same* as the unconditioned response, the only difference being that it was made to a different, formerly neutral stimulus. But when we cease trying to be so inflexibly "objective," we begin to see something of the utmost importance. Perhaps the most salient feature of an *emotion*, as opposed to a behavioral reflex (in Pavlov's

---

[2] For a slightly earlier, and presumably independent, emphasis upon the role of representation in "cognitive processes," see Scheerer (1953).

sense), is its representativeness: for example, the emotion of fear gains its special biological value from the fact that it can be experienced, not only in the absence of its adequate (unconditioned) stimulus, but also *without the pain* (and biological danger) occasioned by the latter. In other words, the fear is a sort of primitive, but very powerful, representation or "image" *of* the pain; and hope, by the some token, is an image of pleasure or gratification (cf. Leeper, 1948). Hull and his followers originally tried to encompass these facts in the notation, r_g, or "anticipatory goal reaction." But the notion was never very satisfactory because of its nonspecificity. Hull, like Pavlov, was trying to avoid recourse to anything so subjective as an emotion and, in consequence, threw up a quite unnecessary barrier to further progress. But, as we have already seen (Mowrer, 1960, Chapter 11), Amsel (1958), in dealing with the problem of extinction, has recently transcended this bias, and probably no one would today defend it very strongly.

Once the reality of emotion, as a sort of intermediary between the organism and the "real thing," has been acknowledged, it is quickly discovered that emotions, of several kinds, can be conditioned to (a) external stimuli, giving rise to approach and avoidance behavior, and (b) to response-correlated stimuli, giving rise to response facilitation (habit) and inhibition. More than this, in phenomena such as vicarious trial and error (Hull's pure-stimulus acts), we see that living organisms sometimes perform actions solely because of their informative, cognitive, or feedback function, thus further enlarging our understanding of mediation and representation.

And, finally (in Chapters 4 and 5), our analysis has forced upon us the necessity of recognizing representativeness in yet another form: sensations, it seems, are also conditionable and thus provide the basis for what may be termed *images proper*. Here, as we have seen, is the basis for both memory and imagination, as they have been traditionally and popularly conceived.

Perhaps, in his emphasis upon representation, Professor Nuttin has not yet told us what consciousness *is;* but he has given us an excellent lead as to one of the things it *does:* it enables us to function *abstractly* or, as Hull suggested, in the "not here and not now." In an unconscious (sleeping) organism, such "mental life" is absent—or at least vastly reduced (cf. the dream). Later in this chapter we shall revert to this useful line of thought; but we have pursued it as far as practicable for the moment, and turn to what may at first seem to be an unrelated set of considerations.

III. Learning Theory and Servomechanisms

Prodded on the one side by recent neurological findings (Section I) and, on the other by the inherent weaknesses of classical stimulus-response models (Section II), contemporary students of learning have been increasingly intrigued and challenged by those developments in engineering and machine design known as servotechnology or cybernetics. Campbell (1956b) has recently published a perceptive paper in this connection which will here serve as our point of departure (see also English, 1954). Campbell notes, first of all, that in the past efforts to conceptualize the phenomenon of "habit" have moved along two different lines: "One of these is to define the response in terms of the body's own coordinates, in terms of muscle contractions or movements. The second alternative, equally operationally specifiable, has been to define the learned response in terms of a change in the relationship between organisms and environment. Responses defined in these terms become objective moves, places reached, regions entered, etc." (p. 105).

Here we at once recognize the distinction, previously noted (Mowrer, 1960, Chapter 8), between so-called *response* learning and *place* learning; and Campbell then points out that although the *fact* of place learning is indisputable, "the most popular and best developed learning theories have ignored this fact and have gone ahead assuming the adequacy of defining response in isolated motor or muscle terms" (p. 105).

A major reason for this resistance is that accepting the validity of the second definition of responses presents the learning theorist with a much more difficult problem, a problem which cannot readily be encompassed by the anatomically reinforced conceptualization of the simple reflex arc, with discrete afferent and efferent neural transmission pathways. A second reason for resistance lies in the fact that those who, like Tolman (1932) and Lashley (1929), have pointed out the adaptive, object-consistent nature of learned responses, have not presented plausible mechanistic theories of how such responses could be achieved, and have used language implying purpose, thus raising the ghost of metaphysical issues which had been important at the time when psychology was freeing itself from philosophy. Recent attention to the engineers' achievement of self-regulating machines, the behavior of which is consistent to uniform ends achieved through variable intermediate steps (as in the thermostat and governor at the most simple level and as in the aiming and tracking devices for anti-aircraft artillery at a more complicated level), has supplied a mechanistic model of adaptive, habitual response mechanisms. While we cannot say that adopting a steady state of homeostatic model will solve at the psychological or physiological level the problem of how such responses are achieved by the organism, it does at least give a deterministic model for facing squarely one of the toughest aspects of the actual phenomena of habit (p. 106).

Because of the implication of the passage just quoted and because repeated allusion has already been made in this book to similar concepts, it is desirable at this juncture to develop a more explicit understanding of just what is involved in the self-regulation achieved by the so-called servomechanisms. No better survey of this field can be found than that provided by a small book recently published under the title, *Automatic Control*. It consists of several brief and lucid articles which initially appeared in the *Scientific American*, the first two of which are especially relevant for our immediate purposes. One of these, entitled "Self-Regulation," is by Ernest Nagel (1955a) and begins thus:

Automatic control is not a new thing in the world. Self-regulative mechanisms are an inherent feature of innumerable processes in nature, living and nonliving. Men have long recognized the existence of such mechanisms in living forms, although, to be sure, they have often mistaken automatic regulation for the operation of some conscious design or vital force. Even the deliberate construction of self-regulating machines is no innovation: the history of such devices goes back at least several hundred years.

Nevertheless, the preacher's weary cry that there is nothing new under the sun is at best a fragment of the truth. The general notion of automatic control may be ancient, but the formulation of its principles is a very recent achievement. And the systematic exploitation of these principles—their subtle theoretical elaboration and far-reaching practical application—must be credited to the twentieth century. When human intelligence is disciplined by the analytical methods of modern science, and fortified by modern material resources and techniques, it can transform almost beyond recognition the most familiar aspects of the physical and social scene. There is surely a profound difference between a primitive recognition that some mechanisms are self-regulative while others are not, and the invention of an analytic theory which not only accounts for the gross facts but guides the construction of new types of systems (p. 2).

And the second article, by Arnold Tustin (1955), takes up the story and carries it on as follows:

For hundreds of years a few examples of true automatic control systems have been known. A very early one was the arrangement on windmills of a device to keep their sails always facing into the wind. It consisted simply of a miniature windmill which could rotate the whole mill to face in any direction. The small mill's sails were at right angles to the main ones, and whenever the latter faced in the wrong direction, the wind caught the small sails and rotated the mill to the correct position. With steam power came other automatic mechanisms: the engine-governor, and then the steering servo-engine on ships, which operated the rudder in correspondence with movements of the helm. These devices, and a few other such as simple voltage regulators, constituted man's achievement in automatic control up to about twenty years ago.

In the past two decades necessity, in the form of increasingly acute problems arising in our ever more complex technology, has given birth to new families of such devices. Chemical plants needed regulators of temperature and flow; air warfare called for rapid and precise control of searchlights and anti-aircraft guns; radio required circuits which would give accurate amplification of signals.

Thus the modern science of automatic control has been fed by streams from many sources. At first, it now seems surprising to recall, no connection between these various developments was recognized. Yet all control and regulating systems depend on common principles. As soon as this was realized, progress became much more rapid. Today the design of controls for a modern boiler or a guided missile, for example, is based largely on principles first developed in the design of radio amplifiers.

Indeed, studies of the behavior of automatic control systems give us new insight into a wide variety of happenings in nature and in human affairs. The notions that engineers have evolved from these studies are useful aids in understanding how a man stands upright without toppling over, how the human heart beats, why our economic system suffers from slumps and booms, why the rabbit population in parts of Canada regularly fluctuates between scarcity and abundance.

The chief purpose of this essay is to make clear the common pattern that underlies all these and many other varied phenomena. This common pattern is the existence of feedback, or—to express the same thing rather more generally—interdependence.

We should not be able to live at all, still less to design complex control systems, if we did not recognize that there are regularities in the relationship between events—what we call "cause and effect." When the room is warmer, the thermometer on the wall reads higher. We do not expect to make the room warmer by pushing up the mercury in the thermometer. But now consider the case when the instrument on the wall is not a simple thermometer but a thermostat, contrived so that as its reading goes above a chosen setting, the fuel supply to the furnace is progressively reduced, and, conversely, as its reading falls below that setting, the fuel flow is increased. This is an example of a familiar control system. Not only does the reading of the thermometer depend on the warmth of the room, but the warmth of the room also depends on the reading of the thermometer. The two quantities are interdependent. Each is a cause, and each an effect, of the other. In such cases we have a closed chain or sequence—what engineers call a "closed loop" [Fig. 7–1].

In analyzing engineering and scientific problems it is very illuminating to sketch out first the scheme of dependence and see how the various quantities involved in the problem are determined by one another and by disturbances from outside the system. Such a diagram enables one to tell at a glance whether a system is an open or a closed one. This is an important distinction, because a closed system possesses several significant properties. Not only can it act as a regulator, but it is capable of various "self-excitatory" types of behavior—like a kitten chasing its own tail.

The now-popular name for this process is "feedback." In the case of the thermostat, the thermometer's information about the room temperature is fed back to open or close the valve, which in turn controls the temperature. Not all automatic control systems are of the closed-loop type. For example, one might put the thermometer outside in the open air, and connect it to work the fuel valve through a specially shaped cam, so that the outside temperature regulates the fuel flow. In this open sequence system the room temperature has no effect; there is no feedback (Fig. 7–1). The control compensates only that disturbance of room temperature caused by variation of the outdoor temperature. Such a system is not necessarily a bad or useless system; it might work very well under some circumstances. But it has two obvious shortcomings. Firstly, it is a "calibrated" system; that is to say, its correct working would require careful preliminary testing and special shaping of the cam to suit each particular application. Secondly, it could not deal with any but standard conditions. A day that was windy as well as cold would not get more fuel on that account.

Fig. 7–1. Feedback loop (at bottom) contrasted with open control sequence (top). In a hypothetical heating system, the outside temperature (To) might be employed to actuate the thermostat control (Th) on the furnace (F) to adjust room temperature (T). But there is no provision for determining whether the room temperature has attained the level desired. This self-regulating principle is uniquely provided by the feedback circuit. Here the variable which is to be controlled, the room temperature, itself actuates the thermostat. It thus controls the performance of the furnace (Tustin, 1955, p. 12).

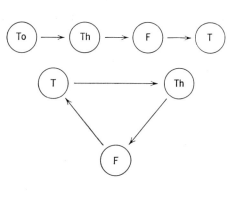

The feedback type of control avoids these shortcomings. It goes directly to the quantity to be controlled, and it corrects indiscriminately for all kinds of disturbance. Nor does it require calibration for each special condition.

Feedback control, unlike open-sequence control, can never work without *some* error, for the error is depended upon to bring about the correction. The objective is to make the error as small as possible. . . .

The principle of control by feedback is quite general. The quantities that it may control are of the most varied kinds, ranging from the frequency of a national electric-power grid to the degree of anesthesia of a patient under surgical operation. Control is exercised by negative feedback, which is to say that the information fed back is the amount of departure from the desired condition (pp. 10–14).[3]

The relevance of all this to our present concerns is clear. Self-regulation has previously been regarded as one of the most important yet mystifying characteristics of living organisms. Various global concepts such as "intelligence," "consciousness," and "knowledge" have been invoked as explanations, but not to good effect. Radical behaviorism was a movement of protest which was pointed in the right direction but, because of certain rigid, self-imposed limitations, was handicapped in what would otherwise have been its normal development. Now, however, it has proved possible to construct *machines* with impressive capacity for *self*-regulation; and since there can be no imputation of "subjectivism" here, such machines and the principles they embody have inspired new attempts to account for the adaptive capacities of living organisms along "objective" lines.

IV. Law of Effect, Feedback, and "Knowledge of Results"

In one sense, the Law of Effect may be said to have postulated the principle of "feedback" long before the current interest in cybernetics. It has held, from the beginning, that the consequences of a response, whether good or bad, *act back upon* that response (really upon *the organism*) in such a way as to increase or decrease the likelihood of its future occurrence. Through time, from "trial to trial," the organism's behavior is thus automatically controlled, regulated, adapted in a way that is of the utmost importance to its continued existence (cf. Hilgard, 1956, pp. 469 ff.).

In *Learning Theory and Behavior* it has been shown (as was already sufficiently apparent from common experience) that if the "feedback" from a response is punishing, that response tends to be "weakened" (made less probable of future occurrence); whereas, if the feedback is rewarding, the response tends to be strengthened (made *more* probable of occurrence). In Chapter 10 it is shown, moreover, that if the feedback from a response—be that feedback either punishing or rewarding—is delayed rather than immediate, the rate and amount of learning are correspondingly reduced. And in Chapter 11 we have seen that learning can be reversed, not only by the introduction of an op-

---

[3] The term "inverse feedback" (McCulloch, 1951) seems preferable to "negative feedback." It implies equally well that the system is error-actuated and does not conflict with the use of "positive" and "negative" feedback in the sense of hopes and fears.

posed type of reinforcement, but also (though more gradually) by the mere withdrawal of reinforcement. These principles were all appreciated by Thorndike and are especially clear in situations where the consequences of a response are in the nature of *primary* reinforcements, decremental or incremental. These principles are, of course, also easily demonstrable, particularly in human beings, when the reinforcements are derived, secondary.

It has been shown many times over (again by Thorndike—see below) that human subjects learn decidedly better with than without a "knowledge of results," a fact which accentuates the principle of effect and minimizes the importance of such factors as "repetition," "frequency," "use," and the like. Under the heading of "Information and Effect," McGeoch & Irion (1952) have a lucid discussion of this topic, which is reproduced here:

In many studies of human learning, information (knowledge of results) has been the source of reinforcement. Such information may be inherent in the learning task itself, as when the subject observes the results of his own behavior in the pursuit-meter situation, or the information may be given by the experimenter by means of some signal. Usually, information depends upon past experience and transfer of training, since the subject must be able to interpret the informative cues. The use of information also depends upon the subject's motivation, at least to a certain extent. Thus, the learner must want to make the correct response before the informative signals of *Right* and *Wrong* can have much efficacy.

Information can vary in degree of specificity or precision. In a repetition of one of Thorndike's line-drawing experiments (1927), Trowbridge and Cason (1932) have found that learning increases with increasing precision of the information given. The subjects drew only three-inch lines, but drew them under four different conditions in a counterbalanced order. The conditions were: (1) the control, in which the experimenter said nothing after the drawing of each line; (2) a nonsense-syllable condition, in which the experimenter spoke a different nonsense syllable when the subject had finished drawing each line; (3) a "right" and "wrong" condition, in which the experimenter announced *Right* or *Wrong* after each drawing (as Thorndike had done); and (4) an exact information condition, in which the subject was told the amount and direction of his error.

The major results may be seen [in Table 7–1]. There is no learning under the control condition and none when a nonsense syllable is spoken after each line. Announcement of *Right* or *Wrong* leads to a sharp reduction of error, but exact information about the amount and direction of errors both minimized them early in practice and reduced them as practice went on. The percentages of correct responses (not given in the table) for the four conditions are: control, 13.6; nonsense-syllable, 5.1; Right-Wrong, 22.6; and exact information, 54.8. These percentages corroborate the average error scores in demonstrating that increased precision of information about the results of responses is accomplished by increasing amounts of learning.

This is the usual result. Without information, little or no learning results. On the other hand, when information of results is given, learning occurs and becomes more efficient over wide limits as the precision of the useful information increases. The more exact the information, the more exact can the standard become and the more precise may be the selection among responses. It may be questioned whether *all* information about the results of an act can be excluded from a subject as complexly motivated as the human being. Information concerning the relation of an act to the experimenter's standard can be excluded, but the subject may still obtain some information about the relation of the act to a standard of his own. In estimating the lengths of strips of paper without information from the experimenter, he may form an opinion about the accuracy of his estimate, which then functions as if it were information. In drawing lines he has kinaesthesis, on the basis of which he can estimate the relation of the line drawn to his own conceptual standard of the length of line he tried to draw. Some of Thorndike's (1932) results on line-drawing without formal information of results show an approach to a stable value which presumably represented the subject's own standard which he approached with the aid of informal information available to him (pp. 265–268; cf. Seashore & Bavelas, 1941).

TABLE 7–1

Average Errors in Units of $\frac{1}{8}$ Inch when Each Condition Appeared in the Initial Position of the Practice Order

(From Trowbridge and Cason, 1932, p. 253)

Groups of Trials	Condition			
	Control	Nonsense	Right-Wrong	Exact Information
First 30	5.97	8.87	7.33	1.93
Middle 40	6.85	8.57	5.35	1.12
Last 30	6.40	8.43	3.90	.97

What, precisely, do these findings mean in terms of our present analysis? They show that actions may be influenced by their effects, not only when these effects take the form of primary rewards and punishments, but also when they take the form of mere "knowledge." But this knowledge is not "purely cognitive": it is an evaluative knowledge—a knowledge, so to say, of Good and Evil, of Right and Wrong. And our earlier discussions prepare us immediately to transform such "knowledge" into *secondary reinforcements*, type-D and type-I.

What these observations come down to, ultimately, is this: In order for responses to be facilitated or inhibited they have to be reinforced, positively or negatively, primarily or secondarily. There must, that is to say, be a "feedback" of some sort, an experienced effect or consequence. But the particular type of feedback involved is a comparatively slow one, occurring only *after* a particular response is completed; and it is therefore capable of influencing only *later* actions. Thus, as far as the organism's total behavior is concerned, we are dealing with a closed-loop system; but as far as *any particular action* or response is concerned, the system is decidedly open. Here, it seems, is one of the critical weaknesses in much earlier theorizing about the phenomenon of habit, a weakness which has been corrected in the current conception which stresses, not "bonds" or reflex "arcs," but complete circuits which are constantly active while a given act is in progress. This concept will be more explicitly considered in the next section.

V. Revised Two-Factor Theory as a Cybernetic Analogue

As just indicated, there is inherent in the Law of Effect a kind of feedback, or "servo," principle. But that principle, as postulated, is of such a nature as to influence or control, not a response as it occurs, but rather the response or behavior of the organism in the same (or a similar) situation *on some future occasion*. The Law of Effect has often been criticized for making living organisms, at least per theory, "blind" and stupid. They can, according to this law, adaptively modify their behavior *after* an action has occurred; and in this sense they are granted, by the law, a kind of intelligence. But many observers insist that living organisms also have the capacity to alter their actions *while they are occurring* and that this capacity delivers them from the blind bumbling which the Law of Effect seems to demand of them. As it turns out, in our attempt to discover how variation and control of a given response are achieved, we hit upon a new and apparently better way of explaining how it is that control, in the sense of alterations in subsequent behavior, is brought about, i.e., *what* learning is and *how* it occurs.

As earlier sections of this chapter have shown, there is nothing radically new about either the concept, or indeed the application, of automatic control. However, it remained for Norbert Wiener (1948) to suggest a colorful and inclusive term to cover a broad range of related phenomena in this area [4] and to point out a number of interest-

---

[4] Says Wiener: "We have decided to call the entire field of control and communication theory, whether in the machine or in the animal, by the name *Cybernetics*, which we get from the Greek χυβερνήτης or *steersman*. In choosing this term, we wish to recognize that the first significant paper on feed-back mechanisms is an article on governors, which was published by Clerk Maxwell in 1868, and that *gov-*

ing parallels in nature. The one of greatest use to us at the moment has been put in these words:

Now, suppose that I pick up a lead-pencil. To do this I have to move certain muscles. However, for all of us but a few expert anatomists, we do not know what these muscles are; and even among anatomists there are few if any who can perform the act by a conscious willing in succession of the contraction of each muscle concerned. On the contrary, what we will is *to pick the pencil up*. Once we have determined on this, our motion proceeds in such a way that we may say roughly that the amount by which the pencil is not yet picked up is decreased at each stage. This part of the action is not in full consciousness.

To perform an action in such a manner, there must be a report to the nervous system, conscious or unconscious, of the amount by which we have failed to pick the pencil up at each instance. If we have our eye on the pencil, this report may be visual, at least in part, but it is more generally kinaesthetic, or to use a term now in vogue, proprioceptive. If the proprioceptive sensations are wanting, and we do not replace them by a visual or other substitute, we are unable to perform the act of picking up the pencil, and find ourselves in a state of what is known as *ataxia*. An ataxia of this type is familiar in the form of syphilis of the central nervous system known as *tabes dorsalis*, where the kinaesthetic sense conveyed by the spinal nerves is more or less destroyed [cf. Mowrer, 1960, Chapter 7, Section VIII].

However, an excessive feed-back is likely to be as serious a handicap to organized activity as a defective feed-back. In view of this possibility, Mr. Bigelow and myself approached Dr. Rosenbleuth with a very specific question. Is there any pathological condition in which the patient, in trying to perform some voluntary act like picking up a pencil, overshoots the mark, and goes into an uncontrollable oscillation [as a too refined servomechanism does in "wild oscillation" or "hunting"]? Dr. Rosenbleuth immediately answered us that there is such a well-known condition, that it is called purpose tremor, and that it is often associated with injury to the cerebellum.

We thus found a most significant confirmation of our hypothesis concerning the nature of at least some voluntary activity. It will be noted that our point of view considerably transcended that current among neurophysiologists. The central nervous system no longer appears as a self-contained organ, receiving inputs from the senses and discharging into the muscles. On the contrary, some of its most characteristic activities are explicable only as circular processes, emerging from the nervous system into the muscles, and re-entering the nervous system through the sense organs, whether they be proprioceptive or organs of the special senses. This seemed to us to mark a new step in the study of that part of neurophysiology which concerns not solely the elementary process of nerves and synapses but the performance of the nervous system as an integrated whole (pp. 14–15).

---

ernor is derived from a Latin corruption of χυβερνήτης. We also wish to refer to the fact that the steering engines of a ship are indeed one of the earliest and best developed forms of feed-back mechanisms" (p. 19).

On later pages of his book, Wiener speaks of "learning," "memory," and the "conditioned reflex"; but he does not tie up these phenomena in any systematic way with the discussion just quoted. The connection, if pursued, is basic and illuminating. What the foregoing passages emphasize most pointedly is that the first "effect" of a bit of behavior on the part of living organisms is to stimulate, to inform, to *feed back* knowledge to the subject about the direction, extent, speed, and general nature of the behavior itself. This we have called response-dependent stimulation. There then follows a *second, subsequent effect* in the nature of success or failure of the behavior to satisfy the felt need or motive which originally prompted it. It is, of course, this latter occurrence which Thorndike and other proponents of the Law of Effect have stressed—but stressed in such a way, or in such a context, as to cause the first type of *effect* to be largely neglected.

The reason for this neglect or oversight is obvious. As we have seen in the first chapter of this book (see also Mowrer, 1960), "habit," as conceived by Thorndike, was merely a modifiable reflex, a "bond" or connection extending from some sense organ, *straight through* the organism, one may say, to the muscles involved in a particular pattern of movement. And volition, consciousness, control had nothing to do with the situation. This, of course, is the misconception which the above quotation from Wiener so effectively corrects. But Wiener's analysis does not provide us, explicitly, with an alternative theory, although it points the way to such a theory.

In reverting to the fact that responses characteristically have *immediate* and then somewhat *later* effects, one is reminded of the possibility that the *immediate* effects of a response, i.e., the proprioceptive and other sensory stimulation produced thereby, are in an ideal position to become *conditioned stimuli* for the detachable, conditionable components of the reactions elicited by the later effects, i.e., the gains or losses, rewards or punishments which result from the subject's behavior in relation to the external world. In other words, what Thorndike saw as the more or less exclusive effect of an action may be thought of as the *unconditioned stimulus,* some part of the reaction to which becomes connected, through Pavlovian conditioning, to the first and most immediate "effects" of the reaction. When we put what Thorndike saw together with the Wiener insight, we thus obtain a remarkably good theory (cf. Miller, 1958).

Such a theory, couched in the terms just used, may seem somewhat novel; but from the standpoint of common sense it is, again, "old hat." What it says, in the more usual vernacular, is that "experience" shapes our "expectations" and that our expectations then, in turn, control or govern our behavior. If the objective and the subjective, the technical and the commonplace approaches to the psychology of learning thus merge and fuse, it can hardly be an occasion for regret.

As a result of his dismissal of conditioning as an unimportant if not, indeed, a nonexistent form of learning, Thorndike by-passed this possibility. Because Pavlov, on the other hand, was only passingly interested in habit formation (see Mowrer, 1960, Chapter 3), he also overlooked it. While Hull came close to the conception, for reasons which are not entirely clear he, too, failed to develop its full potentialities. In some ways, Tolman, Lewin, and Freud were closer still; but they also only approximated this formulation. Can it be that the cyberneticists have given us the clue to a truly powerful and unifying view of the matter?

VI. Sluckin and Ashby on Minds and Machines

Not only have psychologists become interested in the newer types of self-regulatory machines, as possible models for an improved understanding of mind; engineers, on the basis of the intelligence and apparent "purposiveness" of their machines, have also become interested in psychological problems. But at once a difference has been apparent: although machines have been built with remarkable capacities for self-regulation, they are not ordinarily able to *learn*. Their intelligence is "wired in," and they just go ahead doing, automatically, the often quite remarkable things they are supposed to. Living organisms, by contrast, are capable of developing, from "experience," their *own* rules, goals, concepts, and ideas (Sinnott, 1952); and this is a feat which has fascinated and challenged the engineer.

In 1954 an English writer, W. Sluckin, with training in both engineering and psychology, published a small book in which a number of automata, simulating living organisms, are briefly described. Typical of the earlier machines of this kind is the one described by Sluckin as follows:

Some thirty years ago an interesting little toy enjoyed a good deal of popularity. It was known as the mechanical "beetle." When wound up, it could move on toothed wheels across a table. The "beetle" was provided with a pair of "feelers," one of which slid along the table top. On reaching the edge of the table, the sliding feeler would drop; this would operate the toy's mechanism in such a way that the beetle would change the direction of its movement to that parallel with the table edge. It would again move on until on reaching the corner, it would change its direction once more, and so on. The mechanism was quite simple. The behaviour of the "beetle" was no more complex than that of many other mechanical devices which respond automatically to certain signals, clues, or stimuli.

Sluckin then describes a number of "conditioned-reflex models" and "maze-running machines," but the most serious attempt, to date, to construct a learning machine has been made by Ashby and reported in his book, *Design for a Brain* (1952). Preliminary to his discussion of this apparatus, which he calls the "homeostat," Ashby makes the following interesting observations:

The organism affects the environment, and the environment affects the organism: such a system is said to have "feedback." . . .

The same feature is shown by the example of . . . the kitten and the fire. The various stimuli from the fire, working through the nervous system, evoke some reaction from the kitten's muscles; equally the kitten's movements, by altering the position of its body in relation to the fire, will cause changes to occur in the pattern of stimuli which falls on the kitten's sense-organs. The receptors therefore affect the muscle (by effects transmitted through the nervous system), and the muscles affect the receptors (by effects transmitted through the environment). The action is two-way and the system possesses feedback.

The observation is not new:

"In most cases the change which induces a reaction is brought about by the organism's own movements. These cause a change in the relation of the organism to the environment: to these changes the organism reacts. The whole behavior of free-moving organisms is based on the principle that it is the movements of the organism that have brought about stimulation." (Jennings.)

The good player of a quick ball game, the surgeon conducting an operation, the physician arriving at a clinical decision—in each case there is the flow from signals interpreted to action carried out, back to further signals and on again to more action, up to the culminating point of the achievement of the task." (Bartlett.)

"Organism and environment form a whole and must be viewed as such." (Starling.)

It is necessary to point to the existence of feedback in the relation between the free-living organism and its environment because most physiological experiments are deliberately [done] with spinal reflexes, a stimulus is applied and the resulting movement recorded; but the movement is not allowed to influence the nature or duration of the stimulus. The action between stimulus and movement is therefore one-way. A similar absence of feedback is enforced in the Pavlovian experiments with conditioned reflexes: the stimulus may evoke salivation, but the salivation has no effect on the nature or duration of the stimulus.[5]

[5] Cf. the example, cited earlier in this chapter, of a thermostat mounted on the *outside* of a house and connected to the furnace within.

Such an absence of feedback is, of course, useful or even essential in the analytic study of the behaviour of a mechanism, whether animate or inanimate. But its usefulness in the laboratory should not obscure the fact that the free-living animal is not subject to these constraints.

Sometimes systems which seem at first sight to be one-way prove on closer examination to have feedback. Walking on a smooth pavement, for instance, seems to involve so little reference to the structures outside the body that the nervous system might seem to be producing its actions without reference to their effects. *Tabes dorsalis*, however, prevents incoming sensory impulses from reaching the brain while leaving the outgoing motor impulses unaffected. If walking were due simply to the outgoing motor impulses, the disease would cause no disturbance to walking. In fact, it upsets the action severely, and demonstrates that the incoming sensory impulses are really playing an essential, though hidden, part in the normal action (pp. 36–38).

Ashby discusses learning, which he exemplifies with his homeostat, under the heading of *ultra-stability;* and as background for that discussion he introduces and defines the concept of *stability.* By this he means essentially what others have called automatic control and homeostasis. This is achieved by means of feedback, but feedback of a particular kind, namely *negative* or error-reducing feedback. By contrast,

Instability in such systems is shown by the development of a "runaway." The least disturbance is magnified by its passage round the circuit so that it is incessantly built up into a larger and larger deviation from the resting state. The phenomenon is identical with that referred to as a "vicious circle" (p. 52).

In order to sharpen this distinction, Ashby makes the following comparison:

The automatic pilot is a device which, amongst other actions, keeps the aeroplane horizontal. It must therefore be connected to the ailerons in such a way that when the plane rolls to the right, its output must act on them so as to roll the plane to the left. If properly joined, the whole system is stable and self-correcting: it can now fly safely through turbulent air, for though it will roll frequently, it will always come back to the level. The homeostat, if joined in this way, would tend to do the same. . . .

So far they show no difference; but connect the ailerons in reverse and compare them. The automatic pilot would act, after a small disturbance, to *increase* the roll, and would persist in its wrong action to the very end. The homeostat, however, would persist in its wrong action only until the increasing deviation made the step-functions start changing. On the occurrence of the first suitable new value, the homeostat would act to stabilize instead of to overthrow; it would return the plane to the horizontal; and it would then be ordinarily self-correcting for disturbances.

There is therefore some justification for the name "ultra-stable"; for if the main variables are assembled so as to make their field unstable, the ultrastable system will change this field till it is stable. The degree of stability shown is therefore of an order higher than that of the system with a single field (pp. 99–100).

There is thus inherent in Ashby's discussion the useful distinction between what he calls *stability*, or mere homeostatic self-regulation (as manifested by many reflexive mechanisms and physical machines), and the concept of *ultra-stability*, which he equates to learning. Ashby's further analysis of the latter phenomenon makes good reading; but, in the end, one feels that nothing very important has been added to our knowledge of learning, except to show that learning-like functions can be performed by machines. There is, moreover, this fundamental oversight. It will be recalled, from Section IV of this chapter, that a *kind* of feedback is the distinguishing feature of the Law of Effect; but it is feedback from the environment (generally), after an act is completed, and not from the organism's own receptors while the act is in progress. Despite the excellent case which Ashby makes for feedback of the latter kind (see pp. 270–271), when he comes to the hypothetical analysis of learning, he ignores the more immediate type of feedback and refers only to the remote "feedback" which is implied by the very term "effect" in the Law of Effect.[6] Like Sluckin's analysis, previously cited, that of Ashby falls down precisely where one might expect it to make its most telling point. These and other writers on cybernetics have apparently been so strongly influenced by traditional habit theory that, despite their expert understanding of feedback principles, they fall into the stereotyped pattern of thought about S—R bonds as the basis of learning or unlearning.

So striking and so puzzling is this oversight that one is moved to caution and doubt concerning the reasonableness of the alternative hypothesis which is fundamental to the present book. If this hypothesis is sound, it would seem likely that it would have been independently articulated by various writers, and particularly by those with concerns jointly covering cybernetics and learning. However, at least a cursory survey of the available literature (Jeffress, 1951; von Foerster, 1950, 1953) gives no lead to any parallel statement, a fact that certainly should suggest more than the usual degree of tentativeness in advocating or accepting such a view.

[6] This is all the more puzzling because the passage from Bartlett, which was quoted by Ashby (p. 271), obviously refers to feedback of the first rather than of the second kind.

VII. Can Feedback and Representation Be Combined?

In this chapter we have now examined two quite different approaches to those complex, highly organized activities which are subsumed under the concept of consciousness. Following the suggestion of Nuttin, we have explored the notion that what he calls "representation" lies at the heart of such activities; and we have also reviewed the basic principles which are incorporated in those self-regulatory machines which most nearly approximate the higher (mental) capacities of living organisms. The question we must now consider is whether these two approaches are essentially independent, perhaps even inconsistent, or whether they are capable of being combined into a still more powerful and comprehensive conceptual model. This is a question whose answering calls for specialized competence which is beyond that of the present writer; but it is our good fortune that a research team, consisting of W. T. Powers, R. L. McFarland, and R. K. Clark (1957), of the Chicago VA Research Hospital, have tackled precisely this problem and have kindly made available an advance copy of a paper entitled "A General Feedback Theory of Human Behavior" in which they give the results of some years of thought and experimentation.[7] Despite its highly synoptic style, this paper runs to fifty typescript pages and obviously cannot be substantively summarized in the course of a few pages. What can be done—and for our purposes will suffice—is to describe the *strategy* of the authors' efforts and the *direction* in which they are attempting to move.

These writers begin by remarking:

> To those readers already well-acquainted with electronic feedback theory we can state the essence of what we have to present here in a few words: we have observed that human feedback systems can be governed by control of their reference-levels. Using this insight we have found it possible to build up a hierarchical assembly of feedback systems in which control is accomplished thru a higher system's setting the reference-levels for lower systems. These concepts appear to constitute a new organizing principle for psychology. We hope that this may be one of the results which many people have been seeking since the birth of cybernetics (p. 1).

Much is being said or implied here which becomes fully comprehensible only as one reads on into the Powers-McFarland-Clark paper; but the general notion which the writers wish to present will be clear

[7] For an account of somewhat similar enterprises, see Fairbanks (1954), Jacobson (1955), J. G. Miller (1955), and Osgood (1957).

to the reader if only one "translation" is made. Later in the paper it becomes apparent that by "reference-levels" the writers mean something very similar to what Nuttin refers to as the *representation function* and to what we have denoted by such terms as image, mediator, and (perhaps) emotion (see also Fairbanks' notion of a "comparator," 1954). Thus the integration of feedback theory and the concept of representation becomes an explicit objective. The writers continue their introductory remarks as follows:

What our model will do, we hope, is to make such diverse points of view *make sense in terms of each other;* in other words, we consider our model to be first of all an organizing principle, an overall description of human organization, that may lead to some of the *basic* theory that has been lacking in behavioral science for so long. Such a statement may seem somewhat immodest: let us add that none of the authors has any illusions about the sources of our ideas. We have only attempted to organize what has been done by others (p. 2).

The authors then pursue their analysis by observing that:

Feedback concepts have been used in behavioral theories for (literally) centuries, in the form of various "self-correcting" aspects of psychological models. The concept that all behavior is designed to minimize stimuli [error activation, in cybernetic terms] is an elementary feedback idea, as is the concept of homeostasis as applied to the human system by Cannon (p. 3).

However, before such general notions can be maximally useful they must be exemplified in more specific detail; and it is here that the real difficulty is encountered. Those machines which are capable of the most strikingly "intelligent" performances are, of course, the giant computers, of which there are two principal varieties: *digital* computers and *analogue* computers. Since the former operate electrically (by means of relays) or electronically (by means of vacuum tubes or transistors) and are usually both more accurate and more rapid than the latter (which, in the typical instance, operate on some mechanical principle), the tendency has been to take the digital computer as the model for mental operations (cf., for example, Von Neumann, 1958; Newell, Shaw, & Simon, 1957, 1958). But despite ingenious attempts to liken the laws of neuronic action to digital-computation principles (see, e.g., McCulloch & Pitts, 1948), the would-be union has not been a happy or fruitful one; and Powers, McFarland, and Clark are well advised in their selection to the *analogue* computer as their model. They say:

An analogue computer is inherently less precise than a digital computer, because instead of relying on counting techniques (which can be carried to any desired degree of accuracy) based on exact equations, it depends on setting up a system whose properties are analogous to the properties of the equation or the physical system under study. But fortunately the analogue computer has several great advantages over the digital computer as far as our use of it is concerned: it provides a technique for representing a system in terms of its *functions*, which need be defined only as the problem requires, and in terms of the signals which are handled by these functions. It gives us a representation of relationships within the system under study such that we can often get an intuitive grasp of the system's operation. Given a system which can validly be looked upon as an analogue computer, the feedback concepts inherent in this approach make it possible to make moderately precise predictions of the behavior of the whole system. Perhaps one final advantage of the analogue techniques should be mentioned: to analyze the organization of human behavior in this way requires only a knowledge of the *functions* performed by the person, whereas the digital approach as exemplified in cybernetics demands ultimately a complete knowledge of the structure of the nervous system, neurone by neurone. Of course the digital techniques can be "smoothed" so that they come to resemble analogue techniques, and may eventually lead to more precise and complete knowledge, but at the moment even moderately precise knowledge more easily gained has an essential place in our study of behavior (pp. 5–6).

When one comes to think of it, *analogy* and *representation* are strikingly similar concepts: both imply a *likeness* between two different objects, events, or processes. Thus, we can say, readily enough, that fear is the *analogue* of pain and still mean that the pain is *represented*, functionally, by the fear. The very term *image* implies an analogy or likeness; and in order for one event to *mediate* another, there must in some sense be an equivalence.[8] Thus, by the happy choice of the in some ways "inferior" analogue computer as their conceptual model, Powers, McFarland, and Clark avoid what, thus far, has been a blind alley for others. But even here they are quick to acknowledge the priority of others. They note that Ashby's Homeostat also functions on the analogue rather than the digital principle; but their approach differs from that of Ashby in the following ways:

The fundamental difference between our approach and Ashby's is in the "tightness" of feedback control involved in our model. Whereas Ashby conceives of human systems as being rather slow-acting and compliant to external forces, we conceive of the opposite, that most human feedback systems stay very close to the "resting state," and that small deviations result in immediate and strong corrections, thus rendering direct environmental forces relatively ineffectual except under extreme circumstances. Behavior, then, we say results from an alteration of the resting state within

[8] This equivalence may be either inherent or arbitrary. In the latter case we speak of *coding*.

the limits of a variable behavioral field, and that this alteration takes place *as a result of information received by the organism.* When the organism is driven past the limits of its abilities to maintain the prescribed momentary resting states, we assume with Ashby that some adaptive change in the system must occur. However we do not insist that the adapting function be random; our treatment of an organizing function allows for the possibility that the chief factor may be random, but we redefine "random" in relativistic terms (pp. 7–8).

It is evident that at this point the argument is becoming involved and technical to a degree which makes it impractical to try to follow it, in detail; but one aspect thereof deserves special notice:

> There is implied in all feedback systems a *reference-level* for the feedback signal, such that if the feedback signal moves above or below this level, the deviation is corrected. Therefore we introduce [into our conceptual system] a signal which carries the information defining this reference-level, and call it the Reference-Signal. Thus the Output Function acts on the difference between the Feedback and Reference-Signals, not on the Feedback Signal alone. It acts to keep this difference small. Since the Output Function must act on a signal much smaller than either the Reference or Feedback Signal, it must be sufficiently sensitive to produce a large Output Signal on the basis of a relatively small difference between Reference and Feedback Signals (pp. 10–11).

Here the reader will at once be reminded of many earlier allusions to this principle. For example, in Chapter 12 of *Learning Theory and Behavior*, the phenomenon of *skill* is analyzed in terms, not of "motor" fitness or refinements, but of highly trained *discriminations*, between the feedback from actual performance of an activity and a *standard* of performance which has already (by example, instruction, or past experience) been established. The parallelism to Feedback Signals and Reference Signals, as used by the authors cited, will be evident.

Or, take the case of the autism theory of word learning (Chapter 3). Here it is assumed that a human infant or "talking" bird becomes able to *say* a word by virtue of the fact that he already "knows" what it *sounds like* and can practice the response against the model which already exists (in memory or "imagination").

These, of course, are not isolated or unusual examples: they typify the *general* conception of response selection and performance which is basic to our analysis as a whole; and it is believed that this conception is strikingly congruent with the theoretical model elaborated by Powers *et al.* In concluding, these writers say that their next concern will be in "relating feedback theory to other theories of human behavior, and to that end our next papers will be directed" (p. 50). It is hoped that, in those papers, they too will see this same congruence. But, in any event, their approach is off to a good start empirically in that it has enabled these investigators to devise (or suggest) a number of practical procedures or experiments, of which the following is representative.

The analysis of the first four orders of control may prove to be a very useful clinical tool; it has been pointed out that clonus oscillations and the oscillations seen in certain neural disorders are at a frequency we would assign to the first-order systems. By our method of artificially unstabilizing the control-systems by use of negative damping, we can emphasize tendencies to oscillations before they might otherwise become clinically noticeable (p. 48).

The system obviously has "power" and we may look forward to its further development and application with high expectation.[9]

VIII. Some Guideposts to Research

The present section was part of a preliminary draft of this chapter which was written before the work of Powers, McFarland, and Clark had come to the author's attention. It therefore made no allusion to

---

[9] The writer is indebted for a recent letter from Dr. Clark who, with his colleagues, has been good enough to read a manuscript copy of this chapter. While expressing general agreement with the present analysis, Dr. Clark suggests this refinement in the interpretation of the Powers-McFarland-Clark system: "The concept of 'reference-level' is based on the way information is used in a feedback system rather than on what variables this information represents. Whenever any kind of 'stored' information functions to determine the equilibrium state of the feedback system (remember that this means the reference level to which that system brings its *input* information), we refer to it as the reference-signal. We have formally postulated that these reference-signals are replayed recordings of past feedback (input) signals, and so are quite properly considered as memories or 'images.' In this sense, our 'reference-signal' is what Nuttin calls a 'vicarious presence' of perception, but we differ sharply from him in that we suppose that the system's input signals are also 'representations' of environmental variables, and are *not at all* those variables themselves. (We find it rather hard to imagine how the nervous system can perceive anything until it is represented by a neural signal.)" The notion that performance represents an attempt to match a standard or "reference level" of some sort can be given greater generality, and familiarity, by recalling the Lewinian notions, already widely current in psychological literature, of "level of aspiration" and "performance level" and the Freudian concepts of ego and superego. In sociology there is also the notion of actual behavior and "ideal pattern" or "role expectation." *Discrepancy* between the ideal and the actual, in all these systems, is assumed to be motivating and self-correcting. For a somewhat similar attack upon this type of problem, see Jacobson (1955).

Reference Signals and Feedback Signals, as Powers *et al.* employ these terms; but it now develops that this section nevertheless provides two rather dramatic instances of their applicability. In the first procedure here described, we are obviously dealing with a situation in which the Reference Signals are maintained intact but where the Feedback Signals which would normally be operative are excluded. Thus all basis for comparison (the authors cited speak of a Comparator Function, pp. 11 ff.) is eliminated, and it is not surprising that performance (presumptively) becomes chaotic (see also Fairbanks, 1954).

In the second set of observations reported we have the interesting situation where two different sources of sensory feedback, which ordinarily vary together in an orderly, predictable way, are rendered incompatible and discordant (see also Riggs *et al.*, 1953). Here, too, are possibilities for further research (which are at least in part anticipated by the reference of Powers *et al.* to the phenomenon of *conflict* in their system).

With this preamble, the section follows, very much as originally written.

When the author recently made a summary presentation of the revised two-factor interpretation of learning at a neighboring university, a question was asked which went as follows:

> You posit that "habit" is—or at least *may* be—entirely a matter of the meanings that get associated with response-correlated stimuli; and from this it follows that if all such stimuli could be eliminated the "habit" would automatically be shorn of its "strength." Isn't such reasoning somewhat academic? For if you eliminate all the response-correlated stimuli or sensory "feedback," you also eliminate the stimuli that *initiate* the response.
>
> For example, take a rat in a Skinner box. Some of the stimuli which are correlated with bar pressing on the part of the rat are visual, i.e., the rat *sees* his paw as he places it on the bar and this constitutes a part of the feedback on which you assume habit strength depends. But you can't eliminate the rat's view of his paw, for experimental purposes, without also eliminating his view of the bar as well. And if the rat can't see the bar, then, of course, one wouldn't expect him to try to press it, no matter how strongly instigated he might be to press it when the bar was normally visible.

This is a good argument and one for which no adequate rejoinder was immediately forthcoming. However, a few days later the writer remembered an apparatus note, entitled, "A Device for Studying Eye-Hand Coordination without Visual Guidance," which was published more than twenty-five years ago (Mowrer, 1935). The following paragraphs are quoted therefrom:

In the manual localization or manipulation of a seen object, three distinct stimulus-factors are ordinarily involved: (1) visual stimulation from the object; (2) visual stimulation from the hand and arm; and (3) kinaesthetic (at times also cutaneous) stimulation from the hand and arm. An analysis of the extent to which each of these three factors contributes to the development and efficient performance of eye-hand reactions is of considerable importance. It is obvious, however, that neither the second nor the third factor can be studied in isolation from the first; for with the elimination of vision of the object, reactions made to it cease to be eye-hand reactions. In Ss in whom the kinaesthetic (and cutaneous) sensitivity of the hand and arm is absent, either as a result of neural lesion or local anaesthetization, the first and second simulus factors may simultaneously be studied, independently of the third (Lashley, 1917). But so far as the writer is aware no entirely satisfactory method has previously been devised for eliminating the second factor (visual stimulation from the hand and arm) in such a manner as to make possible the study of eye-hand reactions with

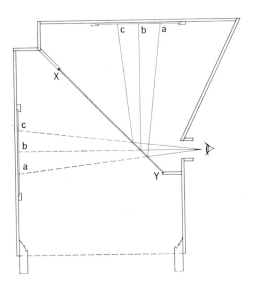

Fig. 7–2. Diagram of apparatus for testing eye-hand co-ordination without visual guidance. The diagonal partition (X–Y) consists of a plain mirror so situated as to cause the reflected image of the top of the upper compartment, as seen by subject through the indicated aperture, to appear in the position occupied by the back of the lower compartment. The lower compartment has no floor; and the central area of the front, below the shelf supporting the mirror, is also open, so that the subject, by extending his arm, can easily touch the back of the apparatus and reproduce, by drawing, the figure projected there from the top of the apparatus.

only the first and third (or only the first) factor operative.[10] The apparatus here described [see Fig. 7–2] was constructed with this end in view. . . .

The apparatus . . . should be found useful not only as a means of ex-

---

[10] Direct vision of the hand and arm is usually eliminated in mirror-drawing experiments, but the hand and arm can always be seen in the mirror (for illustration see G. M. Whipple, 1915, p. 122). In the Miles two-story maze all vision of the hand and arm is effectively eliminated, but the seen (top) maze is not spatially congruent with the explored (bottom) maze. For illustration of Miles' apparatus see W. Miles, 1927, p. 369; also C. M. Cox, 1928, facing p. 542.

ploring and demonstrating the role of visual guidance in the eye-hand co-ordination of adults, but also as a means of studying the development of this type of response in children. It may likewise facilitate the investigation of the effect of various positions of the eyes and head upon the tonus of the extremities. Again, it may be employed in the clinical diagnosis of certain subtle disorders of coordination (notably those arising from impaired kinaesthetic sensitivity). As an instrument for studying the effects of practice without knowledge of results its utility is obvious. Finally, by using Ss in whom the kinaesthetic sensitivity of the hand and arm is reduced or lacking, it should be possible with this apparatus to study eye-hand coordination at its simplest level, i.e., with vision of the object as the only stimulus-factor; such an investigation should provide significant information regarding the fundamental character of spatio-motor integration (pp. 493–495).

The excerpts just quoted were written well in advance of the cybernetics vogue, and even before the second version of two-factor learning theory had been clearly articulated by anyone. Nevertheless, they seem to offer a good way of demonstrating the role of information "feedback" in so-called habit. In Chapter 7 of *Learning Theory and Behavior* we have seen the effects upon speech that are produced by slightly delaying auditory feedback. In the apparatus just described, it is possible, in the case of eye-hand coordinations, or "habits," to eliminate visual feedback without interfering with the visual field in which the action is to occur; and, by means of afferent nerve blocks, it should be possible to eliminate all cutaneous and proprioceptive backlash as well, thus leaving, presumably, no feedback at all. At least one physiological psychologist, to whom the question has been put, has confidently predicted that, under the conditions described, "performance would go completely to pot."

If "habit" is a matter of stimulus-response bonds, of the kind postulated by Thorndike and later implicitly assumed by Hull (see Chapter 1), then, given proper motivation and the visual field in the above example, established "habits" ought to run off smoothly enough. Such does not seem at all likely to occur. However, research rather than argument is what we need here most urgently (cf. Slack, 1955).

In the apparatus note just alluded to, the strategy for showing the role of feedback in habit involves the *elimination* of one or more modalities of information. Let us now ask what happens if two modalities of feedback, which are normally congruent, are rendered *incongruent*. In postural and locomotor "habits," gravitational and visual cues are normally anchored in a relatively invariant manner. Because both stationary and moving objects in our environment have to maintain certain characteristic positions if they are to preserve their "balance," we are accustomed to certain visual stimuli, e.g., the vertical lines of buildings, being parallel to the direction of gravity as it impinges upon our bodies. Therefore, one wonders what happens under those relatively abnormal circumstances where there is a discrepancy between visual and gravitational cues. Such a discrepancy may be noted, in a limited way, as one rounds a curve on a train; but a much more dramatic and instructive instance has been reported by Gibson & Mowrer (1938):

A striking opportunity to observe the influence of centrifugal force upon the perception of the vertical (and one which, so far as the writers are aware, has not previously been taken advantage of) is that afforded by the so-called "motordrome," where vehicles travel around the inside wall of a large vertical cylinder.

In order to obtain some notion concerning the sensory impressions of persons who perform in these motordromes, one of the writers has questioned several such persons and on two occasions has accompanied one of them. In a "drome" with a diameter of 40 feet, a motorcycle traveling around the vertical sidewall at a speed of 35 m.p.h. is acted upon by a horizontal centrifugal force equal to approximately 3.9 times gravity. Naturally one's "weight" under such conditions is relatively tremendous; the task of lifting a hand (which feels as if it might be made of lead) involves exorbitant effort. At still greater speeds the blood is centrifuged from the head, with ensuing cerebral enemia and loss of consciousness, the occurrence of which is presaged by what the riders refer to as "going blind." Following a ride in a motordrome there is also an interesting form of postrotational nystagmus which, however, cannot be pertinently discussed here.

Without exception performers in a motordrome report the feeling that they are riding in a virtually upright position, with the motordrome lying on its side and rolling along barrel-fashion. The actually vertical wall of the motordrome 'beneath' them is perfectly horizontal. Therefore, since the vector resultant formed by centrifugal force and gravity is not quite perpendicular to the wall of the motordrome (deviating about 14° at a speed of 35 m.p.h. in a "drome" of the size indicated), a motorcycle rider will feel that he is tilted slightly away from his perceived vertical, which is perpendicular to the wall. Experienced riders learn to accept this unnatural position, but for the neophyte it is extremely disconcerting, causing him continually to be trying to "straighten up" (i.e., sit in an actually horizontal position) which of course interferes with the balancing of the motorcycle.

On the first occasion when the writer accompanied a professional rider in a motordrome, the only describable experience was one of complete spatial disorientation. Movement was clearly perceptible but it was impossible to give it any definite directional reference. It was as if a complexly integrated perceptual mechanism had completely broken down; and this, we conjecture, is precisely what had happened. Visual and postural factors were thrown into such violent conflict that no stable perceptual organization could emerge. However, on the occasion of the second ride (which occurred only a few minutes after the first), this confusion disappeared, and the spatial illusion by veteran riders was vividly experienced.

Here it is significant to note that although this illusion, that the motor-drome is lying on its side and revolving in this position, clearly reveals the predominance of what we have called gravitational factors over visual factors, nevertheless visual factors exert some influence on the perceived vertical. If the g-factors were the sole determinants in this situation the rider's apparent vertical would deviate just 76° from the real vertical, coinciding with the vector resultant. As it is, the rider's vertical deviates 90° from the real vertical, presumably under the influence of a visual tendency for the sidewall to determine the rider's horizontal. In other words we are accustomed to ride in a visually upright position on a horizontal surface, and within limits this visual factor exerts its own influence. A new perceptual integration is achieved, in which gravitational factors are the primary determinants, but which is also influenced to some degree by visual cues (pp. 316–318).[11]

The observations just cited raise some interesting questions, only a few of which we can consider here. First let us ask: How can we account, in terms of learning theory, for the dominance of gravitational cues over visual cues? It would appear that when the two are first dissociated, there is a period of profound conflict; but then, remarkably quickly, the subject "learns" to orient on the basis of gravity rather than vision. Why so? Because, presumably, the consequences of giving gravity priority are more rewarding, less punishing than are the consequences of giving vision priority and disregarding gravity. In other words, it is more *important*, in the total economy of an organism, to "obey" gravitational cues than it is to obey certain visual ones; and one can reasonably infer that the issue is decided (quite quickly) upon the basis of simple rewards and punishments.

But then one wonders if the observations just cited have any unique or differential bearing upon the assumptions underlying revised two-factor theory. Perhaps not, in any way that is immediately apparent. But further attention to the problem may suggest some researchable inferences.

IX. Response Initiation and Related Problems

Although the preceding sections of this chapter may convey the impression that we are at last "closing in" on some of the most recalcitrant of psychological problems, there is no denying that sizable

---

[11] It must be kept in mind that the intensity of the total mass acceleration acting upon the body in a motordrome is several times greater than normal gravity. Because of this augmentation of intensity, it is possible that spatial perception is here influenced somewhat more by what we have called gravitational factors than would be the case if the direction of gravity could be changed without its magnitude also being altered (cf. the "haunted-swing" illusion).

mysteries are still at large. One of these is the mystery of response initiation. This problem does not, of course, arise in a strict S—R psychology: a stimulus impinges upon the organism and, because of a direct (innate or learned) neural connection therewith, a particular response ensues. But as soon as this hypothetical connection is broken— as it obviously must be—by the introduction of *central* (intervening) processes, the whole question of response selection and control re-emerges in acute form. The assertion that the *person, self,* or *ego* chooses, decides, wills what to do, while corresponding to common perception, does not provide a scientific solution to the problem. Does cybernetics substantially advance our understanding here?

Slack (1955), to cite only one of many contemporary theorists who have been much influenced by cybernetic thought, has taken the position "that we do not know what the stimulus is unless we know what the response is and we do not know what the response is unless we know what the stimulus is" (p. 267). This view, of course, is predicated on the assumption that we are here dealing, not with open-circuit reflexes, but with closed-circuit, voluntary, self-regulated re-sponses of the sort we have identified as "habitual." Without benefit of constant sensory feedback *from* the response, *as* it is occurring, the response is assumed to be impossible.

After half a century of radical behaviorism (S—R psychology), this all sounds quite daring and new. But it is not. We have already seen (in Chapter 5) that in 1896 Dewey clearly perceived the difference between a reflex *arc* and the total neural *circle* involved in actual be-havior. And in his *Principles of Psychology*, published in 1890, in the chapter on "Will" (in Vol. II), William James even more explicitly anticipated present-day developments. For full realization of how truly remarkable this chapter is, in light of contemporary thinking, it must be read in its entirety; but perhaps its most remarkable feature is the extent to which the author makes sensory feedback from action es-sential to the continuation, and even initiation, thereof. James cites clinical reports on a number of individuals in whom kinesthetic impulses were lacking or seriously impaired, and shows that here voluntary movement was possible only with visual guidance. For example, he quotes the following passage from a report by Strümpell concerning "his wonderful anaesthetic boy, whose only source of feeling were the right eye and the left ear" (p. 489):

"One could observe how his eye was directed first to the object held before him, then to his own arm; and how it never ceased to follow the latter during its entire movement. All his voluntary movements took place under the unremitting lead of the eye, which as an indispensable guide, was never untrue to its functions" (pp. 491–492).

And when, in such a case, vision is eliminated, it is often impossible for the individual even to *start* a particular movement.

Thus Dr. Strumpell relates how turning over the boy's hand made him bend the little finger instead of the forefinger [as directed], when his eye was closed. "Ordered to point, e.g., toward the left with his left arm, the arm was usually raised straight forward, and then wandered about in groping un- certainty, sometimes getting the right position and then leaving it again. Similarly with the lower limbs. . . . The turning of the head, too, from right to left, towards certain objects known to the patient, only ensued correctly when the patient, immediately before his eye was bandaged, specially refreshed his perception as to what the required movement was to be" (p. 491).

"This," says James after reviewing much similar evidence, "is perhaps all that need be said about the existence of passive sensations of move- ment and their indispensableness for our voluntary activity" (p. 492). He was clearly convinced that response without concomitant stimula- tion was highly inefficient, if not altogether impossible; and he quite energetically opposed the notion, then current, of a *"feeling of innerva- tion."* The only *feeling* of movement or action, James argued, comes from the kinesthetic and other sensations which the movement itself produces (see also Mead, 1934, pp. 70–71).

Moreover, James anticipated present-day developments in positing a notion very similar to that implied by Powers, McFarland, and Clark in the use of their term "Reference Signals." He said:

One has only to play tenpins or billiards, or throw a ball, to catch his will in the act, as it were, of balancing tentatively its possible effects, and ideally rehearsing various muscular contractions nearly correct, until it gets just the right one before it, when it says "Now go!" This premonitory weighing feels so much like a succession of tentative sailings forth to power into the outer world, followed by correction just in time to avoid the irrevocable deed, that the notion that *outgoing* nerve-currents rather than mere vestiges of former passive sensibility accompany it, is a most natural [but erroneous] one to entertain (p. 493).

We may consequently set it down as certain that, *whether or not there be anything else in the mind at the moment when we consciously will a certain act, a mental conception made up of memory-images of these sensa- tions, defining which special act it is, must be there* (p. 492; italics added).

The implications of this way of thinking for *skill* learning did not escape James, and we find him saying:

So in acquiring any art or voluntary function, the marksman ends by thinking only of the exact position of the goal, the singer only of the perfect sound, the balancer only of the point of the pole whose oscillations he must counteract. The associated mechanism has become so perfect in all these persons that each variation in the thought of the end is functionally correlated with the one movement fitted to bring the latter about (p. 497).

But despite the shrewdness of these observations (and of similar ones by Dewey), they fell among stones and were not to get a congenial hearing for more than half a century. Why, one must ask, was this the case? The answer undoubtedly is complex; but we may conjecture that one important element in the situation was the lack, in James' account, of a proper emphasis upon motivation or dynamics. If our analysis is sound, a particular course of behavior is selected, or "willed," because its image, or anticipated occurrence, arouses hope; whereas its nonoccurrence or incorrect occurrence arouses no hope, or even fear. There is presumably, as James implies, a kind of *scanning* of various possibilities which occurs in connection with response selection (cf. Jeffress, 1951; Adrain *et al.*, 1954); and here *symbolic* behavior seems to play a crucial role. But this way of thinking about the problem only raises the anterior question: How is the appropriate scanning or symbolic behavior itself selected? Why, for example, does a rat at a choice point move its head (in VTE) laterally, rather than vertically— or why does it move its head at all? Or, in the case of a human being confronted by a particular problem, why do *relevant*, rather than purely random, symbols "occur" to him? Admission of connectionism, at *this* level, might solve the problem; but, having rejected it at the level of gross, overt behavior, one is loath to admit it at the symbolic level. Perhaps this is a mistake; perhaps connectionism holds for symbolic behavior. There must, after all, be a limit to this positing of higher and higher mechanisms of control (cf. Powers, McFarland, and Clark) and to the introduction of more and more intervening ("central") factors. Otherwise one explains nothing and ends in an infinite regress.[12]

[12] Or the solution might go as follows. A hungry boy who has never before eaten an apple sees one and samples it. It is pleasant tasting and satisfies his hunger. Conceivably the sight, smell, and taste of the apple and the other sensations (proprioceptive and the like) associated with the act of eating become *conditioned to the hunger drive*, so that when the hunger subsequently recurs, the boy will "think of" apple eating, i.e., he will have *images* derived from the earlier experience. The hope (secondary reinforcement) which was conditioned to the sensations will now generalize to the images; and, lacking conflicting impulses, the boy will start trying to find another apple. Here we are making a number of assumptions which are highly unorthodox as far as conventional learning theory is concerned; but they may nonetheless be valid. Thorndike by-passed any such thinking on the premise that, in the situation described, a bond is forged *directly*

Or perhaps the solution lies in the notion of an even more elaborate and comprehensive type of scanning. Many electronic devices (e.g., television and radar) employ extensive "sweep circuits"; and it is conceivable that similar activities go on constantly in the brain, during consciousness (cf. Pitts & McCulloch, 1947; Walter, 1954; Ellingson, 1956) and that our images and other symbolic reactions are selected by a process whereby the *needs* of the moment either concentrate the scanning process in certain "areas" or produce a differential sensitivity of some sort.[13] Here we are obviously still in a no-man's-land; but the

---

between hunger and apple-seeking and apple-eating behavior. The difficulties inherent in this view are well known. In Pavlovian parlance, one might speak of some reaction elicited by the apple (e.g., salivation) getting conditioned to some stimulus experienced just before (or as) the apple was eaten (e.g., the sight or smell of the apple); but one would *not* be inclined to think of the *hunger drive* becoming a conditioned stimulus. This is precisely what the foregoing analysis presupposes, that the hunger becomes the conditioned stimulus for arousing an image of apple and apple eating, to which has also been conditioned the emotion of hope which, for reasons previously considered in this book, would put the individual into more or less appropriate action. In Section VII of this chapter some importance has already been attached to the concept of "reference level," image, or standard toward which an error-actuated servo-system always moves. Perhaps if images (of objects and of actions) get conditioned to drives, the program of "scansion" and "search" is solved. Moreover, there is already a considerable literature suggesting a relationship between drive, or need, and imagery. In a recent review of that literature, Noël Jenkins (1957) refers to the "relationship between need-state and such processes as imagery, association, and problem solving" (p. 107) and goes on to summarize the views of McClelland (1951) thus: "Motivation is presumed to have different effects at different intensity levels. When it is weak, in the 'wish fulfillment' stage, goal images occur. As it increases, a 'push toward reality' is experienced, in which *deprivation* imagery tends to replace goal imagery" (p. 108). In some ways the hypothesis under examination here is reminiscent of the older notion of the "association of ideas," but the defect there was lack of the concept of reinforcement; and much the same comment can be made with respect to so-called S—S contiguity theory (Tolman, 1932; Birch & Bitterman, 1951). This note is written just as this book goes to press; otherwise an effort would be made to integrate the above analysis into the text and to explore further its systematic implications. But from this preliminary examination, it seems to have considerable promise as a means of extricating ourselves from the dilemma into which our analysis up to this point has led us. (For a somewhat similar attack upon this problem, see Miller, 1958; also Dollard & Miller, 1952; cf. footnote 4, Chapter 5 of this volume; Fairbanks, 1954; Mowrer, 1960, Chapter 8, Section VII.)

[13] How, one wonders, has this problem been solved in the great self-regulatory machines? Or *has* it been solved? An operator still has to "wire in" the instructions, i.e., *make* certain connections before the machine can operate. In living organisms there is likewise a certain minimum of fixed connections; but there is also an apparent indeterminancy which does not exist in the machine.

clinical phenomenon of *aphasia* offers some unique opportunities for trenchant inquiry. The author is indebted to Professor M. D. Steer, of Purdue University, for this observation by N. C. Kephart: "The trouble with the mentally retarded child is that he has his marbles but doesn't have enough of them, whereas the brain-injured [aphasic] child has all his marbles but can't find them." Once the aphasic individual is *reminded* of the name of the object in question, he can utter the word quite readily; the trouble, truly, is one of locating, finding it. Osgood, sensing the special theoretical importances of aphasia, has recently instituted an intensive program of investigation; but, in a less dramatic way, everyone is familiar with the problem in terms of momentary inability to "get" just the right word, to recall a name, and like experiences. Whether these functional failures are dynamically determined (blocked), as Freud (1920) has maintained, or have some other explanation is not immediately important; but they function, in any case, quite admirably to remind us that *selection* occurs in thought as well as in deed and that both success and failure in respect to these functions pose problems for future inquiry (see Schuell & Jenkins, 1959).

X. Learning and the Unconscious

The only other problem to which we shall address ourselves in this chapter has to do with the role of *un*conscious activities in mental life, and more particularly the question of their relationship to learning. As we have repeatedly seen, both living organisms and machines can "behave" in highly complex and "intelligent" ways without necessarily exhibiting the phenomenon of learning. And learning may be found in relatively simple organisms; and at least its analogue can be exhibited by even simple machines (Sluckin, 1954). Therefore, psychologists have been moved to ask: Is consciousness necessary for learning? Under the heading of "incidental learning," "learning without awareness," and the like, various writers (McGeoch & Irion, 1952; Postman & Jarrett, 1952; Scheerer, 1953; Eriksen, 1958; McConnell, Cutler, & McNeil, 1958; and others) have dealt with this issue in interesting and ingenious ways; but, from one point of view, the question is already answered, and categorically so. *All* learning, it seems, is "unconscious." As noted elsewhere (Mowrer, 1960, Chapter 1), there is *never* any sensation or awareness of learning as such. We see the *results*, in our own behavior and that of others, of learning; and we can deliberately put ourselves into a position or situation *to learn*. But this, presumably, is not quite the point in the studies cited.

Perhaps the problem will take on greater tangibility if we get down to cases. Suppose a human being is used as a subject in an experiment on the conditioning of fear, as measured by the psychogalvanic response (PGR), and that a tone and an electric shock are the CS and UnCS, respectively. After a few paired presentations of these two events, the subject will report: "The tone is followed by the shock and so makes me afraid." But how does he *know* this? If the learning involved only the conditioning of fear, then the tone might well evoke this response, but the subject would not know what he was *afraid of*. Normally, along with the fear conditioning, there will be a cognitive, or imaginal, conditioning: the tone will call up, not only the emotion of fear, but also an image of the shock, thus enabling the individual to "know" *why* he is afraid—he is afraid *of* the shock (see Chapter 5).

It is not uncommon, however, for human beings (and quite possibly other organisms) to experience emotions and *not* know why. Here, apparently, the emotional conditioning "comes through" but the imaginal conditioning (memory) does not. Consider this instance. A friend of the writer's normally eats and sleeps well, but for a few days he noted slight disturbances with respect to both these functions and a vague feeling of uneasiness. And before going to bed on the night in question, he sat quietly for half an hour or so trying very hard to discover the source of his "anxiety." Finally, without success, he went to bed and shortly to sleep; but later in the night he woke in a "cold sweat" and upon getting up to dry himself off had a clear perception of the cause of his difficulties. Two days hence he was to read a paper at a scientific meeting. The paper was already written, and he had rather looked forward to presenting it. So, superficially at least, there was "nothing to worry about." But, as the time approached for the actual presentation, his "unconscious" had become apprehensive about the presentation, considerably in advance of his knowing consciously *why* he was emotionally aroused. Perhaps it is observations of this kind that have prompted Lacey (1956) to refer to the emotions as "the voice of the unconscious" (see also Section I). When we have the affects without the appropriate imagery, we are likely to say that our unconscious is "bothering" us; whereas, if the appropriate imagery is present, the same emotional disturbance will be referred to in quite different terms.[14]

[14] The writer is indebted to Dr. Herbert Lansdell (1958) for first calling his attention to the possibility that emotional responses can be conditioned (through thalamic centers of the brain) without concomitant cognitive learning (presumably in the cortex) and thus suggesting a neuroanatomical locus for "the unconscious." In support of the notion that "learning without fine discrimination" occurs in the

Usually the assumption, in cases such as the one cited, is that the "ideational content" that ought to accompany the emotion has been "repressed" or otherwise dynamically obstructed. And in Chapter 10 we shall revert to this line of thought. But here we are more particularly concerned with those efforts that have been made to study this sort of phenomenon experimentally. In a well-known experiment reported by Divin in 1937, words were passed in review on a memory drum before human subjects; and on each occurrence of the word "barn," the subjects received an electric shock. Later it was found that the words such as "cow" and "chickens" also produced emotional reactions, as objectively measured by the PGR, without the subjects' awareness. Here, obviously, was a form of "unconscious generalization," which was being mediated by a concept which the subjects had not made explicit to themselves.

In the controversial Greenspoon experiment (already cited in Chapter 3), human subjects, under appropriate conditions of social reinforcement (minimal "grunts" of approval), show an increased tendency to produce, for example, plural nouns without being "aware" that the experimenter has been differentially reinforcing this category of responses (cf. Mandler & Kaplan, 1956). It would seem that, not fear, but *hope* (and resulting habit strength) has been conditioned to a certain class of verbal responses without the subject having a clear image of that class, category, or concept. Here it can hardly be a question of repression, since there is nothing unpleasant or embarrassing about the situation. Perhaps, since the "unconditioned stimulus" is a complex one, i.e., a *concept* rather than just a specific word, the difficulty is rather one of forming a clear image of it. The rather astonishing thing is that such categories can be identified *emotionally*, before they are intellectually! Can this be the primitive basis for imputation of "creativeness" to the unconscious (cf. Sachs, 1942; Jung, 1958)? [15]

---

reticular formation, Lansdell cites MacLean (1955), Sharpless & Jasper (1956), Jasper (1956), Himwich (1958), and somewhat earlier sources (e.g., Morgan & Stellar, 1950, pp. 271 and 447). For exploration along similar lines, see Bunch (1958); see also the discussion in Section I of this chapter of the distinction between wakefulness ("arousal") and consciousness ("cognition").

[15] Had it been available earlier, a new paper by Dulany (1960) could have altered and, quite possibly, simplified some of the foregoing discussion (see also Chapter 2, especially footnote 4). The Greenspoon type of experiment is so interesting and, for revised two-factor learning theory, embarrassing because it purports to show learning of a word class without conscious occurrence or use of any word or phrase on the part of the subject for this class. Said otherwise, the dilemma is this: How is it possible for a human being to develop an in-

Guthrie has criticized Tolman's version of learning as cognition without motivation. Normally, if our views are valid, learning involves *both* a cognitive (imaginal) and a motivation (emotional) aspect. Although both occur, it seems, by means of conditioning, they are apparently mediated by two rather different mechanisms. Certainly there is no *a priori* reason why these two forms of learning should always function in a strictly coordinated manner; and if the emotional reaction, so to say, gets ahead of the ideational reaction (or if the latter is dynamically inhibited), then we would have the condition typically described as "unconscious motivation," i.e., feelings of depression, elation, or apprehension which are not, so far as the subject can see, realistically justified. Perhaps the "justification" is there but is simply not perceived. The discovery or recovery of such ideation often constitutes the experience commonly termed "insight." [16]

---

creased tendency to utter, for example, plural nouns without the use of any word or phrase or concept to *mediate* the transfer of reinforcement from uttered words to unuttered words of this class? A rat learns to press a bar because there is a sameness about the patterns of sensory feedback which are followed by reward, and which therefore take on the capacity to arouse (or "mediate") secondary reinforcement. In other words, the habit of pressing the bar for food develops because there is so much *in common* between all bar-pressing responses. But *men* is not at all "the same" as *turnips* or *boxes*, and it is not immediately apparent how rewarding the subject for saying "men" will increase his tendency to say "turnips" or "boxes" or other plural nouns, unless the *class* of words which brings reward is discovered, verbalized, and used as a guide to the selection of such words. The Greenspoon type of experiment seems to show that such learning is nevertheless possible—and has been especially congenial to those investigators who, following B. F. Skinner's lead, have largely rejected the concept of mediation (i.e., mediated generalization). The Dulany paper is highly pertinent at this juncture, for it provides an alternative way of interpreting the Greenspoon effect along quite different lines, which are compatible with reinforcement principles. Because Dulany's analysis is slightly involved, we shall not attempt to reproduce it in detail. But two or three sentences will catch the general tenor: "If we can even speak of learning here, Ss learned or insightfully grasped an often confirmed hypothesis, an hypothesis that 'Umhmm' followed upon associating in a series. They did not learn to respond with plural nouns; the increase in plural nouns is better credited directly to the transfer of a complex verbal habit" (p. 7). "If associating after plural nouns brings more plural nouns with a set to continue a series than with a set to find a new category, the present verbal reinforcement effect could be ascribed to the mediation hypothesis that cue prior verbal habits" (p. 8). It seems that Dulany is well on the way to dissolving a very troublesome paradox and to opening the way to the further development and consolidation of systematic learning principles (cf. Staats, 1959b; Maltzman, Brook, Bogartz, & Summers, 1958; and Dulany and Eriksen, 1959).

[16] For a collection of interesting papers on "unconscious motivation," see Stacey & DeMartino (1958); also J. G. Miller (1942).

The foregoing discussion is admittedly fragmentary and far from logically rigorous; but the question of conscious and unconscious factors in learning and behavior control is so important that it cannot be ignored merely because it is still perplexing. This morning the author had the experience, as not infrequently happens, of waking up precisely at his usual rising time, slightly in advance of the ringing of the family alarm clock. He was dreaming about some difficulties connected with the completion of this chapter, and they were sufficiently disturbing to disrupt sleep. How, within the framework of learning theory, as presently conceived, can we account for this type of phenomenon?

Or, take the remarkable effects that can be produced by means of hypnosis—or that occur spontaneously in various pathological states of dissociation: fuges, multiple personality, and the like. These phenomena are so tangible and yet so baffling that at least one erstwhile student of learning (Hilgard, 1958) has decided that in the whole area of psychology, *they* offer the most important and crucial research possibilities and challenges. In a volume such as the present one, it is not possible or, at this stage of knowledge, appropriate to give much attention to this sort of thing; but in Chapter 10 we shall briefly return to it, from a somewhat different vantage point. In the meantime, we shall explore another of the many directions in which modern learning theory ramifies.[17]

[17] The writer has just had occasion to review a remarkable book-length manuscript entitled *The Mind of Robots*, by J. T. Culbertson (1960). In it the author argues that it is now possible, at least theoretically, to produce the phenomenon of consciousness synthetically. Other students of automation have, of course, often commented upon the parallels between the accomplishments of computers and of minds, but only by a far stretch of the imagination can the former be said to be "conscious." Now, by a new set of assumptions and principles (including those of "nerve nets"), Dr. Culbertson believes that *bona fide* consciousness can be *created artificially*. This is a bold proposal and, if substantiated, will constitute another major breakthrough in man's attempt to understand his Universe. (Had it been possible, this footnote would have appeared, as indicated, on p. 253).

8

Learning, Causality, Probability, and Statistics

This chapter and the next one stem from the following, somewhat anomalous circumstances. If one reads the writings of mathematicians on the subject of statistics and probability, one finds frequent allusion to certain "psychological problems" which are at least tacitly disavowed. And if one follows the work of psychologists, one discovers that for certain purposes they resort, quite freely, to mathematical procedures, with the intimation that the problems involved are non-psychological or at least metapsychological.

If one could be sure that this interaction represented a genuine division of labor and competence, all would be well. But there are indications that some of the problems which the mathematicians say are *psychological* are the same as, or at least not very different from, the problems which psychologists take to be *mathematical*, with the result that these problems are tossed back and forth, in the manner of the proverbial "hot potato," and thus remain very much "up in the air." Here our attempt will be to try to get a firmer grasp on some of these issues and to try to think them through psychologically rather than wish them off on the mathematicians. After all, ultimate reality is presumably unitary—and the distinction between mathematics and psychology arbitrary.

I. The Problem Stated and Exemplified

This chapter has been written, discarded and rewritten three times; and were it not that the rest of this book has already gone to press, it is entirely possible that, after due criticism and reconsideration, the present version would suffer a similar fate.[1] Therefore, what is to follow is offered with no great confidence, and certainly with no intimation of finality. But something has surely been gained from earlier explorations and the over-all nature of the underlying problem or problems more precisely identified. Moreover, developments in the psychology of learning which have been reviewed in *Learning Theory and Behavior* and in antecedent chapters of the present volume suggest a much more natural linkage with probability theory than did earlier behavioristic and reflexological approaches; and if we do not here fully succeed in our attempt to explicate this relationship, others, profiting from our mistakes, eventually will.

Gradually, from the earlier efforts to write this chapter, one generality has emerged which can be set forth with something like assurance, namely, that all scientific endeavor is, in the final analysis, concerned with the ascertainment of *causal connections*. Of late it has been fashionable in some quarters to deny the validity of the whole notion of causation; but here we shall continue to accept both the validity and the necessity of this concept and will assume, further, that it is the *sine qua non* for all practical prediction and control (cf. Bolles & Messick, 1958; Boole, 1854; Fisher, 1956; Mandler, 1959; Peirce, 1878b; and von Mises, 1957; also Sections II and VII).

In the history of the race and in the development of each individual, many cause-effect relationships are so obvious, and so quickly "learned" (see also Chapter 9), that no refined form of inquiry or "proof" is needed. For example, it is so readily and so universally discoverable that a sharp object pressed into the skin will (normally) *cause pain* that there is not the least doubt about it and no one needs to set about elaborately investigating and establishing this "effect." And so far as is known, there has likewise never been much doubt or controversy about the superiority of round wheels over square ones.[2] But there

---

[1] For illuminating comments on an earlier draft of this chapter, the writer is much indebted to his colleagues, Dr. Lee J. Cronbach, Dr. William E. Kappauf, and Dr. Lloyd G. Humphreys, and to Dr. Leonard J. Savage of the Department of Mathematics at the University of Chicago. While these gentlemen cannot be held accountable for what is said in the present version of this chapter, they at least deserve credit for protecting the reader from earlier, more primitive false starts and errors.

[2] Bilodeau (1952) makes the point well when he says: "Of the countless hypotheses which are set up every day by scientist and layman alike, most do not undergo the rigors of a statistical test. Regardless of the nature and quantity of data available, most of our decisions are made—hypotheses are retained or rejected —without recourse to mathematical formulation or development" (p. 271).

are many other situations where causality is much less clear and good practice correspondingly less certain; and here we have resorted and are still resorting to those specialized techniques which, hopefully, help make the "evidence" less equivocal and are conducive to general agreement.

One of the most rudimentary and important of scientific devices is, of course, that of "controls" or "checks." If, for example, on the basis of casual observation, someone develops the hypothesis that fish will helpfully fertilize growing corn, and if one then applies fish to all the corn planted in a given year and if the corn does indeed grow unusually well that year, there is a *presumption* that the hypothesis is valid. But a skeptic might cogently argue that the good yield was due to "something else"—perhaps some concomitant variation in cultivation, unusually abundant or propitious rainfall, or some other "confounded" (coincidental) variable. So the sensible thing to do is to apply the special treatment to certain hills of corn and not to others. If, now, it is found that the treated hills produce a perceptibly larger yield than do the untreated ones, one cannot attribute the effect to some *general* (confounded) condition, such as cultivation or rainfall, and has to admit that the effect is *probably* due to the special treatment.[3]

But why is one here disposed to say "probably" rather than "certainly"? Systematic error (confounding) has been eliminated, so why is not the causal relationship unambiguous and sure? In some ways this question is pedantic; for without having a precise answer to it, primitive "scientists" and men of affairs made innumerable important discoveries and demonstrated them to others with sufficient cogency to effect many new and improved ways of doing things.[4] Nevertheless, the question is interesting; and as late as 1876 we find Charles Darwin

[3] For discussion of modern refinements in the use of experimental controls, especially in agriculture, see Fisher (1937).

[4] Writing in 1956, Newman remarked that "It is three hundred years exactly since Pascal and Fermat conducted their famous exchange of letters dealing with a question proposed by the gambler Chevalier de Meré. The question concerned the division of stakes at games of dice, and the answer to it, contained in the correspondence of the two great French mathematicians, is generally regarded as the foundation of the theory of probability." But in a footnote Newman shows that "the Italian mathematician Jerome Cardan (Gerolamo Cardano), of Milan (1501–1576), was the real pioneer in this field" (p. 1319). In any case, it is clear that *science* did not have to wait upon the emergence of probability theory and statistics but is a much older enterprise. In fact, some sciences (viz. physics and astronomy) long spurned statistics and even now sometimes look askance at this discipline.

(see Fisher, 1937) posing it to his cousin, Sir Francis Galton, in the following context. Having, with others, casually noted the superior vigor of cross-fertilized plants, Darwin set out to establish or "prove" the relationship scientifically. Thus he sprouted and grew several cross-fertilized seeds of certain plants along side of self-fertilized seeds of the same species, under as nearly identical conditions as he could achieve. The results obtained for a variety of wheat, *Zea mays*, are shown in Table 8–1 (adapted from Fisher, 1937).

TABLE 8–1

Heights (in inches) of Crossed and Self-fertilized Wheat Plants as Transmitted by Mr. Darwin to Mr. Galton

Pot	Crossed	Self-fert.
I	$23\frac{4}{8}$	$17\frac{3}{8}$
	12	$20\frac{3}{8}$
	21	20
II	22	20
	$19\frac{1}{8}$	$18\frac{3}{8}$
	$21\frac{4}{8}$	$18\frac{5}{8}$
III	$22\frac{1}{8}$	$18\frac{5}{8}$
	$20\frac{3}{8}$	$15\frac{2}{8}$
	$18\frac{2}{8}$	$16\frac{4}{8}$
	$21\frac{5}{8}$	18
	$23\frac{2}{8}$	$16\frac{2}{8}$
IV	21	18
	$22\frac{1}{8}$	$12\frac{6}{8}$
	23	$15\frac{4}{8}$
	12	18

From merely inspecting these two arrays of numbers, one quickly gets the *impression* that the cross-fertilized plants were, in general, taller than the self-fertilized ones; and the simple mathematical procedure of obtaining the *mean* height of the plants in the two arrays (20.1 inches vs. 17.5 inches) amply confirms this impression; but, in light of the marked *variability* in the heights of both the crossed and the self-fertilized plants, it is not hard to imagine that the difference in the two means could be due to "chance" and therefore not reflect the influence of cross-fertilization at all. In other words, with the amount of "spontaneous" variability which occurs in both sets of plants, it is clear that the means for various other sets of 15 plants, drawn at random from *either* of the two "parent populations" (all crossed and all self-fertilized *Zea mays* imaginable), would themselves show considerable variability. Therefore, one is left with the disturbing possibility that the difference between the two means actually obtained in Mr. Darwin's experiment was *not* due to cross-fertilization but to an "error" or "accident" of sampling. And what Darwin wished to know was how to interpret and evaluate this possibility, precisely.

That Mr. Galton did not know any very satisfactory solution to the problem thus posed is indicated by the fact that his principal analytic device was to arrange the plants in two arrays in the order of tallest to shortest, as shown in Table 8–2, and note the difference (in the third column) between each corresponding pair.

TABLE 8–2

Heights of Mr. Darwin's Wheat Plants (see Table 8–1) Rearranged in Descending Order of Magnitude, with Differences Shown

Crossed	Self-fert.	Difference
$23\frac{4}{8}$	$20\frac{3}{8}$	$-3\frac{1}{8}$
$23\frac{2}{8}$	20	$-3\frac{2}{8}$
23	20	-3
$22\frac{1}{8}$	$18\frac{5}{8}$	$-3\frac{4}{8}$
$22\frac{1}{8}$	$18\frac{5}{8}$	$-3\frac{4}{8}$
22	$18\frac{3}{8}$	$-3\frac{5}{8}$
$21\frac{5}{8}$	18	$-3\frac{5}{8}$
$21\frac{4}{8}$	18	$-3\frac{4}{8}$
21	18	-3
21	$17\frac{3}{8}$	$-3\frac{5}{8}$
$20\frac{3}{8}$	$16\frac{4}{8}$	$-3\frac{7}{8}$
$19\frac{1}{8}$	$16\frac{2}{8}$	$-2\frac{7}{8}$
$18\frac{2}{8}$	$15\frac{4}{8}$	$-2\frac{6}{8}$
12	$15\frac{2}{8}$	$+3\frac{2}{8}$
12	$12\frac{6}{8}$	$+0\frac{6}{8}$

It is apparent, when the data are thus re-arranged, that the self-fertilized plants exceed the crossed plants in only two of the 15 cases or comparisons; and from a common-sense point of view, such evidence certainly seems favorable to the hypothesis under examination, that cross-pollinated plants are more vigorous than self-pollinated ones. But Mr. Galton had no way of precisely stating or estimating the degree of relationship thus prevailing, as is indicated by the fact that the best he could do, in returning the data to Darwin, was to append the words, "very good." Almost anyone, after examining Darwin's data would share the impression that these findings do indeed favor the hypothesis in question; but what is manifestly lacking is a method of stating the *degree* or *amount* of the association or relationship between mode of pollination and plant vigor, or even the assurance or confidence that there *is* such an association, with greater accuracy than is implied by such expressions as "favorable" or "very good."

In other words, causal relationships are often suspected (as in the example cited) but are not clear-cut; and the whole thrust of modern "statistics," it will here be argued, has been to try to find a method or model of some sort for designating the phenomenon of association, correlation, or causation in definite, quantifiable units of measurement.

II. Causality and the Concept of Chance

In a situation such as the one last described in the preceding section, there is a temptation to speak of the *causal* relationship prevailing between cross-fertilization (the so-called independent variable) and plant size (the dependent variable or effect) and to differentiate this relationship, categorically, from the operation of so-called *chance* factors in the situation. In one respect such a distinction is important; for what we want to know, in practice, is whether the obtained results, in any given instance, could be due to "chance factors" or are properly attributable to some systematic influence such as that hypothesized by Mr. Darwin. But before we can profitably pursue this problem, it is essential that we carefully scrutinize the assumptions underlying the phenomena which we commonly denote by the word "chance."

In both the crossed and the self-fertilized wheat plants which were grown by Mr. Darwin, there was considerable intragroup variability. Let us begin our analysis by supposing that there had been no such variability and that all the plants in each of the two groups had been, in respect to height, absolutely identical. In other words, let us suppose not only that the mean of the self-fertilized plants was 17.5 inches but that all the individual plants constituting this group were also of precisely this height. And let us similarly suppose not only that the mean height of the crossed plants was 20.1 inches but that all of the individual plants comprising the group were exactly this same height. In such a situation no "statistical" problem would exist. If, in other words, each cross-pollinated plant invariably grew to be 2.1 inches taller (at a certain age) than each self-pollinated plant, there would be no question whatever concerning the "relationship" between the pollination process and plant vigor.

When working with biological materials, such an outcome is, of course, most unusual; but the suppositious illustration is by no means absurd, for in many mechanical systems such relationships regularly exist and occasion no surprise. For example, one can easily construct a machine such that if a given quantity of lead (or any other homogeneous substance) is placed at one point on the machine it will invariably cause a pointer to move a certain distance on a calibrated scale. Here the relationship between "cause" and "effect" is so clear and uncomplicated that no one bothers to ask if the movement of the pointer could be "due to chance." Here our direct perceptions are deemed to be completely unambiguous and trustworthy.[5] But if the pointer "spontaneously" moved around a good deal regardless of whether the piece of lead was present ("experimental" condition) or absent ("control" condition), we would then obviously have a problem and would be hard-put to ascertain or "weigh" the effect of the piece of lead. If we applied the lead and the pointer moved, we could not be sure but that it would have "moved anyway"; or if we applied the lead and the pointer did *not* move, there would always be the possibility that the effect had been counteracted by the random, uncontrolled forces operating on the machine.

So we now have an analogue of the circumstances under which the practical need for "statistics" arises: namely, circumstances wherein *the dependent variable fluctuates markedly*, regardless of whether we apply the particular independent variable, or cause, in which we are interested. If all of Darwin's self-fertilized plants had grown to precisely one height and all the cross-fertilized plants to a precisely different height, he would not have needed to consult Mr. Galton, the statistician: the "effect" would have been perfectly clear and unambiguous to direct inspection. But when, as we say, *chance* factors are also operating (as concomitant, uncontrolled causes), the evaluation of a specific "effect" becomes very difficult;[6] and in some quarters

[5] There may, to be sure, be some slight variability in the place at which the pointer comes to rest when the piece of lead is placed on the machine ("scales") on successive "trials," and we may, therefore, wish to use as our estimate of the *true* "weight," impact, or effect of the lead the average for several such readings. But this is not to say that we have the slightest doubt as to what made the pointer move in the first place. In other words, the main cause-effect relationship is perfectly unambiguous; and we ascribe the variations noted to "lost motion" or other imperfections in the machine.

[6] The effect produced by the independent variable may be precisely the same in both cases; but where there is so-called spontaneous variation in the dependent variable, the specific effect is so "blurred" that confidence is much reduced. "Statistics" is an attempt to restore this confidence.

the notion has arisen that cause and effect and "chance" are radically different orders of events and must be treated accordingly. But our example suggests (and validly so) that "chance factors" are just those "causes" which we cannot accurately identify and precisely control.

Let us revert, once again, to Mr. Darwin's wheat plants. It is obvious that the spontaneous variation in plant height was relatively great in both the crossed and the self-fertilized specimens: $23\frac{4}{8}$ inches to 12 inches in the former, $20\frac{3}{8}$ inches to $12\frac{6}{8}$ inches in the latter. We must, of course, ask: Now what caused *this?* And we are inclined to answer, "Well, nothing in particular—this variability was just *due to chance.*" This is misleading. A more exact answer would go something like this: "There were undoubtedly many pertinent factors operating in the situation over which Mr. Darwin had no control: e.g., germination vigor of individual seeds, amount and quality of nutrient stored therein, adventitious differences in moisture and nutrient in the surrounding soil, minor inequalities in available light, and so on." In other words, the so-called spontaneous variations in the height of the plants were presumably just as definitely "caused" as was the systematic difference which was attributable to cross-fertilization; but since the sources of the so-called spontaneous variability were not identifiable and controllable, we tend to lump them under the somewhat mystical category of "chance." This so-called "error variance" is now often, and quite properly, said to be due, not to "chance," but to our *ignorance* and *impotence*. If we *knew* all and could *do* all, our experiments with even plants and animals could have the same precision as does the weighing of a piece of lead on a mechanical balance. (But then, of course, we wouldn't need to "experiment," would we?)

Although we may think of this view of "chance" as very sophisticated and modern, it is actually quite old. For example, Laplace (1749–1827), although one of the founders of modern statistical theory, was firm in his insistence upon the universality of causation. For example, writing in 1814, he said:

All events, even those which on account of their insignificance do not seem to follow the great laws of nature, are a result of it just as necessarily as the revolutions of the sun. In our ignorance of the ties which unite such events to the entire system of the universe, they have been made to depend upon final causes or upon hazard, according as they occur and are repeated with regularity, or appear without regard to order; but these imaginary causes have gradually receded before sound philosophy, which sees in them only the expression of our ignorance of the true causes (Newman, 1956, p. 1325).

And that other great French mathematician and scientist, Henri Poincaré (1854–1912), makes the point equally emphatically when he says:

We have become absolute determinists. . . . Every phenomenon, however minute, has a cause; and a mind infinitely powerful, infinitely well-informed about the laws of nature, could have foreseen it from the beginning of the centuries. If such a mind existed, we could not play with it at any game of chance; we should always lose.

In fact for it the word chance would not have any meaning, or rather there would be no chance. It is because of our weakness and our ignorance that the word has a meaning for us. And, even without going beyond our feeble humanity, what is chance for the ignorant is not chance for the scientist. Chance is only the measure of our ignorance. Fortuitous phenomena are, by definition, those whose laws we do not know. (Reproduced from Newman, 1956, p. 1380.)

So we may say, again, that the whole problem of or need for "statistics" arises because so many situations which we wish to understand and control more adequately are, despite our best efforts, still pretty "messy"; and we very much need some means of sorting out, if we can, the effect of the independent variable which we have deliberately introduced from the effects of variations which are due to *other* "independent" variables or causes over which we have (as yet) no control. The task is by no means a simple one, and it should not surprise us if we find that in both theory and practice "statistics" is considerably less than a finished discipline.

III. Chance (Randomness) as a Psychological Phenomenon

Since scientific interest in probability theory (on which all statistical procedures are admittedly founded) started in the study of games of chance, it will be useful for our purposes to scrutinize such games with some care. There is a common assumption to the effect that the element of chance or randomness in such games is somehow inherent in the *objects*—coins, dice, cards, roulette wheels, etc.—which are used for gaming. For example, this assumption is repeatedly expressed in Levinson's 1950 book, *The Science of Chance:*

The coin is an inanimate object, and the reason that it is as likely to show heads as to show tails is its symmetrical construction, not any choice or fancy on its part. Now the construction of the coin, which alone determines its behavior, remains exactly the same, whether there have been ten straight heads, or ten straight tails, or one hundred straight trials, for that matter.

On each toss there is always the same chance for heads as for tails (p. 34).

The best way to grasp this fundamental point—that in tossing a coin the chance of heads is exactly equal to the chance of tails, regardless of how the preceding tosses have come out—is to see that every other theory is absurd in itself and leads to absurd consequences (p. 35).

And later this author stresses the same point in speaking of the performance of dice:

In throwing a die it is the symmetrical construction of the die that leads us to believe that its sides are equally likely to turn up. If the die is "loaded," which means that it is not symmetrical, this is no longer true, as many craps players have found out, sometimes a little late. Or imagine a die of uniform material with six flat sides which are *unequal*. This mechanical change has knocked our definition completely out, for there are no equally likely cases into which the situation can be analyzed (p. 47).

So, if the source of the variability or chance is inherent in the physical object or objects thus employed, the phenomenon would certainly seem to be more subject to mathematical than psychological treatment. But there is another way of thinking about this problem.

As already indicated, the common assumption is that the source of randomness in dice throwing or coin tossing is in the objects themselves. In reading the following passage from a monograph by Neyman (1952), it occurs to one that perhaps we ought instead to look for it *in the throw or toss* which puts the object or objects into motion.

We may construct a special machine to toss coins. This machine may be very strong, driven by an electrical motor so as to impart a constant initial velocity to the coin. The experiments may be carried on in a closed room with no noticeable air currents; the coin may be put into the machine always in the same way; and even then I am practically certain that the results of the repeated experiments will vary. Perhaps very frequently we may get heads, but from time to time the coin will fall tails. The experimenter may be inclined to think that these cases arise from "error of experimentation" (p. 25).

Neyman uses this illustration, actually, to argue for the irreducible reality of "chance," but what it does more forcibly is to call attention to the possibility that if all other elements in the situation were held strictly constant, the ultimate reason for variability in outcome would have to be traced to *slight differences in the intensity of the impulsion.* And from this it would follow that if the magnitude of the impulsion could be controlled with sufficient refinement, it might be possible to replace the random behavior of a tossed coin with perfect (or at least near-perfect) control thereof. As much is, in fact, implied by Neyman himself when he says that, by tightening up on the conditions of experimentation, we might be able to get a preponderance of heads, and only a few tails. And the occurrence of any tails at all must, of necessity, be due to failure on our part to control the experimental situation with sufficient precision; "chance," it seems, is indeed some "error of experimentation."

This idea that a perfectly precise (but adjustable) machine which flipped a coin or spun a roulette wheel under absolutely uniform conditions would introduce absolute control and abolish "chance" may be a new one to many readers (as it was to the present writer); but a little further perusal of the probability literature shows that the notion has been about for some time. For example, it turns out that Poincaré (cf. also Section II) understood all this quite well, and wrote lucidly and fully about it:

> To find a better definition of chance we must examine some of the facts which we agree to regard as fortuitous, and to which the calculus of probabilities seems to apply; we then shall investigate what are their common characteristics.
>
> The first example we select is that of unstable equilibrium; if a cone rests upon its apex, we know well that it will fall, but we do not know toward what side; it seems to us chance alone will decide. If the cone were perfectly symmetrical, if its axis were perfectly vertical, if it were acted upon by no force other than gravity, it would not fall at all. But the least defect in symmetry will make it lean slightly toward one side or the other, and if it leans however little, it will fall altogether toward that side. Even if the symmetry were perfect, a very slight tremor, a breath of air could make it incline some seconds of arc; this will be enough to determine its fall and even the sense of its fall which will be that of the initial inclination.
>
> *A very slight cause, which escapes us,* determines a considerable effect which we cannot help seeing, and then we say this effect is due to chance. . . . Here again we find the same contrast between a very slight cause, unappreciable to the observer, and important effects, which are sometimes tremendous disasters (pp. 1381–82).
>
> The game of roulette does not take us as far as might seem from the preceding example. Assume a needle to be turned on a pivot over a dial divided into a hundred sectors alternately red and black. If it stops on a red sector I win; if not, I lose. Evidently all depends upon *the initial impulse I give the needle.* The needle will make, suppose, ten or twenty turns, but it will stop sooner or not so soon, according as I shall have pushed it more or less strongly. It suffices that the impulse vary *only by a thousandth or a two thousandth* to make the needle stop over a black sector or over the following red one. These are differences *the muscular sense cannot distinguish* and which elude even the most delicate instruments. So it is impossible for me to foresee what the needle I have started will do, and this is why my heart throbs and I hope everything from luck. The difference in the cause is imperceptible, and the difference in the effect is for me of the highest importance, since it means my whole stake. (Reproduced from Newman, 1956, p. 1383, italics added.)

It is therefore of special interest that we differentiate between "games of skill" and "games of chance." A game of skill is one in which special talent, motivation, and practice can make a systematic difference in the outcome. For example, in tennis one can *learn to sense* (discriminate) the difference between a stroke which will send the ball out of the court and a stroke that will keep it in. The control is, of course, not perfect, but it is dramatically better for the experienced player than for the beginner. By contrast, a game of chance is, by its very nature, such that skill avails nothing. And the explanation, as implied in the passages from Poincaré, is based on a well established psychological principle, commonly designated as the Weber-Fechner function. As between two objects of equal size which, however, weigh two ounces and three ounces, respectively, a person with normal touch and kinesthesis can easily discriminate the heavier from the lighter. But as between two objects of equal size which weigh, respectively, 19 and 20 ounces, the individual is quite helpless to make a systematic discrimination, although the *absolute* difference in the weight of these two objects is no greater (namely, one ounce) than the difference between the two lighter objects which are perfectly differentiated.

In other words, what the Weber-Fechner law says is that our discrimination between two sensations is a function of the *ratio* of the difference to the absolute magnitude or intensity of the two sensations, rather than of the absolute difference between them. And the point (or region) beyond which a difference ceases to be discriminable is known as the difference "threshold."

Now, to return to games of chance, we can say that they always operate in such a way that different outcomes are dependent on such small differences in *effort* that they cannot be perceived, i.e., fall well *below* the discrimination "threshold," with a resulting *loss of control* over the outcome. With a little practice, one can reach the point that he can always make a coin fall in a certain way *if* he flips it so gently that it will turn over, let us say, only three times. In other words, a person can discriminate between the effort necessary to make the coin turn over three times and that required to make it turn over two times or four times. But in coin tossing on which wagers are placed, this type of performance is ruled out as "unfair"; and the individual is required to make the coin spin 15 or 20 times at the very least. Now the difference in effort that will mark the difference between heads and tails becomes *so small* that it cannot be discriminated, even by the most practiced gamblers. The discrimination, and therefore the control, is lost "below the threshold," and the effects or results become relatively, if not absolutely, "random." But this is not because causation has ceased to operate; it is simply that, in most life situations, we do not need and do not have the capacity for such fine discriminations as exact control would here presuppose. Thus we "lose control" of the performance of the coin, not because of *its* structural characteristics but *ours;* and so, if we choose, we may "play" with this phenomenon, but we cannot *work* with it.[7]

At the risk of digressing unduly, it is perhaps also worth noting that this view of games of chance may provide an important insight into one of the sources of fascination which gambling has for some people. Even though the winner in a game of chance rationally knows that he won "by chance," still there is a tendency to assume that *skill* somehow got into the situation; and if one can *do* something which others obviously wish to do but cannot (as when one *wins*), there is undoubtedly a form of "ego income" which goes beyond the purely financial gain. Perhaps this is why games of chance can be "fun" even when betting is not involved—and why habitual gambling is often an expression of "neurosis."

Now in what has been said in this section, it is not at all implied that randomness is exclusively a psychological phenomenon. The pattern in which raindrops fall is often cited as a good illustration of randomness, which is certainly completely impersonal, nonpsychological. And the behavior of genes and atoms provides many more subtle examples of a similar kind. But since so much inspiration for modern statistical methods has been drawn from the games of chance, it is not amiss to remind ourselves that we are here dealing with familiar psychological principles and are by no means solely in the realm of physics and "pure mathematics."

IV. The Mathematical Approach to Probability and the Problem of Statistics

In the preceding section we have seen that, contrary to a prevailing opinion, the phenomenon of randomness in games of chance arises not

[7] Levinson (1950, p. 41), like various other writers, alludes briefly to the difference between games of skill and games of chance; but the most extensive discussion of this topic known to the present writer is to be found in von Mises (1957, pp. 136–138). It may also be pertinently noted that just as games of chance involve a loss of control through a failure of discrimination, the loss of control which occurs when behavior is very rapid (see Mowrer, 1960, Chapter 12) is due to the fact that such behavior "gets ahead" of the sensory feedback therefrom. In both cases, "errors" result, but for different reasons.

so much from the nature of the objects thus employed as from an inescapable lack of "skill" (sensory acuity) in the manipulation of these objects. This discovery, illuminating as it is in some ways, does not, however, bring us appreciably nearer to a solution to the "statistical" problem as defined in Sections I and II.

There is an old saying among scientists that in research you can't lose: If, in the course of trying to study one phenomenon, you encounter a difficulty, you can always turn and study *it*. In a sense, this is the strategy that has brought the discipline of statistics into existence: If spontaneous fluctuations in the dependent variable obscure the effect of some deliberately introduced independent variable, then—for the time being at least—let us study spontaneous fluctuations. And when we do, the first thing we discover is that such fluctuations often (though by no means always) tend to be "normally distributed," i.e., most specimens will be intermediate or "average" with respect to the attribute in question (such as height of wheat plants), with the number of specimens decreasing as one moves out toward each of the two extremes of the distribution continuum. Thus, if Mr. Darwin had taken, not 15, but 500 ordinary self-pollinated wheat plants and measured their heights at a given stage of growth, he would very likely have obtained a distribution which approximated the contours of a bell, or the so-called normal curve. And with this discovery, one is reminded of certain mathematical functions and of the results of various games of chance.

If two or more events are, by definition (or by physical arrangement), equally likely or probable of occurrence (the postulate of equally-occurring events), this fact can be represented mathematically by a ratio: e.g., $1/2$ (as in coin tossing), $1/6$ (as in dice), or $1/52$ (in drawing any particular card from a standard deck). What the ratio means (and this *is* the mathematical definition of probability) is that if there are N *possibilities* (which are equally likely), the *probability* of the occurrence of any one of these (equally likely) possibilities is $1/N$. Thus, if a coin (which has two sides and thus two possible ways of landing) is tossed, the probability of its falling heads up is $1/2$; and the very same value, of course, also holds for the probability of its falling tails up. And since $1/2$ plus $1/2$ equals 1, these two physical possibilities are mathematically (and logically) exhaustive. Or, similarly, if a die (which has six sides and thus six possible ways of landing) is thrown, the probability of any one of the six numbered sides "coming up" is supposedly $1/6$; and six times this fraction equals one, which again is logically exhaustive. From this way of mathematically stating "simple" probabilities, all manner of more complex probabilities or expectations can be derived. For example, the expectation of obtaining *two* heads from two tosses of an "ideal" coin is no longer 1/2 but 1/2 x 1/2 or 1/4; the expectation of obtaining *three* heads from three tosses is 1/2 x 1/2 x 1/2 or 1/8; etc.[8] Or the expectation of rolling two sixes (or any other two numbers) on a "fair" pair of dice is 1/6 x 1/6 or 1/36. And it has been found that if all the possible combinations of, let us say, heads and tails on 10 successive tosses of a coin (or simultaneous tosses of 10 coins) are computed (or actually tested), the resulting distribution turns out to be the normal, bell-shaped curve already alluded to (precisely, if computation is used, approximately in an empirical test). Thus, in pure randomness it is found that there are certain lawful relationships, the so-called *laws of chance;*[9] and so the hope of a science of statistics arose and has been applied, among other ways, as follows.

From the type of mathematical model here described, it is, of course, possible to say just how likely a given outcome is *if* "chance alone" is operating. If, therefore, in a situation wherein an independent variable has been deliberately introduced the results are such that they might easily be attributed to "chance alone," then we do not consider that anything has been "proved"; but if a result is obtained which would be expected only one time in a thousand (P = .001) under "chance alone," then we still do not say that the influence of the deliberately introduced variable has been "proved" (the obtained result might *still* have happened "by chance"); but we can say, and with confidence, that it would be *very unlikely* (only one "chance" in a thousand). This is the logic of the so-called *null* hypothesis, i.e., the hypothesis that the result obtained (for the difference between two, or more,

---

[8] Common logic shows that if a coin is tossed twice, there are four possible outcomes: two heads, a head and then a tail, a tail and then a head, and two tails. And if the coin is tossed three times there are eight possible outcomes: HHH, HHT, HTH, THH, TTH, THT, HTT, and TTT. The general formula which is applicable here is, of course, the familiar binomial theorem from elementary algebra, $(a + b)^n$, where "a" represents the chance of obtaining heads on a given trial, "b" the chance of obtaining tails, and "n" the number of actual trials.

[9] " 'How dare we speak of the laws of chance? Is not chance the antithesis of all law?' So says Bertrand at the beginning of his *Calcul des probabilities.* Probability is opposed to certitude; so it is what we do not know and consequently it seems what we could not calculate. Here is at least apparently a contradiction, and about it much has already been written" (Poincaré, Newman, 1956, p. 1380). Although individual events are not predictable ("knowable"), the paradox is resolved by noting that the so-called laws of chance are based upon "averages" or the behavior of "large numbers." (Cf. also later sections of this chapter.)

groups) is *not* caused by the deliberately introduced independent variable but is due entirely to an error or accident of sampling from what is really just one (homogeneous) distribution, or "universe." So what evidence does then, in effect, is not to "prove" some *positive* hypothesis (*that* is logically impossible because, no matter how good the evidence, there is always some room for doubt) but to progressively "disprove," in the sense of *discredit*, the null hypothesis, i.e., the hypothesis of no "real" (deliberately produced) difference.

Now what has obviously happened here is that we have moved from vague, impressionistic terms such as "favorable" or "very good" (see the Darwin experiment) to a precise, mathematical continuum, extending from 1.0 to .0000?.[10] Thus we can say that if the dependent variable in question were *not* effective, the expectation of obtaining any particular result would be: 1/2, 2/33, 7/100, 1/1,000, etc. Here we have moved from such vague verbal phrases as those just mentioned to precise mathematical expressions, which would seem to be a very important advance. For example, to refer again to the Darwin experiment, such a procedure permits one to say (after some comparatively simple calculations—see Fisher, 1937, p. 35 ff.) that the expectation of obtaining a difference such as that actually reported between two samples of 15 plants if the null hypothesis were true, i.e., if cross fertilization did *not* make any difference in plant vigor, would be 3/100 or .03. Or, said differently, if chance alone were operating and if 100

[10] This objective of statistical procedures has been stressed by various writers. "Galton's great gift lay in his awareness, which grew during his life, of the vagueness of many of the phrases in which men tried to express themselves in describing natural phenomena. He was before his time in his recognition that such vagueness could be removed, and a certain precision of thought attempted by finding quantitative definitions of concepts fit to take the place of such phrases as "the average man," "variability," "the strength of inheritance," and so forth, through the assembly of objective data, and its systematic examination. That the methods he himself used were often extremely crude, and sometimes seriously faulty, is, indeed, the strongest evidence of the eventual value to the progress of science of his unswerving faith that objectivity and rationality were accessible, even in such elusive fields as psychology, if only a factual basis for these qualities were diligently sought" (Fisher, 1956, pp. 1–2; see also Section I). Neyman, in 1952, wrote: "The objects in a real world, or rather our sensations connected with them, are always more or less vague, and since the time of Kant it has been realized that no general statement concerning them is possible. The human mind grew tired of this vagueness and constructed a science from which anything that is vague is excluded— this is mathematics. But the gain in generality must be paid for, and the price is the abstractness of conceptions with which mathematics deals and the hypothetical character of the results" (p. 23). And Savage (1956) says, quite simply, that statistics is "the art of dealing with vagueness" (p. 154).

double sets of 15 plants were selected at random, only three of them ought to show a difference as large as or larger than the one obtained. Here we see, once again, that where "chance" is operating, "anything" *can* happen, theoretically; but some combinations of events are much *more* and others much *less* probable, predictable, expectable.

Thus, it would seem that we have arrived at a highly exact, albeit somewhat round-about, means of *measuring causation,* in situations in which a given effect is being masked by the action of other concurrently operating causal ("chance") factors. In situations in which the "channel" is quiet (to use the language of "information theory"), the "message" (from a deliberately introduced cause or "signal") comes through unambiguously; but when there is "noise" in the channel, it is much more difficult for the message to "get through," and it is here that the statistical methods just described may help us decide whether we have really "heard something" or not. Such a service, if it does what it purports to, is no small accomplishment.

V. Has the "Statistical" Problem Really Been Solved?

We can now, it seems, *define* the fundamental "statistical" problem quite clearly: It is the problem that arises when we try to see if one variable produces a change in another variable in a situation where the latter *spontaneously* changes, or "fluctuates," due to the action of other causal factors which are commonly termed "chance." It is, however, less certain that we have found the *solution* to this problem. From reading some writers, it would appear that there is not the slightest doubt on this score. But a more catholic perusal of the literature on probability theory and statistics reveals long-standing and continuing doubt and reservation. Writing in 1878, Charles Sanders Peirce evaluated the field thus:

> This branch of mathematics is the only one, I believe, in which good writers frequently get results entirely erroneous. In elementary geometry the reasoning is frequently fallacious, but erroneous conclusions are avoided; but it may be doubted if there is a single extensive treatise on probabilities in existence which does not contain solutions absolutely indefensible (Peirce, 1878a, p. 608).

That the situation is today not materially improved, despite some much-heralded "advances," is suggested by the following quotations. Writing in 1956, in an introduction to a paper by Ernest Nagel, Newman observes:

It is remarkable, as Laplace wrote, that "a science which began with the considerations of play has risen to the most important objects of human knowledge." But it is in a sense even more remarkable that despite the attention bestowed on this science, and its enormous influence, mathematicians and philosophers are quite unable to agree on the meaning of probability. Their disagreement is less easily explained than that of the three men describing the elephant. For in this case the observers are not blind and the creature is of their own design (p. 1395).

And in a letter to Dr. Henry F. Kaiser, under date of May 1, 1958, Professor L. J. Savage has said: "This is a tough time to be teaching elementary statistics, for the state religion seems to be crumbling rapidly and the new faith has not yet been hammered out." [11]

Now we must ask: From what sources of difficulty do these expressions of skepticism arise? Among those that appear to be most obvious, we can identify the following:

1. *The assumption of homogeneity of variance.* It will be remembered that the solution to the statistical problem most widely accepted since about 1940 involves a comparison of the results actually obtained, from an experimental group and a control group, with the results that might be expected if two samples of the same size were drawn from a single population in which the "variance" or spontaneous variation is known to be "normally distributed." In other words, starting with a *mathematical model* for random variation, we ask what the chances are of drawing two separate samples whose mean difference is as great or

---

[11] Not *all* professional statisticians see this degree of chaos in their field. For example, Levinson (1950) says: "If the theory of chance had grown up to be a black sheep in the scientific fold, we might hold the gamblers responsible for it and tell them that they should have kept their difficulties to themselves. But it is not a black sheep. It is a well-behaved member of the mathematical family and has rendered conspicuous service to many of that large group of subjects to which mathematics has been fruitfully applied. Among these subjects are not only many sciences, but many businesses as well, including insurance—one of the largest of all" (p. 15). *Analytical* or *descriptive* statistics is undoubtedly useful in helping us *see* what the data are; but here our concern is rather with *inferential* statistics, which purportedly helps us make practical decisions. To the best of the present writer's knowledge, there is no published evidence that we do any better, practically, with than without inferential statistics. In fact, Bilodeau (1952) has shown that in at least one experimental situation human subjects make every bit as good decisions without the aid of "significance tests" as they would with them, reaching decisions at what would be the .05 to .01 level of confidence (P-value) without the aid of any such statistic. This appraisal may be unfair to inferential statistics, but the Bilodeau study points in the right direction: the value of inferential statistics should not be taken on faith and needs to be empirically demonstrated.

greater than the mean difference obtained from an actual experiment. If, as noted earlier, the chances are small—say one in a hundred—of obtaining a difference of this magnitude from two random samples from the same parent population, we are impressed with the likelihood that the actual difference is due to the influence of the independent variable which was deliberately introduced into the experiment; but if this likelihood is considerably greater (say, one in five or one in ten), we dismiss the difference as easily due to chance. Of course, this reasoning involves the assumption that the variance in the population (or populations) with which we are dealing in an actual experiment is also normal, i.e., like that of the mathematical model. If it is not—and it often *is* not, then the justification for the comparison is seriously impugned.[12]

[12] This point hardly needs extensive documentation. Perhaps the following excerpt from Hotelling (1958) will supply all that is necessary: "There are indeed situations in which valid information about probabilities can be deduced from rather broad conditions, as in ergodic theory and in the various limit theorems specifying particular forms, such as the normal law for the distribution of functions of a large number of variates, with an approximation that improves as the number of constituent variates increases. These supply some warrant for using the normal law as a tentative approximation for particular variates, but the normal law is often negated by the facts, and in the absence of adequate factual investigation the common practice of imputing a normal distribution to almost everything may lead to serious mistakes. . . . As in all physical, biological and social sciences, we can go some way with theoretical models, but do not remain satisfied without observational checks on our deductions at as many points of the structure as possible" (p. 11). In other words, whenever a statistical procedure is predicated on the "normal law," we must remind ourselves that this law provides only a *mathematical model* which does not (as once supposed) correspond to some great universal, unvarying principle but is, rather, created by certain selected *definitions* (including the assumption of equally-occurring events). Therefore, deductions made from these definitions (constituting the model) apply strictly and precisely only to data which conform, strictly and precisely, to these definitions; and such natural conformity is rare. Therefore, as Professor Hotelling properly notes, we must remember that our statistical inferences must be thought of as mere "approximations," which must be empirically checked as closely as possible. Also useful is his point that data follow the normal law best when, in our terms, the number of uncontrolled independent (chance) variables affecting the dependent variable is large. And this is not always the case in practice. Suppose that the error variance (as opposed to that introduced by the experimental variable) were due entirely to one or two uncontrolled variables, which operated in discrete amounts, quantum-wise. Here ordinary tests of significance would be totally unwarranted; and to the extent that the assumption of perfect randomness (homogeneity of variance) is not met, to that extent are statistical inferences drawn from a model which involves such an assumption questionable, over and beyond the element of doubt or uncertainty which is inherent in *all* statements of probability (see also Neyman, 1952).

In an effort to circumvent this problem, tests of significance have recently been introduced which make no assumption about the homogeneity or normality of variance; but these tests—the nonparametric tests, so-called—are admittedly less sensitive and their justification, on other grounds, is still open to doubt (cf. Section VII).

2. *Limitations of the "null" hypothesis.* As background for the discussion which is to follow next but, also, because of the inherent importance of the problem, let it be noted that although the null hypothesis is the one commonly tested by the "new statistics," other hypotheses are logically possible within the same framework and are also of practical interest. What a test of significance, as thus far defined, does is to tell us (assuming homogeneity of variance) how likely a mean difference of the size obtained would be if the two samples were randomly drawn from a master population having the characteristics of the postulated mathematical model. In other words, the resulting P-value indicates how likely the obtained result would be *if* the postulated cause-and-effect relationship, or hypothesis in question, were *not* true and *if* the error variance in the situation were "normally" distributed.

But sometimes this is not what we wish to know. Perhaps it is already sufficiently evident to direct inspection that there is a "real" difference (rather than just a "chance" one) between two means and that what we wish to know instead is *how much* the difference is. Now it is possible to postulate or hypothesize, not only that there is *no* "real" difference between the two obtained means (the null hypothesis), but that there *is* a difference and that it is of some specified magnitude. Then the question becomes: If the two samples in question (constituting the results from the experimental and the control groups) are, respectively, from two larger (parent) populations whose means differ by the amount specified, what are the probabilities of obtaining, by means of random sampling from these two populations, two comparable groups whose means differ as much as or more than the means of the two actual samples?

This liberalization in the type of hypothesis that can be "statistically" tested is undoubtedly an advance in some ways, yet the fact is that these developments do not bear upon the problem of homogeneity of variance, already alluded to; and, if anything, they even exacerbate the problem which will be considered next.[13]

3. *Hypothesis "acceptance" or "rejection," a false issue.* Several genera-

[13] For an introduction to the literature pertinent to the foregoing, see Fisher (1956), especially his discussion of "fiducial limits" (p. 51 ff.) and "likelihood ratios" (p. 66 ff.). See also von Mises (1957, p. 135 ff.) and Neyman (1952, p. 229 ff.).

tions of graduate students, in various disciplines, have been taught that in doing research one must always decide, before collecting any data whatever, upon the P-value at which the null hypothesis is going to be "rejected" and some alternative positive hypothesis "accepted." And, as a corollary, one must also decide in advance precisely how many subjects (observations) are to be involved in the experiment (see Paragraph 4). Thus, it was reasoned, the investigator is protected against the danger of simply running subjects until, through random fluctuation, he gets a P-value which "suits him," and then stopping. Having, in other words, set in advance both the P-value at which the null hypothesis is to be "rejected" and the number of subjects to be used, the experimenter is presumably prevented from, consciously or unconsciously, "fudging."

Now, on the face of it, this seems like a high, moral principle. But it does not stand scrutiny and many detailed arguments can be advanced against it, which come to focus in the following incident. A few years ago the writer participated in the final oral examination of a Ph.D. candidate (in another department) who, along with thousands of other graduate students, had been trained to believe that in research you must always set the criterion of "significance" for your results in advance of doing an experiment. Therefore, in the summary of his findings, this student had dutifully written, "The results of this experiment provide no basis for believing that the hypothesis in question is true." The fact was that the results provided quite a lot of "evidence" in favor of the hypothesis; but because the student had in advance set a P-value of .05 and actually obtained a P-value of .07, he was compelled, by this singular logic, to report "*no* evidence." How much better it would have been if this man had simply carried out his experiment, reported whatever P-value he obtained, and then let *the reader* make whatever use of this information he saw fit.

For *some* purposes a P-value of .07 is quite sufficient, whereas for other purposes one may wish to insist upon a P-value of .01 or even .001. And it would seem obvious that since a researcher cannot foresee all the varied circumstances in which his findings may be relevant, he has no right to prejudge the case. Editors of scientific journals may, if they wish, set a policy of *not publishing* experimental results which do not meet some specified level of "significance" (e.g., the .05 level); but we should be quite clear that such a policy represents a practical (and perhaps entirely justified) *decision* and not a sacred dividing line between abstract truth and error, or evidence and "no evidence."

4. "Statistics" and the problem of decision. A few months ago the writer participated in the training of a group of educators—principals, teachers, and school-board members—in research and statistical methods that might be applicable to problems commonly encountered in primary and secondary schools. And at one point he asked the members of the group what service or function they expected statistics to perform for them. The reply given by one person (with nodded assent from a number of others) was memorable. She said: "*We want statistics to tell us what to do.*" Most specialists in the field now cringe when they hear this sort of statement; but it was not long ago that this interpretation was at least implicitly advocated in our leading textbooks. When the logic of the null hypothesis was at the height of its popularity, the scientific investigator was counseled as follows: First you decide upon the P-value at which you will *reject* the null hypothesis, and if this value is reached or exceeded in actual experimentation, your mind is, so to say, automatically "made up" for you: you have "proved" the alternative hypothesis and must presumably now act upon it in whatever way is relevant to the practical situation. But, as we have already seen, "circumstances alter cases," and what is sufficient evidence for *one* decision may not at all be sufficient for another; and it clearly exceeds the investigator's right and responsibility to try to fix a decision point in advance of experimentation to control all contingencies (see also Section VI).

In other words, "truth" is a *relative* matter, in two ways: (1) it is relative in the sense that it is never absolute, i.e., the evidence at our disposal is always partial, incomplete; and therefore our judgments, if wise, always have some measure of tentativeness or uncertainty about them; and (2) it is relative because evidence that is "true" (good enough) for one purpose may not be at all sufficient for another. This is not to say, of course, that the ultimate principles according to which the Universe functions are unreliable, indefinite, or variable; the point is that *our knowledge* of these principles, based as it is upon limited observation, is partial and (ideally) tentative—and that decision and action will vary, not only as a function of the degree of our conviction or doubt (based on the evidence), but also as a function of the magnitude of the danger, or risk, that would be involved (subjectively) if we made a mistake, a misjudgment. Whether we like it or not, we are therefore concerned here, not only with epistemology (the problem of knowledge, or *cognitive* learning) but also with value theory and the problem of choice (*affective* learning). And the notion that we can, by statistics or other "purely objective" methods, arrive at the ultimate (absolute) truth and therefore make infallible decisions is an illusion. The organismic, or psychological, element can, without question, be somewhat "reduced" or "standardized"; but it cannot, in the final analysis, be eliminated (cf. Nagel, 1955).

5. *Level of significance and number of subjects.* The final difficulty with which we shall here be concerned is not a particularly subtle one, yet it has been slow to gain general recognition. In many situations it is found that the difference between a "reliable" and an "unreliable" difference between the experimental and control group means depends upon the number of subjects (or specimens) used, so that the investigator, if of a mind to, can determine in advance whether a hypothesis will be accepted or rejected (at some predetermined "level of confidence") by the simple expedient of running relatively many or relatively few subjects. Suppose, for example, that the independent variable which is under investigation makes a real but slight difference in the dependent variable. Now statistical formulae being what they are, the larger the number of subjects used in the two groups receiving different treatment in an experiment, the greater the likelihood of obtaining a difference that is "reliable" at some specified P-value. Therefore, if one wishes to discredit a given hypothesis, all one needs to do is to run a number of subjects which would be "reasonable" if dealing with a more potent variable but not sufficient to produce an "acceptable" P-value in the present case; and, by the same token, if one is particularly intent upon supporting a given hypothesis, a causal relationship (if present at all) can be substantiated if one deals with very large numbers of subjects (see Bolles & Messick, 1958; also Section VII).

Obviously this difficulty, taken in conjunction with the others reviewed in this section, constitutes a major weakness in the theory and application of the newer and supposedly definitive statistical procedures.

VI. Statistics, Decision Theory, and Ordinary Choice

In their book *Decision Processes,* Thrall, Coombs, & Davis (1954) remark:

Any system may be a "model." It may, for instance, in some remarkable case, be only a model for itself. In general, the same system may provide a model for many other systems in being a realization of each *either* under "interpretation" *or* "abstraction." . . . Thus "mathematical model" here means simply "formal deductive system"; a mathematical model together with a given interpretation of the model in the "real world" constitutes a "theory," while "real world" itself is a term intended to denote . . . whatever your form of epistemology will buy (p. 6).

Now if our discussion up to this point establishes anything with clarity, it is that the "model" on which most statistical tests of significance are based, while purporting to provide "a model for many other systems," in point of fact comes perilously close to being "only a model for itself." In the preceding section we have seen how questionable is the assumption of homogeneity of variance with respect to actual, empirical data; and even in games of chance, where the assumption is most nearly met, some discrepancy is to be expected, on both empirical and theoretical grounds. In a classical experiment with dice, W. F. R. Weldon (cited by Yule, 1919, p. 258) threw 12 dice 4096 times and found that although the results approximated those predicted by the "laws of chance," they did not by any means conform perfectly (Fig. 8–1). And Bolles & Messick (1958) argue as follows:

> Might not the null hypothesis always be rejected if sufficiently powerful significance tests were used? Even in the classical situation with a tossed coin, are there ever any really unbiased coins, or are all coins in real life smoother or heavier on one side than on the other? [Cf. also Section III.] If the null hypothesis might, in fact, not be exactly tenable, especially when continuous measures are used, then what about the theory of significance tests? An extreme expression of skepticism has been recently summarized by Savage (1957), who asserts that "Exclusive reliance on tests of significance obscures the fact that statistical significance does not imply substantive significance. . . . Null hypotheses of no difference are usually known to be false before the data are collected; when they are, their rejection or acceptance simply reflects the size of the sample and the power of the test, and is not a contribution to science" (p. 223).

Thus has there arisen the surmise that, even after the most careful statistical treatment and interpretation, data which are contaminated to begin with (see Sections I and II) *remain* contaminated and that conclusions with respect to them must be drawn with double caution: (a) caution arising from the very nature of probability, even as mathematically idealized (in models), and (b) caution prompted from recognition of the almost certain discrepancy between mathematical models and the "real world." The result, quite naturally, has been a shift in interest on the part of many investigators from statistical techniques as such to what is now generally (and somewhat pretentiously) termed *decision theory*. Gradually it has been realized that statistical procedures *cannot* "tell us what to do" (cf. Section V–4); that doing presupposes *deciding;* and that deciding is contingent not only upon the available *evidence* but also upon the nature of the *risks* (of gain and loss), or *values*, which are involved.

Edwards (1954) has cogently pointed out that "Economists and a

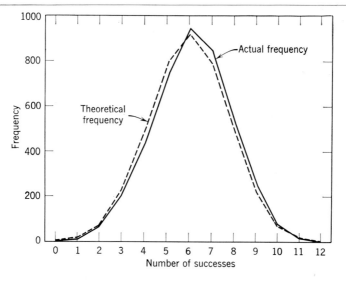

Fig. 8–1. Two curves showing the relationship between the theoretically expected and the obtained frequencies in a dice-throwing experiment carried out by Weldon (reported by Mills, 1924, p. 525). The somewhat angular contour of the curve representing the theoretical frequency of various combinations on the dice is determined by the fact that a finite number of dice (12) were involved in each throw. If a very large or infinite number of dice had been used, the curve would be smooth, bell-shaped. The results actually obtained closely approximate but do not exactly match the theoretical (mathematical) expectation. A "success," it should be said, was counted in this experiment whenever a 4, 5, or 6 spot came up on a die; 1, 2, and 3 spots were not counted. Thus, on any given throw, it was possible to obtain anywhere from 0 to 12 successes (the extremes being represented by a 4, 5, or 6 spot showing on none of the 12 dice and by a 4, 5, or 6 spot on all of them). The most commonly expected occurrence would, of course, be six dice showing successes or counters and six dice showing noncounters.

few psychologists have produced a large body of theory and a few experiments that deal with individual decision making" and that "This literature is almost unknown to psychologists, in spite of sporadic pleas in both psychological and economic literature for greater communication between the disciplines" (p. 390). The reluctance of contemporary psychologists to face the problem of decision making undoubtedly has its roots in Behaviorism, for this conception of psychological science held that nothing so subjective and "internal" as choice and "will" was to be countenanced; and it would have fitted very nicely into the general behavioristic plan and strategy if we could have passed the whole process of decision back upon something as conveniently objective and impersonal as a statistical formula. But this has not proved possible; and the current effort to shift the problem from "statistics" to "decision theory" represents a last desperate effort to retain the fiction of objectivity and impersonality. This struggle is rather wistfully implied in the following quotation from Wallis & Roberts (1956):

> Decision theory in this broad sense is not yet ready for practical application, except perhaps in special circumstances. The term "decision theory" has, of course, great appeal, for everyone has to make decisions, and everyone hopes for some magic formula by which to make them; as a result, more has sometimes been claimed for decision theory than it can yet produce in practice. Already, however, decision theory has resulted in clarification of the standard significance testing procedure. That is, it illuminates the nature, uses, and limitations of significance tests (p. 385).

Thrall, Coombs, & Davis (1954) and their collaborators, while vigorously pursuing the search for mathematical models for the "decision processes," nevertheless frankly recognize the clearly psychological dimensions of the problem. And the analysis has been pushed still further along these lines by Feather (1959) in an article entitled "Subjective Probability and Decision Under Uncertainty." We cannot here be concerned with the details of this article, but its over-all objectives are so clearly stated in the author's introduction and are so pertinent to present considerations that this part of the article will be quoted in its entirety.

> In this paper it is intended to review generally five approaches which relate to the analysis of behavior in a choice situation where a decision is made between alternatives having different subjective probabilities of attainment. The present discussion is mainly concerned with the way in which the concept of subjective probability has been incorporated into each model.
> The five contributions to be reviewed are: (a) the Lewin, Dembo, Festinger, and Sears (1944) analysis of level of aspiration behavior; (b) Tolman's (1955) discussion of the principles of performance; (c) Rotter's (1954) basic equation in his social learning theory; (d) Edwards' (1954, 1955) discussion of the SEU model from decision theory; and (e) Atkinson's (1957) risk-taking model.
> The remarkable fact about these five approaches is their similarity with respect to concepts employed and equations advanced. Recently Siegel (1957) has noted the close similarity between the level of aspiration analysis by Lewin *et al.* (based on the earlier work of Escalona [1940] and Festinger [1942] and the SEU decision model). The *first* main aim of this paper is to show that the parallel may be taken further to include the analyses by Tolman, Rotter, and Atkinson. This parallel is all the more interesting and significant in that these models have developed from different areas of research. Lewin *et al.* are concerned with goal-setting in the level of aspiration situa-

tion, Tolman's analysis is related to animal experimentation, Rotter's social learning theory is applied to clinical problems, the Edwards SEU model relates to research in decision theory, and Atkinson is concerned with the effect on risk-taking behavior of individual differences in motive strength. It would appear, then, that interpretations of research from diverse areas are converging upon a similar type of model.

Despite this parallel, however, there is a discrepancy in the way in which subjective probability is included in the different analyses. The *second* main aim of this paper is to bring this discrepancy to light. The discrepancy concerns whether or not concepts which are akin to utility in the various models are taken to be *independent* of subjective probability. In other words, are utilities, valences, reinforcement values, and similar concepts related to subjective probability in these models, or are they assumed to be independent? It will be argued that this question can be approached experimentally, and an experimental study (Feather, in press) testing hypotheses, derived from assumptions about the effects of past learning on behavior in choice situations, will be outlined in an attempt to resolve some of the disagreement. (p. 150).

The reader who may have been very much "at sea" in earlier sections of this chapter will now begin to recognize some familiar landmarks. The problem of decision making obviously articulates with the contents of Chapters 6 and 7; and anyone who is also familiar with *Learning Theory and Behavior* (Mowrer, 1960) will recognize almost all of the writers referred to in the passage just quoted from Feather. Here, in order that the reader may feel even firmer ground beneath him, let it be recalled that the whole thrust of revised two-factor learning theory has been to re-introduce the problem of choice (where it had been quite abolished by the reflexology of Pavlov and the stimulus-response "bonds" of Thorndike); to show that hopes and fears (which are the dynamic conditioners of choice) themselves imply not only "probabilities" (cf. Chapter 9) but also the nature and magnitude of risks (promises and threats); and to provide, generally, a conceptual and explanatory framework of scope and power. However, our journey is not yet at an end and we must push on through some more unexplored—and "rugged"—territory.[14]

VII. Causation and Correlation

This chapter is predicated on the assumption that in science we are mainly concerned with the discovery of cause-and-effect relation-

[14] The reader who wishes to explore the literature on this general subject more thoroughly will find that Wasserman & Silander (1958) have published a very useful monography, "Decision-Making: An Annotated Bibliography." And for a discussion of theory, see Janis (1959).

ships. But, as we quickly found, the perception and interpretation of such relationships is often obscured (a) by the phenomenon of confounding, which (happily) can nearly always be eliminated by appropriate experimental design, and (b) by random (as opposed to systematic) errors, which "statistics" supposedly helps us deal with. And the discussion thus far has been largely concerned with the question of whether and to what extent this latter supposition is, in fact, valid.

Our conclusions must be tentative; but the moral of our discussion up to this point seems to be as simple as it is painful: Despite tremendous effort and ingenuity, the statistical problem is still very far from having an elegant mathematical solution, and it may even be doubted that such a solution is, in principle, possible. The task which modern statistical inquiry has set for itself may be likened to that of devising a means for making a meaningful signal, which is transmitted over a noisy communications channel, more intelligible without reducing the noise/signal ratio. B. F. Skinner (1938) has long since abandoned statistical analysis and sought to improve the "clarity" of experimental findings in learning research by gaining better control over irrelvant variables and thus reducing spontaneous variations in subject performance. His contention is, in effect, that regardless of the mathematical transformation employed, contaminated data are still contaminated and that the only way to draw sound inferences is to insist upon clear-cut raw data (cf. Mowrer, 1960, Chapter 8).

But perhaps we have not given the statistical approach a fair trial. Perhaps there are other possibilities that have not yet been examined. As far as the now conventional "tests of significance" are concerned, it would seem (if our preceding analysis has been sound) that we are nearing the "end of the line." But imbedded in the common language used in our discussion is an intimation that is well worth noting. Almost synonymously, we have used the terms, causation, connection, association, and *correlation*. And there is a well developed literature on statistical methods of dealing with "correlation" which, in point of fact, considerably antedates the work on "significance tests." Therefore, let us turn back to an older book, such as that of Mills (1924), and re-examine this area of statistical development. This author begins his discussion of correlational techniques by asking the following question:

> If it is possible in dealing with time series [discussed by Mills in earlier chapters] to secure a definite mathematical equation for the relation between time and the normal values of the items in a given series, cannot the same device be employed in studying the relationship between other variables?

Can we not measure, mathematically, the relation between cotton production and the price of cotton, between corn yield and rainfall, between earnings and the output of labor? If this can be done, it will place in the hands of the economist a very powerful tool, giving his methods something of the precision which attaches to the work of the physical scientist (pp. 363–364).

And as a further example, Mills reproduces data on "taxable personal incomes and motor vehicle registration in forty-three states, 1921" in tabular form, which he then translates into the scatter diagram shown in Fig. 8–2. At first blush, these data seem to be very different from

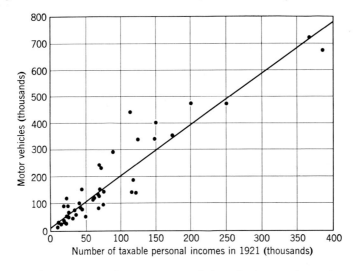

Fig. 8–2. A simple scatter diagram, or correlation chart, reproduced from Mills (1924, p. 366). A so-called coefficient of correlation is a single value, ranging from 0.0 to +1.0 or −1.0, which indicates how precise or close the association or correlation between two variables is. If the correlation is perfect (and "linear"), all values lie along a straight, diagonal (ascending or descending) line (as is the case, for example, of the weight of an object and the distance it causes the pointer on a good set of scales to move). The line shown in the above figure is given only as an approximation of the trend shown in the actual data. The coefficient of correlation for the data in this exhibit is .935.

the Darwin-Galton data; but further analysis will show some very fundamental similarities. In both cases there are *two* major variables: the independent variable or cause (mode of pollination, number of taxable personal incomes) and the dependent variable or effect (plant vigor, incidence of motor cars). But, it can be objected, in the Darwin experiment there were only two values for the independent variable (self-pollination and cross-pollination), whereas in the Mills example the independent variable is continuous (taxable incomes of nothing to $400,000). However, even this difference can be minimized if we note that the Mills data *might*, if we wished, be limited to just two values for the independent variable, let us say states with 5,000 to 10,000 taxable incomes and states with 50,000 to 60,000 taxable incomes. (Or smaller ranges could be used if such a procedure did not too seriously attenuate the data). Here the situation would be essentially the same as in the Darwin experiment; but since we have a lot more 'information" in this situation than Mr. Darwin had in his, we might as well use all of it if we can. Therefore, we will permit continuous variation in the independent variable and will return again to the scatter diagram. As Mills observes:

It is clear from this diagram that there is a relationship between the two variables [indicated by the upward slope of the line]. In general, the states with a large number of taxable personal incomes are also those having a large number of motor vehicles. The relationship, however, is not perfect. Thus both Kentucky and Oklahoma had 69,000 taxable personal incomes in 1921, yet the former had 126,000 motor vehicles registered, while the latter had 221,000. Were the relationship perfect a single value of the Y-variable [motor cars] would always be paired with a single variable of the X-variable [number of taxable incomes] (p. 364).

We therefore face the same problem that existed in Mr. Darwin's data. In other words, if the value of the dependent variable was always the same for a given value of the independent variable, the causal relationship, connection, or correlation would be perfect; it would be obvious to ordinary inspection; and there would be no "statistical" problem. But in both situations it is clear that factors other than the stipulated independent variable are affecting the dependent variable, so that an element of ambiguity is present in both cases. Although it seems unlikely, it is still conceivable that, the world-over (or through time), there is no real relationship between high incomes and prevalence of motor cars and that our sample is in some way a biased one, reflecting an "error of sampling." Therefore, basically the same questions of reliability and significance arise as exist in ordinary experimental situations. Mills epitomizes these questions as follows:

A mathematical expression has now been secured for the relation between the two variables being studied, the number of taxable personal incomes, by states, and the number of motor vehicles registered. The former is the independent or X-variable in the equation, the latter the dependent or Y-variable. This equation constitutes a measure of the functional relationship between these two variables, but it is only an expression of *average* relationship. How significant is the equation? If the relationship were perfect, and the plotted points all lay on the line describing this relationship, the equation could be used with confidence as an accurate instrument for determining the value of one variable from a value of the other. But a line with a definite equation may be fitted to points which depart very widely from it, which are widely dispersed. In such a case the equation may have the appearance of describing a precise relationship but the variation is so great that it cannot be used with confidence. It is the same problem as that which arises when an average is employed. We must know how significant the average is, how great the concentration about it, before we may use it intelligently. So the equation of relationship between variables means little unless we know to what extent it holds in practical experience. We must have a measure of the dispersion about the line we have fitted.

In describing the frequency distribution, it has been found, the standard deviation is the best general measure of the variation. It is, obviously, the measure we need in determining the reliability of the equation of average relationship. The standard deviation about this line will not only serve as a general index of the significance of this equation but will enable us to measure the degree of accuracy of estimates based upon the equation (pp. 367–368).

For our present purposes, we have now pursued this argument far enough. We see that conventional correlational procedures, in practice, run into exactly the same difficulties as are encountered when we attempt to deal with "averages" and that basically similar statistical devices have been suggested for dealing with them. Therefore, if we have found these devices less than thoroughly satisfactory for dealing with the problem of averages, we question them equally in the context of correlation.

But now appears an article by Bolles and Messick (1958) entitled "Statistical Utility in Experimental Inference," in which a new tack is made on this old problem. The authors begin by saying:

The majority of statistical procedures carried out in conjunction with psychological research are tests of significance. Typically, the researcher wants to know whether his data reflect a "real" difference between control and experimental groups, or whether the observed difference could have arisen by chance. Two points may be brought out: one is the concept of power and the other concerns the distinction between real and chance differences. A powerful test is one which gives a high probability of claiming a real difference when one actually exists in the population. Since the researcher is mainly concerned with finding real differences, he uses the most powerful tests at his disposal (p. 223).

There then follows the expression of dissatisfaction with present tests of significance which has already been quoted, in Section VI, after which the authors say:

The polemical point of this paper is that the fundamental obligation of *E* is to account for variation; obtaining significance differences is only incidental to his task of controlling, predicting, and explaining (p. 224).

To summarize so far, there are two properties of significance tests which limit their usefulness in psychological research: (a) they are dependent upon the power of the test in general and the sample size in particular [see Section V-5]; (b) the empirical situation of controlled and uncontrolled variables does not precisely correspond to the statistical inference model which involves real and chance effects [Section V-1]. Thus, the null hypothesis may or may not be true in the model, but in empirical situations, except under the conditions noted above, and possibly when crude discrete measures are used, it is almost certainly false. It would seem, then, that an index of utility is called for which can be used to supplement significance tests. In this connection we propose the label "coefficient of utility" for the class of statistics which describe the partitioning of variance (p. 225).

The interested reader can consult the Bolles-Messick article in the original for the details of the exact method employed; but what is pertinent here is the fact that it is based upon a *correlational* procedure.

Equation 3 means that *U* can be interpreted in terms of the correlation between the independent and dependent variables. Such a correlation is analogous to the biserial correlation in that it is dichotomous for one variable. *U* is also closely related to Fisher's inter-class correlation and to Kelley's unbiased correlation ratio (p. 226).

It should be noted that the concept of statistical utility is applicable to non-normal populations and may be used to supplement non-parametric significance tests (p. 226).

The author is not competent to evaluate the Bolles-Messick method from a technical standpoint; but it is obvious that this method is centrally concerned with exactly those problems which have held our attention in preceding sections and is also congruent with our supposition that causation is basically a matter of correlation, association, connection. And with this point now apparently well established, we turn to what may be regarded as the second half of our discussion of this general topic, which will be continued in the next chapter.

9

Learning, Causality, Probability, and Statistics (continued)

In the preceding chapter we have seen that the efforts to handle the "statistical" problem by means of tests of significance have encountered serious difficulties; that it is too early to tell how far the Bolles-Messick "coefficient of utility" may deliver us from these difficulties; and that, in any case, there is growing interest in "decision theory," which brings psychological processes more directly into the picture than they have previously been. In this chapter we shall therefore look at the problem from a frankly psychological standpoint—more specifically, that of revised two-factor learning theory—and see what new perspectives or insights can thus be gained.

I. Learning and Causation

Some years ago the author gave a seminar jointly with I. A. Richards, in the course of which Professor Richards conjectured that learning, when finally understood, would turn out to be related, perhaps rather closely, to the phenomenon of causality. And if one pursues the point, one discovers that, although largely neglected by contemporary learning theorists, this relationship was discussed by David Hume, with clarity and penetration, more than two hundred years ago. In his *Treatise of Human Nature* (1738), Hume approached the problem as follows:

The qualities, from which this association [of ideas] arises, and by which the mind is after this manner convey'd from one idea to another, are three, viz., *Resemblance, Contiguity* in time or place, and *Cause and Effect* (p. 319).

'Tis sufficient to observe, that there is no relation, which produces a stronger connexion in the fancy, and makes one idea more readily recall another, than the relation of cause and effect betwixt their objects (p. 320).

Hume's language is different from that usually employed today, but the translation is not difficult. "Resemblance" is presumably what we now term *generalization* (on the basis of similarity; see Mowrer, 1960, Chapter 12); and contiguity refers to the conjunction of stimuli which constitutes the familiar paradigm of *conditioning*. But what of cause and effect?

A few days ago the furnace in the writer's home was being repaired, and one of the workmen suddenly stepped back and jostled an ornamental bird cage which was hanging on a tall metal stand. The stand and cage started to fall, and the writer called out a warning; but it was too late for the workman to catch them and they crashed to the floor, breaking a part of the cage. The workman's ill-considered movement *caused* the pedestal to fall, and the fall *caused* the cage to break.

Now a knowledge of causal relationships is obviously important to living organisms, since it enables them to *prepare* for events in advance of their occurrence, or to *interrupt* or *precipitate* them. So the question arises as to whether our theory, which reduces all learning to conditioning, is able to account for learning of this particular kind. Causation is commonly stated in terms of if-this, then-that. *If* the workman bumps the stand, with sufficient force, it and the cage will *fall*. *If* the cage falls, it will (probably) *break*. Here there is always a sequence of *two events*, so-called cause *and* effect; and we immediately perceive the possibility that the cause (coming first) may function as a conditioned stimulus and the effect (or consequence) as the unconditioned stimulus. Damage to a valuable object usually evokes a reaction of dismay; and the fact that the writer cried out when he saw the pedestal and cage *falling* suggests that he was, in fact, conditioned to react to falling objects much as one does to the object *after* the fall.[1]

If this analysis is valid, then the conditioning process is well suited to capture the essence of cause-and-effect relationships. We are, in fact, already quite accustomed to think of an unconditioned stimulus as an *effect*, a consequence, an outcome, a reinforcer (positive or nega-

---

[1] From a high-school English class the writer recalls a piece of drollery entitled, "Darius Green and His Flying Machine." After his machine had crashed, Darius was asked how he liked the fall. His reply was that the *fall* was pleasant enough but that he had not enjoyed the *landing*. Thus, falling presumably qualifies as "an initially neutral stimulus" which, however, becomes fear-arousing because it is so likely to be followed by incremental reinforcement, or pain.

tive). If this, then *that!* But the notion of a cause, i.e., the *this,* serving as a conditioned stimulus is more novel—and perhaps doubtful. At once one will think of many conditioned stimuli which manifestly are *not* causes or causal. One would hardly say that a ticking metronome, in a Pavlovian experiment on salivary conditioning, *causes* the food to appear or that a buzzer which warns a rat of impending electric shock *causes* the shock. These are *signs,* we say, not causes. But, as we have seen, a sign may *also* be a cause. Thus we arrive at the conclusion that the causal relationship, as psychically apprehended, is *a special case of the more general phenomenon of conditioning or learning by contiguity.* All causes, when they are known, act as conditioned stimuli, but not all conditioned stimuli are causes; and contemporary psychologists have largely overlooked the special case for the reason that in laboratory studies the relationship between CS and UnCS is nearly always arbitrary rather than necessary. There is, however, no reason to doubt that conditioning would occur quite as readily in the one case as in the other. One could easily arrange a situation in which the ticking of a metronome would, in fact, *cause* food to appear or, equally, the sound of a buzzer cause shock to come on. The experimenter himself is, of course, very much interested in discovering necessary or causal sequences (what causes or controls what); but his tacit assumption that his subjects have no such capacity or interest has blinded him to the full scope and implication of the learning process.[2]

Arbitrary signs and true causes are, of course, in practice often very much alike, especially if one uses them merely in preparing for the inevitable, as for instance with respect to the weather. There used to be (perhaps still is) a saying in the rural area of North Missouri where the writer lived as a child to this effect: "Evening red and morning gray sends the traveler on his way; but evening gray and morning red brings

[2] An exception to this general neglect of the causal relationship is the work of Michotte (1946), which recently inspired Gruber, Fink, and Damm (1957) to perform an ingenious experiment on what they call the "perception of causality." They say: "The stimulus event was the collapse of a 'bridge' following the removal of one of its vertical members. A very definite and striking impression of causality is reported if the time between the removal of this upright and the collapse of the bridge is sufficiently short. As the time interval increases, S reports such an impression less and less frequently" (p. 89). Here removal of the support may be thought of as the CS and the collapse of the bridge as the UnCS; and such an interpretation is strengthened by the finding that as the interval between these two events is increased, the "impression of causality"—conditioning?—decreases (cf. Mowrer, 1960, Chapter 10). When two such events will be perceived as causally related and when not (aside from the question of temporal relationship) will be explored in the paragraphs which follow.

rain upon the traveler's head." Clearly, a gray evening (cloudy sunset) is here regarded as a *sign* of rain; but is it also a *cause* thereof? Actually it is difficult to know, and one readily sees why primitive peoples were often confused about signs and causes and why the distinction between superstition and magic, on the one hand, and more rational beliefs and practices, on the other, was often vague in their minds. Perhaps by means of smoke or steam, which would make the sunset "gray" (or cloudy), one *could* make it rain! Only in those areas where natural signs can be reproduced by human intervention do we quickly discover the distinction between signs which are truly causal and signs which are not. Otherwise, as is generally true of "the weather," observation and inference of a much more detailed and subtle kind is required—and, even then, our understanding of the situation may not be very precise.

II. David Hume on Causality and Learning

Having in the preceding section quoted Hume and having then shown how much further an analysis of the cause-and-effect relationship can be carried, let us allow Hume to speak again for himself:

The idea, then, of causation must be deriv'd from some *relation* among objects; and that relation we must now endeavour to discover. I find in the first place, that whatever objects are considered as causes or effects, are *contiguous*; and that nothing can operate in time or place, which is ever so little remov'd from those of its existence. Tho' distant objects may sometimes seem productive of each other, they are commonly found upon examination to be link'd by a chain of causes, which are contiguous among themselves, and to the distant objects; and when in any particular instance we cannot discover this connexion, we still presume it to exist. We may therefore consider the relation of *contiguity* as essential to that of causation; at least may suppose it such, according to the general opinion, till we can find a more proper occasion to clear up this matter, by examining what objects are or are not susceptible of juxtaposition and conjunction (pp. 377-378).

Having thus discover'd or suppos'd the two relations of contiguity and succession to be essential to cause and effects, I find I am stopt short, and can proceed no farther in considering any single instance of cause and effect. Motion in one body is regarded upon impulse as the cause of motion in another. When we consider these objects with the utmost attention, we find that the one body approaches the other; and that the motion of it precedes that of the other, but without any sensible interval. 'Tis in vain to rack ourselves with *further* thought and reflection upon this subject (p. 379).

Hume here shows a nice understanding of the gradient of reinforcement according to which conditioning weakens as the temporal interval between CS and UnCS increases (see footnote 2); and he is also quite explicit in noting, as we also have been, that cause-and-effect is not a distinct phenomenon, psychologically, but a special case of learning by contiguity. But perhaps Hume did not see the distinction between conditioned stimuli which are causes and those which are merely signs? Immediately following the passage last quoted, he says:

> Should any one leave this instance, and pretend to define a cause, by saying it is something productive of another, 'tis evident he would say nothing. For what does he mean by *productive?* Can he give any definition of it, that will not be the same with that of causation? If he can; I desire it may be produc'd. If he cannot; he here runs in a circle, and gives a synonymous term instead of a definition.
>
> Shall we then rest contented with these two relations of contiguity and succession, as affording a complete idea of causation? By no means. An object may be contiguous and prior to another, without being consider'd as its cause. There is a NECESSARY CONNECTION to be taken into consideration; and that relation is of much greater importance, than any of the other two above mention'd (p. 379).

But surely we have made an advance over Hume in that we have given up the "association of ideas" in favor of the more objective and operational emphasis upon behavior and behavior change. Actually, as will be recalled from earlier chapters of this book, the natural course of Behaviorism has been such as eventually to force back upon us a recognition of something very much like the association of ideas (conditioning of images; Chapter 5); and Hume himself was by no means without an appreciation of what was to be gained by the objective approach. Already in the *Treatise of Human Nature* there was a section entitled "Of Reason in Animals"; and in *An Enquiry Concerning Understanding* (1777), there is the following more extended and explicit discussion:

> *First,* it seems evident, that animals, as well as men, learn many things from experience, and infer, that the same events will always follow from the same causes. By this principle they become acquainted with the more obvious properties of external objects, and gradually, from their birth, treasure up a knowledge of the nature of fire, water, earth, stones, heights, depths, etc., and of the effects which result from their operation. The ignorance and inexperience of the young are here plainly distinguishable from the cunning and sagacity of the old, who have learned, by long observation, *to avoid what hurt them, and to pursue what gave ease or pleasure.* . . .
>
> This is still more evident from the effects of discipline and education on animals, who, by the *proper application of rewards and punishments,* may be taught any *course of action,* and most contrary to their natural instincts and properties. Is it not experience, which renders a dog *apprehensive of pain,*

when you menace him, or lift the whip to beat him? Is it not even experience, which makes him answer to his name, and infer, from such an arbitrary sound, that you mean him rather than any of his fellows . . . ?

In all these cases, we may observe, that the animal infers some fact beyond what immediately strikes his senses; and that this inference is altogether founded on past experience, while the creature expects from the present object the same consequences, which it has always found in its observation to result from similar objects (pp. 110–111, italics added).

Here we see clearly Hume's first main objective, namely that of showing that knowledge is *not innate*, that we acquire our "ideas" through experience, through learning, and that Hume does not mean his theory to apply to ideas alone, but as well to *actions*. Here, in the latter instance, it is not merely continuity that counts but also reinforcement, in both the decremental and incremental sense.

Having shown that "ideas" are not innate, Hume proceeds to argue that they are, in general, likewise derived not from reason, but from *experience*. Here surely was the Manifesto of Empiricism, empiricism in a double sense: Empiricism as *induction*, rather than deduction, as the royal road to knowledge; and empiricism in the sense of opening up the possibility for studying "mental processes," not subjectively and "logically," but objectively, behaviorally. The historical and logical importance of the work of Hume (and associated thinkers) can therefore hardly be exaggerated. His books can certainly be read by contemporary students of the psychology of learning with respect and profit—though it is somewhat deflating to see how little advance, in certain ways, there has been over what a bright young man was able to say about these matters more than two centuries ago!

III. Learning and the "Causal Texture of the Environment"

As already indicated, contemporary behavior theorists have given comparatively little attention to the relationship between causation and learning. But in 1935, Tolman & Brunswik published a paper entitled "The Organism and the Causal Texture of the Environment," which was destined to alter this situation. Here an interesting and important issue was raised. It was pointed out that most laboratory studies had, up to that time, involved the learning of living organisms under "constant" conditions. Thus, if a rat ran through a maze once and found food in the goal box, it was the experimenter's (if not also the rat's) expectation that food should *always* be found there. This sort of constancy or regularity was assumed to be an inherent part of the scientific method. But Tolman & Brunswik very persuasively argued that such uniformity of reward does not parallel the natural environment of living organisms, where success and satisfaction are exceedingly chancy matters. As Brunswik (1955) later observed, "The environment to which the organism must adjust presents itself as semi-erratic and . . . therefore all functional psychology is inherently probabilistic" (p. 193). Hence it would follow that if one wants to study learning in a more realistic setting, one should provide rewards intermittently rather than continuously.

It is true that, prior to 1935, considerable work had been done on the extinction of learned responses, under conditions of nonreward, following acquisition with reward. This, to be sure, was a kind of variability or inconsistency; but the reward was usually consistently given up to a point, beyond which it was, again consistently, withheld. In the conditioning experiments carried out in Pavlov's laboratory the strength of a conditioned salivary response would sometimes be tested, as training proceeded, by withholding the reinforcing (unconditioned) stimulus now and then, thus providing, inadvertently, a small element of intermittency in the acquisition schedule. But no systematic research or theorizing emerged in this connection; and it was really the Tolman-Brunswik paper that raised the issue of "probabilistic learning" for the first time in fully explicit form.

This paper stimulated two important lines of subsequent research; but before we explore them, it will be useful to look at the "common sense" of this problem in a little greater detail.

It goes without saying that if life were *not* chancy, *learning* would be unnecessary. If life were simple and if experiential sequences were stable and certain, then the solutions to all problems could be "wired in," as reflexes and instincts. Such an arrangement actually exists in certain limited areas. Because it is invariably useful to diminish the intensity of the light striking the retina of the eye when the intensity exceeds a certain maximum, it is highly adaptive to have a mechanism which "automatically," i.e., with mechanical certainty, reacts to light in such a way as to control and limit its intensity. One cannot think readily, if at all, of any circumstance in which such a protective device would not be advantageous; and, conveniently enough, we are normally born equipped with just such an arrangement. We call it the "pupillary reflex."

Or, lacking reflexive solutions to its problems, an organism, in an environment of the kind described, could have a mechanism for extremely rapid learning ("insight," in the sense in which some Gestalt psychologists have used the term). Assuming conditions to be constant, invariant, *one* experience in a given situation would be as good as a hundred, as far as the "information" derived would be concerned, so learning might as well be complete and absolute, in *one trial*. Actually, as we well know, learning is usually a more gradual process;[3] and the indications are that this progressive, rather than all-or-none, nature of learning is not just stupidity on the part of organisms. Instead, it appears that life is indeed chancy, that many events *are* "purely coincidental," and that *the truth*, i.e., genuine causal relationship, is a matter of probability and can be established only on the basis of *repetitive occurrences*. Therefore, it is presumably by design, rather than by default, that the nervous system of living organisms changes gradually rather than precipitously. An organism can, of course, learn *too slowly*, in which event we speak of its possessor as being really "stupid." But an organism could, in theory at least, also be too smart for its own good. If it learned *too rapidly*, then it would be regarded as credulous, naive, superstitious. Its difficulty, to borrow an old quip, would be that it knew so much that "ain't so."

The best formulation of this problem known to the present writer is one to be found in a paper entitled, "The Brain Analogy: A Discussion," by H. E. Coburn (1952), who, interestingly enough, is an engineer, rather than a psychologist. This paper should be consulted in the original for its full import; but its relevance to the present discussion is suggested by the following quotation, which is the opening paragraph of a section entitled "Optimum Learning Rate."

It is probable that the interaction of various mutations and natural selection has established a rate of conditioning which closely approximates the theoretical optimum. While slow learning is obviously detrimental, extremely fast learning may likewise be injurious when we recall that one or two sensory samples do not determine an answer but merely establish a hypothesis. *The brain has no way of "knowing" which elements of the stimulus situation are significant.* It must accept and condition to all S [stimuli], automatically, and in accordance with probability. The *appearance* of purpose is due solely to the fact that systematic S result in *stable* conditioning (p. 456).

And, in conclusion, this author says:

The foregoing discussion must necessarily be considered heuristic, and, as always with science, provisional. It seems reasonable to conclude, however,

---

[3] Krechevsky (1932) has conjectured that in a trial-and-error situation, living organisms make trial responses in the manner of "hypotheses," holding that such a response, when it occurs, occurs, so as to say, "full strength," and is then confirmed or refuted, but not "strengthened" or "weakened." Guthrie's conception of learning (Mowrer, 1960, Chapter 8) is somewhat similar. See also Hudson's monograph on "One-Trial Learning in the Domestic Rat" (1950).

that the importance of evolution for behavior theory has been demonstrated. The author would also like to believe that the nature of reinforcement, probably the outstanding problem in psychological theory, has been clarified a little (p. 459).

In short, then, we can perhaps say that an organism, to have an optimal capacity for "adjustment" to its environment, must be neither too "trusting" nor too "skeptical" (cf. statistical errors, type I and type II, as discussed by Wald, 1950, and others). Its confidence ought, ideally, (through learning) to come to match "the causal texture of the environment." Therefore the way to study learning most realistically, Tolman & Brunswik held, is to have an experimental environment in which events, such as reward, nonreward, or punishment are *more or less probable*, rather than absolutely consistent and certain.[4]

IV. Learning with the Probability of Reinforcement Less than Unity: "Probabilistic Learning"

The theoretical considerations advanced by Tolman and Brunswik opened up two new lines of empirical inquiry. Heretofore it had been assumed that if, in laboratory experimentation, a given response on the part of a subject (for example, the negotiation of a maze by a rat) produced, or "caused," reward on one trial, it should *always* produce reward and that if a given signal (as in Pavlovian conditioning) was followed by ("caused") a given unconditioned stimulus (or reinforcement) on one trial, it should have the same effect on *all* trials. At least these were the rules which were tacitly accepted for that portion of an experiment in which learning (acquisition) was supposed to occur, although they could be changed if one wished to study the course of extinction (Mowrer, 1960, Chapter 11); but here again, if conditions were changed from reinforcement to nonreinforcement, the latter was likewise supposed to be absolutely uniform, consistent. However, as Tolman & Brunswik pointed out, these are *not* the conditions which ordinarily prevail in a state of nature; and living organisms must therefore be capable of learning "the causal texture" of an environment, not only when cause-and-effect relationships are uniform and consistent, but also when they are irregular and inconsistent, i.e., under conditions wherein reinforcement is not certain but merely more or less *probable*.

These theoretical considerations opened up two new lines of empirical inquiry, one of which has already been extensively reviewed

[4] For an extreme development of this, or at least a related line of thought, see Estes (1950, 1955a, 1955b); also Mowrer, 1960, pp. 287–292.

elsewhere (Mowrer, 1960, Chapter 12) under the heading of "intermittent reinforcement," and the other, commonly referred to as "probabilistic learning," will be discussed in this and the following section. However, it should be noted that when first embarked upon, both of these lines of investigation led to paradoxical findings, which seemed to constitute serious threats to the whole reinforcement (reward-and-punishment) approach to learning. But now it has been shown that by means of the revisions in reinforcement theory which have been systematized in *Learning Theory and Behavior* (and summarized in the first chapter of this volume), the results of intermittent reinforcement can be accommodated very comfortably within this framework. And we shall now see that although the work on probabilistic learning also presents certain seeming difficulties for revised two-factor learning theory, these, too, can be nicely resolved by the same basic assumptions and principles and that, in the process, we gain some important insights into the problem of probability and statistics in general.

In intermittent reinforcement, it will be recalled, there is only *one* "correct" response and it is correct (effective) only *part* of the time. But suppose, now, that an organism is presented with a problem, e.g., hunger, which can be solved by either of *two different* responses and that the likelihood of reward for these two responses is not the same. A simple T-maze provides such a situation, physically; and a reinforcement schedule of, let us say, 75% reinforcement for going to the goal box in the right wing of the maze and 25% reinforcement for going to the goal box in the left wing of the maze provides the desired psychological conditions.

A priori, the results are not difficult to predict. In the beginning, the subjects (i.e., rats) might be expected to show an equal, or 50–50, tendency to turn right and to turn left at the choice point in the maze. But right turning would be reinforced 75% of the time and left turning only 25% of the time, so the right-going tendency ought to build up more rapidly than the left-going tendency, and eventually the subjects ought to go right 100% of the time. This outcome would not only be expected from the fact of differential reinforcement; it would also be a "logical" solution to the problem since it would *maximize* reward. As long as a subject went to the right on all trials, he would be assured of reward on three-fourths of these trials; and any departure from 100% preference for the right side would, on the average, cause the ratio of reinforcement to drop somewhat below three times in four. However, in some experiments thus far reported, a seemingly different kind of result has, in fact, been obtained.

It cannot be our purpose here to review all of the researches which have now been carried out along the lines just indicated. Instead, we shall cite only enough of these to indicate what appears to be trends. We shall begin with a study reported by Brunswik, in 1939, which the author summarized as follows:

As a contribution to what might be called the "psychophysics of probability," five groups of 48 rats each were rewarded on the two sides of a choice situation different proportions of times. . . . A training of 24 trials failed to establish a discriminatory response in only one of the groups, for which the chances of reward on the two sides were ⅔ against ⅓ (group "67:33"). In contrast to that, groups "100:50," "75:25" and "50:0" were significantly above the "threshold of probability" in an increasing order. For the last of these groups, "50:0," the difference with control group "100:0" which represented the traditional unambiguous type of training dropped below significance ("threshold of certainty") (pp. 194–196).

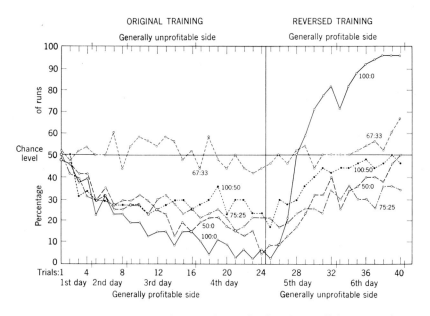

Fig. 9–1. Graphic presentation of the results obtained by Brunswik in an experiment on "probability learning."

The results of the part of Brunswik's experiment which is of major interest to us here are shown in Fig 9–1. It is to be noted, in the first place, that all groups of subjects began the experiment with an evenly divided (50–50) preference for the right and left wings of the T-maze.

The group that was consistently rewarded in one wing and consistently not rewarded in the other wing (100:0) moved steadily, as the lower curve in the graph shows, toward a "one-sided" choice. In contrast, the ratio of 67% reinforcement on one side and 33% reinforcement on the other was not readily discriminated by the subjects from a purely chance (50:50) pattern of reinforcement. However, toward the end of the original training period (24 trials), there is some evidence that discrimination was beginning to occur; and, in the reversal period that followed, there is rather clear evidence of discrimination. As will be seen in Fig. 9–1, the other ratios of reinforcement, falling between 67:33 and 100:0, gave intermediate results.

Taken as they stand, these results seem to favor the notion that, in an experiment of the kind described, rats tend, in their choice between two alternative goals (which differ only in frequency of "pay-off") to *match* the objective probabilities rather than to maximize the possibility of reward (cf. Heron, 1942). Such an interpretation might seem, at first glance, to support the notion that learning is a special sort of *cognitive* process rather than one determined by *reinforcement*. Certainly, the behavior of Brunswik's rats seems to reflect more strongly the nature of *reality* than their own needs or self-interest (cf. Woodworth, 1958).

There are, however, two considerations which warrant some reservation in this connection. In the first place, the initial training was stopped after only 24 trials, at a point where all groups were still moving in the direction of greater preference for the "more profitable" side. It is, of course, entirely possible that if the subjects had been given a more extended experience in this situation, they would have arrived at a "maximizing" rather than "matching" solution to the problem. In other words, it is possible that *all* groups would have eventually developed substantially a 100% preference for the more profitable side and a 0% preference for the less profitable side. Therefore, as far as this important theoretical question is concerned, these data are incomplete and inconclusive (see Brand, Woods, & Sakoda, 1956).

Moreover, the procedure used in Brunswik's investigation was such as to be, in one respect, decidedly unfavorable to the maximizing solution. Whenever an animal went to one or the other side of the maze and found no food there, it had to "correct" its errors by turning around and going to the *other side* of the maze, where food (in most groups) would now be found. This meant that on those comparatively rare occasions when a rat found no food on the generally "more profitable" side, it would be *required* to leave this side and go to the less profitable side. This procedure insured continued reinforcement on the less profitable side and worked against 100% selection of the more profitable side.

Hence, it is evident that for a clear-cut answer to these issues, a new experiment needs to be carried out which would be, in general, similar to Brunswik's but different from it in that (1) a noncorrection rather than correction method would be used and that (2) the training would be continued for a sufficient number of trials to show unequivocally what the subjects' stable, final adjustment would be. To the best of the present writer's knowledge, no one has carried out an experiment of this sort, with animal subjects.[5]

There has, however, been a considerable amount of research done on probabilistic learning with human subjects which we can now profitably examine. Fortunately, this work has been admirably summarized in an article by Grant (1953), which we shall here follow.[6] Says Grant:

> The writer's interest in this problem arose in connection with the problem of extinction in conditioning. Extinction implies the discrimination of a change in the sequence of stimuli. The problem becomes acute in the situation of partial reinforcement where the subject is randomly reinforced on only 25%, 50%, 75%, or some other percentage of the trials.
>
> In the subsequent extinction the subject may require quite a large number of trials before a clear-cut discrimination of the change in stimulus conditions occurs. . . . The discriminability of the change in stimuli during extinction has been the explicit or implicit basis of interpretations of extinction proposed by several investigators (Grant, Hake, & Hornseth, 1951; Humphreys, 1939b; Jenkins & Stanley, 1950; Mowrer & Jones, 1945; Virginia Sheffield, 1949; and Skinner, 1953a) (p. 19).

Grant then describes the apparatus with which several of his own researches have been carried out. It is similar to a device originally employed by Humphreys, consisting of a board with two electric lamps mounted on it, one at the left and the other at the right. When the lamp at the left is illuminated, the subjects are then to *guess* whether the lamp at the right will or will not also be turned on. On successive

[5] Since the above was written, an unpublished study by Stanley (1950) has been called to the writer's attention which appears to meet these two conditions, of noncorrection and extended training. The results of this experiment have not yet been seen, but indirect reports are to the effect that given these conditions, the subjects (rats) tended to maximize rather than match. The same finding seems to have been obtained in the study by Bush & Mosteller (1951), which again, has not yet been examined in the original. See also Estes (1959).

[6] For a different attack upon the problem, see Bruner, Goodman, & Austin (1956, Chapter 7).

trials, the signal light (at the left) can be "confirmed" (by light at the right) on any desired percentage of the total number of the trials; and the experimenter can see, from the subjects' records, how well they approximated in their guessing the actual pattern of confirmation or "reinforcement." In Fig. 9–2 we see the results obtained from such a procedure.

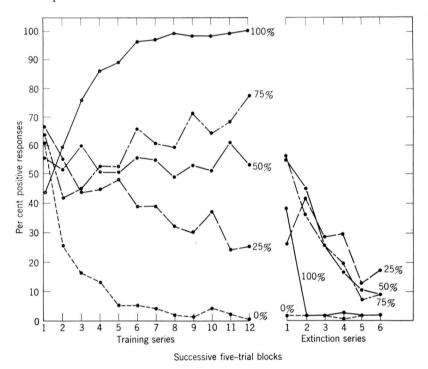

Successive five-trial blocks

Fig. 9–2. Data reproduced from Grant, Hake & Hornseth (1951) showing how closely the guessing of human subjects approximates the actual ratio of confirmed and nonconfirmed stimulus sequences.

At first it may appear that the procedure just described is not strictly comparable to that employed by Brunswik with rats as subjects. In the Brunswik procedure, the subjects had two alternative routes to reinforcement, each of which might be either right or wrong on any given trial. In the Grant experiment, on the other hand, no such response alternative is seemingly present. The procedure would appear rather more like that where there is a single correct response, with some trials rewarded and others not. But, actually, in the Grant (Humphreys) procedure, the subject does have two alternatives available to him on each trial: he may guess either *Yes* or *No,* and he may be right or wrong *either way.* He may guess that the signal light will be confirmed (followed by the other light) on a given trial, and it may or may not be; or he may guess that it will not be confirmed, and it may or may not be.[7] Thus, as in the Brunswik T-maze procedure, a "hit" or a "miss" can occur in either case, which is *not* true when an animal, in a conventional partial-reinforcement procedure, is running a straight alley or pressing a single Skinner bar. In the latter type of situation there is *only one* possibility of success and one of failure.

There is, however, one thing that can be done with the T-maze procedure which cannot be done with the flashing lights. In the maze, one can have any desired ratio of reinforcement and nonreinforcement on either side; whereas, with the lights, there is necessarily a reciprocal relationship between the ratio of confirmation and nonconfirmation of Yes guesses and No guesses. But otherwise, the two procedures are comparable; and the fact that they lead to ostensibly different results, in rats and in human beings, poses a special problem, which will be considered in the next section.

V. Probabilistic Learning in Rats and Men Compared

In connection with the preceding analysis of the Brunswik experiment, it has been suggested that, given an opportunity, rats will tend to maximize reinforcement; whereas, in experiments of the type reported by Grant, there is a good deal of evidence that human beings, by contrast, stabilize at a level of guessing which matches the objective ratios, instead of maximizing the absolute number of "hits." For example, if the light on the left (in the Humphreys-Grant apparatus) is confirmed, let us say, 75% of the time, then one could

---

[7] Recent reports have begun to appear in the literature on "probabilistic discrimination learning," which Estes, Burke, Atkinson, and Frankmann (1957) describe as follows: "Consider a standard two-choice discrimination apparatus (e.g., a Grice box or a Lashley stand) with two discrimination cues available, say a light and a tone. To set up a classical discrimination problem, one might present either the light or the tone on each trial and reinforce responses to the right door when the light is present. To set up a probabilistic discrimination problem, one might assign to the tone and light the probabilities .8 and .4, respectively, of occurring on trials when the left response is reinforced and the probabilities .4 and .8, respectively, of occurring on trials when the right response is reinforces" (p. 233). Here, too, a matching rather than maximizing solution is adopted by human subjects.

be unfailingly right 75% of the time by guessing confirmation 100% of the time. And every guess of nonconfirmation is likely to reduce this level of success because whenever the subject predicts nonconfirmation his chances of a hit are only one in four or 25%. However, human subjects, in their guessing, tend to approximate and stay remarkably near the objective ratio.

In Fig. 9–2, the 75% and 25% curves are still pointing in the direction of a maximizing solution when the experiment is ended; so, on the basis of these data alone, one might wonder if, given a sufficient number of additional trials, the subjects might not arrive, eventually, at the 100% and 0% levels of prediction. But to this Grant says:

> It might be mentioned parenthetically that in other experiments at Wisconsin and John Hopkins (Hake & Hyman, 1953) it has been found that the 75% and 25% assymptotes will be held for as long as 240 trials (pp. 21–22).
> Increasing the proportion of positive responses when the proportion of positive trials is above .5 will increase the percentage of hits, but the subject must increase the proportion of positive responses to 1.00 in order to *maximize* the expected number of hits. Instead of doing this he apparently stops increasing the rate of emission of positive responses when P_r [response probability] is equal to P_s [stimulus probability] (p. 24).

It is apparent, then, that either we are not justified in inferring that rats, given favorable conditions, will maximize or else we must conclude that there are factors operative in human subjects in a situation of this kind that are not to be found in rats.

In the paper which is here under discussion, Grant goes on to describe the results of extensive experiments which were inspired by the Shannon-type of "information theory." However, these studies are extremely intricate and, for our purposes, not directly relevant. Nevertheless, Grant concludes his paper with some remarks which are easily grasped and well worth noting.

> Inasmuch as the final stable solution does not maximize hits or reinforcements the question arises—what does it do? Concentration of attention on single trials was shown above to reveal very little from the point of view of information analysis. If, however, the stimulus *rate* is called "the response," then an interesting relationship becomes clear (pp. 40–41).
> In other words, the subject actually maximizes the transmission of information by his performance. Rather than maximizing reinforcements on single trials, the subject regularizes his behavior so as to minimize the stimulus-response variability. Lest this finding be taken to support contiguity theory one must recall that the result does not deal with single responses. It is likely that a statistical contiguity theory such as that of Estes (1950) could handle the situation, but the older forms of contiguity and reinforcement theories must be doctored to cover this case. Thus, the fact remains that what the

subject does do and what he does achieve is the maximization of information transfer when the stimulus is defined as a rate and when the response is defined as a rate (p. 42).

Granted the essential soundness of Grant's analysis of the behavior of human beings in a situation of this kind, it does not necessarily follow that rats function in the same way. The *goal* of human subjects, in such a situation, may be quite different from those of rats. For example, it is entirely possible that, as Grant suggests, human subjects conceive *their* task, in situations of this kind, to be precisely that of matching their behavior to the stimulus probabilities. Merely adopting the solution that would maximize hits may seem entirely too simple and obvious to them. Something else, they infer, is required of them. But the rat, oblivious of any such considerations, would be expected, given the right conditions and enough trials, to maximize. Support for this type of thinking comes from a study reported by Wyckoff & Sidowski (1955). It begins thus:

> The study of the reactions of human S_s, when confronted with ambiguous situations, is of considerable theoretical and practical importance. One aspect of this problem has been investigated in a number of experiments referred to as verbal conditioning experiments, which have utilized a paradigm originated by Humphreys (1939b) and others (Grant, Hake & Hornseth, 1951; Jenkins and Stanley, 1950). In these experiments S was required to select one of two responses on each of a large number of trials. Each response was considered "correct" by S a certain percentage of the time in a random sequence, and S was given some signal to indicate correct responses. We will refer to the percentage of times that a given response was "correct" as the *yield* of that response. . . .
>
> All of these experiments have placed S in a situation where his assigned task has been to make a series of guesses or predictions. The responses to be made were essentially verbal in nature, requiring no skill. Recognition of this feature is illustrated by the use of the term "verbal conditioning" (Estes & Straughn, 1954; Grant, Hake, & Hornseth, 1951; Humphreys, 1939). Similarly the reinforcements have been simple cues which indicated that the response was correct or not correct. These charactertistics appear to have set the stage for *a kind of problem-solving attitude on the part of S that is illustrated by the typical attempts of S to find a pattern in the sequence* (p. 225, italics added).

We shall make no attempt to describe or reproduce the results of the Wyckoff-Sidowski experiment, except to say that here there was a clear tendency for the subjects to *maximize* rather than to match. Of this the authors say:

> Reasons for the difference between the present results and previous results are considered in detail. Our interpretation includes the notion that the

decreased tendency to interpret the task as a guessing or problem-solving task eliminates certain factors which otherwise interfere with the approach to an optimal solution. These factors are related to past experience with guessing and problem solving (p. 231).

Still remaining to be performed, it seems, is an experiment in which human subjects would be assigned, or would spontaneously assume, the task of getting as high a "yield" as possible. Let us imagine, for example, a "slot-machine" which operated as follows. Each trial or "play" costs, let us say, ten cents. The player has a choice on each play of throwing a lever to the right or to the left. The machine is rigged so that a left throw "pays off" with twenty cents one time in four, while a right throw pays off by the same amount three times in four. With this arrangement, the player, if he chose the left throw consistently, would lose twenty cents every four trials (on the average); whereas, if he made the right throw consistently, he would (on the average) *gain* twenty cents every four trials. And intermediate patterns of response would result in intermediate patterns of loss or gain.

Suppose, now, that such a machine were installed on a street corner or in a factory or club locker room. Can there be any doubt what would happen? It would seem a foregone conclusion that players would soon start making *all throws to the right,* with resulting profit to themselves and considerable loss to the owner of the machine.[8]

Here is an apparent conflict: in one situation (discussed by Grant) human subjects match rather than maximize, while in the other situation we may confidently infer that they maximize rather than match. Grant and Wyckoff & Sidowski have already provided a possible cue for the resolution of this difficulty, and the same line of thought is further extended in a paper by Edwards (1954) entitled, "The Theory of Decision Making." The latter points out that the notion that human beings, in all their behavior, are endeavoring to "maximize something" is widely accepted by economists. And to this he then adds:

[8] Since the above was written a partial empirical confirmation has been reported by Edwards (1956). "Using real money rewards," this investigator obtained results which "raise doubts about the familiar generalization which says that in probability learning situations the asymptotic probability of choice is equal to the probability of reward" (p. 177). In other words, this investigator, using human subjects, found a tendency to maximize reward rather than merely match probabilities. See also a series of experiments recently carried out by Stevenson & Zigler (1958), Stevenson & Weir (1959), Stevenson & Weir (1960a), and Stevenson & Weir (1960b).

This notion of maximization is mathematically useful, since it makes it possible for a theory to specify a unique point or a unique subset of points among those available to the decider. It seems to me psychologically unobjectionable. So many *different kinds of functions can be maximized* that almost any point actually available in an experimental situation can be regarded as a maximum of some sort. Assumptions about maximization only become specific, and therefore possibly wrong, when they specify *what is being maximized* (italics added, p. 382).

If, as in the example of the specially constructed slot machine, the motivation or "set" of the subject is purely economic, then "maximizing" will lead to one sort of behavior. But if, as suggested by Wyckoff & Sidowski and by Grant, the subject is trying to show someone else (or himself) that he can discern the *ratio* or *pattern* of confirmation and nonconfirmation in a given situation, then we can expect a different kind of performance. But in neither case is the principle of "maximizing," or reinforcement, violated: In the one situation the subject is trying to maximize *money* and in the other he is trying to maximize *matching*. It all seems to be a matter of the subject's *motivation*.[9]

VI. Two Other Facets of the Probability Problem

We may now usefully revert to two considerations relevant to studies of probability learning in animals. It has already been suggested that, in a favorably designed experiment, hungry rats may be expected to maximize the food obtained rather than to match, in their choice behavior, the objective probabilities of reward in one or the other of

[9] The fact that both human and animal subjects, in food or money maximizing situations, develop a clear-cut preference for a response with high-reinforcement probability over one with a low-reinforcement probability has important systematic implications. Such a preference would indicate, unequivocally, that a habit which is reinforced relatively often is stronger than a habit which is reinforced less often. Yet we have seen that habit strength, as measured by resistance to extinction, is ostensibly greater when a habit has been built up by relatively *in*frequent, rather than frequent, reinforcement. This dilemma, together with other considerations previously advanced, suggests that we have probably erred in assuming that resistance to extinction is necessarily a valid index of habit strength. It now appears that, by the technique of intermittent reinforcement, what we do is *not* augment habit strength, properly speaking, but *diminish the effectiveness of extinction* (in contrast to its effectiveness following continuous reinforcement). This conclusion is consistent with a point of view gradually evolved in *Learning Theory and Behavior* (see especially Chapters 11 and 12) and in Chapter 5 of this book; see also Mason (1957).

two different places (as in a T-maze). In conversation, Dr. Norman Ginsburg has made a quite pertinent observation in this connection. In a situation where, let us say, the ratio of reinforcement for two different responses is $75\%:25\%$, it is a comparatively simple matter for a rat to discover that one response, or choice, is *better* than the other, so that the rat will "favor," i.e., go predominantly to, one side rather than the other. But it might be actually quite difficult, if not impossible, for the rat to discover that the maximizing solution (100% choice of the 75% reinforcement alternative) would be "better" than the mere matching choice. If, in this situation, a rat maximized, it would obtain food 6/8ths of the time, whereas if it *matched*, it would do almost as well, receiving food 5/8ths of the time. It is therefore possible that the rat would simply *fail to discriminate* such a relatively small probability difference.[10] Moreover, the rather mysterious tendency toward "spontaneous" response variability (Mowrer, 1960, pp. 336–342) might, quite independently, operate against a consistent, 100% selection of the 75% alternative. (Indeed, one does not get absolutely consistent selection of even a 100:0 alternative.)

The other point to be noted in passing is this. In this and the companion volume we are exploring the hypothesis that there are two kinds of reinforcement, decremental and incremental; and in the preceding discussion we have been concerned exclusively with the former. So one may be prompted to ask: What is the course of "probability" learning, where incremental rather than decremental reinforcement is involved? As we know, *nonoccurrence* of an expected reward acts somewhat like a punishment (Mowrer, 1960, Chapters 11 and 12). Therefore, in a situation ostensibly involving some specific ratio of reward and nonreward, we actually have a ratio of reward and "punishment." But the further question remains as to how choice behavior in lower animals would be affected if punishment of a more active sort were introduced. In the investigation already cited, Brunswik (1939) ran two additional groups of subjects in which reward and nonreward was supplemented by "an electric shock in each case of an unsuccessful choice" (p. 183). The reinforcement ratios used were 75:25 and 100:50. In both groups the rate of learning (to discriminate against an original equal preference for the two goals) was accelerated and the tendency toward maximizing, as opposed to matching, was clearly evident. Says Brunswik:

[10] Cf. the inability of the rats in Brunswik's 1939 experiment to "discriminate" (within 24 trials at least) between a 67:33 ratio of reinforcement in a T-maze and a 50:50 ratio.

Learning then increases with an increase of the probability ratio of punishment. Apparently the avoidance of punishment becomes a stronger motive as compared with the anxiousness of the animal to reach food as quickly as possible. . . . Discrimination of probabilities tends to increase with the increase of the ratio of the probability of *emphasis* on the two sides of the probability discrimination problem (p. 185).

Being, along with Tolman, reluctant to take a reinforcement position, Brunswik interprets punishment, not as incremental reinforcement, but as providing "emphasis." However, despite this interpretation, there is nothing in Brunswik's *data* that goes against a two-factor reinforcement interpretation. It is true that incremental (negative) reinforcement has, to date, been very little employed in studies on probability learning, although, as Edwards notes, the economic theory of maximization (or "reinforcement") is clearly two-sided.[11] Economic man is assumed "to seek pleasure and avoid pain," in either an immediate or some future sense of those terms.

There are many other facets of the probability-learning problem that invite exploration, but enough has been said to show that there is no basic incompatability between the empirical facts in this domain and our assumptions concerning the two-fold nature of reinforcement and behavior change (or choice, cf. Chapter 6).

VII. Knowledge, Learning, and Reality

In this section we shall be dealing with certain matters which are sometimes regarded as essentially "philosophical" and thus, perhaps, beyond the scope of scientific endeavor; but, as we shall find, they are not without practical and, for our purposes, highly relevant implications. Our thesis, specifically, will be that "knowledge" is a sort

---

[11] At the writer's instigation, Mr. Mohammed Akhtar (1959b) has carried out a study with laboratory rats in which it has been found that expectations generated by prior studies of intermittent reinforcement or, as we may now equivalently say, intermittent *frustration* are also met when one introduces active *punishment* (electric shock) in place of or as a supplement to nonreward frustration. These findings confirm our supposition that nonreward is itself a *form* of punishment and that what happens in intermittent reinforcement is not that greater habit strength results but that the "sting" is taken out of nonreward frustration, as experienced during acquisition, so that it is less effective during extinction proper. This is presumably why Mr. Akhtar finds that active punishment (shock) is similarly less effective in inhibiting bar-pressing behavior during extinction if the punishment has frequently occurred and been followed by reward during acquisition (cf. Tsushima, 1959).

of *replica* of the real world and that it is through *learning* that this "isomorphism" is established.

David Hume, writing in 1777, has already been quoted as saying:

> It seems evident, that animals, as well as men, learn many things from experience, and infer, that the same events will always follow from the same causes. By this principle, they become acquainted with the more obvious properties of external objects, and gradually, from their birth, treasure up a knowledge of the nature of fire, water, earth, stones, heights, depths, etc., and of the effects which result from their operation (p. 110).

Here the key phrase is *treasure up a knowledge,* of external objects and events. This can only mean, surely, that Hume saw learning as a process whereby living organisms, in physically confronting (experiencing) the real world, reproduce within themselves a sort of conception or picture thereof which they thereafter in some sense "carry around" with them, i.e., "treasure up" as knowledge. The same view has been expressed, in varying ways, by many other writers but nowhere better than by Vinacke (1952) in his book, *The Psychology of Thinking,* in a chapter with the graphic title, "The Internalization of Experience." Here we read:

> Various titles have been suggested for the fact that the individual incorporates in his own system characteristics originally external to himself, such as symbolic representations of environmental objects, the norms of his culture, and the real or ideal traits of persons with whom he has close emotional ties. We shall call this progressive absorption process the "internalization of experience." It has its basis both in the specific, recognizable learning processes which are studied extensively in the psychological laboratory and in more gradual, subtle learning processes, which, as yet, are comparatively little understood. The effects of this latter kind of learning are becoming increasingly clear with intensive study of cultural differences, selective factors in perceptions and memory, and the evidence furnished by the clinic in the inner dynamics of personality (pp. 262–263).

Here one will think, immediately, of the process of imitation (Chapter 3) or "identification," as it is sometimes called, wherein "habits" or "traits" of others are taken over, "incorporated," quite literally and totally, by the subject. But one will think also of a more rudimentary type of phenomenon. Punishment and rewards are ordinarily conceived of as external events, things that happen *to* us. But, as we have repeatedly seen in this and the companion volume, through learning living organisms "incorporate" both punishments and rewards, in a very useful and predictable way. If a stimulus has preceded a punishment, that stimulus takes on the capacity to cause the organism to *punish itself,* i.e., to *be afraid;* and if a stimulus has preceded a reward, that stimulus takes on the capacity to cause the organism, likewise, to *reward itself,* i.e., to be *relieved, hopeful.* Hence, it is a simple matter to articulate Vinacke's thesis with even the most rudimentary forms of learning as we now understand them. But its applicability is perhaps most strikingly evident when we examine the phenomenon of *imagery,* which has forced itself upon our attention in this book. A physical *stimulus* gets inside us first as a *sensation;* but the latter is normally coterminus with the stimulus itself and, at best, provides the basis for what is called a *perception,* but it does not as such constitute *memory* or *knowledge.* As we have seen in Chapter 5, however, a sensation can be *conditioned* (in attenuated form) to other psychological events and may therefore be reactivated, as *an image,* in the absence of the original stimulus, thus providing the basis for what has traditionally been known as the "association of ideas." Here we see "internalization" in a particularly dramatic form which, as indicated in Chapters 6 and 7, has far-flung implications.

The import of these considerations for the present discussion is, specifically, this: that we must assume that probability has, first of all, a basis in the real world which, by means of learning can be gradually reproduced in the nervous system so as to give a sense of *conviction,* or set of expectations, which corresponds fairly precisely (one would hope) to prevailing external reality. Thus, of necessity, we assume an external reality (probability) and an internal (personalistic) one; and learning is the process whereby the latter comes to match the former. This is the essence, it seems, of knowledge, wisdom, realism (cf. Section IX; also Polanyi, 1958).

VIII. Causality and Human Behavior

In Section II of the preceding chapter Laplace and Poincaré have been represented as holding, with impeccable logic, that the universe is consistently and inexorably deterministic; and our whole analysis of the concept of "chance" was predicated upon this assumption. But this view now leads us to the familiar contradiction existing between such strict determinism and man's apparent or at least presumed *freedom.* Does our specialized knowledge of the principles of learning provide any sort of resolution of this paradox?

In 1952 there appeared in the *American Scientist* an article by Adolf Grunbaum entitled "Causality and the Science of Human Behavior" which admirably sets the problem just alluded to. Here the author says:

It is not uncommon to find that even those who have complete confidence in the continued success of the scientific method when applied to inanimate nature are highly skeptical of its applicability to the study of human behavior. . . .

Several important arguments have been offered against the hypothesis that cause-effect relationships exist in human behavior. . . . In this article I shall attempt to show that the arguments in question are invalid and that there are good reasons for accepting the causal hypothesis against which they are directed. . . .

If human behavior, both individual and social, does not exhibit cause-effect sequences, then the scientific method is essentially irrelevant to the elucidation of the nature of man, and both scientific psychology and the social sciences are permanently barred from achieving the status of sciences (p. 665).

Dilthey and his followers in the *Geisteswissenschaften* movement insist on the methodological autonomy of psychology and the social sciences, claiming that intelligent goal-seeking, which is so characteristic of man, calls for a method differing *toto genere* from that of the physical sciences. . . . Rules for managing individuals and nations can be based only on causal laws which tell us that *if* such and such is done, it is likely that the outcome will be thus and so, either in all cases or in an explicitly stated percentage of cases. It is useless to bemoan the great gap between our mastery of physical nature and our scientific understanding of man, if one denies the existence of the conditions which alone would make a scientific analysis of man possible. Only if human behavior does display some kind of causal law is it significant to emphasize the need for closing the dangerous gap between man's control over physical nature and his scientific knowledge of himself lest he destroy himself (pp. 665–666).

The author of this article concedes that "the assumption that causal laws are discoverable" for human behavior involves some rather staggering difficulties, but the nature of his ultimate faith in this connection is already apparent. However, in his attempt to implement this faith, he does not see the problem in the light which, from the standpoint of our present analysis, would seem to make it most manageable. As our inquiries in this and the preceding book have shown, about 60 years ago American psychology adopted a radically new program and philosophy which very nicely agreed with the premises of the physical sciences concerning cause and effect. The basic formula was: stimulus (cause) produces response (effect). All was strictly determined. The individual had no spontaneity, no freedom, no self-determination, no choice; he was strictly a machine which reacted only when in some way stimulated. But, as we have now seen, this approach encountered some very serious difficulties. Application of the if-this, then-that formula, as the basis for deriving scientific laws, was beset with the stubborn reality of *behavioral variability. This*, it was found (and as everyone knew already), produces *that* in some individuals, but *something else* in others; and the attempt to build up trustworthy inductions concerning simple stimuli-response correlations got nowhere. Almost at once it was evident that the analysis would have to be pitched at a higher level, namely, one that would take the source of this variability, namely *learning*, into systematic account; and this is why the theories of Pavlov and Thorndike came so immediately to the forefront in behavior theory. Here were different, but equally plausible, attempts to show that, for psychology at least, the *this* (independent variable) must not be conceived of simply as a stimulus but rather as the *conditions* under which *behavior* (the *that*, or dependent variable) changes. For Pavlov the secret of "reinforcement" (behavior change) was contiguity of stimuli (of a specified kind, in a specified sequence), whereas for Thorndike it was "effect," in the sense of reward or punishment; and much effort, in this book and the companion volume, has gone into the comparison, elaboration, and integration of these two positions as they have developed over the years.

First we had to discover the (surely obvious) fact that the behavior of most living organisms is by no means merely a matter of fixed reflexes. If behavior is initially made up of reflexes, the latter are modifiable either in the way suggested by Pavlov or in the way suggested by Thorndike or in both ways. But then, as investigation proceeded, it became apparent that reflexology simply would not do. The linkage between stimulation and response is much *looser*, we found, than the concept of the reflex allows. Hopes and fears were, to be sure, reflexes and subject to modification in precisely the way Pavlov had postulated; but these reactions are emotions, not behavior, and their "coupling" to behavior is by no means rigid and reflexive. Most, if not all, life situations involve some element of conflict; and by means of operations considered in earlier chapters, living organisms consider, compare, and integrate these competing inner forces into something called a *decision* (cf. Chapter 8, Section VI) which then and only then eventuates in action.

Moreover, as our analysis proceeded we found that in order to have anything like an adequate conception of the decision-making or problem-solving process, we had to take symbols and meanings into account; and here we encountered the necessity for introducing into our system the concept of imagery or memory, to provide the *cognitive* counterpart to the *affectivity* already posited. Thus there emerges a conceptual scheme in which "determinism" is not denied but *elabo-*

rated in such a manner as to grant to man and other higher organisms the measure of freedom and flexibility which they obviously possess. (The rigid and "stupid" determinism which early Behaviorism demanded is gone, and we now have a theoretical model which is at least beginning to approximate the realities as we intuitively know them. Yet our labors have not simply brought us back to common sense and Faculty Psychology. In positing that man (and, to a lesser extent, other organisms), on the basis of values (emotions) and memories of the past and images of the future, is capable of choice and more or less "rational" decision, we have not reverted to the doctrine of "free will" and *in*determinism. We have instead concluded that behavior is *very complexly* determined, first by the conditions that govern learning (the principles of reinforcement) and then by symbolic operations in which learning, so to say, supplies the raw data but not the final solution. Commonly we say that an individual learns to *do* this or that. This is inaccurate. The individual learns certain facts and certain emotions and then *decides* "what to do."

This is not to suppose for a moment that both learning and decision making do not obey laws which are just as much a part of the eternal scheme of things as are physical or chemical principles. But it *is* to insist that within this framework the individual has or may achieve "freedom" in a very real and meaningful sense of the term.

A few years ago, in response to an article by Wilbur G. Katz (1953) entitled "Freedom and Responsibility: A Difficulty of Relating Christianity and Law," the present writer published a paper entitled, "Freedom and Responsibility: A Psychological Analysis" (Mowrer, 1953). Here the foregoing argument was recapitulated and somewhat expanded as follows:

Up to this point our analysis has been strictly scientific and deterministic. But it has proceeded along lines which promise to lead us to a clearer conception of "freedom and responsibility" as it applies no less in religion and law than in psychology and psychiatry. In order to move forward in this regard, let us look first at what the word "freedom" does or does not imply. It does *not* imply caprice or lawlessness. Instead, in its most profound meaning, it implies the *capacity to change*, when circumstances change and old actions need to be replaced by new ones. Inanimate objects, like stones, are the least free, most bound, fixed. If you tap a rock with a hammer it may "change" in the sense of flaking or cracking but it will not change in the sense of becoming more or less resistant to our blows; much less will it change its "behavior" in the sense of "going away" or "fighting back" as opposed to "staying put" passively and thus subject continually to our assault. To make the point at issue without undue elaboration, we may note that living organisms do a good deal better than stones and other inanimate objects. Even the lowliest of creatures have at least a small repertoire of variable responses they can make to noxious stimulation; and the higher ones can carry over their experiences from one situation to another. In short, they can *learn*, and in so doing they achieve a still higher level of "freedom," non-fixity. And man, by the use of language, attains to a loftier position still in that he can learn *vicariously*, thus avoiding in many instances even a single direct encounter with the situation to which the learning is relevant.

It is thus sufficiently clear that man, in his "right mind," has the greatest freedom of all. He is least determined, least doomed to stupid repetitiveness, and most versatile, flexible, adaptive. But man is no less lawful in his behavior than are other living organisms—or, for that matter, nonliving things; it is just that in him we see *the laws of learning* most fully and ingeniously developed. Behavior thus remains lawful but it makes the individual "free" in the only sense in which this term is meaningful, or "freedom" itself worth while or desirable! (pp. 67–68).

Certainly an individual who is functioning well and is "happy" *feels* free and self-determining, regardless of what his philosophical presuppositions may be. And, by the same token, we know that when the reverse situation prevails the individual feels helpless, trapped, hopeless, driven, doomed. As one neurotic woman once said to the author, "I'm not sick; I'm just *unfree*." So our concern is not with the question: Is man, in some ultimate and enduring sense, free or under compulsion? The fact is, man may be *either*, depending upon circumstances. The real question, therefore, is: Why is man sometimes, in the experiential sense, free and sometimes not? The answer is to be found, it seems, only if one views man as a *social* creature, and this will be a part of our purpose in Chapter 10 (see also Mowrer, 1959a).

IX. Two Conceptions of "Probability"

It may at first appear that, while bearing upon the relationship between learning and causation, the preceding discussion in this chapter is not particularly relevant to statistics and probability theory. The relevance lies here. Science is concerned with the discovery of "truth," particularly in the realm of cause and effect (as opposed to the more descriptive concerns of certain other disciplines, such as history). Cause and effect is apprehended, we now believe, by the familiar process of learning through contiguity (or perceived correlation). But the data from which such relationships are inferred (learned) may, as we saw in Chapter 8, be either clear-cut and unambiguous or more or less obscured by the operation of unintended and (very commonly) unidentified factors in the situation other than the one under specific examination (as *the* cause or independent variable).

Now if causal relationships are obvious and undebatable, we have no need for "statistics"; direct perception or "experience" suffices. But where data are equivocal, efforts have been made to invoke certain mathematical models as aids to our inferential efforts. And here is where the trouble starts, both in theory and in practice. As indicated in Chapter 8, serious practical difficulties arise in connection with the use of such models; and besides, there is a general, theoretical issue which should now be considered. In briefest form it can be stated thus: Mathematical models are deductive; learning and scientific inquiry are, in general, inductive; therefore, the introduction of statistical methods (mathematical models), it is sometimes argued, is a *tour de force* and an impertinence.

For example, Jeffreys (1939) has put the matter this way:

> The mathematical proof [used in statistics] is deductive, and induction in the scientific sense is simply unintelligible to the pure mathematician—as such; [although] in his unofficial capacity he may be able to do it very well. Consequently little attention has been paid to the nature of induction, and apart from actual mathematical technique the relation between science and mathematics has done little to develop a connected account of the characteristic scientific mode of reasoning. . . . Running through the whole is the tendency to claim that scientific method can be reduced in some way to deductive logic, which is the most fundamental fallacy of all: it can be done only by rejecting its chief feature, induction (p. 2).

In Chapter 8 (Section V) we have already seen how permeated the whole history of probability theory and statistics has been with disagreement and controversy; and a good deal of the difficulty has undoubtedly arisen from the attempt to combine or "mix" the inductive methods of science (and ordinary observation) with the purely deductive rules of formal mathematics. Whitehead once tried to resolve this difficulty by observing: "There is a tradition of opposition between adherents of induction and of deduction. In my view it would be just as sensible for the two ends of a worm to quarrel" (quoted from Newman, 1956, p. 1341). And in Chapter 6 of this volume we have found a complementary and harmonious relationship between ordinary learning (as induction) and reasoning or insight (as deduction). Certainly both are real and useful. But as far as the theory and application of statistics are concerned, these two facets of the problem have only recently been clearly identified.

In an article on "The Meaning of Probability" which was published in 1935, Ernest Nagel made the following attack upon this problem. On the premise that it is not "the philosopher's task to legislate away any of the meanings which 'probability' may have," he did, however, attempt "to *distinguish* between different meanings" of this term (p. 12). What is for our purpose the heart of Nagel's analysis of this problem reads as follows:

With these methodological principles in mind, I turn now to an analysis of the meaning of probability. Lack of time, to say nothing of lack of competence, does not permit an adequate survey of the innumerable contexts in which propositions about probabilities occur. I wish, however, to distinguish five broad type of contexts in which they do occur, consider three analyses of the meaning of the term "probability," and indicate the bearings of the above methodological considerations upon each.

Statements involving probabilities are to be found in (1) every-day discourse, (2) in the field of applied statistics and measurements, (3) within the context of physical and biological theories, (4) in the comparison of theories with each other for their respective degrees of probability, and (5) in the branch of mathematics known as the calculus of probability. Examples of each type of statement will appear in due course, in the discussion of the three major interpretations of probability with which I wish to concern myself. To these I now turn.

The first interpretation is the classic one, associated with the historical development of the mathematical theory of probability. It has been expounded with vigor by the English logician and mathematician De Morgan. According to him, the word "probable" refers to the state of mind with respect to an assertion for which complete certainty or knowledge does not exist. Hence the degree of certainty of a proposition, its "probability," is the degree of belief with which it is held. For certainty has degrees and all grades of "knowledge," it is claimed, are capable of being quantitatively conceived. It is possible, therefore, to apply the calculus of probability to the degrees or strength of belief, if probability is defined algebraically as the ratio of the number of alternatives "favorable" to an "event" to the total number of equiprobable alternatives. The transition from this definition to the previous one is mediated by the principle of sufficient reason or indifference, according to which two propositions are equally probable if the strength of our belief is equally divided between them.

The second interpretation of probability is professed by certain English logicians like the economist Keynes. According to it, any two propositions are related not only by the relations usually studied in traditional logic, such as implication, but also by a directly intuitable relation called probability. This relation is not analyzable, although it is capable of having degrees. However, while any two propositions will each have some degree of probability with respect to a third, the degrees of probability are not in general comparable or measurable. Hence it is not always possible to apply the calculus of probability in order to explore the implications of compound assertions of probability relations. But whenever the calculus is applicable, the application is carried on in terms of a modified principle of indifference.

The third interpretation of probability is already implicit in Aristotle, but has become prominent only within the last century as a consequence of applying the probability calculus to a statistics and physics. Its central idea is that by the probability of a proposition or an "event" is meant the relative frequency of the "event" in an indefinite class of events. A more precise statement of this view will be given presently. It is sufficient at this point to emphasize the fact that on this interpretation every statement involving probabilities is a *material proposition* whose truth or falsity is to be discovered by examining objective relative frequencies (pp. 14-16).

Now before we discuss the Nagel analysis, it will be useful to place along side of it another attempt, more recently made by Savage (1954), to provide a similar "taxonomy" of the meanings of the term, probability. This writer says:

> It is unanimously agreed that statistics depend somehow on probability. But, as to what probability is and how it is connected with statistics, there has seldom been such complete disagreement and breakdown of communication since the Tower of Babel (p. 2).

> I would distinguish three main classes of views on the interpretation of probability, for purposes of this book, calling them objectivistic, personalistic, and necessary. . . .

> *Objectivistic* views hold that some repetitive events, such as tosses of a penny, prove to be in reasonably close agreement with the mathematical concept of independently repeated random events, all with the same probability. According to such views, evidence for the quality of agreement between the behavior of the repetitive event and the mathematical concept, and for the magnitude of the probability that applies (in case any does), is to be obtained by observation of some repetitions of the event, and from no other source whatsoever.

> *Personalistic* views hold that probability measures the confidence that a particular individual has in the truth of a particular proposition, for example, the proposition that it will rain tomorrow. These views postulate that the individual concerned is in some ways "reasonable," but they do not deny the possibility that two reasonable individuals faced with the same evidence may have different degrees of confidence in the truth of the same proposition.

> *Necessary* views hold that probability measures the extent to which one set of propositions, out of logical necessity and apart from human opinion, confirms the truth of another. They are generally regarded by their holders as extensions of logic, which tells when one set of propositions necessitates the truth of another.

> After what has been said about the intensity and complexity of the controversy over the probability concept, you must realize that the short taxonomy above is bound to infuriate any expert on the foundations of probability, but I trust it may do the less learned more good than harm (p. 3).

Upon reading either Nagel's or Savage's analysis alone, without the other, one might be somewhat uncertain as to precisely what is implied by the three definitions, or types, of probability which each of these writers lists. But if one puts these discussions together, they usefully complement each other and give us three relatively clear-cut and distinct conceptions. Let us begin by looking at what Savage calls the *objectivistic* view and Nagel's "third interpretation of probability," to which he gives no descriptive name but characterizes by saying that "on this interpretation every statement involving probabilities is a *material proposition* whose truth or falsity is to be discovered by examining objective relative frequencies" (p. 1404). It is evident that both writers are referring here to what might be called the *true* value of a probability, i.e., the value that would be obtained if our observations were exhaustive. If one had a trainload of black and white marbles, all mixed together, the *true* ratio of black marbles to all marbles (if we counted them) might turn out to be 29/104. So the true, or *objective*, "probability" of one's blindly selecting a black marble (assuming a homogeneous mixture) would be 29 in 104, or 29/104*ths*.

But let us assume that it isn't practical to make an exhaustive count of the marbles in this population (or "universe") as a means of determining how many black and how many white marbles there are but that we still want to get *some* idea of what the ratio is. Our procedure will be to take a *sample*, large or small, depending upon how accurate we wish our impression, or *estimate*, to be, and selectively count the marbles therein. Suppose that we decide to use a sample of 1,000 marbles and that 250 of them turn out to be black. The assumption or belief which will be most reasonable in this situation is that the ratio of black marbles to all marbles is 250/1,000 or $\frac{1}{4}$. This is the best guess or most informed "hypothesis" one can make on the basis of the available information. This is presumably what Nagel calls the *classical* view of probability and what Savage calls the *personalistic* one. In this connection Nagel speaks of a "state of mind," "certainty of a proposition," "degree of belief," "knowledge," whereas Savage speaks of "degree of confidence in the truth of a proposition."

Thus we may say that the *objectivistic* definition of probability is based upon an exhaustive examination of the pertinent data; but such an examination is often impossible (or at least impractical) and so leaves this value as an unknown, an abstraction, an "ideal." The *personalistic* definition, on the other hand, involves a *belief* concerning this abstraction which has been established on the basis of evidence, or experience, which is partial, fragmentary, nonexhaustive. In situations where an exhaustive examination of the facts has been made, the objective and the personalistic conceptions of probability coincide; but when the reverse is true, i.e., when the examination has *not* been exhaustive (when we have merely "sampled"), it is necessary to distinguish between the "true" and the "obtained" ratio, accepting the latter as the best available estimate of the former.

An *estimate* of a probability is obviously psychological, in the sense that it represents what some one or more persons have learned and thus believe about some state of affairs; hence the term "personalistic." In the ultimate analysis, the true ("objective") state of affairs is also psychological or "personalistic" in that it, too, involves knowledge which is inside someone's head. But, by its very nature, it is projected or perceived as being "out there" and so may appropriately be termed "objectivistic" (cf. Polanyi, 1958).

What, now, of the third conception of probability which our authors list? Savage identifies this as the *necessary* view, which holds that "one set of propositions, out of logical necessity and apart from human opinion, confirms the truth of another"; and Nagel, who particularly associates the name of John Maynard Keynes with this position, characterizes it by saying that "any two propositions are related not only by the relations usually studied in traditional logic, such as implication, but also by a directly intuitable relation called probability." In bold relief, we can term this the *logical* or *inferential* conception of the probable, or probability. Suppose that we know something about the origin or the intended use of the trainload of marbles. Then we can make either very exact deductions or more or less plausible guesses about the ratio of black marbles to all marbles. Such a conception of or way of arriving at a "probability" is obviously different from the two approaches first mentioned. *They* are both empirical, the one exhaustively so, the other involving an estimate or approximation; whereas the so-called "necessary" view is logical, inferential, deductive.

Although we have made no direct attack in this volume upon the topic of logic or inference, we have approached it a number of times tangentially and can now suggest that it depends crucially upon the phenomenon of mediation (see especially the discussion of "reasoning" in Chapter 6). Inference is obviously very important; but although one can see why Nagel and Savage refer to the inferential (or "necessary") approach to probability, it is not what most statisticians and researchers have in mind when they speak or think about probability. When a psychologist performs an experiment, he first reports his *findings*, quite objectively and accurately, and subjects them to whatever statistical treatment he thinks is appropriate; but he keeps all this separate from his conjectures and qualifications and interpretations which he may offer in that portion of his report which he very likely heads "Discussion." Here, under the heading of "Discussion," one lets himself go a bit, somewhat disregards the constraints of statistical conventions and plays out his "hunches," talks "horse sense." Here one is again discussing what is "probable," but probable in the sense of taking *other* considerations into account, not just the delimited experimental evidence (and its "statistical" interpretation). This is presumably what Savage and Nagel have in mind in suggesting their third definition or conception of "probability."

Clarifying as the reader may find the foregoing threefold definition of "probability," he will nevertheless sense—if he has followed the discussion here and in earlier parts of this chapter at all closely—an ambiguity, a looseness, a disjunction. Where, precisely, does it lie? It lies in the policy pursued here, and in most discussions of probability theory, of selecting as an illustration a situation which is *static* (something that *is*, like the ratio of black marbles to all marbles in a given population) as opposed to a more *dynamic* situation, wherein one is concerned with the question of what *causes* what, of something not merely being but *becoming*. And if we ponder this distinction a moment longer, we see that there is a fundamental inconsistency between the notion of causation and so-called probability. Causation implies *necessity* in the relationship between two events; whereas probability, by its very nature, denies necessity and substitutes the notion of uncertainty, chance, possibility.

It is true that our information or knowledge is very often incomplete or possibly unreliable and that we do well to qualify our statements, our "conclusions." But when we thus say that *this* "probably causes" *that*, it can be very misleading. It isn't that the causation (or lawful relationship) is "probable." Instead, it is our understanding of and control over the situation that is "probable" and problematic, i.e., permeated with ignorance and possible error. As we have seen earlier (Sections I–III of Chapter 8), the whole occasion for statistics arises from the confounding and multiplicity of "causes" operating in a situation; and, remarkably enough, statistics "work best" when these extraneous causes are *most numerous* (so as to insure a near-normal distribution in the values of the dependent variable). When we know precisely what we are doing and, as a result, have virtually perfect control of the situation, statistics simply are not necessary. And this is why B. F. Skinner, for example, has dedicated so much of his research effort to the refinement of controls and the standardization of experimental conditions, rather than trying to "justify" (as he might say) slip-shod experimentation with elaborate statistical manipulations.

When the writer began work on this chapter and the preceding one, his attitude toward statistics was considerably more positive and his respect greater than they now are. Either we have deluded ourselves into thinking better of statistics than we ought, or else the present analysis is in some way seriously defective. The writer would welcome informed arguments in the direction of either of these possibilities.

This is not to say, of course, that tests of significance and other commonly employed statistical devices are of no value whatever and should be discarded. Even though one accepts all the reservations which have been advanced in the preceding discussion, one still tends to be grateful to the author of a research report for "using statistics," in both their descriptive and inferential forms. P-values, no less than graphs, are an aid to communication; and we are not here necessarily suggesting their abandonment, at least not until "something better" is available. But what can be emphasized, with considerable conviction, is that what we now have, in the way of inferential statistics, is not very good. We should constantly remind ourselves that such techniques involve *mathematic models* which operate according to certain definitions and rules which apply only very approximately to most of the empirical situations to which we liken them. In ordinary computation, our mathematical models work exceedingly well, yea, perfectly; but it is a serious error, it seems, to assume that *all* mathematical models have this same degree of pertinency and efficiency.

Or, let us consider an alternative way of viewing the situation. Perhaps the fundamental difficulty lies, not in "statistics," but in the fact that we ask them to perform an essentially impossible task. As we have seen, despite some sophistry to the contrary, the basic objective in science is the ascertainment of causal relations; and perhaps there *is* no way to be sure of such relations in situations which are "noisy," i.e., situations in which there is a great deal of uncontrolled variance, or error. Perhaps Skinner is right and that the only thoroughly satisfactory solution to the problem is to have "clear channels," i.e., to exclude more effectively than we commonly do the operation of extraneous variables, so that the effect of the experimental variable can "come through" so clearly that we do not need "statistics." This is a perception which the author did not have a few months ago. He will be interested to learn how generally shared his misgivings are—or, if they are ill-founded, how they can be corrected.

10

Social Learning
and Human Personality

Typically, the experiments already reported in this book have involved an organism in either classical conditioning or in an attempt, on the part of the organism, to solve a "physical" problem of some sort. Here the opportunities for the experimenter to control the situation and to obtain clear-cut results are relatively good; and it is understandable that much of the research on learning has been of this general nature. It goes without saying, however, that *social* learning is also of very great importance—of *supreme* importance at the human level —and that our scientific as well as practical concern must be extended in this direction. Occasionally, in preceding chapters, we have alluded to situations involving the interaction of two or more subjects (see, for example, the discussion of imitation in Chapter 3); but this emphasis has been decidedly incidental. Now, at length, we turn to a more direct consideration of the problem.

We shall start with both laboratory and field observations on social learning in animals and then examine some of the special social demands and advantages which human beings experience. Here, against the background of the earlier systematic discussions, we shall also briefly consider human personality and psychopathology. But a word of caution: Many earlier attempts have been made to "apply" learning theory to education, delinquency, neurosis, psychotherapy, and the like, with only limited success. In this book we have seen how transient and continually evolving our conceptions of learning have been. While it is hoped that the psychology of learning is at last coming of age, past experience suggests caution and tentativeness in this connection. Our primary task is still that of adequate conceptualization.

I. Representative Experiments on Social Learning in Animals

A number of experiments on the "social conditioning" produced in hunger-motivated rats, under a variety of situations, have been carried out by students working with the present writer. Severe competition and fighting, it was found (Mowrer, Kornreich, & Yoffe, 1940), produce well defined and quite stable "dominance hierarchies." If three hungry litter-mate rats are put into a small transparent plastic cylinder and given a single pellet of food, they will, for a time, be equally energetic, confident, and aggressive in competing for it (Fig. 10–1a). However, as the experiment proceeds, the rats will experience unequal degrees of reward and punishment, with the result that one rat will emerge as clearly "dominant," one as thoroughly subordinated, and one somewhat intermediate in the "pecking order" (Fig. 10–1b).[1] So effective may be the punishment inflicted by one rat upon the other during the competitive struggles and fights that the defeated one may become afraid to eat food in the experimental situation even though alone and extremely hungry (Fig. 10–1c) (cf. Fredericson, 1951; Kohn, 1951; and Pavlov & Scott, 1956). The investigators cited—Mowrer, Kornreich, & Yoffe—originally planned to see to what extent this type of inhibition and incapacity would generalize to other problem-solving situations, but the contemplated experiments were never carried out. (For a somewhat similar study, with mice, see Scott & Marston, 1953; also Scott, 1958c, Grant & Chance, 1958, and Miller & Murphy, 1956a.)

On the other hand, rats which have been reared from birth in a situation where they have to eat from a single pellet find that they can eat more rapidly and more continually if they stop tugging on and trying to escape with the common piece of food (Mowrer, 1938b). Provided they are not too seriously deprived, rats under these conditions, learn to "share" (Fig. 10–1d) (cf. Fredericson, Fink, & Parker, 1955).

There is a temptation to speak, in connection with the last-described experiment, of "co-operation." But this would probably involve a too general, too loose use of the term. The word can more justifiably be applied to an experiment carried out by Crawford (1937, 1941) and admirably summarized by Nissen (1951):

---

[1] This term comes from Schjelderup-Ebbe's (1922) study of the dominance hierarchy that spontaneously emerges in domestic chicken hens.

In a laboratory experiment, Crawford first trained young chimpanzees individually to pull in a weighted box, by means of an attached rope, in order to obtain the food reward on the box. Then the weight of the box was increased (so that one animal could not move it). Next, two ropes were attached, the box was baited with two portions of reward, and two

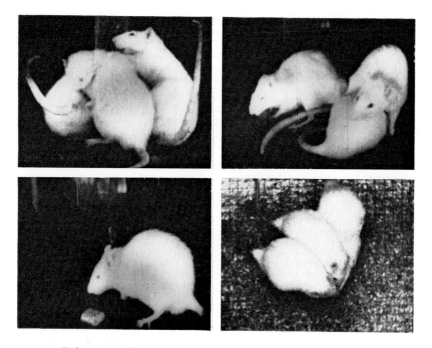

Fig. 10–1. Enlargements from a motion picture (Mowrer, Kornreich, & Joffe, 1940) showing various stages of competition and cooperation in rats. Fig. 1a (upper left) shows three hungry rats so busy fighting over food that the food itself lies unnoticed in the right foreground. In Fig. 1b (upper right) the same three rats are shown after their fighting (during the course of two or three half-hour sessions) has established one rat as dominant (at the left with food in mouth) and has intimidated the other two. Of the latter, the more subordinated, or "submissive," animal is shown in Fig. 1c (lower left). Note that the social punishment received for trying to eat in the competitive situation has been so severe, and effective, that although now entirely alone (and safe), this animal is still inhibited. Although quite hungry, this rat does not dare touch the pellet of food lying directly in front of him. In this group of rats the problem of competition and fighting over food has been "solved" (after a fashion) by the establishment of a dominance-submission hierarchy. A very different type of solution, involving sharing, is shown, with a different set of rats, in Fig. 1d (lower right). These rats, as a result of long experience (beginning at an early age), have found that by sharing each rat gets all the food it wants—and doesn't have to fight. The markedly different "social structure" in the two groups is manifestly a result of learning.

animals were put in the cage. At first each chimpanzee pulled without any reference to his partner's actions; only by chance did the two pull at the same time and so move the box. It was necessary for the experimenter to give a signal, which the partners had individually associated with initiating the pull, to get them to pull together. Once the temporal coordination of effort had been established in this way, the extraneous signal could be omitted. One of the partners, A, usually watched the other, B, and was ready to add her pull as soon as B started heaving the rope. Sometimes it was arranged that B was satiated when the experiment began; A would then urge and direct B to pull. Eventually B would pull, although she had no desire for the food reward. In these circumstances A often reaped the entire material benefits of the teamwork.

In a later experiment by Crawford one animal was trained to push against four colored plaques, arranged around the sides of a cage, in a certain order. The cage was then divided into two sections by a partition of bars; the colors to be pushed first and third were on one side, the colors to be pushed second and fourth were in the other part of the cage. The trained animal was then put on one side, and her partner, who knew the mechanics of pushing the plaques but not the correct order, was put on the other side of the partition. The trained animal X watched her partner's actions and pushed the color available to her after Y had pushed the color preceding it in the sequence; X sometimes solicited her partner, using begging gestures . . . that were spatially directed toward the particular color on her partner's side that was the next one in order (p. 540).[2]

Another type of social problem solving has been studied by the present author (Mowrer, 1939b) as part of the series of investigations already referred to. Individually, hungry rats were placed in a box 24 inches long, 18 inches wide, and 18 inches high. It was open at the top, and the floor consisted of hardware cloth. At one end of the box was a "Skinner bar," located at a convenient height for operation by a rat; and at the *other end* was a food trough into which a small pellet of food would roll each time the bar was pressed. This arrangement meant that in order to obtain food, the hungry rat had to shuttle between bar and food trough, pushing the bar, going for the food, returning to push the bar, etc. After this type of performance was well established in each of three rats, they were put into the apparatus simultaneously, thus creating an acute "social problem."

The difficulty was, of course, that whenever a given rat went to push the bar, one or perhaps both of the other rats, being nearer the food trough when the food-delivery mechanism was activated, would get to the trough first and appropriate the pellet. As a result, the bar-

---

[2] For an annotated bibliography on the literature on competition and cooperation up to 1937, see Allport, Murphy, & May.

pressing activity went unrewarded and tended to extinguish, while remaining near the trough and waiting for some *other* luckless fellow to push the bar was reinforced. Needless to say, the production of pellets during the first session of one hour during which the rats were together was very low (Fig. 10–2a and 10–2b).

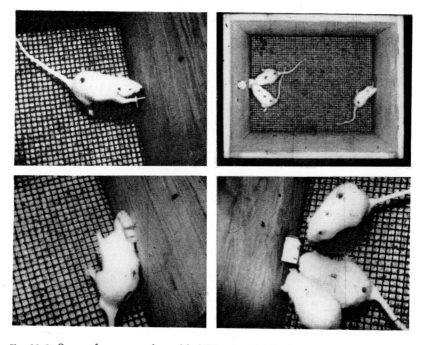

Fig. 10–2. Scenes from a movie entitled "An Artificially Produced Social Problem in Rats" (Mowrer, 1939b). By pushing a bar at one end of a box, a rat (Fig. 2a, upper left) can cause a pellet of food to be delivered in a little trough on the opposite side of the box. Now when three animals which have learned, individually, to "make a living" in this way are put together, the "social problem" shown in Fig. 2b (upper right) arises: the rat that does the "work" no longer gets the reward. Finally, after much confusion and frustration, one of the three animals (in this particular group it happened to be No. 3) gets so desperate (mad!) that it "attacks" the bar, biting and shaking it as shown in Fig. 2c (lower left). The result is that in this way one animal produces so many pellets that some are still uneaten by the other two rats when he gets back to the food trough. A "class society" thus emerges: a "worker" and two "parasites." These developments are shown graphically in Fig. 10–3.

However, between this first session together and the second one, at the same time next day, the rats were given no supplementary food.

In other words, a sink-or-swim policy was adopted with respect to their learning to "support" themselves in the experimental situation. Usually, on the third day, one of the rats in a group of this kind would solve the problem. Being now extremely hungry and also *frustrated*, one of the rats would have a tendency to seize the bar with its teeth, gnaw on it, rattle it, and thus cause it to move up and down a great many times in rapid succession (Fig. 10–2c). If the rat was then

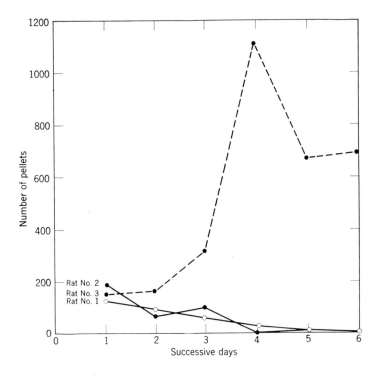

Fig. 10–3. "Production curves" for the three rats depicted in Fig. 10–2. On the first day, in this social-problem situation, all three rats, having previously been trained, alone, to obtain food in this apparatus, do a certain amount of bar pressing but far too little (during the one-hour test period) to sustain them, because the animal that presses the bar does not get the pellet thus produced. Again on the second day, production remains low. On the third day, with all three rats now extremely hungry, the solution begins to emerge. By the fourth day, rat No. 3, by the technique shown in Fig. 10–2, is "supporting" the entire group. Because they were so hungry, it took over 1,100 pellets to satisfy the group on this day; but thereafter only about 600 (200 per animal) were required. Note that as rat No. 3 became increasingly proficient as the worker, the other two rats progressively abandoned their productive efforts. Here, once more, we see the emergence of a social structure, or "system," as a result of social interaction and learning.

quick about it, he could get back to the food trough before the supply of pellets thus produced had been consumed by the two idlers (Fig. 10–2d). Finding food after such a performance tended, of course, to cause a rat to repeat it; and when the multiple pressing of the bar became habitual, the problem was solved. The typical pattern of pellet production for a group of three rats under the conditions just described is shown in Fig. 10–3. Of several sets of rats run in this experiment, in only one did a "worker" fail to emerge; here the experiment had to be discontinued in order to prevent all three animals from starving.

An experimental attack upon another type of social interaction in rats was reported by Davitz & Mason in 1955. By way of introduction they say:

> The purpose of this study was to investigate the effect of one animal's presence on the strength of a fear response exhibited by another animal. A study by Masserman (1943) suggested that a cat's fear of eating was reduced by observing a nonfearful cat eating; and a recent experiment by Liddell (1950a) demonstrated that presence of a mother goat increased the tolerance of kids to withstand environmental stress. Therefore, generalizing from the results of these previous studies, we predicted that presence of one rat would tend to reduce the strength of a fear response exhibited by another rat.
>
> The experimental population of the present study was divided into "Fearful" and "Nonfearful" Ss, and the experiment was designed to compare the strength of a fear response exhibited by Fearful Ss tested individually, Fearful Ss tested with another Fearful animal, and Fearful Ss tested with a Nonfearful animal (p. 149).

Davitz & Mason summarize their study thus:

> The purpose of this study was to investigate the effect of one rat's presence on the strength of a fear response exhibited by another rat. The Ss were 48 male albino rats. After 30 trials on which blinking light and electric shock were paired, the degree of fear associated with the blinking light and the apparatus was tested using an activity measure as the behavioral index of fear. Fearful Ss were tested individually; Fearful Ss were tested with another fearful rat; Fearful Ss were tested with a Nonfearful rat; Nonfearful Ss were tested with a fearful rat; Nonfearful Ss were tested with another Nonfearful rat; Nonfearful Ss were tested individually. The results [Fig. 10–4] indicate that the presence of a Nonfearful rat reduced the strength of a fear response exhibited by a Fearful S and that the presence of another Fearful rat influenced behavior in the same direction but to a degree just short of significance. These results were interpreted in terms of two opposing drive states: curiosity and fear (p. 151).

Liddell's finding that a kid is less likely to become panicky if the mother goat is present fits well with learning principles: If the mother has acquired secondary-reinforcing (fear-reducing) properties for the kid, a stimulus which would otherwise arouse strong fear would be expected to arouse significantly less fear with the mother present. And the same is true for Masserman's observations: If certain of the sounds and possibly sights associated with a cat's own eating have taken on secondary reinforcement (see Mowrer, 1960, Chapter 4), we would expect similar sounds and sights provided by the eating of another cat to have much the same influence; and if, as assumed, secondary reinforcement consists of fear reduction, the effect noted by Masserman would follow as a matter of course (cf. Stone's 1954 review of presence and absence of human "mothering").

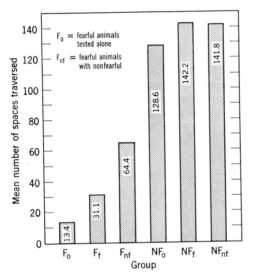

Fig. 10–4. Bar diagram showing the difference in exploratory behavior of fearful rats tested alone (F_o) and fearful rats tested with a nonfearful rat (F_{nf}). The purpose of the other groups represented in the diagram is explained in the text. Reproduced from Davitz and Mason (1955, p. 150).

What the explanation of the findings reported by Davitz and Mason is cannot be so readily determined. It may be that the mere sight and proximity of members of their own species is likewise reassuring and comforting to rats; but the authors point to other possibilities. They say:

Although there is limited experimental evidence on the social factors which might influence fear and activity of rats, it does not seem unreasonable to hypothesize that the differences in activity observed in the present study were a function of two opposing drive states. One of the drive states, curiosity, leads to active exploration of the test apparatus and the partner rat; the other, fear, leads to inactivity and freezing. In terms of our response measure, these two drives are incompatible, and factors which produce a change in either drive state would tend to influence the activity measure. For example, the introduction of another animal or of a distracting stimulus would increase the number of new stimulus elements to be explored; this might serve to implement the curiosity drive and lead to increased activity. On the other hand, the introduction of another animal might also serve to make the testing situation less similar to the training situation [in which only *one* rat was present at a time]; thus, the fear of Ss tested with another rat may have been less than the fear of Ss tested individually as a result of differential generalization (from training to testing situation) of the secondary drive stimuli and mediating cues which elicited fear. It is also possible that the curiosity and fear interact in such a way that introduction of another rat would increase the number of new stimuli in the test situation, distract the attention of the fearful S from the fear-producing and fear-mediating cues (i.e., blinking light and crouching), and thus lead to a reduction of the fear response (p. 151).

Although the inference that another member of the same species can provide secondary reinforcing cues and thus counteract the effect of fear cues is not unreasonable in the case of either the Masserman or Liddell experiment, or even the Davitz-Mason experiment, the alternative interpretations suggested by the latter still need to be kept in mind and perhaps used as the basis of subsequent inquiry (cf. Holder, 1958).

For many years it has been known that gentle, docile laboratory rats usually do better in an experiment than do wild, apprehensive ones. A paper published by John B. Watson in 1916 has already been cited (Mowrer, 1960, Chapter 10) in which the author says: "Two groups of animals (rats), closely similar in age, *docility*, body weight, etc., were chosen" (italics added, p. 77). And in recent years, many experimenters have made a regular practice of "gentling" animal subjects before starting any kind of laboratory work with them.

A number of related studies, carried out in the Psychology Laboratory at McGill University, show that "intelligence" in an animal is a function of the variety of his social and environmental experience generally. Summarizing this work, Hebb & Thompson (1954) say:

Experimental studies have shown clearly that when the postnatal environment is held constant the level of learning capacity and problem solving in the rat is innately determined (Heron, 1935; Tryon, 1940; Thompson and Bindra, 1952); that is, one can breed rats that will be brighter, or duller, when brought up in the same environment. But they show equally clearly that when heredity is held constant between experimental groups, by the split-litter method, infant experience determines the level of adult problem solving (Hymovitch, 1952; Bingham and Griffiths, 1952; Forgays and Forgays, 1952). The rat brought up in a "free environment," or even with almost no freedom of bodily movement but with wide and extensive perceptual experience, is the better problem solver at maturity. For the rat, then, adult intelligence depends both on heredity and on the stimulating action of the postnatal environment (p. 533).

Various other experiments, similar to those cited in the foregoing pages, could be described here; but the ones mentioned are representative and will serve to indicate both the limitations and value of experimental work on social learning in animals. The results are often interesting, but their scientific worth is sometimes questioned. Many words have been spent in debating the *human* relevance or "transferability" of such findings; and one of the most trenchant, yet conservative, appraisals of the problem is that made by Hebb & Thompson, in these words:

> Thus the first point we make in citing this work is that animal experiment may clarify a human problem without "proving" anything. It may draw attention to facets of human behavior one has not noticed; it may point to a troublemaking but implicit assumption; it may suggest a new principle of human behavior. Furthermore, animal experiment in the past has repeatedly shown that the treatment of some human problem or other has been oversimplified. But in all these cases, the relevance of the animal work is strictly dependent on whether, when applied to man, it does clarify the human problem (p. 533).

Granted that experiments involving two or more animal subjects are likely to be both intuitively interesting and also suggestive, the fact remains that the results thus far obtained do not "add up" very impressively, i.e., have not given rise to any generally accepted *theoretical system*. This fact has been cogently pointed out and a suggestion made for further progress in a paper by Sears (1951). Here we read:

> In the main, . . . in spite of their long prepossession with social influences on the individual, psychologists think monadically. That is, they choose the behavior of one person [or animal] as their scientific subject matter. For them, the universe is composed of individuals. These individuals are acted upon by external events, to be sure, and in turn the external world is modified by the individuals' behaviors. But the universal laws sought by the psychologist almost always related to a single body. They are monadic laws, and they are stated with reference to a monadic unit of behavior (pp. 478–479).
> But if personality and social behavior are to be included in a single theory, the basic monadic unit of behavior must be expandable into a diadic one. A diadic unit is one that describes the combined actions of two or more persons. (Although the prefix means "two," the term is used here simply as the minimal instance of multiplicity. Similar principles would hold whether the interactions were two or more.) A diadic unit is essential if there is to be any conceptualization of the *relationships* between people, as in the parent-child, teacher-pupil, husband-wife, or leader-follower instances. To have a science of interactive events, one must have variables and units of action that refer to such events. While it is possible to systematize some observations about individuals by using monadic units, the fact is that a

large proportion of the properties of a person that compose his personality are originally formed in diadic situations and are measurable only by reference to diadic situations or symbolic representations of them. Thus, even a monadic description of a person's action makes use of diadic variables in the form of social stimuli (p. 479).[3]

There could hardly be a clearer, more concise statement of the existing status of behavioral science or a more persuasive call for the extension of systematic theory and experimentation from the isolated subject to the subject-in-relationship. However, as of this writing, there is nothing to be reported in the way of achievement along these lines at all comparable to what has been and is still being accomplished by way of developing "monadic" behavior theory. Rotter's recent (1954) book, *Social Learning and Clinical Psychology*, lists a set of "basic postulates for a social learning theory of personality," but the continuity between these postulates and the principles which have emerged from animal research is, perhaps of necessity, tenuous. Says Rotter:

We refer to this point of view as a *social learning theory of personality*. This approach as now developed makes only limited use of many specific "laws" of learning developed on subhuman species. It seeks to use only psychological constructs in prediction without recourse to physiological concepts. It is a social learning theory because it stresses the fact that the major or basic modes of behaving are learned in social situations and are inextricably fused with needs requiring for their satisfaction the mediation of other persons (p. 84).

It appears that a good deal more research and theory construction will be needed before the kind of material presented in the present volume can rigorously articulate with the level of analysis represented by Rotter's work (cf. Hare, Borgatta, & Bales, 1955; Scott, 1950, 1956; Sidowski, Wyckoff, & Tabory, 1956; Sidowski, 1957; Vinacke, 1954).

II. Unlearned Social Behavior in Animals

As the preceding section indicates—and as we abundantly know from common observation, animal behavior is manifestly modifiable under the impact of experience with other organisms. Also we know that social situations arise naturally in lower animals or can be experimentally created which afford suggestive parallels to humanly relevant problems of a social, economic, and political nature. And, as we shall later see in this chapter, the end is not yet as far as fruitful research

[3] For a good summary of social behavior and social organization in animals, see Chapter 8 of Scott's (1958) book, *Animal Behavior*. Here one finds one type of attempt to systematize social behavior.

along these lines is concerned. However, it is well at this point to remind ourselves of a major, and quite remarkable, limitation. Social behavior in some infrahuman organisms, in its most intricate and exquisite forms, *is not learned* but is dependent upon mechanisms which have been variously named but which all involve a large factor of innateness.

This fact constitutes both a severe limitation and a marvelous advantage: it gives to some animal societies and to individual existence therein a static quality, a fixity, a rigidity, a predetermination which we human beings disdain and abhor; but it also constitutes a sort of guarantee of social and biological adequacy, born of thousands, even millions of years of evolutionary trial-and-error, which we human beings have lost. *We* depend almost exclusively upon *culture*, which is a learned phenomenon, both historically and individually speaking; and while culture, as a way of life and guide to action, has certain advantages over nativistic, built-in problem solutions, the situation is such that we can, on occasion, fall flat on our collective face. We pride ourselves on our flexibility and freedom, but the attendant responsibility and risk are also great.

In a work such as the present one, it is not our task to explore those innate mechanisms which insure social competence in certain of the lower organisms. In fact, by their very nature these mechanisms are antithetical to the phenomenon we know as learning. But we must recognize their reality and, more than this, have some appreciation of what a momentous thing it was when our progenitors made the transition from this sort of animal world into our distinctively human one. This is not to say that this transition was necessarily sudden or in any sense absolute; but it was nonetheless tremendous and deserves our deep interest and respect.

There was a period, some decades back, when the concept of instinct was so over-worked, especially by unjustified extension into human affairs, that it came into general disrepute. However, there is a current revival of interest therein on a much more modest, and therefore sounder, scale. Among modern students of the problem, none is more articulate and astute than Professor N. Tinbergen, of Oxford University; and we shall rely heavily upon Chapter V of his 1953 book, *Social Behavior in Animals,* for the summary knowledge of this field with which we shall here have to be content. By way of reviewing earlier chapters, Tinbergen says:

> In the preceding chapters I have tried to show that social co-operation serves a great variety of ends. Mating behaviour is not merely the act of coition, but is preceded by long preliminaries. These preliminaries, or court-

ship, have very distinct functions. It is necessary that the two partners are brought together. Their activities must be synchronized. The reluctance against bodily contact must be overcome. Inter-specific matings must be prevented. The female must appease the male's aggressiveness. We have seen that all these functions are served by a signalling system, by which one individual can influence the other's behavior. In family life, the behaviour of the parents has to be co-ordinated so that they take turns in guarding the eggs or young. When the young are to be fed, or when they must be warned against a predator, close co-operation, often involving mutual signalling, is necessary. Several of the relationships of family life extend beyond that into group life, and here again we found that co-operation was based on signalling. Finally, I argued that fighting, and especially reproductive fighting, although in some respects a disadvantage to the individual, is of great use to the species, because it effects spacing out and thus tends to prevent harmful over-crowding. Since actual fighting inflicts damage as well as effecting spacing-out, a signalling system such as exists in most species, where damage is reduced to a minimum while the intimidating effect is retained, is to the species' advantage. Threat display reduces fighting in two ways: if shown by an owner (of a territory, a female, a hole, etc.) it intimidates rivals. If shown by a trespasser, it marks the latter out for attack, and thus enables an owner to leave harmless intruders alone. Again, these functions depend on signals.

The signalling system has been studied in a number of cases. Although much more work has still to be done, some general conclusions are already possible.

We have seen that the parent Herring Gull feeds the chicks by regurgitating some food, and presenting part of it to the young, keeping it between the tips of the bill. The young gull is first roused by the "mew call" of the parent, then it pecks at the bill tip, clearly guided by visual stimuli, until it gets the food in its bill, when it swallows it. The various signals, auditory and visual, are given by the parent and reacted to by the chick. In discussing such signalling systems, I will call the individual presenting the stimuli the actor, and the individual responding to the stimuli the reactor (pp. 72–73).

The observations just cited are of great importance and fit well with earlier discussions in this volume. For example, one is immediately reminded of the passages quoted in Chapter 4 from G. H. Mead concerning the difference between *signals* and *symbols;* and it is noteworthy that Tinbergen speaks of the former, in connection with his animal studies, but does not allude to the latter concept at all. In Chapter 2 and 4 we have seen that lower animals are capable of making and responding to simple mediating responses ("pure-stimulus acts") and of thus showing foresight and even insight (see Chapter 6) of a limited kind; but it is also clear that there is, in the general social interaction of living organisms in a state of nature, a system of communication which is surprisingly direct in its action and which involves, it would seem, virtually no mediation. In order for language and the higher mental processes as we know them in human beings to emerge, it is as if the very basis on which animal "language" has developed had to be abandoned and a "new start" made, along radically different lines. As noted in Chapter 2, there is a limited sense in which even an emotion is a mediator; but in Chapters 4 and 5 we discovered that in order to have human language, representational mediators, in the form of *images*, must also be freely available. Is *this* the development which made human mentality uniquely possible? There is some evidence of imagery in lower animals, so the difference here is apparently one of degree rather than kind; and we are left with no sure understanding of precisely what it is that preserves that subtle, yet impenetrable, barrier between the human and the nonhuman.

Tinbergen continues his analysis as follows:

Turning now to the reactor's behavior, we find again that it is innate. The Herring Gull chick aims its pecking response at the parent's bill tip from the first, without having to learn it. The male Stickleback raised in isolation reacts to other males by fighting, to females by courting. It could not have learnt this. In other words, it is not only the capacity to perform these motor patterns that is innate, but their sensitivity to special releasing and directing stimuli as well (p. 78).

In many of the other animals that have been studied we find that the reactor, just like the gull chick, responds to a few selected stimuli provided by the actor. As we have seen, the fighting of the Robin is released by the red breast more than by any other bodily character. The male Stickleback's fighting is released by the red underside more than by anything else. The male "moustache" of the Flicker overrides the influence of any other character, and so on. It seems as if such colors, shapes, calls, movements, have but one function: the release of fitting responses in the reactor. This idea was first clearly put forward by Lorenz (1935) [see also 1937], who pointed out that social responses are often released by such features, which seemed to be specially adapted to this function. Such organs he called releasers. Lorenz described this concept of releaser in the following words: "The means evolved for the sending out of key stimuli may lie in a bodily character, as in special colour design or structure, or in an instinctive action, such as posturing, "dancing" and the like. In most cases they are to be found in both, that is, in some instinctive acts which display colour schemes or structures that were evolved exclusively for this end. All such devices for the issuing or releasing stimuli, I have termed releasers (*Auslöser*), regardless of whether the releasing factor be optical or acoustical, whether an act, a structure, or a colour."

The evidence which is now accumulating through the work of a number of workers in this field seems to confirm Lorenz's hypothesis in the main. In a very few cases is the evidence complete enough, and much more work remains to be done, but on the whole the principle of releasers seems to be a very useful one for understanding the mechanisms of social co-operation (pp. 80–81).

After a detailed review of releasers which involve sounds, chemical signals, and touch and visual stimuli, Tinbergen concludes his analysis thus:

> So far as our present knowledge goes, social co-operation seems to depend mainly on a system of releasers. The tendency of the actor to give these signals is innate, and the reactor's responses are likewise innate. Releasers seem always to be conspicuous, and relatively simple. This is significant, because we know from other work that the stimuli releasing innate behaviour are always simple "sign stimuli." It seems therefore as if the structures and behaviour elements acting as releasers are adapted to the task of providing sign stimuli. When releasers serve, in addition, the function of reproductive isolation, they are specific as well, that is, different from releasers in other species. This specificity cannot always be attained by one single releaser, but a sequence of releasers, each in itself not very specific, can in its entirety be highly specific.
>
> Not all communication, however, is based on releasers; there are certain complications. As we have seen, many social animals respond to the species' social releasers only when provided by certain individuals, which they know personally. In such cases personal connexions, established through learning processes, confine the reactor's responses to signals from one or a few individuals only; they still respond to the releasers of the species, but only after they have narrowed their attention to particular members of the species.
>
> The reactor's responses are sometimes immediate and simple movements. Often, however, they are internal responses; the signal in such cases changes the reactor's attitude and prepares it for a more complicated and variable activity.
>
> We see therefore that a community functions as a result of properties of its members. Each member has the tendency to perform the signal movements releasing the "correct" responses in the reactor; each member has specific capacities that render it sensitive to the species' signals. In this sense the community is determined by the individuals. (pp. 85–86).

Tinbergen extends his analysis to include the signalling that occurs not only within a given species but also between different species and elaborates this general approach in other illuminating ways. However, for our purposes these are not directly relevant and cannot be pursued in this context. But it would be a mistake in a chapter of this kind not to make at least passing acknowledgment to the very substantial work which has been done in this area and to the realities with which this work has very properly been concerned.

III. Imprinting and "Critical Periods"

From time to time in this and the antecedent volume, reference has been made to the phenomenon of *instinct,* as a type or pattern of be-

havior whose occurrence is evidently dependent upon the mere maturation or growth of the nervous system, quite apart from experience or
learning; and it has been conjectured that such behavior is most likely
to be present either (a) where the environment is extremely constant or
(b) where biological issues are at stake which are so vital that they
cannot be left to the vicissitudes of individual learning. Within the past
century, a somewhat intermediate phenomenon has been discovered
which is of special relevance to the social life of living organisms. This
is the phenomenon of *imprinting* (Beach & Jaynes, 1954).

In a now classic paper, published in 1937, Konrad Lorenz dates his
career as a naturalist from one Easter when, as a small boy, he was given
a baby duck. Somewhat to his surprise, but delight, he found that the
duckling was soon following him faithfully wherever he went; and
child though he was, he realized that he had become a *bone fide* "mother
substitute" for the little creature. So fascinated was the boy by this
behavior that although he was later educated as a physician, his major
interest and vocation throughout life have remained that of naturalist
and sagacious student of bird behavior (cf. Section II).

As a result of extensive observations, both in the field and under
semi-experimental conditions, Lorenz has developed the concept of
"imprinting," a notion lying somewhere between instinct and learning
(cf. Spaulding, 1873). Many young birds, it seems, have a tendency,
as soon as hatched, to *follow the first moving object they see*. Normally
this is the mother bird; but if the circumstances are *ab*normal, this
object may be a human being, a foster mother of a different species, or
even an inanimate object. Here there can be no question of the behavior
being dependent upon secondary reinforcement—for there has, as yet,
been no *primary* reinforcement. But a learning of sorts is clearly involved, for the initial and somewhat fortuitous attachment to the
"mother" becomes stable and differential. After a short time, the young
bird will respond in this way to *no other* bird or object, and remains
fixated upon the one it has thus "imprinted." However, if separation
from the original mother occurs, a second "imprinting," or "adoption,"
can take place, as the story of Lorenz' Easter duckling indicates. Here
it seems that well known learning principles are involved.[4]

In order to sharpen the concept of imprinting and to avoid the
possible errors of casual or field observations, Jaynes (1956) has made a
careful laboratory study thereof, which he summarizes thus:

[4] For a more detailed discussion of this point, with special reference to the problems involved in getting Seeing-Eye dogs properly attached to their masters, see
Chevigny (1946), also Mowrer (1950, Chapter 24).

Imprinting phenomena were studied in 18 domestic neonate chicks. An apparatus [Fig. 10–5] was used in which the young birds, with no observable reward, developed following and approach responses toward a cardboard object which moved irregularly about a 10-ft. alley. Four experiments were performed to investigate the development of these responses on the first four days after hatching and their generalization. The conclusions reached are as follows:

1. The reaction of neonate chicks to a moving object is not merely a following response, but it is a matrix of responses including attention, vocalization, approaching, and following, usually in this order.

2. The reaction appears suddenly within the first few minutes of exposure, and develops progressively in the first half-hour. Gradual improvement occurs over the first four days, probably due to general maturation.

3. There are innate preferences in neonates of this species, for some objects prove better cues for imprinting purposes than others of approximately the same size.

4. Birds show a decrement in responding upon introduction of a strange object in place of the object with which they were trained.

5. The amount of generalization decrement is somehow dependent upon the characteristics of the stimulus used in training.

6. After four days of training, chicks approach the objects to which they have been trained in preference to other objects in a choice situation, the time taken to do so depending upon how well they have followed the object previously (p. 206).

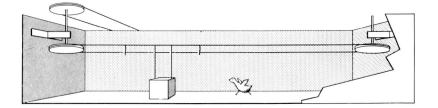

Fig. 10–5. "Apparatus for the study of filial imprinting in birds. An object (a cardboard cube in the figure) is suspended on a pulley system, so that it moves irregularly about a 10-ft. alley. Lengthwise dimensions in this diagram are shortened for purposes of illustration" (Jaynes, 1956, p. 202).

By way of further interpreting his findings, Jaynes says:

The experiments prove that without any observable reward young birds of this species follow a moving stimulus object and very rapidly come to prefer that object to others. The first appearance of this response occurred shortly after exposure to the object and was invariably preceded by distinct changes in vocalization in reaction to it. Thereafter, locomotor responses to the moving object increased in frequency and vigor. Both practice and physiological maturation appeared to be responsible for improvement over the first few days of life. Previous reports that imprinting is suddenly acquired are thus substantiated in part, but that practice plays an important role is indicated by the graphs [shown in Fig. 10–6].

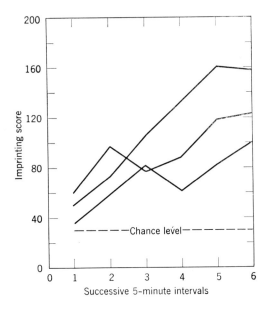

Fig. 10–6. "Three typical curves for the development of imprinting on the first day of life during a ½-hr. session. Scores are the number of seconds spent within a foot of the moving object during a 5-minute interval" (Jaynes, 1956, p. 203).

Imprinting has been called "irreversible," and thereby distinguished from other arrangements for learning. This could mean two things: (a) that it is never forgotten, and (b) that once an object induces the following reaction, other objects cannot do so. The latter is clearly untrue, at least in the neonate period of the species studied, since considerable generalization occurred to quite dissimilar objects (p. 205). [See also Jaynes, 1958a, 1958b.]

Although it is not easy to identify any element of reward in the experimental situations described by Jaynes (see also Moltz & Rosenblum, 1958), there are many other recorded cases (not usually thought of as "imprinting" but manifestly similar) where conventional learning principles may very well apply. One such example has been extensively studied by Scott (1945). This investigator was concerned with the genesis of "leadership" as it is manifested in sheep and other species where the herd or flock characteristically follows a leader. Contrary to what might seem a reasonable expectation, it is not the strongest and most aggressive male that typically plays the role; it is rather, for sheep, the ewe with the largest number of descendants in the group. She, ordinarily, is one of the oldest members of the flock and is perhaps quite feeble in the bargain; but she nevertheless has an emotional value for the other sheep which make them want to follow and be with her.

In the light of what we think we know about the principles of learning, what can we say about this observation? Clearly, as a result of nursing her lambs, a ewe takes on secondary reinforcement, i.e., becomes positively "cathected," for them; but we might expect this situation, of affection and attachment, to be of limited duration. Nutritionally, lambs must eventually be weaned; and we would expect the mother, at this point, to lose her attraction for them. In some species, this appears to be precisely what occurs: the young and the mother may separate or, even though remaining in the same vicinity or even in the same social group, they may later have no special interest in each other. Can it be that the mother sheep, though no longer providing milk, usefully serves as a guide to "greener pastures," water, shelter, and the like? If so, this might keep up the attachment to and dependence upon her for a while; but, ultimately, one would suppose that the lamb would "know it all" and strike out independently.

Or, might it not be that at this point the lamb stays on with the flock for protection? While perhaps a secondary consideration, this is certainly not the primary one, for much the same tendency toward "flocking" will be seen in a protected pasture as on an open, and more problematic, range. That the original nursing situation is somehow crucial is indicated by the observation, also reported by Scott, that bottle-fed and "pet" lambs never become properly integrated with the flock. They will be seen grazing alone, perhaps quite far from their fellows, and seem much more positively oriented toward human beings than toward their own species. At least as far as other sheep are concerned, they are "social isolates." Like birds that are taken from the company of their own kind and induced to "identify" with human beings, at least to the extent of "talking," pet lambs, insofar as they can, seem to act more like people than like sheep. They have been "weaned" from their own kind in a triple sense—nutritionally, emotionally, behaviorally—and "cathected" instead to members of a different species.[5]

Both in imprinting and in instances of cathexis established through obvious rewards there is, however, a tendency for the "impressionable"

[5] See McCulloch & Haslerud's (1939) study, "Affective Responses of an Infant Chimpanzee Reared in Isolation from its Kind." Cf. also Chapter 3.

period to be limited to the early period of life. From this observation has developed a concept of "critical periods," of which Scott (1958b) has recently written:

What is the critical-period hypothesis? In the first place it is in certain respects no longer a hypothesis but a well-established generalization which can be stated as follows: All highly social animals which have been so far studied show early in life a limited period in which the group of animals with which the individual will form positive social relationships is determined. To take a few of many examples, the slave-making ants grow up, they become attached to their captors [much in the manner of children "stolen" by the Comanche Indians] and take care of their young, and no longer recognize their own species. The experiments of Lorenz with newly hatched greyleg geese which quickly form a social bond with the first moving object they see, whether goose or human, have dramatized the findings of Heinroth and others that contact with the young birds in the proper stage of development establishes a strong social relationship regardless of the species concerned. Lambs that are taken at birth and raised on the bottle form social relations with people rather than with sheep and become as a result quite unsheeplike in many respects. The dog is particularly interesting because the process of socialization with human beings is a normal part of its life as a domestic animal. Dogs are more closely attached to people than are many animals, and develop a relationship which is in many ways similar to the human parent-child relationship. Furthermore, the critical period for socialization in the dog does not begin at birth but approximately three weeks later.

The existence of critical periods for the process of primary socialization can therefore be taken as established. Other parts of the critical period hypothesis, namely, that there exist certain periods of sensitivity to psychological damage, still remain as hypotheses and need a great deal more experimental evidence before they are accepted (p. 42) [see Section III].

Although some species (e.g., the African Grey Parrot) can still be tamed and trained at the adult level, taming is certainly vastly easier—and, in some species, possible only—in the young. From the standpoint of familiar learning principles, conjectures have sometimes been made as to why this should be the case (Mowrer, 1950, Chapter 24); but the fact is, the phenomenon is not well understood and may well involve a pre-arranged mechanism ("imprinting") of some sort. Whatever the explanation, this matter of social attachment or fixation is of great importance for group formation and the emergence of sociality in general, as we shall shortly see.

IV. Domestication, Socialization, and Group Life

How did group life evolve? What are its advantages, and disadvantages, in comparison with a solitary existence? What are the mechanisms whereby members of a given (or different) species are inducted into the life of the group? These are questions to which we have at least tentative answers and which are manifestly related to the psychology of learning.

Group life seems to have originated from one or both of the following biological circumstances: parent-offspring and sibling relationships. It has already been noted that group formation (flocking) in sheep follows a matriarchial (ewe-lamb) pattern; and King (1956a), observing the domestic guinea pig under "semi-natural conditions," found that the social group is essentially an extended (polygamous) family, consisting of a male, several females, and offspring. But Scott (1958b) reports a different picture for wolves and the domestic dog:

> In dogs there is a close association between mother and puppies during the first 3 weeks of life, but since the permanent social relations of the puppy are formed after this period and at a time when the mother leaves the litter for long periods, the result is that the strongest relationships are formed with the litter mates. This relationship is in turn the basis of pack organization of adult dogs and wolves (p. 43).

And elsewhere Scott (1954) says:

> The social group of the wolf is the pack, which seems to be based on a litter of animals which grow up together. Occasionally the pack may be founded by a single pair and a litter which stays on as adults, but the young litter ordinarily move out of the territory to form new packs. As described by Murie (1944), the home life of wolves is highly peaceful and cooperative. A certain amount of dominance is exhibited while feeding, but the members of the pack get along well together even when more than one male is present. Strange wolves, however, are violently repulsed and driven off (pp. 742–743).

Here, then, we see the beginnings of what anthropologists call the _in-group_ and its counterpart, the out-group and the _stranger_. King (1954) begins a paper on "Closed Social Groups among Domestic Dogs" thus:

> Many social animals form groups which are closed to other individuals of the same species. Strangers attempting to enter a bee hive (Butler and Free, 1952), an ant colony (Wheeler, 1923), a school of swordtail fish (Noble and Borne, 1940), a chicken flock (Collias, 1944), a group of howling monkeys (Carpenter, 1934), or a wolf pack (Murie, 1944) are driven off, severely beaten, or killed. The repulsion of the stranger may be undertaken by a specialized member of the group or by the united efforts of the entire group. In some species, such as ants, the individuals specialized for excluding strangers may be even morphologically distinct from other members of the group. In other species, such as prairie dogs (King, 1951), all of the group members may cooperate to expel a stranger from the group.

These extremes in morphological and social specialization suggest that the preservation of group integrity is a fundamental adaptive mechanism. The study of closed social groups has been limited principally to life history descriptions of a particular species or to the phenomenon of territoriality [see Howard, 1920], which stresses the defense of an area rather than the preservation of group composition. The former studies have shown that closed societies exist at many phylogenetic levels throughout the animal kingdom (p. 327).

Although the ascendancy-submission hierarchy, or "pecking order," of a social group may at first seem to be inspired completely by competition and hostility, yet there is some evidence that such a hierarchy represents the beginning of social order. As Scott (1958b) has observed, "A dominance order may be thought of as an adaptation for reducing destructive fighting in a group" (p. 159). And the sociologists, Sumner, Keller, & Davie (1928), maintain that even in human society cooperation always has a substratum of "antagonism." On the basis of this type of thinking, King then concludes:

Since [in the dogs observed] the group members formed a social hierarchy by aggressive behavior, they were conditioned to react aggressively toward individuals like themselves. By this process of conditioning of the group members to each other, any socially structured group may be closed to strangers (p. 336).

In other words, the hypothesis is that because of *suppressed* hostility toward each other, the members of a social group immediately feel, by generalization, hostility toward strangers of the same species and variety toward whom there is no restraining affection or mutual fear. The difficulty with this argument is, of course, that it does not explain why the latter emotions do not also generalize. The little-understood mechanism of *jealousy*, if carefully investigated, might bring us closer to the facts of the situation.

Perhaps our best insights concerning the mechanisms whereby the young of a given species normally *socialized*, i.e., prepared for group life among their own kind, come from observations concerning the process commonly known as *domestication*, i.e., the adjustment of an individual or individuals of one species for life in the social group of another species. As we have seen (Chapter 3), certain kinds of birds can be so completely weaned from their own species that they adopt the noises (words, laughter, singing, etc.) of human beings and may even lose sexual interest in their own kind (Mowrer, 1950, Chapter 24). The alienation of "pet" lambs has also been cited in the present chapter. And Scott (1954) has an excellent paper on "The Effects of Selection and Domestication upon the Behavior of the Dog." According to Scott and other authorities the dog sprang (some 8000 years ago) from a domesticated variety of wolf (cf. Lorenz, 1955), under the following reconstructed circumstances:

A primitive hunting tribe in Europe or Asia may very easily have fallen into a commensal relationship with wolves with the latter frequenting the village refuse heap and the human inhabitants finding it profitable to rob the wolf dens at times when food was scarce. At some point, a young wolf puppy was caught and adopted by the people and nursed and fed by them. This animal would consider the human group as its society and would be peaceful and tolerant toward them, and as it grew older would have a tendency to go out and hunt and bring back food to the village. It would reject wild wolves except at the time of mating and in due course other wolf puppies could be raised in the village and be socialized with respect to man (p. 743).

Here mutual dependence is the key to domestication (socialization), and we can assume that some measure of mutual annoyance or resentment will be tolerated by virtue of that dependence. This line of thought has been perhaps most fully and explicitly developed by Carpenter (1952) in his monograph on "Social Behavior of Non-human Primates." Because this study is based upon extensive first-hand field observation and involves theoretical constructs which readily articulate with revised two-factor learning theory, the following extended excerpt is quoted:

Integration of Societies of Non-Human Primates. What are the processes which result in the formation of simian primate societies? What processes cause such associations to persist as identifiable groupings for relatively long periods of time? What are the counter-acting processes which result in individuals leaving the groupings or the division of the societies? Currently it is proposed that answers to these questions may be given in terms of genetics, maturation and growth, motivation and learning.

Generally conceived, there are two clusters of interacting processes which may be defined. *There are those processes which have a centripetal effect on individuals which form groups, and there are those processes which have a centrifugal effect.* When the centripetal process predominates for all individuals, none leave the society; it has a high degree of *cohesion.* When the centrifugal forces predominate for the group, individuals may leave the group; it has a low degree of cohesion. Thus, the centripetal and centrifugal processes interact and result in varying degrees of group cohesiveness and dynamic stability. *It is proposed that the vector sums of the centripetal and centifugal forces equal the degree of group cohesiveness.*

Genetic and maturational processes are conceived to operate to increase to some degree the probability that defined patterns of behavior will occur, as they do occur, and more frequently than on the basis of chance alone. Not only the anatomical but also the associated behavioral patterns like locomotion, grasping, vocalizations and some aspects of perception, are

peculiarly characteristic of some genera, and thus may be said to be principally determined by the process of genetics plus maturation. Furthermore,
the basic or primary needs or drives like temperature demands, intake needs,
prepotent motor responses like sucking, clinging or grasping and sexual
activities, as well as prepotent avoidance responses are initially, basically and
predominately the expression of genetic, maturational and adjustment determiners.

This reasoning leads to the formulation of an important principle for
understanding the dynamics of group integration: Namely, *that the drives,
tensions or needs of one individual which are satisfied by activities of another individual or individuals of a grouping modify the previous adjustments between or among the individuals.* This may be termed the principle
of *reciprocal interaction.*

The following will illustrate this principle: Given a female and her new-
born infant the stage is set for the operation of the process of *reciprocal
interaction.* The female has normally a set of activated needs or drives which
the infant, as a cluster of incentives, appropriately satisfies. Reciprocally,
the infant has at birth a set of activated needs or drives which the female
satisfies as a complex of appropriate incentives. The female eats the placenta
and umbilicus. She licks the amneotic fluids from the infant. She holds
and guards the neonate. The infant is predisposed to cling to the hair or
fur of the female. It responds positively to her warmth and protection. It
avoids moving away from the female. It avoids other animals. Presently it
nurses. Thus, conditioning principles are adequate to explain the building
up and the reinforcement of specific, positive reciprocal interactions between the two organisms: the female and her infant [cf. Harlow, 1958].

As the infant grows it explores more and more. It explores itself, its
mother, nearby space and objects. It explores other young monkeys and
they respond positively or negatively to it. Play, first individual, then social,
emerges. Both positive and negative responses to an increasing number of
other members of the group are elaborated through reciprocal conditioning
and learning. The young monkey learns to react positively to some individuals and classes of animals and to avoid others. Motor patterns of
offense, defense and escape mature and are exercised. Long before the
young monkey has adequately matured physiologically for primary sexual
behavior, motor aspects of these activities are expressed and exercised. During play the young monkey may frequently be observed mounting and
being mounted. Gradually the infant gains statuses and learns to behave
appropriately with reference to other individuals in their statuses. It becomes
socialized.

If the growing young one is a male, it must compete successfully with
all other males or leave the group. If it is female, its adjustments within the
group are stimulated, facilitated and reinforced by means of sexual and
other varieties of behavior.

Sexual behavior especially affects group integration according to the
principle of *reciprocal interaction.* The estrus female with her activated
drive for copulation provides for the responsive males of a group a set of
incentives which satisfy the drives or reduce the tensions of the males. The
interactional responses involved in primary sexual behavior positively rein-

force these social responses. They may become generalized through conditioning and learning with the effect that the probabilities are increased for the reoccurrence of positive interactional activities other than sexual among the individuals. Conversely, the probabilities are reduced for the occurrence of negative or antagonistic behavior.

Accordingly it is reasonable to assume that the operation of the principle of reciprocal interaction, in a great many kinds of social behavior, results in the development and maintenance of a network or matrix of frequently recurring positive interactions. These integrate the individuals with a structured grouping. These are the centripetal forces which attract the animals to each other, regulate their interactions and cause the society to persist as an identifiable group.

Territorial adaptations and interactions with other groups, i.e., attacking, being attacked or threatened by attacks are conceived to reinforced the over-all integration of non-human primate groups.

Competition, conflicts and various forms of aggression, which are integral processes of the simian primates' social behavior, also operate within the limits of the principle of *reciprocal interaction* to differentiate the statuses of individuals, to create intra-group stresses and to cause some individuals to leave the society. There are also extra-group incentives for individuals which do not have their needs satisfied within the organized indigenous group. These are the centrifugal forces which, when strong enough, result in dispersions of group members or the actual disintegration of the society.

Summary Statement. The integration of societies of non-human primates consists of processes which lead to centripetal and centrifugal effects. It is believed that explanations of the social integrative processes can be stated in terms of genetics, maturation, motivation and conditioning or learning. A general principle of reciprocal interaction is proposed. This principle applies to the interactions of organisms between or among which there are reciprocal satisfactions of needs, drives and tensions. Female-infant interactions, the interactions of young animals during play and male-female primary sexual behavior are cited to illustrate how the principle operates to increase the probabilities of the occurrence of positive interactions. Territorial adaptations and interactions with other groups of the same species are believed also to reinforce group integration. Conflicts and attacks have negative or opposite effects (pp. 243–244).

In Figs. 10–7 and 10–8 we see some of the situations which, according to Carpenter, make for social cohesion or disruptions and, we may add, individual happiness or misery.

Carpenter's analysis lends itself admirably to restatement in terms of revised two-factor learning theory. In fact, it is, in itself, almost such a statement. To begin with, there are the primary rewards and punishments which are mediated by group living. These are, on the one hand, food (especially for the young), shelter and mutual protection, and sexual gratification and, on the other hand, the aggressions which arise as a result of unregulated competition for the available rewards. To the extent that an individual experiences rewards in the group, various forms of stimulation associated with group life take on secondary reinforcement and tend to *hold* the individual in the group. To the extent that an individual experiences punishments in the group, the associated stimuli take on the capacity to arouse fear and tend to *repel*, or "expel," the individual. Hence the image of "centripetal" and "centrifugal" forces acting upon each individual in the group which thus determine, for the group as a whole, its stability or instability.

But it goes without saying that a given individual does not have the

Fig. 10–7. Socially reinforcing behavior in monkeys (courtesy of C. R. Carpenter). Mutual grooming, mothering, and sexual behavior are cohesive forces, tending to preserve group life.

same experiences with each and every member of the group. More or less strongly differentiated reactions from other individuals may be predicted on the basis of sex, age, strength, etc. Hence, each individual learns to react selectively, discriminatingly toward other members of the group, while at the same time establishing attitudes of friendship or enmity on the part of others toward him. All of which leads to what Carpenter has briefly alluded to under the head of "status" and to which might well be added the notion of *role*.

Fig. 10–8. An outcast male monkey (courtesy of C. R. Carpenter). Competition and fighting for food and mates are socially disruptive and sometimes drive individual animals out of a group.

Hence, in a stable, successful social group the total learning associated with life in the group is relatively great. Carpenter, following common practice, has termed this *socialization*. Yet in even the most highly integrated animal groups, both the amount and the "quality" of social learning seems elemental and primitive in comparison with the social learning which occurs at the human level. It is nevertheless useful to see group life and group-mediated learning in its elemental, relatively unelaborated form. For it is presumably out of such a setting that human society, culture, and personality have evolved; and it still provides the rudiments of social, personal, and interpersonal reality.

V. Further Analysis of Social Learning and Group Structure

As between considerations advanced in Sections II and III of this chapter and those just reviewed in Section IV, the reader will no doubt feel some strain and inconsistency. The work of Lorenz, Tinbergen, Jaynes, and others suggests that, at least in a state of nature, social action and organization in animals are mainly determined by innate mechanisms (instincts, releasers, etc.), whereas in the immediately preceding section, considerable evidence is advanced for believing that individual experience and learning are of paramount importance. How can this difference in emphasis be reconciled? Two points should be specifically noted:

1). While stressing innate determination of social responses, Tinbergen does not by any means exclude individual learning; and Carpenter likewise does not say that motivation and learning are exclusively responsible for the shaping of social acts and attitudes. With these variables he also includes "genetics and maturation." Hence, the difference, in any case, is relative rather than absolute.

2). Careful review of Sections II and III and comparison with Section IV will indicate that the writers cited are, by and large, interested in different species, and even phyla. The investigators first mentioned draw heavily upon observations with *birds* and *fishes*, whereas the others are interested mainly in higher *mammals:* sheep, dogs, primates. And it is noteworthy that the studies cited in Section I were likewise concerned, exclusively, with mammals.

Hence we emerge with the plausible induction that although some genetically determined, maturational factors are undoubtedly involved in the development of social life in mammals and that learning somewhat influences the social life of other phyla, such as birds and fishes, there is, nevertheless, a broad difference to be noted here between the *relative* importance of each. And since human beings have a mammalian background and have become very highly specialized in adaptation through learning, this difference in emphasis makes complete sense and shows that already in other mammals there is, so to speak, an anticipation of and preparation for the trend which was to become so outstanding at the human level and is so very different from the nativistic mechanisms of other phyla.

In this section we shall be particularly concerned with certain new experimental techniques and concepts which seem to have special promise for further clarifying and consolidating animal experimentation and learning theory, on the one hand, and human personality and social phenomena, on the other. Let us consider, particularly, two studies recently reported by J. V. Murphy and associates. In 1955, Murphy, Miller, & Mirsky performed an ingenious experiment on what they called "Interanimal Conditioning in the Monkey." By way of introduction they say:

> Dramatic changes in individual and group behavior have been reported in studies of experimentally induced "neurotic behavior." Gantt (1944) has observed such phenomena in his dog Nick. Liddell (1953) made similar observations with sheep, and Masserman (1943, 1953) has reported extensive behavioral changes in cats and monkeys. Although many investigators have been aware of changes in the social interactions of animals after a series of conditioning experiences, it is noteworthy that no controlled experiments on interindividual conditioning have been reported.
>
> Laboratory studies of avoidance conditioning typically have been restricted to conditioned stimuli such as lights and tones. It is not, however, an inherent aspect of the phenomenon which imposes this restriction. The present study was designed to demonstrate that one monkey can be successfully utilized as the stimulus for conditioned avoidance behavior in other monkeys. The specific aim was to develop a technique which could be used to modify interanimal transactions. The demonstration of such a possibility is considered relevant to numerous problems in the area of group functioning and personality theory. This lack of application of conditioning principles to social interaction phenomena is particularly interesting when one recognizes the importance of interindividual transactions in clinical practice (p. 211).

The experimental procedure used by Murphy, Miller, & Mirsky was simple. An apparatus was constructed which consisted, essentially, of two compartments, each of which would comfortably hold a monkey, with a plate-glass partition between them (Fig. 10–9). The experimental animal, in Compartment 1, normally could not see the stimulus animal, in Compartment 2; but by a slight shift in lighting arrangement, the stimulus animal could be made clearly visible. Sight of the stimulus animal was then made the danger signal, or CS, in an ordinary active avoidance learning procedure: i.e., five seconds after exposure of the stimulus animal, a shock was delivered to the grill floor of Compartment 1, unless the experimental animal pushed a response bar which caused the stimulus monkey to disappear and prevented the shock. Compartment 2 was frequently exposed without the stimulus monkey in it, and not associated with shock. Therefore, the experimental animal learned that sight of Compartment 2 was dangerous only if it contained the stimulus monkey, thus focusing attention upon the monkey rather than exposure of the compartment as such.

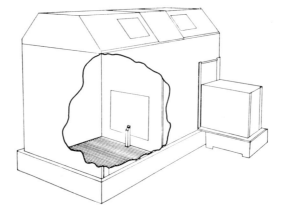

Fig. 10–9. Apparatus used by Murphy, Miller, & Mirsky (1955, p. 212) for the study of "interanimal conditioning in the monkey." The stimulus animal (in the right-hand compartment) becomes visible to the experimental animal (in the left-hand compartment) with a change in illumination. The vertical response lever, by means of which the experimental animal can "turn off" the stimulus animal and thus avert electric shock, can be seen just in front of the plate-glass window separating the two compartments. The small adjacent box (at the extreme right) serves to house the stimulus monkey during neutral trials.

Results obtained from use of this procedure show that, as was to be confidently expected, the appearance of one animal can be made the occasion for a fear reaction and appropriate "avoidance" behavior (bar pressing) quite as readily as can the presentation of some inanimate stimulus such as a buzzer or a light (cf. also the Watson-Raynor experiment described in Chapter 11, Mowrer, 1960). Moreover, the method lent itself admirably to the study of generalization (from the stimulus monkey to other monkeys) and discrimination. (One often wonders to what extent one animal "knows the difference" between other animals of the same species. Here, it would seem, is a way to find out.)

In concluding this article, the authors say:

The social avoidance conditioning technique is particularly challenging when viewed from a "fear reduction" viewpoint. If the sight of the stimulus animal gives rise to "fear" in a conditioned animal, numerous predictions of inter-animal behavior suggest themselves. One application currently under investigation is the experimental modification of the group dominance structure in a group of monkeys.

The modification of interindividual behavior is presumably not restricted to avoidance behavior. It appears equally feasible to establish approach behavior or any combination of avoidance and approach behavior (p. 213).

It was therefore entirely natural that in 1956 Murphy & Miller should have published a sequel to the study just cited, on "The Manipulation of Dominance in Monkeys with Conditioned Fear," which they summarize thus:

Two group-dominance tests were conducted on ten rhesus monkeys. On the basis of these tests five pairs of animals adjacent, or nearly adjacent, in the hierarchy were given an additional five dominance determinations. The animal in each pair which received the greater number of raisins in each of the seven tests between the two animals was designated as dominant. This animal in each pair was subjected to avoidance conditioning with his submissive partner as the conditioned stimulus. After attaining a conditioning criterion, each pair of monkeys was given an additional five dominance tests. After completing this phase two additional group-dominance tests were completed. An additional three pairs were selected as before and subjected to the same procedure. The dominance status was found to be significantly reversed following the completion of conditioning. It was suggested that this observation provides behavioral evidence for the presence of fear in avoidance conditioning which is independent of the conditioning situation (p. 248).

Considering that the fear conditioning occurred in one situation (Fig. 10–9) and that the dominance-submission relationship was tested in a very different one and that the correct (fear-reducing) response in the former situation was bar pressing and in the latter situation deference and withdrawal, the effect here reported is dramatic indeed. The findings show that the attitude of one animal toward another can be altered, not only by punishment administered *by* one animal *to* another, but also by the experience of punishment merely *in the presence* of the other animal. This is a sort of social "latent learning" (Chapter 2) or "putting through" (Mowrer, 1960, Chapter 7). The experimental possibilities which the method suggests, and their theoretical implications, are numerous, as the following paragraph suggests:

The observed modification in interindividual transactions conform very nicely with that suggested by the interpretation of avoidance conditioning which emphasizes the presence of fear as an intervening variable. The modification of dominance provides behavioral evidence for the presence of fear in avoidance learning which is independent of the conditioning situation. Recently completed experiments on interanimal conditioning in which the extinguished response in the previously conditioned animal is reinstated at a high level by observing the stimulus animal undergoing painful shock stimulation will make it possible to establish more definitive evidence for the presence of fear in avoidance conditioning and its communication between animals (p. 247). [See the discussion of "empathy" in Chapter 3.]

It goes without saying that, using the same apparatus, one could also make an experimental animal come to "like" a stimulus monkey by associating the latter with the presentation of food, water, or other decremental primary reinforcement. Here there would be an "un-earned" increment of liking, or "love," just as there is an unearned increment of fear in the situation actually employed by Murphy and associates. Artificial though such situations are, they provide, by this very fact, exceptional opportunities for the experimental manipulation of social relationships.

Gewirtz (1960) has recently reviewed such systematic evidence as there is on the process whereby human infants develop positive emotional ties to parents and others. The most substantial induction from this material is that by virtue of the care and protection which adults provide for infants, the former take on the capacity, as well known learning principles (Mowrer, 1960, Chapters 3–5) would predict, to produce secondary reinforcement of either the type-1 or type-2 varieties or, more probably, both.

Stone (1954) has published a "Critique of Studies of Infant Isolation," which conspire to show the devastating effect, upon both intellectual and social development, of the lack of normally satisfying human con-tacts; and Thompson & Heron, in the same year, reviewed studies on "The Effects of Restricting Early Experience on the Problem-Solving Capacity of Dogs" and certain other animals. While the type of restric-tions alluded to here is somewhat different from the isolation considered by Stone, the net result is much the same: "adverse effects on the problem-solving ability of the adult dog" (p. 29). From the analysis of language learning put forward in Chapter 3 and from the whole conception of approach behavior and habit formation developed in *Learning Theory and Behavior*, these findings occasion no surprise.

VI. Guilt: A Unique Aspect of Human Socialization and Personality

There is, of course, a large and illuminating literature on socialization of the human young, both in our own and other societies; but, in the main, this lies beyond our present scope or interest. Here we shall restrict ourselves to a special problem, which, though central to the socialization process, has been generally neglected from the standpoint of learning theory. This problem is the phenomenon of conscience, character, or the internalized sense of right and wrong.

Much of the training which children receive is rather obviously similar, at least in principle, to teaching and learning procedures studied in the animal laboratory. Children are taught to shun certain objects (avoidance learning), to abstain from certain actions (inhibition), to be attracted by certain objects (approach learning), and to perform certain activities (response selection or habit formation). In the process they, like our laboratory subjects, develop attitudes of fear and hope, experience relief and disappointment, and manifest general patterns of timidity or courage. They make generalizations, develop discriminations and skills and, by principles already considered, learn to talk.

But, with all this, something essentially and distinctively human is still lacking: the capacity to experience that fateful phenomenon known as *guilt*. Around the turn of the century, a number of empirical studies and systematic books were published on the psychology of religion, wherein guilt was naturally given an important place. But the experimental psychology of that era, concerned as it was with sensation and perception, had little to say about and less to contribute to the topic. Gradually, with the ascendance of psychoanalysis, attention was again drawn to the problem but in a way which we now suspect of being basically mistaken (Section VII) and in a language more figurative and poetic than scientific. Like the introspectionists of an earlier day, both Behaviorists and Neobehaviorists, priding themselves on their scientific presuppositions, have left the problem almost untouched; and it is only recently that serious efforts have been made to interrelate the two areas. Of these, one of the most useful is a paper published by Ausubel in 1955 and entitled "Relationships between Shame and Guilt in the Socializing Process."

On the basis of incompletely analyzed field observations, a number of anthropologists arrived at the view that only in those societies embracing the Judeo-Christian tradition is the phenomenon of conscience, or "superego," to be found in fully developed form and that other societies, if they have an orderly moral system at all, depend upon the more superficial reaction know as *shame*. The distinction is, of course, familiar: in shame the individual is uncomfortable only if "found out," "caught"; whereas in guilt there is self-condemnation and self-punishment regardless of the social situation. Many dog lovers report clear evidence of shame in these creatures. For example, a former student of the writer says that his half-grown beagle has very much of a "hang-dog" manner when the master comes home if the dog has chewed or otherwise mutilated household furnishings during the course of the day. The master need not have yet learned of the damage or in any way shown disapproval. The dog himself "knows" he is "guilty." But it is a limited form of guilt and apparently arises only when the situation suddenly changes from master-away to master-at-home. In the former situation the dog is safe; in the latter, he is suddenly in danger, and his behavior changes accordingly. In other words, the dog not only discriminates between master-gone and master-home but also between master-home, situation-good *and* master-home, situation-bad.

This, manifestly, is the shame reaction. Only if the dog, having misbehaved, showed "remorse" or "shame" *before* the master came home could we legitimately speak of guilt in the deeper sense of the term. Here there would presumably have to be a vivid anticipation or fore-image of situation-with-master-home, and it is not certain that lower animals are capable of this degree of representational activity.[6] Of course, the chances are that the young beagle, in the case cited, will eventually abandon the destructive behavior; but we do not know whether it is because his "character" develops *or* because some of his puppish urges (e.g., those occasioned by erupting teeth) simply disappear (cf. Sections VII and VIII).

Now Ausubel, in the paper cited, makes the eminently reasonable point that fully-fledged guilt is almost a certain necessity in the members of any well ordered society and that a so-called shame culture, such as the Navaho, Samoans, and even Japanese are said to have, simply would not be adequate to its purpose. He says:

> Without the aid rendered by guilt feelings, child rearing would be a difficult matter indeed. If children felt no sense of accountability or moral obligation to curb their hedonistic and irresponsible impulses, to conform to accepted social norms, or to acquire self-control, the socializing process would be slow, arduous, and incomplete. . . . And since it is plainly evident that the maintenance of perpetual vigilance is impractical, that fear alone is never an effective deterrent against antisocial behavior, and that the interests of personal expedience are not always in agreement with prescribed ethical norms, a social order unbuttressed by a sense of moral obligation in its members would enjoy precious little stability (p. 378).

> We might expect that guilt feelings would be found universally; and, hence, the burden of proof regarding their alleged absence in a given culture more properly rests with the investigator making the allegation (p. 379).

[6] A nice appreciation of this point is shown by Boisen (1936) when he says: "In language and imagination we rehearse the responses of others just as we dramatically enact other consequences. We foreknow how others will act, and the foreknowledge is the beginning of judgment passed on action. We know *with* them: there is conscience" (p. 171).

But how, precisely, is it that such a "watchdog" (Ausubel's term—others have spoken of an internal "gyroscope") is established in the growing child? Ausubel's statement that guilt is "a special kind of negative self-evaluation . . . a self-reaction to an injured conscience" is a good one; and he goes on to suggest that conscience is "an abstraction referring to a feeling of obligation to abide by all internalized moral values. The injury consists of a self-perceived violation of this obligation" (p. 379). But there is still need for a mechanism, a *dynamic* whereby such internalization occurs. This Ausubel adduces as follows:

Behavior can first be regarded as manifesting moral properties when a sense of obligation is acquired. The central hypothesis of the present formulation is that this development typically takes place in children who are accepted and intrinsically valued by parents, and who thereby acquire a derived or vicarious status in consequence of this acceptance. By the fiat of parent acceptance they are provided with intrinsic feelings of security and adequacy despite their manifest dependency and incompetence to fend for themselves. They accordingly become disposed to accept parental values implicitly and unconditionally out of loyalty to the individuals to whom they owe their status and self-esteem (p. 380).

In other words, out of his *perceived dependency* the child decides that in hurting significant others (being "bad") he is really hurting himself; and by this route the values of parents and of the larger social group are internalized, introjected, incorporated. Sometimes it is said that the child develops good character by "identifying" with others; but this formulation is, at best, rather inexplicit and, at its worst, verges on circularity: to identify with is to become *like* others and this is precisely what is to be explained. The notion of dependency clearly suggests obligation; and when we are obligated to others their welfare becomes, quite literally, *our own.*[7]

And Boisen (1936) puts the same thought succinctly when he says:

The individual judges himself by the standards of those to whom he gives allegiance and with whom he wishes to be identified, and to be unable to stand before the inner tribunal means for him isolation and destruction (p. 174).

Could capacity for guilt, as thus conceived, be created and studied in the laboratory with animal subjects? Internalization is by no means

[7] Boder (1949) relates that a small gypsy boy, in a Nazi concentration camp, was permitted to accompany his father as he went about the *Lager* administering beatings to inmates who had displeased the authorities. Soon the small boy was observed to have found a club for himself and to be "helping" his father. Here, obviously, was identification or conscience formation which was psychologically natural but socially monstrous.

a new concept to us. Fear has been alluded to as "internalized" trauma; Vinacke has characterized learning in general as "internalization of experience"; and Sidman, Schaefer, and others (Mowrer, 1960, Chapter 12) have shown that rats and other laboratory animals are capable of responding to internal temporal cues. But what, exactly, is it that is internalized as conscience? It is an awareness of and concern for the welfare of others; and in our laboratory researches we usually see to it that the experimental situation is as *impersonal* as possible. Typically the reports of experiments read: "The experiment was conducted with the subject in an isolation chamber . . . a one-way observation mirror was used . . . contact with the experimenter was excluded, etc." And, of late, B. F. Skinner has spear-headed a drive toward the complete automation ("programming") of experimentation, so that the investigator merely throws a switch and leaves the subject alone with a preset, pre-instructed machine. While extremely useful for some purposes, this type of research (Skinner, 1958b, has suggested a modified version for classroom instruction) is not likely to tell us much about either the operation or formation of conscience. Those designedly "unscientific" and highly *personal* procedures whereby we care for young children or make "pets" of the young of other species are far more likely to yield relevant insights.

It may well be, of course, that even with the closest intimacy between man and animal, only the grossest rudiments of conscience can be established. Perhaps, in order for certain representational processes presumed to be necessary for conscience to occur, articulate language must be available. However, the loyalty of dogs to their masters is proverbial; and their sense of dependency is clearly manifested, it would seem, in their possessiveness and jealousy. Thus, by the hypothesis advanced by Ausubel, perhaps there *is* the capacity, at least in the dog, not only for shame but also for genuine guilt (cf. Chevigny, 1946) and that it could be precisely investigated in the laboratory if one were but willing to make the necessary investment of time and to disregard some of the rules commonly thought to be essential in animal experimentation (see Sections VII and VIII).

In this book we have repeatedly defended the principle of biological homeostasis, i.e., the assumption that living organisms are basically "selfish" and that they constantly strive to reduce existing drives and to forestall their recurrence. In the present context, however, we find ourselves discussing conscience and concern for the welfare of *others*. Does this not squarely controvert the premises on which much of the earlier discussion proceeded? We should remember that, superimposed on his biological substructure, man has a long history of *social evolution* and that in the process of his individual training he is imbued with values which, though ultimately based on biological considerations, nevertheless transcend them. Here, as conscience, a new form of homeostasis or equilibrium comes into existence: *moral equilibrium*— and its antithesis, disequilibrium. Here conscience, rather than "the flesh," is of more direct concern, but the continuity is evident. Some writers have, in various ways, attempted to deny or break this continuity. For example, the theologian R. C. Johnson (1958), in a series of articles on the Apostle Paul, says: "All would-be Christianity says to us, 'Obey and be free,' . . . ; but the Christian gospel says, 'Be free and obey' " (p. 49). In its setting what this statement means is that one finds contentment and existential meaning, not in the fulfillment of obligation, but from a special gift of grace, out of gratitude for which one then becomes kindly and helpful. If there is validity in this view, it escapes the present writer; and certainly most psychologists would be inclined to agree with Ausubel when he suggests that conscience, as manifest concern for the welfare of others, derives ultimately from the "meaningful threat of withdrawal of love and approval" (p. 281). In this light we can fully acknowledge the imperatives of conscience as the highest expression of the human mind and spirit, without in the least violating the fundamental principles that have guided our exploration of adaptive behavior in lower organisms. Conscience can "hurt" no less than can one's body; and the relief that comes when conscience is "cleared" is equal to, if not greater than, any possible form of organic relief or pleasure. Hence, any account of human motivation and personality that ignores the "moral strivings" of man is grossly incomplete and, by that very fact, misleading and dangerous.

VII. A Possible Laboratory Approach to the Problem of Guilt

After reading a preliminary draft of this chapter, Mr. A. A. Salama suggested a promising methodology for studying "guilt" reactions in lower animals. Let us start with a hungry laboratory rat that has learned to eat pellets of food from a small trough recessed in the wall of a "Skinner box" (a small, experimental compartment). But now we decide that this behavior shall be "taboo," and whenever the rat hereafter takes a pellet from the trough and eats it, we put an electric charge on the floor grill, beneath the animal, and keep it there until the animal presses a little bar located on the side of the box opposite the food trough. The question posed by Mr. Salama is: After a few occurrences of this form of punishment, would the rat, after eating a pellet of food —and feeling "guilty" about having done so—perhaps *show* his guilt by running to the bar and pressing it, even though no shock is present? Such behavior would indicate, at the very least, that the eating behavior had become a sign for the rat of imminent danger, i.e., capable of making the rat *afraid;* and it is not unreasonable to suppose that the rat would now try to deal with this fear by pressing the bar.

The problem would, of course, be how to get enough fear conditioned to the act of eating to make the animal feel "guilty" and yet not *inhibit* the animal from performing the forbidden (punished) act. Ordinarily we think of fear operating *prospectively* in animals: "*If* I do thus and so, I will be punished." Can it also operate *retrospectively?* —"*Since* I have already *done* thus and so, I shall be punished." So far as the writer is aware, no one has previously posed this question, experimentally. Even here the fear itself is, obviously, still prospective, since the punishment lies in the future; but the temporal placement of the *occasion* for the fear is certainly different, in the one case lying in the future ("*If* I do thus and so, . . ."), in the other case lying in the past ("*Since* I have done thus and so, . . ."). Hearnshaw (1956), in a paper previously cited in this book, suggests that it might be worthwhile to note the retrospective aspects of the emotion of guilt, specifically, as they are reflected in the words *regret* and *remorse.* Introspectively, these states are very vivid to most human beings. But it is, of course, questionable as to whether they exist in lower animals. However, the problem can at least be approached in the *operational* terms which Mr. Salama has proposed; and it is hoped that someone will soon initiate work along these lines.

In the meantime, it may be useful to develop some related theoretical considerations. The foregoing discussion seems to introduce a new dimension in the unfolding process of identifying and objectively investigating various emotional states. But, at the same time, it will be noted that previous work provides at least the foundation for this development. In this book and in the companion volume, we have repeatedly had occasion to note that avoidance behavior can take either of two major forms: passive avoidance, wherein fear is conditioned to certain response-correlated stimuli and thus leads to inhibition of the response itself; and active avoidance, wherein fear is conditioned to environmentally presented, independent stimuli and leads to flight from the region in which such stimuli are experienced.

Now it is obvious that our analysis of so-called passive avoidance, or "punished" behavior, has been in one respect incomplete. When an act has been punished and the organism later refrains from repeating the act, we think we have a fairly complete understanding of the principles involved. (Chapter 1; also Mowrer, 1960, Chapters 2, 3, and 11). But we have almost totally neglected the fear that undoubtedly occurs, not only when an organism is merely *tempted* to perform a forbidden act (but refrains), but also when the organism has actually executed the forbidden act and stands in dread of chastisement. Here, no longer able to control (avert) punishment by behaving "properly," the organism is caught in a far more difficult dilemma, i.e., in a "state of sin." And, in like situations, human beings often cry out, "What can I do to be *saved?*" The lower animal, in such a predicament, presumably has a somewhat comparable experience. Ordinarily, when a punishment has not been "successful," i.e., when it has not actually inhibited the behavior in question, it is simply administered again, with little or no regard to how the animal may itself *feel* about the situation. The neat thing about the Salama proposal is that it at least offers the animal a chance to *say*, behaviorally, something on this score. Even though a fear of punishment has not been sufficient to block a goal-directed action (or "habit"), this is not to say that there is no fear present in the situation at all; and *after* the goal in question has been satisfied, the fear may be very considerable. Indeed, we might even expect it to be *greater* at this point because it is precisely here that incremental reinforcement has previously occurred; and the fear that is experienced *in advance* of the performance of an act is always generalized from situation-*following*-act. Thus we arrive at the inference that even though fear of punishment may not be great enough to inhibit an act, that fear may be very lively indeed *after* the act is performed, which is operationally very close to what is ordinarily meant by the emotion or state of *guilt*.[8]

Salama has proposed that we study fear following a tabooed action by providing the organism with an opportunity to perform the same response as has previously been required to terminate the primary punishment. Supposing that, in the delay between the eating behavior

---

[8] It is pertinent at this point to make a distinction between the guilt following an action (a) with and (b) without the expected reward. Intuitively it would seem that guilt would be greater in (a), and the same expectation follows from theory: since the original positive drive is now eliminated (or at least reduced), the fear of punishment would be experienced, so to say, unopposed. Moreover, since it is often not the act itself but the ensuing gratification that is considered "bad," there may be a further basis for a differential reaction in the two situations described.

and grill shock, the animal *did* press the bar, the question would then arise as to whether the shock should now be omitted or occur anyway. If the shock, under these circumstances, were omitted and if the subject showed a tendency to persist in the bar-pressing behavior, one would be tempted to wonder if this were not at least an approximation of *apology* and *expiation:* at the very least it would seem to say, "I'm sorry—don't punish me—I'm punishing myself!"

Finally, a word should be said about some thoughts for which the writer is indebted to Dr. Richard H. Walters, of the University of Toronto. As Dr. Walters has observed, many fears have a "chancy" quality: for example, if a person is crossing a river on thin ice and "makes it," there is no reason to continue to be afraid subsequently. In fact, he will feel vastly relieved and even elated. He has gambled and "won." The element of danger in the situation is in the act itself (i.e., the feared consequence is physical, not social), and there is no subsequent risk of the past "catching up" with the individual. Probably most fears in lower animals are of this character, even the fears associated with other living organisms. If they "get by" with a given action in the immediate situation, they are not likely to be later hunted down and punished. In other words, the concept of *moral responsibility* is largely absent in a state of nature.

But in human experience the situation is very different. If one takes a chance and violates some *social* norm (or law), the fact that he escapes immediate detection and punishment does not at all mean that he is really "in the clear." Objectively, there is always the possibility of subsequent detection; and added to this is the fact that the individual's conscience may also bother him. Thus a human being is likely to *think about* prospective misdeeds somewhat as follows: "Even though I am not objectively caught either at the time of the act or later, still I shall be 'caught,' inescapably, by my continuing insecurity and bad conscience, so the gain is just not worth the loss." [9] Here "punishment," in general terms, is assured, by the very *knowledge of right and wrong;* and the deterring effect is presumably much greater than where the individual, for whatever reason, does not react in this way.

This discussion is admittedly rough, because the terrain over which it moves is, to psychologists, new and unexplored. For example, until recently the writer saw no way at all of getting an operational (situational) purchase on the problem of guilt, and felt that its study in animals and articulation with systematic behavior theory was all but

[9] For a discussion of the effects of intermittent (uncertain) reinforcement, see Tsushima (1958), Mowrer (1960, Chapter 12).

impossible. But now, with the aid of suggestions such as those of Salama and Walters which have been reviewed here, the situation seems by no means hopeless. Actually, the connecting link has been lying right under our eyes and we have not been able to see it, namely, the situation which prevails whenever an organism (animal or human) has performed a previously punished act and is in a state of uncertainty and apprehension as to whether it will *again* be punished. Such an organism is, both objectively and subjectively, guilty in at least the most primitive sense of the term; and our further analysis of the problem can confidently build on this foundation.

VIII. Preliminary Report on Temptation and Guilt in Young Dogs (R. L. Solomon)

After this chapter was in galley proof, the author learned of some highly pertinent studies in progress at Harvard University; and inquiry brought the following full and illuminating statement from Professor Richard L. Solomon, with gracious permission to reproduce it here. This report is particularly gratifying, and exciting, because it shows the "power" of contemporary behavior theory. Operating with shared premises but otherwise quite independently, Dr. Solomon and his associates have moved along theoretical and experimental lines extremely close to those delineated in the preceding section of this chapter. Moreover, this report, preliminary though it is, shows how animal experimentation (cf. Section I) serves to order and clarify our thinking about human phenomena which are commonplace but which may otherwise remain quite imperfectly analyzed.

At the end of this material, some of the most striking similarities between it and the preceding discussion in this chapter will be briefly noted; but the reader can make a sort of game for himself if, as he goes along, he independently watches for these—as well as differences and discrepancies, if any. The report from Dr. Solomon follows:

Yes, we have been carrying on experiments on resistance to temptation and guilt in puppies for the last six years in our laboratory. The work has been a joint enterprize under the authorship of Drs. A. H. Black, R. L. Solomon, and J. W. M. Whiting (with the assistance of Drs. Russell M. Church and Dean Peabody). We have carried out several experiments, but because they have taken a great deal of time, and because the accumulation of enough numbers for certain conclusions has been slow, we have published nothing on our major findings to date. Dr. Black, who is now at McMaster University will publish a short note in the *Canadian Journal of Psychology* concerning some peripheral aspects of the study, but the major study, when it does come out, will be under the authorship of Black, Solomon, and Whiting.

Here is the general nature of our experiments to date. First, we developed what we called a *taboo, training situation* and standardized it as much as possible. The taboo training room was a square room approximately 15 × 15, fairly soundproof, and equipped with a one-way mirror. In one corner of the room was placed a chair and in front of it at each leg of the chair were two small dishes. The trainer sat in the chair and he was equipped with a rolled-up newspaper with which he could swat the subjects on the rump. All experiments were run with six-months-old puppies as subjects. The procedure was as follows: Each puppy was starved for two days and then was brought into the experimental room by one experimenter. The trainer was sitting in the chair. In one of the food dishes was highly preferred boiled horsemeat. In the other dish was a less preferred commercial dog chow (Food X). The dishes could be quickly switched from side to side. The puppy usually chose the horsemeat a few seconds after he was introduced into the room. As he *touched* the horsemeat, he was swatted by the trainer. If the swat was not enough to break up the consummatory behavior, the puppy was swatted again and again until he withdrew from the horsemeat. This usually produced complete, initial negative generalization; but after the passage of time, the puppies usually made another pass at the horsemeat. They were swatted again. Eventually, they shifted their concentration to Food X which they ate without being molested.

We tried several variations on this taboo training procedure, and we finally arrived at one which produced fairly rapid discriminative avoidance learning. We usually carried the puppies along for several days, making sure that they were reliable in avoiding the tabooed horsemeat and that they quickly and avidly ate Food X. We set up an arbitrary learning criterion: after twelve errorless trials the animal had learned the taboo.

Following this, the experiment entered the *temptation-testing* phase. This consisted of starving the puppy for two days and introducing him to the experimental room with the *trainer absent*. In one dish were three Food-X pellets, and in the other dish was a large pile of boiled horsemeat. The three pellets were for the purpose of checking the effect of the change in the feeding situation induced by the absence of the trainer. All puppies gobbled up the three pellets with a short reaction time and then went through various antics in relation to the large dish of horsemeat. Some puppies would circle the dish over and over again. Some puppies walked around the room with their eyes toward the wall, not looking at the dish. Other puppies got down on their bellies and slowly crawled forward, barking and whining. There was a large range of variability in the emotional behavior of the puppies in the presence of the tabooed horsemeat. We measured resistance of temptation as the number of seconds or minutes which passed by before the subject ate the tabooed food. Each puppy was only given a half hour a day in the experimental room in the presence of the horsemeat. If he did not eat the horsemeat at that time, he was brought back to his home cage, was not fed, and a day later was introduced into the experimental room again. This procedure was continued until the puppy finally violated the taboo, or until he became so emaciated and dehydrated from lack of food that we felt that he could not survive the experiment any longer.

In our pilot experiments we found a very great range of resistance to temptation. The shortest period of time it took a puppy to kick over the traces was a little over six minutes, and the longest period of time was sixteen days without eating, after which time the experiment was terminated and the puppy fed in his home cage. This huge range gave us the opportunity to see the effects of some antecedent conditions and some constitutional differences in determining the resistance to temptation scores [cf. "submissive" rat shown in Fig. 10–1c, Section I].

Here are some of the antecedent conditions we have worked with. In every case the consequent condition or dependent variable was resistance to temptation. In our first experiments we studied the difference between hand feeding and watering puppies versus machine feeding and watering them from the time they were weaned up until the taboo training at six months of age. Litters were split into two groups and one group was never fed or watered except when a human being came in and did so, while the other group was never fed and watered unless a machine produced food and water without a human being present at the time. Three separate litters of mongrel puppies were run in this experiment. In the case of each of these experiments, the familiarity of both groups of puppies with the experimenters was held constant and equated. That is, whenever an experimenter came into the living quarters to feed and water the hand-fed group, he also exposed himself to the machine-fed animals and touched them and interacted with them for the same period of time. We kept this familiarity control throughout all of our experiments. All puppies were given their shots by the same person, and the cages were cleaned by the same person. The only difference, then, was the difference between dependence on machines and dependence on human beings for food and water. The first three litters, run over the first three years of our experimentation, contained eight, six, and six puppies, respectively.

The first litter gave us very encouraging results. There was a significant difference in resistance to temptation scores between hand-fed and machine fed groups. Of the eight puppies in the litter there was only one overlapping case, with three of the hand fed puppies clearly outlasting the rest of the field, and three of the machine fed puppies clearly having low resistance to temptation. In the second litter the picture was not so clear, mainly because all of the puppies showed very high resistance to temptation. Four of these puppies failed to touch the horsemeat after 14 days and we had to terminate the experiment. The other two puppies kicked over the traces, and one was in the hand-fed group and one was in the machine-fed group. In the third litter which we ran under the same conditions, none of the puppies violated the taboo. Obviously, we were hitting some kind of a ceiling, and obviously, the temperamental characteristics of the puppies were very important. For example, we found that the best single predictor of resistance to temptation without regard to experimental conditions was our assessment of the timidity of the puppy prior to the experiment. Puppies who are timid in approaching human beings and who are easily frightened by loud noises are also those puppies who resist temptation most effectively. This fits with the observations made by the people at Jackson Laboratories at Bar Harbor, Maine. Paul Scott has reported that Shetland Sheepdogs are especially sensitive to reprimand, and that taboos can be established with just one frightening experience, such taboos being extremely resistant to extinction. On the other hand, the Basenjis seem to be constitutional psychopaths, and it is very difficult to maintain taboos in such dogs.

We also tried some variations on the Freudian notion of ambivalence. We checked to see whether it made a difference if the trainer was the prior nurturing agent or not. I raised a litter of six puppies from weaning to six months of age, under conditions which made them completely dependent upon me for everything they needed. I cleaned their cages, I fed and watered them, and no one else had nurturant interactions with the puppies, although lots of other people came in the room, walked back and forth in front of the cage so that the puppies could be familiarized with other people. Then, at six months of age, I taboo-trained three of the puppies, and another experimenter taboo-trained the other three puppies. We wanted to see whether taboo training was more effective when the nurturing agent was also the punishing agent. Here, again, our taboo training was too effective. All puppies resisted temptation for sixteen days, and the experiment was terminated.

We are now in the midst of another experiment, similar to this one, in which the Freudian notion of ambivalence is being explored with a few more experimental variations. We hope to cut down the effectiveness of our taboo training techniques, and settle for a poorly established aversion for horsemeat, one that will be easier to extinguish. We then hope to check on our prior observations, especially in the hope that our success with the first litter of eight puppies can be repeated with other litters. Litter variance is extremely important, and we have to design our experiments so that it can always be taken into account in such a way that it is not confounded with any other experimental conditions. We haven't reached the stage yet when we want to go the expense of using thoroughbreds, so we use mongrel pups.

Over the long haul our object is to vary systematically those parameters of a socialization process which have been postulated to lead to high resistance to temptation. Note that I am separating *resistance to temptation* from *guilt*, and I am avoiding the use of conscience and superego which may be some sort of a compound of the two manifestations. For example, in the first litter we ran, we found that when a puppy did kick over the traces and eat the horsemeat, he did so with his tail wagging the whole time; and after he ate the horsemeat, when the experimenter came into the room the puppy greeted him with tail wags, and with no obvious distress. On the other hand, in some preliminary work we did, we noticed that some pups showed much more emotional disturbance after they ate the horsemeat than when they were approaching it. We were able to relate this to uncontrolled differences in training techniques. We are now privately *convinced*, although we do *not* have open and shut experimental evidence to prove it, that when puppies are walloped just as they *approach* the taboo food, they build up a high resistance to temptation. However, if and when such puppies do kick over the traces, they don't show any emotional upset following the crime. On the other hand, if you let a puppy eat half of the horsemeat up before you wallop him, you can still establish avoidance of the horsemeat. However, in the case of these puppies, there is a lot more emotional disturbance *following* the crime. This could be called a guilt reaction, and the presence of the experimenter is not required to elicit it. The presence of the experimenter seems to intensify it, when he does finally come in the room after the crime is committed. Therefore, we believe that the conditions for the establishment of strong resistance to temptation as contrasted with the capacity to experience strong guilt reactions, is a function of both the intensity of punishment and the time during the approach and consummatory response sequence at which the punishment is administered.

We feel that delayed punishment is not very effective in producing a high level of resistance to temptation, but it is effective in producing emotional reactions after the commission of the crime. Call these reactions guilt, if you wish, for lack of a better term. On the other hand, it is clear that punishment introduced after the animal eats quite a bit of the horsemeat does operate backward in time, and it does produce aversion and the disruption of approach responses. These approach responses, however, don't seem to be as reliably broken up by such delayed punishment. On the other hand, we have yet to see an emotional disturbance following the crime in a puppy whose approach behavior alone has been punished.

We feel that this observation is important, since it represents two major types of socialization techniques used by parents. In one case the parent traps the child into the commission of a tabooed act so that the child can be effectively punished, the hope being that this will prevent the child from performing the act again. The other technique is to watch the child closely and to try to anticipate when the child intends to do something wrong and punish the child during the incipient stages. Each of these techniques, according to our observations with puppies, should lead to a very different outcome with regard to the components of "conscience."

We assume that "conscience" has two components: the ability to resist temptation, and the susceptability to guilt reactions. We assume that these two components are partially independent, and that by appropriate training procedures we could produce puppies who have high resistance to temptation, but low susceptability to guilt reactions; high resistance to temptation along with high susceptability to guilt reactions; low resistance to temptation along with low susceptability to guilt; and low resistance to temptation along with high susceptability to guilt reactions. It is easy to examine these four classes of outcomes and see four clinically important combinations in the neuroses, as well as the creation of a psychopath.

We are very hopeful about the eventual contribution of these experiments, and Johnny Whiting and I plan to try to keep this research going over the years. It has the continuing support of the Laboratory of Social Relations, and as long as we have students who now and then will be willing to put in their time in assisting us, we will eventually have an interesting story to tell. This research does, however, take a long time to carry out, and we have very little to show for our six years of work.

You may be interested to note that an analogous temptation testing situation has been set up in Johnny Whiting's shop for use with children. They have developed a beanbag game which can be used to measure resistance to temptation (cheating), and they are studying different antecedent con-

ditions as they relate to the cheating score. This work is even more in its
infancy than that of the puppy work, however.

We are also interested in situational determinants of resistance to temptation. It is our theory that when a puppy is constantly nurtured by one person, the following association is established: "When I am hungry, the
experimenter comes; or, when I am thirsty the experimenter comes." According to this line of reasoning, high drive stimulus level leads to the
anticipation of the appearance of the nurturing agent. On the other hand,
if the nurturing agent is also the punisher in the taboo training situation,
then anticipation of the arrival of the nurturing agent, accompanied by
touching the tabooed object or trying to consume it, should lead to intense anxiety reactions. These reactions are quite observable during the
training procedure, and quite often the puppies avoid the experimenter or
vacillate quite a bit in going toward and away from him. When the
puppy is left alone in the room during temptation testing, we assume that
the following mechanisms operate. If the puppy is in a state of high drive,
the following association occurs: "Experimenter will come," because this
is what has been established in the previous nurturant relationship. If there
has not been such a previous nurturance relationship, then the association
will not run itself off. If, under the high drive condition, the association
does occur, and the puppy does expect the experimenter to come, he is
faced with the problem: "If I eat the food and the experimenter comes, I
will get swatted." This leads to an anticipatory anxiety attack and aversive
behavior. For a puppy which has been nurtured by the trainer, the more
it needs the trainer at the time, the more likely it is to stay away from
the taboo food.

Generalizing from this analysis, the child who is reaching into the
tabooed cookie jar will be less likely to touch the forbidden cookies if
the child needs to have his diaper changed at the time, and the punishing
agent is the one who has also been the nurturing agent and the diaper
changer. This part of our analysis leads to experiments on situational determinants of resistance to temptation. We have not yet gone into situational determinants of intensity of guilt reactions, but we hope to do this
job sometime along with the other.

Eventually, when we have established the ease with which the major
phenomena can be produced in the laboratory, we will have to go into
parametric studies. We are certainly not in a position to do this now,
because we haven't even found out how to control our taboo training situation so that it will give us a convenient range of behavioral variability. We
thought we had it under control at one time, but later litters gave us
quite a setback.

Without attempting in any sense to indicate all the rich implications
of the foregoing, we may nevertheless make special note of the following considerations:

1). The work of Dr. Solomon and his colleagues, like the analysis
suggested in Sections VI and VII, leads to a distinction between *guilt*
as the fear that arises *after* a previously punished act has been com-

mitted, and *temptation* as the fear and conflict which occur *before* a forbidden act occurs. Thus, to point to only one of many possible ramifications of this distinction, we may note that what is ordinarily called guilt, or guilt feeling, in Freudian psychoanalysis is more properly speaking temptation, or temptation fear. As observed elsewhere (Mowrer, 1950), orthodox analytic theory really has no place in it (at least in the genesis of neurosis) for the phenomenon of guilt *per se*.

2). Note the assumption, in both places, that conscience, in order to qualify as such, must operate *in the absence* of the external authority or source of punishment, thus differentiating the resulting emotion from that of *shame*. In this context the reader will find it pertinent to examine a paper by Adams & Romney (1959) entitled "A Functional Analysis of Authority." Also pertinent, at least by title, but not yet available as this book goes to press are two contributions to the *Nebraska Symposium on Motivation for 1959:* Lewin & Baldwin's "Pride and Shame in Children" and Whiting's "Sorcery, Sin, and the Superego: A Cross-Cultural Study of Some Mechanisms of Social Control."

3). In the article by Ausubel (cited in Section VI), it is postulated that conscientiousness and guilt reactions are most readily established when the source of discipline is an individual on whom there is a felt dependence. It is noteworthy that this assumption, at least as a hypothesis, is under examination in the Harvard studies. As soon as the technical difficulties cited are overcome, we may expect some interesting experimental findings on this score.

4). Note the rather nice distinction that emerges in these studies between the type of disciplinary procedure that produces stable resistance to *temptation* and that which results in clear evidence of *guilt* reactions. Ideally, one might suppose that in the training of children, we should be more concerned with the former than the latter, since restraint rather than remorse, as such, is our objective. However, when, for whatever reason, restraint fails, do we not also wish the individual to be capable of remorse? As Solomon observes, it seems that that complex faculty which we call conscience in human beings represents *both* functions.

5). In an era in which a systematic effort has been made to eliminate punishment in education and human relations (and Hell in religion!) and to operate, at least nominally, solely on the basis of reward (and "love"), it is interesting that we seem to arrive at the conclusion that punishment is essential to the establishment of guilt capacity and "character." It might be chastening to members of the love-and-love-alone school of thought to try to set up conscience in puppies *without* punishment, although we hasten to add that punishment is more effective (presumptively) if love (dependence) is also present in the situation.

6). Note that in the Harvard researches, guilt and temptation reactions are tested with the trainer absent but *observing* (through the one-way vision window). Here we are reminded of the proverbial *watching* role of conscience and its symbolization as an *eye* or *eyes*. Undoubtedly one of the great bulwarks of conscience, as an internal agency of control, is the possibility of one's having been "seen," of being "found out" through insufficiently concealed *evidence*. (Cf. the paradoxical, but insightful, quip that conscience is "that inner voice which tells us when someone is watching.")

7). It is no accident that puppies have been used as subjects in the Harvard studies. In terms of its capacity for domestication, the dog, as we know, ranks very high. Certainly one would expect much less success in work of this kind with the Herring Gull or the Stickleback (Section II). Interestingly, the Harvard researchers report striking genetic differences in this capacity even among different breeds of dog. Perhaps, after all, there is a truly constitutional element in the making of a so-called constitutional psychopath (or liar).

8). Finally, though by no means exhausting the parallels and points of special interest here, we may note that the underlying theoretical assumptions are quite congruent with the views set forth in this volume and its companion under the rubric of "revised two-factor learning theory." The roles of hope and fear, and their controlling influence with respect to overt behavior, are easily identifiable; and it would not seem unlikely, if such experimentation were cleverly extended, that it might also bring out, at least inferentially, the role of imagery.

IX. Normal and Pathogenic Ways of Handling Human Guilt and Obligation

Despite the intricate elaboration of theory and the protracted nature of its therapy, Freudian psychoanalysis was predicated on an extremely simple assumption. It held, in essence, that the psychoneuroses occur because, as a child, the individual was too severely disciplined with respect to displays of aggression and of sexual interest and that, for reasons never made fully explicit, the resulting inhibitions could be undone only in the so-called transference relationship developed in analysis. The picture, supposedly, was therefore merely one of a failure of extinction of unrealistic fears and false guilts under ordinary conditions and of its successful occurrence under the extraordinary conditions provided by analysis (Mowrer, 1948; 1953c).

By contrast, the more traditional view had been that human beings sicken in mind and soul because of *real* guilt and its improper management. The Freudian view not only sharply reversed this assumption; to many it seemed to imply that guilt was, in fact, *never* "real"—and was not to be taken seriously even by normal persons. To those who did not live through the "debunking" era of the 1920's and early 30's, such a statement may seem extravagant; but it is documented by Boisen, in his 1936 book, as follows:

> This interjected remark of Dr. Myerson's is representative of a widespread attitude among psychiatrists and others of the humanistic scientists. They profess unconcern over the problem of right and wrong. Among them a prevalent point of view identifies the *normal* with the *average* and some even talk with condescending superiority about "the antiquated good-evil antithesis." . . . To be good is unusual and therefore abnormal. A prominent lecturer on mental health thus talks about eradicating the sense of guilt just as he would a vermiform appendix. By this he apparently means not that what we call sin is an anachronism, . . . but rather, if I understand him aright, that conscience itself is an outgrown appendix and ought to be subjected to the psychoanalytic scalpel (pp. 164–165).

That the psychoanalytic view could be easily restated in learning-theory terminology—the assumption of simple malconditioning and a special technique for extinction—was not, however, any guarantee of its validity. Animal experimentation has shown that, lacking at least occasional reinforcement, all fears move toward extinction (Mowrer, 1960, Chapters 11 and 12) and that "early experience" does not necessarily exert the fateful influence upon adult personality which Freud hypothesized (Stanley & Monkman, 1956; King, 1956b, 1957, and 1958; and Levine, 1957); and the results of educational ventures based upon analytic premises have also been far from reassuring (Aichhorn, 1936; Hoffer, 1945; Anna Freud, 1935). Even the therapeutic accomplishments of analysis have turned out to be far less impressive than was at first assumed, as leading analysts themselves now concede (Freud, 1937; Eysenck, 1952; Kubie, 1956). So it would appear that psychoanalytic premises are not only too simple; they are apparently basically unsound, in a way which no amount of proliferation or apology will remedy.

Gradually, it seems, we are returning to the older view that man is indeed a "sinner," in the sense of recurrently disregarding obligations and rupturing his relatedness, and is obsessed and tortured until he makes amends and redeems himself. The assumptions underlying this view, while admittedly more complex than the psychoanalytic ones, are nevertheless presumed to be consistent with and deducible from an adequate psychology of learning. Ausubel has suggested a logic for deriving conscience and guilt capacity; and we now are faced by the question of whether one can go still further with this type of analysis and find a radically effective "therapy."

One of the basic dilemmas that beset classical psychoanalysis was the assumption that fears, once established during socialization, would continue to exert their unrealistic inhibitory influence indefinitely unless extinguished in the transference relationship (see Dittes, 1957). Unless proper caution is observed, the alternative view just sketched may find itself in a similar predicament. Conscience, we now assume, is an internalized version of "the voice of the community"; but, once internalized, is it as autonomous as inhibitory fears were assumed to be? Or does conscience, in order to continually function, have to be supported and reinforced at least occasionally from without? Here Ausubel's discussion again is helpful.

Shame relies on external sanctions alone. Guilt relies on both internal and external sanctions. The latter sanctions consist of the presumed judgments of others regarding one's lapses with respect to moral obligations and the resulting self-depreciation vis-a-vis the group, as well as the customary social reprisals associated with the misdemeanors arousing guilt. In addition, feelings of guilt have external reference in that they acknowledge accountability for a moral offense against the group (p. 383).

Reinforcing most of the moral sanctions that we customarily assign to the domain of conscience is a parallel set of statutes and group pressures enforced by appropriate public reprisals. Even in cultures where moral obligations are highly internalized, we usually find a policeman on the corner giving a friendly nudge to sluggish consciences or a timely warning to impish consciences pondering a brief vacation from duty (p. 387).

Conscience, then, represents a firm social reality which is always *there*, in case conscience itself falters; and the manifest social purpose of conscience and value to the individual lie precisely in its ability to supply, in token form, the sanctions which must otherwise be applied, full force, by society. But no assumption of "functional autonomy" or inextinguishability is here implied. Conscience, as the internalized agent of organized society, constantly receives community support and endorsement and is thus normally perpetuated and recurrently strengthened. It is, however, possible for a human being to behave in such a way as to circumvent community reinforcement of conscience, and this fact provides a sound beginning for a theory of psychopathology.

In Fig. 10–10 appears a drawing which is designed to show, in broad outline, the nature of social interaction *through time*. Here individual I, at point t_1, performs some act R_x which impinges upon some one or more other persons, O; and O reacts with response R_y, which will impinge upon I at point t_2 in time *if* he is there.[10] Now, obviously,

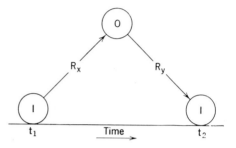

Fig. 10–10. Diagram of social action and reaction, through time. It is conjectured that personal normality or abnormality is largely a function of the expectations generated in I as a result of behavior R_x at t_1 concerning the probable nature of the response of O (R_y) at t_2.

if R_x has been a *good* act and one which is likely to evoke a favorable response from O, it is probable that I will be present at t_2. But suppose that R_x has been a disloyal, damaging, short-sighted act of some sort. I will anticipate an *un*favorable R_y reaction and will be reluctant to be "on the spot" when the "blow falls." In light of this conflict, I may simply not "show up." The wise, normal, and socially healthy individual, on the other hand, is likely to say: "Very well, I have it coming to me so will take my medicine. It may be good for me." By this he is implying that he is willing to submit to the *shame* of having his conscience (guilt capacity) reinforced. He admits having been "at fault," accepts punishment, makes restitution; and goes forth with a heightened resolution to "do better" in the future.

The techniques and strategies for trying to *avert* reinforcement of conscience are, of course, legion. The individual may appear at t_2 but deny act R_x. In short, he *lies*. Or he may admit that he performed R_x but attempt to rationalize, alibi, excuse himself. Here the troublesome question of *intent* arises. The individual may, also, simply "lay low," *hide*. Or, he may show up at t_2 but *defy* his accuser(s).[11] These courses of conduct are all familiar and, though hardly admirable, will

---

[10] The aptness of this kind of spatial analysis is indicated by the common expressions, "going straight" and "being crooked." And Selye (1956) has suggested that nothing so powerfully determines human happiness—and even health—as one's habitual tendency to generate, by his own behavior, an expectation of gratitude or resentment in others.

[11] Cf. the quip: "I deny the allegation and defy the allegator!"

still be perceived as "normal." Suppose, however, that I appears (or is presented) at t_2 but is manifestly "not all there." He apparently thinks and acts as if he is somewhere else. He does not answer questions, or answers them irrelevantly. His manner is "withdrawn," his speech and actions "bizarre." Such a person, we aptly say, is "off." And instead of sentencing him to a prison or other punishment, we say that surely he is *sick* and ought to be "hospitalized" and "treated."

There was a time, not too long ago, when the insane were *not* thought of as sick and were subjected to all manners of punitive and retaliatory measures. The memory of that era is still vivid enough to make us reluctant even to countenance the notion of culpability in any form. But the notion that insanity is an illness and can be treated without any reference to moral considerations has also led to disillusionment; and we are again being forced to explore the possibility that "mental illness" (of the manifestly functional varieties) is really *moral inadequacy* and that only *moral rehabilitation* can, in the final analysis, be therapeutically effective.

After he himself had sojourned for a time in "the wilderness of the lost" and then regained his sanity, Dr. Anton Boisen (1936) argued persuasively that insanity is a moral and spiritual crisis and that, as such, it can be successfully resolved only along moral and religious lines. Theologians gradually began to listen to Boisen, until today the nation's 350,000 clergymen have an outlook upon and interest in acute personality disturbance which contrasts pleasantly with the picture prevailing half a century ago. And it was Boisen, more than any other man, who was responsible for this change! However, it has only been within the last few years that the secular healing professions—psychiatry, clinical psychology, and social work—have begun to entertain this point of view. This trend is indicated, for example, by such books as *Progress in Psychotherapy* (Fromm-Reichmann & Moreno, 1956) and by the fact that many persons other than clergymen are now joining the recently established Academy of Religion and Mental Health. But perhaps the most dramatic and authentic evidence of all has recently come from a 34-year-old man who, at the time of writing, was residing on a closed ward in a mental hospital with a diagnosis of "paranoid schizophrenia." This document has recently been published in full elsewhere (Anonymous, 1958); but the following excerpts will suggest its general thesis and tenor:

> I propose that the motive force of schizophrenic reactions is *fear*, just as fear motivates, according to Freud, neurotic mechanisms—but with this difference: in the case of schizophrenia, the chronic fear is more properly

called terror, or concealed panic, being of the greatest intensity; and second, as is not the case in neurosis, the fear is conscious; third, the fear itself is concealed from other people, the motive of the concealment being fear. In neurosis a sexual or hostile drive, pointing to the future, is defended against. In schizophrenia, by my view, detection by others of a guilty deed, the detection pointing to the past, is defended against (pp. 2–3).

Motivated in the very first place by fear, the schizophrenic psychoses originate in a *break with sincerity*, and not in the classically assumed "break with reality." The patient's social appetite (an instinctive drive in primates, I believe), including love and respect for persons and society, is consciously anticathected or forsaken and ultimately repressed with the passage of time, since full satisfaction of sociality entails, more or less, communicative honesty, faith, and intimacy. Also, the tension set up in interpersonal intimacy by the withholding of emotionally important (although perhaps logically irrelevant) information causes unbearable pain. This repression of sociality accounts for the well-known "indifference" of schizophrenics. But if safety can be achieved by means of "perjury" alone without great discomfort, then no further defenses are adopted. Perjury is here defined as avoiding telling the whole truth and nothing but the truth. If, for many possible reasons, perjury is not an adequate and comfortable guarantee of safety, as it usually is not, then "cutting" of social contacts is progressively pursued—all in the interest of safety in respect to avoiding possible punishment. Suppression and repression of the social appetite or instinct is thus central to schizophrenia. I believe that repression of sexual and hostile drive is *not* primary in schizophrenia, although it is secondary, as will be explained further on (p. 9).

So what is a schizophrenic? In brief, he is a terrified, conscience-stricken crook, who has repressed his interest in people, unavowedly insincere and uncooperative, struggling against unconscious sexual perversion. He is of no mean Thespian ability. And his favorite Commandment is that which one nowadays facetiously calls the Eleventh Commandment, "Thou shalt not get caught."

Attempts to expose him may only drive him further "underground." But a knowledge of his true nature will surely lead, someday, to somebody's discovering a sure, quick, effective and enduring cure (p. 40).

Here is a thoroughly *behavioral* interpretation of so-called mental illness and one which should lend itself to restatement in terms of learning theory. In brief, it holds that the first step in psychopathology is *mis*behavior, which is then compounded by flight from external punishment and conscience strengthening. However, this avoidance strategy is a very costly one in that it drives the individual out of society, physically (as, for example, in vagrancy and hermitism) or psychically (in insanity). In either case, the individual is not responsibly *there* when censure falls or obligations "come due." Simple retribution seems unlikely to reform either the insane or those somewhat less complicated "offenders" whom we do not hesitate to call delinquents or criminals.

But experience also show that excusing the insane as sick is no more justifiable than would be a similar practice (which has sometimes been urged) with respect to criminals. This we know: The "redemption" of wayward individuals is never an easy or simple process. And this fact should be a constant challenge to learning theorists and a warning to those who would propose a spuriously easy and premature solution. In a volume which will appear soon, under the editorship of Eglash (1960), the timely suggestion is made that ordinary criminals are more readily corrected and transformed by *restitution* than by retribution. Perhaps there is a lesson here also for those who are concerned with the insane: but it is a lesson which can be logically assimilated and wisely applied only if we recognize the insane as sinful, rather than "merely sick." While such a judgment may appear harsh, it is also hopeful and may well deliver us from the cul-de-sac into which the concept of illness has here taken us.[12]

X. Dissociation of Image and Affect—The Pathology and Hygiene of Thought

In the preceding section, it is intimated that in psychopathology there may be a larger element of volition and individual accountability than commonly supposed and that the individual is really "all right" except for his deliberately perverse conduct. The time has now come to make a partial correction. The psychotic individual and even the neurotic is obviously not simply malingering, and his disorders of action are usually accompanied, or at least followed, by corresponding disturbances of thought and feeling. Our earlier discussion gives some understanding of the interpersonal and broadly social dynamics of behavior pathology. What can we now say about the pathology of thought?

In Chapter 6 brief reference is made to the fact that, in order for an individual to "know what it is all about," a conditioned stimulus must arouse not only the appropriate affect but also a proper image or memory of the unconditioned stimulus. If the affect occurs but the image does not, we have the prototype of that "disproportionality of affect" which is said to be the hallmark of psychopathology. Here the individual has feelings—often in the nature of fears—which do not seem to be "related to anything." But probably the more apt statement is that such emotions are not disproportionate but *dissociated*. How can such dissociation occur?

---

[12] Recent papers by Manis (1955) and Syz (1957) typify the diverse ways in which this altered point of view is today being expressed and validated. See also Shoben (1957) and Mowrer (1959a and 1960a).

Freud wrote at length on the concept of *repression*, whereby the ego, under the sway of a too harsh superego, supposedly denied certain "evil" impulses (of sex and aggression) access to consciousness and motor expression. Perhaps, alternatively, the picture is one in which the individual, in an attempt to spare himself the anguish of guilt and fear of punishment, consciously or unconsciously suppresses the *memories* that arouse such feelings. For a time, perhaps quite a long time, such a strategy may work: by simply refusing to "think about" those events which make him experience guilt—Sullivan (1945) called it "selective inattention"—the individual remains untroubled. But then, being untroubled, he may continue in old errors, thereby confounding his guilt; or realistic pressures may increase, more heavily taxing his inner resources. The result, very likely, is that "old affects" now recur, despite the continued cognitive dissociation, and the individual feels he is "losing his mind" (cf. Chapter 5, Section XII, and Chapter 7, Section X).

If this picture is the true one, psychotherapy must take a course rather different from that of orthodox psychoanalysis. The latter has typically tried to help the patient discover the denied and rejected *impulses* which, in pressing for recognition and gratification, presumably make the individual anxious or depressed. Here the assumption was that the individual has not *done* anything wrong, he merely *wants* to; and since the thing he wants to do is not really wrong, the path to recovery, at least in theory, is straightforward. By the alternative hypothesis, what is "repressed"? One possible answer is, nothing. It seems entirely likely that in some instances the individual remains, throughout the course of his disorder, entirely conscious of the source of his guilt and fear of punishment (cf. Section VI). Here the therapeutic task is not one of interpretation or "making the unconscious conscious" but instead that of somehow persuading the individual to confess his misconduct, responsibly face the consequences, and make whatever restitution is realistic and practical (Mowrer, 1959a, 1960a).

In other cases, however, real dissociation may have occurred and require special efforts to undo. Certain of the psychoanalytic techniques (e.g., free association), but now employed in a different over-all theoretical framework, may be useful here; but our greatest immediate contribution can be made by means of a more explicit consideration of the process whereby dissociation occurs in the first place.

Let us begin by imagining what may be termed a *failure* of thought. The individual has a problem, perhaps a very urgent and important one, which he thinks and thinks about, but to no avail. There just doesn't seem to *be* an answer! Every possibility he considers is unpromising. All the feedbacks from his tentative, token, symbolic processes are "negative." On the basis of already enunciated principles, what might we expect? As we know (Mowrer, 1960, Chapter 11), any activity which is persistently unrewarding (frustrating) or punishing tends to *extinguish;* so, in the present instance, we would expect the individual, eventually, to just *stop thinking.* Suppose, for example, in the Rawin set discussed in Section III of Chapter 6, that the little "head" (cup) turned and turned and issued orders for the "body" of the apparatus to move now this way, now that, but that the discrepancy or off-target condition (drive state) could not be eliminated. The *machine* would presumably not "care." It would just keep on trying, until it wore out. But *living organisms* are different. They get tired, discouraged, "mad," and tend to stop unavailing activity. This does not, of course, surprise us. The more puzzling question is: What sort of problem could prove to be so urgent and yet so insoluble that the organism will eventually quit trying?

Revised two-factor learning theory suggests that behavior, in general, is made up of *four* elements: approach, avoidance, action, and inhibition. And usually one of these types of adjustment, or some combination thereof, will deal quite adequately with any sort of problem situation. What, then, would be a sufficient cause for an organism to "give up" its problem-solving operations, particularly in a situation where the individual's biological existence is not in jeopardy. If, for example, an organism were in any environment where absolutely nothing edible was to be had, it would eventually get weak, abandon activity, and just "lie down and die." But here our concern is with a different but, alas, not uncommon phenomenon. It is the spectacle of a human being who has "given up" and "quit," ostensibly in the midst of plenty. In short, our problem is that of human psychopathology.

The late Harry Stack Sullivan was fond of saying that, in his long career as a psychiatrist, he had observed that *normal* people deal with a problem situation in one of three ways: they get *on* with it, they get *out* of it, or they get *help* with it. Now getting "on" with a problem means, in our terms, action and approach; and getting "out" means avoidance and inhibition. What about the matter of "help"? This approach to the solution of a problem clearly takes us into the realm of *social psychology* (cf. Sections I–IX).

With these premises established, we are now in a position to state the problem more precisely. Human beings, of all living organisms, are the only species in which psychopathology is endemic. Something like it may be artificially induced in animals, but it is not "natural" to them. Man, on the other hand, is *naturally* disposed to "mental disease." Why? The answer must satisfy two conditions: It must refer to some problem which animals do not normally experience and which man encounters commonly and for which, also commonly, he does not know *how* to seek help. What can such a problem be? There is, apparently, only one answer: It is the problem of *guilt.* Guilt is *not* the kind of problem for which one readily and naively seeks "help," for "help" here would involve publicizing a secret; and this seems not like "help" at all, but rather a step which makes matters *worse.* In fact, the total energies of a guilty individual tend to be directed toward concealment rather than confession. And whose "help" does he need if the inviolate preservation of a *secret* is his main objective. "The less *said* the better!"

It is, presumably, in this context that an individual may conclude that his problem is insoluble, that normal thinking is useless, and may start using his mental powers for purely defensive purposes. Now he is faced by a double danger: the threat of punishment from without and the threat of self-punishment from within. And it need not surprise us if both action and thought are disarticulated from the real world (loss of "contact") and become preoccupied with an inner struggle. The question of the most efficient method of helping an individual find his way out of such an emotional morass is still an open one. But if the correct logic of his predicament could be presented to him, it ought to be possible for patient and therapist, working together, to move little by little from guilt and confusion to confession, expiation, and peace.[13]

We now have what is perhaps a fairly comprehensive understanding of the circumstances under which thought processes may become

---

[13] It should be noted that, in the very act of getting into such a predicament, the individual has cut himself off from established cultural solutions to human problems. Everyone has had the experience of long struggling with some problem and then finding how really simple and rather obvious its solution may be—when someone else shows it to us! "Now why didn't *I* think of that," we say. Which only goes to show that when it comes to the original solving of problems, even the brightest of us are comparatively slow and "stupid." And it is only by virtue of the fact that most of the things we know have been discovered and passed on to us *by others* that we ordinarily appear to be so clever and so competent. Therefore, when an individual stops interacting freely and openly with others and "goes into business for himself," he faces some formidable tasks. Now his is indeed a "private world" in which he is, of necessity, *alone* and wherein he soon becomes lost and helpless. The task of therapy, insofar as it *can* be performed by others, must therefore involve the strategy of somehow inducing the "lost" individual to come back into "contact" with society so that he can again share in and profit from accumulated wisdom and proven practices.

pathological; and we have at least a general notion of how they can, once again, become more normal and wholesome. What can be said about the *hygiene* of thought, i.e., the *prevention* of disorders of the kind already referred to? Folklore, the world over, is full of suggestions in this connection; but perhaps the most systematic attempt to encourage a healthy thought life involves what is commonly known as *meditation* and prayerful *receptiveness*. In even the most normal of persons, memories and obligations sometimes "get lost in the shuffle" of the day's activities; and a "quiet time," regularly observed, provides an opportunity for them to re-emerge into consciousness. Just as the "sick" individual flees from his memories and dreads intimate communication with himself, the healthy person may find pleasure and practical gain from a daily period of "self-examination" in which he ties together the fragmented ends and tatters of his experience, and from which he emerges with *plans* (cf. Chapter 6) for orderly and responsible behavior.

XI. The Uniqueness of the Human "Condition"—Some Existential Issues

Throughout this book and the antecedent one, the attempt has been always to discuss scientific problems in *historical context*. Otherwise, much of the research and theorizing that we have had to examine would appear meaningless or even absurd. Now, in bringing this chapter— and this work as a whole—to a close, we must look at yet another problem in its historical setting.

Psychology, a century ago, was not an independent science or discipline. It was hardly even a word. Much of what is now implied by the term was included under "moral philosophy" and theology; and it was only gradually and often painfully that psychology, as we know it today, became differentiated from related areas. But now, there are many large departments of psychology in colleges and universities the world over, national and even international psychological associations flourish, and the field is also firmly established in the popular mind. Nevertheless, the fact remains that this independent existence was won at the price of deliberately severing some very natural relationships and arbitrarily restricting the range of problems with which the psychologist, as scientist, should be concerned.

No psychologist, as an individual, has ever lost sight of the fact of his own mortality, i.e., the inevitability of his ultimate death; and this fact unavoidably colors the whole course and meaning of human existence. But psychologists, in their *official* role, have been strangely silent in this connection—and the reason is not far to seek. One of the major functions of religion and ethical philosophy has been to help man meet his existential perplexities; and in their attempt to establish and preserve their professional identity, psychologists have tended to ignore not only the traditional solutions but the very problem itself. Typical is the remark of a young clinical psychologist: "Yes, it is certainly true that persons in psychotherapy often speak of death and its personal implications for them, but at this point I keep quiet or else just 'reflect' what they have said."

Within recent decades there has been a tendency to assume that preoccupation with the problem of death is a sign of "morbidity" and that it is of no concern to an emotionally healthy individual. It is indeed true that when life itself is going well, death often seems remote, unreal; and that it looms largest in our thoughts when we are physically ill or emotionally troubled. But death is also a problem for the physically and emotionally healthy person; and one of the reasons that contemporary men and women are again turning to religion in such great numbers seems to be that here death and death fear are recognized as being as normal as they are common.

Thomas Aquinas begins his book, *My Way of Life*, with this statement of what is in many ways *the* human problem:

> The road that stretches before the feet of a man is a challenge to his heart long before it tests the strength of his legs. Our destiny is to run to the edge of the world and beyond, off into the darkness: sure for all our blindness, secure for all our helplessness, strong for all our weakness, gaily in love for all the pressure on our hearts (p. 1).

To what extent can "learning theory," as we now know it, contribute to a better understanding and a more courageous confrontation of this enigma? It is perhaps premature to reply, "Not at all," for this is a matter to which most learning theorists, as such, have given scant attention. Perhaps new and profound insights will indeed be forthcoming here—a possibility to which we must not entirely close our minds. But so long as the investigation of learning mechanisms is tied to the infrahuman organism, just so long, it appears, will we fail to encounter the crisis which has now been with man since the dawn of recorded history—and probably for thousands of years before that.

And what has man done with this problem? With other living organisms he shares many, many characteristics; truly he is a part of the Animal Kingdom. But only man is *religious;* and this characteristic reflects, specifically and uniquely, his efforts at "salvation," following

Adam's "fall." Or, should we say, following man's *rise* to the point of being god-like in his intelligence and awareness, but still all too human in his mortality? (See Fromm, 1955.)

How, then, does religion cope with this problem? It has, for one thing, offered man the hope of survival and immortality in *another world*. However sympathetic and reverent one may be toward this hope, it is not easy to see how psychology, with its present concepts and methods, can articulate with it. That is to say, it cannot give us *evidence* of the validity of this expectation. This is literally a metaphysical solution; and psychology, as science, deals only with the palpable, or at least the observable.

But there is another aspect of religion, the *social* aspect, with which psychology can, if it chooses, articulate. Here the etymology of the word itself is instructive. It comes, we find, from the Latin word, *religio,* meaning "to hold back, bind fast," and from *ligare,* meaning "to bind," the latter giving us such words as *ligament* and *ligature,* meaning a fastening, bandage, or bond (*Webster's Unabridged Dictionary*).

And just how does religion, that "blest tie that binds," operate? It ties, binds, relates man to God and his fellowmen and in so doing *holds back* the intolerable loneliness and despair that otherwise may arise from the fact of his finitude (Tillich, 1953). Due to man's "disobedience," God has withdrawn from his sight, so that man may know Him only indirectly, through prayer and other forms of worship; but the opportunity for loving service to other human beings is tangible and ever-present. How interesting it is that after the account of man's Fall in Genesis comes the story of Cain and Abel, from which we learn that man can survive physically *and psychologically,* only if he becomes his "brother's keeper," concerned, compassionate, generous, helpful, related.

In the pursuit of relatedness man is counseled to do many things which, from a biological frame of reference, sound paradoxical. He is told that he does not "live by bread alone," that he must "turn the other cheek" and "go the second mile." He must be reconciled with his neighbor before the sun goes down; and he must give generously and be a doer of good works. He must love his neighbor as himself and —most enigmatic of all—must "lose himself to find himself."

Psychoanalysis, while under Freud's own leadership, was not only implacable in its opposition to religion as practice; it even denied its implicit premises. Death was not the ultimate test of human character and courage; man was said to have an "instinct" *for* it. But, from the beginning, this doctrine was questioned by otherwise faithful followers of Freud; and among latter-day neo-Freudians one finds many taking a position that seems much closer to the "illusion" which Freud thought had such an unpromising future than to Freud's own conjectures. For example, in Erich Fromm's book, *The Sane Society* (1955), we find this poetic and insightful passage:

> The aim of life is to live it intensely, to be fully born, to be fully awake. To emerge from the ideas of infantile grandiosity into the conviction of one's real though limited strength; to be able to accept the paradox that every one of us is the most important thing there is in the universe—and at the same time not more important than a fly or a blade of grass. To be able to love life, and yet to accept death without terror; to tolerate uncertainty about the most important questions with which life confronts us— and yet to have faith in our thought and feeling, inasmuch as they are truly ours. To be able to be alone, and at the same time one with a loved person, with every brother on this earth, with all that is alive; to follow the voice of our conscience, the voice that calls us to ourselves, yet not to indulge in self hate when the voice of conscience was not loud enough to be heard and followed. The mentally healthy person is the person who lives by love, reason and faith, who respects life, his own and that of his fellow man (p. 204).

If, in the present book, learning theory appears to have achieved some degree of maturity at the level of the "animal model," we must remain modest indeed in face of the larger, infinitely more challenging problem: that of showing the continuity, if continuity there be, between those psychological processes which are common of man and beast and those capacities and concerns which we see only at the human level. It may be that the precepts which have been worked out over the ages for an abundant life of the spirit can be derived, with further analysis, from principles that hold for biological adjustment, thus resolving the numerous paradoxes previously mentioned. But until this is done, our faith that it *can* be done must be tentative; and the assumption that there is really no problem here is one which, however justifiable as a temporary expedient, cannot be indefinitely held by a science that aspires to a comprehensive knowledge of man.

Bibliography and Author Index

Aamodt, Marjorie S. (See Stanley & Aamodt, 1954).

Adams, D. K. (1929) Experimental studies of adaptive behavior in cats. *Comp. Psychol. Monogr.*, **6**, No. 27 [226].

Adams, J. S., & Romney, A. K. (1959) A functional analysis of authority. *Psychol. Rev.*, **66**, 234–251 [405].

Adelman, H. M. (See Maatsch, Adelman, & Denny, 1954).

Adrian, E. D., *et al.* (1954) *Brain mechanisms and consciousness.* Springfield, Ill.: Charles C. Thomas [286].

Aichhorn, A. (1936) *Wayward youth.* New York: The Viking Press [407].

Akhtar, Mohammed (1959a) Preliminary studies on the paradoxical "attractiveness" of danger signals in rats. (Unpublished research report) [192–196].

—— (1959b) The effect of intermittent punishment during acquisition of a habit upon subsequent inhibition thereof by means of consistent punishment. (Unpublished research report) [345].

Allport, F H. (1924) *Social psychology.* Cambridge, Mass.: The Riverside Press [90, 102].

—— (1955) *Theories of perception and the concept of structure.* New York: John Wiley & Sons, Inc. [187].

Allport, G W. (1935) Attitudes. *In Handbook of social psychology.* Worcester, Mass.: Clark University Press [25].

Amatruda, C. S. (See Gesell & Amatruda, 1947).

Ames, Louise B. (1946) The development of the sense of time in the young child. *J. Genet. Psychol.*, **68**, 97–125 [136].

Amsel, A. (1958) The role of frustrative nonreward in noncontinuous reward situations. (Mimeographed paper) [19, 259].

—— (See Wilson, Weiss, & Amsel, 1955).

Anonymous (1958) A new theory of schizophrenia. *J. Abn. & Soc. Psychol.*, **57**, 226–236 [410].

Applezweig, M. H. (1951) Response potential as a function of effort. *J. Comp. Physiol. Psychol.*, **44**, 225–235 [181].

Aristotle [231, 353].

Ashby, W. R. (1952) *Design for a brain.* New York: John Wiley & Sons, Inc. [183, 185, 222, 270, 273, 276–277].

Atkinson, J. W. (1957) Motivational determinants of risk-taking behavior. *Psychol. Rev.*, **64**, 359–372 [318].

—— (See McClelland, Atkinson, Clark, & Lowell, 1953).

Atkinson, R. C. (See Estes, Burke, Atkinson, & Frankmann, 1957).

Austin, G. A. (1953) Tolman's interpretation of vicarious trial and error. *Psychol. Rev.*, **60**, 117–122 [215].

—— (See Bruner, Goodnow, & Austin, 1956).

Ausubel, D. P. (1955) Relationship between shame and guilt in the socializing process. *Psychol. Rev.*, **62**, 378–390 [391–395, 405, 408].

Bacon, F. [231].

Bain, A. [209].

Baker, C. H. (1959) Towards a theory of vigilance. *Canad. J. Psychol.*, **13**, 35–42 [201].

Balas, R. F. (See Hare, Borgatta, & Balas, 1955).

Baldwin, A. L. (See Lewin & Baldwin, 1959).

Baldwin, J. M. (1906) *Thought and things* (Vol. 1.) New York: The Macmillan Co. [248].

—— [114].

Bally, C. (1936) *Le langage et la vie.* Paris, In *An essay on man* by E. Cassirer, 1944, New Haven: Yale University Press [158].

Barber, T. X. (1959) The "eidetic image" and "hallucinatory" behavior: A suggestion for further research. *Psychol. Bull.*, **56**, 236–239 [205].

Bard, P. (1934) On emotional expression after decortication with some remarks on certain theoretical views. *Psychol. Rev.*, **41**, 309–329, 424–449 [255].

Barker, R. (1942) An experimental study of the resolution of conflict by children: Time elapsing and amount of vicarious trial-and-error behavior occurring. In *Studies in personality* (Q. McNemar & M. A. Merrill, eds.). New York: McGraw-Hill [215].

Bartlett, F. (1958) *Thinking, an experimental and social study.* London: Geo. Allen & Unwin, Ltd. [208, 216, 250].

—— [271].

Bartley, S. H. (1957) *Principles of perception* (G. Murphy, ed.). New York: Harper & Bros. [187].

Bavelas, A. (See Seashore & Bavelas, 1941).

Beach, F. A. (1944) Responses of captive alligators to auditory stimulation. *Amer. Nat.*, **78**, 481–505 [127].

Beach, F. A., & Jaynes, J. (1954) Effects of early experience upon the behavior of animals. *Psychol. Bull.*, **51**, 239–263 [374].

Beberman, M. [242].

Beberman, M., Vaughn, H. E., *et al.* (1959) *High school mathematics, Unit 1* (Teachers' Edition). Urbana: University of Illinois Press [243].

Berlyne, D. E. (1958) The influence of complexity and novelty in visual stimuli on orienting responses. *J. Exp. Psychol.*, **55**, 289–296 [191].

Bertrand, J. [307].

Bigelow, J. H. [268].

Bilodeau, E. A. (1952) Statistical versus intuitive confidence. *Amer. J. Psychol.*, **65**, 271–277 [294, 310].

Bindra, D. (See Thompson & Bindra, 1952).

Bingham, W. E., & Griffiths, W. J. (1952) The effect of different environments during infancy on adult behavior in the rat. *J. Comp. Physiol. Psychol.*, **45**, 307–312 [367].

Birch, H. G., & Bitterman, M. E. (1949) Reinforcement and learning: The process of sensory integration. *Psychol. Rev.*, **56**, 292–308 [168].

—— (1951) Sensory integration and cognitive theory. *Psychol. Rev.*, **58**, 355–361 [287].

Birge, Jane S. (1941) *Verbal responses in transfer.* Ph.D. dissertation, Yale University, New Haven, Conn. [62].

Bitterman, M. E. (See Birch & Bitterman, 1949).

—— (See Birch & Bitterman, 1951).

Bitterman, M. E., Feddersen, W. E., & Tyler, D. W. (1953) Secondary reinforcement and the discrimination hypothesis. *Amer. J. Psychol.*, **66**, 456–464 [19].

Bitterman, M. W., Reed, P. C., & Kubala, A. L. (1953) The strength of sensory preconditioning. *J. Exp. Psychol.*, **56**, 178–182 [168].

Bixenstine, V. E. (1956) Secondary drive as a neutralizer of time in integrative problem solving. *J. Comp. Physiol. Psychol.*, **49**, 161–166 [149].

Black, A. H. [399–400].

Blanshard, B. (1940) *The nature of thought.* V. I. New York: The Macmillan Co. [250].

Blanton, R. L. (See Lipman & Blanton, 1957).

Blodgett, H. C. (1929) The effect of the introduction of reward upon the maze performance of rats. *Univ. Calif. Publ. Psychol.*, **4**, 113–134 [30–34, 47, 49–52].

Bloomfield, L. (1933) *Language.* New York: Henry Holt & Co. [119, 121–123, 141].

Boder, D. P. (1949) *I did not interview the dead.* Urbana: University of Illinois Press [393].

Bodmer, F. (1944) *The loom of language.* New York: W. W. Norton & Co. [86].

Bogartz, W. (See Maltzman, Brooks, Bogartz, & Summers, 1958).

Boisen, A. T. (1936) *The exploration of the inner world.* New York: Harper & Bros. [392–393, 407, 410].

Bolles, R. (See Petrinovich & Bolles, 1957).

Bolles, R., & Messick, S. (1958) Statistical utility in experimental inference. *Psychol. Rep.*, **4**, 223–227 [294, 315, 323–325].

Boole, G. (1854) *An investigation of the laws of thought.* New York: Dover Publications, Inc. [294].

Boren, J. J. (See Sidman & Boren, 1957).

Borgatta, E. F. (See Hare, Borgatta, & Balas, 1955).

Boring, E. G. (1929) *A history of experimental psychology.* New York: D. Appleton-Century [167].

Borne, R. (See Noble & Borne, 1940).

Boulding, K. E. (1956) *The image.* Ann Arbor: University of Michigan Press [vii, 165, 171, 180].

Bousefield, W. A. (1959) The significance of partial response identities for the problem of meaning. (Unpublished paper, APA symposium, Cincinnati) [57].

Brady, J. V. (1957) A comparative approach to the experimental analysis of emotional behavior. In *Experimental psychopathology* (Hoch & Zubin, eds.) New York: Grune & Stratton, Inc. [255].

Brand, H., Woods, P. J., & Sakoda, J. M. (1956) Anticipation of reward as a function of partial reinforcement. *J. Exp. Psychol.*, **52**, 18–22 [336].

Brazier, Mary A. B. (1954) The action of anaesthetics on the nervous system with special reference to the brain stem reticular system. In *Brain mechanisms and consciousness*, Springfield, Ill.: Charles C. Thomas [255].

Breed, F. S. (1911) The development of certain instincts and habits in chicks. *Behav. Monogr.*, **1**, 1–75 [102].

Bremer, F. (1954) The neurophysiological problem of sleep. In *Brain mechanisms and consciousness* (J. F. DelaFresnaye, ed.). Springfield, Ill.: Charles C. Thomas [255].

Bridgman, Laura [157].

Brogden, W. J. (1939) Sensory preconditioning. *J. Exp. Psychol.*, **25**, 323–332 [168].

Brooks, L. O. (See Maltzman, Brooks, Bogartz, & Summers, 1958).

Brown, J. S. (1942) Factors determining conflict reactions in difficult discrimination. *J. Exp. Psychol.*, **31**, 272–292 [215].

Brown, R. W. (1955) *Untersuchungen zur Onomatopoiie Language* (A review). *Language*, **31**, 84–91 [96].

———— (1958a) The semantic differential outgrows infancy: Is a boulder sweet or sour? (a review). *Cont. Psychol.*, **3**, 113–115 [160].

———— (1958b) *Words and things.* Glencoe, Ill.: The Free Press [152–154, 159, 173, 257].

Bruner, J. S. (1959) A decade of "New Look" perception: A symposium. *Amer. Psychol.*, **14**, 379 [199].

Bruner, J. S., & Goodman, C. C. (1947) Value and need as organizing factors in perception. *J. Abn. & Soc. Psychol.*, **42**, 33–44 [197].

Bruner, J. S., Goodnow, Jacqueline J., & Austin, G. A. (1956) *A study of thinking.* New York: John Wiley & Sons, Inc. [241, 337].

Brunswik, E. (1939) Probability as a determiner of rat behavior. *J. Exp. Psychol.*, **25**, 175–197 [335, 344].

———— (1955) Representative design and probabilistic theory in a functional psychology. *Psychol. Rev.*, **62**, 193–217 [331, 339, 345].

———— (See Tolman & Brunswik, 1935).

Brutten, M. (See Myklebust & Brutten, 1953).

Bugelski, B. R., Coyer, R. A., & Rogers, W. A. (1952) A criticism of pre-acquisition and pre-extinction of expectancies. *J. Exp. Psychol.*, **44**, 27–30 [59].

Bühler, Charlotte (1930) *The first year of life.* New York: John Day Co. [136].

Bühler, K. (1930) *The mental devolopment of the child.* New York: Harcourt, Brace & Co. [136].

Bunch, M. E. (1958) The concept of motivation. *J. Gen. Psychol.*, **58**, 189–205 [290].

Burke, C. J. (See Estes, Burke, Atkinson, & Frankmann, 1957).

Bush, R. R., & Mosteller, F. (1951) A mathematical model for simple learning. *Psychol. Rev.*, **58**, 313–323 [337].

Butler, C. G., & Free, J. B. (1952) The behavior of worker honeybees at the hive entrance. *Behavior*, **4**, 262–292 [379].

Campbell, D. T. (1956a) Perception as substitute trial and error. *Psychol. Rev.,* **63**, 330–342 [2, 183–185].

—— (1956b) Adaptive behavior from random response. *Behav. Sci.,* **1**, 105–110 [2, 260].

Cannon, W. B. (1932) *The wisdom of the body.* New York: W. W. Norton & Co. [275].

Cardan, J. [295].

Carpenter, C. R. (1934) A field study of the behavior and social relations of howling monkeys. *Comp. Psychol. Monogr.,* **10**, 1–168 [384–385].

—— (1952) *Social behavior of nonhuman primates.* State College, Penn.: Pennsylvania State University [381–386].

—— (1953) A theoretical orientation for instructional film research. *Audio-Visual Communication Rev.,* **1**, 38–52 [142].

Carroll, J. B. (1953) *The study of language.* Cambridge: Harvard University Press [124, 142, 160, 165].

Cason, H. (1936) Sensory conditioning. *J. Exp. Psychol.,* **19**, 572–591 [166].

—— (See Trowbridge & Cason, 1932).

Cassirer, E. (1923) *Philosophie der symbolischen Formen.* Berlin: B. Cassier, 1923–29 [158].

—— (1944) *An essay on man.* New Haven: Yale University Press [vii, 87, 96, 121, 133, 142, 156–157, 160, 164].

Chance, M. R. A. (See Grant & Chance, 1958).

Chevigny, H. (1946) *My eyes have a cold nose.* New Haven: Yale University Press [374, 394].

Chomsky, N. (1959) Verbal behavior (a review). *Language,* **35**, 26–58 [160].

Church, R. M. (1959) Emotional reactions of rats to the pain of others. *J. Comp. Physiol. Psychol.,* **52**, 132–134 [115].

—— [399].

Clark, R. A. (See McClelland, Atkinson, Clark, & Lowell, 1953).

Clark, R. K. (See Powers, McFarland, & Clark, 1957).

Coate, W. B. (1956) Weakening of conditioned bar-pressing by prior extinction of its subsequent discriminated operant. *J. Comp. Physiol. Psychol.,* **49**, 135–138 [59].

Coburn, H. E. (1952) The brain analogy: A discussion. *Psychol. Rev.,* **59**, 453–460 [332].

Cofer, C. H. (See Foley & Cofer, 1943).

Cofer, C. N. (1957) Reasoning as an associative process: III. The role of verbal responses in problem solving. *J. Gen. Psychol.,* **57**, 55–68 [56, 239].

Cole, Marie-Louise W. (See Hunt, Cole, & Reis, 1958).

Collias, N. E. (1944) Aggressive behavior among vertebrate animals. *Physiol. Zool.,* **17**, 83–123 [379].

Conrad, D. G. (See Muenzinger & Conrad, 1953).

Coombs, C. H. (See Thrall, Coombs, & Davis, 1954).

Coppock, H. W. (1954) Stimuli preceding electric shock can acquire positive reinforcing properties. *J. Comp. Physiol. Psychol.,* **47**, 109–113 [191].

Coppock, W. J. (1958) Pre-extinction in sensory preconditioning. *J. Exp. Psychol.,* **55**, 213–219 [168].

Cornsweet, J. C. (See Riggs, Ratliff, Cornsweet, & Cornsweet, 1953).

Cornsweet, T. N. (See Riggs, Ratliff, Cornsweet, & Cornsweet, 1953).

Cotton, J. W. (See Lewis & Cotton, 1958).

Courtney, P. D. (1949) Identification and learning: A theoretical analysis. Ph.D. dissertation, Harvard University [90, 141].

Cox, Catherine M. (1928) The intelligence factor in the solution of space problems with the two story maze. *Amer. J. Psychol.,* **40**, 524–561 [280].

Coyer, R. A. (See Bugelski, Coyer, & Rogers, 1952).

Crannell, C. W. (1940) The effect of equal distribution of runs on "insight" performance in rats. *J. Psychol.,* **9**, 311–321 [238].

Crawford, M. P. (1937) The cooperative solving of problems by young chimpanzees. *Comp. Psychol. Monogr.,* **14**, 1–88 [360–362].

—— (1941) The cooperative solving by chimpanzees of problems requiring serial responses to color cues. *J. Soc. Psychol.,* **13**, 259–280 [360–362].

Cronbach, Lee J. [294].

Crutchfield, R. S. (See Postman & Crutchfield, 1952).

Culbertson, J. T. (1960) *The mind of robots.* (To be published) [292].

Cutler, R. L. (See McConnell, Cutler, & McNeil, 1958).

D'Amato, M. R. (See Kendler, Pliskoff, D'Amato, & Katz, 1957).

Damm, V. (See Gruber, Fink, & Damm, 1957).

Darby, C. L., & Riopelle, A. J. (1959) Observational learning in the rhesus monkey. *J. Comp. Physiol. Psychol.,* **52**, 94–98 [192].

Darwin, C. (1873) *The expression of the emotions in man and animals.* New York: D. Appleton-Century [90, 127–128].

—— (1885) *The descent of man.* New York: Humboldt [127].

—— [2, 295–296, 298–300, 306, 308, 321–322].

Dashiell, J. F. (1938) Part V of symposium on law of effect. *Psychol. Rev.,* **45**, 212–214 [188].

—— (1949) *Fundamentals of general psychology* (3rd ed.). New York: Houghton Mifflin Co. [215].

Davie, M. R. (See Sumner, Keller, & Davie, 1928).

Davis, J. D. (See Grice & Davis, 1958).

Davis, R. L. (See Thrall, Coombs, & Davis, 1954).

Davitz, J. R., & Mason, D. J. (1955) Socially facilitated reduction of a fear response in rats. *J. Comp. Physiol. Psychol.,* **48**, 149–151 [364, 366–367].

Deese, J. (1951) The extinction of a discrimination without performance of a choice response. *J. Comp. Physiol. Psychol.,* **44**, 362–366 [59].

—— (1952) *The psychology of learning.* New York: McGraw-Hill [188].

—— (1955) Some problems in the theory of vigilance. *Psychol. Rev.,* **62**, 359–368 [189].

DeLaguna, Grace (1927) *Speech: Its function and development.* New Haven: Yale University Press [81, 120, 135].

DeMartino, M. F. (See Stacey & DeMartino, 1958).

Dembo, Tamara (See Lewin, Dembo, Festinger, & Sears, 1944).

DeMeré, Chevalier [295].

De Morgan [353].

Denny, M. R. (See Maatsch, Adelman, & Denny, 1954).

De Poncins, G. (1949) *Eskimos.* New York: Hastings House [190].

Desiderato, O. (1956) The interaction of several variables in latent learning. *J. Exp. Psychol.,* **52**, 244–250 [50].

Dewey, J. (1896) The reflex arc concept in psychology. *Psychol. Rev.*, **3**, 357–370 [1, 178, 180, 284, 286].

—— [249].

Dicarlo, L. M. (1958) The effect of hearing one's own voice among children with impaired hearing. Reprint No. 706. Washington, D. C.: The Volta Bureau [84].

Dilthey, W. [348].

Dinsmoor, J. A. (1950) A quantitative comparison of the discriminative and reinforcing functions of a stimulus. *J. Exp. Psychol.*, **40**, 458–472 [187].

—— (1954) Punishment: I. The avoidance hypothesis. *Psychol. Rev.*, **61**, 34–46 [196].

Dittes, J. E. (1957) Extinction during psychotherapy of GSR accompanying "embarrassing" statements. *J. Abn. & Soc. Psychol.*, **54**, 187–191 [408].

Divin, K. (1937) Certain determinants in the conditioning of anxiety. *J. Psychol.*, **3**, 291–308 [290].

Dollard, J. (See Miller & Dollard, 1941).

Dollard, J., & Miller, N. E. (1950) *Personality and psychotherapy.* New York: McGraw-Hill [60, 62, 141, 147, 154–155, 241–242, 287].

Dove, C. C., & Thompson, M. E. (1943) Some studies on "insight" in white rats. *J. Genet. Psychol.*, **63**, 235–245 [238].

Draguns, J. (See Flavell & Draguns, 1957).

Dulany, D. E. (1955) Avoidance learning of perceptual defense and vigilance. Ph.D. dissertation, University of Michigan [77, 197].

—— (1957) Avoidance learning of perceptual defense and vigilance. *J. Abn. & Soc. Psychol.*, **55**, 333–338 [197].

—— (1960) Hypotheses and habits in verbal "operant conditioning." *Psychol. Rev.*, (in press) [77, 290].

Dulany, D. E., & Eriksen, C. W. (1959) Accuracy of brightness discrimination as measured by concurrent verbal responses and GSRs. *J. Abn. & Soc. Psychol.*, **59**, 418–423 [200, 291].

Dulany, D. E., & Tsushima, T. (1959) Operant conditioning of a punished response that avoids a greater punishment. (To be published) [201].

Edwards, W. (1954) The theory of decision making. *Psychol. Bull.*, **51**, 380–411 [316, 318, 342].

—— (1955) The prediction of decisions among bets. *J. Exp. Psychol.*, **50**, 201–214 [318, 319].

—— (1956) Reward probability, amount, and information as determiners of sequential two-alternative decisions. *J. Exp. Psychol.*, **52**, 177–188 [342].

Eglash, A. (1960) *Creative restitution: Guidance and rehabilitation of offenders.* (To be published) [412].

Eisenson, J. [88].

Ellingson, R. J. (1956) Brain waves and problems of psychology. *Psychol. Bull.*, **53**, 1–34 [287].

Ellson, D. G. (1941a) Hallucinations produced by sensory conditioning. *J. Exp. Psychol.*, **28**, 1–20 [166].

—— (1941b) Experimental extinction of an hallucination produced by sensory conditioning. *J. Exp. Psychol.*, **28**, 350–361 [166].

Enc, A. [96].

English, H. B. (1954) *The historical roots of learning theory.* Garden City, N. Y.: Doubleday, Page & Co. [260].

Eriksen, C. W. (1958) Unconscious processes. In *Nebraska symposium on motivation* (M. R. Jones, ed.). Lincoln: University of Nebraska Press [171, 199, 288].

———— (1959) A decade of "New Look" perception: A symposium. *Amer. Psychol.*, **14**, 379 [200].

———— (See Dulany & Eriksen, 1959).

Eroféeva, M. N. [202].

Escalona, Sybille K. (1940) The effect of success and failure upon the level of aspiration and behavior in manic-depressive psychoses. *Univ. Ia. Stud. Child Welf.*, **16**, 199–302 [318].

Estes, W. K. (1950) Toward a statistical theory of learning. *Psychol. Rev.*, **57**, 94–107 [333, 340].

———— (1955a) Statistical theory of spontaneous recovery and regression. *Psychol. Rev.*, **62**, 145–154 [333].

———— (1955b) Statistical theory of distributional phenomena in learning. *Psychol. Rev.*, **62**, 369–377 [333].

———— (1959) Learning theory and the new "mental chemistry." *Amer. Psychol.*, **14**, 440 [337].

Estes, W. K., Burke, C. J., Atkinson, R. C., & Frankmann, J. P. (1957) Probabilistic discrimination learning. *J. Exp. Psychol.*, **54**, 233–239 [339].

Estes, W. K., & Straughan, J. H. (1954) Analysis of a verbal conditioning situation in terms of statistical learning theory. *J. Exp. Psychol.*, **47**, 225–234 [341].

Estrich, R. M., & Sperber, H. (1952) *Three keys to language.* New York: Rinehart & Co. [87].

Evans, S. (1936) Flexibility of established habit. *J. Gen. Psychol.*, **14**, 177–200 [238].

Eysenck, H. J. (1952) The effects of psychotherapy: An evaluation. *J. Consult. Psychol.*, **16**, 319–324 [407].

Fairbanks, G. (1954) Systematic research in experimental phonetics: 1. A theory of the speech mechanism as a servosystem. *J. Speech & Hearing Disorders*, **19**, 133–139 [84, 274–275, 279, 287].

Feather, N. T. (1959) Subjective probability and decision under uncertainty. *Psychol. Rev.*, **66**, 150–164 [318–319].

Feddersen, W. E. (See Bitterman, Feddersen, & Tyler, 1953).

Fermat, P. [295].

Ferster, C. B. (1953) Sustained behavior under delayed reinforcement. *J. Exp. Psychol.*, **45**, 218–224 [67].

Fessard, A. E. (1954) Mechanisms of nervous integration and conscious experience. In *Brain mechanisms and consciousness.* Springfield, Ill.: Charles C. Thomas [252].

Festinger, L. (1942) A theoretical interpretation of shifts in level of aspiration. *Psychol. Rev.*, **49**, 235–250 [318].

———— (1957) *A theory of cognitive dissonance.* Evanston, Ill.: Row, Peterson & Co. [206].

———— (See Lewin, Dembo, Festinger, & Sears, 1944).

Finesmith, S. (1960) Systematic changes in the galvanic skin response during paired associate learning. (In press) [169–170].

Fink, C. D. (See Fredericson, Fink, & Parker, 1955).

———— (See Gruber, Fink, & Damm, 1957).

Fisher, R. A. (1937) *The design of experiments.* London: Oliver & Boyd [295–296, 308].

———— (1956) *Statistical methods and scientific inference*. London: Oliver & Boyd [294, 308, 312].

Flavell, J. H., & Draguns, J. (1957) A microgenetic approach to perception and thought. *Psychol. Bull.*, **54**, 197–217 [208].

Fletcher, F. M. (See Muenzinger & Fletcher, 1936).

Foley, J. P., Jr., & Cofer, C. H. (1943) Mediated generalization and the interpretation of mediated behavior: II. Experimental study of certain homophone synonymous gradients. *J. Exp. Psychol.*, **32**, 168–175 [62, 146].

Forgays, D. G., & Forgays, J. W. (1952) The nature of the effect of free-environmental experience in the rat. *J. Comp. Physiol. Psychol.*, **45**, 322–328 [367].

Forgays, J. W. (See Forgays & Forgays, 1952).

Fowler, H. W. (1926) *A dictionary of modern English usage*. London: Clarendon Press [135].

Frank, L. K. (1923) Suggestions for a theory of learning. *Psychol. Rev.*, **30**, 145–148 [37].

Frankmann, J. P. (See Estes, Burke, Atkinson, & Frankmann, 1957).

Fredericson, E. (1950) Cognitive maps and reinforcement. *J. Genet. Psychol.*, **76**, 253–262 [181].

———— (1951) Competition: The effects of infantile experience upon adult behavior. *J. Abn. & Soc. Psychol.*, **46**, 406–409 [360].

Fredericson, E., Fink, C. D., & Parker, J. R. (1955) Elicitation and inhibition of competitive fighting in food deprived mice. *J. Genet. Psychol.*, **86**, 131–141 [360].

Free, J. B. (See Butler & Free, 1952).

Freides, D. (1957) Goal-box cues and pattern of reinforcement. *J. Exp. Psychol.*, **53**, 361–371 [178].

Freud, Anna (1935) *Psychoanalysis for teachers and parents*. (Barbara Low, trans.) New York: Emerson Books, Inc. [407].

Freud, S. (1911) Formulations regarding two principles of mental functioning. *Collected Papers, Vol. IV*, 13–21. London: Hogarth Press, 1934 [214].

———— (1920) *A general introduction to psychoanalysis*. New York: Liveright Publishing Co. [25, 288].

———— (1937) Analysis terminable and interminable. *Collected Papers, Vol. V*. London: Hogarth Press [407].

———— [270, 277, 418–419].

Fries, C. C. (1952) *The structure of English*. New York: Harcourt, Brace & Co. [137–138, 140–141].

Fromm, E. (1955) *The sane society*. New York: Rinehart & Co. [418–419].

Fromm-Reichmann, Frieda, & Moreno, J. L. (1956) *Progress in psychotherapy*. New York: Grune & Stratton, Inc. [410].

Fuller, H. J. (1934) Plant behavior. *J. Gen. Psychol.*, **11**, 379–394 [185].

Gagné, R. M. (1959) Teaching machines and transfer of training. *Amer. Psychol.*, **14**, 409 [57–58].

Galton, F. [296, 299, 308].

Gantt, W. H. (1944) *Experimental basis for neurotic behavior*. New York: Hoeber [387].

Gardner, R. W., Holzman, P. S., & Siegal, R. S. (1956) Some variables affecting size judgments. *Perceptual and Motor Skills*, **6**, 285–290 [198].

Garner, W. R. (1958) Symmetric uncertainty analysis and its implications. *Psychol. Rev.*, **65**, 183–196 [123].

Garner, W. R., & McGill, W. J. (1956) The relation between information and variance analysis. *Psychometrika*, **21**, 219–228 [123].

Garrett, H. E. (1955) *General psychology*. New York: American Book Co. [236–238].

Gellerman, L. W. (1933a) Form discrimination in chimpanzees and two-year-old children. I. Form (triangularity) *per se. J. Genet. Psychol.*, **42**, 3–27 [215].

—— (1933b) Form discrimination in chimpanzees and two-year-old children. II. Form versus background. *J. Genet. Psychol.*, **42**, 28–50 [215].

Gentry, Evelyn (See Muenzinger & Gentry, 1931).

Gesell, A., & Amatruda, C. S. (1947) *Developmental diagnosis*. New York: Hoeber [92].

Gewirtz, J. L. (1960) The origins of social motivation and emotional attachment. *Current trends in psychological theory* (1959). Pittsburgh: University of Pittsburgh Press [390].

—— (See Rheingold, Gewirtz, & Ross, 1959).

Gibson, E. J. (See Gibson & Gibson, 1955).

Gibson, J. J., & Gibson, E. J. (1955) Perceptual learning: Differentiation or enrichment. *Psychol. Rev.*, **62**, 32–41 [198].

Gibson, J. J., & Mowrer, O. H. (1938) Determinants of the perceived vertical and horizontal. *Psychol. Rev.*, **45**, 300–321 [282].

Ginsburg, N. [222, 344].

Girden, E. (1938) Conditioning and problem-solving behavior. *Amer. J. Psychol.*, **51**, 677–687 [215].

Gleitman, H. (1955) Place learning without prior performance. *J. Comp. Physiol. Psychol.*, **48**, 77–79 [59].

—— (See Tolman & Gleitman, 1949a).

—— (See Tolman & Gleitman, 1949b).

Gleitman, H., Nachmias, J., & Neisser, U. (1954) The S—R reinforcement theory of extinction. *Psychol. Rev.*, **61**, 23–33 [59].

Gloor, P. (See Jasper, Gloor, & Milner, 1956).

Goldstein, K. (1939) *The organism*. New York: American Book Co. [240].

Goodman, C. C. (See Bruner & Goodman, 1947).

Goodnow, Jacqueline J. (See Bruner, Goodnow, & Austin, 1956).

Goss, A. E. (1955) A stimulus-response analysis of the interaction of cue-producing and instrumental response. *Psychol. Rev.*, **62**, 20–31 [64].

—— (1960) Verbal mediating responses and concept formation. *Psychol. Rev.* (in press) [56].

Goss, A. E., & Wischner, G. J. (1956) Vicarious trial and error and related behavior. *Psychol. Bull.*, **53**, 35–54 [215, 218].

Grant, D. A. (1953) Information theory and the discrimination of sequences in stimulus events. In *Current trends in information theory*, 18–46. Pittsburgh: University of Pittsburgh Press [337, 339–343].

Grant, D. A., Hake, H. W., & Hornseth, J. P. (1951) Acquisition and extinction of a verbal conditioned response with differing percentages of reinforcement. *J. Exp. Psychol.*, **42**, 1–5 [337–338, 341].

Grant, E. C., & Chance, M. R. A. (1958) Rank order in caged rats. *J. Animal Behavior*, **6**, 183–194 [360].

Greenaugh, J. B., & Kittredge, G. L. (1906) *Words and their way in English speech.* New York: The Macmillan Co. [138].

Greenspoon, J. (1950) The effect of verbal and non-verbal stimuli on the frequency of members of two verbal response classes. (Unpublished doctor's dissertation, University of Indiana) [77, 290].

Grice, G. R., & Davis, J. D. (1958) Mediated stimulus equivalence and distinctiveness in human conditioning. *J. Exp. Psychol.,* **55,** 565–571 [63, 64, 66].

Griffith, B. C., Spitz, H. H., & Lipman, R. E. (1959) Verbal mediation and concept formation in retarded and normal subjects. *J. Exp. Psychol.,* **58,** 247–251 [56].

Griffith, C. R. (1924) *General introduction to psychology.* New York: The Macmillan Co. [138].

Griffith, J. [41, 202].

Griffiths, W. J. (See Bingham & Griffiths, 1952).

Gruber, H. E., Fink, C. D., & Damm, V. (1957) Effects of experience on perception of causality. *J. Exp. Psychol.,* **53,** 89–93 [327].

Grünbaum, A. (1952) Causality and the science of human behavior. *Amer. Sci.,* **40,** 665–676 [347–348].

Gulliksen, H. (1958) The semantic differential comes of age: How to make meaning more meaningful (a review). *Cont. Psychol.,* **3,** 115–119 [160].

Guthrie, E. R. (1930) Conditioning as a principle of learning. *Psychol. Rev.,* **37,** 412–428 [37].

———— (1952) *The psychology of learning.* (Rev. ed.) New York: Harper & Bros. [3, 216].

———— [171, 332].

———— (See Smith & Guthrie, 1921).

Hagenbrook, L. D. [218, 220].

Hake, H. W. (See Grant, Hake, & Hornseth, 1951).

Hake, H. W., & Hyman, R. (1953) Perception of the statistical structure of a random series of binary symbols. *J. Exp. Psychol.,* **45,** 64–74 [340].

Hakerem, G. (See Sutton, Hakerem, Protnoy, & Zubin, 1960).

Hallowell, A. I. (1950) Cultural factors in the structuralization of perception. (Presented at the Conference on Social Psychology at Cross Roads 1950, University of Oklahoma, April 7, 1950). (Mimeographed paper) [197].

Haney, G. W. (1932) The effect of familiarity on maze performance of albino rats. *Univ. Calif. Publ. Psychol.,* **4,** 319–333 [33].

Hansmann, Eugenia [239].

Hanfmann, Eugenia, & Kasanin, J. (1937) A method for the study of concept formation. *J. Psychol.,* **3,** 521–540 [240].

Hare, A. P., Borgatta, E. F., and Balas, R. F. (eds.) (1955) *Small groups: Studies in social interaction.* New York: Alfred A. Knopf [369].

Hare, Rachel (See Ritchie, Hay, & Hare, 1951).

Harlow, H. F. (1949) The formation of learning sets. *Psychol. Rev.,* **56,** 51–65 [100].

———— (1958) The nature of love. *Amer. Psychol.,* **13,** 613–685 [382].

———— [192].

Hartley, D. (1705–1757) [167].

Hartley, E. L. (See Newcomb, Hartley, et al., 1947).

Hartley, P. H. T. (1950) An experimental analysis of interspecific recognition. In

Symposia of the society for experimental biology. New York: Academic Press, Inc. [131].

Haslerud, G. M. (See McCulloch & Haslerud, 1939).

Haslerud, G. M., & Meyers, Shirley (1958) The transfer value of given and individually derived principles. *J. Educ. Psychol.,* **49,** 293–298 [246].

Hay, Alice (See Ritchie, Hay, & Hare, 1951).

Hayakawa, S. I. (1942) *Language in action.* New York: Harcourt, Brace & Co. [123].

Hayes, Cathy (1951) *The ape in our house.* New York: Harper & Bros. [108 ff., 160, 178].

——— (See Hayes & Hayes, 1951, 1952).

Hayes, K. J., & Hayes, Cathy (1951) The intellectual development of a home raised chimpanzee. *Proc. Amer. Phil. Soc.,* **95,** 105–109 [98, 109].

——— (1952) Imitation in a home-reared chimpanzee. *J. Comp. Physiol. Psychol.,* **45,** 450–459 [108 ff., 160].

Heard, W. G. (See Staats, Staats, & Heard, 1959).

Hearnshaw, L. S. (1956) Temporal integration and behaviour. *Bull. Brit. Psychol. Soc.,* No. 30, 1–20 [396].

Hebb, D. O. (1949) *The organization of behavior.* New York: John Wiley & Sons, Inc. [171, 186, 205, 256].

——— (1953) On human thought. *Canad. J. Psychol.,* **7,** 99–110 [210].

Hebb, D. O., & Thompson, W. R. (1954) The social significance of animal studies. In *Handbook of social psychology* (Gardner Lindzey, ed.). Reading, Mass.: Addison-Wesley Press [367–368].

Heinroth, D. [378].

Helson, H. (1947) Adaptation-level as frame of reference for prediction of psychophysical data. *Amer. J. Psychol.,* **60,** 1–29 [206].

——— (1948) Adaptation-level as a basis for a quantitative theory of frames of reference, *Psychol. Rev.,* **55,** 297–313 [206].

Hendrix, Gertrude (1947) A new clue to transfer of teaching. *Elem. Sch. Jour.,* **68,** 197–208 [246].

——— (1950) Prerequisite to meaning. *Math. Teacher,* **48,** 334–339 [246].

Hernandez-Peon, R., Scherrer, H., & Jouvet, M. (1956) Modification of electric activity in cochlear nucleus during "attention" in anesthetized cats. *Science,* **123,** 331–332 [204].

Heron, W. T. (1935) The inheritance of maze learning ability in rats. *J. Comp. Psychol.,* **19,** 77–89 [367].

——— (1942) The effects of a differential rate of reinforcement of responses to two levers. *J. Comp. Physiol. Psychol.,* **33,** 87–96 [336].

——— (See Thompson & Heron, 1954).

Hess, W. R. (1954) The diencephalic sleep centre. In *Brain mechanisms and consciousness.* Springfield, Ill.: Charles C. Thomas [254].

Hilgard, E. R. (1951) The role of learning in perception. In *Perception—An approach to personality* (Blake and Ramsey, eds.). New York: Ronald Press Co. [197].

——— (1956) *Theories of learning.* New York: Appleton-Century Crofts [230, 234, 264].

——— (1958) Unconscious processes and human rationality. Lecture, University of Illinois [292].

Hilgard, E. R., & Marquis, D. G. (1940) *Conditioning and learning.* New York: Appleton-Century Crofts [56, 244].

Hill, F. S. (See Keller & Hill, 1936).

Himwich, H. E. (1958) Psychopharmacologic drugs. *Science,* **127**, 59–72 [290].

Hoffer, W. (1945) Psychoanalytic education. *Psychoanal. Stud. the Child,* **1**, 293–307 [407].

Holder, Elaine E. (1958) Learning factors in social facilitation and social inhibition in rats. *J. Comp. Physiol. Psychol.,* **51**, 60–64 [367].

Hollingworth, H. L. (1928) *Psychology: Its facts and principles.* New York: D. Appleton-Century [94, 136].

Holt, E. B. (1931) *Animal drive and the learning process.* Vol. I. New York: Henry Holt & Co. [8–9, 102, 104, 171].

Holzman, P. S. (See Gardner, Holzman, & Siegal, 1956).

Honzik, C. H. (1931) Delayed reaction in rats. *Univ. Calif. Publ. Psychol.,* **4**, 307–318 [226–227].

——— (See Tolman & Honzik, 1930).

Honzik, C. H., & Tolman, E. C. (1936) The perception of spatial relations by the rat. *J. Comp. Psychol.,* **22**, 287–318 [50].

Hornseth, J. P. (See Grant, Hake, & Hornseth, 1951).

Hotelling, H. (1958) The statistical method and the philosophy of science. *J. Amer. Stat. Assoc.,* **12**, 9–14 [311].

Hovland, C. I. (See Sears & Hovland, 1941).

Hovland, C. I., & Sears, R. R. (1938) Experiments on motor conflict: I. Types of conflict and their modes of resolution. *J. Exp. Psychol.,* **23**, 477–493 [215].

Howard, E. (1920) *Territory in bird life.* London: John Murry (also, London: Collins, 1948) [380].

Hudson, B. B. (1950) One trial learning in the domestic rat. *Genet. Psychol. Monogr.,* **57**, 173–180 [332].

Hull, C. L. (1929) A functional interpretation of the conditioned reflex. *Psychol. Rev.,* **36**, 498–511 [37].

——— (1930a) Simple trial-and-error learning: A study in psychological theory. *Psychol. Rev.,* **37**, 241–256 [37].

——— (1930b) Knowledge and purpose as habit mechanism. *Psychol. Rev.,* **37**, 511–525 [37, 56, 136, 154, 214, 227].

——— (1931) Goal attraction and directing ideas conceived as habit phenomena. *Psychol. Rev.,* **38**, 487–506 [37–39].

——— (1932) The goal gradient hypothesis and maze learning. *Psychol. Rev.,* **39**, 25–43 [37].

——— (1943) *Principles of behavior.* New York: Appleton-Century Crofts [3, 11, 22, 24, 26, 47, 60, 101, 104, 107, 141, 167, 175, 177, 181, 210].

——— [25, 61, 152, 223, 259, 270, 281].

Hume, D. (1738) *Treatise of human nature.* Green & Gros, eds. New York: Longmans, Green & Co. [325, 328 ff.–329].

——— (1777) *An enquiry concerning human understanding.* Oxford: Clarendon Press [329–330, 346].

Humphrey, G. (1921) Imitation and the conditioned reflex. *Ped. Sem.,* **28**, 1–21 [101, 114].

Humphreys, L. G. (1939a) Acquisition and extinction of verbal expectations in a situation analogous to conditioning. *J. Exp. Psychol.,* **25**, 294–301 [18].

———— (1939b) The effect of random alternation of reinforcement on the acquisition and extinction of conditioned eyelid reactions. *J. Exp. Psychol.*, **25**, 141–158 [337, 341].

———— [294].

Hunt, J. McV. (1960) Experience and motivation: some reinterpretations. *Child Devel.* (to be published in September [205–207].

Hunt, J. McV., Cole, Marie-Louise W., & Reis, Eva E. S. (1958) Situational cues distinguishing anger, fear, and sorrow. *Amer. J. Psychol.*, **71**, 136–151 [23].

Hunter, W. S. (1913) The delayed reaction in animals and children. *Animal Behavior Monogr.*, **2**, 1–86 [226–227].

———— (1928) *Human behavior*. Chicago: University of Chicago Press [136].

Hurwitz, H. M. B. (1955) Response elimination without performance. *Quart. J. Exp. Psychol.*, **7**, 1–7 [59].

Hyman, R. (See Hake & Hyman, 1953).

Hymovitch, B. (1952) The effects of experiential variations on problem-solving in the rat. *J. Comp. Physiol. Psychol.*, **45**, 313–321 [367].

Irion, A. L. (See McGeoch & Irion, 1952).

Jackson, H. [158, 160].

Jacobsen, E. (1955) Controls in man: Methods of self-direction in health and disease. *Amer. J. Psychol.*, **68**, 549–561 [274].

———— [153].

James, W. (1890) *Principles of psychology* (two volumes). New York: Henry Holt & Co. [247, 284–286].

———— (1902) *Varieties of religious experience*. New York: Henry Holt & Co. [256].

———— [248].

Janis, I. L. (1959) Motivational factors in the resolution of decisional conflicts. In *Neb. symposium*. Lincoln: University of Nebraska Press [319].

Jarrett, R. F. (See Postman & Jarrett, 1952).

Jasper, H. (See Sharpless & Jasper, 1956).

Jasper, H., Gloor, P., & Milner, B. (1956) Higher functions of the nervous system. *Ann. Rev. Physiol.*, **18**, 359–386 [290].

Jaynes, J. (1956) Imprinting: The interaction of learned and innate behavior: I. Development and generalization. *J. Comp. Physiol. Psychol.*, **49**, 201–206 [374–376].

———— (1958a) Imprinting: The interaction of learned and innate behavior: III. Practice effects on performance, retention, and fear. *J. Comp. Physiol. Psychol.*, **51**, 234–237 [376, 386].

———— (1958b) Imprinting: The interaction of learned and innate behavior: IV. Generalization and emergent discrimination. *J. Comp. Physiol. Psychol.*, **51**, 238–242 [376, 386].

———— (See Beach & Jaynes, 1954).

Jeffress, L. A. (ed.) (1951) *Cerebral mechanisms in behavior*. New York: John Wiley & Sons, Inc. [273, 286].

Jeffreys, H. (1939) *Theory of probability*. Oxford: Clarendon Press [352].

Jefrey, W., & Kaplan, R. J. (1957) Semantic generalization with experimentally induced associations. *J. Exp. Psychol.*, **54**, 336–338 [56].

Jenkins, J. J. (See Schuell & Jenkins, 1959).

Jenkins, N. (1957) Affective processes in perception. *Psychol. Bull.*, **54**, 100–127 [198, 287].

Jenkins, W. O., & Stanley, J. C. (1950) Partial reinforcement: A review and critique. *Psychol. Bull.*, **47**, 193–234 [337, 341].

Jennings, H. S. [271].

Johnson, D. M. (1950) Problem solving and symbolic processes. *Ann. Rev. Psychol.*, **1**, 297–310 [212].

—— (1955) *The psychology of thought and judgment.* New York: Harper & Bros. [250–251].

Johnson, R. C. (1958) The theology of Paul. *Crossroads*, **8**, 23–53 [395].

Johnson, W. (1946) *People in quandaries.* New York: Harper & Bros. [160].

—— (1956) *Your most enchanted listener.* New York: Harper & Bros. [160].

Jones, Helen M. (See Mowrer & Jones, 1943, 1945).

Jouvet, M. (See Hernandez-Peon, Scherrer, & Jouvet, 1956).

Jung, C. G. (1958) *The undiscovered self.* London: Little, Brown, & Co. [290].

Kaiser, H. F. [310].

Kalish, D. (See Tolman, Ritchie, & Kalish, 1947).

Kant, E. [308].

Kaplan, R. J. (See Jefrey & Kaplan, 1957).

Kaplan, W. K. (See Mandler & Kaplan, 1956).

Kappauf, W. E. [294].

Kardash, Kaya [243–246].

Karwoski, T. F. (See Stagner & Karwoski, 1952).

Kasanin, J. (See Hanfmann & Kasanin, 1937).

Katz, S. (See Kendler, Pliskoff, D'Amato, & Katz, 1957).

Katz, W. G. (1953) Freedom and responsibility: A difficulty in relating Christianity and Law. *J. Legal Educ.*, **5**, 269–285 [350].

Keehn, J. D. (See Mowrer & Keehn, 1958).

Keller, A. G. (See Sumner, Keller, & Davie, 1928).

Keller, F. S., & Hill, F. S. (1936) Another "insight" experiment. *J. Genet. Psychol.*, **48**, 484–489 [238].

Keller, Helen (1902) *The story of my life.* New York: Doubleday, Page & Co. [85, 157].

Kellogg, W. N. (1958) Echo ranging in the porpoise. *Science*, **128**, 982–988 [186].

Kelly, G. A. (1955) *The psychology of personal constructs* (two volumes). New York: W. W. Norton & Co. [207].

Kendler, H. H. (1947) An investigation of latent learning in a T-maze. *J. Comp. Physiol. Psychol.*, **40**, 265–270 [45].

—— (1959) Learning. *In Annual review of psychology.* Stanford, Calif.: Annual Reviews, Inc. [55, 57].

Kendler, H. H., & Mencher, H. C. (1948) The ability of rats to learn the location of food when motivated by thirst—An experimental reply to Leeper. *J. Exp. Psychol.*, **38**, 82–88 [45].

Kendler, H. H., Pliskoff, S. S., D'Amato, M. R., & Katz, S. (1957) Nonreinforcements versus reinforcements as variables in the partial reinforcement effect. *J. Exp. Psychol.*, **53**, 269–276 [178].

Kephart, N. C. [288].

Keynes, J. M. [353, 356].

King, J. A. (1951) Social behavior, social organization, and population dynamics in a black-tailed prairiedog town in the Black Hills of South Dakota. Ph.D. dissertation, No. 3519, University of Michigan [379].

——— (1954) Closed social groups among domestic dogs. *Proc. Amer. Phil. Soc.,* **98,** 327–336 [379].

——— (1956a) Social relations of the domestic guinea pig living under semi-natural conditions. *Ecology,* **37,** 221–228 [379].

——— (1956b) Sexual behavior of C57BL/10 Mice and its relation to early social experience. *J. Gen. Psychol.,* **88,** 223–229 [407].

——— (1957) Relationships between early social experience and adult aggressive behavior in inbred mice. *J. Gen. Psychol.,* **90,** 151–166 [407].

——— (1958) Parameters relevant to determining the effect of early experience upon the adult behavior of animals. *Psychol. Bull.,* **55,** 46–58 [407].

Kittredge, G. L. (See Greenaugh & Kittredge, 1906).

Kleitman, N. (1957) Sleep, wakefulness, and consciousness. *Psychol. Bull.,* **54,** 354–359 [254].

Klüver, H. (1933) *Behavior mechanisms in monkeys.* Chicago: University of Chicago Press [215].

Kohler, W. (1921) Zur Psychologie des Schimpansen. *Psychologische Forschung,* **1,** 2–46 [158].

——— (1927) *The mentality of apes.* New York: Harcourt, Brace & Co. [158, 231–236].

Kohler, W., & Wallach, H. (1944) Figural after-effects: An investigation of visual process. *Proc. Amer. Phil. Soc.,* **88,** 269–357 [256].

Kohn, M. (1951) Satiation of hunger from stomach versus mouth feeding. *J. Comp. Physiol. Psychol.,* **44,** 412–422 [360].

Konorski, J. (1950) Mechanisms of learning. In *Psychological mechanisms in animal behavior.* Cambridge, England: Academic Press (New York: Academic Press, Inc.) [66].

——— (1958) Trends in the development of physiology of the brain. *J. Ment. Sci.,* **104,** 1100–1110 [209, 256].

——— [77].

Kornreich, J. S. (See Mowrer, Kornreich, & Yoffe, 1940).

Korzybski, A. (1933) *Science and sanity.* Lancaster, Pa.: International Non-Aristotalian Library Pub. Co. [123].

Krechevsky, I. (1932) 'Hypotheses' in rats. *Psychol. Rev.,* **39,** 516–532 [332].

Kubala, A. L. (See Bitterman, Reed, & Kubala, 1953).

Kubie, L. S. (1956) Some unsolved problems of psychoanalytic psychotherapy. In *Progress in psychotherapy* (Fromm-Reichmann & Moreno, eds.). New York: Grune & Stratton, Inc. [407].

Kuenne, Margaret R. (1946) Experimental investigation of the relation of language to transposition behavior in young children. *J. Exp. Psychol.,* **36,** 471–490 [243–246].

Kunberger, Dorothy [243, 246].

Kuo, Z. Y. (1937) Forced movement or insight? *Univ. Calif. Publ. Psychol.,* **6,** 169–188 [238].

Lacey, J. I. (1956) The evaluation of autonomic responses: Toward a general solution. *Ann. N. Y. Acad. Sci.,* **67,** 123–164 [289].

Langer, Susanne K. (1951) *Philosophy in a new key.* New York: Pelican Books [121–123].

Lansdell, H. (1958) The impact of some recent neurophysiological research on psychological thinking (unpublished manuscript) [289].

Laplace (1749–1827) [300, 310, 347].

Lashley, K. S. (1917) The accuracy of movement in the absence of excitation from the moving organ. *Amer. J. Physiol.*, **43**, 169–194 [280].

—— (1918) A simple maze with data on the relation of distribution of practice to the rate of learning. *Psychobiology*, **1**, 353–367 [30, 33].

—— (1929) *Brain mechanisms and intelligence.* Chicago: University of Chicago Press [260].

—— (1951) The problem of serial order in behavior. In *Cerebral mechanisms in behavior: The Hixon Symposium* (L. A. Jeffress, ed.). New York: John Wiley & Sons, Inc. [256].

—— (1956) Personal communication [170].

Lawicka, W. (1957a) The effect of the prefrontal lobectomy on the vocal conditioned reflexes in dogs. *Acta Biologiae Experimentalis*, **17**, 317–325 [77].

—— (1957b) Physiological analysis of the disturbances of the delayed responses in dogs after prefrontal ablation. *Bulletin de L'Académie Polonaise des Sciences*, **4–5**, 107–110 [229].

Lawrence, D. H. (1949) Acquired distinctiveness of cues: I. Transfer between discriminations on the basis of familiarity with the stimulus. *J. Exp. Psychol.*, **39**, 770–784 [63].

—— (1950) Acquired distinctiveness of cues: II. Selective association in a constant stimulus situation. *J. Exp. Psychol.*, **40**, 175–188 [63].

Leeper, R. W. (1948) A motivational theory of emotion to replace "emotion as disorganized response." *Psychol. Rev.*, **55**, 5–21 [259].

—— (1951) Cognitive processes. In *Handbook of experimental psychology* (S. S. Stevens, ed.). New York: John Wiley & Sons, Inc. [250].

Leuba, C. (1940) Images as conditioned sensations. *J. Exp. Psychol.*, **26**, 345–351 [166, 207].

Levine, S. (1957) Infantile experience and consummatory behavior in adulthood. *J. Comp. Physiol. Psychol.*, **50**, 609–612 [407].

Levinson, H. C. (1950) *The science of chance.* New York: Rinehart & Co. [301, 305, 310].

Levy, N. J. (See Seward & Levy, 1949).

Lewin, K. (1936) *Principles of topological psychology.* New York: McGraw-Hill [25].

—— (1942) Field theory of learning. *Yearb. Nat. Soc. Stud. Educ.*, **41** (Part II), 215–242 [170].

—— [270, 278].

Lewin, K., & Baldwin, A. L. (1959) Pride and shame in children. In *Nebraska symposium on motivation* (pp. 138–173). Lincoln: University of Nebraska Press [405].

Lewin, K., Dembo, Tamara, Festinger, L., & Sears, Pauline S. (1944) Analysis of level of aspiration behavior. In *Personality and the behavior disorders* (J. McV. Hunt, ed.). [318].

Lewis, D. J., & Cotton, J. W. (1958) Partial reinforcement and nonresponse acquisition. *J. Comp. Physiol. Psychol.*, **51**, 251–254 [61].

Lewis, M. M. (1948) *Language in society: The linguistic revolution and social changes.* New York: Social Science Publishers [92].

—— (1951) *Infant speech: A study of the beginnings of language.* New York: Humanities Press [136].

Liddell, H. (1950a) Some specific factors that modify tolerance for environmental stress. *Res. Publ. Assoc. Nerv. & Ment. Dis.*, **29**, 155–171 [364–367].

―――― (1950b) The role of vigilance in the development of animal neurosis. In *Anxiety* (Hoch & Zubin, eds.). New York: Grune & Stratton, Inc. [190].

―――― (1953) Dynamics of experimental neuroses. In *Comparative conditioned neuroses* (R. W. Miner, ed.). *Ann. N. Y. Acad. Sci.*, **56**, 164–170 [387].

Lindsley, D. B. (1957) Psychophysiology and motivation. In *Nebraska symposium on motivation* (R. M. Jones, ed.). Lincoln: University of Nebraska Press [204].

Lipman, L., & Blanton, R. L. (1957) The semantic differential and mediated generalization as measures of meaning. *J. Exp. Psychol.*, **54**, 431–437 [56, 207].

Lipman, R. E. (See Griffith, Spitz, & Lipman, 1959).

Lippitt, R. O. (See Spence & Lippitt, 1946).

Liu, In-Mao [171].

Lorenz, K. (1935) Der Kumpan in der Umwelt des Vogels. *Jour. f. Ornithol.*, **83**, 137–213 and 289–413 [372].

―――― (1937) The companion in the bird's world. *Auk*, **54**, 245–273 [372, 374].

―――― (1955) *Man meets dog*. Boston: Houghton Mifflin Co. [381].

―――― [378, 386].

Lorge, I. (1936) Irrelevant rewards in animal learning. *J. Comp. Psychol.*, **21**, 105–128 [89].

Loucks, R. B. (1931) Efficiency of the rats' motor cortex in delayed alternation. *J. Comp. Neurol.*, **53**, 511–567 [227].

Lowell, E. L. (See McClelland, Atkinson, Clark, & Lowell, 1953).

Luchins, A. S. (1960) A variational approach to empathy. In *The phenomenological problem* (A. E. Kuenzli, ed.). New York: Harper & Bros. [115].

Lumsdaine, A. A. (1939) Conditioned eyelid responses as mediating generalized finger reaction. *Psychol. Bull.*, **36**, 650 (abstract) [56, 146].

Lyman, B. (1959) Signal vigilance level and conditioned avoidance acquisition in the goat. *J. Comp. Physiol. Psychol.*, **52**, 89–91 [192–193].

McCarthy, Dorothea (1954) Language development in children. In *Manual of child psychology* (L. Carmichael, ed.; 2nd ed.). New York: John Wiley & Sons, Inc. [136–137].

McClelland, D. C. (1951) *Personality*. New York: William Sloane Associates [287].

―――― (1955) The psychology of mental content reconsidered. *Psychol. Rev.*, **62**, 297–303 [172].

McClelland, D. C., Atkinson, J. W., Clark, R. A., & Lowell, E. L. (1953) *The achievement motive*. New York: Appleton-Century-Crofts [206].

McConnell, J. V., Cutler, R. L., & McNeil, E. B. (1958) Subliminal stimulation: An overview. *Amer. Psychol.*, **13**, 229–242 [288].

McCord, F. (1939a) The delayed reaction and memory in rats: I. Length of delay. *J. Comp. Psychol.*, **27**, 1–37 [226].

―――― (1939b) The delayed reaction and memory in rats: II. An analysis of the behavioral dimension. *J. Comp. Psychol.*, **27**, 175–210 [215].

McCulloch, T. L., & Haslerud, G. M. (1939) Affective responses of an infant chimpanzee reared in isolation from its kind. *J. Comp. Psychol.*, **28**, 437–445 [377].

McCulloch, W. S. (1951) Why the mind is in the head. In *Cerebral mechanisms in behavior: The Hixon Symposium* (L. A. Jeffress, ed.). New York: John Wiley & Sons, Inc. [221–264].

────── (See Pitts & McCulloch, 1947).

McCulloch, W. S., & Pitts, W. (1958) The statistical organization of nervous activity. *J. Amer. Stat. Assoc.*, **4**, 91–99 [275].

McFarland, R. L. (See Powers, McFarland, & Clark, 1957).

McGeoch, J. A., & Irion, A. L. (1952) *The psychology of human learning.* New York: Longmans, Green & Co. [265, 288].

McGill, V. J. (1954) *Emotions and reason.* Springfield, Ill.: Charles C. Thomas [216].

McGill, W. J. (See Garner & McGill, 1956).

McKeller, P. (1957) *Imagination and thinking.* New York: Basic Books, Inc. [205].

McNeil, E. B. (See McConnell, Cutler, & McNeil, 1958).

McNemar, Olga W. (See Taylor & McNemar, 1955).

Maatsch, J. L., Adelman, H. M., & Denny, M. R. (1954) Effort and resistance to extinction of the bar-pressing response. *J. Comp. Physiol. Psychol.*, **47**, 47–49 [181].

MacCorquodale, K. (See Meehl & MacCorquodale, 1953).

MacCorquodale, K., & Meehl, P. E. (1948) On a distinction between hypothetical constructs and intervening variables. *Psychol. Rev.*, **55**, 95–107 [68].

MacLean, P. D. (1955) The limbic system ("visceral brain") in relation to central gray and reticulum of the brain stem: Evidence of interdependence in emotional processes. *Psychosom. Med.*, **17**, 355–366 [290].

Maddi, S. R. (See Moltz & Maddi, 1955).

Magoun, H. W. (1954) The ascending reticular system and wakefulness. In *Brain mechanisms and consciousness* (DelaFresnaye, J. F., ed.). Springfield, Ill.: Charles C. Thomas [253].

Maier, N. R. F. (1929) Reasoning in white rats. *Comp. Psych. Monogr.*, **6**, No. 29, 1–93 [23].

────── (1931) Reasoning and learning. *Psychol. Rev.*, **38**, 332–346 [230].

────── (1938) A further analysis of reasoning in rats. II. The integration of four separate experiences in problem solving. III. The influence of cortical injuries on the process of "direction." *Comp. Psych. Monogr.*, **15**, 1–43 [215].

────── (1940) The behavior mechanisms concerned with problem-solving. *Psychol. Rev.*, **47**, 43–58 [215].

Malinowski, B. (1938) The problem of meaning in primitive languages. In *The meaning of meaning* (by Ogden & Richards). New York: Harcourt, Brace & Co. [140].

Maltzman, I., Brooks, L. O., Bogartz, W., & Summers, S. S. (1958) The facilitation of problem solving by prior exposure to uncommon responses. *J. Exp. Psychol.*, **56**, 399–406 [291].

Mandler, G. (1959) Stimulus variables and subjective variables: A caution. *Psychol. Rev.*, **66**, 145–149 [294].

Mandler, G., & Kaplan, W. K. (1956) Subjective evaluation and reinforcing effect of a verbal stimulus. *Science*, **124**, 582–583 [290].

Manis, M. (1955) Social interaction and the self concept. *J. Abn. & Soc. Psychol.*, **51**, 362–370 [412].

Markey, J. F. (1928) *The symbolic process and its integration in children.* London: Kegan Paul, Trench, Trubner & Co., Ltd., [249].

Marquis, D. G. (See Hilgard & Marquis, 1940).

Marston, Mary-'Vesta (See Scott & Marston, 1953).

Mason, D. J. (1957) The relation of secondary reinforcement to partial reinforcement. *J. Comp. Physiol. Psychol.,* **50**, 264–268 [353].

——— (See Davitz & Mason, 1955).

Masserman, J. H. (1943) *Behavior and neurosis.* Chicago: University of Chicago Press [364–367, 387].

——— (1953) Neuroses in monkeys. In *Comparative conditioned neuroses* (R. W. Miner, ed.). *Ann. N. Y. Acad. Sci.,* **56**, 253–265 [387].

Maxwell, J. C. [267].

Mead, G. H. (1934) *Mind, self, and society.* Chicago: University of Chicago Press [vii, 114, 155–156, 161, 249, 285, 371].

Meehl, P. E. (See MacCorquodale & Meehl, 1948).

Meehl, P. E., & MacCorquodale, K. (1953) Drive conditioning as a factor in latent learning. *J. Exp. Psychol.,* **45**, 20–24 [50–51].

Mencher, H. C. (See Kendler & Mencher, 1948).

Messick, S. (See Bolles & Messick, 1958).

Meyers, Shirley (See Haslerud & Meyers, 1958).

Michotte, A. (1946) *La perception de la causalité.* Louvain: L'Institut supérieur de Philosophie [327].

Miles, W. (1927) The two story duplicate maze. *J. Exp. Psychol.,* **10**, 369 [280].

Miller, G. A. (1951) *Language and communication.* New York: McGraw-Hill [160].

Miller, G. A., Galanter, E., & Pribram, K. H. (1960) *Plans and the Structure of Behavior.* New York: Henry Holt & Co. [173].

Miller, J. G. (1942) *Unconsciousness.* New York: John Wiley & Sons, Inc. [291].

——— (1955) Toward a general theory for the behavioral sciences. *Amer. Psychol.,* **10**, 513–531 [154].

Miller, N. E. (1935) A reply to 'Sign-gestalt or conditioned reflex?' *Psychol. Rev.,* **42**, 280–292 [38–39, 41–44, 46–48, 51, 59, 62, 154].

——— (1944) Experimental studies of conflict. In *Personality and the behavior disorders,* Vol. I. (J. McV. Hunt, ed.). New York: Ronald Press Co. [18, 215].

——— (1948) Studies of fear as an acquirable drive: I. Fear as motivation and fear-reduction as reinforcement in the learning of new responses. *J. Exp. Psychol.,* **38**, 80–101 [196].

——— (1958) Central stimulation and other new approaches to motivation and reward. *Amer. Psychol.,* **13**, 100–108 [18, 255, 269, 287].

——— (1959) Liberalization of basic S—R concepts: Extensions to conflict behavior, motivation, and social learning. In *Psychology: A study of a science* (S. Koch, ed.). New York: McGraw-Hill [173].

——— (See Dollard & Miller, 1950).

Miller, N. E., & Dollard, J. (1941) *Social learning and imitation.* New Haven: Yale University Press [22, 98, 102–107, 114, 181].

Miller, R. E. (See Murphy, Miller, & Mirsky, 1955).

——— (See Murphy & Miller, 1956).

Miller, R. E., & Murphy, J. V. (1956a) Social interactions of rhesus monkeys: I.

Food-getting dominance as a dependent variable. *J. Soc. Psychol.*, **44**, 249–255 [360].

—— (1956b) Social interactions of rhesus monkeys: II. Effects of social interaction on the learning of discrimination tasks. *J. Comp. Physiol. Psychol.*, **49**, 207–211 [241].

Miller, R. E. Murphy, J. V., & Mirsky, I. A. (1959) Nonverbal communication of affect. *J. Clin. Psychol.*, **15**, 155–158 [115].

Mills, F. C. (1924) *Statistical methods.* New York: Henry Holt & Co. [317, 320–321].

Milner, B. (See Jasper, Gloor, & Milner, 1956).

Mirsky, I. A. (See Miller, Murphy, & Mirsky, 1959).

—— (See Murphy, Miller, & Mirsky, 1955).

Moltz, H. (1955) Latent extinction and the reduction of a secondary reward value. *J. Exp. Psychol.*, **49**, 395–400 [59].

—— (1957) Latent extinction and the fractional anticipatory response mechanism. *Psychol. Rev.*, **64**, 229–241 [59–60].

Moltz, H., & Maddi, S. R. (1955) Reduction of secondary reward value as a function of drive strength during latent extinction. (Unpublished manuscript) [59].

Moltz, H., & Rosenblum, L. A. (1958) Imprinting and associative learning: The stability of the following response in Peking ducks. *J. Comp. Physiol, Psychol.*, **51**, 580–583 [376].

Monkman, J. A. (See Stanley & Monkman, 1956).

Montague, W. P. [251].

Moorehead, A. (1957) A reporter in Africa. The birds and the beasts were there. *The New Yorker*, May 25, p. 45 ff. [190].

Moreno, J. L. (See Fromm-Reichmann & Moreno, 1956).

Morgan, C. L. (1900) *Animal behavior.* London: E. Arnold [209].

Morgan, C. T., & Stellar, E. (1950) *Physiological psychology.* New York: McGraw-Hill [290].

Morgan, L. [185].

Morkovin, B. V. (1960) *Through the barriers of deafness and isolation* (in press). New York: The Macmillan Co. [82].

Morris, C. W. (1946) *Signs, language, and behavior.* New York: Prentice-Hall, Inc. [141, 152].

—— (1958) Language in the objective mode: Words without meanings (a review). *Cont. Psychol.*, **3**, 212–214 [160].

Mosteller, F. (See Bush & Mosteller, 1951).

Mowrer, O. H. (1935) A device for studying eye-hand coordination without visual guidance. *Amer. J. Psychol.*, **47**, 493–495 [279].

—— (1938a) Preparatory set (expectancy)—A determinant in motivation and learning. *Psychol. Rev.*, **45**, 61–91 [200–201].

—— (1938b) Animal studies in the genesis of personality. *Trans. New York Acad. Sci.*, **56**, 273–288 [360].

—— (1939a) A stimulus-response analysis of anxiety and its role as a reinforcing agent. *Psychol. Rev.*, **46**, 553–565 [196, 362–363].

—— (1939b) *An artificially produced social problem in rats* (film). State College, Penn.: Psychological Cinema Register [362–364].

―――― (1940) Preparatory set expectancy—Some methods of measurement. *Psychol. Monogr.*, **52**, No. 2, 1–43 [201].

―――― (1947) On the dual nature of learning: A reinterpretation of "conditioning" and "problem solving." *Harv. Educ. Rev.*, **17**, 102–148 [3].

―――― (1948) Learning theory and the neurotic paradox. *Amer. J. Orthopsychiat.*, **18**, 571–610 [407].

―――― (1950) *Learning theory and personality dynamics.* New York: Ronald Press Co. [73, 84, 94, 112, 134, 230, 234, 374, 378, 380, 405].

―――― (1952) The autism theory of speech development and some clinical applications. *J. Speech & Hearing Disorders*, **17**, 263–268 [79, 82].

―――― (1954) The psychologist looks at language. *Amer. Psychol.*, **9**, 660–692 [53, 56, 88, 93, 132, 134, 148, 161, 223, 407].

―――― (1956) Two-factor learning theory reconsidered, with special reference to secondary reinforcement and the concept of habit. *Psychol. Rev.*, **63**, 114–128 [12, 112].

―――― (1957) Symbolic transformation—in two keys (a review). *Cont. Psychol.*, **2**, 57–59 [160].

―――― (1958) Hearing and speaking: An analysis of language learning. *J. Speech & Hearing Disorders*, **23**, 143–152 [86].

―――― (1959a) Changing conceptions of the unconscious. *J. Nerv. & Ment. Dis.*, **129**, 222–234 [412–413].

―――― (1959b) The dean of American psychology takes a stand (a review). *Cont. Psychol.*, **4**, 129–133 [190].

―――― (1960) *Learning theory and behavior.* New York: John Wiley & Sons, Inc. [1, 9, 11–12, 23–24, 26, 28–29, 31, 35, 37, 41, 47–49, 51–52, 54–55, 58, 60, 67–68, 74–75, 84, 100, 104, 107, 113, 114, 124, 143, 159, 163–164, 168, 171, 175–176, 181, 183, 185, 189, 192, 196, 201, 208, 210, 213, 231, 235–236, 256–257, 259–260, 264, 268–270, 277, 287–288, 294, 305, 319–320, 326–327, 332–334, 343–344, 366–367, 388–390, 394, 397–398, 407, 414].

―――― (1960a) *The crisis in psychiatry and religion: An analysis of the moral issues in mental illness.* Princeton, N J.: D. Van Nostrand Co. [412–413].

―――― (See Gibson & Mowrer, 1938).

Mowrer, O. H., & Jones, Helen M. (1943) Extinction and behavior variability as functions of effortfulness of task. *J. Exp. Psychol.*, **33**, 369–386 [181–182].

―――― (1945) Habit strength as a function of the pattern of reinforcement. *J. Exp. Psychol.*, **35**, 293–311 [19, 337].

Mowrer, O. H., & Keehn, J. D. (1958) How are inter-trial "avoidance" responses reinforced? *Psychol. Rev.*, **65**, 209–221 [191, 193].

Mowrer, O. H., Kornreich, J. S., & Yoffe, Isabelle (1940) *Competition and dominance hierarchies in rats* (film). State College, Penn.: Psychological Cinema Register [360–361].

Mowrer, O. H., Palma, Florence, & Sanger, Marjorie (1948) Individual learning and 'racial experience' in the rat, with special reference to vocalization. *J. Genet. Psychol.*, **85**, 29–43 [126–128].

Mowrer, O. H., & Ullman, A. D. (1945) Time as a determinant of integrative learning. *Psychol. Rev.*, **52**, 61–90 [215].

Muenzinger, K. F. (1938) Vicarious trial and error at a point of choice: I. A general survey of its relation to learning efficiency. *J. Genet. Psychol.*, **53**, 75–86 [215].

——— (1946) Reward and punishment. *Univer. Colorado Studies, General Series* (A), **27**, 1–16 [212].

——— [188, 215, 217].

Muenzinger, K. F., & Conrad, D. G. (1953) Latent learning observed through negative transfer. *J. Comp. Physiol. Psychol.*, **46**, 1–8 [51].

Muenzinger, K. F., & Fletcher, F. M. (1936) Motivation in learning. VI. Escape from electric shock compared with hunger-food-tension in the visual discrimination habit. *J. Comp. Psychol.*, **22**, 79–91 [215].

Muenzinger, K. F., & Gentry, Evelyn (1931) Tone discrimination in white rats. *J. Comp. Psychol.*, **12**, 195–205 [212–213].

Murie, A. (1944) The wolves of Mount McKinley. *U. S. Dept. Int. Fauna Ser.*, No. 5, Washington, D. C.: Government Printing Office [379].

Murphy, G., & Solley, C. M. (1957) Learning to perceive as we wish to perceive. *Bull. Menninger Clinic*, **21**, 225–237 [197].

Murphy, J. V. (See Miller & Murphy, 1956a, 1956b).

——— (See Miller, Murphy, & Mirsky, 1959).

Murphy, J. V., & Miller, R. E. (1956) The manipulation of dominance in monkeys with conditioned fear. *J. Abn. & Soc. Psychol.*, **53**, 244–248 [389, 390].

Murphy, J. V., Miller, R. E., & Mirsky, I. A. (1955) Interanimal conditioning in the monkey. *J. Comp. Physiol. Psychol.*, **48**, 211–214 [387–388, 390].

Myerson, A. [407].

Myklebust, H. R., & Brutten, M. (1953) A study of the visual perception of deaf children. *Acta Oto-Laryngologica*, Suppl. 105 [85].

Nachmias, J. (See Gleitman, Nachmias, & Neisser, 1954).

Nagel, E. (1935) The meaning of probability. *J. Amer. Stat. Assoc.*, **31**, 10–30 [352–354, 356–357].

——— (1955a) *Self-regulation in automatic control.* New York: Simon & Schuster; originally published in *Scient. Amer.*, 1952, **187**, 44–47 [261].

Nash, H. (1959) The behavioral world. *J. Psychol.*, **47**, 277–288 [205].

Neisser, U. (See Gleitman, Nachmias, & Neisser, 1954).

Newcomb, T. M., Hartley, E. L., *et al.* (1947) *Readings in social psychology.* New York: Henry Holt & Co. [81].

Newell, A., Shaw, J. C., & Simon, H. A. (1957) Empirical explorations of the logic theory machine: A case study in heuristic. *Proceedings of the Western Joint Computer Conference.* Los Angeles, Calif.: February, 1957 [275].

——— (1958) Elements of a theory of human problem solving. *Psychol. Rev.*, **65**, 151–166 [275].

——— (1958b) *The process of creative thinking* (mimeographed). Santa Monica, Calif.: The Rand Corp. [247].

Newman, J. R. (1956) *The world of mathematics* (four volumes). New York: Simon & Schuster [295, 300, 303, 307, 309–310, 352].

Neyman, J. (1952) *Lectures and conferences on mathematical statistics and probability.* Washington, D. C.: Graduate School, U. S. Dept. Agr. [302, 308, 311–312].

Nissen, H. W. (1951) Social behavior in primates. In *Comparative psychology* (C. P. Stone, ed.; 3rd ed.). New York: Prentice-Hall, Inc., pp. 423–457 [360–362].

Noble, C. E. (1958) Emotionality (e) and meaningfulness (m). *Psychol. Rep.*, **4**, 16 [164].

Noble, G. K., & Borne, R. (1940) The effect of sex hormones on the social hierarchy of *Xiphophorus helleri* (Abstract No. 257). *Anat. Rec.,* **78**, (Suppl. p. 147) [379].

Nuttin, J. (1955) Consciousness, behavior, and personality. *Psychol. Rev.,* **62**, 349–355 [257–259, 274–275].

Ogden, C. K., & Richards, I. A. (1923) *The meaning of meaning.* New York: Harcourt, Brace & Co. [140].

Osgood, C. E. (1953) *Method and theory in experimental psychology.* New York: Oxford University Press [53, 55, 63, 140–141, 146, 152, 188, 209–210, 214, 226–229].

———— (1957) Motivational dynamics of language behavior. In *Nebraska symposium on motivation* (R. M. Jones, ed.). Lincoln: University of Nebraska Press [274].

———— (1958) Language in the objective mode: The question of sufficiency (a review). *Cont. Psychol.,* **3**, 209–212 [160].

———— (1960) Report of an interdisciplinary seminar and conference held at the Boston Veterans Administration Hospital, June 15 to July 30, 1958. (Mimeographed—to be published) [288].

Osgood, C. E., & Suci, G. J. (1955) Factor analysis of meaning. *J. Exp. Psychol.,* **50**, 325–338 [71, 164].

Osgood, C. E., Suci, G. J., & Tannenbaum, P. H. (1957) *The measurement of meaning.* Urbana: University of Illinois Press [160].

Paget, R. (1930) *Human speech.* New York: Harcourt, Brace & Co. [88].

Palma, Florence (See Mowrer, Palma, & Sanger, 1948).

Parker, J. R. (See Fredericson, Fink, & Parker, 1955).

Pascal, B. [295].

Pavlov, I. P. (1927) *Conditioned reflexes* (C. V. Anrep, trans.). London: Oxford University Press [2, 11, 13, 22, 25–26, 38, 167, 179, 192, 202, 210, 258, 331].

———— [4, 6–7, 16, 171, 202, 211, 259, 270, 319, 349].

Pawlowski, A. A., & Scott, J. P. (1956) Hereditary differences in the development of dominance in litters of puppies. *J. Comp. Physiol. Psychol.,* **49**, 353–358 [360].

Peabody, D. [399].

Pei, M. (1948) *The story of language.* New York: J. B. Lippincott Co. [138].

Peirce, C. S. (1878a) The doctrine of chances. *Pop. Sci. Monthly,* **12**, 604–615 [309].

———— (1878b) The probability of induction. *Pop. Sci. Monthly,* **12**, 705–718 [309].

Penfield, W. (1954) Studies of the cerebral cortex of man: A review and an interpretation. In *Brain mechanisms and consciousness.* Springfield, Ill.: Charles C. Thomas [255].

Perkins, C. C., Jr. (1955) The stimulus conditions which follow learned responses. *Psychol. Rev.,* **62**, 341–348 [188].

Perky, C. W. (1910) An experimental study of imagination. *Amer. J. Psychol.,* **21**, 422–452 [166].

Perloe, S. (1959) A decade of "New Look" perception: A symposium. *Amer. Psychol.,* **14**, 379 [200].

Peterson, G. (1955) An oral communication model. *Language,* **31**, 414–427 [74].

Petrinovich, L., & Bolles, R. (1957) Delayed alternation: Evidence for symbolic processes in the rat. *J. Comp. Physiol. Psychol.,* **50**, 363–365 [178].

Phillips, L. W. (1958) Mediated verbal similarity as a determinant of the generalization of a conditioned GSR. *J. Exp. Psychol.,* **55**, 56–62 [207].

Piaget, J. (1926) *The language and thought of the child* (M. Warden, trans.). New York: Harcourt, Brace & Co. [94].

——— (1951) *Play, dreams and imitation in children* (Gattegno & Hodgson, trans.). New York: W. W. Norton & Co. [103–104].

——— (1952a) *The language and thought of the child.* New York: Humanities Press [160].

——— (1952b) *The origins of intelligence in children.* New York: International Universities Press [206].

Pillsbury, W. B. (1950) Knowledge in modern psychology. *Psychol. Rev.,* **57,** 328–333 [209].

Piotrowski, Z. A. (1957) *Perceptanalysis.* New York: The Macmillan Co. [197].

Pitts, W. (See McCulloch & Pitts, 1958).

Pitts, W., & McCulloch, W. S. (1947) How we know universals: The perception of auditory and visual forms. *Bull. Math. Biophys.,* **9,** 127–147 [287].

Plato [141, 217].

Pliskoff, S. S. (See Kendler, Pliskoff, D'Amato, & Katz, 1957).

Poincaré, H. (1854–1912) [301, 303–304, 307, 347].

Polanyi, M. (1958) Towards a post-critical philosophy. Chicago: University of Chicago Press [347, 356].

Postman, L. (1958) Mediated equivalence of stimuli and retroactive inhibition. *Amer. J. Psychol.,* **71,** 175–185 [29].

Postman, L., & Crutchfield, R. S. (1952) The interaction of need, set, and stimulus-structure in a cognitive task. *Amer. J. Psychol.,* **65,** 196–217 [198].

Postman, L., & Jarrett, R. F. (1952) An experimental analysis of "learning without awareness." *Amer. J. Psychol.,* **65,** 244–255 [288].

Powers, W. T., McFarland, R. L., & Clark, R. K. (1957) A general feedback theory of human behavior. (Mimeographed paper.) [69, 274–276, 278–279, 285–286].

Pringle, J. W. S. (1951) On the parallel between learning and evolution. *Behaviour,* **3,** 175–215 [183, 185].

Prokasy, W. F. (1956) The acquisition of observing responses in the absence of differential external reinforcement. *J. Comp. Physiol. Psychol.,* **49,** 131–134 [187–188].

Protnoy, M. (See Sutton, Hakerem, Protnoy, & Zubin, 1960.

Pumphrey, R. J. (1950) Hearing. In *Symposia of the Society for Experimental Biology.* Part IV. *Physiological mechanisms in behavior.* New York: Academic Press, Inc. [186].

——— (1951) *The origin of language.* Liverpool: University Press [87].

Rappaport, D. (1951) *The organization and pathology of thought.* New York: Columbia University Press [250].

Ratliff, F. (See Riggs, Ratliff, Cornsweet, & Cornsweet, 1953).

Razran, G. H. S. (1939b) A quantitative study of meaning by a conditioned salivary technique (semantic conditioning). *Science, N. S.,* **90,** 89–90 [56, 148].

——— Personal communication [140].

Ray, W. S. (1958) Generalization among meaningful relations in problem solving. *Amer. J. Psychol.,* **71,** 737–741 [57].

Reed, P. C. (See Bitterman, Reed, & Kubala, 1953).

Reichlin, B. (See Taylor & Reichlin, 1951).

Reis, Eva E. S. (See Hunt, Cole, & Reis, 1958).

Révész, G. (1940, 1941) Die menschlichen Kommunikationsformen und die sogenannte Tiersprache. *Proceedings of the Netherlands Akademie van Wetensschappen,* **43,** Nos. 9, 10; **44,** No. 1 [157].

Révész, G., *et al.* (1954) Thinking and speaking: A symposium. *Acta Psychologica* (Amsterdam), **10**, No. 1 [250].

Rheingold, Harriet L., Gewirtz, J. L., & Ross, Helen W. (1959) Social conditioning of vocalization in the infant. *J. Comp. Physiol. Psychol.*, **52**, 68–73 [83].

Richards, I. A. [325].

———— (See Ogden & Richards, 1923).

Riggs, L. A., Ratliff, F., Cornsweet, J. C., & Cornsweet, T. N. (1953) The disappearance of steadily fixated visual test objects. *J. Opt. Soc. Amer.*, **43**, 495–501 [279].

Rigrodsky, S. R. (1958) Application of Mowrer's autistic theory to the speech rehabilitation of mentally retarded pupils. Paper presented at the 34th Annual Convention of the American Speech and Hearing Association (New York City) [82].

Riopelle, A. J. (See Darby & Riopelle, 1959).

Ritchie, B. F. (1947) Studies in spatial learning: III. Two paths to the same location and two paths to two different locations. *J. Exp. Psychol.*, **37**, 25–38 [215].

———— (See Tolman, Ritchie, & Kalish, 1947).

Ritchie, B. F., Hay, Alice, & Hare, Rachel (1951) Studies in spatial learning: IX. A dispositional analysis of response performance. *J. Comp. Physiol. Psychol.*, **44**, 442–449 [215].

Roberts, H. V. (See Wallis & Roberts, 1956).

Rogers, C. R. (1951) *Client-centered therapy*. Boston: Houghton Mifflin Co. [207].

Rogers, W. A. (See Bugelski, Coyer, & Rogers, 1952).

Romney, A. K. (See Adams & Romney, 1959).

Rosenbleuth, A. [268].

Rosenblum, L. A. (See Moltz & Rosenblum, 1958).

Ross, Helen W. (See Rheingold, Gewirtz, & Ross, 1959).

Rotter, J. B. (1954) *Social learning and clinical psychology*. New York: Prentice-Hall, Inc. [318–319, 369].

Rozeboom, W. W. (1956) Mediation processes in learning. Unpublished doctoral dissertation, University of Chicago [57].

———— (1957) Secondary extinction of lever-pressing behavior in the albino rat. *J. Exp. Psychol.*, **54**, 280–287 [59].

———— (1958) "What is learned?"—An empirical enigma. *Psychol. Rev.*, **65**, 22–33 [55].

Russell, B. (1927) *Philosophy*. New York: W. W. Norton & Co. [71, 231].

———— (1948) *Human knowledge—Its scope and limits*. New York: Simon & Schuster [142, 165].

———— [152].

Russell, W. A. (1959) Associative models for transfer. *Amer. Psychol.*, **14**, 432 [57].

Sachs, H. (1942) *The creative unconscious*. Cambridge, Mass.: Sci-Art Press [290].

Sakoda, J. M. (See Brand, Woods, & Sakoda, 1956).

Salama, A. A. [395, 399].

Sanger, Marjorie D. (See Mowrer, Palma, & Sanger, 1948).

Sanger, Marjorie D. (1955) Language learning in infancy: A review of the autistic hypothesis and an observational study of infants. *Harv. Educ. Rev.*, **25**, 269–271 [82].

Sapir, E. (1921) *Language*. New York: Harcourt, Brace & Co. [158].

——— (1933) Language. In *Encyclopedia of social science*, pp. 155–169. New York: The Macmillan Co. [121].

Savage, I. R. (1957) Nonparametric statistics. *J. Amer. Stat. Assoc.*, **52**, 331–344 [316].

Savage, L. J. (1954) *The foundations of statistics*. New York: John Wiley & Sons, Inc. [308, 354, 356–357].

——— Personal communication [294, 310].

Schaefer, V. H. (1959) Differences between strains of rats in avoidance conditioning without an explicit warning signal. *J. Comp. Physiol. Psychol.*, **52**, 120–122 [394].

Scharlock, D. P. (1954) The effects of a pre-extinction procedure on the extinction of place and response performance in a T-maze. *J. Exp. Psychol.*, **48**, 31–36 [59].

Scheerer, M. (1953) Personality functioning and cognitive psychology. *J. Personality*, **22**, 1–16 [258, 288].

Schein, E. H. (1954) The effect of reward on adult imitative behavior. *J. Abn. & Soc. Psychol.*, **49**, 389–395 [107].

Scherrer, H. (See Hernandez-Peon, Scherrer, & Jouvet, 1956).

Schjelderup-Ebbe, T. (1922) Beiträge zur sozial-Psychologie des Haushuhns. *Zeit. F. Psychol.*, **88**, 225–252 [360].

Schlosberg, H., & Solomon, R. L. (1943) Latency of response in a choice discrimination. *J. Exp. Psychol.*, **33**, 22–39 [190–215].

Schneirla, T. C. (1950) Basic correlations and coordinations in insect societies, with special reference to ants. *Colloques Internationaux du Centre National de la Recherche Scientifique*. XXXIV. Structure et physiologie des Sociéties animales. Paris: March. [133].

Schoenfeld, W. N. (1950) An experimental approach to anxiety, escape, and avoidance behavior. In *Anxiety* (H. Hoch & J. Zubin, eds.). New York: Grune & Stratton, Inc. [196].

Schonbach, P. (1958) Cognition, motivation, and time perception. (Technical report No. 2, Naval research contract No. N8 onr-66216, mimeographed, University of Minnesota) [171].

Schuell, H., & Jenkins, J. J. 1959 The nature of language deficit in aphasia. *Psychol. Rev.*, **66**, 45–67 [288].

Scott, J. P. (1945) Social behavior, organization and leadership in a small flock of domestic sheep. *Comp. Psychol. Monogr.*, **18**, 1–29 [376–377].

——— (1950) The social behavior of dogs and wolves: An illustration of socio-biological systematics. *Ann. N. Y. Acad. Sci.*, **41**, 1009–1021 [369].

——— (1954) The effects of selection and domestication upon the behavior of the dog. *J. Nat. Cancer Inst.*, **15**, 739–758 [379–380].

——— (1956) The analysis of social organization in animals. *Ecology*, **37**, 213–221 [369].

——— (1958a) *Animal behavior*. Chicago: University of Chicago Press [369].

——— (1958b) Critical periods in the development of social behavior in puppies. *Psychosom. Med.*, **20**, 42–53 [378–380].

——— (1958c) *Aggression*. Chicago: University of Chicago Press [360].

——— [401].

——— (See Pawlowski & Scott, 1956).

Scott, J. P., & Marston, Mary-'Vesta (1953) Nonadaptive behavior resulting from a series of defeats in fighting mice. *J. Abn. & Soc. Psychol.*, **48**, 417–428 [360].

Sears, Pauline S. (See Lewin, Dembo, Festinger, & Sears, 1944).

Sears, R. R. (1951) A theoretical framework for personality and social behavior. *Amer. Psychol.*, **6**, 476–483 [368].

—— (See Hovland & Sears, 1938).

Sears, R. R., & Hovland, C. I. (1941) Experiments on motor conflict: II. Determination of mode or resolution by comparative strengths of conflicting responses. *J. Exp. Psychol.*, **28**, 280–286 [215].

Seashore, H., & Bavelas, A. (1941) The functioning of knowledge of results in Thorndike's line-drawing experiment. *Psychol. Rev.*, **48**, 155–164 [266].

Selye, H. (1956) *The stress of life*. New York: McGraw-Hill [409].

Seward, J. P. (1947a) The minimum requirement for learning a maze discrimination. *Amer. Psychol.*, **2**, 409 [46].

—— (1947b) A theoretical derivation of latent learning. *Psychol. Rev.*, **55**, 83–98 [47].

—— (1949) An experimental analysis of latent learning. *J. Exp. Psychol.*, **39**, 177–186 [47–51, 59–60].

Seward, J. P., & Levy, N. J. (1949) Sign learning as a factor in extinction. *J. Exp. Psychol.*, **39**, 660–668 [58–60].

Shannon, C. E., & Weaver, W. (1949) *The mathematical theory of communication*. Urbana: University of Illinois Press [138].

Sharpless, S., & Jasper, H. (1956) Habituation of the arousal reaction. *Brain*, **79**, 655–680 [290].

Shaw, J. C. (See Newell, Shaw, & Simon, 1957).

—— (See Newell, Shaw, & Simon, 1958).

—— (See Newell, Shaw, & Simon, 1958b).

Sheehan, J. G. (1953) Theory and treatment of stuttering as an approach-avoidance conflict. *J. Psychol.*, **36**, 27–49 [84].

Sheehan, J. G., & Voas, R. B. (1954) Tension patterns during stuttering in relation to conflict, anxiety-binding, and reinforcement. *Speech Monogr.*, **21**, No. 4 [84].

Sheffield, Virginia F. (1949) Extinction as a function of partial reinforcement and distribution of practice. *J. Exp. Psychol.*, **39**, 511–525 [175, 177, 337].

Sherrington, C. S. (1906) *Integrative action of the nervous system*. New Haven: Yale University Press [221, 256].

Shipley, W. C. (1933) An apparent transfer of conditioning (abstract). *Psychol. Bull.*, **30**, 541 [53–55].

—— (See Spence & Shipley, 1934).

Shoben, E. J. (1957) Toward a concept of the normal personality. *Amer. Psychol.*, **12**, 183–189 (412).

Sidman, M. (1953) Two temporal parameters of the maintenance of avoidance behavior by the white rat. *J. Comp. Physiol. Psychol.*, **46**, 253–261 [394].

Sidman, M., & Boren, J. J. (1957) A comparison of two types of warning stimulus in an avoidance situation. *J. Comp. Physiol. Psychol.*, **50**, 282–287 [195–196].

Sidowski, J. B. (1957) Reward and punishment in a minimal social situation. *J. Exp. Psychol.*, **54**, 318–326 [369].

—— (See Wyckoff & Sidowski, 1955).

Sidowski, J. B., Wyckoff, L. B., & Tabory, L. (1956) The influence of reinforcement and punishment in a minimal social situation. *J. Abn. & Soc. Psychol.*, **52**, 115–119 [369].

Siegal, R. S. (See Gardner, Holzman, & Siegal, 1956).

Siegel, S. (1957) Level of aspiration and decision making. *Psychol. Rev.*, **64**, 253–262 [318].

Silander, F. S. (See Wasserman & Silander, 1958).

Silverman, S. R. (1954) Teaching speech to the deaf—The issues. Reprint No. 654. Washington, D. C.: The Volta Bureau [84].

Simmons, R. (1924) The relative effectiveness of certain incentives in animal learning. *Comp. Psychol. Monogr.*, **2**, 1–79 [30].

Simon, H. A. (See Newell, Shaw, & Simon, 1957).

——— (See Newell, Shaw, & Simon, 1958).

——— (See Newell, Shaw, & Simon, 1958b).

Sinnott, E. W. (1952) The biology of purpose. *Amer. J. Orthopsychiat.*, **22**, 457–468 [270].

Skinner, B. F. (1938) *The behavior of organisms.* New York: Appleton-Century-Crofts [18, 51, 187, 320].

——— (1953a) Some contributions of an experimental analysis of behavior to psychology as a whole. *Amer. Psychol.*, **8**, 69–78 [183, 337, 357–358].

——— (1953b) *Science and human behavior.* New York: The Macmillan Co., [196].

——— (1957) *Verbal behavior.* New York: Appleton-Century-Crofts [57, 92, 135, 142, 152, 160].

——— (1958a) Reinforcement today. *Amer. Psychol.*, **13**, 94–99 [92, 255].

——— (1958b) Teaching machines. *Science*, **128**, 969–977 [57, 394].

Slack, C. W. (1955) Feedback theory and the reflex arc concept. *Psychol. Rev.*, **62**, 263–267 [281, 284].

Sluckin, W. (1954) *Minds and machines.* Middlesex, England: Pelican Books [270, 288].

Smith, Mr. and Mrs. G. William [133].

Smith, S., & Guthrie, E. R. (1921) *General psychology in terms of behavior.* New York: D. Appleton–Century [37].

Solley, C. M. (See Murphy & Solley, 1957).

Solomon, R. L. (1948) Effort and extinction rate: A confirmation. *J. Comp. Physiol. Psychol.*, **41**, 93–101 [182].

——— Personal communication [399–406].

——— (See Schlosberg & Solomon, 1943).

Spaulding, D. (1873) Instinct, with original observations on young animals. *Macmillan's Magazine*, **27**, 282–293 [374].

Spence, K. W. (1937) The differential response in animals to stimuli varying within a single dimension. *Psychlo. Rev.*, **44**, 430–444 [244].

——— (1951) Theoretical interpretations of learning. In *Comparative psychology* (C. P. Stone, ed.; 3rd ed.). New York: Prentice-Hall, Inc. [51].

——— (1956) *Behavior theory and conditioning.* New Haven: Yale University Press [51, 60].

Spence, K. W., & Lippitt, R. O. (1946) An experimental test of the sign-gestalt theory of trial and error learning. *J. Exp. Psychol.*, **36**, [45].

Spence, K. W., & Shipley, W. C. (1934) The factors determining the difficulty of blind alleys in maze learning by the white rat. *J. Comp. Psychol.*, **17**, 423–436 [39].

Sperber, H. (See Estrich & Sperber, 1952).

Spinoza, B. [217].

Spitz, H. H. (See Griffith, Spitz, & Lipman, 1959).

Spitz, R. A. (1958) *No and yes.* New York: International Universities Press [164].

Spragg, S. D. S. (1934) Anticipatory responses in the maze. *J. Comp. Psychol.,* **18,** 51–73 [39].

Staats, A. W. (1959a) Meaning and word associates: Separate processes. *Amer. Psychol.,* **14,** 432 [57].

—— (1959b) Verbal habit-familities, concepts, and the operant conditioning of word classes. Technical Report No. 10, Naval Research Contract Nonr 2794 (02), mimeographed Arizona State University (Tempe) [207, 291].

—— (See Staats & Staats, 1957).

Staats, A. W., Staats, Carolyn K., & Heard, W. G. (1959) Language conditioning of meaning to meaning using a semantic generalization paradigm. *J. Exp. Psychol.,* **57,** 187–192 [147].

—— Language conditioning of denotative meaning. Technical Report No. 13, Naval Research Contract Nonr 2794 (02), mimeographed. Arizona State University (Tempe) [207].

Staats, Carolyn K., & Staats, A. W. (1957) Meaning established by classical conditioning. *J. Exp. Psychol.,* **54,** 74–80 [57, 148].

Staats, Carolyn K. (See Staats, Staats, & Heard, 1959, 1960).

Stacey, C. L., & DeMartino, M. F. (eds.) (1958) *Understanding human motivation.* Cleveland, Ohio: Howard, Allen, Inc. [291].

Stagner, R., & Karwoski, T. F. (1952) *Psychology.* New York: McGraw-Hill [199].

Stanley, J. C., Jr. (1950) The differential effects of partial and continuous reward upon the acquisition and elimination of running response in a two-choice situation. Ed.D. thesis: Harvard University [337].

—— (See Jenkins & Stanley, 1950).

Stanley, W. C., & Aamodt, Marjorie S. (1954) Force of responding during extinction as a function of force required during conditioning. *J. Comp. Physiol. Psychol.,* **47,** 462–464 [181–182].

Stanley, W. C., & Monkman, J. A. (1956) A test for specific and general behavioral effects of infantile stimulation with shock in the mouse. *J. Abn. & Soc. Psychol.,* **53,** 19–22 [407].

Starling, E. H. [271].

Stellar, E. (See Morgan & Stellar, 1950).

Steer, M. D. [288].

Stevenson, H. W. (See Weir & Stevenson, 1959).

Stevenson, H. W., & Weir, M. W. (1959) Variables affecting children's performance in a probability learning task. *J. Exp. Psychol.,* **57,** 403–413 [342].

—— (1960a) Developmental changes in the effects of reinforcement and non-reinforcement of a single response. (To be published) [342].

—— (1960b) Probability learning in children as a function of incentive conditions and probability of reinforcement. (To be published) [342].

Stevenson, H. W., & Zigler, E. F. (1958) Probability learning in children. *J. Exp. Psychol.,* **56,** 185–192 [342].

Stewart, G. R. (1946) *Man, An autobiography.* New York: Random House [86, 134–136, 159, 161].

Stewart, P. A. (See Thomas & Stewart, 1957).

Stone, L. J. (1954) A critique of studies of infant isolation. *Child Devel.,* **25,** 9–20 [365, 390].

Straughan, J. H. (See Estes & Straughan, 1954).

Strumpell, A. I. [284–285].

Suci, G. J. (See Osgood & Suci, 1955).

———— (See Osgood, Suci, & Tannenbaum, 1957).

Sullivan, H. S. (1945) Conceptions of modern psychiatry. Washington: William Alanson White Psychiatric Foundation. (Reprinted from *Psychiatry*, **3**:1 and **8**:2 [413].

———— [414].

Summers, S. S. (See Maltzman, Brooks, Bogartz, & Summers, 1958).

Sumner, W. G., Keller, A. G., & Davie, M. R. (1928) *The science of society*, 4 vols. New Haven: Yale University Press [89, 380].

Sutton, S., Hakerem, G., Protnoy, M., & Zubin, J. (1960) The effect of shift of sensory modality on serial reaction time: A comparison of schizophrenics and normals. *Amer. J. Psychol.*, (submitted for publication) [204].

Switzer, S. A. (1934) Anticipatory and inhibitory characteristics of delayed conditioned reactions. *J. Exp. Psychol.*, **17**, 603–620 [38].

Syz, H. (1957) An experiment in inclusive psychotherapy. In *Experimental psychopathology*. New York: Grune & Stratton, Inc. [412].

Szymanski, J. S. (1918) Versuche über die Wirkung der Factoren, die also Antrieb zunn Erlernen einer Handlung dienen konnen. *Pflüger's Archiv f. d. gesamte Psyciologie*, **171**, 374–385 [30].

Tabory, L. (See Sidowski, Wyckoff, & Tabory, 1956).

Tannenbaum, P. H. (See Osgood, Suci, & Tannenbaum, 1957).

Taylor, D. W., & McNemar, Olga W. (1955) Problem solving and thinking. In *Annual Rev. Psychol.*, **6**, 455–477 [212].

Taylor, J. G., & Reichlin, B. (1951) Vicarious trial and error. *Psychol. Rev.*, **58**, 389–402 [215].

Thistlethwaite, D. (1951) A critical review of latent learning and related experiments. *Psychol. Bull.*, **48**, 97–129 [34, 51].

Thomas Aquinas (1274) *Summa theologica*. Translated (by W. Farrell, & M. J. Healy) as *My Way of life* (1952). Brooklyn, N. Y.: Confraternity of the Precious Blood [417].

Thomas, G. J., & Stewart, P. A. (1957) The effect on visual perception of stimulating the brain with polarizing currents. *Amer. J. Psychol.*, **70**, 528–540 [256].

Thompson, G. G. (1952) *Child psychology, Growth trends in psychological adjustment*. Boston: Houghton Mifflin Co. [134].

Thompson, M. E. (See Dove & Thompson, 1943).

Thompson, W. R. (See Hebb & Thompson, 1954).

Thompson, W. R., & Bindra, D. (1952) Motivational and emotional characteristics of "bright" and "dull" rats. *Canad. J. Psychol.*, **6**, 116–122 [367].

Thompson, W. R., & Heron, W. (1954) The effects of restricting early experience on the problem-solving capacity of dogs. *Canad. J. Psychol.*, **8**, 17–31 [390].

Thorndike, E. L. (1898) Animal intelligence: An experimental study of the associative processes in animals. *Psychol. Monogr.*, **2**, No. 4 (whole No. 8) [89, 98–101, 104, 210].

———— (1911) *Animal intelligence*. New York: The Macmillan Co. [210].

———— (1913) *Educational psychology, Vol. II. The psychology of learning*. New York: Teachers College, Columbia University [179].

———— (1927) The law of effect. *Amer. J. Psychol.*, **39**, 212–222 [265].

———— (1931) *Human learning*. New York: D. Appleton-Century [11].

—— (1932) *The fundamentals of learning.* New York: Teachers College, Columbia University [11, 266].

—— (1935) *The psychology of wants, interests and attitudes.* New York: D. Appleton-Century [25].

—— (1943) *Man and his works.* Cambridge, Mass.: Harvard University Press [72, 87–88, 91, 117–118, 121–123].

—— [2, 4–6, 16, 61, 146, 170–171, 185, 211, 223, 258, 265, 269–270, 281, 286, 319, 349].

Thorpe, W. H. (1956) *Learning and instinct in animals.* London: Methuen & Co. [74, 222].

Thrall, R. M., Coombs, C. H., & Davis, R. L. (1954) *Decision processes.* New York: John Wiley & Sons, Inc. [315, 318].

Tillich, P. (1953) *The courage to be.* New Haven: Yale University Press [418].

Tinbergen, N. (1953) *Social behavior in animals.* London: Methuen & Co.; New York: John Wiley & Sons, Inc. [128, 370–373, 386].

Tinklepaugh, O. (1928) An experimental study of representative factors in monkeys. *J. Comp. Psychol.,* **8,** 197–236 [226].

Titchener, E. B. (1909a) *Lectures on the experimental psychology of the thought processes.* New York: The Macmillan Co. [174].

—— (1909b) *Textbook of psychology.* New York: The Macmillan Co. [204].

Tolman, E. C. (1926) A behavioristic theory of ideas. *Psychol. Rev.,* **33,** 252–269 [215].

—— (1927) A behavioristic definition of consciousness. *Psychol. Rev.,* **34,** 433–439 [215].

—— (1932) *Purposive behavior in animals and man.* New York: Appleton-Century-Crofts [1–3, 11, 47, 68, 215, 236, 260, 287].

—— (1933a) Sign-gestalt or conditioned reflex? *Psychol. Rev.,* **40,** 246–255 [34–38, 41, 43, 47].

—— (1938) The determiners of behavior at a choice point. *Psychol. Rev.,* **45,** 1–41 [181, 215].

—— (1939) Prediction of various trial and error by means of the schematic sowbug. *Psychol. Rev.,* **46,** 318–336 [215].

—— (1941) Discrimination vs. learning and the schematic sowbug. *Psychol. Rev.,* **48,** 367–382 [215].

—— (1948) Cognitive maps in rats and men. *Psychol. Rev.,* **53,** 189–208 [215].

—— (1955) Principles of performance. *Psychol. Rev.,* **62,** 315–326 [318].

—— [25, 69, 152, 171, 183, 216, 270, 319, 345].

—— (See Honzik & Tolman, 1936).

Tolman, E. C., & Brunswik, E. (1935) The organism and the causal texture of the environment. *Psychol. Rev.,* **42,** 43–77 [330–331, 333].

Tolman, E. C., & Gleitman, H. (1949a) Studies in spatial learning: VII. Place versus response learning under different degrees of motivation. *J. Exp. Psychol.,* **39,** 653–659 [215].

—— (1949b) Studies in learning and motivation: I. Equal reinforcements in both end-boxes, followed by shock in one end-box. *J. Exp. Psychol.,* **39,** 810–819 [44–48, 51, 59].

Tolman, E. C., & Honzik, C. H. (1930) Introduction and removal of reward and maze performance in rats. *Univ. Calif. Publ. Psychol.,* **4,** 257–275 [47].

Tolman, E. C., Ritchie, B. F., & Kalish, D. (1947) Studies in spatial learning: V.

Response learning versus place learning by the non-correction method. *J. Exp. Psychol.*, **37**, 285–292 [215].

Troland, L. T. (1928) *The fundamentals of human motivation.* New York: D. Van Nostrand & Co. [209].

Trowbridge, M. H., & Cason, H. (1932) An experimental study of Thorndike's theory of learning. *J. Gen. Psychol.*, **7**, 245–258 [265–266].

Tryon, R. C. (1940) Genetic differences in maze learning ability in rats. *Yearb. Nat. Soc. Stud. Educ.*, **39**, 111–119 [367].

Tsushima, T. (1958) The effects of combination of positive and negative reinforcement: An experimental analogue of child-rearing practice. M. A. thesis, University of Illinois: Urbana; (see also *Scientific Reports of Kyoto Prefectural University*, 1959, **3**, 147–154) [345, 398].

—— (See Dulany & Tsushima, 1959).

Tustin, A. (1955) Feedback. In *Automatic control*. New York: Simon & Schuster; originally published in *Scient. Amer.*, 1952, **187**, 48–55 [261].

Tyler, D. W. (See Bitterman, Feddersen, & Tyler, 1953).

Ullman, A. D. (See Mowrer & Ullman, 1945).

Underwood, B. F. (1949) *Experimental psychology.* New York: D. Appleton-Century [215].

Urban, W. M. (1939) *Language and reality—The philosophy of language and the principles of symbolism.* New York: McGraw-Hill [138].

Vaughn, H. E. (See Beberman, Vaughn, *et al.*, 1959).

Verplanck, W. S. (1956) The operant conditioning of human motor behavior. *Psychol. Bull.*, **53**, 70–83 [77].

Vinacke, W. E. (1952) *The psychology of thinking.* New York: McGraw-Hill [346–347, 394].

—— (1954) *The miniature social situation.* University of Hawaii, Psychological Laboratory [369].

Voas, R. B. (See Sheehan & Voas, 1954).

von Foerster, H. (ed.) (1951) *Cybernetics. Transactions of seventh conference.* New York: Josiah Macy Foundation [74, 273].

—— (1953) *Cybernetics—Circular causal and feedback mechanism in biological and social systems. Transaction of tenth conference on cybernetics.* New York: Josiah Macy Foundation [273].

Von Frisch, K. (1950) *Bees: Their vision, chemical sense, and language.* Ithaca, New York: Cornell University Press [132–133].

von Mises, R. (1957) *Probability, statistics, and truth.* (Original German ed., 1928). London: Geo. Allen & Unwin, Ltd. [294, 305, 212].

von Neumann, J. (1958) *The computer and the brain.* New Haven, Conn.: Yale University Press [275].

Wald, A. (1950) *Statistical decision functions.* New York: John Wiley & Sons, Inc. [333].

Walker, E. L. (1948) Drive specificity and learning. *J. Exp. Psychol.*, **38**, 39–49 [45].

Wallach, H. (See Kohler & Wallach, 1944).

Wallis, W. A., & Roberts, H. V. (1956) *Statistics: A new approach.* Glencoe, Ill.: The Free Press [318].

Walpole, H. (1941) *Semantics: The nature of words and their meanings.* New York: W. W. Norton & Co. [123].

Walter, W. G. (1954) The electrical activity of the brain. *Sci. Amer.*, **190**, 54–63 [287].

Walters, R. H. Personal communication [398–399].

Wasserman, P., & Silander, F. S. (1958) *Decision-making: An annotated bibliography*. Ithaca, New York: Graduate School of Business and Public Administration [319].

Watson, J. B. (1914) *Behavior: An introduction to comparative psychology*. New York: Henry Holt & Co. [2, 209].

—— (1916) The effect of delayed feeding upon habit formation (abstract). *Psychol. Bull.*, **13**, 77 [367].

—— (1919) *Psychology from the standpoint of a behaviorist*. Philadelphia, Pa.: J. B. Lippincott Co. [2].

—— [171–173, 249, 257].

Weaver, W. (See Shannon & Weaver, 1949).

Weinreich, U. (1958) Travels through semantic space (a review). *Word*, **14**, 346–366 [160].

—— (1959) Techniques of lexicography: syllabus and basic bibliography. Mimeographed: Columbia University [124].

Weinstock, S. (1954) Resistance to extinction of a running response following partial reinforcement under widely spaced trials. *J. Comp. Physiol. Psychol.*, **47**, 318–322 [20, 175–177, 189].

Weir, M. W. (See Stevenson & Weir, 1959, 1960a, 1960b).

Weir, M. W., & Stevenson, H. W. (1959) The effect of verbalization in children's learning as a function of chronological age. *Child Devel.*, **30**, 143–149 [245].

Weiss, E. J. (See Wilson, Weiss, & Amsel, 1955).

Weldon, W. F. R. [316–317].

Wertheimer, M. (1959) *Productive thinking*. New York: Harper & Bros. [247].

Wheeler, R. H. (1929) *The science of psychology*. New York: T. Y. Crowell Co. [90].

Wheeler, W. M. (1923) *Social life among the insects*. New York: Harcourt, Brace & Co. [379].

—— (1928) *The social insects: Their origin and evolution*. New York: Harcourt, Brace & Co. [222].

Whipple, G. M. (1915) *Manual of mental and physical tests: Complex processes*. Baltimore: Warwick & York, Inc. [280].

Whitehead, A. N. [352].

Whiteis, U. E. (1956) Punishment's influence on fear and avoidance. *Harv. Educ. Rev.*, **26**, 360–373 [200–201].

Whiting, J. W. M. (1959) Sorcery, sin, and the superego: A cross-cultural study of some mechanisms of social control. In *Nebraska symposium on motivation* (R. M. Jones, ed.). Lincoln: University of Nebraska Press [405].

—— [399–400, 403].

Whorf, B. L. (1952) Sciences and linguistics. In *Collected papers on metalinguistics*. Washington, D. C.: Dept. of State, Foreign Service Institute [137].

—— (1956) *Language, thought, and reality* (J. B. Carroll, ed.). New York: John Wiley & Sons, Inc. [160].

Wiener, N. (1948) *Cybernetics*. New York: John Wiley & Sons, Inc. [12, 267].

Williams, K. A. (1929) The conditioned reflex and the sign function in learning. *Psychol. Rev.*, **36**, 481–497 [37].

Wilson, K. (1954) In *Psycholinguistics—A survey of theory and research prob-*

lems. (C. E. Osgood & T. A. Sebeok, eds.) Bloomington: University of Indiana Press [123].

Wilson, Wilma, Weiss, Elizabeth J., & Amsel, A. (1955) Two tests of the Sheffield hypothesis concerning resistance to extinction, partial reinforcement, and distribution of practice, *J. Exp. Psychol.*, **50**, 51–60 [175].

Wilson, W. R. (1924) Principles of selection in trial-and-error learning. *Psychol. Rev.*, **31**, 150–160 [37].

Winthrope, H. (1946) Semantic factors in the measurement of personality integration. *J. Soc. Psychol.*, **24**, 149–175 [124].

Wischner, G. J. (1952a) Anxiety-reduction as reinforcement in maladaptive behavior: Evidence in stutterers' representations of the moment of difficulty. *J. Abn. & Soc. Psychol.*, **47**, 566–571 [84, 202].

—— (1952b) An experimental approach to expectancy and anxiety in stuttering behavior. *J. Speech & Hearing Disorders*, **17**, 139–154 [84].

—— (See Goss & Wischner, 1956).

Wissemann, H. (1954) *Untersuchungen zur Onomatopoiie.* Heidelberg: Carl Winter, Universitatsverlag [96].

Wolff, C. (1945) *The psychology of gesture.* London: Methuen & Co. [90].

Woods, P. J. (See Brand, Woods, & Sakoda, 1956).

Woodworth, R. S. (1958) *Dynamics of behavior.* New York: Henry Holt & Co. [7, 19, 173, 190, 336].

Wyatt, Gertrude L. (1960) *Speech and interpersonal relations in childhood.* (In preparation) [135].

Wyckoff, L. B. (1952) The role of observing responses in discrimination learning. Part I. *Psychol. Rev.*, **59**, 431–442 [187].

—— (See Sidowski, Wyckoff, & Tabory, 1956).

Wyckoff, L. B., & Sidowski, J. B. (1955) Probability discrimination in a motor task. *J. Exp. Psychol.*, **50**, 225–231 [341–343].

Yerkes, D. N. (See Yerkes & Yerkes, 1928).

Yerkes, R. M. (1943) *Chimpanzees, A laboratory colony.* New Haven: Yale University Press [228].

Yerkes, R. M., & Yerkes, D. N. (1928) Concerning memory in the chimpanzee. *J. Comp. Psychol.*, **8**, 237–271 [226].

Yoffe, Isabelle (See Mowrer, Kornreich, & Yoffe, 1940).

Yule, G. U. (1919) *An introduction to the theory of statistics.* London: C. Griffin & Co., Ltd. [316].

Zener, K. (1937) The significance of behavior accompanying conditioned salivary secretion for theories of the conditioned response. *Amer. J. Psychol.*, **50**, 384–403 [8, 325].

Zigler, E. F. (See Stevenson & Zigler, 1958).

Zimmerman, D. W. (1957) Durable secondary reinforcement: Method and theory. *Psychol. Rev.*, **64**, 373–383 [21].

—— (1958a) Sustained performance based on secondary reinforcement: An improved method with added controls. Ph.D. thesis: University of Illinois [21].

—— (1958b) An unsuccessful attempt, based on the autism theory of language learning, to teach dogs to bark instrumentally. (Unpublished research) [78].

—— (1959) Sustained performance in rats based on secondary reinforcement. *J. Comp. Physiol. Psychol.*, **52**, 353–358 [177].

Zipf, G. K. (1949) *Human behavior and the principle of least effort.* Cambridge, Mass.: Addison-Wesley Press [90, 160].

Zubin, J. (See Sutton, Hakerem, Protnoy, & Zubin, 1960).

Subject Index